R_m	Market rate of return
ROA	Return on assets
ROE	Return on shareholders' equity
S_P	Sharpe's index of portfolio performance (reward-to-volatility measure)
σ	Standard deviation
T_P	Treynor's index of portfolio performance
t	Time
TV	Time value of an option
σ^2	Variance
V_n	Accumulated value of an investment at the end of *n* periods
YTM	Yield to maturity

NOTICE
FOR YOUR PROTECTION
BEFORE YOU OPEN THE DISKPACK,
READ THE SOFTWARE LICENSE AGREEMENT
ON THE LAST PAGE OF THIS BOOK.

**Opening the diskpack indicates your acceptance
of the Software License Agreement.**

E3–119

INVESTMENTS

INVESTMENTS

RICHARD K. SMITH
University of Montana

DENNIS PROFFITT
Grand Canyon College

ALAN A. STEPHENS
Utah State University

WEST PUBLISHING COMPANY
St. Paul   New York   Los Angeles   San Francisco

WEST'S COMMITMENT TO THE ENVIRONMENT

Interior Design: Barbara Bauer
Artwork: Rolin Graphics
Copyeditor: Patricia Lewis
Composition: Graphic World
Cover Image: David Bishop
Cover Design: Three Fish Design
Production, Prepress, Printing and Binding by West Publishing Company

Copyright © 1992 By WEST PUBLISHING COMPANY
      50 W. Kellogg Boulevard
      P.O. Box 64526
      St. Paul, MN 55164–0526

99 98 97 96 95 94 93 92   8 7 6 5 4 3 2 1 0

Library of Congress Cataloging-in-Publication Data

Smith, Richard K. (Richard Kay), 1917-
    Investments / Richard K. Smith, Dennis L. Proffitt, Alan A.
Stephens.
      p.   cm.
    Includes bibliographical references and index.
    ISBN 0-314-89339-3 (hard)
    1. Securities—United States. 2. Stock-exchange—United States.
3. Investment analysis. I. Proffitt, Dennis L. II. Stephens, Alan
A. III. Title.
HG4963.S6 1992   91-29417
332.6—dc20   CIP

To our wives and children . . .

Prudence, Richard, Stephen, and Prudence Anne

Judy, David, and Karen

Patricia, Audrey, Laura, Matthew, and Erica

BRIEF CONTENTS

CONTENTS

ix

APPENDICES

PREFACE

A first course in investments offers both a stimulating intellectual challenge and a chance to learn the practical art of intelligent investing. Fact and theory are combined. Theory is needed to explain the pricing of securities and to enable the student to learn how securities are assembled into optimal portfolios. Facts are needed to explain the many types of securities on the market and to show how they can be used in long-term investing, speculating, and hedging. Investing without sufficient knowledge of theory and fact often causes otherwise intelligent people to make regrettable mistakes.

This book has a number of features helpful to students and teachers alike. First, it is comprehensive. All widely-traded marketable securities are described and explained; and all leading investment theories are examined and evaluated. Second, it is timely. For example, it deals with the newest types of investment media, such as options on futures; it discusses current developments, such as international diversification; and it examines new market theories, such as the one that sees a connection between positive feedback strategies and rational destabilizing speculation. Third, the book explains investment concepts clearly and concisely, often with examples. Real-world flavor is added by numerous boxed-off "sidelights" from sources such as the *Wall Street Journal, Forbes,* and *Business Week.* Fourth, mathematical presentations are used where necessary for clear exposition, but only to that extent. Fifth, the book contains numerous chapter-end questions and problems that are thought-provoking and helpful to students in mastering the material. And, finally, the book is supplemented by a package of software and data with which students can apply the knowledge they have gained from the text and classroom presentations.

The software package is fully documented in an appendix to the book. One program allows the user to calculate returns, means, variances, standard deviations, covariances, and correlations. Another program performs simple regression analysis. The programs designed specifically for investment analysis and planning permit the user to: value stocks with three dividend discount models; determine bond prices, yields, and durations; evaluate bond swaps; solve for the optimal portfolio; estimate option prices; calculate the implied volatility of a stock, given the option premium; determine the sensitivity of an option price to time, volatility, and the risk-free rate; determine the profit profiles for various option strategies; determine the cheapest or most likely bond to be delivered under a Treasury bond futures contract; and determine the results of program trading strategies.

The 23 chapters of the book are organized into six parts. Part 1 (Background Information) begins with an explanation of the principal factors that should be taken into account in making investment decisions. These include the investor's tolerance for risk, the tradeoff between risk and return, the efficiency of the markets, income taxes, and the benefits of diversification. Chapter 2 describes the principal types of marketable and nonmarketable securities and explains how to read newspaper quotations for stocks, bonds, and Treasury bills. Chapter 3 explains how new issues are brought to the market and how previously-issued securities are traded. It describes various types of buy and sell orders, short selling, margin trading, and the essentials of securities regulation. Chapter 4 describes numerous sources of investment information, computerized as well as printed. It is important to know the kinds of information that are available and where the information can be found.

Part 2 (Risk and Return: Theory and Evidence) provides essential information about methods of measuring risk and return, and it explains and evaluates three kinds of investment theories: capital market theory (or asset pricing), portfolio theory, and efficient market hypothesis. As explained in chapter 6, the two principal capital market theories are the capital asset pricing model (CAPM) and the arbitrage pricing theory (APT). Tests of these theories are discussed in chapter 7.

Portfolio theory is organized around the concept of portfolio efficiency. An efficient portfolio is one that provides the highest expected return at a given level of risk, or, alternatively, the least amount of risk at a given level of expected return. It is from these efficient portfolios that individual and institutional investors can find their optimal portfolios.

Efficient market theory, in its broadest form, holds that securities prices accurately reflect all information and adjust immediately to reflect any new information. In a perfectly efficient market, securities are never over- or underpriced. Chapter 8 reviews a number of interesting studies that have tested various levels of this theory.

Part 3 (Analysis and Selection of Common Stocks) deals with four kinds of issues: how fundamental information, such as earnings and dividends, can be used to value stocks (chapter 9); how estimates of earnings and dividends can be made (chapter 10); how investors use fundamental information in their attempts to find undervalued stocks (chapter 11); and how technical methods (for example, analysis of past price patterns) are used in attempts to find undervalued stocks or to predict the trend of the market (chapter 12).

Part 4 (Analysis of Fixed-Income Investments) is a three-chapter sequence dealing with fixed-income securities such as U.S. Treasury securities, municipal securities, and corporate notes and bonds. Chapter 13 expands on chapter 3's explanation of various types of fixed-income securities. Chapter 14 explains yield measurement, bond risks, and the term structure of interest rates. Chapter 15 (Fixed-income Strategies) explains several strategies by which fixed-income investors attempt to earn abnormally high returns. These include bond swaps and riding the yield curve.

Part 5 (Speculative Investments and Hedging) deals with so-called derivative securities, the values of which are largely determined by the prices of one or more underlying assets. These include futures (chapter 16), options (chapter 17), warrants, convertibles and options on futures (chapter 18), and advanced strategies for trading options and futures (chapter 19). Derivative securities have become extremely important for two diametrically different kinds of activity: speculation and hedging. Speculators attempt to take advantage of expected future price changes, while hedgers attempt to protect themselves from the adverse effects of such changes.

In Part 6 (Portfolio Theory and Management) chapter 20 explains how an investor can select an optimal portfolio. Chapter 21 deals with the important matter of measuring how well a portfolio has performed, and it explains various methods by which measurement can be made. Chapter 22 explains that for many investors the most practical method of selecting an optimal portfolio, or some portion of an optimal portfolio, is by investing in mutual funds. Chapter 23 explains that by investing a portion of one's portfolio in foreign securities it may be possible to assemble a portfolio with a higher level of efficiency (that is, with a higher expected return at a given level of risk) than is obtainable when investments are limited to domestic securities.

The Instructor's Manual for the text contains outlines for courses that will cover only certain parts of the book. The manual also provides a large bank of challenging multiple choice questions and problems, in addition to solutions to all end-of-the-chapter questions and problems.

ACKNOWLEDGMENTS

Many people have helped us in preparing this book. We are especially grateful to Wolfgang Ametsbichler, Peter M. Ellis, Newell Gough, Allen D. Kartchner, Robert Mechem, Howard Puckett, Paul A. Randle, Neil Seitz, Clifford R. Skousen, David B. Stephens, Philip R. Swenson, and our students. We are also deeply indebted to Robert Horan, editor, Janine Wilson, editor, and Tad Bornhoft, production editor, of West Publishing Company, and to Patricia Lewis, copy editor, all of whom have given us many ideas, considerable help, and much encouragment. Finally, we want to thank the following reviewers for their many constructive suggestions, which are reflected throughout the book: Michael L. Austin, University of Nevada; W. Scott Baumann, Northern Illinois University; Randall Billingsley, Virginia Polytechnic Institute and State University; Gerald Blum, University of Nevada; Alyce Campbell, University of Oregon; D. Gary Carman, Southwest Texas State University; John H. Crockett, George Mason University; Ted Day, Vanderbilt University; Mike Devaney, Southeast Missouri State University; John Ellis, Colorado State University; Thomas Eyssell, University of Missouri, St. Louis; John Gerppert, University of Nebraska; James A. Greenleaf, Lehigh University; Douglas Hearth, University of Colorado; Elizabeth Hennigar, University of San Diego; Leo P. Mahoney, Bryant College; Andreas G. Merikas, Mississippi State University; John Miller, San Jose State University; Robert E. Nelson, Western Kentucky University; John P. Olienyk, Colorado State University; James A. Overdahl, University of Texas at Dallas; David R. Peterson, Florida State University; Murray Sabrin, Ramapo

College of New Jersey; Mary Jean Scheuer, California State University–Northridge; Pochara Theerathorn, Wichita State University; Alan Weatherford, California Polytechnic State University–San Luis Obispo; Richard E. Williams, Wright State University; and John Wingender, Oklahoma State University.

INVESTMENTS

PART 1   BACKGROUND INFORMATION

1 INVESTMENT GOALS AND STRATEGIES

This is a book about investment theories and investment practices. It emphasizes *common stocks, bonds, stock options,* and *future contracts,* but the basic principles covered here apply to investments of all kinds. One of the keys to successful investing is a careful assessment of the potential risks and rewards. In this book you will learn about the tools needed to make these assessments. You will see how professionals manage large portfolios and how you can manage your own assets to achieve well-planned investment goals. This chapter introduces a number of factors that should be considered in making investment decisions.

INVESTMENT MANAGEMENT AND TOLERANCE FOR RISK

Much of the investment theory is based on the notion that investors want to earn the highest possible return at an acceptable level of *risk*. It is quite properly assumed that the market offers a trade-off between risk and return. This trade-off exists because most individuals are unwilling to take on riskier projects unless they offer the possibility of greater gains. Riskier securities are unattractive unless they offer higher *expected returns*. No one would purchase common stocks rather than *U.S. government bonds* if stocks did not offer a chance for greater income.

TOLERANCE FOR RISK

Acceptable levels of risk vary widely among individuals, and for any one individual the acceptable level usually depends on the expected return. Most investors are willing to assume more risk, up to a point of maximum tolerance, for a higher expected return. Differences in *risk tolerance* exist for several reasons, notably the following:

1. Psychological makeup
2. Wealth and stability of income
3. Financial obligations and responsibilities
4. Age and health
5. Future cash needs

3

The last item merits further comment. The sooner an investment might have to be sold to obtain cash, the safer and more liquid it should be. Securities with volatile prices, such as common stocks and even long-term U.S. government bonds, should not be purchased by anyone with a short investment horizon.

Investors should think carefully about their own tolerance for risk. Anyone who is unwilling to think about *risk tolerance* or the relative risks and expected returns of different investments is likely to invest either too cautiously and sacrifice potential income or too aggressively and sustain large losses.

TIME AND ABILITY TO MANAGE INVESTMENTS

Many individuals with the ability to manage their own investments do not have sufficient time, and others with the time do not have the ability. Individuals who lack either the time or ability to manage investments should consider well-diversified *mutual funds* or go to professionals for assistance. Although mutual fund investing still leaves the problem of which of the hundreds of funds are best suited for the investor's needs, it is easy to find information about the funds' investment policies and past performance. Other types of pooled investments (where cash supplied by many individuals, corporations, and others is invested in a single portfolio of assets) include *annuities, unit investment trusts,* and *closed-end investment companies.*

CHARACTERISTICS OF SECURITIES

During the past 20 years, there has been a remarkable increase in the variety of securities available to investors. A monograph issued by the Financial Analysts Research Foundation in 1985 described 34 new financial instruments introduced between 1970 and 1985.[1] Later, an article in *Financial Management* described a large number of new investment securities, including 14 innovative consumer-type financial instruments introduced through 1988.[2] Among the new securities are numerous options and futures contracts that can be used either for speculating or for hedging against changes in stock prices or interest rates. Since options and futures are very important to investors, they are analyzed in considerable depth in later chapters.

One of the latest proposals, which may be a reality by the time you read this, is for the creation of a security representing a large bundle of stocks (such as all stocks in the *Standard & Poor's 500 Index*) that can be traded on the exchanges as though it were a single stock. Options and futures on bundles of securities have been traded for a number of years.

New securities will continue to be created as long as the securities exchanges, securities firms, and others are able to develop new instru-

[1]Michael D. Atchison, Richard F. DeMong, and John L. Kling, *New Financial Instruments: A Descriptive Guide* (Charlottesville, Va.: The Financial Analysts Research Foundation, 1985).

[2]John D. Finnerty, "Financial Engineering in Corporate Finance: An Overview," *Financial Management* 17, no. 4 (Winter 1988): 14–33.

ments that seem to provide opportunities for increasing income or lowering the cost of capital. The principal types of investment securities now available are described in Chapter 2.

HISTORICAL RISK-RETURN TRADE-OFF

One of the most important historical facts about investments is the positive relationship between risk and the rate of return when both are averaged over a long period of time. With risk measured by the standard deviation of the annual returns, common stocks have proved to be riskier than bonds and, on the whole, have provided higher returns. Similarly, government and high-grade *corporate bonds* have been riskier than *U.S. Treasury bills* and, more often than not, have earned a higher return.

Figure 1-1 shows the relationship of *nominal and real returns* to risk

---

|||| **FIGURE 1-1**

Stocks, Bonds, and Treasury Bills: Compound Annual Returns and Risk, 1926–1990

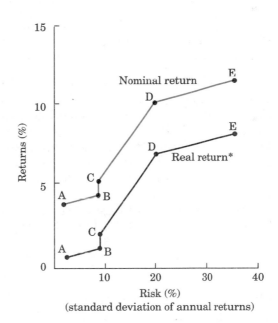

A   Treasury bills
B   Long-term U.S. Government Bonds
C   Corporate bonds
D   Large common Stocks
E   Small common Stocks

---

*Nominal return Minus Inflation Rate.

SOURCE: *Data from Stocks, Bonds, Bills and Inflation: 1991 Yearbook* (Chicago: Ibbotson Associates, Inc., 1991).

|||| SIDELIGHT
History May Hold Clues to Future Investment Returns

How large a return should investors expect from stocks, bonds, and other securities? After the October 1987 crash, many began to think stocks were a poor investment. But others have continued to expect returns of 20% a year, a little above the average for the years 1985–1988.

From 1926 to 1988, the stock market (as represented by Standard & Poor's 500 Index) provided a compound annual return of 10.0%, assuming dividends were reinvested. But results varied widely over shorter periods.

Steven Einhorn of Goldman Sachs expects average returns of 11% for stocks, 9% for bonds, and 7% for Treasury bills for the coming decades, and he foresees an inflation rate of 5%.

Bond returns have been low since World War II because of the upward trend of interest rates, which has depressed bond prices.

A standard asset mix for pension funds is 60% stocks, 30% bonds, and 10% cash equivalents. Most individuals probably earn lower returns than pension funds because they have too much invested in bank accounts and short-term securities.

SOURCE: Adapted from Karen Slater, "History May Hold Clues to Future Investment Returns," *The Wall Street Journal*, February 21, 1989, p. C1. Reprinted by permission of *The Wall Street Journal*, © Dow Jones & Company, Inc. (1989). All Rights Reserved Worldwide.

---

for five different types of securities for the years 1926 through 1990.[3] Treasury bills, the most stable of the five investments, earned the lowest average return, while small common stocks, the most volatile of the group, earned the highest return. Bonds and large common stocks fell between the two extremes. Whether the average return on stocks will be higher than the return on bonds over the next 10 or 20 years no one can know, but as noted in the Sidelight, a number of professionals expect that to happen.

The real returns of Figure 1-1 were calculated by deducting the average *inflation rate* of 3.1% from the nominal returns. The average real return over the period of 65 years was less than 1% for Treasury bills, between 1% and 2% for Treasury bonds, a little over 2% for corporate bonds, about 7% for large common stocks, and 8.5% for small common stocks.

Results over Shorter Periods

Risk-return relationships over periods shorter than the 65 years of Figure 1-1 are often strikingly different from the longer-term results. For example, the lower line in Figure 1-2 shows that over the 10-year period

[3]The data on risk and returns in this chapter are from *Stocks, Bonds, Bills and Inflation: 1991 Yearbook* (Chicago: Ibbotson Associates, Inc., 1991). The average returns are geometric means of the annual returns. They reflect increases and decreases in market values as well as dividends and interest income. The risk associated with each series of annual returns is measured by the standard deviation.

ending with 1980 the average return on Treasury bills was higher than the returns on government and corporate bonds and nearly as high as the average return on large common stocks. Far above all others was the average return for small common stocks, which was twice the return for larger stocks.

Relative returns for the 10-year period ending with 1990 were much different from those of the previous decade. Bonds became much more volatile and provided returns as high as the returns on large stocks. Small stocks remained highly volatile, but their returns dropped precipitously, almost down to the average yield for Treasury bills.

Returns by Years

Additional perspective is provided by Figure 1-3, a graph of the annual returns on which the average returns for large common stocks, corporate bonds, and Treasury bills in Figures 1-1 and 1-2 are based. It shows, for example, that while the annual return for large common stocks was above

---

|||| **FIGURE 1-2**

Stocks, Bonds, and Treasury Bills: Compound Annual Returns and Risk, 1971–1980 and 1981–1990

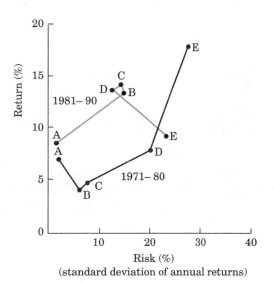

A   Treasury bills
B   Long-term U.S. government bonds
C   Corporate bonds
D   Large common stocks
E   Small common stocks

SOURCE: Data from *Stocks, Bonds, Bills and Inflation: 1991 Yearbook* (Chicago: Ibbotson Associates, Inc. 1991).

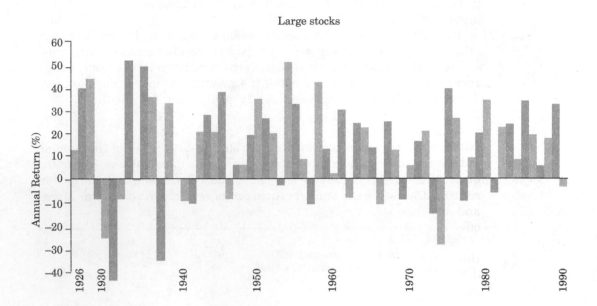

FIGURE 1-3

Annual Returns: Large Stocks, Long-Term Corporate Bonds, and U.S. Treasury Bills, 1926–1990

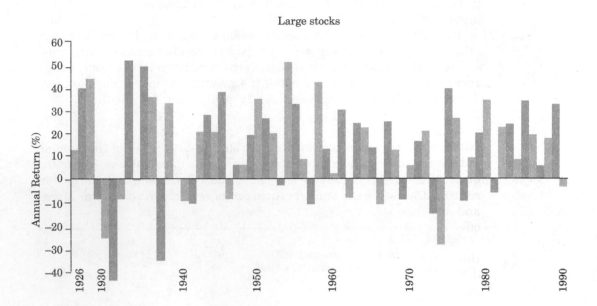

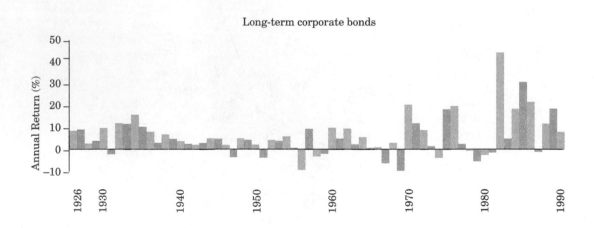

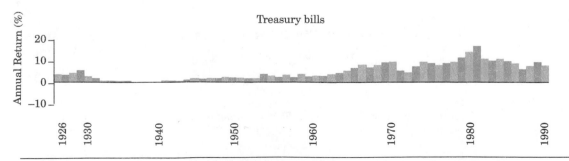

SOURCE: *Stocks, Bonds, Bills and Inflation: 1991 Yearbook* (Chicago: Ibbotson Associates, Inc. 1991).

30% nearly one-fourth of the time, it was negative about one-third of the time. In contrast, the Treasury bill return rarely moved up or down more than a few percentage points from one year to the next and was never negative. The corporate bond return was between the returns for common stocks and Treasury bills in a majority of the years and was negative about one-fifth of the time. Bond returns became considerably more volatile in the 1970s and 1980s, reflecting wider fluctuations in interest rates.

It is important to remember that even though, on the whole, higher-risk securities have provided higher returns, risk does not cause returns. The addition of riskier assets to a portfolio does not necessarily increase the return. It only creates the possibility of a higher return.

Risk and the Expected Return

It is clear that actual returns on riskier assets are sometimes—in fact, quite often—lower than the actual returns on safer assets. Expected returns are a different matter. Most investors have an aversion to risk and are therefore willing to acquire riskier assets only if they seem to offer the possibility of higher returns.[4]

The lowest acceptable expected return for an investment is known as the *required return*. At any given time, it varies among assets due to differences in taxability and risk, and for any given asset, it varies over time due to changes in interest rates, as well as changes in the perceived riskiness of the asset, or in the premium required by investors for a given amount of risk. Since investors are free to choose among many different assets, the rate required for any one asset is influenced by the expected returns for all others. For example, the returns required for stocks are influenced by the returns for bonds. When bond yields move substantially higher, stock prices fall to levels at which stocks will continue to offer expected returns high enough to compete with bonds.

When the market for an income-producing asset, such as a common stock, is efficient (in the sense that all information bearing on its value is reflected appropriately in its price), the expected return and required return are equal. If the expected return rises above the required return (for example, asset X in Figure 1-4), which can happen if investors do not respond immediately to favorable new information, the price of the asset will be bid up until the expected return falls to the level of the required return. Or, if the expected return drops below the required return, indicating that the price of the asset is too high (asset Y), sellers must lower the price to bring the expected return up to the level of the required return.

Composition of the Expected Return

The expected return for any risky asset is the sum of the *risk-free rate* of interest and a *risk premium,* as shown in Equation 1-1:

$$E(R_{it}) = R_{ft} + RP_{it} \qquad (1\text{-}1)$$

---

[4]The widespread aversion to significant financial risks can be seen, for example, in the demand for insurance against risks of many kinds.

where

$$E(R_{it}) = \text{expected return for asset } i \text{ at time } t$$
$$R_{ft} = \text{risk-free rate of interest at time } t$$
$$RP_{it} = \text{risk premium for asset } i \text{ at time } t$$

The risk premium is the compensation required by investors for the risk associated with a particular asset at a particular time. Risk premiums change over time as a result of changes in the perceived riskiness of assets and changes in the attitude of investors toward risk.

No investment is entirely free of risk, but U.S. Treasury bills come close. Therefore, it is customary to use the 30-day Treasury bill rate as a proxy for the risk-free rate, which is composed of the *real risk-free rate* and an inflation premium:

$$R_{ft} = r_t + p_t \qquad (1\text{-}2)$$

where

$$R_{ft} = \text{risk-free rate at time } t$$
$$r_t = \text{real rate at time } t$$
$$p_t = \text{inflation premium at time } t$$

The real risk-free rate, which is not observable in the market, can be approximated by subtracting an estimate of the expected short-term inflation rate from the yield on 30-day Treasury bills. For example, if the 30-day bill rate is 6.5% and the expected short-term inflation rate is estimated at 5.0%, the estimated real rate is approximately 1.5%.

Risk and the Required Return

A stylized plot of required returns for various types of financial assets is shown in Figure 1-5. Treasury notes and bonds are somewhat riskier than Treasury bills because of greater price fluctuations in response to changes in interest rates. Corporate bonds are riskier than Treasury bonds for various reasons, including the possibility of default.

Inflation and Taxes

Investment planning requires consideration of both inflation and taxes. Investment income increases the investor's wealth only to the extent that the nominal return exceeds the *inflation rate* plus the product of the tax rate and the nominal before-tax return on the investment. Consider Example 1-1.

EXAMPLE 1-1 AFTER-TAX REAL RETURN

Nominal before-tax return on a taxable investment	9%
Rate of inflation	6%
Income tax rate	30%

|||| **FIGURE 1-4**

Expected and Required Returns

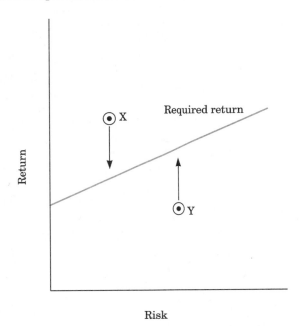

X   Underpriced: expected return too high
Y   Overpriced; expected return too low

A nominal return of 9% may seem attractive, but after allowing for inflation and taxes, the after-tax real return is only 0.3%.

Unadjusted return	9.0%
Less approximate adjustment for inflation*	(6.0)
Less taxes (.30 × 9%)	(2.7)
After-tax real return	0.3%

*More precisely, if the unadjusted return is r and the rate of inflation is i, the adjusted before-tax return is $(1 + r)/(1 + i) - 1$. In this example, the inflation-adjusted, before-tax return is $(1.09)/(1.06) - 1$, or 2.8%, which makes the more accurately calculated inflation adjustment 6.2% (9.0% − 2.8%) and the after-tax real return, 0.1%.

The investor pays tax on the nominal return of 9% even though the before-tax real return is only about 3% (9% − 6%). ||||

Due to the uncertainty of the inflation rate, no securities are entirely riskless. U.S. Treasury bills are completely free of default risk, and they are relatively immune to price fluctuations resulting from changes in market interest rates, but they are not perfectly safe. Even with Treasury bills, an unexpected increase in the rate of inflation can cause the real

|||| **FIGURE 1-5**
Required Return and Risk

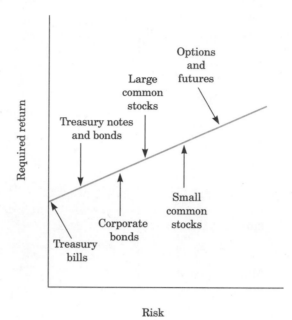

return to be lower than expected. If, for example, a Treasury bill is purchased at a yield of 8% when the expected inflation rate is 5%, the expected before-tax real return is 3% (8% − 5%), the actual before-tax real return will be only 1% if the inflation rate turns out to be 7% instead of 5%.

MARKET EFFICIENCY

No idea in the field of investments has created more controversy or been the subject of more empirical research than the idea that the money and capital markets are efficient. In a perfectly efficient market, stock and bond prices reflect all relevant information in an unbiased manner. This implies that the prices of securities are equal to their *economic values;* that is, the prices are equal to what the securities are worth in light of their riskiness and the cash income they are expected to provide.

Logic and empirical evidence both give reason to believe that the market for most widely traded stocks and bonds is quite efficient most of the time. Efficiency arises from the actions of many well-informed, profit-seeking investors who are competing with one another in an effort to earn the highest possible return at a given level of risk. It is easy to believe that investors often react quickly when prices of securities diverge materially from their economic values. Yet, as explained in Chapter 8, there is considerable evidence that stock prices do not always reflect new information promptly, nor do they always represent a rational assessment of the available information. Historical evidence indicates, for example, that common stock investors have a tendency to overreact to new information, bidding prices up too high when the information is favorable, and depressing prices too much when it is unfavorable.[5]

Most tests of *market efficiency* are based on the performance of common stocks. For example, studies are made to determine whether stocks with one or more common (special) characteristics, such as a low ratio of price to earnings per share, have provided abnormally high returns. The returns of the special stocks are compared to the returns of a diversified portfolio of stocks after adjusting for the difference in risk. If it turns out that the *risk-adjusted returns* of the special stocks are significantly higher than the returns of the diversified portfolio, it is sometimes concluded that the special stocks have earned abnormally high returns. However, there is always another possibility. Since any estimate of risk is necessarily crude, the apparent abnormality of the special-stock returns may simply reflect an improper allowance for the difference in risk.

Active and Passive Investment Strategies

Market inefficiencies may be reflected in either the mispricing of individual issues relative to one another or in the mispricing of stocks as a whole relative to bonds or other kinds of assets. Thus, investors attempting to earn abnormal returns may use two active strategies: the selection of seemingly mispriced individual issues and *market timing,* a scheme that involves moving funds into and out of stocks and other securities on the basis of expectations about the future trend of the market. Since any active strategy involves greater costs than a passive strategy, it can be successful over a long period of time only if the market is in fact inefficient, and the investor is able to find enough inefficiencies to make the search worthwhile.

In an efficient market, the best common stock strategy is a passive one, which involves buying and holding a portfolio of widely diversified stocks. For example, one might select stocks from all issues traded in a given market, such as the New York Stock Exchange, or from all stocks represented in a given market index, such as Standard & Poor's 500, the Wilshire 5000, or the Capital International World Index, which is based on stocks from 19 different countries.

Diversifying over Time

Investors who believe it is virtually impossible to earn abnormal returns by timing the market often use a dollar-cost averaging strategy. This simple plan calls for purchasing stocks or shares in a mutual fund in more or less equal dollar amounts at regular, frequent intervals of no longer than several months. The objective is to avoid making too many

[5]Werner F. M. De Bondt and Richard Thaler, "Does the Stock Market Overreact?" *The Journal of Finance* 40, no. 3 (July 1985): 793–805; and "Further Evidence on Investor Overreaction and Stock Market Seasonality," *The Journal of Finance* 42, no. 3 (July 1987): 557–81.

purchases when prices are unusually high. It also assures the investor that at least some of his or her purchases will be made when prices are down.

DIVERSIFICATION AND RISK

The overall risk of an investment is evidenced by the volatility of its return, which is generally about the same as the volatility of its price. The greater the volatility, as measured by the *standard deviation* of the return, the more difficult it is to predict what the future return will be. On the whole, stocks are riskier than bonds, and bonds are riskier than Treasury bills because the returns are less predictable. For the same reason, a single common stock is riskier than a diversified portfolio of stocks. With a diversified portfolio, price changes of individual stocks are to some degree offsetting, which causes the standard deviation of the portfolio to be smaller than a weighted average of the standard deviations of the individual securities.

The risk-reduction effects of diversification can be explained in terms of its impact on unsystematic, or *firm-specific, risk,* which is that portion of total risk that arises from unexpected developments affecting an individual firm or its industry. Examples of such firm-specific or industry-specific developments are raw material shortages, changes in customers' needs or desires, and changes in competitive conditions.

An investor who holds only one stock is exposed to all of the risk that may arise from unexpected adverse developments affecting that stock. But for an investor who owns stocks in two or more largely unrelated industries, there is always the chance that negative developments in one will be offset by positive developments in another. In general, the greater the number and diversity of the stocks being held, the greater the chance that positive and negative developments peculiar to individual firms or industries, or even peculiar to an entire national economy, will offset one another. For that reason, some investors now include foreign stocks in the common stock portion of their portfolios.

If a portfolio of stocks is a representative sample of all stocks in the market, it will perform like the market, and the only risk is *systematic,* or *market, risk.* Any unexpected increases or decreases in the return are solely the result of market-wide factors, such as an unexpected change in interest rates or in the outlook for corporate profits.

FINANCIAL LEVERAGE

When funds can be borrowed at an interest rate lower than the expected return on the assets to be purchased with the borrowed funds, investors have an incentive to finance investments in part with borrowed money. However, when borrowed funds are used, the range of the investor's possible returns widens, and there is greater chance of a loss. *Leverage* has a positive effect if the return on the securities is higher than the interest rate on the borrowed money, but a negative effect if the rate of return on the securities is lower than the interest rate on the borrowed funds. Thus, decisions about leverage involve a trade-off between risk and return. In deciding whether to use leverage, it is important to calculate the returns under a number of possible outcomes, including the worst along with the best that can be imagined.

|||| SUMMARY

Successful investing requires careful consideration of a number of factors, among the most important of which are the investor's objectives and tolerance for risk. Anyone who is unwilling to think about objectives, risk tolerance, or the relative risks and expected returns of different investments is likely to invest too cautiously and sacrifice potential income or too aggressively and sustain large losses.

Investing involves a trade-off between risk and the expected return. Riskier investments usually offer the possibility of higher returns, which makes them attractive to many investors. However, the actual returns on riskier assets are sometimes lower than on safer investments for extended periods of time. Investing in stocks, bonds, and other securities requires an understanding of their risk-return characteristics. Only if one has this knowledge, is it possible to make intelligent investment decisions. Inflation and taxes must also be taken into account because the return is not a meaningful figure until it has been adjusted for these factors.

The market for most widely traded securities is quite efficient most of the time. On the whole, prices do not differ widely from economic values for extended periods. Thus, it is difficult to earn extraordinary returns by selecting individual issues that seem to be underpriced or by timing the market, which involves moving funds between stocks, bonds, and other assets on the basis of forecasts of their future relative returns. However, the securities markets are not perfectly efficient. Prices do not always respond promptly to new information, and they are sometimes driven too high or too low by investors' overreaction to positive or negative developments affecting individual firms, industries, or the economy.

The most appropriate investment strategy for most individuals is to buy and hold a well-diversified portfolio of assets. Diversification eliminates unsystematic risk and thereby reduces fluctuations in the value of a portfolio and the possibility of large losses. With a fully diversified portfolio, only systematic, or market, risk remains.

A popular method of trying to earn above-average returns is to invest partly with borrowed money. Leveraging a portfolio can either increase or decrease the return on the investor's equity, depending on whether the return on the assets is higher or lower than the interest rate on the borrowed funds. In any case, it increases the range of possible outcomes and thereby increases the risk.

|||| # QUESTIONS

1. Describe the historical relationship between risk and the rate of return for large and small common stocks, corporate bonds, U.S. Treasury bonds, and U.S. Treasury bills.

2. Explain the relationship between risk and the expected return.

3. Explain the relationship between the expected return and the required return.

4. Explain what is meant by the trade-off between risk and return.

5. What two adjustments must be made to the nominal return to determine an investor's "true" return? How are they made?

6. Explain how the following are related: expected return, risk-free rate, real rate, inflation premium, and risk premium.

7. Aside from empirical evidence, why should one believe that the securities markets in this country are quite efficient?

8. Explain how investors seek abnormal returns through stock selection and market timing. What assumptions underly the use of these active strategies?

9. Why does diversification reduce risk?

10. What is systematic risk? Why does diversification not reduce this kind of risk?

11. What should be considered in deciding whether to leverage a portfolio of common stocks?

|||| # SELECTED REFERENCES

Atchison, Michael D., Richard F. DeMong, and John L. Kling. *New Financial Instruments: A Descriptive Guide*. Charlottesville, Va.: The Financial Analysts Research Foundation, 1985.

De Bondt, Werner, and Richard Thaler. "Does the Stock Market Overreact?" *The Journal of Finance,* 40, no. 3 (July 1985): 793–805.

————, "Further Evidence on Investor Overreaction and Stock Market Seasonality." *The Journal of Finance* 42, no. 3 (July 1987): 557–81.

Finnerty, John D. "Financial Engineering in Corporate Finance: An Overview." *Financial Management* 17, no. 4 (Winter 1988): 14–33.

Stocks, Bonds, Bills and Inflation: 1991 Yearbook. Chicago: Ibbotson Associates, Inc., 1991.

2 STOCKS, BONDS, AND OTHER SECURITIES

How can a person learn to make wise choices from the bewildering variety of investment media currently available? Certainly, the first step is to gain an awareness of the principal kinds of investments and to develop an understanding of their basic characteristics. The purpose of this chapter is to introduce you to a number of financial investments, with primary emphasis on marketable securities. Many of the securities discussed in this chapter are analyzed in considerable depth in later chapters.

TYPES OF SECURITIES

As Table 2-1 shows, securities can be broadly classified into two groups: marketable and nonmarketable. The most important nonmarketable securities are nonnegotiable *certificates of deposit* (issued by commercial banks and thrift institutions), *U.S. saving bonds,* cash value life insurance, and annuities. A potential disadvantage of nonmarketable securities is their relative illiquidity. They cannot be sold, and an interest penalty is sustained if they are surrendered for cash before maturity.

Marketable securities are classified into three groups: *money market,* capital market, and *derivative securities*. Money market securities are debt instruments that mature in one year or less. On the whole, they are safe and highly liquid. Included are U.S. Treasury bills, *negotiable certificates of deposit, commercial paper, bankers' acceptances,* and *Eurodollar certificates of deposit*. Since most money market securities are in denominations of $10,000 or more, many individuals invest in these securities indirectly through money market mutual funds.

Capital market securities include common stocks and all fixed-income securities that either have no maturity or mature in more than one year. Thus, *preferred stocks,* notes and bonds with maturities of more than one year, and mortgage-backed securities are all classified as capital market securities. A derivative security is one whose value is determined by the expected future value of another security or group of securities. Derivative securities include *stock purchase warrants,* stock options, *stock index options, interest rate futures,* and *options on futures*. Trading of options and futures has grown dramatically over the last two decades.

|||| **TABLE 2-1**
Financial Assets (Partial List)

Nonmarketable assets
    Savings certificates
    U.S. savings bonds
    Cash value life insurance policies
    Annuities
Marketable assets
    Money market securities
        U.S. Treasury bills
        Commercial paper
        Negotiable certificates of deposit
        Bankers' acceptances
        Eurodollar certificates of deposit
    Capital market securities
        U.S. Treasury notes and bonds
        Agencies (notes and bonds of government-sponsored or-
            ganizations)
        Municipal bonds
        Corporate notes and bonds
        Mortgage-backed securities
        Common stock
        Preferred stock
        Convertible securities
            Convertible bonds
            Convertible preferred stock
Derivative securities
    Stock purchase warrants
    Exchange-traded options on individual stocks
    Options on stock indexes
    Financial futures
        Stock index futures
        Interest rate futures
    Options on futures

DEBT AND EQUITY SECURITIES OUTSTANDING

Table 2-2 shows the amounts of debt and equity securities of U.S. issuers outstanding at December 31, 1985, and June 30, 1990.[1] The amounts reported for debt securities are the amounts owed; equity securities are shown at market values. The large increases in bonds and other debt securities reflect a growing reliance on debt financing by governments as well as business corporations. From the end of 1985 to mid-1990, debt securities as a whole grew almost twice as fast as the gross national product. By far the fastest growing debt, as Figure 2-1 shows, were *mortgage-backed issues* and corporate bonds.

In the remainder of this chapter, the various securities are discussed in the order in which they are listed in Table 2-1.

[1]Except for U.S. savings bonds, the debt securities in Table 2-2 exclude nonmarketable issues.

NONMARKETABLE SECURITIES

Securities that can be converted to cash only by submission to the issuer for redemption are among the most important investments for individuals. Two of these, *savings certificates* and U.S. savings bonds, are discussed briefly in the following paragraphs. Although cash value life insurance and annuities are also very important investment media, they are outside the scope of this book. It is worth noting, however, that insurance and annuity contracts can be analyzed using techniques similar to those we will be examining for bonds and other fixed-income securities.

Savings Accounts

Table 2-3 shows the average annual rates offered by large commercial banks and thrift institutions (primarily savings and loan association and mutual savings banks) on certain accounts and savings certificates on January 2, 1991, compared to the maximum rate on U.S. savings bonds at that time. One advantage of savings certificates over a number of other investments is that if issued by an insured institution, they, together with deposits, are protected up to a total of $100,000 for any one investor. However, the yields tend to be lower than the yields for marketable U.S. Treasury securities of comparable maturities. Further, if a savings certificate is redeemed early, the holder sacrifices some of the accrued interest. For that reason, certificate holders who are in need of immediate

---

||| **TABLE 2-2**

Debt and Equity Securities of U.S. Issuers, 1985 and 1990

	Amount (Billions)		Percentage Increase	Percentage of Total	
	12/31/85	6/30/90		1985	1990
Debt securities					
U.S. Treasuries	$1,597	$ 2,366	48%	25.1%	23.5%
Agencies[a]	258	379	47	4.0	3.8
State and local governments	474	637	34	7.5	6.3
Corporate bonds	747	1,461	96	11.8	14.5
Mortgage-backed[b]	369	936	154	5.8	9.3
Open market paper[c]	325	536	65	5.1	5.3
Total	3,770	6,315	68	59.3	62.7
Equity securities (excluding mutual funds)	2,584	3,752	45	40.7	37.3
Total debt and equity	6,354	10,067	58	100.0	100.0
Gross national product[d]	4,015	5,443	36		

[a]Agencies are debt securities issued by corporations, such as the Federal National Mortgage Association, that were created but are not owned by the federal government.

[b]Mortgage-backed securities are debt instruments issued with the backing of residential real estate loans.

[c]Open market paper (excluding U.S. Treasury bills, which are included in U.S. Treasuries) consists of bankers' acceptances, negotiable certificates of deposit, and commercial paper.

[d]Gross national product for 1990 is the seasonally adjusted annual rate for the second quarter.

SOURCE: *Federal Reserve Bulletin.*

|||| **FIGURE 2-1**

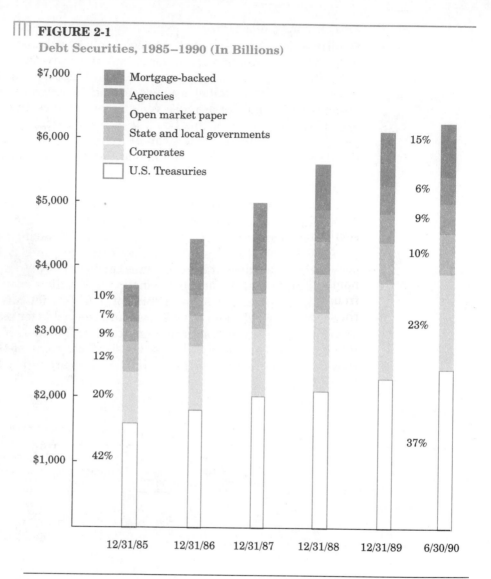

Debt Securities, 1985–1990 (In Billions)

SOURCE: *Federal Reserve Bulletin.*

funds often pledge their certificates as collateral for a loan from the issuing bank or thrift institution. The interest rate on such loans is typically about two percentage points above the rate on the pledged certificates.

United States Savings Bonds

The U.S. Treasury issues two kinds of savings bonds, series EE and series HH. The series EE bonds, with a maturity of 12 years, are issued at 50% of face value and can be redeemed at a higher price at any time after six months. The series HH bonds, which can be acquired only in exchange for EE bonds, are issued at face value and pay interest semiannually. In early 1991 the annual rate for HH bonds was 6%. The effective interest rate on an EE bond depends on the length of the holding period; if the bond is held for more than five years, the rate may also be affected by the rates on U.S. Treasury securities during the period the bond has been held.

For the first five years, the nominal rate on EE bonds increases with the holding period, starting with 4.16% after six months and increasing to 6.00% if held for the full five years. Interest is compounded semiannually, which makes the effective rate 6.09%. If series EE bonds are held for more than five years, the nominal rate is the higher of 6% or 85% of the average annual rate on five-year U.S. Treasury securities during the investor's holding period. Thus, if the average rate on five-year U.S. Treasury securities during the investor's holding period was 8.0%, the bond would earn 6.8% (.85 × 8%), which is an effective rate of 6.92% with semiannual compounding.

Series EE savings bonds are sometimes more attractive than savings certificates issued by banks and other financial institutions, even if the nominal interest rate is lower. Not only is savings bond interest exempt from state income taxes, but federal income taxes can be deferred until the bonds have matured if the holder so chooses. Also, if interest rates are expected to decline materially, an investor may feel it is advantageous to lock in a minimum rate of 6% for a period of 12 years. In addition, for some taxpayers, the interest received on redemption of a series EE bond is excluded from taxable income to the extent that the taxpayer has paid expenses for higher education during the year for himself or herself, for his or her spouse, or for a dependent. On the other hand, if series EE bonds are held only a few years, the rates are much lower than the rates on savings certificates.

For many investors, U.S. savings bonds are not as attractive as marketable Treasury securities. Not only are the rates on marketable issues generally higher, but the marketable issues can be pledged as collateral for a loan. Nevertheless, for various reasons, individuals hold series EE and HH bonds with a total redemption value of about $100 billion. They offer a potential tax advantage over the marketable issues and greater certainty as to the cash value at any future time. Unlike marketable issues, the cash value of a savings bond does not decline with an increase in interest rates.

|||| **TABLE 2-3**

Consumer Savings Rates, January 2, 1991

Money market deposits	5.74%
Six-month savings certificates	7.03
One-year savings certificates	7.09
Thirty-month accounts	7.20
Five-year savings certificates	7.44
U.S. savings bonds	7.19*

*Guaranteed minimum 6%.

SOURCE: *The Wall Street Journal,* January 3, 1991.

MARKETABLE SECURITIES

Money Market Securities

If you want an investment that may be almost as safe and liquid as a bank account, depending on the issuer, you may find money market securities attractive. They are short-term marketable debt securities issued by the U.S. government, state and local governments, bank holding companies, and corporations of many kinds as well as thrift institutions and certain other entities.

Treasury Bills The safest and most liquid of all money market securities are the Treasury bills (T-bills) of the U.S. government. They are issued on a discount basis (that is, for less than face value), and the holder receives the face amount at maturity. Since 1982, all Treasury bills have been issued in book-entry form and thus exist only on a computerized record. The investor receives a receipt rather than an engraved Treasury bill. With rare exceptions, U.S. Treasury bills mature in 12, 26, or 52 weeks (3, 6, or 12 months).

Treasury bills offer slightly lower yields than other money market securities because they are free of default risk, and the interest is exempt from state and local income taxes. Due to the extremely large volume of trading and relatively stable prices, government securities dealers require only a small spread between the prices at which they offer to buy (the bid price) or sell (the asked price) a particular issue. Thus, transaction costs in the Treasury bill market are low.

Treasury bills can be purchased either at the time of issuance or later in the secondary market. New three-month and six-month bills are auctioned every Monday by the Federal Reserve, acting as agent for the Treasury. New one-year bills are auctioned on the fourth Thursday of each month. Bids for new bills may be submitted through any of the 12 Federal Reserve Banks. Bids are of two kinds: competitive and noncompetitive. Competitive bidders are required to state the amount they wish to purchase and the yield at which they are willing to buy. Noncompetitive bidders need only state the amount of bills they wish to purchase. All noncompetitive bids are accepted at a price equal to a weighted average of the accepted competitive bids.

Bank Discount Yield Quotations for Treasury bills in the *Wall Street Journal* and other papers are in terms of yields rather than prices, as shown in Figure 2-2. Three kinds of yields are calculated for Treasury bills. The bid and asked quotations are stated in terms of the *bank discount yield;* the figure in the right-hand column is the *bond equivalent yield*. A third measure, not shown in Figure 2-2, is the *effective, or compounded, yield*. The following are the January 10, 1991, quotations for the bills due May 30, 1991:

Quotation Date	Maturity Date	Bid	Asked	Yield
1/10/91	5/30/91	6.26%	6.24%	6.48%

|||| **FIGURE 2-2**

Treasury Bill Quotations, January 10, 1991

Maturity	Days to Mat.	Bid	Asked	Chg.	Ask Yld.
TREASURY BILLS					
Jan 17 '91	3	5.28	5.20	−0.56	5.27
Jan 24 '91	10	5.26	5.20	−0.57	5.28
Jan 31 '91	17	5.40	5.36	−0.26	5.45
Feb 07 '91	24	5.45	5.41	−0.21	5.50
Feb 14 '91	31	5.64	5.62	−0.13	5.73
Feb 21 '91	38	5.98	5.96	−0.08	6.08
Feb 28 '91	45	6.00	5.98	−0.14	6.11
Mar 07 '91	52	6.07	6.05	−0.12	6.19
Mar 14 '91	59	6.15	6.13	−0.08	6.28
Mar 21 '91	66	6.17	6.15	−0.06	6.31
Mar 28 '91	73	6.17	6.15	−0.05	6.31
Apr 04 '91	80	6.20	6.18	−0.04	6.35
Apr 11 '91	87	6.21	6.19	−0.04	6.37
Apr 18 '91	94	6.20	6.18	−0.02	6.37
Apr 25 '91	101	6.28	6.26	−0.05	6.46
May 02 '91	108	6.25	6.23	−0.03	6.44
May 09 '91	115	6.26	6.24	−0.03	6.46
May 16 '91	122	6.26	6.24	−0.06	6.46
May 23 '91	129	6.26	6.24	−0.06	6.47
May 30 '91	136	6.26	6.24	−0.06	6.48
Jun 06 '91	143	6.20	6.18	−0.05	6.42
Jun 13 '91	150	6.26	6.24	−0.02	6.50
Jun 20 '91	157	6.28	6.26	−0.04	6.53
Jun 27 '91	164	6.21	6.19	−0.05	6.46
Jul 05 '91	172	6.31	6.29	−0.02	6.57
Jul 11 '91	178	6.28	6.26	−0.03	6.55
Aug 01 '91	199	6.28	6.26	−0.06	6.56
Aug 29 '91	227	6.28	6.26	−0.06	6.57
Sep 26 '91	255	6.21	6.19	−0.05	6.50
Oct 24 '91	283	6.30	6.28	−0.07	6.62
Nov 21 '91	311	6.30	6.28	−0.06	6.64
Dec 19 '91	339	6.24	6.22	−0.04	6.61

SOURCE: *The Wall Street Journal*, January 11, 1991. Reprinted by permission of *The Wall Street Journal*, © Dow Jones and Company, Inc. (1991). All Rights Reserved Worldwide.

The *bid* of 6.26% is the bank discount yield based on the price at which dealers were buying; the *asked quotation* of 6.24% is the bank discount yield based on the price at which dealers were selling. Dealers require a slightly higher yield (lower price) on the bills they are buying than on the bills they are selling. The yield of 6.48% in the right-hand column is the bond equivalent yield based on the asked price. You will note that the bond equivalent yield is 0.24% (6.48 − 6.24), or 24 basis points, higher than the asked bank discount yield.

The formula for calculating the bank discount yield is

$$BDY = (D/F) \times (360/N) \tag{2-1}$$

where

BDY = bank discount yield

D = amount of discount for $10,000 of face value

F = face value of $10,000

N = number of days to maturity

To determine any Treasury bill yield, it is necessary to know the amount of the discount, which can be calculated with the following equation derived from Equation 2-1:

$$D = BDY \times 10,000 \times (N/360) \tag{2-2}$$

Given the bank discount yield of 6.24% on the asked side of the market and $N = 140$ (the number of days from January 10 to May 30), the amount of the discount for a $10,000 bill was $242.67, calculated as follows:

$$D = .0624 \times 10{,}000 \times 140/360$$
$$= 624 \times .38889$$
$$= \$242.67$$

Thus, the asked price was $9,757.33 ($10,000 − $242.67).

The price at which dealers were buying a $10,000 Treasury bill due May 30, based on the bid of 6.26%, was $9,756.55:

$$D = .0626 \times 10{,}000 \times 140/360$$
$$= 626 \times .38889$$
$$= \$243.45$$
$$P = 10{,}000 - D$$
$$= 10{,}000 - 243.45$$
$$= \$9{,}756.55$$

Note that the dealer's spread per $10,000 of face value (the asked price minus the bid price) was $0.78 ($9,757.33 − $9,756.55). This is .0078% of face value and would amount to $78 on bills of $1,000,000.

The formula for calculating the bond equivalent yield is

$$BEY = (D/P) \times (365/N)$$

where

$$BEY = \text{bond equivalent yield}$$
$$P = \text{price}$$

For the bill maturing May 30, 1991, on which the discount based on the asked price was $242.67, and the asked price itself was $9,757.33, the bond equivalent yield of 6.48% is calculated as follows:

$$BEY = \left(\frac{242.67}{9{,}757.33}\right) \times \left(\frac{365}{140}\right)$$
$$= .02487 \times 2.60714$$
$$= .0648 \text{ or } 6.48\%$$

The bond equivalent yield is 24 basis points (6.48 − 6.24) higher than the bank discount yield for two reasons: the formula for BEY relates the discount to the price of the bill rather than to its face value, and it annualizes the yield with 365 days rather than 360.

The effective, or compounded, yield (EY) is calculated as follows:

$$EY = [1 + (D/P)]^{365/N} - 1$$

For the bill maturing May 30, 1991, the effective yield is 6.61%:

$$EY = \left(1 + \frac{242.67}{9{,}757.33}\right)^{365/140} - 1$$

$$= 1.02487^{2.60714} - 1$$
$$= 1.0661 - 1$$
$$= .0661, \text{ or } 6.61\%$$

Compounding raises the yield from 6.48% to 6.61%, or by 13 basis points.

Commercial Paper Many finance companies, bank holding companies, and other large corporations do much of their short-term borrowing with unsecured notes, which are referred to as commercial paper. The notes are in bearer form and may be either on a discount basis, like Treasury bills, or an interest-bearing basis. Typically, individual notes are for more than $100,000. Large firms sell their paper directly to investors, while smaller companies sell through commercial paper dealers, which are generally investment banking firms. Dealers buy the notes of smaller issuers, add a markup of perhaps one-eighth of 1%, and sell the notes to investors.

Most commercial paper is backed either by a commercial bank open line of credit—a strong moral commitment by a bank to make loans to the issuer up to a stated maximum amount—or by a bank letter of credit, which is a legal commitment by a bank for which the issuer pays a fee. Most individual investing in commercial paper is done indirectly through money market mutual funds.

A large proportion of all commercial paper is rated by at least one of the bond rating agencies. Although commercial paper issuers pay the rating agencies for this service, it is unlikely that such payments result in any bias in the ratings since the success of a rating agency depends upon its ability to issue credible ratings. Investors would soon recognize any bias, and the ratings would become meaningless.

No matter how strong the issuer and how good the backing, there is some credit risk with any commercial paper. Because of this risk and the taxability of the interest by state and local governments, yields on high-quality commercial paper are a little higher than the yields on U.S. Treasury bills.

Negotiable Certificates of Deposit All of the large money center banks and approximately 200 regional banks and thrift institutions issue negotiable certificates of deposit (CDs), which are essentially short-term, unsecured notes. Some are sold directly to investors, while others are distributed through dealers, who also buy and sell previously issued CDs in the secondary market. Negotiable CDs of the larger and stronger issuers can be sold almost as readily as U.S. Treasury bills.

Most negotiable CDs mature within one year. They are usually issued in bearer form and, unlike Treasury bills, are issued on an interest-bearing rather than discount basis. Some CDs are issued with a floating rate, which is usually tied to a specified Treasury bill rate or to the composite rate for the negotiable CDs of major banks. As with commercial paper, the yields on negotiable CDs are invariably somewhat higher than Treasury bill yields because of the default risk and taxability of the interest by state and local governments. In recent years, the spread between

CD and Treasury bill yields has generally ranged between 50 and 100 basis opints, or from 0.5 to 1%. However, as Figure 2-3 shows, it has sometimes been much larger, reflecting an increase in the perceived riskiness of CDs, an increase in the risk aversion of investors, or a combination of the two.

Bankers' Acceptances   Typically, acceptances are created by banks to finance imports or exports. They are issued on a discount basis, and the yields are comparable to the yields on negotiable CDs and the highest-grade commercial paper. From an investor's perspective, a bankers' acceptance is similar to a negotiable CD since both are debt instruments issued by a bank. However, there are two differences: first, an acceptance is "two-name paper," and as such, it is a primary liability of the accepting bank and a secondary liability of the drawer of the acceptance; second, bankers' acceptances are not covered by FDIC insurance. Since acceptances are generally for large amounts, the market is dominated by institutional investors.

Eurodollars   Dollar-denominated deposits in banks outside the United States (including foreign branches of U.S. banks) and in branches of foreign banks in the United States are called Eurodollars. Most Eurodollars are either nonnegotiable time deposits or negotiable CDs, and

|||| **FIGURE 2-3**

Spread between Three-Month CD and Treasury Bill Rates, September 1976–June 1990

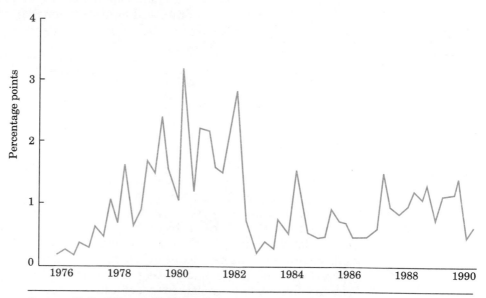

SOURCE: *Federal Reserve Bulletin.*

they are usually large. While Eurodollars were first created in Europe, many are now issued by banks in other places, including, for example, Canada, Japan, Hong Kong, Singapore, and the Bahamas.

Rates on Eurodollar CDs are often slightly higher than the rates on domestic CDs in the United States. Issuers of Eurodollar CDs are able to pay higher rates because Eurodollar deposits are free of FDIC insurance premiums and need not be backed by legal reserves.

Capital Market Securities

Long-term debt securities (e.g., notes, bonds, and mortgage-backed securities), common stocks, preferred stocks, *convertible bonds,* and *convertible preferred stocks* are referred to as capital market securities. Since they either have a long maturity or no maturity, capital market securities tend to be held for long periods. In this chapter, we will examine them briefly, reserving more detailed discussions for later chapters.

Marketable U.S. Treasury Notes, Bonds, and STRIPS Marketable long-term securities issued by the U.S. government include *Treasury notes,* Treasury bonds, and *STRIPS.*[2] The latter are zero-coupon issues derived from Treasury notes and bonds with maturities of 10 or more years.

The original maturities of Treasury notes range from 2 to 10 years, and the maturities of Treasury bonds are usually from 15 to 30 years. The longer maturities make the prices of notes, bonds, and STRIPS more sensitive than Treasury bills to changes in interest rates.

The interest payments on bonds are referred to as the coupons, or *coupon payments*. Thus, Treasury notes and bonds, which pay interest twice a year, are coupon issues. STRIPS are *zero-coupon securities* since they are issued at a discount, pay no periodic interest, and are redeemed at face value at maturity. Interest on all U.S. Treasury securities is exempt from state and local income taxes, but not from the federal income tax.

Virtually all Treasury note and bond issues are sold at auctions, which are less frequent than the auctions for Treasury bills. The minimum denomination for notes and bonds is $1,000.

Treasury securities are usually traded in the over-the-counter market, where investors buy from and sell to securities dealers rather than other investors. Dealers for Treasury securities include several large securities firms and a number of major banks. Treasury bonds are listed on the New York Stock Exchange, but few are traded there.

Price Quotations Published quotations for Treasury securities are representative prices obtained from the Federal Reserve Bank of New

---

[2]STRIPS is the acronym for Separate Trading of Registered Interest and Principal of Securities. Since January 1985, all new U.S. Treasury note and bond issues with maturities of at least 10 years are transferable in their component pieces (that is, pieces of each interest payment and the principal payment) on the Federal Reserve wire system. The buyer of a STRIP acquires ownership of a piece of a future interest payment or a piece of the principal payment for a particular bond issue.

York, and they are based on data supplied by dealers for transactions of $1 million or more. Prices of Treasury notes, bonds, and STRIPS are quoted in 32nds. For example, the asked price of 98.16 for the 8.00% notes maturing in August 1999, reported in Figure 2-4, means 98 and $^{16}/_{32}$, indicating a price equal to 98.50% of face value, or $985 for a $1,000 note. With the bid price at 98.12 and the asked price at 98.16, the dealer's spread is $^4/_{32}$, or 0.125%, which amounts to $125 on a round lot of 100 bonds with a total face value of $100,000. On odd-lot transactions, dealers add a service charge or price adjustment. Investors can buy odd lots through banks or brokerage firms.

Any STRIP with a long maturity sells at a very large discount. For example, the asked price for the issue maturing May 2009 was $20^{30}/_{32}$, or 20.9375% of face value, which is $209.38 for a STRIP with a maturity value of $1,000. If a STRIP is held by a taxable investor and is not in a tax-deferred account (such as an IRA), the interest is subject to federal income tax as it accrues, even though no interest is received until the STRIP matures or is sold.

As with Treasury bills, the quoted yields for notes and bonds are on the asked side of the market. For example, the yield of 8.25% on the 8% notes of August 1999 is the *yield to maturity* at the asked price of $98^{16}/_{32}$.[3] For issues that are callable prior to final maturity, such as the $11^3/_4$'s of February 2005-10 that mature in 2010 but are callable in 2005, the yield is figured to the call date if the price is above par and to the final maturity if the price is at a discount.

Securities of Government-Sponsored Organizations Securities of a number of enterprises that were created, and in some cases originally owned, by the federal government, are known as *agency issues*. The outstanding agency debt is roughly 15% as large as the U.S. Treasury debt. The five principal issuers and the amounts of their outstanding obligations on June 30, 1990, are shown in Table 2-4.

Three of the five largest issuers of agency securities (Federal Home Loan Banks, Federal National Mortgage Association, and Federal Home Loan Mortgage Corporation) were created to promote home ownership by increasing the availability of housing credit. The other two large issuers, the Farm Credit Banks and the Student Loan Marketing Association, were set up to provide agricultural credit and to encourage student loans, respectively.

None of the five largest issuers of agency securities are owned by the federal government, and none of their obligations are guaranteed by the government. Two of the five, the Federal National Mortgage Association (or Fannie Mae) and the Student Loan Marketing Association (or Sallie

---

[3]Yield to maturity is the compound annual rate of return an investor will earn if the security is purchased at the quoted price and held to maturity, assuming annual reinvestment of the interest payments at a rate equal to the yield to maturity. It is like the internal rate of return for a capital expenditure.

FIGURE 2-4

U.S. Treasury Notes and Bonds, January 9, 1991

TREASURY BONDS, NOTES & BILLS

Wednesday, January 9, 1991

Representative Over-the-Counter quotations based on transactions of $1 million or more.

Treasury bond, note and bill quotes are as of mid-afternoon. Colons in bid-and-asked quotes represent 32nds; 101:01 means 101 1/32. Net changes in 32nds. n-Treasury note. Treasury bill quotes in hundredths, quoted on terms of a rate of discount. Days to maturity calculated from settlement date. All yields are to maturity and based on the asked quote. For bonds callable prior to maturity, yields are computed to the earliest call date for issues quoted above par and to the maturity date for issues below par. *-When issued.

Source: Federal Reserve Bank of New York.

U.S. Treasury strips as of 3 p.m. Eastern time, also based on transactions of $1 million or more. Colons in bid-and-asked quotes represent 32nds; 101:01 means 101 1/32. Net changes in 32nds. Yields calculated on the bid quotation. ci-stripped coupon interest. bp-Treasury bond, stripped principal. np-Treasury note, stripped principal.

Source: Bear, Stearns & Co. via Street Software Technology Inc.

GOVT. BONDS & NOTES

Rate	Maturity Mo/Yr	Bid	Asked	Chg.	Ask Yld.
11 3/4	Jan 91n	100:02	100:04	− 1	0.24
9	Jan 91n	100:04	100:06	....	5.33
7 3/8	Feb 91n	100:01	100:03	....	6.20
9 1/8	Feb 91n	100:07	100:09	....	5.93
9 3/8	Feb 91n	100:10	100:12	− 1	6.31
6 3/4	Mar 91n	99:30	100:00	− 1	6.62
9 3/4	Mar 91n	100:19	100:21	− 1	6.50
12 3/8	Apr 91n	101:12	101:14	− 1	6.52
9 1/4	Apr 91n	100:23	100:25	− 1	6.49
8 1/8	May 91n	100:14	100:16	....	6.55
14 1/2	May 91n	102:19	102:23	....	6.25
8 3/4	May 91n	100:23	100:25	....	6.60
7 7/8	Jun 91n	100:16	100:18	− 1	6.62
8 1/4	Jun 91n	100:22	100:24	....	6.59
13 3/4	Jul 91n	103:15	103:17	....	6.61
7 3/4	Jul 91n	100:17	100:19	+ 1	6.64
7 1/2	Aug 91n	100:13	100:15	+ 1	6.69
8 3/4	Aug 91n	101:03	101:05	....	6.74
14 7/8	Aug 91n	104:22	104:26	....	6.52
8 1/4	Aug 91n	100:26	100:28	+ 1	6.82
8 3/8	Sep 91n	101:01	101:03	....	6.79
9 1/8	Sep 91n	101:18	101:20	+ 1	6.77
12 1/4	Oct 91n	103:30	104:00	+ 1	6.76
7 5/8	Oct 91n	100:18	100:20	....	6.81
6 1/2	Nov 91n	99:21	99:23	+ 1	6.85
8 1/2	Nov 91n	101:09	101:11	....	6.84
14 1/4	Nov 91n	105:31	106:03	+ 1	6.71
7 3/4	Nov 91n	100:21	100:23	+ 1	6.90
7 5/8	Dec 91n	100:21	100:23	+ 1	6.85
8 1/4	Dec 91n	101:08	101:10	+ 1	6.83
11 5/8	Jan 92n	104:16	104:18	+ 1	6.88
8 1/8	Jan 92n	101:05	101:07	....	6.91
6 5/8	Feb 92n	99:18	99:20	....	6.99
9 1/8	Feb 92n	102:05	102:07	+ 1	6.99
14 5/8	Feb 92n	107:27	107:31	+ 1	6.95
8 1/2	Feb 92n	101:18	101:20	+ 1	6.99
7 7/8	Mar 92n	100:31	101:01	+ 1	6.98
8 1/2	Mar 92n	101:22	101:24	+ 2	6.98
11 3/4	Apr 92n	105:17	105:19	+ 1	7.03
8 7/8	Apr 92n	102:06	102:08	....	7.04
6 5/8	May 92n	99:14	99:16	+ 1	7.02
9	May 92n	102:13	102:15	+ 2	7.04
13 3/4	May 92n	108:14	108:16	+ 1	7.01
8 1/2	May 92n	101:26	101:28	+ 1	7.06
8 1/4	Jun 92n	101:20	101:22	+ 1	7.02
8 3/8	Jun 92n	101:24	101:26	+ 1	7.06
10 3/8	Jul 92n	104:18	104:20	+ 1	7.09
8	Jul 92n	101:08	101:10	+ 1	7.09

Rate	Maturity Mo/Yr	Bid	Asked	Chg.	Ask Yld.
7 3/8	May 96n	97:18	97:22	− 11	7.91
7 7/8	Jul 96n	99:20	99:24	− 12	7.93
8	Oct 96n	100:02	100:06	− 12	7.96
7 1/4	Nov 96n	96:17	96:21	− 12	7.98
8	Jan 97n	99:28	100:00	− 11	8.00
8 1/2	Apr 97n	102:05	102:09	− 9	8.03
8 1/2	May 97n	102:02	102:06	− 11	8.05
8 1/2	Jul 97n	102:30	102:02	− 13	8.09
8 5/8	Aug 97n	102:19	102:23	− 13	8.09
8 3/4	Oct 97n	103:07	103:09	− 14	8.11
8 7/8	Nov 97n	103:26	103:30	− 13	8.11
8 1/8	Feb 98n	99:29	100:01	− 14	8.12
7	May 93-98	93:19	93:27	− 16	8.13
9	May 98n	104:12	104:16	− 16	8.17
9 1/4	Aug 98n	105:27	105:31	− 14	8.18
3 1/2	Nov 98	93:04	94:04	....	4.39
8 7/8	Nov 98n	103:20	103:24	− 16	8.22
8 7/8	Feb 99n	103:17	103:21	− 18	8.25
8 1/2	May 94-99	101:03	101:11	− 12	8.03
9 1/8	May 99n	105:00	105:04	− 18	8.26
8	Aug 99n	98:12	98:16	− 18	8.25
7 7/8	Nov 99n	97:14	97:18	− 17	8.27
7 7/8	Feb 95-00	97:11	97:15	− 19	8.28
8 1/2	Feb 00n	101:08	101:12	− 18	8.28
8 7/8	May 00n	103:21	103:25	− 18	8.29
8 3/8	Aug 95-00	100:24	100:28	− 13	8.14
8 3/4	Aug 00n	102:29	102:31	− 20	8.30
8 1/2	Nov 00n	101:21	101:23	− 20	8.24
11 3/4	Feb 01	123:01	123:09	− 21	8.30
13 1/8	May 01	132:31	133:07	− 19	8.28
8	Aug 96-01	98:11	98:19	− 21	8.20
13 3/8	Aug 01	135:01	135:09	− 25	8.30
15 3/4	Nov 01	151:23	151:31	− 24	8.37
14 1/4	Feb 02	141:20	141:28	− 28	8.38
11 5/8	Nov 02	123:21	123:29	− 26	8.40
10 3/4	Feb 03	117:06	117:14	− 24	8.42
10 3/4	May 03	117:08	117:16	− 25	8.44
11 1/8	Aug 03	120:08	120:16	− 25	8.45
11 7/8	Nov 03	126:06	126:14	− 27	8.46
12 3/8	May 04	130:24	131:00	− 27	8.46
13 3/4	Aug 04	141:29	142:05	− 30	8.47
11 5/8	Nov 04	125:00	125:04	− 28	8.50
8 1/4	May 00-05	100:02	100:06	− 21	8.22
12	May 05	128:10	128:14	− 38	8.53
10 3/4	Aug 05	118:07	118:11	− 27	8.53
9 3/8	Feb 06	107:26	107:30	− 26	8.44
7 5/8	Feb 02-07	93:13	93:17	− 22	8.36
7 7/8	Nov 02-07	95:15	95:19	− 21	8.37
8 3/8	Aug 03-08	99:14	99:18	− 22	8.42

U.S. TREASURY STRIPS

Mat.	Type	Bid	Asked	Chg.	Bid Yld.
Feb 91	ci	99:13	99:13	....	6.38
May 91	ci	97:24	97:24	+ 1	6.74
Aug 91	ci	96:03	96:04	+ 1	6.80
Nov 91	ci	94:16	94:17	+ 1	6.81
Feb 92	ci	92:25	92:26	+ 1	6.95
May 92	ci	91:07	91:08	+ 2	6.97
Aug 92	ci	89:13	89:14	+ 1	7.15
Nov 92	ci	87:27	87:29	− 1	7.15
Feb 93	ci	86:01	86:02	− 1	7.32
May 93	ci	84:12	84:14	− 3	7.38
Aug 93	ci	82:24	82:26	− 2	7.43
Nov 93	ci	81:19	81:21	− 2	7.29
Feb 94	ci	79:08	79:10	− 3	7.66
May 94	ci	77:19	77:22	− 4	7.73
Aug 94	ci	76:01	76:03	− 4	7.77
Nov 94	ci	74:18	74:20	− 6	7.79
Nov 94	np	74:12	74:14	− 7	7.86
Feb 95	ci	72:27	72:30	− 6	7.89
Feb 95	np	72:25	72:28	− 7	7.91
May 95	ci	71:12	71:15	− 7	7.92
May 95	np	71:11	71:14	− 8	7.93
Aug 95	ci	69:29	70:00	− 8	7.94
Aug 95	np	69:29	70:00	− 8	7.94
Nov 95	ci	68:27	68:30	− 8	7.86
Nov 95	np	68:18	68:21	− 8	7.95
May 99	np	50:15	50:18	− 10	8.37
Aug 99	ci	48:27	48:31	− 12	8.51
Aug 99	np	49:14	49:17	− 10	8.37
Nov 99	ci	47:26	47:30	− 12	8.52
Nov 99	np	48:12	48:16	− 11	8.38
Feb 00	ci	46:21	46:25	− 12	8.56
Feb 00	np	47:13	47:17	− 10	8.38
May 00	ci	45:22	45:26	− 12	8.56
May 00	bp	46:13	46:17	− 11	8.39
Aug 00	ci	44:25	44:29	− 12	8.55
Aug 00	np	45:13	45:17	− 11	8.40
Nov 00	ci	44:05	44:09	− 12	8.48
Feb 01	ci	42:25	42:29	− 12	8.59
May 01	ci	41:26	41:30	− 12	8.61
Aug 01	ci	40:30	41:02	− 12	8.61
Nov 01	ci	40:02	40:06	− 12	8.62
Feb 02	ci	39:01	39:05	− 14	8.66
May 02	ci	38:05	38:09	− 13	8.68
Aug 02	ci	37:11	37:15	− 13	8.68
Nov 02	ci	36:18	36:22	− 13	8.68
Feb 03	ci	35:22	35:26	− 12	8.70
May 03	ci	34:29	35:01	− 12	8.71
Aug 03	ci	34:05	34:09	− 12	8.71
Nov 03	ci	33:15	33:19	− 13	8.71
Feb 04	ci	32:21	32:25	− 12	8.73
May 04	ci	31:31	32:03	− 12	8.73
Aug 04	ci	31:09	31:13	− 12	8.73
Nov 04	ci	30:21	30:24	− 11	8.73
Nov 04	bp	30:19	30:23	− 12	8.74
Feb 05	ci	29:29	30:01	− 12	8.75
May 05	ci	29:09	29:13	− 12	8.75
May 05	bp	29:10	29:14	− 12	8.74
Aug 05	ci	28:21	28:25	− 11	8.75
Aug 05	bp	28:22	28:26	− 12	8.74
Nov 05	ci	28:11	28:15	− 11	8.68
Feb 06	ci	27:14	27:18	− 12	8.75
Feb 06	bp	27:29	28:00	− 11	8.64
May 06	ci	26:28	27:00	− 11	8.75
Aug 06	ci	26:10	26:13	− 11	8.75

SOURCE: *The Wall Street Journal,* January 10, 1991. Reprinted by permission of *The Wall Street Journal,*

|||| **TABLE 2-4**

Principal Issuers of Federal Agency Securities and Their Debt Outstanding, June 30, 1990 (In Billions)

Federal Home Loan Banks	$123
Federal Home Loan Mortgage Corporation	31
Federal National Mortgage Association	118
Farm Credit Banks	53
Student Loan Marketing Association	32
Total	$357

SOURCE: *Federal Reserve Bulletin.*

Mae), are owned publicly, and their stocks are listed on the New York Stock Exchange. The other three are owned by participating organizations, such as savings and loan associations and federal land banks.

Although the federal government does not guarantee agency securities, the goals of the agencies have received government endorsement to such an extent and are considered so important to housing, agriculture, and higher education, that it is thought unlikely Congress would allow the agencies to fail. Since investors believe these securities are almost as safe and liquid as U.S. Treasury obligations, they are traded at yields only slightly higher than the yields on Treasury securities.

Municipal Securities Securities issued by states, counties, cities, and various entities created by those governments (such as airport authorities and water districts) are called *municipals*. With certain exceptions, the interest on municipals is exempt from federal income taxes and from state income taxes in the state of issuance. The value of the exemption depends on the investor's marginal tax rate. Thus, municipal securities are often attractive to individuals in higher tax brackets but unattractive to organizations exempt from federal income taxes.

Municipals backed by the full taxing power of the issuer are known as *general obligation bonds* (GOs), while those backed only by revenues from the project for which they were issued (such as a toll bridge or university dormitory) are called *revenue bonds*. General obligation bonds are usually safer than revenue bonds issued by the same unit of government.

The Tax Reform Act of 1986 eliminated the Federal income tax exemption for certain kinds of municipal securities issued after August 6, 1986. No longer exempt are bonds issued to finance capital assets for a private business or to finance a private activity such as a sports stadium. Also, if the bonds are issued for purposes such as low-income housing or student loans, the interest is a "tax preference" item and becomes taxable if the investor is liable for the "minimum tax."

Taxable investors often have occasion to compare the yields on taxable and *tax-exempt bonds*. This can be done by calculating either the after-tax yield of the taxable bonds or the *equivalent taxable yields* of the tax-exempt bonds. If *BTY* is the before-tax yield of a fully taxable bond and

T_t is the investor's marginal tax rate (federal and state taxes combined), the investor's after-tax yield *(ATY)* can be calculated as follows:

$$ATY = BTY(1 - T_t) \qquad (2\text{-}5)$$

If *ATY* is lower than the yield on the tax-exempt municipal investment *(MY)*, the municipal investment is the more attractive of the two, unless its yield advantage is offset by other factors.

The equivalent fully taxable yield *(EFTY)* of a fully exempt municipal bond is calculated as follows:

$$EFTY = MY/(1 - T_t) \qquad (2\text{-}6)$$

If *EFTY* is greater than *BTY,* the municipal investment is the more attractive of the two, other factors aside.

Example 2-1 compares the yields of a fully taxable bond and a tax-exempt bond on a before-tax and after-tax basis.

EXAMPLE 2-1   COMPARISON OF TAXABLE AND TAX-EXEMPT
　　　　　　　 YIELDS

Facts:
　Before-tax yield of fully taxable bond *(BTY)* — 9%
　Yield of tax-exempt bond *(MY)* — 6%
　Investor's marginal tax rate, federal and state combined (T_t) — 40%
Before-tax comparison:
　Before-tax yield of fully taxable bond — 9%
　Equivalent fully taxable yield of tax-exempt bond [*EFTY* =
　　$MY/(1 - T_t)$] = [6%/(1 − .40)] = — 10%
After tax comparison:
　After-tax yield of taxable bond
　　$ATY = (BTY)(1 - T_t) = (9\%)(1 - .40) =$ — 5.4%
　Yield of tax-exempt bond — 6.0%

||||

Corporate Notes and Bonds Corporate debt securities are considerably more complicated and difficult to analyze than U.S. Treasuries. As a rule, Treasury bonds and Treasury notes are all alike except for denomination, *coupon rate,* and maturity. Corporate notes and bonds are much more diverse. Besides denomination, coupon rate, and maturity, they may differ in a number of other ways, including the characteristics of the issuer, degree of seniority or subordination, amount of default risk, callability, convertibility, and asset backing.

Corporate bonds have many names. Unsecured bonds are known as debentures, and if they are subordinated to other obligations of the issuer, they are *subordinated debentures.* Secured bonds are called *mortgage bonds* if the security is real estate, *equipment trust bonds* if the security is equipment, or *collateral trust bonds* if the backing is in the form of marketable securities. Bonds that are convertible into other securities are known as convertibles; others are *straight bonds.* Bonds that pay interest periodically are called *coupon bonds;* and bonds that can be called by the issuer before maturity are *callable bonds*. Any one bond may have a number of characteristics; for example, a common type of corporate bond is a callable subordinated convertible debenture.

Newspaper Quotations Figure 2-5 is a partial listing of corporate bonds traded on the New York Exchange, as reported in the *Wall Street Journal*. The du Pont 8½s of 16 (coupon rate 8½%, maturity 2016) are an example. The closing price of 91¼ indicates a price equal to 91.25% of the face, or par, value. For a $1,000 bond, the price was $912.50. The *current yield* of 9.3% is, to the nearest tenth of 1%, the annual interest on the bond ($85) divided by the closing market price of $912.50. Note two important differences between the quotations for corporate bonds and Treasury bonds. First, the quoted yield for corporate bonds is the current yield; for Treasury bonds it is the yield to maturity. (For long-term investors, yield to maturity is more meaningful than current yield because it reflects compounding and takes into account the prospective capital gain or loss on a bond that is selling at a discount or premium, assuming it is held to maturity and redeemed at face value.) Second, the prices of corporate bonds are expressed in 8ths, 4ths, and halves, whereas the prices of Treasury notes and bonds are expressed in 32nds.

Mortgage-Backed Securities Total mortgage debt on one- to four-family homes in the United States has increased recently at a rate of approximately $200 billion a year. A large portion of this increase in mortgage debt has been acquired by investors through the purchase of mortgage-backed securities that are issued against pools of residential real estate mortgage loans. Each security is a claim against the mortgages that have been set aside, in a pool, as backing for the set of securities to which it belongs.

A substantial portion of all mortgage-backed securities are guaranteed by the U.S. government through the Government National Mortgage Association (GNMA). These securities, with a minimum denomination of $25,000, are called *"Ginnie Mae Pass-throughs,"* or "Ginnie Maes." They are known as pass-throughs because the principal and interest payments received monthly on the mortgage loans are passed through to the holders of the securities.

Many individuals invest in Ginnie Maes indirectly through mutual funds. Since mortgage loans are often fully repaid before final maturity, there is no way to determine how quickly a pass-through security will be retired. Largely because of this uncertainty about the timing of the payments (referred to as *"repayment risk"*), Ginnie Maes offer slightly higher expected yields than U.S. Treasury securities of comparable maturities.

Common Stocks The common stockholders of a corporation are its owners. As owners, they are the residual claimants against the corporation's income and assets. If the corporation's profits are higher than expected, the shareholders' returns are apt to be high as well, but if profits are lower than expected, shareholder returns are almost sure to be low. If worst comes to worst and the corporation fails, the shareholders are last

FIGURE 2-5

Corporate Notes and Bonds, January 9, 1991

Quotations as of 4 p.m. Eastern Time
Wednesday, January 9, 1991

Volume $58,210,000

	Domestic		All Issues	
Issues traded	Wed.	Tue.	Wed.	Tue.
Issues traded	639	638	646	638
Advances	229	215	231	215
Declines	274	280	279	280
Unchanged	136	143	136	143
New highs	32	25	34	25
New lows	15	21	16	21

SALES SINCE JANUARY 1
(000 omitted)

1991	1990	1989
$254,172	$240,677	$162,940

Dow Jones Bond Averages

	−1990− High Low	−1991− High Low		−1991− Close Chg. %Yld	−1990− Close Chg.
20 Bonds	93.04 88.44	92.01 91.54		91.63 +0.09 9.51	92.83 +0.02
10 Utilities	94.48 89.23	94.21 93.60		93.99 +0.39 9.34	94.36 +0.08
10 Industrials	91.60 86.43	89.68 89.28		89.28 −0.20 9.68	91.30 −0.04

[Detailed corporate bond quotation tables follow — Bonds, Cur Yld, Vol, Close, Net Chg. columns — reproduced from The Wall Street Journal.]

in line, which means they receive nothing until all creditors and the preferred shareholders, if any, have been paid in full. In that respect, corporate stockholders are in the same position as owners of sole proprietorships or the partners in a partnership. But corporate shareholders have one distinct advantage: they are not personally liable for the debts of the corporation. Partly because of this freedom from liability, it is often much easier to sell shares in a corporation than to sell a proprietorship or an interest in a partnership.

Voting Rights Except for the holders of certain classified stock, common shareholders have the legal right to control a corporation by electing the directors and voting on certain other matters, including proposed mergers. However, a person's legal rights and effective rights are often quite different, and that is apt to be true with respect to corporate control. Shareholders vote for the directors, but in many instances the only persons running are the group selected by management. Most voting is by *proxy,* which means the shareholders sign a form (a proxy) that authorizes someone to vote in their stead at the annual meeting. Unless shareholders request otherwise, votes are cast in accordance with the recommendations of the directors as set out in the proxy. Shareholders have a real choice only if someone decides to wage a proxy battle and provides an alternative slate of directors.

Preemptive Rights A number of state statutes and corporate charters give shareholders a *preemptive right,* or the right to subscribe to any new shares in proportion to the number of shares they already hold. When shareholders have this right, new stock is issued in a *"rights offering,"* with each shareholder receiving stock rights (options to purchase the new stock) equal to the number of shares held. The terms of the offering determine how many rights and how much cash are required to purchase a new share. Stockholders can either exercise or sell their rights.

Par Value and No-Par Stock Common stock must have either a *par value* or, if it is no-par stock, a stated value. Neither par value nor stated value has any real significance. Largely ineffective are the state laws that provide that if stock is issued for less than par value and the corporation fails, the shareholders can be held personally liable for the corporation's debts in the amount that the issue price was below par. Corporations easily shield their shareholders from any such liability by issuing no-par stock or stock with a low par value. Par values ranging from one cent to one dollar are common. The par value of a stock has no influence on the market value. Market values depend on what investors think a stock is worth, not on an arbitrary value assigned to the stock by the corporation.

Common Stock Quotations The common stocks of most large corporations and many smaller companies are traded on one or more stock exchanges, in the over-the-counter market, or both. Figure 2-6 is a small portion of the quotations for New York Stock Exchange stocks on one day. The quotations show the high and low price of the stock for the last 52 weeks; the annual dividend rate in dollars and cents; the *dividend yield,* which is the annual dividend divided by the closing price of the stock; the *price/earnings (P/E) ratio,* which is the ratio of the closing price of

|||| **FIGURE 2-6**

New York Stock Exchange Common Stock Transactions, April 3, 1991

Quotations as of 4:30 p.m. Eastern Time

52 Weeks Hi	Lo	Stock	Sym	Div	Yld %	PE	Vol 100s	Hi	Lo	Close	Net Chg
		-A-A-A-									
30⅛	9⅛	AAR	AIR	.48	3.4	13	305	14½	13⅞	14⅛	+ ⅛
n 9⅜	7¾	ACM OppFd	AOF	1.03e	11.4	...	96	9⅛	9	9	− ⅛
11⅛	8¾	ACM Gvt Fd	ACG	1.26	11.5	...	1107	11⅛	11	11	...
n 8¼	6½	ACM MgdIncFd	AMF	1.01	12.6	...	575	8⅛	8	8	− ⅛
12⅝	10	ACM MgdMultFd	MMF	1.50	12.1	...	153	12½	12¼	12⅜	...
10⅞	8⅝	ACM SecFd	GSF	1.26	12.0	...	1806	10⅝	10⅜	10½	+ ⅛
9	7¼	ACM SpctmFd	SI	1.01	11.4	...	352	9	8¾	8⅞	...
26⅜	17	AL Labs A	BMD	.16	.6	21	692	26¼	26⅛	26⅛	− ⅛
3	1	AM Int	AM	...	...	...	536	1⅝	1½	1½	− ⅛
16⅞	4⅝	AM Int pf		2.00	18.6	...	226	10¾	10⅜	10¾	+ ¼
10¼	8⅝	AMEV Sec	AMV	1.05a	10.6	...	27	10	9⅞	9⅞	...
70¼	39¾	AMR	AMR	...	...	...	2749	58⅝	57½	58½	+1¼
24⅝	22¼	ANR pf		2.12	9.1	...	1	23¼	23¼	23¼	− ⅛
44¼	29¾	ARCO Chm	RCM	2.50	6.2	13	386	40⅜	40⅛	40⅛	− ¼
4	1¼	ARX	ARX	...	...	...	941	2½	2⅜	2½	+ ¼
56¼	38¼	ASA	ASA	3.00	6.5	...	484	45¾	45½	45¾	+ ¼
4	1⅞	ATT Cap yen wt		...	...	...	255	3⅞	3⅜	3⅞	+ ¼
s 49⅞	32⅝	AbbotLab	ABT	1.00	2.0	22	9673	49⅞	47¼	49⅞	+2⅞
14	9⅞	Abitibi g	ABY	.50	...	...	25	13	13	13	+ ⅛
9⅞	4½	AcmeCleve	AMT	.40	6.0	19	79	6⅝	6⅜	6⅝	+ ⅛
9⅛	4¾	AcmeElec	ACE	...	...	2	121	5	4⅞	5	+ ⅛
s 39	22	Acuson	ACN	...	...	28	473	38	36⅝	37¾	+ ½
17⅛	14⅝	AdamsExp	ADX	1.72e	10.3	...	229	16⅝	16½	16⅝	...
14½	7	AdobeRes	ADB	...	...	...	25	7¾	7⅝	7¾	...
19⅞	16	AdobeRes pf		1.84	10.8	...	8	17	17	17	− ⅛
21⅝	18⅝	AdobeRes pf		2.40	12.1	...	24	19⅞	19⅞	19⅞	...
11¾	3⅝	AdvMicro	AMD	...	...	...	9596	10¾	10⅛	10⅝	+ ½
32⅜	13	AdvMicro pf		3.00	10.1	...	541	29⅞	29½	29⅝	+ ⅛
5½	1⅝	Advest	ADV	...	...	...	270	4	3¾	3⅞	...
54⅜	29	AetnaLife	AET	2.76	6.0	8	1732	46½	46	46¾	+ ⅛
10⅞	6¼	AffilPub	AFP	.24	2.4	29	929	10⅛	9⅞	10⅛	+ ¼
22½	10⅝	Ahmanson	AHM	.88	4.9	11	3437	18	17⅜	18	+ ½
▲ 4⅜	1⅝	Aileen	AEE	...	...	8	944	5	4⅝	4⅞	+ ½
69⅝	42⅝	AirProduct	APD	1.44	2.1	16	1079	67⅝	66¼	67⅝	+1⅛
s 27	13½	AirbornFrght	ABF	.30	1.4	12	1537	21⅝	20⅛	21⅝	+1⅜

52 Weeks Hi	Lo	Stock	Sym	Div	Yld %	PE	Vol 100s	Hi	Lo	Close	Net Chg
31	22¼	AvonPdts pf		2.00	6.6	...	295	30¼	30⅛	30¼	+ ⅛
▲ 20¼	10	Aydin	AYD	.50e	2.4	14	105	20⅝	20⅛	20⅝	+ ⅝
		-B-B-B-									
37⅞	30¼	BCE Inc g	BCE	2.56	...	...	1384	35⅞	35¼	35¾	...
19⅞	7¾	BET	BEP	1.27e	10.5	7	494	12¼	12	12⅛	+ ¾
n 29⅝	18¼	BJ Svc	BJS	...	...	16	508	26¼	26	26¼	+ ⅛
11¾	3⅛	BMC	BMC	...	...	17	163	6	5⅝	5¾	+ ¼
35½	26⅝	BP Prudhoe	BPT	4.17e	13.8	8	346	30⅝	30	30¼	...
28¾	22⅝	BRE Prop	BRE	2.40	8.3	14	41	28¾	28⅝	28¾	+ ⅛
11⅝	2⅝	BRT RltyTr	BRT	...	...	...	24	3⅝	3⅜	3⅜	− ⅛
8⅞	3¾	Bairnco	BZ	.20	2.3	...	601	8⅞	8⅜	8⅞	+ ½
20¾	14¼	BakrFentrs	BKF	1.95	11.6	...	56	16¾	16½	16¾	...
34⅜	20⅜	BakrHughs	BHI	.46	1.7	24	4565	26¾	26⅜	26¾	+ ¾
21¾	15⅝	BaldorElec	BEZ	.48	2.4	14	101	20¼	19⅞	20	+ ⅛
34⅛	25⅝	Ball Cp	BLL	1.16	4.4	13	950	26½	26⅛	26⅝	+ ¼
13⅛	1⅞	BallyMfg	BLY	...	...	...	5472	5⅛	4⅝	5⅛	+ ⅜
15¾	3¾	BaltimrBcp	BBB	.60	6.9	28	1145	8⅞	8¼	8¾	+ ⅜
30⅝	24⅝	BaltimrGE	BGE	2.10	7.2	14	481	29⅛	28½	29⅛	+ ⅝
36½	19	BancOne	ONE	1.16	3.3	13	3070	35¼	34¾	35	+ ⅛
6½	2⅝	BancFla	BFL	...	...	...	45	4¼	4	4¾	+ ⅛
36⅜	23⅝	BancoBilV	BBV	1.57e	5.1	9	4	31	31	31	+ ¼
55⅞	34	BancoSantdr	STD	1.96e	3.6	9	102	53⅝	53¼	53⅝	+ ⅝
▲ ¾	⅛	BancTexas	BTX	...	...	...	903	¹³⁄₁₆	⅝	⅝ − ¹⁄₁₆
100⅛	66	Bandag	BDG	1.10	1.1	17	112	96¾	96	96⅛	− ¾
x 15¾	3	BankBost	BKB	.40	4.4	...	x6340	9⅛	8¾	9⅛	+ ¾
31⅞	11¼	BankBost pfA		3.56e	12.9	...	4	27¾	27½	27½	+ ¼
30⅛	10¾	BankBost pfB		3.44e	13.2	...	31	26	25¾	26	+ ⅝
53	16	BankBost pfC		6.32	13.5	...	z270	46¾	46½	46¾	− ¼
39¼	13¼	BankNY	BK	2.12	7.6	7	2760	28	27½	27⅝	− ⅜
34	24⅛	BankNY adj pfA		3.55e	10.5	...	3	33⅞	33½	33¾	− ⅛
▲ 37	17½	BankAmer	BAC	1.20	3.2	10	10820	37¾	36⅜	37⅞	+1
38	30½	BankAmer pf		3.42e	9.0	...	16	37⅜	37⅜	37⅜	...
66¼	55¼	BankAmer pf		6.00	9.2	...	62	65⅜	65	65¼	...
48¾	28½	BankTrst	BT	2.54	6.0	5	1735	42¼	42¼	42½	+ ½
n 14⅝	6¾	BannerAero	BAR	...	...	...	42	10⅛	10	10⅛	+ ⅛
s 36	22	Barclays	BCS	2.15i	6.7	17	595	32½	31¾	32¼	+1¼
25¾	21	Barclays pr		2.78	11.2	...	132	24⅝	24⅝	24¾	− ⅛
25	20⅝	Barclays prB		2.72	11.0	...	83	24¾	24⅝	24¾	+ ¼
25¼	21	Barclays pfC		1.90e	7.7	...	28	25	24¾	24¾	− ¼

13¾	8¾	LongvwFibr	LFB	.52a	4.0	14	531	13½	13⅛	13⅛	− ⅛
40⅞	24⅛	Loral	LOR	.88	2.3	12	893	39⅛	38¾	38⅞	+ ⅛
53⅝	34¼	LaLandExpl	LLX	1.00	2.5	21	491	40	39¼	39⅞	+ ½
45¼	20¼	LaPacific	LPX	1.08	3.5	13	870	30⅞	30⅜	30⅞	+ ½
x 29½	26¼	LaP&L pf		3.16	11.3	...	x3	28⅛	28	28	− ¼
49⅞	18⅜	Lowes Cos	LOW	.52	1.6	17	1690	31¾	30⅞	31¾	+ ⅝
59⅛	34⅞	Lubrizol	LZ	1.52	2.9	10	876	52⅞	52¼	52¾	+ ⅝
s 21¼	15⅝	LubysCafe	LUB	.46	2.3	17	1059	20¼	19¾	20	+ ⅛
45¼	28	Lukens Inc	LUC	1.48	3.4	9	205	43½	42¼	43½	+1⅝
▲ 29¼	15⅝	LuxottGp	LUX	.68e	2.3	15	467	29½	28	29¼	+1½
34⅜	21⅝	Lydall	LDL	...	...	11	65	32¼	32	32¼	...
23½	13⅛	Lyondell	LYO	1.60a	7.4	5	717	22	21½	21¾	− ¼
		-M-M-M-									
7¾	3¼	M/A Com	MAI	...	...	11	195	6⅞	6⅝	6⅞	+ ⅛
3¼	½	MAI Sys	MCO	...	...	...	45	⅞	¹³⁄₁₆	¹³⁄₁₆	− ¹⁄₁₆
45⅝	19⅜	MBIA	MBI	.56	1.5	11	340	36⅜	35½	36⅜	+ ¾
n 28⅛	22¹⁵⁄₁₆	MBNA Cp	KRB	.40e	1.5	...	2143	27½	26¾	26¾	− ⅜
22¼	18⅛	MCN	MCN	1.64	7.9	15	203	20⅝	20½	20¾	...
1⅛	³⁄₃₂	MDC Cp	MDC	...	...	...	142	¹³⁄₁₆	¹³⁄₁₆	¹³⁄₁₆	+ ¹⁄₁₆

▲ 19¼	16½	NiaMoPwr pf		1.79e	9.0	...	2	20	20	20	+ ¾
104½	98½	NiaMoPwr pf		10.60	10.2	...	z10	103½	103½	103½	...
15¼	11½	NiaShare	NGS	1.40e	10.2	...	93	14	13¾	13¾	− ⅛
12	8⅝	NichApIgte	GEF	.09e	.8	...	740	12	11¾	12	+ ⅛
17⅜	6	Nicolet	NIC	...	...	20	310	13	12⅞	12⅞	+ ⅛
47	34¾	NICOR	GAS	2.24	5.4	11	526	41¼	40⅝	41¼	− ⅛
s 54½	26	Nike B	NKE	.56	1.2	12	2544	46⅛	45	45¾	+ ¼
19⅛	13¼	NobleAffil	NBL	.16	1.2	21	645	13⅞	13⅝	13¾	...
20	5⅞	NordRes	NRD	...	...	...	50	1007	10½	9⅞	10½ + ½
47¼	35	NorflkSo	NSC	1.60	3.6	13	1430	45⅛	44¾	45	+ ¼
32¼	30	NSoRIwy pf		2.60	8.1	...	1	32	32	32	...
41¾	26⅝	Norsk	NHY	.62e	2.1	12	1643	29¾	29¼	29⅝	+ ½
4⅝	1⅝	Nortek	NTK	.03j	...	...	134	3½	3⅜	3½	− ⅛
19	14⅛	NoEuroOil	NET	1.41e	9.2	11	15	15⅜	15⅛	15⅜	...
15	4⅞	NorthForkBcp	NFB	.45	6.2	...	352	7¼	7⅛	7¼	+ ¼
6⅜	1¼	NoeastFed	NSB	...	...	...	67	3¼	3⅛	3⅛	− ¼
13	4⅝	NoeastFed pf		...	...	...	8	7½	7¾	7¾	− ⅛
21½	17¾	NoeastUtil	NU	1.76	8.6	11	1188	20½	20⅛	20½	+ ¼
x 37¼	26⅞	NoStPwr	NSP	2.32	6.7	12	x4810	34½	34	34¾	...
44½	37¼	NoStPwr pf		3.60	8.5	...	z10	42¼	42¼	42¼	...

the stock to reported earnings per share for the last four quarters; the high, low, and closing price for the day; and the change in the price from the close of the previous day.

A shareholder's return in a dividend-paying company has two components: the dividend and the *capital gain or loss* (i.e., the increase or decrease in the price of the stock). If, for example, the dividend yield is 5% and the price of the stock has increased 7% during the year, the return for the year is 12%.

Dividends   Most large, publicly traded corporations pay quarterly cash dividends. The dividend declaration of the board of directors specifies the amount of the dividend, the *date of record,* and the payment date. On the whole, dividends are paid to those who are on the shareholder list on the record date. An exception is made with respect to shares traded shortly before that date. The fourth day before the record date is designated the *ex-dividend date.* Those who purchase shares before the ex-dividend date receive the dividend whether they are shareholders of record on the record date or not; those who purchase on or after the ex-dividend date do not receive the dividend. For example, if a board were to designate Friday, August 10, as the dividend record date, the ex-dividend date would be Monday, August 6, four days before the record date. Anyone purchasing the stock on or after August 6, the ex-dividend date, would not receive the dividend.

Classified Common Stock   Some corporations have more than one class of common stock. For example, it is not unusual for small companies to issue class A stock to outside investors and class B to the founders of the firm. The class A shareholders may receive all of the dividends for a specified number of years, while the class B shareholders have all of the voting power during that period.

Ford Motor Company and General Motors are two of the few large corporations that have more than one class of common. Ford's class A stock is, for the most part, owned by the general public, and the class B is owned by members of the Ford family. The class B stock was created so the family can maintain control of the company by retaining 40% of the total voting power regardless of the number of shares of class A stock outstanding. Only the class A stock is traded on the New York Stock Exchange.

General Motors has three classes of common stock: the original General Motors shares, General Motors E stock, and General Motors H stock. The E and H shares were issued to the stockholders of Electronic Data Systems and Hughes Aircraft when General Motors acquired those companies in 1984 and 1985. Dividends on the E and H shares depend on the earnings of those two divisions of the company. All three classes of General Motors stock are traded on the New York Stock Exchange.

Preferred Stock   The common stockholders of a corporation are its owners, the bondholders are creditors, and preferred stockholders are somewhere in between. Preferred stocks are similar to bonds in some respects and similar to common stocks in others. Like bonds, preferred stocks promise fixed periodic payments (called dividends in the case of preferred stock), and, in some cases, the issuer promises to retire the stock on a specified maturity date. Like common stocks, preferred shares are not a debt security; therefore, failure to pay preferred dividends is not grounds for bankruptcy. Preferred shareholders have some voting rights, but they are nearly always more limited than the rights of the common shareholders. Generally, preferred shareholders are permitted to vote only if the company has failed to pay the preferred dividends. In the event of bankruptcy, the claims of preferred shareholders are inferior to bondholder claims but take precedence over the claims of common stockholders.

Preferred stocks are rarely attractive to individual investors because preferred shares offer lower returns than bonds of comparable risk. This strange phenomenon is due to a provision in the federal tax laws that excludes from a corporation's taxable income 70% of any dividends it receives from another corporation. Thus, corporate investors are willing to buy preferred stocks at lower yields than fully taxable bonds. This drives preferred yields down to levels that are quite unattractive to individual investors.

Convertible Securities Many corporate bonds and preferred stocks are, at the holder's election, convertible into a predetermined number of shares of stock of the issuing company. In effect, a convertible owner has both a fixed-income security and an option on the company's stock that can be exercised by surrendering the convertible. When the conversion privilege is worth little, the price of a convertible depends largely on its value as a fixed-income security. But when the value of the stock for which a convertible can be exchanged is well above the value of the convertible as a bond, the price of the convertible depends largely on the price of the stock. Convertibles often sell at lower yields than straight bonds of similar quality because investors place a value on the conversion privilege.

Derivative Securities

One reason for the popularity of derivative securities is the leverage they offer. Typically, the prices of warrants, options, and futures are small in relation to the value of the underlying assets. Thus, profits and losses are large relative to the amount invested. Because of the leverage, derivative securities are widely used for both speculation and hedging. They are very risky when used speculatively, but can be quite safe when used as a hedging device.

Stock Purchase Warrants A warrant is a security that gives the holder the right to buy a specified number of shares of stock from the issuing company at a fixed price over a stated period of time. Bonds are sometimes issued with warrants attached. Most warrants that are attached to bonds can be detached and traded separately. To a large degree, the value of a warrant depends on the relationship between the price of the underlying stock and the price (called *the exercise price*) at which the stock can be purchased by exercising the warrant. Another important influence on warrant values is the length of time until expiration. The longer the remaining life of a warrant, the greater the possible increase in the price of the stock before the warrant expires.

Exchange-Traded Options On a typical day, close to one million option contracts on individual stocks and stock indexes are traded on the various stock and options exchanges in the United States. These options should not be confused with the nontransferable options issued by companies as compensation to their employees. Exchange-traded options are issued by option writers—not by the corporation whose stock is involved. Many call options are written by stockholders to supplement the income from their stock portfolios. Options are also written by speculators.

Publicly traded options are of two kinds: *calls* and *puts*. A call is an option to buy, and a put is an option to sell. Each specifies the price (called the strike price) at which the option can be exercised and the date on which the option expires. Since a call option is an option to buy at a set price, the option holder makes a profit if there is a large enough increase in the price of the underlying stock. Holders of put options make a profit if there is a large enough decrease in the price of the stock.

An option may be on a specific stock or on a large "basket of stocks." The latter are called *index options*. Just as the price of an option on an individual stock is influenced by changes in the price of the stock itself, the price of an index option is affected by changes in the prices of the stocks in the index.

Options provide a convenient vehicle for either *hedging* or speculating. Holders of common stocks can hedge against a decline in the market by purchasing put options on individual stocks or on a market index. Since a put is an option to sell at a set price, the value of the option tends to increase when stock prices decline. For example, if the strike price of a put is $40 and the price of the stock declines from $38 to $36, the price of the option will increase because of the increase in the spread between the price at which the holder of the put can buy the stock on the market and the price at which it can be sold under the option. By hedging with puts, an investor's stock losses in a declining market may be offset, at least in part, by profits on the options.

Relatively small percentage changes in stock prices can result in large percentage changes in option prices. For example, if the price of a stock is $42, investors or speculators might be willing to pay $3 a share for a four-month option to buy the stock for $40. If the price of the stock were to increase $4.20 (10%) in a month, the price of the option might increase about $4.20 as well. Ignoring transaction costs, that would be a gain of 140% on the option [(4.20/3.00) × 100], compared to the gain of 10% on the stock.

Financial Futures The tremendous growth in trading of *financial futures* (principally contracts on stock indexes and U.S. Treasury securities) has been one of the most significant developments in the financial markets in the past 20 years. More than 200,000 contracts are traded on a typical day.

In a futures contract, one party agrees to buy and the other agrees to sell a stated quantity of a designated asset at a specified price on a specified future date. Futures contracts cover a wide variety of commodities (e.g., corn, wheat, soybean oil, coffee, cotton, orange juice, heating oil, and lumber) as well as certain intangibles, including stock market indexes and U.S. Treasury securities.

A *stock index futures contract* is a futures contract whose value moves up and down with a specific index of stock prices. An interest rate futures contract is a contract whose value moves up and down with interest rates. Among the most heavily traded are contracts for the delivery of U.S. Treasury bills, notes, or bonds.

You can become a party to a U.S. Treasury bond futures contract for securities with a face value of $100,000 by depositing a small fraction of that amount as margin. If the price goes against you, however, additional margin must be supplied. In any case, you will probably elect to close out your position before the delivery date arrives, as most futures traders do. This is done by taking an offsetting position, which means selling if you have previously bought, or buying if you have previously sold.

One party to a futures contract may be hedging, while the other is speculating. For example, a farmer who is planning to harvest wheat in September might sell September wheat futures in June for protection against a decline in the price of wheat between June and September. The other party to the contract—the buyer of September futures—might be either a speculator who is betting that the price of wheat will go up or a user of wheat who wants protection against an increase in its price. In any case, the farmer can close out his position either by delivering wheat or by purchasing September wheat futures before the delivery date. If the price of wheat declines materially between June and September and the farmer closes out his position by purchasing September futures, his profit on the futures will at least partially offset the decline in the value of his crop.

|||| ## STOCK MARKET INDEXES

Keeping track of the market's performance is of interest to nearly everyone who invests in common stocks. One way to judge how well your own stocks are performing is to compare their percentage price changes, or total returns, with similar figures for one or more stock market indexes, a number of which are listed in Table 2-5.

DOW JONES INDUSTRIAL AVERAGE

Over 100 years ago, Charles H. Dow, a financial journalist in New York City, developed the first indicator of the level of stock prices. It was based on the prices of 11 stocks he considered representative of the market as

|||| **TABLE 2-5**
Stock Market Averages and Indexes (Partial List)

Dow Jones Averages
  Industrials (DJIA)
  Transportation
  Public utilities
  Financial
  Composite
Standard & Poor's Indexes
  500 stocks (S&P 500, or Composite, Index)
  400 industrials
  40 utilities
  40 financial companies
  20 transportation companies
  250 over-the-counter stocks
  103 capital goods stocks
  25 high-grade common stocks
  20 low-priced common stocks
  Separate indexes for a large number of industrial, public utility, and financial
    groups
Five New York Stock Exchange indexes, including the New York Stock Exchange
  Composite
American Stock Exchange Market Value Index and 16 subindexes
Six NASDAQ indexes, including the NASDAQ Composite
Wilshire 5000 Equity Index for all stocks on which daily quotations are available
Russell 1000, Russell 2000, and Russell 3000*
London Financial Times 100
Tokyo Nikkei Index
Toronto TSE Composite

*The Russell 1000 is based on the market values of the 1,000 most valuable U.S. companies, as determined by *Business Week*. The Russell 2000 is based on the market values of the next 2,000 companies, and the Russell 3000 includes all 3,000 companies.

a whole, 9 of which were the stocks of railroad companies. Gradually, the composition of the average was changed, and after being revised and expanded by an editor of the *Wall Street Journal* in 1928, it became the *Dow Jones Industrial Average,* or DJIA, of 30 stocks.

A stock market index can be characterized by the number and types of stocks it includes and the method used to calculate the index value. The DJIA is unique in its small number of stocks (only 30), the size of the companies (all very large), and the method of calculation. It is a price-weighted, divisor-adjusted average, calculated as follows:

$$\text{DJIA} = \sum_{i=1}^{30} \frac{P_i}{\text{divisor}} \tag{2-7}$$

The weight given each stock is based solely on its price, and the divisor, originally 30, is adjusted downward whenever a company's outstanding shares are increased as a result of a stock dividend or split. On January 8, 1991, the divisor was 0.50543.

Since the DJIA is based on prices alone, rather than aggregate market values, stock dividends and stock splits would cause it to decline if the divisor were not adjusted. Example 2-2, in which it is assumed that the DJIA is composed of just two stocks, A and B, illustrates the point.

The prices of A and B at the end of a certain day are $60 and $40, respectively, making the average $50. Then stock B is split two-for-one; the split reduces its price to $20 and would lower the average to $40 [(60 + 20)/2] if the divisor were not adjusted. To avoid such a result, the divisor must be lowered to 1.6 as shown below.

	Before Split	After Split Unadjusted	After Split Adjusted
Price of A	$60	$60	$60
Price of B	$40	$20	$20
Sum of prices	$100	$80	$80
Divisor (N)	2	2	1.6
DJIA	50	40	50

||||

The DJIA is the indicator of stock prices most individuals hear about or read about each day. Movements of the DJIA are assumed to represent movements of the market as a whole. To keep the average reasonably representative of American business (excluding public utilities, transportation companies, and financial corporations, which are in separate Dow Jones averages), its composition has been changed a number of times. However, it was not until 1979 that IBM and Merck were included, bringing office equipment and drugs into the average for the first time. More recent additions include American Express, Boeing, Coca-Cola, and McDonalds.[4] The 30 companies in the DJIA as of January 8, 1991, are listed in Table 2-6.

The DJIA would be a better measure if its stocks were weighted according to their relative importance as indicated by their aggregate market values instead of their prices. As it is, a change of a given percentage in the price of a relatively high-priced stock has more weight than a change of the same percentage in the price of a lower-priced stock, even if the lower-priced stock has greater total value. For example, in early 1991 the aggregate market value of AT&T was more than five times the aggregate value of International Paper, but because the price of International Paper stock was 75% higher than the price of AT&T, a 1% change in the price of International Paper had 75% more impact on the average than a 1% change in the price of AT&T.

Another shortcoming of the DJIA is the small number of stocks involved. Nevertheless, since the aggregate market value of the 30 stocks

[4]Several of the 30 DJIA companies are not industrial companies in the usual meaning of the word. Three of the companies—American Express, Coca-Cola, and McDonalds—have been added in recent years to make the average more representative of the economy. A fourth, Primerica, was in the average for many years as the American Can Company, a major producer of containers. Along with the change in name, the company changed its principal activities and is now primarily a financial services firm.

|||| **TABLE 2-6**
Dow Jones Industrial Average, January 8, 1991

	Closing Price 1/8/91
Allied Signal	$ 26.88
Aluminum Company of America	55.13
American Express	19.50
AT&T	29.88
Bethlehem Steel	13.50
Boeing	44.00
Chevron	71.50
Coca-Cola	44.00
du Pont	34.63
Eastman Kodak	39.63
Exxon	50.75
General Electric	54.25
General Motors	31.75
Goodyear	17.63
IBM	109.00
International Paper	52.38
McDonalds	27.50
Merck & Co.	83.25
Minnesota Mining and Mfg.	80.13
Navistar	2.75
Philip Morris	48.75
Primerica	22.88
Procter & Gamble	81.88
Sears Roebuck	25.13
Texaco	59.00
Union Carbide	16.38
United Technologies	45.00
USX	28.88
Westinghouse	25.00
Woolworth	27.38
Total	1,268.32
Divisor	0.50543
Average	2,509.4

is more than one-third of the total value of the 500 largest U.S. industrial companies, the DJIA tends to provide a reasonably good picture of what is happening overall to the prices of large industrial stocks.

Value-Weighted Indexes

All stock market indexes, other than indexes for individual sectors of the market and the Dow Jones Averages, are based on large numbers of stocks, with each weighted according to its aggregate market value. A stock with an aggregate market value of $10 billion has 100 times the weight of a stock valued at a total of $100 million. Since changes in such indexes are based on changes in aggregate market values, rather than simply changes in prices, no adjustment needs to be made for stock splits or stock dividends.

Standard & Poor's 500 (Composite) Index

The formula for a typical value-weighted index is

$$\text{index} = \left(\frac{\sum_{i=1}^{n} P_{i1}Q_{i1}}{\sum_{i=1}^{n} P_{i0}Q_{i0}} \right)(B) \qquad (2\text{-}8)$$

where

n = number of stocks in the index

P_{i1} = current price of stock i

Q_{i1} = current number of stock i shares outstanding

P_{i0} = average price of stock i during base period

Q_{i0} = average number of stock i shares outstanding during base period

B = base number (usually 10 or 100)

When the base number *(B)* is 10 (as it is for the Standard & Poor's 500 Index), the formula states that the current value of the index is 10 times the ratio of the current aggregate market value of the stocks in the index to their average aggregate market value during the base period. Thus, on January 18, 1991, when the S&P 500 was 328, the ratio of the aggregate market value of the 500 stocks in the index to their average aggregate market value during the base period (1941–1943) was 328/10, or 32.8.

NASDAQ Composite Index

At the end of 1989, the value-weighted NASDAQ Composite Index was based on the prices of 4,113 stocks, mostly common, with an aggregate market value of $386 billion. While the aggregate value of an average NASDAQ stock was only $94 million, the 50 largest stocks (including, for example, Apple Computer, Intel Corporation, Microsoft, and Nordstrom) had an average value of $2.3 billion and accounted for 30% of the total of all NASDAQ stocks. Thus, the NASDAQ index reflects the prices of certain large stocks as well as the prices of a large number of small stocks.

Comparative Performance of Three Indexes

Figure 2-7 shows the year-to-year changes and overall trend of the Dow Jones Industrial Average, NASDAQ Composite Index, and Standard & Poor's 500 Index for the years 1972 through 1990, with 1971 as the base year.[5] Over this 19-year period, the DJIA rose about 200%, and the other two indexes gained between 220% and 230%.[6] Annual fluctuations of the NASDAQ index were often greater than those of the DJIA and S&P 500.

---

[5]Since the graph is semilogarithmic, equal vertical distances represent equal percentage changes.

[6]The DJIA is referred to as an index even though technically it is an average rather than an index.

|||| **FIGURE 2-7**

Stock Indexes, December 31, 1971, to December 31, 1990
(1971 = 100)

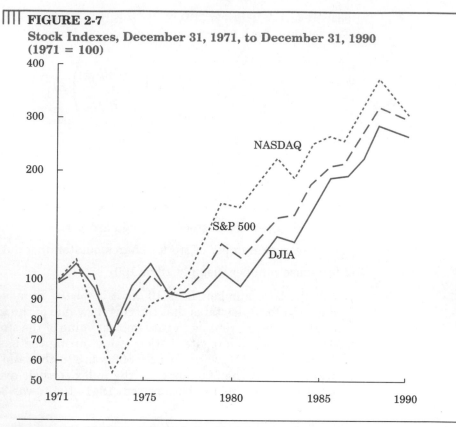

SOURCE: *The Wall Street Journal;* Standard & Poor's Statistical Service; *NASDAQ Fact Book.*

On the average, NASDAQ stocks clearly outperformed the others from 1977 through 1983, but underperformed in the more recent years.

If the indexes were adjusted for inflation, the graph would show that in constant dollars all three declined slightly from the end of 1971 to the end of 1990. Nominally, the indexes rose at average annual rates ranging from 5.9% to 6.4%, but those increases were more than offset by the average inflation rate of 6.5%. Overall, investors' returns were nevertheless positive because of the cash dividends received.

|||| **SUMMARY**

Many securities investments, including U.S. savings bonds, nonnegotiable certificates of deposit, and annuity contracts, are nonmarketable. Although such securities cannot be sold, they can be surrendered for cash before maturity if the holder is willing to accept an interest penalty.

Interest on savings bonds and other U.S. Treasury securities is exempt from state income taxes. The before-tax yields on savings bonds are lower than the yields on marketable Treasury securities of comparable maturities, but the marketable issues are subject to the risk of price fluctuation caused by changes in market interest rates.

Money market securities, including U.S. Treasury bills, commercial paper, short-term negotiable CDs, bankers' acceptances, and Eurodollar deposits, are debt instruments that mature in one year or less. Capital market securities consist of long-term debt instruments (notes, bonds, and mortgage-backed securities), common stocks, and preferred stocks. Long-term U.S. Treasury securities include notes, bonds, and STRIPS. Prices of long-term Treasuries are quoted in 32nds, and the yield reported in the *Wall Street Journal* is yield to maturity.

Securities issued by certain government-sponsored enterprises are known as agency issues. Yields are slightly higher than on U.S. Treasuries because of some credit risk and lower liquidity.

Municipal securities are issued by state and local governments and various entities created by those governments. Many municipals are exempt from the federal income tax as well as state income tax in the state of issuance.

Corporate notes and bonds are considerably more complicated than U.S. Treasury issues because of differences in the issuers themselves as well as variations in protective covenants, risk of default, callability, collateral, and convertibility. Corporate bond prices are quoted in 8ths, 4ths, and halves rather than 32nds, and the yield reported in the *Wall Street Journal* is the current yield rather than yield to maturity.

Holders of mortgage-backed pass-through securities receive monthly principal and interest payments, the amounts of which are difficult to predict because of mortgage prepayments. Overall, yields on government-guaranteed Ginnie Mae pass-throughs are a little higher than yields on U.S. Treasury securities, largely because of the uncertainty as to how rapidly the mortgages will be paid off.

Common stockholders are the owners of a corporation and, as such, are residual claimants against the corporation's income and assets. The return on a common stock consists of the dividend yield and the percentage change in the price of the stock.

Owners of preferred stock have a claim superior to that of common shareholders but inferior to the claims of the corporation's creditors. Preferred stock is generally unattractive to individual investors because the yields are generally lower than yields on bonds of comparable risk. Corporate investors are willing to buy preferreds at comparatively low before-tax yields because corporations can exclude from taxable income 70% of dividends received.

Convertible bonds and convertible preferred stock are fixed-income securities that can be converted, at the holder's option, into a specified number of shares of common stock. Derivative securities include warrants, options, futures, and options on futures. All tend to be highly leveraged. They are used for hedging purposes as well as speculation.

The price levels and price changes of groups of stocks are measured with stock market averages and indexes. Perhaps the best known is the narrowly based Dow Jones Industrial Average. Among the broader stock market indicators, the Standard & Poor's 500 Index is widely used as a benchmark for measuring the relative performance of individual stock portfolios.

|||| **QUESTIONS**

1. Distinguish between money market securities and capital market securities.

2. What are the advantages and disadvantages of series EE U.S. savings bonds relative to marketable U.S. Treasury bonds of similar maturity?

3. What are the advantages and disadvantages of a five-year insured savings certificate relative to a U.S. Treasury bond that will mature in five years?

4. What are the similarities and differences between U.S. Treasury bonds and U.S. Treasury bills?

5. What are the advantages and disadvantages of an insured 270-day savings certificate relative to a 270-day Treasury bill?

*6. A primary advantage of U.S. Treasury bonds is:
   a. high liquidity.
   b. favorable state and local tax treatment.
   c. low credit risk.
   d. all of the above.

*7. Corporate bonds secured by other marketable securities are:
   a. collateral trust bonds.
   b. equipment trust bonds.
   c. income bonds.
   d. mortgage bonds.

*8. The call feature of a bond means that the:
   a. investor can call for payment on demand.
   b. investor can call only if the firm defaults on its interest payments.
   c. issuer can call the bond issue prior to its maturity.
   d. issuer can call the issue during the first three years.

*9. Which of the following sets of features most accurately describes a Ginnie Mae pass-through security?

	Average Life	Payment Frequency	Credit Risk
a.	Predictable	Monthly	High
b.	Predictable	Semiannual	Low
c.	Unpredictable	Monthly	Low
d.	Unpredictable	Semiannual	Low

Note: All questions and problems preceded by an asterisk are from Chartered Financial Analyst (CFA) examinations.

*10. The nominal yield of a bond is the:
   a. annual coupon as a percentage of the current price.
   b. annual rate earned including the capital gain or loss.
   c. rate earned giving consideration to coupon reinvestment.
   d. coupon rate.

*11. Which of the following types of U.S. municipal bonds would be most likely to have the highest rating?
   a. Charitable hospital revenue bonds
   b. Airport revenue bonds
   c. State general obligation bonds
   d. Major city general obligation bonds

*12. A bond analyst at Omnipotent Bank (OB) notices that the number of prepayments on his holdings of high-coupon GNMA issues has been moving sharply higher. This indicates that:
   a. interest rates are falling.
   b. the loans comprising OB's pools have been experiencing lower default rates.
   c. the pools held by OB are older issues.
   d. all of the above.

*13. U.S. corporations are attracted to preferred stocks because much of the income received is generally:
   a. increased during the life of the preferred.
   b. nontaxable.
   c. higher than bonds of equivalent quality.
   d. recognized as an increase in deferred income.

*14. A call provision on a corporate bond benefits the:
   a. issuer.
   b. bondholders.
   c. trustee.
   d. government regulators.

*15. The highest dollar volume of secondary market trading in U.S. corporate bonds occurs on the:
   a. American Exchange.
   b. New York Exchange.
   c. Pacific Exchange.
   d. over-the-counter market.

*16. Which of the following is *not* a characteristic that differentiates nonconvertible preferred stock from common stock? Nonconvertible preferred stock has:
   a. precedence over common stock with respect to the payment of dividends.
   b. a predetermined dividend rate, whereas common stock dividends may vary.
   c. preferential voting rights.
   d. a preferential call on the assets of the company.

*17. The major difference between a warrant and a call option is that:
   a. call options are typically written by investors on existing shares, whereas warrants are issued directly by companies as a means of selling new securities.
   b. call options trade on various options exchanges, whereas warrants trade only on the New York and American Stock Exchanges.
   c. call option valuation models such as Black-Scholes cannot be used to value common stock warrants.
   d. none of the above.

*18. Explain why the following are, or are not, suitable indexes on which to base an index fund.
   a. Dow Jones Industrial Average
   b. Standard & Poor's 500 Index

19. With respect to corporate dividends, explain the declaration date, ex-dividend date, and date of record.

20. Distinguish between a general obligation municipal bond and a revenue bond.

21. Explain why callable bonds sell at higher yields than similar non-callable bonds.

22. Why does a call option have value even if the strike price is higher than the price of the stock?

23. Why do you suppose yield to maturity is figured to the call date if the price is above par and to the final maturity if the price is at a discount from par value?

24. Explain why the DJIA is called a price-weighted, divisor-adjusted average.

25. Explain how the Standard & Poor's 500 Index is calculated.

|||| **PROBLEMS**

1. If the asked price for a $10,000 Treasury bill maturing in 152 days is $9,652, what are the following?
   a. Bank discount yield
   b. Bond equivalent yield
   c. Effective, or compounded, yield

*2. A 120-day Treasury bill is priced at 97 and has a bank discount yield of 9.00%. Its bond equivalent yield is:
   a. 9.00%.
   b. 9.12%.
   c. 9.28%.
   d. 9.41%.

*3. The dollar value of a U.S. Treasury bond quoted at 92.24 is:
   a. $92.24.
   b. $922.40.

    c. $927.50.

    d.   none of the above.

*4. Interest on $500 invested for one year at an annual interest rate of 12% and compounded quarterly is:

    a. $58.33.

    b. $60.00.

    c. $62.75.

    d.   none of the above.

*5. A 30-day U.S. Treasury bill is selling at a 12% yield on a discount basis. Its approximate bond equivalent yield is:

    a.   6.0%.

    b.   11.7%.

    c.   12.0%.

    d.   12.3%.

*6. The taxable equivalent yield on a 6% yield tax-exempt bond for an individual in a 28% tax bracket is:

    a.   4.32%

    b.   7.68%.

    c.   8.33%.

    d.   none of the above.

*7. An 8.6% coupon tax-exempt bond sells for $1,000. What coupon rate on a corporate bond selling at $1,000 par value would produce the same after-tax return to the investor as the tax-exempt bond if the investor is in the 28% marginal tax bracket?

    a.   10.19%

    b.   11.94%

    c.   12.25%

    d.   14.63%

8. One of the securities listed in Figure 2-4 is a U.S. Treasury bond with a coupon rate of 11⅛% that matures in August 2003. Assuming that the face value of the bond is $1,000:

    a.   what is the bid-asked spread in dollars?

    b.   what is the current yield?

    c.   what is the yield to maturity?

    d.   why is the current yield higher than the yield to maturity?

    e.   what was the dollar change in the bid price from the previous day?

9. The bid and asked rates for the Treasury bill with a maturity of June 20, 1991, in Figure 2-2 are 6.28% and 6.26%, respectively. What are the corresponding prices, and what is the bid-asked spread in dollars?

10. Find the following for certain securities listed in Figure 2-6:

    a.   The par value of Acme Electric and Affiliated Publications stocks.

    b.   The terms of the Allen Group preferred stock.

c.   The reason, or reasons, Adobe Resources was not paying a dividend in early 1991.

Note: The answers to Question 10 are not in Figure 2-6.

11.   How can you be sure that the exercise price of the Safeway warrants required to buy one share of stock (Figure 2-6) was at least $9.00? Why would anyone pay $2.38 for the warrants, knowing that the actual exercise price was $13.50?

12.   Suppose an investor's marginal federal tax rate is 28%, her marginal state tax rate is 10%, and each tax is deductible in calculating taxable income for the other. The investor is looking at a U.S. Treasury bond (before-tax yield 9%), the income from which is subject to federal tax but not to state tax, and at a municipal security issued in another state (before-tax yield 7%), the income from which is exempt from federal tax but subject to state tax. Calculate and compare the yields after taking into account federal and state income taxes on the investment income and any tax benefits arising from deduction of those taxes against other taxable income.

|||| SELECTED REFERENCES

Cook, Timothy Q., and Timothy D. Rowe, eds. *Instruments of the Money Market*. Richmond, Va.: Federal Reserve Bank of Richmond, 1986.

CBOT Financial Instruments Guide. Chicago: Chicago Board of Trade, 1987.

Handbook of Securities of the United States Government and Federal Agencies. New York: The First Boston Corporation, 1990.

3 SECURITIES MARKETS AND TRANSACTIONS

Business firms and the federal, state, and local governments raise enormous amounts of cash by issuing securities to the investing public. This would be impossible without sophisticated markets in which stocks, bonds, and other types of securities can be issued and traded. Securities are issued in the primary market and subsequently traded on the exchanges (such as the New York and American Stock Exchanges) and in the over-the-counter market.

This chapter deals primarily with the issuing and trading of stocks and bonds and with federal and state regulation of the securities markets. It first explains the nature of *primary and secondary markets* and the procedures for issuing stocks and bonds. Next, certain important features of the *stock exchanges* and the *over-the-counter market* are examined. Attention is then given to *market orders, limit orders,* and *stop orders,* the three kinds of orders used by investors in buying stocks. Investing with borrowed funds *(margin trading)* and short selling are also explained. Finally, the chapter concludes with an overview of certain federal and state securities laws and regulations that have been adopted for the protection of investors.

PRIMARY AND SECONDARY MARKETS

Markets are often thought of as places where items are bought and sold. In a narrow sense that definition is correct. The New York Stock Exchange is a market, the Chicago Board of Trade is a market, and so is a local auction house. In a broader sense, the term "market" is less concrete. It refers to the interactions between buyers and sellers with respect to any kind of asset or service. It is in this broader sense that a distinction is made between primary and secondary markets for stocks, bonds, and other securities.

The primary market is the market in which new issues of stocks and bonds are offered to the public through *investment banking firms*. The sale of securities in a primary market is referred to as a primary offering. The issuer may be a business corporation, a government, or some other legal entity (such as a hospital or power authority) that needs to raise funds. If the securities are offered to the general public, the issue is called a *public offering*. If they are sold only to a single investor, such as an insurance company, or to a small group of investors, the issue is referred to as a *private placement*.

The secondary markets are the markets in which previously issued securities are bought and sold. Although some secondary market transactions are executed directly between buyers and sellers, the majority are made through securities firms, either on a stock exchange or in the over-the-counter (OTC) market. In the OTC market, a securities firm buys and sells stocks and bonds for its customers without using the facilities of a stock exchange. The firm may be acting as either a *broker* or a *dealer*. When acting as a broker, the firm is an agent for its customer in making a trade with a third party. When acting as a dealer, it is buying or selling for its own account; that is, the firm is buying for or selling from its inventory of securities, just as a grocery store buys for and sells from its inventory of groceries.

||||
PRIMARY OFFERINGS THROUGH INVESTMENT BANKERS

The traditional role of investment banking firms is to assist corporations and governments in raising funds through the issuance of securities.[1] The terms on which the firms provide these services are established either through negotiation or competitive bidding. With competitive bidding, the issuing firm invites investment banking firms to bid for the securities it has decided to offer. In a negotiated offering, the investment bankers advise the issuing firm with respect to the type of securities to issue, the terms of the securities, the timing of the issue, and the price.

When the task of floating a stock or bond issue is awarded to a group of investment banking firms through competitive bidding, the successful firms buy the securities from the issuer and assume the risk of selling them at a satisfactory price to investors. When the arrangements are made through negotiation, the investment bankers may either *underwrite* the issue, thereby assuming the risk of a successful sales effort, or agree only to market the securities on a best-efforts basis. With a *best-efforts offering,* the banking firms agree to do their best to sell the securities, but they guarantee nothing.[2]

Large offerings are usually underwritten by a group of firms, called an *underwriting syndicate,* which is assembled by the managing, or lead, underwriter. It is not uncommon for a syndicate to be composed of 50 or more firms. Additional firms may join the underwriters to form the selling group that markets the issue. Figure 3-1 illustrates the relationships

---

[1]Another major activity of investment banks involves promoting, negotiating, and financing corporate mergers and acquisitions. A number of investment banking firms also operate as brokers and dealers in the secondary market.

[2]Issues are offered on a best-efforts basis under either of two circumstances: management of the issuing firm believes that the cost of underwriting is too high for the amount of risk involved, or the investment bankers are unwilling to assume the risk of underwriting because of substantial uncertainty about the price at which the securities can be sold.

|||| **FIGURE 3-1**

Underwriting and Distributing a Securities Issue

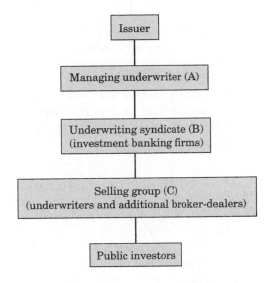

A—Managing underwriter: advises issuer; forms underwriting and selling groups; buys securities from issuer; sells to public and to members of selling group not in underwriting syndicate. B—Underwriting syndicate: buys securities from issuer; sells to public and to members of selling group not in underwriting syndicate. C—Selling group: sells securities to public.

among the various parties involved in making a large public offering.

If an underwritten issue of stock or bonds is successful, the spread between the price paid by investors and the price paid to the issuer by the underwriters is large enough to pay for all of the following:

1. Services performed by the lead underwriter in designing the issue and forming the underwriting syndicate.
2. The risk assumed by the underwriters.
3. The cost of marketing the issue, including commissions paid to brokers.

AN EXAMPLE OF A LARGE UNDERWRITING

In the American Telephone and Telegraph (AT&T) offering of $1 billion of common stock in 1981, Morgan Stanley was the managing underwriter, and some 255 other investment banking firms were in the underwriting syndicate.[3] A selling group composed of the underwriters and an addi-

---

[3]*New York Times,* June 10, 1981, p. D1.

tional 50 firms was responsible for marketing the issue. The underwriters agreed to buy the stock from AT&T at $57 a share (less the fees for managing, underwriting, and selling the issue) no matter what happened to the price of the stock during the offering period. The offering was successful, with the entire issue being sold at $57 in a period of three days. Two factors in particular contributed to the success of the offering: (1) a provision in the securities regulations that permits brokers to "show" an issue to their clients before the Securities and Exchange Commission (SEC) has approved the registration statement, and (2) a regulation that permits the lead underwriter to enter the market as a buyer during the offering period in an effort to stabilize the price. These two aspects of primary offerings are discussed in the next sections.

REGISTRATION STATEMENT AND PROSPECTUS

For all securities issues that are not exempt from registration, the issuer must file a *registration statement* with the SEC describing the offering, outlining the nature of the company's business and its competitive environment, providing information about the company's officers and directors, and containing a set of financial statements. Along with the registration statement, the company must file a copy of the *prospectus,* which is a summary of the essential information contained in the registration statement. Though often ignored by investors, prospectuses provide information that can be very useful, as explained in the Sidelight.

Securities subject to registration cannot be offered for sale to prospective investors before the registration statement has become effective, which can be no sooner than 20 days after the filing and is usually somewhat later than that. However, after the registration statement has been filed and before it has become effective, securities salespersons are permitted to give prospective buyers a preliminary prospectus. On the face of the preliminary prospectus (popularly known as a *"red herring"*), a statement in red ink explains that the registration statement has not yet become effective and that information contained in the prospectus is subject to change. The securities may not be sold nor may offers to buy be accepted before the registration statement becomes effective. Generally, the only facts contained in the final prospectus that do not appear in the red herring are the offering price, the underwriters' fees, and the offering date.

PRICE STABILIZATION DURING OFFERING PERIOD

Under the provisions of the Securities Exchange Act of 1934, it is generally unlawful to attempt to peg, fix, or stabilize the price of a security. However, the SEC is permitted to make exceptions to this rule, and it has done so with respect to the marketing of new issues. To minimize price fluctuations that could hurt an offering, underwriters are allowed to make "stabilizing trades," but they are not allowed to raise the price through such activities, and the trades must be disclosed. The reason for allowing

---

||| SIDELIGHT
Red Flags: Putting a Company in Its Proper Prospectus

Many people who buy new stock and bond offerings live to regret it. Although companies' problems are often impossible to predict, the information contained in a prospectus may give those who read it an inkling of the trouble ahead.

The October 1986 prospectus of ZZZZ Best Co., a carpet cleaning firm founded by 20-year-old Barry J. Minkow, is a good example. It disclosed that 87% of the company's revenues in a recent three-month period had come from a single firm, and that the company was being sued by a man from whom the company had borrowed money at a usurious rate. A year later the company filed for protection from creditors under chapter 11 of the federal bankruptcy laws, with losses to shareholders of as much as $70 million. Minkow was sentenced to 25 years in prison for securities fraud and other offenses.

Another example of a prospectus that should have alerted investors to coming trouble was that of Crazy Eddie, Inc., an electronics retailer. The prospectus revealed that the company had founded a medical school in the Caribbean, invested in oil and gas limited partnerships, and made interest-free loans to the chairman of the board and members of his family.

SOURCE: Adapted from Georgette Jasen, "Red Flags: Putting a Company in its Proper Prospectus," *The Wall Street Journal,* September 7, 1989, p. C1. Reprinted by permission of *The Wall Street Journal,* © Dow Jones & Company, Inc. (1989). All Rights Reserved Worldwide.

---

such trades is to reduce the risks and cost of underwriting. In the 1981 AT&T offering, Morgan Stanley purchased a large number of shares during the first day of the offering and was able to maintain the price on the New York Stock Exchange at exactly $57 a share for the entire day. By the end of the three-day offering period, the price had risen to 58⅞.

THE SPREAD

In addition to legal and accounting fees, three types of investment banking fees are involved in a public issue: the managing underwriter's fee, a fee for each member of the underwriting syndicate, and a selling fee. All fees are deducted from the offering price to arrive at the amount paid by the underwriters to the issuer. The difference between the offering price of a stock or bond and the amount received by the issuer is called the *spread;* the portion of the spread received by the underwriters is called the underwriters' spread. Underwriting fees are generally much higher for stocks than for bonds because of greater uncertainty as to the price. Also, because of the fixed costs involved, fees for small issues tend to be higher as a percentage of the offering price than those for large issues.

AN EXAMPLE OF A SMALL, HIGH-RISK UNDERWRITING

Morgan Stanley, the lead underwriter in the $1 billion AT&T stock offering in 1981, was the sole underwriter of a $25 million note issue by Oxoco, Inc., in 1984.[4] After making a credit analysis of Oxoco, Morgan Stanley agreed to underwrite and market the $25 million offering for a fee of $1 million. The notes were not well received. Six months after the initial offering date, Morgan Stanley still held over $18 million of the notes, and Oxoco had stopped making the quarterly payments to investors. Observers estimated that Morgan Stanley's ultimate loss on the Oxoco notes was much greater than the $1 million fee the firm received.

SHELF REGISTRATION

Two months or more often pass between the time a company decides to issue securities and the time the offering actually takes place. Because of this time lapse and the large fixed costs associated with registering an issue, major companies have been inclined to make their securities offerings large and infrequent. The adoption of SEC Rule 415 in 1982, however, has made it possible for corporations to shortcut the registration process through a procedure known as *shelf registration.*

With shelf registration, a company that makes numerous public offerings is required to file a detailed registration statement only once every two years. It then files a brief amendatory statement at the time of each new issue. The amendments consist largely of details about the specific security being offered. By using this procedure, a company can take a new issue to market in a matter of days instead of weeks or months.

|||| SECONDARY MARKETS

As noted earlier, stocks and bonds are bought and sold in two principal kinds of secondary markets: the organized exchanges (the New York Stock Exchange, the American Stock Exchange, and seven regional exchanges) and the over-the-counter, or OTC, market.[5] The exchanges have trading floors where the orders of buyers and sellers come together. In the OTC market, orders are executed by direct communication between securities firms.

IMPORTANCE OF GOOD SECONDARY MARKETS

Without good secondary markets, no well-developed primary market for securities would exist. Few investors would be willing to buy new issues of stocks or bonds if they were not resalable. *Liquidity* is important. The

---

[4]Allan Sloan, "Red Faces at Morgan Stanley," *Forbes,* July 29, 1985, p. 43.

[5]In addition to the primary and secondary markets, there are a third market and a fourth market. The third market consists of over-the-counter trading of large blocks of exchange-listed stocks by institutions, with securities firms acting as intermediaries. The fourth market consists of direct trading of large blocks of stocks by institutions, with no brokers or dealers involved.

stock exchanges and OTC market provide some assurance that actively traded securities can be sold promptly at a price close to the price on the latest transaction. Through the actions of their market makers (*specialists* on the stock exchanges and dealers in the OTC market), the established markets are sometimes able to cushion the impact of excessive supply or demand on securities prices.[6]

Because of their importance to investors, liquid securities markets are essential to a healthy economy. Corporations require large amounts of outside funds to finance increases in working capital and fixed assets. The willingness of investors to supply this financing is greatly enhanced by their confidence in the liquidity of the stock and bond markets.

In addition to providing liquidity, the secondary markets promote economic efficiency. If the management of a company is making poor use of its resources, the price of the stock is likely to fall below its potential value. When that happens, outsiders have an incentive to acquire control of the company to put the assets to better use, either by managing the company differently or by selling the assets to other firms.

STOCK EXCHANGES

Of the two million public and private corporations in the United States, only about 12,000 to 15,000 have common stocks that are actively traded. Of those, approximately 1,600 are traded on the New York Stock Exchange, 900 on the American Stock Exchange, and 4,400 in the NASDAQ over-the-counter system.[7] The remaining 5,000 to 8,000 are traded either on the regional stock exchanges or over the counter but not in the NASDAQ system. Some stocks are traded in more than one market. For example, nearly 90% of the volume on the regional stock exchanges is in New York Stock Exchange listed stocks. Also, many listed stocks are traded over the counter.

By any measure, the New York Stock Exchange is the largest stock market in the United States, as indicated by the share and dollar volumes reported in Table 3-1.[8] Although trading of the 1,600 common stocks on the New York Stock Exchange is by far the most important activity in that market, the Exchange also handles transactions in preferred stocks, corporate bonds, stock purchase warrants, stock options, and (through its subsidiary, the New York Futures Exchange) stock index futures and options on futures. Trading on the American Stock Exchange involves a similar assortment of financial products.

---

[6]Sometimes the number of persons who want to sell is so great and buyers are so few that the market makers are unable to prevent prices from collapsing, as on October 19, 1987, when stock prices on the New York Stock Exchange fell more than 20% in a single day.

[7]NASDAQ is the acronym for National Association of Securities Dealers Automated Quotation System.

[8]The New York and Tokyo Stock Exchanges are the two largest in the world. Their relative sizes, in terms of the dollar value of the securities traded, change from time to time for various reasons, including changes in the dollar-yen exchange rate.

|||| **TABLE 3-1**
Stock Traded in 1989

	Shares (Billions)	Percentage of Total
New York Stock Exchange	41.7	48.7%
NASDAQ	33.5	39.2
Regional exchanges (1987)	7.3	8.5
American Stock Exchange	3.1	3.6
Total	85.6	100.0

	Dollar Amount (Billions)	Percentage of Total	Per Share
New York Stock Exchange	$1,543.0	68.0	$37.00
NASDAQ	431.4	19.0	12.87
Regional exchanges (1987)	249.0	11.0	34.11
American Stock Exchange	44.4	2.0	14.83
Total	$2,267.8	100.0	

SOURCES: *Securities and Exchange Commission Annual Report, 1988; New York Stock Exchange Fact Book, 1990; NASDAQ Fact Book, 1989;* and *American Stock Exchange Fact Book, 1989.*

Listing Requirements

The several stock exchanges and NASDAQ have *listing requirements* that are largely based on the size of the company and the amount of public interest in its stock. The purpose of the requirements is to exclude stocks that are apt to be highly illiquid. Some of the listing requirements are shown in Table 3-2.[9]

Every year a number of companies that were previously traded only on NASDAQ or on the American Stock Exchange or on one or more of the other stock exchanges list their securities on the New York Stock Exchange. Others that could list on the "Big Board" elect not to do so. Apparently, they believe that listing on the New York Stock Exchange would not improve the market for their shares. They may be right. One cannot be sure that listing a stock on the New York Stock Exchange will improve its marketability. Thus, the shares of a number of sizable companies (including, for example, Alexander & Baldwin, Apple Computer, Consolidated Papers, Intel, MCI Communications, and Standard Register) are traded through the NASDAQ system rather than on one or more of the exchanges. Nearly 1,000 new stocks were listed on the New York Stock Exchange during the 10 years ending with 1989. However, the new listings were to a considerable extent offset by removals from the Exchange as a result of corporate mergers, insufficient trading, or other reasons. The result was a net increase of 137 stocks.

[9]The NASDAQ requirements shown in Table 3-2 are the requirements for admission to NASDAQ's National Market System. The requirements are lower for other NASDAQ stocks.

Growth in Trading Volume

The volume of common stock trading has been growing at a remarkable rate. The average daily volume on the New York Stock Exchange grew from 32 million shares in 1979 to 165 million shares in 1989, an increase of more than 400%. The NASDAQ growth was even greater, with an increase of more than 800% during the same period. The increase in trading on the New York Stock Exchange was facilitated by the electronic order-routing system (SuperDot), which enables member firms to transmit a high percentage of all orders directly to the post where the securities are traded. After the order has been executed, the report of execution is sent to the member firm's office over the same electronic circuit that brought the order to the floor. In 1989 some 149,000 orders moved through this system on a typical day.

Block Trading

The tremendous influence of large institutional investors on the stock market is indicated by the number of large blocks (10,000 shares or more) that are traded in the various markets. In 1989 there were 873,000 trades of large blocks on the New York Stock Exchange involving a total of more than 21 billion shares, which was 51% of the total volume on the Exchange. In the NASDAQ system, the 533,000 *block trades* in stocks of the National Market System accounted for 43% of the trading in those stocks.

Bond Trading

Although 3,000 bond issues of nearly 800 companies and governments are listed on the New York Stock Exchange, bond trading on the Exchange is small. The average daily volume of $35 million in 1989 was insignificant compared to the average daily stock trading of more than $7 billion. Most trading of corporate bonds, as well as U.S. Treasury securities and the bonds of state and local governments, is in the OTC market.

|||| **TABLE 3-2**
Sample of Listing Requirements

	New York Stock Exchange	American Stock Exchange	NASDAQ
Net tangible assets (millions)	$16	$4	$2
Earnings before federal taxes (millions)	$2.5	$.750	$.200
Number of round lot shareholders (100 shares or more)	2,000	800	300
Market value of publicly held shares (millions)	$16	$3	$2

SOURCES: *New York Stock Exchange Fact Book; American Stock Exchange Fact Book;* and *NASDAQ Fact Book.*

STOCK EXCHANGE MEMBERS AND THEIR FUNCTIONS

On the stock exchanges, buy and sell orders are transmitted to members who have a seat on the exchange. At the end of 1989, the New York Stock Exchange had a total of 1,426 members, of whom 1,366 owned "seats" and thereby had access to the trading floor. Four types of members are required to have a seat on the Exchange: commission brokers, specialists, floor brokers, and registered competitive market makers.

Commission Brokers

Brokers receive buy and sell orders, execute the orders if possible, and keep track of unfilled orders. *Commission brokers,* representing brokerage firms on the floor of the exchange, have the task of executing orders received from the firms' registered representatives. Orders are taken to the post where the stock is traded, and unless a price is specified that makes immediate execution impossible, the broker seeks the best available price through an auction process with other brokers, the specialist, or both. If an order specifies a price that is too high or too low for immediate execution, it is left with the specialist for possible future execution.

Specialists

As one would expect, the demand for a stock or bond in the secondary markets is often either stronger or weaker than the supply at the current price. The greater the imbalance, the stronger the upward or downward pressure on the price. To some degree the impact of these imbalances is lessened by the buying and selling of specialists on the stock exchanges and dealers in the over-the-counter market, both of whom have a responsibility for "making a market" for the stocks in which they have agreed to become specialists or dealers.

On the New York Stock Exchange, there is only one specialist for each stock, although some specialists are responsible for more than one stock. Specialists have three roles. First, they act as a brokers' broker, keeping a record of all orders that cannot be executed immediately (known as away-from-the-market orders) and executing them later, if possible.[10] Second, they work as facilitators, bringing together commision brokers who represent buyers and sellers on the floor of the exchange. Finally, and perhaps most important, they operate as dealers, buying and selling for their own account when there are no buyers or sellers willing to trade at a price close to that of the latest transaction.

A significant portion of all orders that come to the floor of the New York Stock Exchange are handled by the specialists, either as agents for commission brokers or for their own account. Specialists on the New York Stock Exchange buy and sell more than 15 million shares a day in trans-

---

[10]Away-from-the-market orders may be either limit orders or stop orders, as explained later in the chapter.

actions involving their own funds. These transactions account for about 10% of the total trading on the Exchange.

Stock exchange rules impose an obligation on specialists to maintain fair and orderly markets for all stocks assigned to them. This does not mean that they are expected to prevent drastic price changes from occurring. That would be impossible. It does mean that specialists must make a reasonable effort to see that price changes, in the absence of material new information, are no more than a small fraction of a point from one transaction to the next. When supply and demand are out of balance, the specialist is expected to go against the trend of the market, buying when there is a shortage of buyers and selling when there is a shortage of sellers in order to maintain price continuity. If there is a shortage of sellers and the specialist does not have any stock in inventory, he is expected to sell short.[11] While specialists are not required to go bankrupt, they are expected to make every reasonable effort to keep the price changes on successive transactions small and to keep the spread between their bid and asked prices narrow.

Specialists are, of course, constrained by various regulations of the stock exchanges. Among the most important is the requirement that they execute orders for others before buying or selling for their own account. If, for example, there is a limit order on the specialist's book to buy 1,000 shares of a stock at 34 and the price drops down to that level, the specialist must fill the limit order before buying any stock for himself at a price of 34 or lower.

Personnel of the stock watch divisions of the exchanges analyze the price and volume patterns to determine how well the specialists have been performing. Poor performance can result in severe penalties, including the assignment of a stock to a different specialist.

Floor Brokers and Registered Competitive Market Makers

The stock exchanges have a number of members called *floor brokers* whose sole function is to execute orders for commission brokers who have more orders than they can handle. At one time, floor brokers were called $2.00 brokers because they received $2.00 for each 100-share transaction they handled.

The smallest group of members on the floor are the *registered competitive market makers* (RCMMs), who were called *floor traders* on the New York Stock Exchange until 1977. Prior to that time, they were on the floor solely to earn a profit by trading for their own accounts. However, regulations of the SEC and the stock exchanges now require these members to assist the specialists in maintaining fair and orderly markets.

---

[11]A short sale is a sale of stock that has been borrowed by the seller. Short sales for speculative purposes are made with the expectation that the price of the stock will soon decline, making it possible for the short seller to cover his or her short position (that is, replace the borrowed stock) with stock purchased at a lower price. Short selling is explained in greater detail later in the chapter.

NASDAQ AND THE OVER-THE-COUNTER MARKET

Introduced in 1970, NASDAQ has vastly improved the performance of the over-the-counter market for the more than 4,000 stocks in the NASDAQ system. Before NASDAQ, brokers could obtain quotations on OTC stocks only from the "pink sheets" published by the National Quotation Bureau or by calling dealers on the telephone. With NASDAQ, brokers have immediate access through the terminals on their desks to the best bid and asked prices on all stocks in the system. Also, through the Small Order Execution System, which was installed in 1984, brokers can execute orders for the purchase or sale of up to 1,000 shares of NASDAQ stock. This system has greatly reduced the effort required to process small trades of OTC stocks.

NASDAQ stocks are divided into two categories: those in the *National Market System* and all others. To be included in the National Market System, a stock must have at least 350,000 publicly owned shares, compared to a minimum of 100,000 shares for other NASDAQ stocks. Newspaper listings of the National Market stocks show the results of the day's trading, including the number of shares traded and the high, low, and closing prices. Listings for the other NASDAQ stocks show only the number of shares traded and representative bid and asked prices.

The market-making function of NASDAQ and other OTC stocks is performed by several hundred broker-dealer firms, many of which are also in the investment banking business. Broker-dealers are involved as principals in a high percentage of all transactions. Some large national firms make a market for hundreds of different stocks and other securities. The responsibilities that go with market making include publication of realistic bid and asked prices and a readiness to buy and sell at those prices in specified, limited quantities.

Levels of NASDAQ Service

NASDAQ provides three levels of service. Level I, which is supplied to about 130,000 brokers, reports the highest bid and the lowest asked price (the so-called inside quotations) for any NASDAQ stock. These two quotes are often from different firms. Suppose, for example, that the four dealers who are making a market in stock X have published the following quotations:

Dealer	Bid	Asked	Shares (Hundreds)
A	30	30¼	5–10
B	30	30½	5–10
C	29¾	30¼	10–15
D	29½	30⅛	10–10

The numbers in the right-hand column indicate how many hundred shares the dealer is willing to buy or sell at the quoted prices. Level I terminals will show the highest bid, 30, and the lowest asked price, 30⅛.

If a broker has an order to buy, she will purchase the stock from dealer D, who has the lowest asking price. If she has an order to sell, she will sell to either A or B, the two dealers with the highest bid.

The terminals for levels II and III, which are considerably more expensive to operate than level I, display the quotes of all the maket makers, listing the bids in descending order and the asked price in ascending order so the best prices are shown at the top. Level III also has an entry capability with which the 500 or so market makers in the NASDAQ system can keep their own stock quotations current.

NASDAQ Versus the Stock Exchanges

In 1980 the SEC partially eliminated the restriction against over-the-counter trading by stock exchange members of securities listed on the exchanges. Under the new rule, member firms can trade in the OTC market any stocks that were not listed on an exchange prior to April 27, 1979. With this change, several hundred stocks can be traded both over the counter and on one or more exchanges. The response to the 1980 ruling by companies in the NASDAQ system has been mixed. Some have decided to list their stocks on an exchange, knowing that such listing no longer excludes their stocks from being traded over the counter. Others have elected not to list, probably because they believe that listing on an exchange would not improve the market for their stocks.

Without question, NASDAQ has made the OTC market more competitive with the stock exchanges. Price quotations are now immediately available on over 4,000 stocks, and the average stock is represented by seven or eight market makers, many of which are large firms with memberships on one or more stock exchanges.

Dealers that make markets in NASDAQ securities are governed by three basic rules:

1. They must enter both bid and asked quotations on any securities for which they are making a market and must be willing to buy or sell at least 100 shares at the prices they have quoted.

2. They must not withdraw from the market, even temporarily, without obtaining permission.

3. Their quotations must be reasonably related to the prices at which the securities have been trading.

Spread between Bid and Asked Prices

As a rule, the smaller the volume of trading in a stock, the greater the spread between the bid and asked prices. Sometimes the spread for low-volume stocks is very large, as the Sidelight points out (see next page). A dealer can operate with smaller markups on fast-moving stocks because the risk is less and the inventory carrying costs are lower relative to the dealer's revenues. NASDAQ has resulted in more competition among dealers and higher volumes of trading, both of which have tended to produce smaller spreads.

|||| SIDELIGHT
Why Are Some OTC Spreads So Big? Shouldn't Small
Investors Get a Break? Are Markups Excessive?

Suppose you want to sell 300 shares of Farmer Brothers, a coffee distributor based in Torrance, California. Your broker reports that the best quotes from the handful of market makers in this over-the-counter stock are a bid of 47 and an offer to sell at 51. That $4 markup is a rapacious 8.5% of the bid price. It comes on top of the brokerage commissions that both you and the seller pay—say, about another $1 a share at a full-service broker.

Why does a market maker need a $1,200 fee for moving 300 shares through his computer terminal? Because his capital is at risk, says the National Association of Securities Dealers (NASD), which sets rules for OTC trading. Farmer Brothers averages only 500 shares a day of trading. Maybe the dealer takes the 300 shares off your hands and can't get rid of them. Maybe you know something he doesn't.

Fair enough. But suppose you are in no hurry to sell. So you put in a sell order at 49, smack in the middle of the spread.

Meanwhile, as it happens, a patient retail buyer is looking to pick up 300 shares. He puts in a buy at 49.

It should now be easy for brokers to fill your order at the price you want. There would be no need for a risk-taking dealer in the middle. The brokers would still get their buying and selling commissions.

Still no trade. Why? With few exceptions, both you and the would-be buyer would be told that market orders at 49 are unrealistic and cannot be executed unless the market moves in your favor.

Plenty of OTC stocks have fat spreads like this. They are, to be sure, thinly traded stocks, but slow trading is no excuse for big markups when both buyer and seller are willing to wait.

Does the world have to work like this? Not at all. Take the same situation in an exchange's public auction market and your offer to sell 300 shares at 49 will be posted—where the buyer at 49 will get a crack at it through his broker.

Indeed, smart retail customers doing a Big Board trade often put in a market order between the bid and offer quoted from the floor if the spread is ¼ point or more. Suppose you want to buy 100 Bell Atlantic

|||| **DOING BUSINESS WITH A BROKER**

Securities brokers handle many different kinds of investment vehicles—so many, in fact, that no individual broker can possibly keep well informed on all of them. For that reason, brokers tend to specialize. Some concentrate on stocks and bonds, others on options, commodities, or financial futures. There is often further specialization within each of these areas. Brokers naturally gravitate toward those things they find most interesting and profitable to handle.

shares quoted at 69½ bid, 69¾ ask. You can put in a buy order at 69⅝, right in the middle. There's no guarantee your order will be executed, but exchange rules demand that it be executed ahead of the 69½ bid (which is probably from a specialist or other professional).

The NASD has made much fanfare of the supposed efficiency of its OTC trading system and, indeed, has succeeded in retaining a lot of stocks that in years past would have migrated to the NYSE or the American Exchange. But what works fairly well for Genentech (typical bid/ask spread: ¼ point) is no bargain for many of the more than 10,000 other OTC issues.

There is hope of salvation, however, for individual investors. Within a few months the Midwest Stock Exchange in Chicago intends to start trading 25 NASDAQ stocks in an auction market. Later in the year the American Exchange plans to begin trading a small set of NASDAQ stocks. The experiment will begin with better-known stocks, so the likely effect for the time being will be to shave ⅛ point off the Genentech spread while doing nothing for the Farmer investor. But it's a start.

"I don't want to predict this is manna from heaven, but we need to try this experiment," says Aulana Peters, an SEC commissioner. "I hope it will benefit the individual investor by giving his order more exposure."

Predictably, the market makers oppose letting the public into the spreads through the exchanges. There's a lot of money involved for them. Securities firms' annual revenues from dealer markups in OTC stocks exceed $1.7 billion, according to Perrin Long of Lipper Analytical Securities Corp. "You're removing my incentive to put capital at risk and provide liquidity," complains Patrick Ryan, head of trading at Johnston, Lemon & Co. and chairman of the NASD Advisory Council.

No question, the dealers with risk capital provide a useful service for investors who want to trade in a hurry. But some patient investors don't want full-service trading. Isn't it time they had a no-frills option?

SOURCE: Adapted from David Henry, "Excessive Markups?" *Forbes*, January 26, 1987, p. 98. Reprinted by permission.

Brokerage firms can be classified into two major categories: full-service firms and discount houses. The principal difference between the two is that full-service firms provide research and investment advice. Both execute buy and sell orders for their customers; offer cash and margin accounts; provide IRA and Keogh accounts; hold customers' securities in safekeeping or allow them to be registered in street name (that is, in the brokerage firm's name); collect dividend and interest payments; and invest cash balances in a money market fund. The type of firm an investor chooses usually depends upon how much he or she values the research and investment advice provided by a full-service firm. The difference between a discount broker's commission of, say, $60 and a full-service broker's commission of $170 to buy 300 shares of stock at a total cost of several thousand dollars may seem small in relation to the amount invested and the value of the information and advice received from a full-service broker. Still, for many people using a discount broker makes good sense, and there are a number of firms to choose from.

OPENING AN ACCOUNT

Opening a brokerage account is a simple process of filling out an application that provides the brokerage firm with a list of credit references and indicates the services the customer would like to receive. Most firms do not require a deposit or an initial purchase of securities. Customers who do not plan to borrow from the firm or do any short selling open a cash account rather than a *margin account*. With a margin account, the customer can borrow with the securities as collateral.

An investor has three choices with respect to custody of the securities: they can be registered in the investor's name and held by the investor, registered in the investor's name and held by the brokerage firm in safekeeping, or registered in the brokerage firm's name (street name) and held by the firm. Registration in street name has the advantage of eliminating the need to endorse the securities and deliver them to the brokerage firm when they are sold.

COMMISSIONS

By far the largest cost involved in buying and selling securities, other than income taxes on any gains, is the broker's commission. The commission of a full-service broker on the purchase or sale of 100 shares of stock is usually between 1.5% and 2.5% of the cost of the stock. The higher the price of the stock and the greater the number of shares traded, the lower the commission as a percentage of the total value. Typical commissions for a full-service broker and a discount broker are shown in Table 3-3.

PROTECTION IF THE BROKER FAILS

Following the failure of a large number of brokerage firms in the late 1960s, Congress created the Securities Investor Protection Corporation (SIPC), a private nonprofit organization for the protection of customers of broker-dealer firms. The SIPC, under the supervision of the SEC, administers an insurance fund that is financed by assessments against broker-dealer members.

The SIPC protects customers of failed firms up to a total of $500,000 per customer, of which up to $100,000 can be the cash balance in the customer's account. The stock exchanges, the National Association of Securities Dealers (NASD), and the SEC are required to report to the SIPC the names of any member firms that are in financial difficulty. If the SIPC decides that customers of the firm need protection, it can bring

ⅠⅠⅠ **TABLE 3-3**

Brokerage Commissions for Full-Service (FS) and Discount (D) Brokers

Number of Shares	$20 per Share Cost of Stock	Commission Amount	Percentage of Total	$50 per Share Cost of Stock	Commission Amount	Percentage of Total
100 (FS)	$ 2,000	$ 50.44	2.52%	$ 5,000	$ 84.47	1.69%
100 (D)	2,000	40.00	2.00	5,000	40.00	0.80
200 (FS)	4,000	92.19	2.30	10,000	168.00	1.68
200 (D)	4,000	40.00	1.00	10,000	53.90	0.54
500 (FS)	10,000	195.13	1.95	25,000	354.60	1.42
500 (D)	10,000	61.73	0.62	25,000	113.89	0.46

SOURCE: Survey by author.

action in federal district court for the appointment of a trustee to liquidate the firm. Sometimes the accounts of failed firms are transferred to other broker-dealers. To date, customers of well over 100 failed brokerage firms have benefited from SIPC protection.

The SIPC's experience in 1981 was especially bad, with a total of 10 liquidations. In that year, a drastic decline in the number of new issues caused the failure of several firms specializing in underwriting low-priced, speculative stocks.

Protection provided by the SIPC has been very good, but far from perfect. Sometimes the records of bankrupt firms are so bad it takes many months to sort out the customers' accounts. In the meantime, the accounts are frozen in place, and the customers are powerless to sell any of their securities.

ORDERS TO BUY AND SELL

Securities are bought and sold with market orders, limit orders, and stop orders.

Market Orders

Most investors buy and sell stocks with a market order, which is an order to buy or sell at the market price. It is the broker's responsibility to execute the order promptly at the best available price. Brokers assume that the customer intends to place a market order unless a different type of order is requested.

Limit Orders

A limit order is an order to buy or sell securities at a specified price or better. Limit orders are used when the investor is either concerned about the possibility of an unfavorable change in the price before the order can be executed or wants to buy or sell at a better price than is currently available. If a limit order cannot be executed immediately, it is entered in the specialist's book. In placing a limit order, the customer must indicate whether it is to be good for just one day or for a specified longer period, such as one week, or until the customer decides to cancel it. The last alternative is known as a GTC (good 'til canceled) order.

Except where the price of a stock is unusually volatile, the use of limit orders in buying stocks would seem to be inadvisable for individuals who intend to hold their investments for long periods of time. Suppose that the price of XYZ stock is $30 and an investor places a GTC limit order to buy the stock at $27, hoping to acquire it for 10% less than the current price. If he or she is lucky, or exceptionally wise, the price of the stock will soon drop to $27 or a little lower and then start a long trend upward after the order has been filled. In the absence of such luck or unusual wisdom, however, the investor may find that the limit order is never executed. In that case, the cash that was set aside, perhaps in a money market fund, to buy the stock may have earned a much lower return than if the stock had been purchased using a market order.

Stop Orders

A stop-sell order is an order to sell stock the investor owns at a price lower than the current market price. It becomes a market order once the price of the stock reaches the stop order price. It will then be executed at the best price available, which may be the same as the stop order price or somewhat higher or lower.

Stop orders can be used either to protect the profit in a stock or to limit the amount of any loss.

EXAMPLE 3-1   STOP ORDER TO PROTECT A PROFIT

Price paid for stock	$25
Current market price	45
Stop order price	42

Instead of selling the stock for $45, the investor has decided to hold it for possible further gains. If the price were to fall to $42 or lower, the order would be executed at the best price available, which might be either higher or lower than $42. ||||

EXAMPLE 3-2   STOP ORDER TO LIMIT A LOSS

Stop order placed:
Price paid for stock	$45
Price when stop order was placed	45
Stop order price	42

The result:
Stop order executed two months later at	$42
Lowest price during next 12 months	40
Price one year later	75

Anyone placing a stop order should be aware of the fact that whether it is to protect a profit or limit a loss, the order may be triggered by a price decline that is only temporary. When that happens, the result may be quite unfavorable.||||

|||| INVESTING WITH BORROWED FUNDS

Brokerage firms and banks accept qualified stocks and bonds as collateral for loans. Thus, investors can usually borrow a portion of the cost of any securities being purchased by using those securities as collateral for the loan.[12] The maximum amounts that can be borrowed against various types of securities are determined by the initial margin requirements, which are set by the Federal Reserve Board.

The initial *margin* requirement is the amount, or percentage, of the purchase price that must come from sources other than borrowings against the securities. For example, if the initial margin requirement is 60% and the cost of the securities is $10,000, the investor must supply $6,000 of the purchase price and can borrow only $4,000 against the securities. The $6,000 could come from borrowings against other securities in the customer's account. The initial margin requirement for common stocks has been 50% for over 15 years and has ranged between 50% and 90% since 1950.[13] Initial margin requirements for other securities are 50% for convertibles, 5% for U.S. government securities, 25% of the market value of qualified corporate bonds, and the lesser of 15% of the principal amount or 25% of the market value of municipal securities.

ACTUAL MARGIN

The actual margin in an investor's account at any time is the amount of his or her equity (that is, the value of the assets minus the loan balance) divided by the value of the assets:

$$\text{Margin} = (MVA - LB)/MVA \qquad (3\text{-}1)$$
$$= E/MVA$$

where

$$MVA = \text{market value of assets}$$
$$LB = \text{loan balance}$$
$$E = \text{equity}$$

---

[12]To borrow from a broker, the investor must have a margin account. If the brokerage firm is a member of the New York Stock Exchange, a deposit of at least $2,000 in cash or securities is required to open such an account; and the owner of the account must authorize the brokerage firm to loan out, or pledge as collateral, any securities in the account. Much of the money brokerage firms loan to margin customers is borrowed from commercial banks, with customers' securities pledged as collateral. Since the interest rate on such borrowings, known as the "broker call rate," is normally lower than the prime bank rate, brokers can usually offer attractive rates to their margin customers.

[13]Not all stocks are marginable. Over-the-counter stocks are marginable only if they are deemed to have characteristics similar to those of stocks registered on national exchanges. More than 2,500 OTC stocks are on the approved list.

If the actual margin falls below the initial margin requirement, the customer's account becomes *restricted*. For example, if stocks costing $50,000 are purchased on a 50% margin, the customer's initial margin and loan are both $25,000. If the value of the stocks falls to $40,000, the customer's equity declines to $15,000 ($40,000 − $25,000), and the actual margin becomes 37.5% ($15,000/$40,000).

Account restriction has two consequences: First, as long as the restriction remains in effect, the customer is not permitted to purchase any more securities on margin. Second, Federal Reserve Board regulations require the broker to retain and apply to the customer's loan balance a portion of the proceeds from the sale of any securities held in the account. With the initial margin requirement at 50%, the broker must retain and apply 50% of the proceeds to the customer's loan.

UNDERMARGINED ACCOUNT

Under New York Stock Exchange regulations, the margin in a securities account is not allowed to fall below a minimum of 25%, called the *maintenance margin*. A number of brokerage firms have "house rules" that set the maintenance margin higher than 25%. If the actual margin falls below the maintenance margin, the account is said to be *undermargined,* and the brokerage firm makes a margin call on the customer. If the customer is unable to comply with the firm's request for additional margin, securities will be sold out of the account in an effort to bring the margin up to an acceptable level. Forced sales of this kind are most likely to occur after a substantial drop in prices, which is usually the worst time to be selling.

It is, of course, important when buying on margin to know how far the price of the stock could fall before a margin call would be made. This can be calculated by solving for P in Equation 3-2, which is derived from Equation 3-1:

$$MM = (MVA - LB)/MVA$$
$$MM = (100P - LB)/100P$$

$(3\text{-}2)$

where

MM = maintenance margin

P = price of stock when actual margin equals maintenance margin

$100P$ = value of 100 shares when actual margin equals maintenance margin

For example, if the maintenance margin is 30% and 100 shares of stock are purchased for $100 a share, with an initial margin of $6,000 and initial loan balance of $4,000, the price at which the actual margin will equal the maintenance margin is $57.14:

$$(100P - \$4,000)/100P = 30\%$$
$$100P - \$4,000 = .30(100P)$$
$$70P = \$4,000$$
$$P = \$57.14$$

POSITIVE AND NEGATIVE LEVERAGE

Securities are purchased on margin with the aim of increasing the return on the investor's equity. The result of using such leverage depends upon two factors: the amount of leverage used and the difference between the rate of return on the margined securities and the interest rate on the borrowed funds.

The range of the investor's possible returns with different amounts of leverage, different rates of return on the purchased securities, and different interest rates on the borrowed funds can be calculated with Equation 3-3:

$$ROIE = ROS + [(1 - MP)/MP](ROS - r) \qquad (3\text{-}3)$$

where

$ROIE$ = return on the investor's equity

ROS = rate of return on the securities[14]

MP = margin percentage, the percentage of the purchase price coming from nonborrowed funds

$1 - MP$ = percentage of the purchase price being borrowed

r = rate of interest on the borrowed funds

The expression $(1 - MP)/MP$ can be viewed as a leverage multiplier. The smaller the margin percentage (that is, the smaller the amount of funds supplied by the investor), the larger the multiplier, and the greater the impact on the investor's return on equity. Example 3-3 shows the range of possible returns on an investor's equity when MP is 50%, r is 6%, and ROS ranges from $+20\%$ to -20%.

EXAMPLE 3-3   IMPACT OF LEVERAGE ON RANGE OF RETURNS

	A	B	C	D
1. ROS (return on securities)	$+20\%$	$+6\%$	0%	-20%
2. MP (margin percentage)	50%	50%	50%	50%
3. $1 - MP$ (percentage borrowed)	50%	50%	50%	50%
4. r (interest rate on borrowed funds)	6%	6%	6%	6%
5. $ROS - r$ = #1 − #4	14%	0%	-6%	-26%
6. $(1 - MP)/MP$ = #3/#2	1	1	1	1
7. $[(1 - MP)/MP](ROS - r)$ = #6 × #5	14%	0%	-6%	-26%
8. $ROIE = ROS + [(1 - MP)/MP](ROS - r)$ = #1 + #7	$+34\%$	$+6\%$	-6%	-46%

With no leverage, the investor's return ranges from $+20\%$ to -20%. With 50% margin, the range widens, with a high of $+34\%$ and a low of -46%. With a greater amount of borrowing, the range of the return on equity would be still wider. For example, with margin of 25% and the return on

[14] The rate of return on securities *(ROS)* for a single period is the cash income (interest or dividends) plus or minus the change in price, all divided by the beginning price.

assets ranging from $+20\%$ to -20%, the return on the investor's equity could be as high as $+62\%$ and as low as -98%.||||

Notice in Example 3-3 that the impact of leverage is asymmetrical—it has greater effect on negative returns than on positive returns. The 50% leverage increases the positive return by 14 percentage points $(34 - 20)$, but increases the size of the negative return by 26 percentage points $(46 - 20)$. This occurs because interest expense, by itself, reduces the size of a positive return and increases the size of a negative return.

|||| ## SELLING SHORT

Selling short is the opposite of taking a long position. Instead of buying and holding a stock with the intention of selling it sometime later, stock is sold with the intention of buying it later. About 7% of all sales on the New York Stock Exchange are short sales, and about 40% of those are by specialists who are selling short to meet a heavy influx of buy orders. Another 25% of short selling is by other members of the Exchange, and the remaining 35% is by the public.

A *short sale* is made by borrowing stock from, or through, a broker and immediately selling it. Short sales are made for speculative purposes as well as hedging. In either case, if the seller later closes out his or her short position (replaces the borrowed stock) with stock purchased at a lower price, there will be a gross profit on the short sale. For example, if stock is borrowed and sold for $50 a share, and the borrowed stock is later replaced with stock purchased for $30, the short seller makes a profit of $20 a share before costs and taxes.

OBLIGATIONS OF A SHORT SELLER

Short sellers have four obligations: (1) to supply margin to the broker in the form of cash or securities; (2) to turn over the proceeds of the sale to the broker as *cash collateral*; (3) to make payments to the lender of the stock in lieu of any dividends paid while the stock is on loan; and (4) to repay the loan of the stock.[15] The short seller can replace the stock at any time, but must replace it when requested by the lender. If the lender demands repayment before the short seller is ready to close out his or her short position by purchasing replacement stock, the short seller may be able to borrow shares from another investor to repay the first loan. If that cannot be done, the short seller's only alternative is to purchase the stock needed to pay back the loan.

The lender of the stock for a short sale may be the short seller's broker, a customer of the broker, or some third party with whom the broker has arranged the loan. Often, the lender is an investor who has purchased the stock on margin. Margin buyers are required to register their stock in the broker's name (street name) and leave it with the broker as collateral. The broker is authorized to loan the stock to others.

---

[15]The broker holds the cash collateral and receives any earnings from investing it.

Example 3-4, in which the lender of the stock is the broker and the margin is assumed to be Treasury bills of the short seller, illustrates a profitable short sale.

EXAMPLE 3-4   A PROFITABLE SHORT SALE

Facts:

Number of shares sold short	100
Price received on short sale	$50
Cash collateral (100 × $50)	$5,000
Margin (50%, in the form of Treasury bills)	$2,500
Amount of dividends paid on stock before loaned stock is replaced	$200
Amount paid for replacement stock (price $30)	$3,000
Commissions:	
On sale of borrowed stock	$100
On purchase of replacement stock	$80

Cash flows:

	Short Seller	Broker
Proceeds from sale of stock	$5,000	
Cash collateral	(5,000)	$5,000
Commission on sale	(100)	100
Payments in lieu of dividends	(200)	200
Cost of replacement stock	(3,000)	
Commission on purchase	(80)	80
Recovery of cash collateral	5,000	(5,000)
Net cash inflow	$1,620	$380

The short seller has earned a before-tax profit of $1,620. The brokerage firm has earned commissions of $180, received $200 in lieu of the dividends it would have received if the stock had not been loaned to the short seller, and has received any income from investment of the cash collateral. ||||

CALCULATION OF SHORT SALE MARGIN

Margin for a short sale is similar to margin for a purchase of securities. The margin requirement is intended to discourage "excessive" speculation and to provide protection for the lender, who in the case of a short sale is the supplier of the stock. The short seller's margin percentage at any time is his or her equity in the account divided by the amount of the short position, which is the current market value of the borrowed securities. The short seller's equity is the margin plus any decrease in the value of the stock from the time of the short sale, or minus any increase in the value of the stock. That is,

$$MP = \frac{\text{equity}}{\text{short position}}$$
$$= \frac{M + (SP - MV)}{MV} \qquad (3\text{-}4)$$

where

$$MP = \text{margin percentage}$$
$$M = \text{margin}$$
$$SP = \text{sales proceeds}$$
$$MV = \text{market value of securities}$$

For example, if 100 shares are sold short at \$60 and the required margin is 50%, the initial margin is \$3,000 (.50 × \$60 × 100). If the price of the stock rises to \$65, making the market value \$6,500, the margin drops to 38.5%, calculated as follows:

$$MP = \frac{\$3,000 + (\$6,000 - \$6,500)}{\$6,500}$$
$$= 38.5\%$$

If the maintenance margin is 30%, the price (P) of the stock at which the actual margin will be just equal to the maintenance margin is \$69.23:

$$.30 = \frac{\$3,000 + (\$6,000 - 100P)}{100P}$$
$$130P = \$9,000$$
$$P = \$69.23$$

SHORT SALE BY A SPECIALIST

Selling volatile stocks short is a highly risky business, as illustrated in the Sidelight, which describes an experience of Francis Santangelo, an American Stock Exchange specialist. Ultimately, he was correct: the Home Shopping Network stock was overpriced. Not long after Santangelo closed out his short position at a huge loss, the price of the stock plummeted, falling far below the prices at which he had made a number of short sales. Too bad he wasn't able, or willing, to maintain his short position a while longer.

REGULATION OF SHORT SALES

An SEC regulation makes it unlawful to sell a stock short if its price is declining. The purpose of the regulation, called the *"uptick rule,"* is to prevent short sellers from putting downward pressure on the price of a stock that is already weak. More specifically, the regulation requires that the price on a short sale be higher than the price on the last transaction unless the price on that transaction was itself higher than the first preceding different price. If the price on the last transaction was higher than the first preceding different price, the short sale price must be no lower than the price on the last transaction. The following examples will illustrate how the regulation is applied.

|||| **SIDELIGHT**
Speculation by a Specialist:
Frannie Santangelo's Horror Story

In May 1986, Francis Santangelo, a specialist on the American Stock Exchange, was granted the right to handle Home Shopping Network, a new listing on the exchange. Investors clamored for the stock when two million shares were offered at $18 on May 13. By the end of the day, it was being traded for $40, and Santangelo was selling short in accordance with his obligation as a specialist to supply stock under those circumstances. During the next few days, he continued to sell short, all the way up to $57 a share. Finally, after going short about 390,000 shares, he began to buy, but at prices far higher than those at which he had been selling. The result was an estimated loss of $5.8 million for Santangelo in just a little over one week.

Any specialist in a rapidly rising stock would be expected to sell short, but observers believe that Santangelo went much farther than most specialists would. He was sure that when the price went from $18 to $40 and more, it would soon fall back down. One reason the price didn't fall immediately is that two growth-oriented mutual funds had bought a large number of shares at $18 and were holding on to them.

SOURCE: Adapted from Diana Henriques, "Frannie Santangelo's Horror Story— He Was Short One of the Great Winners of 1986," *Barron's*, November 3, 1986. Reprinted by permission of *Barron's*, © Dow Jones & Company, Inc. (1986). All Rights Reserved Worldwide.

Example	First Preceding Different Price	Price on Last Transaction	Permissible Short Sale Price
A	40	39⅞	40
B	40	40⅛	40⅛

In example A, where the first preceding different price of 40 was higher than the last price of 39⅞, a short sale can be made only on an uptick, which means a price of at least 40. In example B, where the price of 40⅛ on the last sale was higher than the first preceding different price of 40, the short sale price does not have to be any higher than the price on the last transaction.

|||| **A NATIONAL MARKET SYSTEM**

In 1975 Congress instructed the SEC to promote a fully competitive *national market system* for securities trading. Although that goal has not yet been achieved, significant steps have been taken in the right direction. Four changes were needed to make the stock market a truly national market and to make the brokerage business truly competitive:

1. Abolition of fixed brokerage commissions
2. Creation of a central reporting system for all transactions
3. Establishment of a centralized system for quotations and order execution
4. Provision of national protection for limit orders

The following paragraphs review the progress that has been made in each of these four areas.

NEGOTIATED COMMISSIONS

Until May 1, 1975, the New York Stock Exchange had required its member firms, which included all of the major securities firms in the country, to charge commissions that were no lower than the minimums set by the Exchange. The Exchange control over rates ended May 1, 1975—known as "May Day" in the securities business—when the SEC banned fixed minimum commissions. Since that time, the commissions on large transactions have been greatly reduced, and a number of discount brokers have entered the securities business. Discount brokers now handle an estimated 20% of all shares traded by individual investors.

CENTRAL REPORTING SYSTEM

Two important steps have been taken toward the development of a centralized system for reporting transactions. The first was the adoption of the Consolidated Tape for all New York Stock Exchange listed stocks. With minor exceptions, the tape prints all transactions in stocks listed on the New York Stock Exchange, whether they occur on the Exchange itself, on one of the seven regional exchanges, or in the OTC market. In 1989, trading on the Exchange accounted for 84% of the trading in listed stocks; the regional exchanges accounted for 13%, and the over-the-counter market, 3%.

The second major development in transaction reporting is the NASD system for reporting all transactions in NASDAQ National Market System stocks as the transactions occur. There are now more than 2,000 stocks in this system.

QUOTATIONS AND ORDER EXECUTION

The goal is a system that will assure the execution of each order at the best price available anywhere in the country. The stock exchanges made a significant step in this direction with the creation of the Intermarket Trading System (ITS) in 1978. The ITS is an electronic communications network that links eight markets—the New York, American, Boston, Cincinnati, Midwest, Pacific, and Philadelphia Stock Exchanges and NASDAQ.

The 2,082 issues eligible for trading on the ITS at the end of 1989 represented most of the stocks traded on more than one exchange, including 1,633 listed on the New York Stock Exchange and 449 on the American Stock Exchange. The ITS has increased competition among the specialists on the exchanges and between the specialists and the dealers in the OTC market.

PROTECTION OF LIMIT ORDERS

The only way to assure that limit orders are executed at the best price available anywhere in the country is to have a central limit-order book, referred to as CLOB. With CLOB, limit orders from all markets would be recorded in one book, and the priority of execution would be based on their prices and time of entry. At the present time most limit orders for New York Stock Exchange stocks are filled by the Exchange specialists. With CLOB, the specialists would lose some of this business. The Exchange has not favored the proposed change.

|||| REGULATION OF SECURITIES MARKETS

The issuance and trading of securities are regulated by a large number of federal and state statutes as well as by regulations of the Securities and Exchange Commission, Federal Reserve Board, Commodity Futures Trading Commission, securities commissions of the states, the several stock exchanges, options exchanges, commodity exchanges, and the National Association of Securities Dealers.

The first securities law in this country was enacted by the state of Kansas in the year 1911. Its stated purpose was to protect investors against fraud and misrepresentation in the sale of stocks and bonds. In upholding a similar Ohio statute in 1917, the United States Supreme Court stated that the law had been passed to prevent "speculative schemes which have no more basis than so many feet of blue sky."[16] Hence, state securities acts are often referred to as "blue sky laws."

UNIFORM STATE LAWS

In the mid-1950s, the National Conference of Commissioners on Uniform State laws approved a Uniform Securities Act that has been adopted by most states. Generally, the state laws provide for three kinds of regulation:

1. Antifraud provisions, which make it unlawful for any person, in connection with the offer, sale, or purchase of any security, or in advising others for consideration as to the value of securities, to employ any scheme or device to defraud other parties.

2. Registration of dealers, salespersons, and investment advisers.

3. Registration of securities that are to be issued.

[16]Hall v. Geiger-Jones Co., 242 U.S. 539 (1917).

FEDERAL STATUTES

The principal federal securities laws are based on a different premise than most state statutes. Federal laws assume that full disclosure of the facts relating to a proposed new securities issue is adequate protection for investors. The SEC has no authority to deny registration if the issuer supplies all of the information required in a registration statement. Under state laws, administrators are given authority to deny registration for various reasons, including a belief that sale of the securities would tend to work a fraud upon the purchasers.

Securities Act of 1933

The first two, and perhaps most important, federal securities laws are the Securities Act of 1933 and the Securities Exchange Act of 1934. The 1933 act, sometimes called the "Truth in Securities Law," has two principal objectives:

1. To require companies issuing securities to provide full disclosure of all material information about the company and the securities.
2. To prohibit fraud and misrepresentation in the issuance and sale of securities.

If a securities issue is not exempt from registration, the securities cannot be sold to the public until an appropriate registration statement has been filed with the SEC and the statement has become effective.[17] The law requires that customers be given a prospectus that contains all salient data from the registration statement so they can evaluate the securities and make informed investment decisions. Prospectuses given to customers before the effective date of the registration statement (called "red herrings") must clearly state four things in red ink on the front cover: (1) the prospectus is preliminary; (2) the registration statement has not yet become effective; (3) the information is subject to change; and (4) the securities may not be sold prior to the time the registration statement becomes effective.

The registration requirements are not intended to insure investors against losses in buying new securities. The purpose of the law is simply to require issuers to disclose to prospective investors the facts needed to evaluate the securities. If the facts are properly disclosed in the registration statement and prospectus, the SEC cannot deny registration simply because the commissioners believe that the price is unfair or the issuing company does not have a reasonable chance of success. However, if the registration statement and prospectus are deficient because of misstatements or material omissions, and if the registration nevertheless becomes effective because the errors were not discovered prior to the effective date, any buyers of the securities who sustain losses may have a cause of action against the issuer, and possibly against other parties

---

[17]The 1933 statute provides a number of exemptions, including intrastate offerings, private offerings, and securities of banks, common carriers, charitable organizations, and federal and state governments.

who were involved in preparing the registration statement or selling the securities. If the errors were intentional, the culpable parties are also subject to fines and imprisonment.

Securities Exchange Act of 1934

Market manipulation and trading on the basis of inside information were commonplace in the 1920s and earlier years. Individuals formed syndicates that pooled large sums of money to push the price of a stock up or down to their own advantage. Corporate directors, officers, and major shareholders purchased shares of their own company just before highly favorable information, such as a large dividend increase or discovery of a new ore deposit, was announced to the public. Or, they sold shares of their own company just before the announcement of highly unfavorable information.

The principal objectives of the Securities Exchange Act of 1934 were to eliminate unfair trading practices and make the stock market less speculative. The statute requires directors, officers, and major shareholders to compensate their company for any profits they have made through buying and selling its shares within a six-month period; and it prohibits them from selling the stock short. Also, it requires the directors, officers, and major shareholders to file a report with the SEC for any month in which they have changed their holdings of the compay's stock. These monthly reports are summarized in a monthly SEC report called *The Official Summary of Transactions*.

In an effort to prevent unfair trading and market manipulation, the stock exchanges have adopted elaborate rules to regulate trading on the exchanges; the NASD has done the same for the over-the-counter market. The SEC has given these organizations wide latitude in policing their members.

Insider Trading Although the 1934 act does not deal explicitly with *insider trading* (other than to prohibit short sales and require payment to the company of any profits obtained by insiders through buying and selling its stock within a six-month period), the courts have held that the provisions dealing with fraudulent practices apply to anyone who profits from an unfair informational advantage. For example, it is illegal for corporate officers or directors to buy stock in their own company knowing that favorable information will soon be announced to the public. Less obvious are cases in which parties who are not affiliated with the company acquire inside information and either make trades on the basis of such information themselves or give it to others to exploit.

Over a period of years, the courts have adopted a doctrine that holds it illegal for anyone to trade on material, nonpublic information that has been misappropriated or obtained through a breach of fiduciary duty. Thus, it is illegal for an employee of an accounting firm or law firm representing a company to use nonpublic information about the company to make a profit on its stock. Also, if an investment banker gives an arbitrager inside information about a pending takeover of a company, both the investment banker and the arbitrager may be criminally liable.

Market Surveillance by the NASD

The NASD has a Market Surveillance Section in Washington, D.C., that monitors the quotations and trading activity of NASDAQ securities for the purpose of maintaining fair and orderly markets. The section examines market makers' quotations to see if they are reasonably in line with others and scrutinizes transaction prices and trading volumes for any unusual activity. It can call a temporary halt in trading if time is required to provide the public with new information.

Investment Company Act of 1940

Mutual funds and closed-end investment companies are corporations that invest in other companies and offer their own securities to the investing public. Both are regulated by the Investment Company Act.

The act emphasizes full disclosure and the avoidance of conflicts of interest and unfair dealing by investment company officers and directors. It requires companies to explain their investment policies to prospective and existing shareholders, and since policy changes can materially alter the risk characteristics of a fund, it requires shareholder approval before any investment policy can be changed.

Investment Advisers Act of 1940

Several years ago a *Wall Street Journal* headline stated that "Almost Anyone Can Peddle Stock Advice," and that is still true today. Investment advisers are regulated, but not very rigorously, by the Investment Advisers Act of 1940. The law defines an investment adviser as anyone who is compensated for advising others, orally or through letters or other publications, as to the value of securities or the advisability of buying or selling securities. Specifically exempted are banks and such professionals as lawyers, accountants, and brokers and dealers, where the performance of investment advisory services is incidental to the practice of their principal business or profession. Those who are not exempted are required to register with the SEC, supplying information relating to their education, experience, and criminal record. Of those three factors, only the criminal record can be considered by the SEC in deciding whether a person's registration shall be approved. Prior conviction of certain types of crimes, including violation of the mail fraud statutes or willful violation of any federal securities law, can be the basis for denying registration.

Probably the most important provisions of the Investment Advisers Act are those that make it unlawful for advisers to engage in fraudulent, deceptive, or manipulative acts, either in advertising their services or in making recommendations to their customers. The act also (1) prohibits advisers from basing their compensation on the investor's profits; (2) requires advisers to maintain certain books and records and to file periodic reports with the SEC; and (3) prohibits advisers from trading with their clients as principals or as agents of someone else without the client's permission. SEC regulations relating to advertising by investment advisers prohibit any claim that a graph, chart, formula, or other device offered by the adviser can, by itself, be used to determine which securities to buy or sell or when to buy or sell them. Over the years, the SEC has revoked or suspended the registration of a number of investment advisers who have used false and misleading advertising or deceived their customers in other ways.

|||| SUMMARY

Securities are issued in the primary market and traded in the secondary markets, which consist of the stock exchanges and the over-the-counter market. A good primary market requires the support of well-developed secondary markets because the willingness of investors to buy stocks and bonds depends on the existence of a market in which they can later be sold.

The supply and demand for a stock or a bond at a price close to the price on the latest transactions are often unequal. When that is the case, specialists on the stock exchanges and securities dealers in the over-the-counter market are expected to buy or sell for their own account in an effort to maintain an orderly market.

Investors usually buy and sell securities through brokerage firms. Full-service brokers (many of which are also securities dealers) offer investment advice as well as execute customer orders. Discount brokers offer no investment advice but charge lower commissions for executing orders.

Most investors buy and sell stocks with a market order, which is an order to buy or sell at the market price. Brokers are expected to execute market orders promptly at the best available price. A limit order is used when the investor wants to specify the price at which he or she is willing to make a trade. A stop order is used to protect the profit or limit the loss on shares that are owned or have been sold short.

Investors can leverage their position by purchasing stocks and bonds on margin. The initial margin is the portion of the purchase price that comes from the investor's own funds. An investor's actual margin at any time is his or her equity in the account (market value of the assets minus the unpaid balance of the loan) divided by the market value of the assets. If the actual margin falls below the maintenance margin, which is the minimum allowable margin, the investor receives a margin call. If the requested additional margin is not supplied, securities are sold from the account, and the proceeds are used to reduce the unpaid balance of the loan. Margin trading works to an investor's advantage only if the return on the securities is higher than the interest rate on the borrowed funds.

Investors can bet on a future decline in the price of a stock, or hedge against a future decline in the price of a stock, by selling the stock short. If the price drops far enough, the short seller makes a profit. Until the borrowed shares have been replaced, the short seller is obligated to maintain cash collateral and margin with the broker and to make payments in lieu of any dividends that are paid on the borrowed stock.

Many changes are occurring in the securities industry as the stock exchanges and NASDAQ move toward the congressionally mandated "National Market System." It is expected that Congress and the Securities and Exchange Commission will continue to put pressure on the securities industry until this goal is achieved.

Congress and state legislatures have enacted many statutes for the protection of investors. State laws require the registration of securities firms and new issues of securities. Their primary purpose is to prevent fraudulent practices. The Securities Act of 1933 requires issuers of securities to provide prospective investors with a considerable amount of information. Similar provisions apply to the shares of mutual funds under the Investment Company Act of 1940.

A prime objective of the Securities Exchange Act of 1934 is to eliminate market manipulation and the use of nonpublic information in securities trading. Congress and the Securities and Exchange Commission rely heavily on the stock exchanges and the National Association of Securities Dealers to police the actions of their own members.

|||| QUESTIONS

1. Explain the importance of well-developed secondary markets.

2. Describe the procedure by which investment banking firms underwrite and distribute large issues of corporate securities.

3. Explain the difference between the broker and dealer functions of a securities firm.

4. Comment on the reasons for minimum listing requirements and the nature of those requirements.

5. Explain the two principal functions of stock exchange specialists. Why is their role a controversial one?

6. What is the meaning of "a fair and orderly market"?

7. What factors seem to determine the amount of spread between the bid and asked prices for a stock?

8. What are the potential advantages of a national market system?

9. What are the advantages and disadvantages of having one's securities registered in street name?

10. Comment on the protection given investors by the Securities Investor Protection Corporation.

11. What are the broker's responsibilities in handling a market order?

12. What are the pros and cons of buying and selling stock with limit orders?

13. What is a stop order? Compare it with a limit order. What are the pros and cons of using stop orders?

14. What are the responsibilities of a short seller?

15. SEC regulations prohibit short selling a stock whose price is declining. Explain exactly what this means. Illustrate with prices.

16. Most state securities laws provide for three kinds of regulation. What are they?

17. An arbitrager expects that company A will make an offer to acquire company B in an exchange of stock on terms that will give a premium to B's shareholders. Explain how the arbitrager might attempt to take advantage of this possible merger, using a short sale to hedge against a decline in the value of A's stock. Explain why the attempted hedge might result in a loss if the merger does not take place. Illustrate with a numerical example.

18. What are the principal objectives of the Securities Act of 1933?

19. Explain the meaning and purpose of a "red herring" prospectus.

20. Explain the SEC regulations against the use of nonpublic information to gain an advantage in securities transactions.

21. What is the principal objective of the Securities Exchange Act of 1934, and, in general, how is that objective being pursued?

22. What are the principal purposes of the Investment Company Act of 1940?

23. What are the most important provisions of the Investment Advisers Act of 1940?

||| PROBLEMS

1. If four market makers are quoting the following prices for a certain NASDAQ stock, which quotes will appear on the screen of a broker who has level I of the NASDAQ service?

Broker	Bid	Asked	Shares (Hundreds)
A	25⅞	26¼	10–15
B	25¾	26⅛	5–10
C	25¾	26⅛	5–10
D	25⅝	26	15–20

2. Illustrate the impact of positive and negative leverage on an investor's return on equity, using Equation 3-3:

$$ROIE = ROS + [(1 - MP)/MP](ROS - r)$$

3. Prepare a cash flow statement for a short seller, given the following information, and assuming securities are supplied as margin:

Number of shares sold short	500
Price received on short sale	$60
Cash collateral provided by short seller (500 × $60)	$30,000
Amount of dividends paid by the company before the loaned	
stock is replaced	$500
Price paid for replacement stock	$55
Transaction costs	$400

4. Using the following facts, calculate the investor's current actual margin as a percentage:

Amount paid for the stock	$8,000
Initial margin (60%)	4,800
Current market value of the stock	6,800

5. Calculate the stock price at which any further decrease in the price would put the investor's actual margin below the maintenance margin. Assume that the only asset in the account is 1,000 shares of the Highfly Company, which were purchased on margin.

Amount paid for 1,000 shares of Highfly	$15,000
Initial margin (60%)	$9,000
Maintenance margin, as a percentage	30%

6. Calculate the investor's return on equity, given the following information:

ROS	16%
MP	60%
r	12%

What would the *ROE* be if *ROS* turned out to be 8% instead of 16%?

*7. You wish to sell short 100 shares of XYZ common stock. If the last two transactions were at 34⅛ followed by 34¼, you can sell short on the next transaction only at a price of:
a. 34⅛ or higher.
b. 34¼ or higher.
c. 34¼ or lower.
d. 34⅛ or lower.

8. If 100 shares of stock were purchased at $40 on 50% margin, and the price of the stock is now $36, how much farther could it fall, as a percentage of the present market price, before falling below the maintenance margin, assuming a 30% maintenance margin?

Note: Problems preceded by an asterisk are from Chartered Financial Analyst (CFA) examinations.

‖‖‖‖ **SELECTED REFERENCES**

American Stock Exchange Fact Book. New York: American Stock Exchange (annual).

Bae, Sung C., and Haim Levy. "The Valuation of Firm Commitment Underwriting Contracts for Seasoned New Equity Issues: Theory and Evidence." *Financial Management* (Summer 1990): 48–59.

Bower, Nancy L. "Firm Value and the Choice of Offering Method in Initial Public Offerings." *The Journal of Finance* (July 1989): 647–662.

Glosten, Lawrence R. "Insider Trading, Liquidity, and the Role of the Monopolist Specialist." *Journal of Business* (April 1989): 211–235.

NASDAQ Fact Book. Washington, D.C.: National Association of Securities Dealers (annual).

New York Stock Exchange Fact Book. New York: New York Stock Exchange (annual).

Stoll, Hans R. "The Stock Exchange Specialist System: An Economic Analysis." Monographs Series in Finance and Economics, Graduate School of Business Administration, New York University, 1985.

Tinic, Seha M. "Anatomy of Initial Public Offerings of Common Stock." *The Journal of Finance* (September 1988): 789–822

U.S. Securities and Exchange Commission Annual Report. Washington, D.C.: U.S. Government Printing Office.

4 INVESTMENT INFORMATION

To make sound investment decisions, it is necessary to have good information and know how to use it. One reason for reading a book like this is to learn how to distinguish between relevant and irrelevant information. The purpose of the present chapter is to explain how and where various types of useful data can be found. Later chapters dealing with the analysis of stocks, bonds, and other securities will provide further details.

Evaluation of securities often requires consideration of general economic conditions and the overall outlook for stock and bond prices as well as the prospects for various industries and individual companies. Accordingly, many of the information sources described in this chapter are discussed in the first four sections, dealing with the economy, the stock market, industries, and individual companies, respectively. Publications that do not fill well into any of these four categories are discussed in later sections.

Some publications are discussed in more than one section. For example, *Standard & Poor's Statistics* is examined in the economy section as well as in the stock market section. Publications such as the *Wall Street Journal, Business Week,* and *Dow Jones News/Retrieval* provide so many different kinds of information that they are classified according to the type of publication rather than by the kinds of information they contain.

THE ECONOMY

This section describes a number of publications that contain macroeconomic data, economic forecasts, or both. Much of this information is available in free or low-priced publications of the federal government and the 12 Federal Reserve Banks. Other sources of economic data and macroeconomic forecasts include *Standard & Poor's Statistics, Value Line Investment Survey,* publications of major brokerage firms and banks, and magazines such as *Fortune* and *Business Week.*

ECONOMIC REPORT OF THE PRESIDENT

Prepared by the President's Council of Economic Advisers and published in January of each year, the *Economic Report of the President* is available through the Superintendent of Documents. It contains commentary on recent economic developments as well as macroeconomic forecasts. It also contains an extensive set of statistical tables covering a wide variety of economic times series.

SURVEY OF CURRENT BUSINESS

Published monthly by the U.S. Department of Commerce, the *Survey of Current Business* provides monthly data on many of the same economic series for which annual data are published in the *Economic Report of the President*. These include, for example, industrial production, personal income, manufacturers' sales, manufacturers' new and unfilled orders, inventories, business failures, prices, housing permits and starts, construction costs, a wide assortment of labor statistics, and a number of series dealing with money and banking, corporate finance, the stock and bond markets, and foreign trade. Typically, the *Survey* contains two or three articles dealing with the economy.

BUSINESS CONDITIONS DIGEST

The *Business Conditions Digest* is also prepared by the Department of Commerce. It contains an elaborate collection of graphs and supporting tables dealing with all aspects of the economy, with emphasis on the leading, coincident, and lagging indicators. These include, for example, a graph of the index of the 12 leading economic indicators, similar graphs for the indexes of roughly coincident and lagging indicators, and an individual graph for each of the 22 components of these three indexes.

The *Business Conditions Digest* also contains graphs of a number of diffusion indexes that indicate the pervasiveness of a development or trend by showing the percentage of the items included in an index that have moved up or down. For example, the diffusion index for new orders of durable goods shows the percentage of the 34 durable goods industries in which new orders have increased. Other features of this publication include graphs showing stock prices and consumer prices for a number of foreign countries.

ECONOMIC INDICATORS

The President's Council of Economic Advisers publishes *Economic Indicators* monthly for the Joint Economic Committee of the Congress. It is composed entirely of graphs and supporting tables, which are an excellent source of information on trends in the general economy and the financial markets.

FEDERAL RESERVE BULLETIN

Published monthly under the auspices of the Federal Reserve Board, the *Bulletin* usually contains recent statements of Board members before congressional committees, latest rulings of the Board, a few articles dealing with money and banking, and a set of statistical tables covering banking, the financial markets, and a wide variety of other economic time series.

U.S. INDUSTRIAL OUTLOOK

The *Industrial Outlook,* which is prepared by the Bureau of Industrial Economics of the U.S. Department of Commerce, is published in January of each year. It contains projections more detailed than the forecasts in the *Economic Report of the President.* For example, personal consumption expenditures are broken down into durables, nondurables, and services. Durables are then subdivided into motor vehicles, motor vehicle parts, and other durable goods.

STANDARD & POOR'S STATISTICS

Standard & Poor's publishes an exceptionally comprehensive set of monthly statistics on the economy and the financial markets. In addition to covering such things as the gross national product (GNP), industrial production, employment and unemployment, weekly labor-hours, index of help-wanted ads, retail sales, consumer installment credit, and business failures, it contains a complete set of Standard & Poor's stock indexes.

VALUE LINE INVESTMENT SURVEY

In addition to providing financial and other information on approximately 1,700 companies, *Value Line Investment Survey* publishes macroeconomic projections four times a year. These include the components of GNP, as well as forecasts of prices and wages, housing starts, car sales, the unemployment rate, bond yields, stock prices, disposable income, savings, and corporate profits.

OTHER PUBLICATIONS ON THE ECONOMY

A number of major brokerage firms and commercial banks publish economic analyses and forecasts, and most of the 12 Federal Reserve Banks publish a monthly, bimonthly, or quarterly economic review containing a wide variety of articles. Also very useful to anyone interested in economic trends is the *Historical Chart Book,* published annually by the Board of Governors of the Federal Reserve System. It contains over 100 pages of charts relating to many aspects of the economy, including the stock and bond markets.

|||| THE STOCK MARKET

Several of the publications cited earlier contain historical common stock prices, usually in the form of market indexes of various kinds. The following paragraphs list additional sources of information relating to stock prices and the volume of trading.

SECURITIES AND EXCHANGE COMMISSION ANNUAL REPORT

The annual report of the Securities and Exchange Commission (SEC) deals largely with the regulatory work of the commission, including any enforcement actions it has taken. The statistical portion of the report contains data on such things as the number of securities registered on each exchange, the aggregate value of the securities, the volume of trading, and the aggregate values of new SEC registrations of each type of security.

STANDARD & POOR'S STATISTICS

Standard & Poor's Statistics contains a *Security Price Index Record* that provides a historical record of nearly 100 stock indexes published by Standard & Poor's. These include the composite index (Standard & Poor's 500), industrial index (400 stocks), utilities index (40 stocks), transportation index (20 stocks), financial index (40 stocks), and 88 indexes for individual industries.

NEW YORK STOCK EXCHANGE FACT BOOK

An annual publication of the New York Stock Exchange (NYSE), the *Fact Book* contains nearly 100 pages of information about the Exchange itself and the securities industry, much of it in the form of statistical data. Among other things, the data include trading volumes (stocks, bonds, and warrants, plus options and futures on the New York Futures Exchange), stock price changes, new listings, mergers, name changes, stock splits, margin debt, amount of new issues (public and private), foreigners' purchases and sales of U.S. stocks, U.S. transactions in foreign stocks, numbers and sizes of large block transactions, odd-lot volume, amount of trading in NYSE shares on other exchanges, sales and assets of all corporations versus sales and assets of NYSE listed companies, number of companies and issues listed on the Exchange, and volume of short sales by members and nonmembers.

AMERICAN STOCK EXCHANGE FACT BOOK

The *Amex Fact Book* is similar to the *NYSE Fact Book,* but places more emphasis on options trading because that is a much larger part of total trading on the American Stock Exchange than on the New York Stock Exchange.

NASDAQ FACT BOOK

The *NASDAQ Fact Book* explains new developments in the NASDAQ system and contains a number of interesting statistics about NASDAQ securities. For example, the *1990 Fact Book* indicates that at the end of 1989 the 5,000 NASDAQ securities included approximately 4,000 common stocks of domestic companies, 100 preferred stocks, 200 foreign securities,

100 American Depository Receipts (ADRs), 100 debenture bonds, 300 stock purchase warrants, and the units of 200 unit investment trusts.

|||| INDUSTRIES

STANDARD & POOR'S ANALYST'S HANDBOOK

The *Standard & Poor's Analyst's Handbook* contains data such as sales, operating profit, earnings, dividends, and book value on a per-share basis for a number of Standard & Poor's stock indexes. It also reports the operating margin, net profit margin, dividend payout, dividend yield, and price/earnings ratio. With this data, it is easy to compare the performance of individual companies with the average performance of various large groups of companies on a quarterly and annual basis.

FTC AND SEC QUARTERLY FINANCIAL REPORT

The Federal Trade Commission (FTC) and Securities and Exchange Commission publish a quarterly report containing condensed income statements and balance sheets for a number of industries based upon reports received from individual companies. The income statements show sales, depreciation and amortization, other operating costs and expenses, operating profit, nonoperating income or expense, profit before taxes, income taxes, profit after taxes, and dividends. The balance sheet shows almost as much detail as a typical balance sheet in a corporate annual report. This industry information can be used in evaluating the financial condition and operating results of individual firms.

INDUSTRY FINANCIAL RATIOS

Two sources of industry-average financial ratios are *Annual Statement Studies,* published by Robert Morris Associates, and *Troy's Almanac of Business and Industrial Financial Ratios,* published by Prentice-Hall. Data for *Annual Statement Studies* are supplied by bank lending officers around the country; data for the *Almanac* come from the Internal Revenue Service. Both publications contain a number of financial ratios for each industry and for a number of size classes within each industry.

BUSINESS WEEK

About 45 days after the end of each of the first three quarters and 75 days after the end of the year, *Business Week* reports the operating results for 900 large companies, arranged by industry. The figures reported are sales, net income, profit margin, return on equity, earnings per share, and the price/earnings ratio. While this report provides industry information more promptly than either the *FTC and SEC Quarterly Financial Report* or *Standard & Poor's Analyst's Handbook,* it contains considerably less detail.

VALUE LINE INVESTMENT SURVEY

The *Value Line Investment Survey* provides a brief quarterly analysis of each industry, including composite financial statistics for the industry as a whole. The figures are annual and include four past years as well as forecasts for the current year, the succeeding year, and an average for the years three to five years ahead. These industry analyses sometimes include macroeconomic data of special importance to the particular industry, such as mortgage rates for the building industry.

STANDARD & POOR'S INDUSTRY SURVEYS

Standard & Poor's prepares analyses for approximately 35 industry groups. One basic survey and three supplemental reports are published for each industry each year. Methods of analysis vary with the factors that influence product demand, prices, and costs. The end results are forecasts of gross revenues, costs and expenses, and net income for the industry. Each industry analysis contains comparative financial data for the companies in the industry.

U.S. INDUSTRIAL OUTLOOK

The annual *Industrial Outlook* prepared by the Bureau of Industrial Economics of the U.S. Department of Commerce contains analyses and projections for 200 industries. The industry forecasts are prepared after arriving at a consensus forecast of the gross national product.

TRADE PUBLICATIONS

Each forecast in the *U.S. Industrial Outlook* includes a list of references, many of which are trade publications. For example, references for the pulp, paper, and paperboard industries include the following trade journals: *Pulp and Paper; Pulp and Paper International; Paper Trade Journal; Boxboard Containers; Paper, Film and Foil Converter;* and *Paperboard Packaging.* Trade journals such as these, along with various yearbooks and specialized guides listed in the *Industrial Outlook,* are good sources of information about new developments in an industry.

|||| COMPANIES AND INDIVIDUAL STOCKS

Careful analysis of a company's financial condition and profitability often requires an examination of the notes to the financial statements to determine the company's accounting policies and the status of its pension fund. This kind of information is seldom provided by *Standard & Poor's Stock Reports* or *Value Line Investment Survey.* For most companies with publicly traded stocks, complete financial statements can be found in at least four places: the annual report to shareholders, the annual report to the SEC (Form 10–K), *Moody's Manuals,* and *Standard & Poor's Corporation Records.* Also, if a company has made a recent public issue of stock or bonds, its financial statements can be found in a copy of the prospectus.

ANNUAL REPORT TO SHAREHOLDERS AND FORM 10–K

Most companies with publicy traded stocks will send their annual report to anyone on request. In reading annual reports, one should understand that they are essentially public relations documents. Their principal purpose is to sell the company and its products to present and prospective shareholders, customers, and other interested parties. As a rule, the letter of the chairman and president in the annual report should not be viewed as an objective evaluation of the firm's past accomplishments and future profit potential.

The Form 10–K annual report to the SEC sometimes contains information that is not included in the annual report to shareholders. A copy of this form can usually be obtained from the company. Many libraries and investment firms obtain microfiche copies of Form 10–Ks from Disclosure, Inc., on a subscription basis. Disclosure supplies microfiche copies of reports filed by approximately 11,000 publicly owned companies.

MOODY'S MANUALS AND STANDARD & POOR'S CORPORATION RECORDS

These two services are not investment advisory publications and, in that respect, differ from a service like *Value Line Investment Survey,* which, in addition to providing historical data, analyzes a company's present condition and weighs its prospects for the future.

Subscriptions to *Moody's Manuals* and *Standard & Poor's Corporation Records* include a current news service (semiweekly in the case of Moody's and daily in the case of Standard & Poor's) in which condensed interim financial statements are published along with news items about management changes, new products, mergers and acquisitions, expansion plans, financings, and other items of interest. Since *Moody's Manuals* and *Standard & Poor's Corporation Records* are similar to each other, the present discussion will be limited to a description of Moody's several manuals:

Moody's Industrial Manual covers more than 3,300 companies, including all companies with stocks listed on the New York or American Stock Exchange or any regional exchange. Figures for the larger companies are taken from reports filed with the SEC. The coverage for many companies includes annual income statements and balance sheets for a period of seven years, in addition to condensed quarterly income statements for the past two years. The *Manual* also contains a brief history of the business, a description of its products and properties, a list of the officers and directors, the company address and telephone number, past prices of the company's stock, and detailed terms of any outstanding issues of debt and preferred stock.

Moody's OTC Industrial Manual contains reports of about 3,500 industrial companies whose stocks are traded, in most cases, over the counter. Generally, the *OTC Manual* contains considerably less information about a company than the *Industrial Manual*.

Moody's Transportation Manual covers approximately 1,000 companies, including airlines, railroads, bus lines, trucking companies, steamship and barge lines, tank car companies, and oil pipelines, among others. The information is similar to that found in the *Industrial Manual* except for differences due to the nature of the business.

Moody's Public Utility Manual covers approximately 600 utilities, including electric and gas utilities, gas transmission companies, telephone companies, and water companies.

Moody's Bank and Finance Manual covers over 10,000 financial institutions, including approximately 7,500 commercial banks, along with savings and loan associations, insurance companies, mutual funds, other investment companies, real estate investment trusts, broker-dealer firms, and finance companies, among others.

STANDARD & POOR'S STOCK REPORTS

Standard & Poor's Stock Reports contain two-page summaries of financial and other information about each company included in the service. The complete service includes all stocks on the New York Stock Exchange, all stocks on the American Stock Exchange, and about 2,000 over-the-counter stocks. The reports are revised three or four times a year. An example of a Standard & Poor's stock report is shown in Figure 4-1. Although most of the information in these reports is historical, the service does include earnings forecasts for some companies.

Standard & Poor's assigns a letter grade, ranging from A+ to D, to many of the stocks. These rankings are based largely on the growth and stability of the firm's earnings and dividends over the past 10 years and are not intended to indicate the relative attractiveness of the stocks.

VALUE LINE INVESTMENT SURVEY

The *Value Line Investment Survey* covers the common stocks of approximately 1,700 companies, including most of the stocks listed on the New York Stock Exchange, about 200 that are traded only over the counter, 100 from the American Stock Exchange, 20 from the Toronto Stock Exchange, and a few that are listed only on a regional stock exchange. Value Line issues a new report each week covering approximately one-thirteenth of the stocks in the survey. Thus, the report for each company is revised four times a year. Figure 4-2 is an example of a Value Line report.

The Value Line reports provide a number of facts, figures, and forecasts not contained in *Standard & Poor's Stock Reports*. These include sales and the profit margin for each of the company's principal lines of business (where such information is included in the company's annual report); a graph of the relative price strength of the stock; the number of decisions by insiders and institutions to buy or sell the stock; an itemi-

|||| **FIGURE 4-1**

Standard & Poor's Stock Report: Procter & Gamble

Procter & Gamble   1868

NYSE Symbol PG Options on ASE (Jan-Apr-Jul-Oct)   In S&P 500

Price	Range	P–E Ratio	Dividend	Yield	S&P Ranking	Beta
Nov. 9'90	1990					
80⁵/₈	91¹/₄–61³/₄	18	2.00	2.5%	A	0.91

Summary

This leading consumer products company primarily markets household and personal care products in over 140 countries throughout the world. Acquisitions have been an important driver of growth in recent years. Earnings gains are expected to continue in 1991 and beyond, fueled by further production efficiency improvements and aggressive expansion in overseas markets.

Current Outlook

Earnings for the fiscal year ending June 30, 1991 are projected at $5.05 a share, up from fiscal 1990's $4.49.

The dividend was raised 11%, to $0.50 quarterly from $0.45, with the November, 1990 payment.

Sales for fiscal 1991 should remain in a solid uptrend, fueled primarily by unit volume growth. Margin expansion is expected to slow due to projected higher raw material costs, costs of vigorous overseas expansion, and less pricing flexibility in more competitive domestic markets, but further production efficiency improvements bode well for sustained earnings progress. Recent acquisitions may be modestly dilutive.

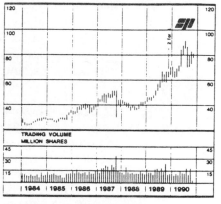

TRADING VOLUME
MILLION SHARES

| 1984 | 1985 | 1986 | 1987 | 1988 | 1989 | 1990 |

Net Sales (Billion $)

Quarter:	1990-91	1989-90	1988-89	1987-88
Sep.	6.65	5.72	5.27	4.66
Dec.	---	6.03	5.27	4.84
Mar.	---	6.12	5.43	4.86
Jun.	---	6.22	5.43	4.97
	---	24.08	21.40	19.34

Sales for the three months ended September 30, 1990 rose 16%, year to year, primarily due to unit volume growth. In the absence of an $81 million ($0.23 a share) onetime gain from litigation settlement, net income was down 1.6%, to $1.57 a share from $1.59.

Common Share Earnings ($)

Quarter:	1990-91	1989-90	1988-89	1987-88
Sep.	1.57	1.59	1.18	1.05
Dec.	E1.18	0.98	0.96	0.76
Mar.	E1.37	1.14	0.93	0.77
Jun.	E0.93	0.78	0.50	0.41
	E5.05	4.49	3.56	2.98

Important Developments

Oct. '90— PG reported plans to market a disposable diaper that would decompose into carbon dioxide, water, and compost within 14 days, and that it had invested $20 million in research toward the development of municipal waste-composting facilities.

Sep. '90— PG agreed to form a joint venture in Italy with the Fater Group under which PG's Pampers diapers business would be combined with Fater's diaper, sanitary napkin, adult incontinence products, and Fameccanica machinery businesses.

Aug. '90— PG and Rhone-Poulenc Rorer Inc. received notification from The Department of Justice on their strategic alliance to develop and market drug products. The Justice Department said that certain provisions of the pact violate anti-trust laws.

Next earnings report expected in late January.

Per Share Data ($)

Yr. End Jun. 30	1990	1989	1988	1987	1986	1985	¹1984	¹1983	1982	1981
Tangible Bk. Val.	11.30	8.98	12.97	12.00	12.00	15.75	15.21	13.88	12.59	11.67
Cash Flow	6.97	5.62	4.85	2.61	3.43	3.00	3.67	3.55	3.15	2.74
Earnings[2]	4.49	3.56	2.98	0.94	2.10	1.90	2.68	2.61	2.35	2.02
Dividends	1.75	1.50	1.37½	1.35	1.31¼	1.30	1.20	1.12½	1.02½	0.95
Payout Ratio	39%	41%	46%	144%	63%	69%	45%	43%	44%	47%
Prices—High[3]	91¹/₄	70³/₈	44	51³/₄	41¹/₄	35⁷/₈	30	31⁵/₈	30³/₄	20¹/₄
Low[3]	61³/₄	42¹/₈	35³/₈	30	31⁷/₈	25¹/₄	22⁷/₈	25¹/₄	19¹/₂	16³/₈
P/E Ratio—	20–14	20–12	15–12	55–32	20–15	19–13	11–9	12–10	13–8	10–8

Data as ong. reptd. Adj. for stk. div(s). of 100% Nov. 1989, 100% Feb. 1983. 1. Reflects merger or acquisition. 2. Bef. spec. item(s) of -0.23 in 1981. 3. Cal. yr. E-Estimated.

Standard NYSE Stock Reports
Vol. 57/No. 224/Sec. 21

November 19, 1990

Standard & Poor's Corp.
25 Broadway, NY, NY 10004

SOURCE: Standard & Poor's Stock Reports (New York: Standard & Poor's Corporation, November 19, 1990). Reprinted by permission of Standard & Poor's Corporation.

||| **FIGURE 4-1 continued**

1868

The Procter & Gamble Company

Income Data (Million $)

Year Ended Jun. 30	Revs.	Oper. Inc.	% Oper. Inc. of Revs.	Cap. Exp.	Depr.	Int. Exp.	3Net Bef. Taxes	Eff. Tax Rate	4Net Inc.	% Net Inc. of Revs.	Cash Flow
1990	24,081	3,161	13.1	1,300	859	445	2,421	33.8%	1,602	6.7	2,414
1989	21,398	2,727	12.7	1,029	688	398	1,939	37.8%	1,206	5.6	1,878
1988	19,336	2,429	12.6	1,018	633	332	1,630	37.4%	1,020	5.3	1,642
1987	17,000	2,177	12.8	990	565	361	617	47.0%	327	1.9	881
1986	15,439	1,753	11.4	1,102	448	286	1,175	39.7%	709	4.6	1,152
1985	13,552	1,343	9.9	1,141	367	202	1,004	36.8%	635	4.7	1,002
11984	12,946	1,717	13.3	926	330	149	1,427	37.6%	890	6.9	1,220
11983	12,452	1,840	14.8	622	311	112	1,550	44.1%	866	7.0	1,177
1982	11,994	1,632	13.6	635	267	106	1,399	44.5%	2777	6.5	1,044
1981	11,416	1,438	12.6	589	237	2111	1,186	43.7%	668	5.9	905

Balance Sheet Data (Million $)

Jun. 30	Cash	Assets	Curr. Liab.	Ratio	Total Assets	Ret. On Assets	Long Term Debt	Common Equity	Total Inv. Capital	% LT Debt of Cap.	% Ret. on Equity
1990	1,407	7,644	5,417	1.4	18,487	8.9%	3,588	6,518	12,364	29.0	25.7
1989	1,587	6,578	4,656	1.4	16,351	7.9%	3,698	5,215	11,248	32.9	21.1
1988	1,065	5,593	4,224	1.3	14,820	7.1%	2,462	6,337	10,121	24.3	16.7
1987	741	4,981	3,458	1.4	13,715	2.4%	2,524	5,740	9,670	26.1	5.5
1986	565	4,632	3,523	1.3	13,055	6.2%	2,457	5,704	9,532	25.8	12.8
1985	478	3,816	2,589	1.5	9,683	6.8%	877	5,272	7,094	12.4	12.3
1984	741	3,656	2,374	1.5	8,898	10.4%	630	5,080	6,524	9.7	18.3
1983	940	3,468	2,078	1.7	8,135	11.1%	783	4,601	6,057	12.9	19.7
1982	578	3,113	1,912	1.6	7,510	10.7%	846	4,164	5,598	15.1	19.4
1981	616	3,052	1,730	1.8	6,961	9.9%	846	3,863	5,231	16.2	17.9

Data as orig. reptd. 1. Reflects merger or acquisition. 2. Reflects accounting change. 3. Incl. equity in earns. of nonconsol. subs. 4. Bef. spec. item(s) in 1981.

Business Summary

Procter & Gamble markets a wide range of personal care and consumer household products. Contributions by business segment in fiscal 1990:

	Sales	Profits
Laundry/cleaning products ..	32%	29%
Personal care products	48%	49%
Food and beverage products	13%	11%
Pulp and chemical s	7%	11%

Foreign business contributed 39% of sales and 26% of net income in fiscal 1990.

Among the more popular laundry and cleaning brands are Bounce, Cascade, Cheer, Comet, Dash, Downy, Era, Ivory Snow, Ivory Liquid, Mr. Clean, Solo, Spic and Span, Tide and Top Job. Personal care products include Camay, Ivory and Zest bar soaps, Bounty, Charmin, Puffs and White Cloud paper tissue products; Pampers and Luvs disposable diapers; Always feminine hygiene products; Sure, Secret and Old Spice deodorants; Crest toothpaste; Head & Shoulders, Prell, Ivory and Vidal Sasson hair care products; Oil of Olay, Noxzema, Cover Girl and Clearasil skin care products; Pepto-Bismol and the Vicks line of cough and cold medicines; and pharmaceuticals. Disposable

diapers accounted for 18% of total sales in fiscal 1990.

Food items include Crisco oil, Duncan Hines cake mixes, Folgers's coffee, Tender Leaf tea, Jif peanut butter, Pringle's potato chips, and Hawaiian Punch, Citus Hill and Sun Drop juice drinks. Other products include cellulose pulp and chemicals.

Dividend Data

Dividends have been paid since 1891. A dividend reinvestment plan is available.

Amt of Divd. $	Date Decl.	Ex-divd. Date	Stock of Record	Payment Date
0.45	Jan. 9	Jan. 12	Jan. 19	Feb. 15'90
0.45	Apr. 10	Apr. 16	Apr. 20	May 15'90
0.45	Jul. 10	Jul. 16	Jul. 20	Aug. 15'90
0.50	Oct. 9	Oct. 15	Oct. 19	Nov. 15'90

Next dividend meeting: early Jan. '91.

Capitalization

Long Term Debt: $3,588,000,000.

5% Conv. Preferred Stock: $1,000,000,000. Held by ESOP.

Common Stock: 346,294,159 shs. (no par). Institutions hold approximately 46%. Shareholders of record: 102,516.

Office— 1 Procter & Gamble Plaza, Cincinnati, Ohio 45202. Tel—(513) 983-1100. Chrmn & CEO—E. L. Artzt. Pres—J. E. Pepper. VP-Secy —A. L. Ford. VP-Treas & Investor Contact—G. Gibson. Dirs—D. M. Abshire, E. L. Artzt, N. R. Augustine, T. F. Brophy, G. V. Dirvin, R. J. Ferris, R. A. Hanson, B. J. Hintz, D. I. Jager, J. R. Junkins, J. Lederberg, W. F. Light, J. W. Nethercott, J. E. Pepper, D. M. Rodenick, J. G. Smale, R. D. Storey, D. S. Swanson, M. v. N. Whitman. Transfer Agent—Procter & Gamble Co., Cincinnati, OH. Registrar—Central Trust Co., Cincinnati. Incorporated in Ohio in 1905. Empl—89.000.

Kenneth A. Shea

|||| **FIGURE 4-2**

Value Line Report: Procter & Gamble

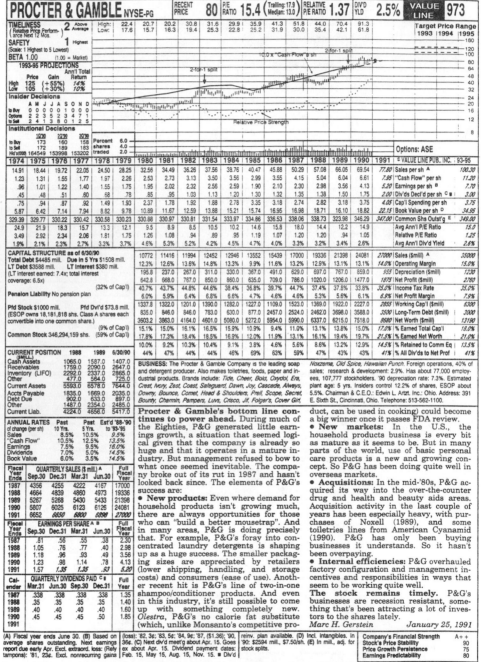

SOURCE: *The Value Line Investment Survey*, January 25, 1991. Reprinted by permission of Value Line, Inc. All rights reserved.

zation of current assets and current liabilities; the method of accounting for inventories; past growth rates of sales, cash flow, earnings, dividends, and book value, all on a per-share basis; Value Line's projections of average annual growth rates for about four years ahead; and a projected price range for the stock three to four years ahead under certain hypothesized economic conditions.

The Value Line ranking system is considerably more ambitious than Standard & Poor's. Every stock is assigned a timeliness ranking, ranging from 1 to 5, and a separate rank for safety. The timeliness ranking reflects Value Line's prediction of a stock's relative performance over the next 12 months, while the safety ranking reflects a company's financial strength and the stability of its stock price. Only the top 100 stocks (about 6% of the total) are ranked "1" for timeliness.

In addition to providing a one-page analysis for each company, the Value Line service includes a weekly summary and a 10 to 12 page supplement called *Selection and Opinion*. The weekly summary contains a number of key figures for each stock, including current timeliness and safety rankings, estimated beta, and the latest quarterly earnings and dividends compared with the levels of a year before.

The Value Line summary also includes a number of screens, or lists, which may be helpful in selecting stocks. Among these are the 100 most timely stocks, stocks offering the highest dividend yields, stocks that, in the opinion of Value Line, have the greatest appreciation potential over the next three to five years, stocks with the lowest price/earnings ratios, companies that have earned the highest rates of return on common equity, and companies that have generated the greatest amount of free cash flow over the past five years. *Free cash flow* is the excess of cash flow (earnings plus depreciation) over the sum of capital expenditures and dividends.

The weekly *Selection and Opinion* section of the Value Line report contains a review of recent developments in the stock and bond markets, comments on the outlook for business and the economy, a recommended investment strategy, a list of stocks whose timeliness or safety ranking has changed, and an analysis of one stock selected by Value Line for highlighting that week.

STANDARD & POOR'S OUTLOOK

Standard & Poor's Outlook is a weekly service of about 12 pages that analyzes current market conditions, makes forecasts of interest rates and market trends, analyzes a number of stocks, comments on recent developments in certain companies and industries, recommends portfolio strategies, and provides up-to-date information on one or more stocks in the S&P supervised list.

Standard & Poor's supervised list consists of about 40 stocks, divided into four groups: high long-term capital gains, promising growth prospects, cyclical and speculative, and high dividend yield. The *Outlook* also contains articles dealing with subjects such as out-of-favor stocks and new investment vehicles. From time to time, it contains computer-generated screens that list groups of stocks with certain characteristics, such as high dividend yields, low price earnings ratios, and fast-growing earnings and dividends.

VALUE LINE OTC SPECIAL SITUATIONS SERVICE

Value Line's *OTC Special Situations Service* is issued semimonthly and recommends a different stock in each issue. Quarterly follow-up analyses are provided for each stock previously recommended until Value Line recommends that it be sold. Each semimonthly report also contains a list of all 48 stocks recommended during the past two years, with a report on their performance, plus a list of all previously recommended stocks that are still "especially recommended" for purchase.

STOCK GUIDES AND HANDBOOKS

For quick and easy reference, Moody's and Standard & Poor's both publish a monthly *Stock Guide* covering over 5,000 common and preferred stocks. Moody's also publishes a quarterly *Handbook of Common Stocks,* which covers more than 900 stocks, and a *Handbook of OTC Stocks.* Information in the stock guides includes the stock's ranking, a brief description of the company's business, past stock prices, and earnings and dividends. Moody's handbooks provide most of this information, plus comments on recent developments in the company and its future prospects and a 15-year graph of the stock price and trading volumes.

EARNINGS FORECASTS

Earnings forecasts for individual companies are compiled by Lynch, Jones, and Ryan *(Institutional Brokers Estimate System,* or *IBES),* Standard & Poor's *(Earnings Forecaster),* and Zacks *(Zacks Investment Research Corporate Earnings Estimator).* The forecasts are obtained from the analysts of a large number of securities firms, and they can be accessed by computer or computer terminal in various ways.

STOCK MARKET NEWSLETTERS AND SECURITIES FIRMS' RESEARCH REPORTS

It is estimated that 1,000 or more stock market newsletters are published in the United States. In addition, many securities firms issue research reports on individual stocks, usually indicating whether the stock is recommended for purchase. *Barron's* publishes brief summaries of 20 to 40 such reports each week.

Newsletters and advisory services come from three kinds of sources: individuals (for example, Stan Weinstein's *Professional Tape Reader* and Martin Zweig's *Zweig Report);* investment information and advisory services (for example, *Standard & Poor's Outlook* and the *Value Line Investment Survey);* and a number of securities firms. Typically, the newsletters and advisory services attempt to predict the trend of the market as well as the relative performance of individual stocks. Performance of the newsletters themselves is monitored by Mark Hulbert in the *Hulbert Financial Digest*.

|||| CHART SERVICES

Many analysts and investors rely heavily on charts like *Standard & Poor's Trendlines* in attempting to predict the market and the performance of individual stocks. *Trendlines* is published monthly and contains charts of stock market indexes and certain technical indicators (such as the spread between stock and bond yields) in addition to individual charts for about 1,500 common stocks. Standard & Poor's also publishes an OTC chart manual. Among other things, the *Trendline* manuals identify stocks with certain characteristics, such as fast earnings growth, and they facilitate comparisons of stock price trends.

|||| BOND SERVICES

For fixed-income investors, Moody's publishes two services: a weekly *Bond Survey* and a monthly *Bond Record*. Standard & Poor's publishes a weekly *Fixed Income Investor* and a monthly *Bond Guide*.

MOODY'S BOND SURVEY

Moody's Bond Survey is a weekly loose-leaf service that describes current conditions in the markets for bonds, preferred stocks, and commercial paper. It also lists and describes recent issues and planned future issues of corporate bonds, municipal bonds, Eurobonds, preferred stock, and commercial paper. Another list shows all bonds on which Moody's ratings have been changed. The survey also provides tables of bond yields and discusses topics of special interest to investors, such as changes in yield spreads.

MOODY'S BOND RECORD

The monthly *Bond Record* is primarily a reference volume that describes a large number of bonds, preferred stocks, and issues of commercial paper. The service covers many types of bonds, including U.S. Treasury obligations, federal agency bonds, Canadian government bonds, corporate bonds, municipal bonds, convertibles, industrial development revenue bonds, and pollution control bonds. The *Bond Record* also contains a list of all bonds, preferred stock, and commercial paper on which Moody's ratings have been recently reviewed.

STANDARD & POOR'S BOND GUIDE

Standard & Poor's Bond Guide does for several thousand corporate bonds (straight and convertible) what Moody's and Standard & Poor's stock guides do for about 5,000 common and preferred stocks. It provides easy access to certain key figures that are useful in evaluating securities. For example, the information on straight bonds includes the coupon rate, bond rating, fixed charges coverage, ratio of funded debt to net property, call price, current yield, and yield to maturity.

In addition to covering about 5,000 corporate bond issues, the *Bond Guide* provides data on the following:

1. Corporate and municipal securities on which the S&P ratings were changed during the month.
2. Bond yields, by grade, for various types of bonds.
3. Recent bond issues registered with the SEC and a calendar for new bond offerings.
4. Foreign bonds, Eurobond issues with S&P ratings, industrial revenue and/or lease rental bonds, municipal bonds, and toll revenue bonds.

|||| NEWSPAPERS

WALL STREET JOURNAL

If an investor could have only one source of information, the best choice would probably be the *Wall Street Journal,* which is published five days a week and is delivered the same day in most parts of the country. News articles in the *Wall Street Journal* include information on many matters of interest to investors: the federal budget; Federal Reserve policy and the outlook for interest rates; current economic conditions; developments in the stock and bond markets; changes in the tax laws; selected rulings of the Supreme Court and various administrative agencies; partial coverage of major developments in companies and industries; new types of investments; and various schemes by which large numbers of naïve investors are swindled by unscrupulous promoters each year.

The *Wall Street Journal* also contains a number of features that are of particular interest to investors. These include a monthly report (on about the 20th) of the short interest in New York Stock Exchange, American Stock Exchange, and OTC stocks; a quarterly report of corporate profits, by industry; quarterly earnings reports of many individual companies; and a weekly report of Federal Reserve data relating to changes in member bank reserves and the money supply.

As comprehensive as it is, however, the *Wall Street Journal* does not provide all the information an investor needs. Common stock investors need ready access to industry statistics and historical financial data for individual firms. The *Wall Street Journal* does not routinely provide this kind of information. Moreover, new developments that have an important impact on a company or an entire industry (such as the introduction of new products, changes in customer preferences, technological innovations, and changes in the competitive climate) are often not reported in the *Journal.*

BARRON'S

Published weekly by the same company as the *Wall Street Journal, Barron's* is more strictly focused on the needs and interests of investors. Each issue contains several articles analyzing the past operating results and future prospects of individual companies. A typical issue also contains an interview with, or article about, a leading securities analyst, investment adviser, or investment manager that probes his or her techniques of analysis or investment strategy. Other articles deal with conditions in specific industries, developments in the money and capital markets, and the results achieved with various investment vehicles and strategies.

Barron's also carries weekly columns on the bond market, the real estate industry and real estate markets, the commodities and financial futures markets, and options. Editor Alan Abelson's weekly column is both highly entertaining and informative. Finally, a major portion of every issue of *Barron's* is devoted to extensive coverage of transactions and prices on the securities and commodities markets, as well as many statistics relating to the general economy and the financial markets.

INVESTOR'S DAILY

First published in 1984, *Investor's Daily* competes with the *Wall Street Journal*. It has several unique features, one of which is the daily reporting of an EPS (earnings per share) ranking and a relative strength ranking for every stock on the New York and American Stock Exchanges and all OTC stocks in the National Market System. The EPS ranking (from 0 to 99) is based on the five-year earnings growth rate and the percentage change in EPS for the latest two quarters versus the same quarters a year earlier. The relative strength ranking is a measure of the stock's daily price change compared to others over the last 12 months.

|||| MAGAZINES

BUSINESS WEEK

Like the *Wall Street Journal, Business Week's* coverage is very broad. Many of its issues contain special features. Just before the beginning of each year, *Business Week* publishes a special issue on investments that contains forecasts of the growth rate of real GNP and the rate of inflation by nearly 50 economists and a dozen econometric services. The investments issue also includes articles on the outlook for various industries and the stocks of individual companies and finally, an "Investments Outlook Scoreboard" that covers about 900 companies in 40 industry groups. For each company, the scoreboard shows the market price, book value, price/earnings ratio, dividend yield, percentage change in market value during the latest year, percentage of shares held by institutions, earnings per share for the two latest years, and two forecasts of earnings per share for the coming year. The earnings forecasts include the consensus forecast of security analysts (published by the *Institutional Brokers Estimate System*) and a forecast based on the earnings trend of the last five years.

Early in the year, *Business Week* publishes an "Industry Outlook" issue that contains comments on the prospects for 25 key industries. Four times during the year, the magazine publishes quarterly earnings of 900 companies in a "Corporate Scoreboard" issue. Annual earnings are reported in mid-March. Finally, in April *Business Week* reports on the aggregate market values of the 1,000 largest U.S. companies. The companies are grouped by industry, making it easy to compare each company with others in the same industry.

FORBES

Published biweekly, *Forbes* is one of the leading publications for investors. The majority of its articles deal with companies and industries, but other topics such as accounting practices, corporate mergers, the economic outlook, and new and unusual investment vehicles are also included. Articles about individual companies stress corporate strategy, the quality of management, and marketing practices rather than financial analysis. A typical issue also contains six or eight columns written by security analysts and investment managers.

Forbes publishes a special issue in January called "Annual Report on American Industry," which provides key financial figures for over 1,000 companies and a brief analysis of about 45 industries. The "Annual Directory" issue in May contains key figures for the 500 companies with the largest sales, the 500 companies with the greatest profits, the 500 with the greatest assets, and the 500 with the largest aggregate market value. Each company is then ranked within its industry on the basis of profits per employee. Also shown are the total number of employees and sales and assets per employee.

In August or September, a special issue of *Forbes* analyzes the performance of several hundred mutual funds. Each fund is assigned two ratings: one based on its performance in "up markets" and the other based on its performance in "down markets" over a period of approximately 10 years.

FORTUNE

Published biweekly, *Fortune* is one of the leading business and investment magazines. Its articles are similar in quality and depth to *Forbes*. Both magazines contain articles about industries and individual companies, but where a typical issue of *Forbes* reviews 12 to 15 companies, *Fortune* covers 2 or 3. *Fortune*'s scope, on the other hand, is broader than *Forbes'*, with frequent articles on topics such as monetary and fiscal policies, regulation of business, international trade, labor relations, and mergers and acquisitions.

One of *Fortune*'s regular features is a "Personal Investing" column that usually discussed the prospects for the stocks of one or two industries and includes an interview with a leading investment manager. This column also covers a variety of other topics such as the Japanese stock market, investing in gold, and investing in bonds.

Each issue of *Fortune* contains an economic forecast, usually focused on two or three items, such as consumer spending, employment, industrial production, corporate profits, or the outlook for certain industries. Twice a year—in early January and early July—the magazine makes a more comprehensive forecast covering GNP, industrial production, prices, corporate profits, and employment. *Fortune* publishes special issues on the 500 largest U.S. industrial corporations (ranked on the basis of sales), the 500 largest service companies, and the 500 largest foreign companies.

INSTITUTIONAL INVESTOR

A typical issue of the monthly *Institutional Investor* contains 15 to 20 articles dealing with such topics as management of pension funds, portfolio strategies, and economic developments. Other regular features include lists of new securities issues and the performance records of portfolios managed by or for mutual funds, insurance companies, and commerical banks. An annual feature is the magazine's selection of an All-American Research Team composed of the three "best" analysts for each industry.

OTHER MAGAZINES AND JOURNALS

Other useful magazines and journals include the *AAII Journal* (published by the American Association of Individual Investors), *Fact, Financial World,* and the magazine called *Money.* The *AAII Journal* is somewhat more analytical and scholarly in tone than the others. *Money* is unusual in its strong emphasis on personal financial planning.

|||| ACADEMIC AND PROFESSIONAL JOURNALS

More than 30 academic and professional journals, including publications of the Federal Reserve Banks, carry articles dealing with investment analysis, portfolio management, and capital market theory. Of these, however, only three (the *Financial Analysts Journal,* the *Journal of Portfolio Management,* and the *CFA Digest)* are addressed exclusively to the investment community. The others are in fields such as accounting, economics, financial management, financial theory, management science, and money and banking.

Typically, investment-related academic articles report new theoretical developments or the results of empirical studies. Since financial research often involves the use of mathematical models and applied statistics, many academic articles are beyond the understanding of most investors. However, in one way or another, the results of many academic studies are widely disseminated and used.

FINANCIAL ANALYSTS JOURNAL AND CFA DIGEST

For investors interested in keeping up to date with the results of investment research, as well as current thinking in the fields of economics and accounting, the *Financial Analysts Journal* (bimonthly) and the *CFA Digest* (quarterly) are two excellent sources of information. Both are published by the Association for Investment Management and Research and are aimed primarily at investment analysts and portfolio managers. The *Financial Analysts Journal* usually contains six to eight articles on a wide range of financial topics, in addition to regular columns entitled "Accounting for Financial Analysis," "Securities Law and Regulation," and "Pension Fund Perspective." Each issue of the *CFA Digest* contains 25 to 30 digests of articles dealing with financial analysis, portfolio management, accounting, economics, and professional ethics and regulation. Also included are brief comments on additional journal articles and recently published *Working Papers* of the National Bureau of Economic Research.

JOURNAL OF PORTFOLIO MANAGEMENT

The *Journal of Portfolio Management* contains a wide variety of articles relating to investment theories and practices. Most are written by professors and investment managers.

|||| COMPUTERIZED DATA AND ANALYSIS

Computers have made much information easily accessible that would otherwise be difficult to obtain. And, once the information has been acquired, calculations can be made, graphs and reports prepared, and records kept with relative ease. The largest sources of computerized data are on-line databases, a number of which are accessbile to microcomputers. A considerable amount of information is also available on disks and tapes.

BROAD-BASED ON-LINE INFORMATION SERVICES

Several computerized information services provide on-line access to a number of databases. Among the most widely used are *Compuserve, Dialog, Dow Jones News/Retrieval,* and *The Source. Dow Jones News/Retrieval,* for example, gives the user access to more than 40 databases, one of which is *Dow Jones News,* with articles from the *Wall Street Journal* and *Barron's.* Other databases in this service provide such information as current and historical stock prices, financial data for more than 10,000 companies from SEC filings, corporate earnings forecasts by analysts at 45 brokerage firms supplied by *Zacks Investment Research,* and detailed corporate financial data for more than 3,000 companies and 170 industries from the *Media General Financial Services* database.

DATA SUPPLIED ON DISKS OR TAPES

A number of organizations supply corporate financial data and securities prices on computer tapes, floppy disks, and compact disks. Perhaps the best known are the various *Compustat* services of Standard & Poor's, some of which have been supplied for more than a quarter of a century.

Compustat

The full *Compustat* database includes financial data on over 10,000 companies, with up to 20 years of annual and 10 years of quarterly income statement and balance sheet data, and 10 years of stock prices, earnings, and dividends. Also included are 20 years of annual data and 5 years of quarterly data for each industry, which facilitates comparison of individual companies with industry averages. The data are available on tapes or compact disks. The software generates reports and allows the data to be downloaded to various spreadsheet programs. It also permits the user to screen the stocks on any criteria he or she may select.

Stockpak II

Standard & Poor's *Stockpak II* is a microcomputer screening program and database on floppy disks covering from 1,500 to 4,600 stocks, depending on the subscription. Approximately 75 data items are supplied for each company, including sales, earnings per share, dividends, certain balance sheet items, growth rates, and the Standard & Poor's ranking. Diskettes with new data can be received either once or twice a month.

With *Stockpak II,* the user can screen the data any number of times to find companies that meet various sets of criteria. The user can also look up (on two pages) the financial and other data for the company and prepare reports (numbers and graphs) in which companies are compared with one another.

Value/Screen Plus

Value Line, Inc., offers a microcomputer screening program, *Value/Screen Plus,* which is similar in some respects to *Stockpak II,* although the latter contains more historical financial data. Both have self-contained databases and permit the user to screen a large number of stocks to find those that meet his or her criteria. The *Value/Screen Plus* database, however, consists of data for the 1,700 or so companies in the *Value Line Investment Survey* and includes Value Line's timeliness rankings and earnings forecasts. It also permits the user to maintain a record of his or her portfolio and prepare a number of different types of portfolio reports.

Other Databases

Research involving a study of stock prices or stock returns often requires analysis of daily stock price changes. This information is readily obtained from the *CRSP* tapes of the Center for Research in Security Prices at the University of Chicago. The tapes provide daily prices for stocks on the New York and American Stock Exchanges, as well as some over-the-counter stocks, beginning with the year 1926. The center also furnishes tapes of monthly prices and quarterly dividends. The publishers of *Media General Financial Weekly* offer a database containing stock prices and trading volumes, as well as balance sheet and income statement data, on more than 3,100 stocks. This database is accessible through various broad-based on-line information services, including *Dow Jones News/Retrieval* and *The Source*.

OTHER MICROCOMPUTER PROGRAMS

The fifth edition of *Individual Investor's Microcomputer Resource Guide* lists and describes briefly and uncritically nearly 300 databases and investment software packages for microcomputers.[1] With a few minor exceptions, these data sources and computer programs can be classified as in Table 4-1. In reviewing any list of investment software, one should recognize that the software available for microcomputers changes almost daily, as new programs are introduced and others are discontinued.

Table 4-1 lists two types of programs for selecting common stocks: fundamental analysis and technical analysis. The large number of software packages for technical analysis may reflect two things: (1) that computers are especially useful in recording, processing, and graphing the large quantities of data used in technical analysis; and (2) that many investors are using technical analysis in selecting stocks. As a rule, technical analysts consider only two kinds of data, stock prices and trading volumes. A typical technical analysis program produces various kinds of price and volume graphs, showing such things as trend lines, moving averages, and support and resistance levels. The data can either be en-

---

[1] *The Individual Investor's Microcomputer Resource Guide,* 5th ed. (Chicago: American Association of Individual Investors, 1987).

|||| **TABLE 4-1**
Microcomputer Investment Software and Services

Type of Program or Service	Number of Programs or Services
Evaluation of debt instruments	17
Financial data services	51
Fundamental analysis (common stocks)	14
Options and financial futures	35
Portfolio management	34
Real estate	23
Statistics	10
Tax and financial planning	38
Technical analysis (common stocks)	66
Total	288

The Individual Investor's Microcomputer Resource Guide, 5th ed. (Chicago: American Association of Individual Investors, 1987).

tered manually (a highly impractical procedure if the investor is using daily or weekly data and looking at more than a few stocks) or downloaded from an on-line database. A large number of databases are described in the *Microcomputer Resource Guide.*

Two kinds of programs are available for fundamental analysis of common stocks: screening programs (such as *Stockpak II* and *Value/Screen Plus)* and valuation programs. With a valuation program, the objective is to calculate the "true worth" or "value" of a stock, given such fundamentals as the firm's financial condition and forecasts of earnings and dividends. Generally, it is up to the user of the program to supply the required forecasts. Some valuation programs use more than one model and arrive at more than one estimate of an appropriate value or range of values. The user's manual may or may not explain the models that are being used. Buying a program with an unexplained model (a "black box") is like paying a stranger for a "hot tip" on the next horse race.

The words *portfolio management* have two meanings. To most investment managers and finance professors, they refer to the task of deciding which assets should be in an investor's portfolio at a particular time and in what proportions. To the purveyors and buyers of microcomputer software, they usually refer to the task of keeping a record of an individual's investments. Thus, most of the 34 portfolio management software packages listed in Table 4-1 are programs that deal with record-keeping and the preparation of reports.

Microcomputer financial planning programs come in many shapes and sizes. Some deal strictly with tax planning, estate planning, or retirement planning. Others assist the user with a variety of tasks, such as budgeting and keeping track of investments in addition to tax and retirement planning.

|||| INDEXES TO NEWSPAPERS AND PERIODICALS

NEW YORK TIMES AND *WALL STREET JOURNAL* INDEXES

For anyone who has the time to search through an extensive index for articles of interest and then read the articles on microfilm or on paper copies reproduced from the mircofilm, the *New York Times* and *Wall Street Journal* indexes can be very useful. Both of these newspapers contain many articles of importance to investors. Both indexes contain brief digests of a number of the articles, which sometimes eliminates any need to read the articles themselves. In any case, one can usually determine from the digest whether it would be worthwhile to read the article in its entirety.

PREDICASTS F & S INDEX

The *Predicasts* service is primarily an index of news items about companies and industries. It covers more than 750 business publications and contains about 2,500 entries a week relating to such things as new products, technological developments, capacity additions, product demand, sales, mergers and acquisitions, social and political developments affecting business, and analysts' reports on specific companies as reported in the *Wall Street Transcript*. The index contains two sections: in one, the articles are referenced by industry and in the other, by company. In the industry section of the index, the articles are arranged according to a numerical coding system based on the Standard Industrial Classification System. In the company section, the articles are arranged alphabetically by company name.

Although the *F & S Index* is a very useful means of locating articles about a particular industry or company, the index itself tells little about the content of the articles, in contrast to the *New York Times* and *Wall Street Journal* indexes.

BUSINESS PERIODICALS INDEX

The *Business Periodicals Index* is a monthly index of business-related articles rather than just news items about companies and industries. Still, there is considerable overlap with the *F & S Index*. Both cover trade journals and many popular weekly and monthly business magazines. Nevertheless, there are major differences: the *Business Periodicals Index* covers a number of academic journals, which are not referenced by the *F & S Index,* while the latter covers newspapers, which are not included in the *Business Periodicals Index*.

|||| # SUMMARY

One of the most important steps in investment decision making is collecting the essential information. Learning what kinds of information are actually needed is one reason for taking a course in investments. The present chapter has explained how and where various types of investment information can be found. Later chapters will explain what kinds of information are useful.

Most factual information required for the evaluation of a corporate stock or bond—other than the terms of the security itself—is related to the economy as a whole, to the industry involved, or to the firm itself. Macroeconomic forecasts and industry analyses appear in a number of publications, governmental as well as private. Financial and other information relating to individual companies can be found in annual reports to shareholders, *Moody's Manuals, Standard & Poor's Corporation Records, Value Line Investment Survey,* and various other places. Buy and sell recommendations relating to corporate stocks and bonds are published by securities firms and a number of investment newsletters and services.

Computers have greatly increased the efficiency with which investors can gather information and make decisions. In many cases, computers have made information widely accessible that would otherwise be known only to a few. Once the information has been obtained, computers and appropriate software make it much easier to keep records and prepare reports. Computerized data are available on disks and tapes and from on-line databases, a number of which are accessible to microcomputers.

Anyone using a computer program to evaluate securities should understand that the reliability of the results depends on the quality of the data supplied to the program as well as on the quality of the program itself. Since valuation models generally require the user to supply estimates of some items and forecasts of others, the soundness of the results depends in large measure upon the ability of the user to make or obtain reliable estimates and forecasts.

|||| QUESTIONS

1. Find and compare two forecasts of nominal GNP, the rate of inflation, and real GNP for the current year. Indicate your sources.

2. Find the latest value of the diffusion index for the leading economic indicators. What does it mean?

3. Find the level of Standard & Poor's Composite Index (S&P 500) at the end of each of the past five years. By what percentage was the index for the latest year higher or lower than for each of the four previous years? Indicate your source.

4. Find an estimate of sales of cars and trucks for the U.S. automobile industry (including vehicles manufactured in the United States by foreign firms) for the current year. Compare this figure with actual sales for the previous year. Indicate your source.

5. Find and compare the following ratios for the automobile and food processing industries for a recent year. Indicate your source and the year.
   a. Current ratio
   b. Fixed asset utilization (or turnover)
   c. Average collection period
   d. Ratio of shareholders' equity to total assets
   e. Profit margin
   f. Return on assets
   g. Return on common equity

6. Why do the earnings and EPS figures reported by Value Line sometimes differ from those in Standard & Poor's?

7. List the items found in a Value Line company report that are not found in a Standard & Poor's stock report.

8. List the items found in a Standard & Poor's stock report that are not found in Value Line.

9. Describe the four *Trendline* graphs for companies.

10. What are the principal differences between the kinds of information found in *Moody's Bond Survey* and *Moody's Bond Record?*

11. What is the difference between *Compustat* and a broad-based on-line information service?

12. Find and compare the price/earnings ratio and dividend yield in a recent issue of *Barron's* for the Dow Jones Industrial Average with the corresponding figures for the Standard & Poor's 500 Index. Also, compare the figures for the latest week with the corresponding figures for a year ago.

13. In what sense are *Stockpak II* and *Value/Screen Plus* fundamental analysis programs?

14. What is the difference between a screening program and a valuation program?

15. Describe the *CRSP* tapes.

16. Why do you suppose there are more technical analysis programs for microcomputers than fundamental analysis programs?

17. In what respects does *Stockpak II* seem to be superior to *Value/Screen Plus,* and in what ways does *Value/Screen Plus* seem to be superior to *Stockpak II?*

18. What kinds of information can an investor get from a broad-based on-line information service?

19. Why wouldn't a computerized valuation model almost certainly provide more reliable answers than a noncomputerized model?

20. Why can the *New York Times* index be very useful to an investor?

21. Describe the *Predicasts F & S Index.*

22. Compare the information on Merck & Company in *Moody's Industrial Manual* with the information in *Standard & Poor's Stock Reports.*

PART 2

RISK AND RETURN: THEORY AND EVIDENCE

5   RISK AND RETURN

In Chapter 1, we briefly discussed the positive historical relationship between risk and return. The principal objectives of the present chapter are to examine methods of measuring risk and return and to explore the relationship between the two.

How do investors evaluate the risk of a stock or a bond or a portfolio of assets and determine acceptable rates of return? These are important and fascinating questions about which much has been learned in recent years. We will first examine methods of measuring the rate of return and then turn our attention to risk and the trade-off between risk and return.

MEASURES OF RETURN AND RISK

The returns on stocks and bonds, except for non-dividend-paying stocks and zero-coupon bonds, are composed of two elements: the periodic dividend or interest payments and the change in the value of the asset.[1] The return for a single period, of whatever length, can be expressed as follows:

$$R_1 = (P_1 - P_0 + C_1)/P_0 \qquad (5\text{-}1)$$

where

R_1 = return for period 1

P_1 = value of asset at end of period 1

P_0 = value of asset at beginning of period 1

C_1 = cash payments received in period 1

For example, if the purchase price (P_0) for a share of stock is \$40, the selling price (P_1) is \$46, and the total dividend for the year (C_1) is \$2,

$$R_1 = (\$46 - \$40 + \$2)/\$40$$
$$= \$8/\$40$$
$$= .20 \text{ or } 20\%$$

---

[1] Earnings from reinvestment of interest or dividends must be included if the compound rate of return is to be calculated. The returns in *Stocks, Bonds, Bills and Inflation*, published annually by Ibbotson Associates, include this third element.

In this case, the yield of 20% consists of a dividend yield of 5% ($2/$40) and a capital gain of 15% ($6/$40).[2]

When returns for more than one year are involved, it is often helpful to calculate the average annual return. Two kinds of averages are used: the arithmetic mean and the geometric mean.

ARITHMETIC MEAN RETURN

The arithmetic mean return is a simple average of two or more returns as shown below:

$$R_A = (R_1 + R_2 + \ldots + R_N)/N = 1/N\sum_{i=1}^{N}R_i \qquad (5\text{-}2)$$

where

$$R_A = \text{arithmetic mean return}$$
$$R_i = \text{return for period } i$$
$$N = \text{number of periods}$$

For example, if the returns for years 1, 2, and 3 are 10%, 8%, and 15%, respectively, the arithmetic mean annual return is (10% + 8% + 15%)/3, or 11%.

GEOMETRIC MEAN RETURN

The geometric mean of a series of annual returns that include reinvestment income is the compound annual rate of return. It can be calculated only after the returns have been converted to value relatives. An annual value relative is simply the annual return, R, plus one. For example, the value relative for a return of 15% is 1.15, and the value relative for a return of −15% is .85 [1 + (−.15)]. The relationship between the value relative (VR) and the return can be expressed as

$$VR = (P_1 + C_1)/P_0 = 1 + R \qquad (5\text{-}3)$$

In terms of the value of an investment, the **value relative** is the ratio of the accumulated value at the end of a period to the value at the beginning of the period. For example, if an investor purchased a non-dividend-paying stock for $100 (designated P_0) at the beginning of a period, and the value rose to $120 (designated P_1) at the end of the period, the value relative, (P_1/P_0), would be $120/$100, or 1.20. If the stock paid a dividend of $5 during the year, the accumulated value at year-end (ignoring income from reinvestment of dividends) would be $125, and the value relative would be $125/$100, or 1.25.

With $(1 + R)$ as a value relative, the geometric mean return (R_G) of a set of periodic returns is calculated as follows:

[2] The return for a single period is sometimes referred to as the holding period yield, or *HPY*. The quantity (1 + *HPY*) is then called the holding period return, or *HPR*. Those exressions are not being used in this text. Instead, the return for a single period is simply called the return, symbolized by *R*, and the quantity (1 + *R*) is called a value relative rather than a holding period return.

$$R_G = [(1 + R_1)(1 + R_2)\ldots(1 + R_N)]^{1/N} - 1 \qquad (5\text{-}4)$$

or

$$R_G = \left[\prod_{t=1}^{N}(1 + R_t)\right]^{1/N} - 1 \qquad (5\text{-}5)$$

EXAMPLE 5-1   ARITHMETIC VERSUS GEOMETRIC MEANS

To compare the arithmetic and geometric means, consider an investment in a mutual fund where

$$P_0 = \$10 \qquad P_1 = \$16 \qquad P_2 = \$10$$

Then

$$R_1 = (\$16 - \$10)/\$10 = .60 \text{ or } 60\%$$
$$R_2 = (\$10 - \$16)/\$16 = -.375 \text{ or } -37.5\%$$
$$R_A \text{ (arithmetic mean return)} = (.60 - .375)/2 = .1125 \text{ or } 11.25\%$$

The mutual fund manager may now advertise that the mutual fund provides an average rate of return of 11.25%. However, it is doubtful that investors feel that they have achieved such a return. The geometric mean return provides the true average return achieved by investors:

$$
\begin{aligned}
R_G \text{ (geometric mean return)} &= [(1 + .60)(1 - .375)]^{1/2} - 1 \\
&= [(1.60)(.625)]^{1/2} - 1 \\
&= 0.0
\end{aligned}
$$

This return reflects the actual return the investors achieved over the two-year investment period. The geometric mean of a set of returns is always less than the arithmetic mean unless all of the returns are the same. And the greater the variation in the returns, the greater the difference between the two means. ||||

The figures in Table 5-1, which are based on the returns for Hewlett–Packard Corporation for 18 quarters beginning in 1985, provide another illustration of the relationship between arithmetic and geometric means. During this particular 18-quarter period, Hewlett–Packard's returns were fairly volatile. Consequently, the quarterly geometric mean of 2.7% was 1.1 percentage points below the quarterly arithmetic mean of 3.8%. If Hewlett Packard's returns had been less volatile, a smaller spread would have existed between its geometric and arithmetic means.

Risk

The American Heritage Dictionary defines risk as "the possibility of suffering harm or loss." For investment purposes, a more precise definition is needed—preferably one that permits risk to be measured. Harry Markowitz provided such a definition in his classic treatise on portfolio selection.[3]

---

[3] Harry M. Markowitz, "Portfolio Selection," *The Journal of Finance* 7(March 1952): 77–91; *Portfolio Selection* (New Haven: Yale University Press, 1959).

|||| **TABLE 5-1**

Arithmetic and Geometric Mean Returns for Hewlett-Packard
Corporation Based on Quarterly Returns, 1985–1989

Year–Quarter	End-of-Quarter Share Price	Quarterly Dividend	Return R_i	Value Relative $(1 + R_i)$
1984–4	36.25			
1985–1	37.50	0.055	0.036	1.036
1985–2	31.75	0.055	−0.152	0.848
1985–3	37.88	0.055	0.195	1.195
1985–4	30.25	0.055	−0.200	0.800
1986–1	39.38	0.055	0.303	1.303
1986–2	45.25	0.055	0.151	1.151
1986–3	39.38	0.055	−0.129	0.871
1986–4	39.00	0.055	−0.008	0.992
1987–1	50.13	0.055	0.287	1.287
1987–2	56.00	0.055	0.118	1.118
1987–3	61.13	0.055	0.092	1.092
1987–4	50.13	0.065	−0.179	0.821
1988–1	56.75	0.065	0.133	1.133
1988–2	61.13	0.065	0.078	1.078
1988–3	50.50	0.065	−0.173	0.827
1988–4	50.50	0.085	0.002	1.002
1989–1	57.75	0.085	0.145	1.145
1989–2	56.75	0.085	−0.016	0.984
Sum			0.685	
N			18	18
Arithmetic mean (sum/N)			0.038	
Product of 18 value relatives				1.604
Geometric mean return $(1.604)^{1/18} - 1$				0.027

Markowitz was the first to define risk in terms of the variability of
the return and the first to demonstrate how the risk of a portfolio is
related to the risk of the individual assets it contains. He measured
variability by the variance of the return, or its square root, the standard
deviation. The greater the variability of the return, the greater the uncertainty as to what the future return will be, and the greater the chance
that it will be substantially lower than expected. For example, the nominal
returns on U.S. Treasury bills usually fluctuate within a narrow range,
and they are never negative. Consequently, the risk is small. On the other
hand, common stock returns are highly variable, difficult to predict, and
sometimes negative. The risk associated with common stocks is therefore
quite substantial.

The standard deviation of the return has two distinct merits as a
measure of risk. First, it is expressed in the same units (percentages) as
the returns themselves. Second, if the returns are approximately normally
distributed, the standard deviation indicates how far the actual return
might fall below the expected return, and with what probability. If the
distribution is normal, only about one-sixth of the returns will be more
than one standard deviation below the expected return, and fewer than

3% of the returns will be more than two standard deviations below the expected return.

Historical Risk and Return

Stocks, Bonds, Bills and Inflation, which was discussed briefly in Chapter 1, reports returns for five classes of securities, along with the rate of inflation. Summary figures from the 1991 volume, shown in Table 5-2, reflect a strong positive correlation between total risk, as measured by the standard deviation, and the rate of return.[4] On the average, small stocks, which tend to be highly volatile, have earned higher returns than large stocks; large stocks have earned higher returns than corporate bonds; and so on. Of course, this does not mean that portfolios of high-risk investments always outperform portfolios of lower risk. Often, they do not. For example, in 6 of the 15 years from 1976 through 1990, the returns on large stocks were greater than the returns on small stocks, and in 5 of the 15 years, the returns on large stocks were lower than the returns on corporate bonds.

The mean returns shown in Table 5-2 were calculated using Equations 5-2 and 5-4. The formulas for calculating the variance and standard deviation of the returns are shown in Equations 5-6 and 5-7:

$$V_i = \sigma_i^2 = \sum_{k=1}^{N} (R_{ik} - \overline{R}_i)^2/(N - 1) \tag{5-6}$$

and

$$S_i = \sigma_i = (V_i)^{1/2} \tag{5-7}$$

[4] *Stocks, Bonds, Bills and Inflation: 1991 Yearbook* (Chicago: Ibbotson Associates, Inc., 1991).

|||| **TABLE 5-2**

Mean Returns and Standard Deviations for Five Classes of Securities, and the Inflation Rate, 1926–1990

Securities	Geometric Mean	Arithmetic Mean	Standard Deviation
Common stocks	10.1%	12.1%	20.8%
Small company stocks	11.6	17.1	35.4
Long-term corporate bonds	5.2	5.5	8.4
Long-term government bonds	4.5	4.9	8.5
U.S. Treasury bills	3.7	3.7	3.4
Inflation	3.1	3.2	4.7

Note: "Common stocks" are the 500 large stocks in Standard & Poor's Composite Index. "Small company stocks" are predominantly the stocks of a large number of relatively small companies.

SOURCE: *Stocks, Bonds, Bills, and Inflation: 1991 Yearbook* (Chicago: Ibbotson Associates, Inc., 1991).

where

$$V_i = \sigma_i^2 = \text{historical variance of the return for security } i$$
$$N = \text{number of returns}$$
$$R_{ik} = \text{historical return for stock } i \text{ in period } k$$
$$\overline{R}_i = \text{mean return for stock } i$$
$$S_i = \sigma_i = \text{standard deviation of the return for stock } i$$

Table 5-3 presents the calculations of the variance of returns for Hewlett–Packard Corporation (HP) and the Standard and Poor's Index for 18 quarters between 1984 and 1989. Over that period, the arithmetic mean return for HP was 3.8% while the arithmetic mean return for the S&P 500 was 5.2%. The variance is the sum of squares shown in columns 2 and 4 of Table 5-3 divided by $N - 1$ (18 − 1). The quarterly variance of HP over that period was 0.025% while the quarterly variance of the S&P 500 was 0.010%. Since the S&P 500 provided a higher return for less risk over the 1985–1989 period, an investor would have been better off investing in the market index rather than in Hewlett–Packard.

|||| **TABLE 5-3**

Arithmetic Mean Returns and Variances for Hewlett–Packard and S&P 500 Quarterly Returns, 1985–1989

Year–Quarter	Hewlett–Packard R_i	$(R_i - \overline{R}_i)^2$	S&P 500 R_i	$(R_i - \overline{R}_i)^2$
1985–1	0.036	0.000	0.090	0.001
1985–2	−0.152	0.036	0.070	0.000
1985–3	0.195	0.025	−0.039	0.008
1985–4	−0.200	0.057	0.181	0.017
1986–1	0.303	0.070	0.133	0.007
1986–2	0.151	0.013	0.058	0.000
1986–3	−0.129	0.028	−0.042	0.009
1986–4	−0.008	0.002	0.034	0.000
1987–1	0.287	0.062	0.249	0.039
1987–2	0.118	0.006	0.029	0.001
1987–3	0.092	0.003	0.056	0.000
1987–4	−0.179	0.047	−0.223	0.076
1988–1	0.133	0.009	0.050	0.000
1988–2	0.078	0.002	0.060	0.000
1988–3	−0.173	0.044	0.002	0.002
1988–4	0.002	0.001	0.039	0.000
1989–1	0.145	0.011	0.064	0.000
1989–2	−0.016	0.003	0.124	0.005
Sum	0.685	0.419	0.934	0.166
N	18	18	18	18
Arithmetic mean	0.038		0.052	
Variance $\Sigma\,[(R_i - \overline{R}_i)^2/(N - 1)]$	0.025			0.010
Standard deviation		0.157		0.100

||| SIDELIGHT
Weighing Risk against Return

Estimating the future risk of a particular investment or portfolio involves a great deal of uncertainty. Traditionally, risk has been equated with the volatility of the returns, as measured by the standard deviation or the variance. Volatility and risk are also measured, in relative terms, with beta.

As a practical matter, financial advisers try to construct portfolios that are unlikely to do worse in any single year than the investor can tolerate financially and emotionally. Future risk is often estimated on the basis of past volatility. Or, it can be evaluated by assuming a number of possible economic scenarios for the coming year and estimating how various investments would fare under each scenario. Of course, different practitioners will make different estimates. For many investors, longer-term risk is at least as important as year-to-year fluctuations. After considering how much short-term pain the investor can accept, it is important to evaluate risk in terms of the possible outcomes over a longer period of time. Longer-term risk can be expressed in terms of the probability that a portfolio will achieve the investor's long-term target rate of return.

SOURCE: Adapted from Karen Slater, "Weighing Risk Against Return Can be a Risky Business," *The Wall Street Journal,* August 24, 1989, p. C1. Reprinted by permission of *The Wall Street Journal,* © Dow Jones & Company, Inc. (1989). All Rights Reserved Worldwide.

Estimating Future Risk and the Expected Return

Although the findings of Ibbotson Associates relative to the historic risk of common stocks, bonds, and Treasury bills are interesting, investors are more concerned with the future risk associated with various assets. For anyone who holds more than one asset, the combined risk of all the asets he or she is holding (that is, the risk of the portfolio) is of primary concern. Any estimate of portfolio risk begins with estimates of the risk of the individual assets, usually measured by the variance (or its square root, the standard deviation) of the return.

One method of estimating the future standard deviation of the rate of return is on the basis of the actual standard deviations during various periods in the past. Another, often preferable, method is by preparing a subjective probability distribution of the future returns, perhaps based in part on historical patterns.[5] Methods used by practitioners to assess risk are discussed in the sidelight.

The first step in preparing a probability distribution of returns is to prepare a mutually exclusive and collectively exhaustive set of economic

---

[5]It is also possible to estimate the variance using the option pricing models that will be discussed in Chapter 17.

scenarios and assign a probability to each of these hypothesized states of the economy. The sum of the probabilities must be one. The forecaster is confident that one of the scenarios (or something close to it) will occur, but is uncertain as to which it will be. The second step is to estimate the rate of return for the security under each of the scenarios. The final result is a set of possible rates of return, with a probability assigned to each. With this information, it is easy to calculate the expected return, the variance, and the standard deviation of the return.

Estimating the Expected Security Return Let us suppose that an analyst has estimated the rate of return for two common stocks, i and j, over the next 12 months under five different scenarios, (a) through (e). Scenario (a) assumes a real GNP growth rate of 6%, an inflation rate of 6% and a prime bank rate of 12%. The assumed growth rate, inflation rate, and prime bank rate are somewhat lower for scenario (b), still lower for (c) and (d), and lowest for (e). For scenario (e), the GNP growth rate is -2%, the inflation rate 2%, and the prime bank rate 6%. For stock i, scenario (a) is the most favorable, (b) is next best, and so on down to scenario (e), which is the least favorable. The outlook for stock j, however, is better under conditions (b) and (c) (with a lower GNP growth rate, lower inflation rate, and lower interest rate than [a]) because company j has a large amount of short-term debt. The lower interest rates under (b) and (c) are expected to have a positive impact on j's profits that will more than offset the negative effects of a slower-growing economy. Neither stock is expected to perform very well under conditions (d) and (e).[6] The five scenarios along with the possible returns for stock i and stock j under each scenario are set out in Table 5-4.

The expected returns for stocks i and j in Table 5-4 were calculated with Equation 5-8.

$$E(R_i) = \sum_{k=1}^{N} P_k R_{ik} \qquad (5\text{-}8)$$

[6] To avoid unnecessary complications, we are considering only a few of the factors that might affect the level of the market as a whole or affect stocks i and j differently.

|||| **TABLE 5-4**

Five Economic Scenarios and the Calculation of Expected Return

Scenario k	Probability P_k	Return		Expected Return	
		R_i	R_j	$P_k R_i$	$P_k R_j$
a	.10	60%	10%	6%	1%
b	.20	30	15	6	3
c	.40	10	20	4	8
d	.20	0	0	0	0
e	.10	-20	-10	-2	-1
Expected return				14%	11%

|||| **TABLE 5-5**

Expected Return, Variance, and Standard Deviation of the
Return: Stock i and Stock j

Stock i

(1) Probability (P_k)	(2) Return (R_k)	(3) Expected Return $(P_k R_k)$	(4) Return Minus Expected Return $[R_k - E(R_i)]$	(5) Column 3 Squared $[R_k - E(R_i)]^2$	(6) Calculation of Variance $P_k[R_k - E(R_i)]^2$
0.10	60%	6%	46%	2,116	211.6
0.20	30	6	16	256	51.2
0.40	10	4	−4	16	6.4
0.20	0	0	−14	196	39.2
0.10	−20	−2	−34	1,156	115.6
Expected return		14			
Variance (total of column 5)					424.0
Standard deviation = $(424)^{1/2}$					20.6%

Stock j

(1) Probability (P_k)	(2) Return (R_k)	(3) Expected Return $(P_k R_k)$	(4) Return Minus Expected Return $[R_k - E(R_j)]$	(5) Column 3 Squared $[R_k - E(R_j)]^2$	(6) Calculation of Variance $P_k[R_k - E(R_j)]^2$
0.10	10%	1%	−1%	1	0.1
0.20	15	3	4	16	3.2
0.40	20	8	9	81	32.4
0.20	0	0	−11	121	24.2
0.10	−10	−1	−21	441	44.1
Expected return		11			
Variance (total of column 5)					104.0
Standard deviation = $(104)^{1/2}$					10.2%

where

$E(R_i)$ = the expected return for stock i

N = number of scenarios

P_k = the probability of scenario k

R_{ik} = the rate of return for stock i under scenario k

Estimating the Risk of Securities The estimated variance and standard deviation of the return for an individual security are calculated as follows, given a probability distribution of the return:

$$\sigma_i^2 = \sum_{k=1}^{N} P_k [R_{ik} - E(R_i)]^2 \tag{5-9}$$

and

$$\sigma_i = (\sigma_i^2)^{1/2} \tag{5-10}$$

where

σ_i^2 = estimated future variance of the return for security i

N = number of scenarios

P_k = probability of the occurrence of scenario k

R_{ik} = estimated rate of return for security i under scenario k

$E(R_i)$ = expected return of security i

σ_i = estimated future standard deviation of the return for security i

The procedure for estimating the variance and standard deviation of the return for stocks i and j is shown in Table 5-5. The table also shows that the variance of security i is much greater than the variance of security j. This should be expected given the range of returns of security i (60% to -20%) versus those of security j (20% to -10%).

|||| THE MARKET MODEL

To facilitate the practical application of quantitative portfolio selection techniques, William Sharpe developed a simple but ingenious method that he called the diagonal model but that is now widely known as the *market model*.[7] The model is founded on the assumption that the returns of individual securities or portfolios are correlated with the returns of a market portfolio of securities.

COVARIANCE AND THE CORRELATION COEFFICIENT

The degree of co-movement between any two variables, including the rates of return for a common stock and the market, can be measured either in absolute terms by the covariance or in relative terms by the coefficient of correlation. If the returns are in the form of probability distributions, the covariance is calculated with Equation 5-11. For historical returns, the covariance is calculated with Equation 5-12.

---

[7] William F. Sharpe, "A Simplified Model for Portfolio Analysis," *Management Science* 9 (January 1963): 277–93. Although the model was intended to apply to securities of all kinds, our discussion will be in terms of common stocks.

$$\text{Cov}_{ij} = \sum_{k=1}^{N} (R_{ik} - \overline{R}_i)(R_{jk} - R_j)P_k \tag{5-11}$$

$$\text{Cov}_{ij} = 1/(N - 1) \sum_{t=1}^{N} (R_{it} - \overline{R}_i)(R_{jt} - \overline{R}_j) \tag{5-12}$$

where

N = number of possible returns for each security in Equation 5-11 or number of time periods in Equation 5-12

R_{ik} = estimated return for security i under scenario k

R_{it} = actual return for i in period t

$\overline{R}_i$ = expected return in Equation 5-11 or mean return in Equation 5-12

The stronger the tendency of the two returns to be above their expected return, or mean, at the same time or under the same conditions, the larger the covariance.

Although the covariance shows whether two variables are positively or negatively related, it does not indicate the degree to which they are related. That is, it is not possible to say that two variables with a positive covariance of 200 are more closely related than two variables with a positive covariance of 100.

The correlation coefficient (ρ) is a standardized measure of covariability that expresses the degree of the relationship between two variables. The possible values of the correlation coefficient range between -1.0 (perfect negative correlation) and $+1.0$ (perfect positive correlation). A correlation coefficient of 0 indicates that no relationship exists between the variables in question.

The correlation coefficient is calculated by dividing the covariance by the product of the standard deviations of the two variables. Equations 5-13 and 5-14 show how the covariance and correlation coefficient are related to one another:

$$\rho_{ij} = \text{Cov}_{ij}/\sigma_i\sigma_j \tag{5-13}$$
$$\text{Cov}_{ij} = \rho_{ij}\sigma_i\sigma_j \tag{5-14}$$

where

ρ_{ij} = correlation between the returns of securities i and j

σ_i and σ_j = standard deviations of the returns of securities i and j, respectively

Table 5-6 presents the calculations of the covariance and correlation coefficients using Equations 5-11 and 5-13 and the data for securities i and j presented in Table 5-4.

Table 5-7 presents the calculations of the historical covariance and correlation coefficient for the quarterly returns of Hewlett Packard and

|||| **TABLE 5-6**

Covariance and Correlation Coefficient, Returns of Stocks i and j

(1) Probability P_k	(2) Stock i Return R_i	(3) Stock j Return R_j	(4) Stock i Return Minus Expected Return $(R_i - \overline{R}_i)$	(5) Stock j Return Minus Expected Return $(R_j - \overline{R}_j)$	(6) (1) × (4) × (5) $P_k(R_i - \overline{R}_i)(R_j - \overline{R}_j)$
0.1	60%	10%	46%	−1%	−4.6
0.2	30	15	16	4	12.8
0.4	10	20	−4	9	−14.4
0.2	0	0	−14	−11	30.8
0.1	−20	−10	−34	−21	71.4
E(return)	14.0	11.0			
Standard deviation	20.6	10.2			
Covariance (sum of column 6)					96.0
Correlation coefficient ($\text{Cov}_{ij}/\sigma_i\sigma_j$)					0.46

|||| **TABLE 5-7**

Covariance and Correlation of Hewlett–Packard and S&P 500
Quarterly Returns, January 1985–June 1989

Year–Quarter	Quarterly Returns Hewlett–Packard (1) R_h	S&P 500 (2) R_m	Covariance Calculations (3) $R_h - \overline{R}_h$	(4) $R_m - \overline{R}_m$	(5) (3) × (4)
1985–1	3.60	9.01	−0.20	3.82	−0.78
1985–2	−15.19	6.97	−18.99	1.78	−33.90
1985–3	19.46	−3.91	15.66	−9.10	−142.55
1985–4	−19.99	18.06	−23.79	12.87	−306.27
1986–1	30.35	13.29	26.55	8.10	214.92
1986–2	15.06	5.78	11.26	0.59	6.63
1986–3	−12.86	−4.24	−16.66	−9.43	157.18
1986–4	−0.81	3.36	−4.61	−1.82	8.42
1987–1	28.67	24.91	24.87	19.72	490.27
1987–2	11.83	2.91	8.03	−2.28	−18.29
1987–3	9.25	5.61	5.45	0.42	2.27
1987–4	−17.89	−22.30	−21.69	−27.49	596.29
1988–1	13.35	5.03	9.55	−0.16	−1.54
1988–2	7.82	5.99	4.02	0.80	3.21
1988–3	−17.28	0.21	−21.08	−4.98	105.02
1988–4	0.17	3.89	−3.63	−1.29	4.70
1989–1	14.52	6.41	10.72	1.22	13.13
1989–2	−1.58	12.42	−5.38	7.23	−38.99
Summation	68.48	93.39			1,059.72
Mean	3.80	5.19			
Variance	246.70	97.37			
Standard deviation	15.71	9.87			
Covariance (1,059.72/17)					62.34
Correlation coefficient [62.34/(15.71)(9.87)]					0.40

the Standard and Poor's 500 Index using Equations 5-12 and 5-13. The correlation between the returns was 0.40.

THE REGRESSION MODEL

The market model assumes that the returns on common stocks are related through their common relationship to the return on the market as a whole. More specifically, it states that the return on stock i in period t (designated R_{it}) is a linear function of the return on the stock market as a whole (designated R_{mt}) during the same period. That is,

$$R_{it} = \alpha_i + \beta_{im}R_{mt} + \epsilon_{it} \tag{5-15}$$

Or, in terms of expectations:

$$E(R_{it}) = \alpha_i + \beta_{im}E(R_{mt}) \tag{5-16}$$

where

R_{it} = return on security i in period t

R_{mt} = return of a market portfolio in period t

α_i = the intercept term

β_{im} = the slope coefficient

ϵ_{it} = the regression error term

E = expectation operator

Systematic Return

According to the market model, the return for each common stock has a systematic relationship with the return for the market as a whole, and the measure of that relationship is the stock's *beta coefficient*. The beta (β_{im}) is a measure of the sensitivity of the stock's return to changes in the market return. The return for stock i is shown as a function of the market return in Equation 5-15 ($\beta_{im}R_{mt}$), and the expected return is shown as a function of the expected market return in Equation 5-16 [$\beta_{im}E(R_{mt})$].

A stock's beta coefficient reflects not only the relative volatility of the stock but the degree to which its return is correlated with the market return. this can be seen in Equations 5-17 and 5-18. In Equation 5-17, beta is calculated by dividing the covariance of the stock's return and the market return by the variance of the market return:[8]

$$\beta_{im} = \text{Cov}_{im}/\sigma_m^2 \tag{5-17}$$

When the covariance is expressed as the product of the correlation coefficient and the two standard deviations, as in Equation 5-18, the equation for beta becomes:

$$\beta_{im} = (\rho_{im}\sigma_i\sigma_m)/\sigma_m^2 \\ = \rho_{im}\sigma_i/\sigma_m \tag{5-18}$$

[8]We can now see that the reason β is subscripted with the variables i and m is because β is a correlation-type measure.

The beta of a market portfolio is equal to 1.0.[9] Stocks with betas greater than 1.0 are highly volatile and have a positive correlation with the market. Such stocks are termed aggressive securities because the market portion of their return is magnified by their beta. Thus, if the return on the market is 10% and the true beta for a security is 2.0, the security's systematic return will be two times the market return, or 20.0%. Stocks with betas less than 1.0 are either more stable than the average or have a low correlation with the market, or both. Such stocks are called defensive securities since their systematic return is only a fraction of the market return. For example, if the market return is 10% and a stock's beta is .80, its systematic return will be 80% of the market return, or 8.0%.

The concept of aggressive and defensive securities suggests a very naïve portfolio strategy. If an investor anticipates a market increase, he or she might invest in high-beta securities in order to capitalize on the expected trend. Conversely, if a market decline is anticipated, an investor might invest in low-beta securities in order to reduce the impact of the anticipated market move.

Table 5-7 shows the following relationships between quarterly returns for Hewlett–Packard and the Standard & Poor's 500: correlation, 0.40; Hewlett–Packard standard deviation, 15.71%; Standard & Poor's 500 standard deviation, 9.87%. With those figures, Hewlett–Packard's beta can be calculated with Equation 5-18, as shown below:

$$\beta_{im} = (.40 \times 15.71)/9.87 = .64$$

The relatively low beta of .64 reflects the low volatility of Hewlett–Packard's stock price and the relatively low correlation with the market return.

Unsystematic Return

A common stock's actual return usually differs from the return that might have been expected, given the market return and the historical relationship of the stock's return to the market return. In a regression analysis, the difference between the actual return and the return that might have been expected, given the market return, is called ϵ_{it}, the random-error term, or residual. That is,

$$\begin{aligned} \epsilon_{it} &= R_{it} - E(R_{it}) \\ &= R_{it} - [\alpha_i + \beta_{im}E(R_{mt})] \end{aligned} \tag{5-19}$$

Note that the expected value of ϵ_{it} is zero; therefore, it does not appear in the expected-return Equation 5-16.

SYSTEMATIC AND UNSYSTEMATIC RISK

The market model led to the idea that the total return of a stock or portfolio of stocks is composed of two elements: return associated with

---

[9]The covariance of any random variable with itself is the variance. Therefore from Equation 5-17, $\beta_{im} = 1.0$.

the market as a whole (systematic return) and return associated with the individual firm or its industry (unsystematic return). Since individual stocks have a systematic relationship with the market as a whole, a portion of their risk must arise from factors that cause the market to rise or fall. This portion of the total risk is known as systematic risk, also called market-related or nondiversifiable risk. It is systematic because of the stock's systematic relationship with the market; it is market related because it arises from the various factors that cause the market to move up and down; and it is nondiversifiable because an investor cannot eliminate the risk by combining securities into portfolios. Anyone who holds common stock is exposed to the risk of the market, no matter how many different stocks he or she may hold.[10]

Unsystematic risk, also called residual or diversifiable risk, is that portion of the total risk that is not market related. It is unsystematic because it is that portion of the variation in a security's return that is not systematically associated with variations in the market return; it is residual because it is that part of risk that remains after the systematic or market risk is removed; and it is diversifiable because it can be eliminated by combining securities into portfolios.

As indicated previously, the variance (or its square root, the standard deviation) is the measure of total risk for an individual security or portfolio of securities. With the market model, the variance of a stock's return can be partitioned into systematic and unsystematic risk as follows:

$$\text{Var}(R_i) = \text{Var}(\alpha_i) + \text{Var}(\beta_{im}R_m) + \text{Var}(\epsilon_i) \qquad (5\text{-}20)$$

Since the variance of α_i, a constant, is zero, the variance of $\beta_{im}R_m$ is $\beta_{im}^2\text{Var}(R_m)$, and the variance of the error term is $\text{Var}(\epsilon_i)$, the equation can be restated:

$$\text{Var}(R_i) = \beta_{im}^2\text{Var}(R_m) + \text{Var}(\epsilon_i)$$

$$\sigma_i^2 = \beta_{im}^2\sigma_m^2 + \sigma_\epsilon^2 \qquad (5\text{-}21)$$

$$\frac{\text{total}}{\text{risk}} = \frac{\text{systematic}}{\text{risk}} + \frac{\text{unsystematic}}{\text{risk}}$$

Equation 5-21 makes it clear that a stock's systematic risk is a function of the variance of the market as well as the stock's beta. Since the variance of the market is the same for all stocks, however, beta is the measure of relative systematic risk. The higher the beta, the higher the systematic risk of the stock relative to the systematic risk of other stocks.

Sources of Systematic Risk

Source of systematic risk include broad influences on stock prices, such as changes in interest rates, changes in the outlook for corporate profits, or changes in the psychology of investors. The impact of these factors on the prices of individual stocks depends in part on the operating and financial characteristics of the individual firms.

---

[10]It is possible, however, to hedge against systematic risk by purchasing options or futures, as we shall see in the chapters dealing with those topics.

Firms with high business risk (due to highly variable sales and rigid costs) or high financial risk (due to high financial expenses) are likely to have high beta coefficients, indicating a high degree of sensitivity to factors that move the market as a whole. For example, betas tend to be high in homebuilding, the automotive/truck, and oilfield services industries, where wide fluctuations in customer demand and inflexible costs cause large changes in profits. Betas tend to be low in industries like beverages, food, household products, and electric utilities, where customer demand is quite stable.

Interest Rate Changes   The influence of interest rates on stock prices merits special attention. While the connection between interest rates and bond prices is closer and perhaps more obvious than the influence of interest rates on stock prices, it is clear that changes in interest rates do affect the stock market, sometimes quite dramatically. Changes in interest rates affect stock prices in two ways: through an impact on the required rate of return and through resulting changes in investors' expectations about future corporate profits. Thus, a decrease in interest rates may boost stock prices not only due to a decrease in the required return but because investors expect lower interest rates to produce higher profits. However, since changes in interest rates, or changes in expectations about future rates, are not the only influence on stock prices, they may go up in spite of an increase in rates or down in spite of a decrease in rates.[11]

Changes in the Rate of Inflation   The risk associated with the rate of inflation is usually referred to as purchasing power risk. It is sometimes defined simply as the risk that prices will rise, causing a decline in the purchasing power of future income. That definition, however, fails to take into account the important distinction between anticipated and unanticipated inflation.

Inflation is a source of risk only to the extent that it causes real returns to be lower than investors have expected. If bonds are purchased at a yield of 10% when the expected rate of inflation is 4%, investors will be harmed only if the inflation rate rises above 4%. Or, if common stocks are purchased at an expected real return of 8% (composed, for example, of a dividend yield of 5%, an expected dividend growth rate of 7% and an expected inflation rate of 4%), investors will be harmed by inflation only if it causes the real return to fall below the expected return of 8%. Sometimes higher inflation rates do seem to be the cause of lower returns on common stocks. During the 1970s, higher rates of inflation led to higher nominal interest rates, and stock prices failed to keep up with the general price level. Apparently, higher required returns more than offset any increases in either current or expected future dividends.

[11]Rising interest rates do not always lead to higher required rates of return on common stocks. The increase in interest rates can be offset by a decrease in the perceived riskiness of common stocks.

Sources of Unsystematic Risk

The sources of unsystematic risk are the many events or developments, favorable and unfavorable, that affect the stocks of individual firms or entire industries but do not have a market-wide impact. These include, for example, development of new products and new technologies, changes in consumer tastes, changes in competitive conditions, changes in management, and the operating and financial characteristics of the firm.

The distinction between the sources of systematic and unsystematic risk is not always black and white. Business risk and financial risk, as defined below, affect the sensitivity of a firm's earnings and stock price to market wide factors as well as to factors that are peculiar to the firm or its industry.

Business Risk The principal sources of business risk are instability in the demand for a firm's products and services, instability in the variable cost ratio, and high fixed operating costs. High business risk leads to unstable operating income and, typically, a highly volatile stock price. Even in relatively stable industries, there are significant differences in business risk among firms due to differences in product mix, operating leverage, and other factors that affect the stability of operating profits.

Financial Risk Financial risk arises from the use of borrowed capital and causes earnings after interest expense to be more volatile than operating income. If a firm has both high business risk and high financial risk, its earnings and stock price are apt to be quite volatile. However, if a firm with high financial leverage has a relatively low level of business risk, as in the case of many public utilities, the earnings, dividends, and stock price may be comparatively stable.[12]

---

[12]One way to estimate the combined influence of business and financial risk on the systematic risk of a firm's stock is to regress a measure of the firm's profitability (such as the rate of return on assets) on the same measure of profitability for a large group of firms, using an equation similar to the market model. The following equation is an example:

$$ROA_{it} = \alpha_i + B_i ROA_{mt} + \epsilon_{it}$$

where

ROA_{it} = return on assets for firm i in period t

ROA_{mt} = return on assets for a large group of firms (e.g., all firms in the S&P 500 index) in period t

Betas estimated in this manner are called accounting betas. Studies indicate that accounting betas are closely correlated with historic market betas calculated by regressing stock returns or percentage price changes on market returns or percentage changes in a market index. Usually, the more volatile a firm's earnings, the more volatile the price of its stock. Ned C. Hill and Bernell K. Stone, "Accounting Betas, Systematic Operating Risk, and Financial Leverage: A Risk-Composition Approach to the Determinants of Systematic Risk," *Journal of Financial and Quantitative Analysis* 15, (September 1980):595–637.

ESTIMATING THE MARKET MODEL'S STATISTICS

It is common practice to make preliminary estimates of a stock's beta, as a measure of its relative systematic risk, by regressing its weekly, monthly, or quarterly returns (or, alternatively, the percentage price changes) against the returns (or percentage price changes) for a broad market index.[13] Such estimates have been made for Hewlett–Packard Corporation by regressing quarterly percentage price changes for its stock on quarterly percentage changes in the S&P 500 Index for the 18 quarters from January 1985 through June 1989. Table 5-8 presents the regression output from a standard spreadsheet program along with the statistics necessary to calculate each of the values included in the regression table. The returns shown in columns 1 and 2 of Table 5-8 were calculated using Equation 5-1.

The return equation for Hewlett–Packard is

$$R_i = \alpha_i + \beta_{im}R_{mt} + \epsilon_{it}$$
$$= 0.483 + .640R_{mt} + \epsilon_{it}$$

The estimated beta of .640 indicates that during the 18 quarters on which the estimates were based, the price of this stock was less sensitive than the average to factors that affected the S&P 500 Index. The positive alpha of .483 indicates that if the market had remained unchanged during this period, the quarterly price increases of Hewlett–Packard would have averaged 0.483%.

The expected return and the error term for each quarter are shown in the last two columns in Table 5-8. These figures were calculated with Equations 5-16 and 5-19, respectively. For example, the expected return in the first quarter of 1985, given the market return of 9.01%, is

$$E(R_{i,1985-1}) = .483 + (.640)(9.01\%) = 6.25\%$$

Given the actual return of 3.60%, the error term was

$$\epsilon_{i,1985-1} = 3.60\% - 6.25\% = -2.65\%$$

Using the above equations, the total return for Hewlett–Packard can be partitioned between systematic and unsystematic return. In the first quarter of 1988, when the market return was 5.03% and the Hewlett Packard return was 13.35%, the market-related portion of that return was

$$\beta_{im}R_{mt} = (.640)(5.03\%) = 3.22\%$$

and the nonmarket portion was

$$\alpha_i + \epsilon_{it} = .483 + 9.65\% = 10.13\%.$$

---

[13]Beta estimates are sometimes made by regressing the excess returns for a stock against the excess returns for the market, with the excess return being defined as the amount by which the return on the stock or the market exceeds the risk-free rate. The form of the equation is $(R_{it} - R_f) = \alpha_i + \beta_i(R_m - R_f) + \epsilon_{it}$. The alpha from the risk-premium equation may be used as a performance measure. Chapter 21 on performance measurement provides a more complete description.

|||| **TABLE 5-8**
Regression Statistics: Hewlett–Packard

Year–Quarter	Hewlett–Packard Return R_i	S&P 500 Return R_m	$R_m R_i$	R_i^2	R_m^2	Expected Return $E(R_i)$	Error Term ϵ
1985–1	3.60%	9.01%	32.44	12.96	81.19	6.25%	−2.65%
1985–2	−15.19	6.97	−105.90	230.63	48.63	4.95	−20.13
1985–3	19.46	−3.91	−76.20	378.87	15.32	−2.02	21.49
1985–4	−19.99	18.06	−360.99	399.47	326.22	12.05	−32.03
1986–1	30.35	13.29	403.18	920.95	176.51	8.99	21.36
1986–2	15.06	5.78	87.01	226.81	33.38	4.18	10.88
1986–3	−12.86	−4.24	54.56	165.43	18.00	−2.23	−10.63
1986–4	−0.81	3.36	−2.73	0.66	11.32	2.64	−3.45
1987–1	28.67	24.91	714.03	821.78	620.41	16.43	12.24
1987–2	11.83	2.91	34.42	139.96	8.47	2.35	9.48
1987–3	9.25	5.61	51.85	85.56	31.42	4.07	5.18
1987–4	−17.89	−22.30	398.89	320.04	497.18	−13.79	−4.10
1988–1	13.35	5.03	67.09	178.13	25.27	3.70	9.65
1988–2	7.82	5.99	46.84	61.21	35.84	4.32	3.51
1988–3	−17.28	0.21	−3.57	298.46	0.04	0.62	−17.89
1988–4	0.17	3.89	0.66	0.03	15.17	2.98	−2.81
1989–1	14.52	6.41	93.15	210.97	41.13	4.59	9.94
1989–2	−1.58	12.42	−19.68	2.51	154.34	8.44	−10.02
Summation	68.484	93.394	1,415.051	4,454.435	2,139.842	68.484	0.000
Mean	3.805	5.189				3.805	0.000
Variance	246.70	97.37				42.403	206.79

Regression output:

Constant (α)	0.483%
R_m coefficient (β)	0.640
Standard error of coefficient (σ_β)	0.354
Standard error of expected return (σ_i)	14.380%
R-squared	0.162
Number of observations	18
Degrees of freedom	16

TABLE 5-8
Regression Statistics: Hewlett–Packard — cont'd

R_i = $\alpha + \beta R_m + \epsilon = .483 + (.640)R_m + \epsilon$

σ_{Ri}^2 = $\beta^2\sigma_{Rm}^2 + \sigma_\epsilon^2$; $(.640)^2(97.4) + 206.8 = 246.7$

Beta (β) = $\dfrac{N\sum R_m R_i - \sum R_i \sum R_m}{N\sum R_m^2 - (\sum R_m)^2} = \dfrac{(18)(1415.051) - (68.484)(93.394)}{(18)(2,139.842) - (93.394)^2} = .640$

Alpha (α) = $\overline{R}_i - \beta\overline{R}_m = 3.805 - (.640)(5.189) = .483$

R_i variance (σ_{Ri}^2) = $\dfrac{\sum R_i^2 - N\overline{R}_i^2}{N-1} = \dfrac{4,454.435 - (18)(3.805)^2}{18-1} = 246.7$

R_m variance (σ_{Rm}^2) = $\dfrac{\sum R_m^2 - N\overline{R}_m^2}{N-1} = \dfrac{2,139.842 - (18)(5.189)^2}{18-1} = 97.4$

ε variance (σ_ϵ^2) = $\dfrac{\sum R_i^2 - \alpha\sum R_i - \beta\sum R_m R_i}{N-1} = \dfrac{4,454.435 - (.483)(64.484) - (.640)(1,415.051)}{18-1} = 206.8$

Correlation (ρ) = $\dfrac{N\sum R_m R_i - (\sum R_m)(\sum R_i)}{[N\sum R_m^2 - (\sum R_m)^2]^{.5}[N\sum R_i^2 - (\sum R_i)^2]^{.5}} = \dfrac{18(1,415.051) - (93.394)(64.484)}{[(18)(2,139.84) - (93.39)^2]^{.5}\ \beta[(18)(4,454.44) - (68.5)^2]^{.5}}$

ρ^2 = $(.402)^2 = .162$

R squared = $\dfrac{\beta^2\sigma_{Rm}^2}{\sigma_{Ri}^2} = \dfrac{(.640)^2(97.4)}{246.7} = .162$

β variance = $(\sigma_\beta^2) = \dfrac{\sigma_\epsilon^2}{\sum R_m^2 - N R_m^2} = \dfrac{206.8}{2,139.842 - (18)(5.189)^2} = .125$

The total risk of the Hewlett–Packard return, in terms of the variance, was 246.7, as shown in Tables 5-7 and 5-8. It can be partitioned into its systematic and unsystematic components with equation 5-21.

$$\text{Systematic risk} \quad = \beta_{im}^2 \, \delta_m^2 = (.640)^2 \, (97.4) = \quad 39.9$$
$$\text{Unsystematic risk} = \delta_\epsilon^2 \qquad = \qquad\qquad\qquad \underline{206.8}$$
$$\text{Total } (\beta_{im}^2 \, \delta_m^2 + \delta_\epsilon^2) \qquad\qquad\qquad\qquad 246.7$$

The systematic portion, which arose from association of the Hewlett Packard return with the market return, was 16.2% (39.9/246.7) of the toal.[14] In terms of regression analysis, this quantity, which is the square of the correlation coefficient of .402, is called the coefficient of determination (R^2).

CHARACTERISTIC LINES

A plot of the rate of return for a stock against the return for a market index is known as a characteristic line, the equation for which is 5-15, the market model.

Figure 5-1 shows the quarterly returns for Hewlett–Packard plotted against the quarterly returns of thc S&P 500. The intercept of the line with the Y-axis is alpha ($\alpha_i = .483$). The slope of the line is an estimate of beta ($\beta_{im} = .640$). The distance between any point and the regression line is the error term for the given market return.

The standard deviation of the errors about the regression line is called the standard error of the estimate. In a regression of the returns for a stock against the returns for an index of the market, the standard error measures how widely the actual returns have varied from the returns that might have been predicted, given the returns on the market index and the average relationship between the stock's return and the returns on that index. Thus, the standard error measures the degree to which the returns on a stock have been affected by non-market factors, and by doing this, it provides a measure of the stock's unsystematic risk. The larger the dispersion of the points about the line, the higher the proportion of unsystematic risk relative to total risk and the smaller the coefficient of determination (R^2). The smaller the dispersion of the points around the line, the higher the coefficient of determination (R^2) and the smaller the unsystematic risk relative to the total risk.

From the wide dispersion about the regression line (Figure 5-1), which is reflected in the large standard deviation of the error term of 14.38% and the low R^2 of 16.2% (Table 5-8), it is clear that a point estimate of Hewlett Packard's return based on Equation 5-16 is likely to be substantially wrong. Therefore, it is better to calculate a range (called a prediction interval) within which the return is expected to fall. This kind of prediction assumes constant dispersion about the regression line.

---

[14]Studies have found that on average the market factor explains about one-third of the variation in individual stock returns. The remainder of the variation (in this case, 83.8%) is attributable to factors peculiar to the firm or its industry.

The prediction or confidence interval is given by

$$E(R_i) \pm t_{\kappa/2}\sigma_\epsilon \left[1 + \frac{1}{N} + \frac{(R_m - \overline{R}_m)^2}{\Sigma R_m^2 - (\Sigma R_m)^2/N} \right]^{1/2} \qquad (5\text{-}22)$$

where

$t_{\kappa/1}$ = the κ confidence level t-statistic (interval coefficient) with
$\quad\quad n - 1$ degrees of freedom

R_m = the value of the independent variable in Equation 5-16

Table 5-9 shows the sampling distribution from Figure 5-1. The mean of the distribution is the expected return estimate developed from Equation 5-16, and the prediction interval comes from Equation 5-22.

Equation 5-22 and Table 5-9 show that the prediction interval varies directly with unsystematic risk (σ_ϵ^2) and inversely with R^2. In the case of Hewlett–Packard, the prediction interval is -27.97 to $+36.61$. When σ_ϵ^2 is large and R^2 is small, which they generally are for individual securities, the prediction interval is too wide to be of any practical use. This is not necessarily true, however for a diversified portfolio because di-

---

|||| **TABLE 5-9**
Prediction Interval Assuming a Market Return of 6.0%

Expected market return: 6.0%
Expected security return: $E(R_i) = \alpha_i + \beta_{im}E(R_m)$
$\quad\quad\quad\quad\quad\quad\quad 4.32 = .483 + .640 \times 6.0$

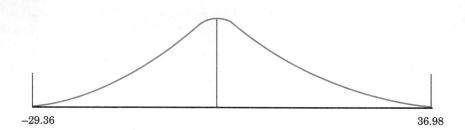

−29.36   36.98

$$E(R_i) \pm t_{\kappa/2}\sigma_\epsilon \left[1 + \frac{1}{N} + \frac{(R_m - \overline{R}_m)^2}{\Sigma R_m^2 - (\Sigma R_m)^2/N} \right]^{1/2}$$

$$4.32 \pm 2.12 \times 14.38 \left[1 + \frac{1}{18} + \frac{(6.0 - 5.189)^2}{2{,}139.84 - (93.4)^2/18} \right]^{1/2}$$

$$4.32 \pm 32.29$$

|||| **FIGURE 5-1**

Characteristic Line: Hewlett–Packard

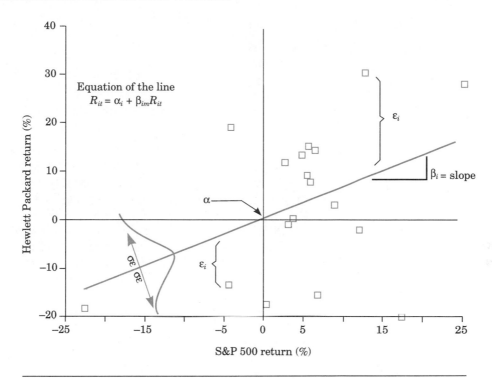

versification can eliminate the unsystematic portion of the total risk, thereby substantially reducing total risk and increasing R^2.

RISK REDUCTION THROUGH RANDOM DIVERSIFICATION

Unsystematic risk can be avoided by holding a well-diversified portfolio. The more closely a portfolio of stocks resembles the market as a whole, the more closely its return will track the market. If a portfolio's return is perfectly correlated with the market return, its unsystematic risk is zero.

If a portfolio contains only a few stocks, it is probably subject to a large amount of unsystematic risk. The addition of a few more randomly selected stocks is likely to cause a sizable reduction in the portfolio's total risk. But risk reduction through the addition of more stocks drops off very quickly. By the time a portfolio contains 15 or 20 well-diversified stocks, little unsystematic risk remains. Further additions will have little effect on the total risk.

The relationship between risk and the number of stocks in a diversified portfolio is illustrated in Figure 5-2. It is based on calculations for

|||| **FIGURE 5-2**

Reducing Risk by Increasing the Number of Securities in a Portfolio

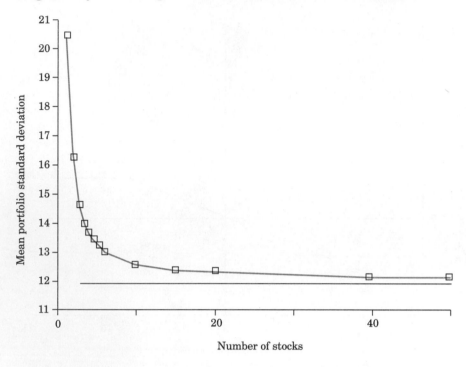

2,400 randomly selected portfolios over 19 semiannual periods.[15] Sixty portfolios contained just 1 stock, 60 contained 2 stocks, 60 had 3 stocks, and so on up to 60 portfolios containing 40 stocks. The stocks for each portfolio were selected at random from the 500 stocks in Standard & Poor's Composite Index. The average systematic risk for all 2,400 portfolios and the relationship between the unsystematic risk and portfolio size were estimated by regressing the standard deviation of the portfolio return (Y) on the reciprocal of the number of stocks in the portfolio ($1/X$), as shown in Equation 5-23:

$$Y = A + B(1/X) \tag{5-23}$$

where

Y = standard deviation of portfolio return

A = average systematic risk of all portfolios

[15]John L. Evans and Stephen H. Archer, "Diversification and the Reduction of Dispersion: An Empirical Analysis," *The Journal of Finance* 23 (December, 1968): 761–67.

B = measure of average relationship between unsystematic risk risk and portfolio size

X = number of stocks in the portfolio

The final estimated equation was

$$Y = .119 + .086(1/X)$$

The average systematic risk for the 2,400 portfolios, in terms of the standard deviation, was 11.9%, and the average unsystematic risk was 8.6% of the reciprocal of the number of stocks in the portfolio. For example, the average total risk of a two-stock portfolio was 11.9% plus 8.6% × 1/2, or 16.2%; and the average total risk for a portfolio of 10 stocks was 11.9% plus 8.6% × 1/10, or 12.8%. The average systematic risk, unsystematic risk, and the total risk (in terms of the standard deviation of the returns) are shown in Table 5-10 for portfolios of various sizes.

|||| **OTHER RISK CONSIDERATIONS**

Risk, as it has been discussed in this chapter, is based on the idea that the risk of an investment is measured by the volatility of its return. Total risk is measured by total variability, and systematic risk is measured by that portion of the total variability that is attributable to one or more systematic factors. As a number of observers have noted, the variability of the return does not have the same significance for all investors. For anyone who holds stocks for long periods of time, even cyclical fluctuations may not be very important. On the other hand, for investors who may want or need to liquidate their holdings in a short period of time, the variability of the return is very important. Thus, the risk of investing in assets such as common stocks varies from investor to investor, depending on the length of their investment horizon.

|||| **TABLE 5-10**
Risk and Portfolio Size

Number of Stocks	Systematic Risk	Unsystematic Risk	Standard Deviation of Portfolio Returns
1	11.9%	8.6%	20.5%
5	11.9	1.7	13.6
10	11.9	0.9	12.8
20	11.9	0.4	12.3
40	11.9	0.2	12.1
100	11.9	0.08	12.0
1,000	11.9	0.008	11.9

SOURCE: Evans and Archer, "Diversification and the Reduction of Dispersion."

The performance of the S&P 500 Index over various periods of time illustrates why the investor's horizon, or planned holding period, has a bearing on the risk of investing in common stocks. In general, the longer the holding period, the smaller the variation among the returns. For example, the range of the S&P 500 returns for all 10-year holding periods from 1961 through 1990 was 1.2% to 17.5%; the range for all 15-year holding periods was 5.4% to 16.6%; and the range for all 20-year holding periods was 7.8% to 11.5%

|||| SUMMARY

The principal objectives of this chapter were to explain various methods of measuring risk and the rate of return and to explore the relationship between these two highly important variables in investment decision making.

The total return from a security consists of the interest or dividend payments plus the increase, or minus the decrease, in the value of the asset, plus reinvestment income. Returns for more than one year are often reduced to a single figure by calculating the arithmetic or geometric mean annual rate of return. The geometric mean annual rate of return, which is the same as the compound annual rate of return if reinvestment income is included, is lower than the arithmetic mean if there is any variation at all in the returns. The geometric mean is a better measure of the investor's "true" return than the arithmetic mean since it represents the rate of increase in the accumulated value of the investment.

The total risk of an asset, according to modern investment theory, is a function of the variability of the return, as measured by the variance or standard deviation. The more variable the return, the more difficult it is to predict future returns, and the greater the chance that the actual return will be substantially lower than the expected return.

Total risk can be partitioned into two components: systematic risk and unsystematic risk. Systematic risk arises from factors, such as changes in interest rates or in the outlook for corporate profits, that cause the market as a whole to move up or down. Unsystematic risk arises from events or developments peculiar to an individual firm or group of firms with similar characteristics. Unsystematic risk can be eliminated by diversifying; systematic risk cannot.

The systematic risk of a common stock relative to that of an average stock is measured by its beta coefficient. Historical betas are calculated by regressing the return of an individual stock on the return for a broad index of the market, such as the S&P 500 Index. The regression equation is known as the market model, and the regression line is called the characteristic line. The slope of the characteristic line is an estimate of the stock's average beta for the period of time covered by the regression analysis.

A stock's beta is a function not only of its volatility relative to the volatility of the market but also the degree to which its return is correlated with the market return. As a measure of relative systematic risk, beta reflects the sensitivity of the stock to various factors that have a market-wide influence. A historical beta of more than 1.0 means that the stock has been more volatile than the market and has been positively correlated with the market. However, a beta of less than 1.0 does not necessarily mean that the stock has been less volatile than the market. A highly volatile stock can have a low beta if its correlation with the market is low.

The assumption that risk is a function of the variability of the return, which underlies the use of the standard deviation as a measure of total risk and beta as a measure of relative systematic risk, seems inappropriate for investors who hold stocks for long periods of time. While it is true that common stocks are quite risky for investors with short investment horizons, if history is any guide, they are not very risky for those who hold diversified portfolios of stocks for a long period of time. During the past 50 years, the range of returns for Standard & Poor's 500 for holding periods as long as 20 years has not been very great.

|||| QUESTIONS

1. Explain how to calculate the geometric mean annual rate of return, given a set of annual returns. Use a simple example to show how the geometric mean is superior to the arithmetic mean as a measure of the return.

2. How is the geometric mean annual rate of return related to the increase in the accumulated value of an investment over a period of n years?

3. Explain why the standard deviation of the return is considered a good measure of risk.

4. Explain how the future standard deviation of a security's return can be estimated with a subjective probability distribution.

5. Explain how the covariance and the correlation coefficient are related. Why is the correlation coefficient easier to interpret?

6. Explain the following equation for the standard deviation of a randomly selected portfolio of common stocks, where X is the number of stocks in the portfolio:

$$Y = .119 + .086 \times 1/X$$

    How were the regression parameters estimated?

7. Comment on the factors that determine how the total risk of a common stock portfolio will be affected by the addition of one more stock.

8. Explain why the coefficient of determination (R^2) is larger in a time-series regression of the returns for a diversified common stock portfolio on the market returns than in a regression of the returns of a single stock on the market returns.

9. Express systematic risk in terms of beta and the variance of the market return.

10. Explain the following equation:

$$\beta_{im} = \rho_{im} \times \sigma_i / \sigma_m$$

11. Why do most common stocks have a positive covariance with other stocks?

12. Define systematic risk and unsystematic risk.

13. Demonstrate how total risk can be decomposed into systematic and unsystematic risk with the market model.

14. Explain why investors should not expect to earn higher rates of return by assuming greater amounts of unsystematic risk.

15. What is a characteristic line?

16. Explain unsystematic risk in terms of the residuals from a regression of an individual stock's return on the market return.

17. What are the characteristics of industries in which common stock betas tend to be high?

18. What can you infer about a security that has a high standard deviation of the return and a low beta?

19. Explain why the standard deviation of the return is not a good measure of risk for all investors.

|||| PROBLEMS

1. Calculate the arithmetic mean and the geometric mean of the following annual returns: 15%, −3%, 12%, 6%, 25%, −8%, 10%, 15%, −30%, 55%

2. Using the following data, calculate the expected return, variance, and standard deviation.

Probabilities	Possible Returns
.10	+.50
.20	+.30
.50	+.20
.15	−.20
.05	−.50

3. Given the following quarterly rates of return for stocks X and Y, calculate the covariance between the returns and the correlation coefficient.

	Quarterly Returns	
Quarter	X	Y
1	2%	5%
2	5	6
3	2	7
4	-3	1
5	6	6
6	3	5
7	7	8
8	2	-1

The following data are to be used with Problems 4–12.

Month	Monthly Returns		Month	Monthly Returns	
	X	S&P 500		X	S&P 500
1	2%	3%	10	5%	3%
2	-10	5	11	-2	1
3	-2	3	12	8	-2
4	5	9	13	-6	-3
5	8	5	14	-2	-5
6	3	2	15	5	2
7	-1	1	16	-3	3
8	5	3	17	18	6
9	6	2	18	6	5

4. Calculate the alpha, beta, R^2, and variance of the error term for stock X.

5. What is the correlation between security X and the market?

6. For each of the 18 months, determine the expected return of security X.

7. In month 18, the market return was 5%. Calculate the market (systematic) and nonmarket (unsystematic) returns that make up the 6% actual return of security X.

8. Determine the total, systematic, and unsystematic risk associated with security X.

9. What percentage of the total risk of security X is due to nonmarket (unsystematic) events?

10. Draw a graph that includes the data points and the characteristic line. Plot the mean return of security X and the market return. Why does this point plot on the characteristic line?

11. On your graph, draw a probability distribution around the characteristic line. Explain how R^2 relates to this probability distribution.

12. Show how diversification would modify your probability distribution. What would happen to R^2?

13. Given that the standard deviation of the error term (σ_e) of a security relative to the market is .0236 and the R^2 is .509, calculate the total risk, systematic risk, and unsystematic risk of the security.

14. Calculate the betas of stocks X and Y, given the following:

$$\sigma_m = 20\% \qquad \sigma_X = 20\% \qquad \sigma_Y = 35\% \qquad \rho_{Xm} = .50 \qquad \rho_{Ym} = .10$$

15. If Cov_{im} is 126 and σ_m^2 is 150, what is β_{im}? If ρ_{im} is .60, what is σ_i?

APPENDIX **5a** # RISK AS DEFINED BY BETA

Recall that systematic risk is the product of beta squared and the variance of the market return. Since the variance of the market is the same for all assets, differences in systematic risk are due entirely to differences in beta. We have also shown that if a portfolio is well diversified, the unsystematic risk is close to zero.[16] Thus, the risk of a well-diversified portfolio depends on its beta, which is a weighted average of the betas of the individual assets contained in the portfolio.

Estimates of future betas for common stocks are usually based, at least in part, on historical betas. And, as noted in Chapter 5, historical betas are typically estimated by regressing monthly returns (or percentage changes in the price) for an individual stock on the monthly returns (or percentage changes in the level) of a market index over a period of years. Obviously, the accuracy of betas estimated on the basis of historical relationships depends upon how stable betas are over time. Thus, there has been a great deal of interest in measuring the stability of betas for individual stocks, as well as the stability of betas for portfolios containing more than one stock.

FACTORS AFFECTING THE STABILITY OF BETA

The stability of calculated betas from one period to the next depends largely upon four factors: (1) the stability of the true beta; (2) the size of the beta; (3) the length of the estimation period; and (4) the length of the prediction period.

STABILITY

To estimate the influence of diversification upon the stability of portfolio betas, Alexander and Chervany formed portfolios of various sizes with stocks selected at random from 160 New York Stock Exchange issues.[17] The original (historical) betas and the forecasted (test) betas were both

---

[16]Recall that a diversified portfolio of even 15 or 20 common stocks has little unsystematic risk.

[17]Gordon J. Alexander and Norman L. Chervany, "On the Estimation and Stability of Beta," *Journal of Financial and Quantitative Analysis* 15 (March 1980): 123–37.

|||| **TABLE 5A-1**

Stability of Beta from One Seven-Year Period to the Next for
Portfolios of Various Sizes

Number of Securities in Portfolio	Mean Absolute Change in Beta from One Seven-Year Period to the Next
1	.27
2	.19
4	.13
7	.12
10	.11
20	.08
35	.07
50	.06

SOURCE: Gordon J. Alexander and Norman L. Chervany, "On the Estimation and Stability of Beta," *Journal of Financial and Quantitative Analysis* 15 (March 1980):123–37.

estimated on the basis of monthly returns over a period of seven years. Table 5A-1 shows that the mean absolute deviation between the original betas of the estimation period and the forecasted betas of the prediction period decreased dramatically as the number of securities in the portfolio increased from 1 to about 20. The deviations decreased still further as the portfolio size was increased to 50 securities. The average amount of error in predicting a seven-year beta for a 20-stock portfolio on the basis of its beta for the preceding seven years was .08.

Portfolio betas are more stable than the betas of individual stocks because changes in individual betas from one period to the next tend to offset one another. The greater the number of stocks in a randomly selected portfolio, the more closely its performance tends to parallel the performance of the universe of stocks from which the portfolio was drawn. At the extreme, if a portfolio contains all of the stocks in the S&P 500 Index in proportion to their aggregate market values, and if betas are calculated by regressing on the percentage changes in the S&P 500 Index, the portfolio beta will be perfectly stable at 1.0 in every period.

SIZE OF BETA

In a major study of the stability and predictability of beta coefficients, Blume made two principal findings: first, the larger the portfolio, the greater the correlation of the portfolio beta from one period to the next (for example, with a portfolio of 50 stocks, the period-to-period beta correlations were approximately 0.98); second, large betas tend to become smaller, and small betas tend to become larger over time.[18] Thus, historical betas are biased estimates of future betas. Blume estimated the amount of the bias by calculating historical betas for a number of stocks for successive seven-year periods. Betas for the second 7-year period were

[18]Marshall E. Blume, "On the Assessment of Risk," *The Journal of Finance* 26 (March 1971): 1–10.

then regressed on betas for the first period to see how closely they were related. The form of the equation was

$$\beta_2 = \gamma_0 + \gamma_1\beta_1 + \epsilon_i \tag{5A-1}$$

A regression of betas for the seven-year period ending in 1968 on betas for the same stocks for the seven-year period ending in 1961 produced the following equation:

$$\beta_2 = 0.399 + 0.556\beta_1$$

With this formula, an historical beta of 0.50 is adjusted upward to 0.68, and a beta of 1.50 is adjusted downward to 1.23. Blume found that when betas for the first of two periods were adjusted in this manner, they became much better estimates of betas for the second period.

Why do betas tend to regress toward the mean? Probably because companies whose earnings are either extraordinarily volatile or extraordinarily stable tend to become more like the average over a period of time. For example, if a stock has an unusually low beta, perhaps due to exceptionally stable earnings and a low ratio of debt to equity, management may increase the firm's debt to gain the advantage of greater financial leverage. The increased leverage may cause the firm's earnings and stock price to become more volatile, which will tend to increase the stock's beta.

LENGTH OF THE ESTIMATION PERIOD

If an investor were to calculate three betas for a firm's stock, one based on monthly returns over the past three years, another based on returns over the past four years, and another based on returns over the past five years, they would almost surely be different. The differences might be quite substantial. Betas tend to change with time for two reasons. First, changes in the operating and financial characteristics of a firm affect the sensitivity of the price of its stock to factors that move the market as a whole. For example, a change in the mix of a firm's products may increase the stability of its sales, earnings, and stock price. Second, stocks have different sensitivities to different external factors. Thus, the amount of change in the price of a stock relative to a change in the market depends upon which factors are moving the market. If a stock is highly sensitive to changes in interest rates, its price will tend to move a great deal when the market moves up or down because of an increase or decrease in interest rates. On the other hand, the price of the stock may not be affected very much when the market is moved by changes in expected corporate profits.

It has been found that betas calculated with 5 to 10 years of monthly data are generally the most stable and provide the best forecasts of future betas. The authors of one study found, for example, that forecast errors were much smaller with a 7-year estimation period than with a 4-year period and were slightly smaller with a 10-year period than with a 7-year period.[19] Other studies have found that a 6-year estimation period is optimal. If the estimation period is too short, the sampling error is apt to be very large. If the estimation period is too long, the calculated beta will reflect conditions, including the characteristics of the firm itself, that no longer prevail.

LENGTH OF THE PREDICTION PERIOD

The historical beta for an individual stock, calculated with monthly data for a period of several years, is apt to be a much better estimate of the stock's beta over the next several years than of its beta over the next year. Table 5A-1 shows that the average absolute change in beta for a single stock from one seven-year period to the next was 27%. In the same study, Alexander and Chervany found that when betas calculated with an estimation period of six years were compared with betas for the next year, the average absolute difference was 81%. Clearly, one should not expect that the average performance of a stock relative to the market over a period of years will provide a good estimate of how it will perform relative to the market in the coming year.

|||| PUBLISHED BETAS

Several organizations, including Merrill Lynch and Value Line, publish betas for large numbers of stocks. Table 5A-2 is a sample of the betas published by Merrill Lynch in April 1991. Merrill Lynch betas are calculated by regressing monthly percentage changes in individual stock prices on the monthly percentage changes in the S&P 500 Index over a period of 60 months, whenever those data are available. The slope of the regression line (the characteristic line) is the stock's beta. The historical betas in Table 5A-2 range from -0.16 to 1.83, and the adjusted betas range from 0.23 to 1.55. Merrill Lynch calculated the adjusted betas with the following formula:

$$\beta_2 = 0.337 + 0.663\beta_1$$

The R^2's in Table 5A-2 represent the proportion of the total variance of a stock's monthly price change that is explained by moves of the S&P 500 Index. Most of the smaller R^2's are for the stocks of the smaller companies. For example, 7 of the 8 R^2's smaller than 0.20 are for stocks with aggregate market values of less than $100 million. The lower the R^2, the greater the variation around the regression line, which means the larger the residuals and the greater the unsystematic risk. In this sample, the smaller stocks tended to have more unsystematic risk than the stocks of the larger firms. Stocks with low R^2's tend to have small betas, since beta is the product of the correlation coefficient (square root of R-squared)

---

[19]Pieter Elgers, Joanne Hill, and Thomas Schneeweis, "Research Design for Systematic Risk Prediction," *Journal of Portfolio Management* 8 (Spring 1982): 43–52.

|||| **TABLE 5A-2**
Merrill Lynch Market Sensitivity Statistics (excluding alpha),
April 1991

Company	Traded	Total Market Value (Millions)	Beta*	Adjusted Beta	R^2	Residual Standard Deviation	Standard Error of Beta
Aileen	NYSE	$ 32	−0.16	0.23	0.01	16.76	0.40
Amplicon	OTC	90	1.36	1.24	0.18	14.64	0.40
Bairnco	NYSE	85	1.55	1.37	0.33	11.87	0.29
Biomet	OTC	1,459	1.46	1.30	0.41	9.30	0.22
Champion Intl.	NYSE	2,418	1.16	1.10	0.53	5.82	0.14
Clark Equipment	NYSE	452	1.23	1.15	0.34	9.16	0.22
Cordis	OTC	438	0.97	0.98	0.14	12.21	0.29
Del Taco Restaurants	OTC	26	0.52	0.68	0.01	16.44	0.40
Elco Industries	OTC	42	0.55	0.70	0.11	7.75	0.19
Fay's Drug	NYSE	217	0.99	0.99	0.28	8.44	0.20
First Bancorp. Ohio	OTC	313	0.61	0.74	0.22	6.07	0.15
General Electric	NYSE	61,816	1.15	1.10	0.75	3.55	0.09
Hexcel	NYSE	86	1.48	1.32	0.37	10.31	0.25
Intelogic Trace	NYSE	12	1.20	1.13	0.11	16.98	0.41
Kenwin Shops	ASE	3	0.53	0.69	0.05	10.74	0.26
Lynch	ASE	22	1.83	1.55	0.51	9.60	0.23
May Dept. Stores	NYSE	6,391	1.40	1.27	0.67	5.33	0.13
NYNEX	NYSE	14,237	0.69	0.79	0.50	3.66	0.09
Peerless Tube	ASE	4	0.81	0.87	0.15	9.93	0.24
Printronix	OTC	28	0.91	0.94	0.27	7.91	0.19
Schering Plough	NYSE	10,656	0.92	0.95	0.57	4.32	0.10
Scientific Atlanta	NYSE	328	1.65	1.43	0.50	8.88	0.21
Stokely	OTC	83	1.26	1.17	0.22	12.48	0.30
Toro	NYSE	212	1.37	1.24	0.42	8.58	0.21
Walgreen Company	NYSE	3,939	1.32	1.21	0.64	5.26	0.13

*Beta estimates are based on S&P 500 Index.

SOURCE: Security Risk Evaluation, April 1991, Merrill Lynch, Pierce, Fenner, & Smith.

and the ratio of the standard deviation of the stock's return to the standard deviation of the market's return as was shown in Equation 5-18:

$$\beta_i = \rho_{im}\sigma_i/\sigma_m \qquad (5\text{-}18)$$

If the correlation coefficient is small, beta is likely to be small even if the standard deviation of the percentage changes in the stock's price is quite large. For example, Del Taco's unadjusted beta was only 0.52 in spite of the fact that the standard deviation of its price was 5.2 times the standard deviation of the S&P 500 Index.[20]

When R^2 is as small as that of Del Taco., one can have little confidence in the estimate of beta. A low R^2 indicates that the price of the stock is

[20]Del Taco Restaurants:

Unadjusted beta	0.52
R^2	0.01
$\rho_{im} = (.01)^{1/2}$	0.10
$\sigma_i/\sigma_m = \beta_i/\rho_{im} = 0.52/0.1 = 5.20$	

about as likely to move against the market as with the market. In that case, a large part of the total risk is unsystematic.

The residual standard deviation (the standard error of the estimate) of Table 5A-2 is the measure of unsystematic risk. In terms of regression analysis, it represents the amount of variation around the regression line. Most of the residual standard deviations in Table 5A-2 are large. For example, the figure of 16.98 for Intelogic Trace indicates that in about one month out of three, the percentage change in the price of the stock was more than 16.98 percentage points greater or smaller than one would expect on the basis of the percentage change in the S&P 500 Index and the stock's adjusted beta of 1.13.

The standard error of beta indicates the amount by which beta might be expected to deviate from the calculated value. For example, the standard error of 0.41 for Intelogic Trace indicates that if the future is like the period covered by the regressions, the unadjusted beta will be within 0.41 of 1.20 about two-thirds of the time.

COMPARISON OF MERRILL LYNCH AND VALUE LINE BETAS

The Merrill Lynch and Value Line betas are similar in that both are based on a regression of the percentage changes in the price of a stock against the percentage changes in a market index over a period of five years. However, they differ in two respects: first, the Merrill Lynch estimates are based on monthly figures whereas the Value Line estimates are based on weekly figures; and, second, the Merrill Lynch estimates are based on the S&P 500 Index, while Value Line uses the New York Stock Exchange Index. Both firms adjust their initial estimates for the tendency of high and low betas to drift toward the mean. The Merrill Lynch equation shown above differs very little from the Value Line equation, which is

$$\beta_2 = 0.350 + 0.670\beta_1$$

A regression estimate of 0.50 would be adjusted to 0.67 by Merrill Lynch and to 0.69 by Value Line, while an estimate of 1.50 would be adjusted to 1.33 by Merrill Lynch and to 1.36 by Value Line.

Table 5A-3 shows Merrill Lynch and Value Line betas for a random sample of 25 stocks as of April 1991. Though there are large differences in the betas for a number of individual stocks, the average betas for the 25 stocks (1.20 and 1.21) are nearly the same.

INDUSTRY BETAS

Table 5A-4 shows that betas tend to be high in the automotive, home-building, and oilfield services industries, where customer demand fluctuates widely and/or rigid cost structures cause the percentage changes in profits to be much greater than the percentage changes in gross revenues. Betas tend to be lower in industries like beverages, foods, household products, and electric utilities, where customer demand is quite stable.

|||| **TABLE 5A-3**

Merrill Lynch and Value Line Betas for 25 Randomly Selected
Value Line Stocks, April 1991

	(A) Merrill Lynch	(B) Value Line	Difference A − B
Allied Signal	0.92	0.95	−0.03
Aydin	1.06	1.05	0.01
Bird	1.11	1.15	−0.04
Campbell Soup	1.06	1.00	0.06
Cincinnati Milacron	1.40	1.30	0.10
Collagen	1.67	1.60	0.07
Delta Air Lines	1.11	1.05	0.06
Farah	1.23	1.15	0.08
GATX	1.05	1.00	0.05
Georgia-Pacific	1.25	1.25	0.00
Horn & Hardart	1.30	1.50	−0.20
Johnson & Johnson	1.00	1.05	−0.05
Lawson Products	0.90	0.95	−0.05
Manor Care	0.85	1.05	−0.20
Millipore	1.26	1.20	0.06
National Service Industries	0.90	1.00	−0.10
Owens-Corning	2.16	1.70	0.46
Phelps Dodge	1.31	1.50	−0.19
Quaker Oats	0.74	0.95	−0.21
SAFECO	0.92	1.10	−0.18
Silicon Graphics	1.59	1.45	0.14
Stone Container	1.74	1.80	−0.06
Timken	1.23	1.20	0.03
Upjohn	1.15	1.10	0.05
Wolverine World Wide	1.16	1.10	0.06
Average	1.20	1.21	−0.01

SOURCE: Value Line Investment Survey and *Merrill Lynch Security Risk Evaluation.*

The range of betas in many industries is strikingly large, indicating great diversity among the firms within a single industry. Differences in business risk, financial risk, and dividend yields among firms that happen to be classified in the same industry are often substantial. For example, the Merrill Lynch betas for companies in the food industry, where the average beta is 1.0, range from 0.50 to 1.70. The industry includes a wide variety of firms that differ as to types of products, production methods, marketing strategies, types of customers, and amounts of financial leverage, all of which can affect the variability of earnings and have an impact on beta. On the average, however, the sales and earnings of food companies are relatively stable, the dividend yields relatively high, and the betas rather moderate.

High dividend yields tend to be associated with relatively stable stocks with below-average betas. The expected dividend growth rates are modest, and a significant portion of the total value of the stock is based on the dividends expected over a relatively short period of time, perhaps the next 10 or 15 years. Investors' expectations about the dividends are likely

|||| **TABLE 5A-4**

Merrill Lynch Betas for Selected Industries, April 1991

Industry	Industry Beta	Range of Betas
Aerospace	1.0	0.5–1.5
Air transport	1.2	0.6–1.9
Autos & trucks	1.3	1.1–1.6
Banking (midwest)	1.0	0.6–1.5
Beverages—Brewers	0.8	0.5–1.0
Chemicals (basic)	1.1	0.5–1.5
Computer software & services	1.4	0.5–1.9
Drugs	1.2	0.8–2.0
Electrical equipment	1.1	0.7–1.4
Electrical utilities (west)	0.5	0.2–0.8
Food processing	1.0	0.5–1.7
Grocery stores	1.0	0.6–1.3
Homebuilding	1.5	1.1–1.9
Household products	1.0	0.8–1.4
Machinery (construction)	1.2	0.8–1.8
Oilfield services/equipment	1.3	0.9–1.9
Paper & forest products	1.3	0.7–2.0
Railroads	1.0	0.7–1.4
Retail stores	1.4	0.6–1.9
Steel industry (general)	1.2	0.7–1.7

Note: Industry betas are averages of Merrill Lynch individual company betas.

SOURCE: Company betas from *Security Risk Evaluation*, April 1991, Merrill Lynch, Pierce, Fenner & Smith.

to be quite stable. As a result, the prices of these high-yield stocks tend to be more stable than the prices of stocks with low dividend yields and high earnings growth rates, where the future dividends are much more uncertain.

BETA FACTOR ANALYSIS

Beta estimates are sometimes based, totally or partially, on analysis of the fundamental factors that are likely to determine a stock's future beta. Multiple regression analysis can be used to determine which factors are important and how much weight each should be given. The forecasting model usually includes a stock's historical beta since there is a tendency for low-beta stocks to retain their low betas and for high-beta stocks to retain their high betas. Another obvious explanatory variable is the industry in which the firm is operating. With a cross-section regression (using data for a number of stocks for the same time period), one can estimate the average relationship between beta and certain characteristics of the firm. For example, the regression model might include the following independent variables:

1. Actual historical beta (calculated with the market model on the basis of monthly price changes over a period of years).

2. Industry classification, using a dummy variable that is set at one for the industry in which the firm is operating and at zero for all other industries.

3. Coefficient of variation of the firm's quarterly earnings per share over a period of years, which reflects the combined effects of business and financial risk on the variability of the firm's profits.

4. Average annual dividend yield over a period of years.

In equation form, the model could be

$$\beta_i = \gamma_0 + \gamma_1 X_1 + \gamma_2 X_2 + \gamma_3 X_3 + \gamma_4 X_4 + \epsilon_i \qquad (5A\text{-}2)$$

The variables to be estimated with the regression are the γ's. The dependent variable, β_i, for each stock is an estimate of its historical beta based on regression analysis with the market model, using, for example, monthly data for the most recent 6-year period (years t-1 through t-6). The variable X_1 can be a similar estimate of the stock's historical beta, but based on data for the six-year period (t-7 through t-12) preceding the most recent period of that same length. Thus, for each industry group, the regression shows how the historical beta for the years t-1 through t-6 is related to the historical beta for the years t-7 through t-12, holding constant the coefficient of variation of quarterly earnings and the dividend yield.

To illustrate how Equation 5A-3 might be applied, suppose that estimates of β_i and the four X's have been made for a number of firms, and the following parameter estimates have been arrived at with regression analysis:

Parameter Estimate		Independent Variable
$\gamma_0 =$	0	
$\gamma_1 =$	0.62	Historical beta, years t-7 through t-12
$\gamma_2 =$	0.50	Industry group (the quantity 0.50 is assumed to be the coefficient for industry group number 1)
$\gamma_3 =$	0.20	Cocfficient of variation, quarterly earnings per share
$\gamma_4 = -0.02$		Dividend yield

Suppose that company A is in industry group number 1, and the values of the independent variables for company A are as follows:

X_1	(beta, years t-7 through t-12)	0.80
X_2	(industry group 1)	1.00
X_3	(coefficient of variation of quarterly earnings per share)	0.30
X_4	(average annual dividend yield)	5.00%

The estimated beta for company A would be

$$(.62 \times .80) + .50 + (.20 \times .30) - (.02 \times 5.0) = 0.956$$

|||| **TABLE 5A-5**
Errors in Predicting Betas of Individual Stocks of Industrial
Firms: Fundamental Betas versus Average of All Betas

Prediction Period (Years)	Mean Absolute Error	
	Fundamental Betas	Average of All Forecasts
1	.598	.635
2	.433	.502
3	.374	.444
4	.352	—

Diana R. Harrington, "Whose Beta is Best?" *Financial Analysts Journal* 39 (July/August 1983):67–73.

As Table 5A-5 shows, Harrington's study of the comparative accuracy of betas published by several different firms indicated that estimates of future betas were somewhat more accurate when based on fundamental betas rather than historical betas, even though the historical betas were adjusted for the tendency to regress toward the mean.[21]

|||| **APPENDIX QUESTIONS**

1. Why are analysts and investors interested in the stability of beta?
2. Why are portfolio betas more stable than betas of individual stocks?
3. Why are historical betas biased estimates of future betas?
4. Why do betas of individual stocks tend to change over time?
5. Comment on the relationship between the length of the prediction period and the stability of beta.
6. What are the implications of a small R-squared in a regression estimate of beta?
7. What is the meaning of the residual standard deviation of 11.87 for Bairnco in Table 5A-2? How is it related to unsystematic risk?
8. How would you interpret the standard error of 0.30 for the estimated beta of Stokely in Table 5A-2?
9. What are the characteristics of industries in which common stock betas tend to be high?
10. Why are there usually wide variations among the betas of firms within a single industry?
11. What is a fundamental beta?
12. Why is a historical beta included as an independent variable in a model for estimating fundamental betas?

[21]Diana R. Harrington, "Whose Beta Is Best?" *Financial Analysts Journal* 39, no. 4 (July/August 1983): 67–73.

|||| SELECTED REFERENCES

Alexander, Gordon J., and Norman L. Chervany. "On the Estimation and Stability of Beta." *Journal of Financial and Quantitative Analysis* 15 (March 1980): 123–37.

Ang, James S., and David R. Peterson. "Return, Risk and Yield: Evidence from Ex Ante Data." *The Journal of Finance* 50 (June 1985): 537–58.

Arnott, Robert D. "What Hath MPT Wrought: Which Risks Reap Rewards?" *Journal of Portfolio Management* 10 (Fall 1983): 5–11.

Blume, Marshall E. "Betas and Their Regression Tendencies." *The Journal of Finance* 30 (June 1975): 785–95.

———. "On the Assessment of Risk." *The Journal of Finance* 26 (March 1971): 1–10.

Dowen, Richard J., and W. Scott Bauman. "A Fundamental Multifactor Asset Pricing Model." *Financial Analysts Journal* 52 (July/August 1986): 45–51.

Elgers, Pieter, Joanne Hill, and Thomas Schneeweis. "Research Design for Systematic Risk Prediction." *Journal of Portfolio Management* 8 (Spring 1982): 43–52.

Estep, Tony, Nick Hanson, and Cal Johnson. "Sources of Value and Risk in Common Stocks." *Journal of Portfolio Management* 9 (Summer 1983): 5–13.

Evans, John L., and Stephen H. Archer. "Diversification and the Reduction of Dispersion: An Empirical Analysis." *The Journal of Finance* 23 (December 1968): 761–67.

Fouse, William L. "Risk and Liquidity Revisited." *Financial Analysts Journal* 33 (January/February 1977): 50–55.

———. "Risk and Liquidity: The Keys to Stock Price Behavior." *Financial Analysts Journal* 32 (May/June 1976): 35–55.

Gahlon, James M., and James A. Gentry. "On the Relationship between Systematic Risk and the Degree of Operating and Financial Leverage." *Financial Management* 11 (Summer 1982): 15–23.

Harrington, Diana R. "Whose Beta Is Best?" *Financial Analysts Journal* 39 (July/August 1983): 67–73.

Hill, Ned C., and Bernell K. Stone. "Accounting Betas, Systematic Risk, and Financial Leverage: A Risk-Composition Approach to the Determinants of Systematic Risk." *Journal of Financial and Quantitative Analysis* 15 (September 1980): 595–637.

Kosnicke, Ralph. "The Limited Relevance of Volatility to Risk." *Journal of Portfolio Management* 13 (Fall 1986): 18–20.

Levy, Haim. "Measuring Risk and Performance over Alternative Investment Horizons." *Financial Analysts Journal* 50 (March/April 1985): 61–67.

Malkiel, Burton G. "Risk and Return: A New Look." National Bureau of Economic Research, Reprint no. 291 (July 1982).

Markowitz, Harry M. "Portfolio Selection." *The Journal of Finance* 7 (March 1952): 77–91.

―――. *Portfolio Selection—Efficient Diversification of Investments* (New Haven: Yale University Press, 1959).

McEnally, Richard W., and David E. Upton. "A Reexamination of the Ex Post Risk-Return Tradeoff on Common Stocks." *Journal of Financial and Quantitative Analysis* 15 (June 1979): 395–519.

Modigliani, Franco, and Gerald A. Pogue. "An Introduction to Risk and Return: Concepts and Evidence." *Financial Analysts Journal* 30 (May/June 1975): 69–86.

Muller, Frederick L., Bruce D. Fielitz, and Myron T. Greene. "S&P Quality Rankings: Risk and Return." *Journal of Portfolio Management* 10 (Summer 1983): 39–52.

Reichenstein, William. "On Standard Deviation and Risk." *Journal of Portfolio Management* 13 (Winter 1987): 39–50.

Shanken, Jay. "Multi-Beta CAPM or Equilibrium APT? A Reply." *The Journal of Finance* 50 (September 1985): 1189–96.

Sharpe, William F. "Capital Asset Prices: Theory of Market Equilibrium under Conditions of Risk." *The Journal of Finance* 19 (September 1965): 525–52.

―――. "Factors in New York Stock Exchange Security Returns 1931–1979. *Journal of Portfolio Management* 8 (Summer 1982): 5–19.

―――. "A Simplified Model for Portfolio Analysis." *Management Science* 9 (January 1963): 227–93.

Sharpe, William F., and Guy Howard B. Sosin. "Risk, Return and Yield: New York Stock Exchange Common Stocks, 1928–1969." *Financial Analysts Journal* 32 (March/April 1976): 33–52.

Sharpe, William F., and Guy M. Cooper. "NYSE Stocks Classified by Risk, 1931–1967." *Financial Analysts Journal* 28 (March/April 1972): 46–54.

Stocks, Bonds, Bills and Inflation: 1991 Yearbook (Chicago: Ibbotson Associates, 1991).

Thompson, Donald J. "Sources of Systematic Risk in Common Stocks." *Journal of Business* 39 (April 1976): 173–88.

6 CAPITAL MARKET AND PORTFOLIO THEORY

Until Markowitz published his classic article on portfolio selection in 1952, there was very little in the investment literature that could be called either portfolio theory or capital market theory.[1] Although investment managers and financial writers recognized the importance of portfolio management and were quite aware of the fact that diversification reduces risk, the literature was virtually devoid of any theory about the measurement of risk, the relationship between risk and return, or the selection of portfolios. For example, in a leading investments text of the late 1930s by Mead and Grodinsky, the authors had little more than the following to say about how to assemble a portfolio of common stocks: "Diversification is a sound and necessary principle of investment, but, to exert its full effect of stabilizing investment values, it should be applied to securities of expanding industries."[2] The authors recommended that risk be taken into account but made no suggestion as to how it might be measured or traded off against the expected return.

During the past 20 to 30 years, financial researchers have made up for the earlier lack of literature on portfolio theory and capital market theory by offering an abundance of articles and textbooks on these closely related subjects. Portfolio theory deals with the selection of portfolios, taking into account risk and the expected return, while capital market theory explains how expected returns are related to risk and other factors of importance to investors. Portfolio theory explains how portfolios should be selected, and is therefore normative, while capital market theory is positive, or descriptive. The Markowitz methodology for portfolio selection is the classic example of portfolio theory. The capital asset pricing model (CAPM) and the arbitrage pricing theory (APT) are the preeminent examples of capital market theory. This chapter on portfolio and capital market theory deals primarily with Markowitz's portfolio theory and the original, single-factor CAPM. Chapter 7 covers two broad topics: tests and modifications of the CAPM and the arbitrage pricing theory.

Since risk is a crucial factor in theories relating to portfolio selection and capital asset pricing, it is the first topic covered in this chapter. Here we will examine the relationship between the risk of a portfolio and the

---

[1]Harry M. Markowitz, "Portfolio Selection," *The Journal of Finance,* (March 1952): 77–91; *Portfolio Selection* (New Haven: Yale University Press, 1959).

[2]Edward Sherwood Mead and Julius Grodinsky, *The Ebb and Flow of Investment Values* (New York: D. Appleton Century, 1939), p. 464.

risk of the individual assets contained in the portfolio. As we will see, a carefully diversified portfolio of common stocks does not have to contain many stocks to eliminate a great portion of the risk of the portfolio. We will also examine the Markowitz theory relating to efficient portfolios and the efficient frontier. Efficient portfolios are those which offer the highest expected return at a given level of risk. The optimal portfolio for an investor is the efficient portfolio that will provide the most satisfying combination of risk and expected return.

|||| **RISK AND RISK MEASUREMENT**

Investment risk depends upon the degree of confidence with which the return on an investment can be predicted. For example, the nominal (as opposed to real) return on U.S. Treasury bills can be predicted with complete confidence, and the risk (except for the rate of inflation) therefore is zero. Common stock returns, on the other hand, are extremely difficult to predict, and the risk is substantial.

One of Markowitz's important contributions to portfolio theory is the idea of measuring risk by the variability of the return, expressed in terms of either the variance or the standard deviation. The greater the variability, the greater the uncertainty about the actual outcome and the greater the chance for a disappointing result.

The standard deviation has two distinct merits as a measure of risk. First, it is expressed in the same units as the returns themselves. Second, if the returns are approximately normally distributed, it indicates how far below *or above* the expected return the actual return might fall. With a normal distribution, two-thirds of the returns will be within one standard deviation, and 95% will be within two standard deviations of the expected return.

The Ibbotson and Sinquefield study of the annual returns on stocks, bonds, and Treasury bills for the years 1926 through 1988 found that the annual returns for large common stocks, small common stocks, corporate bonds, and U.S. Treasury bonds all roughly approximated normal distributions, as shown in Table 6-1.[3] Treasury bill returns were an exception. About 50% of the returns for stocks and bonds were above the mean, with about 50% below; roughly two-thirds were within one standard deviation of the mean, and approximately 95% were within two standard deviations of the mean. However, since each annual return was an average for a large number of securities, it should not be assumed that the returns for each individual security were approximately normally distributed.

An earlier study of the monthly price changes of large numbers of individual stocks found that the standard deviation is highly correlated with other plausible measures of risk, including the range, the mean

---

[3]Roger G. Ibbotson and Rex A. Sinquefield, *Stocks, Bonds, Bills and Inflation: 1989 Yearbook* (Chicago: Ibbotson Associates, Inc., 1989).

|||| **TABLE 6-1**
Annual Returns for Five Classes of Securities, 1926–1988

	Large Stocks	Small Stocks	Corporate Bonds	Government Bonds	Treasury Bills
Arithmetic mean returns	11.4%	18.1%	3.7%	3.1%	3.1%
Standard deviation	21.95	37.3	5.6	5.7	3.1
Range	−43.3	−58.0	−8.1	−9.2	0
	+54.0	+142.9	+18.7	+16.8	+14.7
Percentage above mean	53.6	50.0	42.9	50.0	33.9
Percentage within one standard deviation of the mean	71.4	73.2	58.9	69.6	85.7
Percentage within two standard deviations of the mean	96.4	96.4	94.6	94.6	94.6

SOURCE: *Stocks, Bonds, Bills and Inflation: 1989 Yearbook* (Chicago: Ibbotson Associates, Inc. 1989). Range and percentage figures were calculated by the authors.

absolute deviation, and the semivariance.[4] Since the semivariance measures the dispersion of only those observations that are below the mean, the close correlation between the standard deviation and the semivariance indicates that the standard deviation is a good indicator of the possibility that the return will fall below the mean.

For anyone who holds more than one asset, the combined risk of all the assets he or she is holding (that is, the risk of the portfolio) is of primary concern.[5] The following sections will show how the risk of a portfolio depends not only on the number of individual assets in the portfolio and their risk but also on the degree to which their returns are correlated with one another.

PORTFOLIO RETURN AND RISK

Equation 6-1 shows that the expected return for a portfolio is simply a weighted average of the expected returns for all securities in the portfolio, using the current market values as the weights:

$$E(R_p) = \sum_{i=1}^{N} W_i E(R_i) \tag{6-1}$$

where

$E(R_p)$ = expected return for the portfolio

N = number of securities in the portfolio

[4]Philip L. Cooley, Rodney L. Roenfeldt, and Naval K. Modani, "Interdependence of Market Risk Measures," *Journal of Business*, 50 (January 1977): 356–63.

[5]Any estimate of portfolio risk begins with estimates of the risk of the individual assets, usually measured by the variance (or its square root, the standard deviation) of the return. The concepts of estimating security risk and return were discussed in Chapter 5. If these concepts elude you, Chapter 5 should be reviewed before continuing.

W_i = percentage of total portfolio value represented by security i

$\Sigma W_i = 1.0$

$E(R_i)$ = expected return for security i

If the market values of stocks i and j, the only assets in the portfolio, are $4,000 and $6,000, respectively, and the expected returns are 14% and 11%, the expected return for the portfolio is $(.40 \times 14\%) + (.60 \times 11\%)$, or 12.2%.

Except where the returns of the individual securities in a portfolio are perfectly positively correlated, the standard deviation of the portfolio return is smaller than the weighted average of the standard deviations of the returns of the individual securities. The portfolio return is less variable than the average of the individual returns because fluctuations of the individual returns are partially offsetting. The Sidelight explains the importance of selecting stocks whose returns are not highly correlated.

For a two-security portfolio, Equations 6-2 and 6-3 show that the variability of the portfolio return depends not only upon the variances of the individual securities but upon the degree to which the returns for the assets move together, as measured by either the covariance or the correlation coefficient, as well as the proportion of the total invested in each security.[6]

[6]Procedures for calculating the covariance and correlation coefficient were illustrated in Chapter 5.

||| SIDELIGHT

Portfolios Tango Best when They are Out of Step

To achieve good diversification, one must do more than simply select a hodgepodge of securities.

The secret is to mix investments that do not move in tandem. Stocks in sectors that perform poorly in one period may perform well in the next, and vice versa. Diversification assures that at least part of the portfolio will be in the right place at the right time.

When additions are being made to your portfolio of stocks (or portfolio of mutual funds), it is important to increase your holdings in sectors that have been performing poorly. This will help to rebalance the portfolio.

Experience shows that the odds of outguessing the markets with enough regularity to beat a diversified portfolio are extremely poor. With diversification, you have a better chance of buying some stocks low and selling high over a period of time.

SOURCE: Adapted from Barbara Donnelly, "Portfolios Tango Best When They're Out of Step," *The Wall Street Journal,* September 20, 1989, p. C1. Reprinted by permission of *The Wall Street Journal,* © Dow Jones & Company, Inc. (1989). All Rights Reserved Worldwide.

$$\sigma_p^2 = W_i^2\sigma_i^2 + W_j^2\sigma_j^2 + 2W_iW_j\text{Cov}_{ij} \qquad (6\text{-}2)$$

$$\sigma_p = (W_i^2\sigma_i^2 + W_j^2\sigma_j^2 + 2W_iW_j\text{Cov}_{ij})^{1/2} \qquad (6\text{-}3)$$

where

σ_p^2 = variance of the portfolio return

σ_p = standard deviation of the portfolio return

W_i = proportion of total portfolio value represented by security i

σ_i^2 = variance of the return for security i

Cov_{ij} = covariance of the returns for i and j

σ_i = standard deviation of the return for i

$W_i + W_j = 1.0$

Recall from the discussion in Chapter 5 that the correlation coefficient is a standardized measure of covariance with a value that always lies between -1.0 and $+1.0$ inclusive. It is the covariance divided by the product of the standard deviations of the two variables:

$$\rho_{ij} = \text{Cov}_{ij}/\sigma_i\sigma_j \qquad (6\text{-}4)$$

Since the covariance is the product of the correlation coefficient and the standard deviations of the individual returns,

$$\text{Cov}_{ij} = \rho_{ij}\sigma_i\sigma_j \qquad (6\text{-}5)$$

Equations 6-2 and 6-3 can be restated as follows:

$$\sigma_p^2 = W_i^2\sigma_i^2 + W_j^2\sigma_j^2 + 2W_iW_j\rho_{ij}\sigma_i\sigma_j \qquad (6\text{-}6)$$

$$\sigma_p = (W_i^2\sigma_i^2 + W_j^2\sigma_j^2 + 2W_iW_j\rho_{ij}\sigma_i\sigma_j)^{1/2} \qquad (6\text{-}7)$$

where

ρ_{ij} = correlation coefficient for the returns of i and j

Other things being the same, the smaller the correlation between the returns, the smaller the standard deviation of the portfolio return.

Figure 6-1 shows how the variability of the return for a two-asset portfolio is related to the returns of the individual assets in two extreme situations, perfect positive correlation and perfect negative correlation. With perfect positive correlation, the portfolio standard deviation is a weighted average of the individual standard deviations. With perfect negative correlation, the portfolio standard deviation is zero.

Correlation of Returns and Investment Proportions

Three hypothetical cases and one actual case (based on historical returns of Hewlett–Packard and Kimberly Clark) will illustrate how the standard deviation or risk of a two-security portfolio depends upon the degree of correlation between the returns of the two securities. The returns and variances were calculated using the formulas presented in Chapter 5.

|||| **FIGURE 6-1**

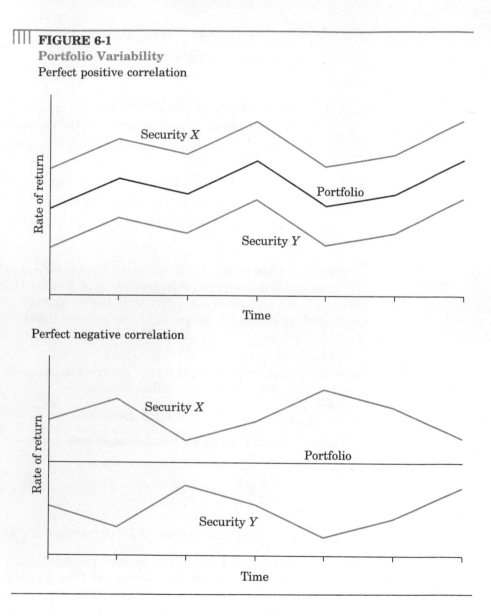

Portfolio Variability

Perfect positive correlation

Perfect negative correlation

Table 6-2 presents standard deviations, correlations, and security weights used in the hypothetical cases.

Perfect Negative Correlation In the first case, shown in column 1 of Table 6-2, the correlation between the returns is perfectly negative ($\rho_{ij} = -1.0$), and the portfolio variance is 0%. The combination of two risky securities results in a portfolio of zero risk. This can be seen by examining Equation 6-6 after substituting -1.0 for ρ_{ij}:

$$\sigma_p^2 = W_i^2\sigma_i^2 + W_j^2\sigma_j^2 - 2W_iW_j\sigma_i\sigma_j \qquad (6\text{-}8)$$

|||| **TABLE 6-2**

Calculation of Variance and Standard Deviation for a Two-
Security Portfolio

	Correlation −1.0	Correlation 0	Correlation +1.0
Given:			
R_i	14.0%	14.0%	14.0%
R_j	6.0%	6.0%	6.0%
σ_i^2	16.0%	16.0%	16.0%
σ_j^2	9.0%	9.0%	9.0%
W_i	42.86%	42.86%	42.86%
W_j	57.14%	57.14%	57.14%
σ_i	4.0%	4.0%	4.0%
σ_j	3.0%	3.0%	3.0%
Calculations:			
1. $W_i^2\sigma_i^2$ (.1837 × 16)	2.94%	2.94%	2.94%
2. $W_j^2\sigma_j^2$ (.3265 × 9)	2.94%	2.94%	2.94%
3. $2W_iW_j$ (2 × .4286 × .5714)	0.490	0.490	0.490
4. ρ_{ij}	−1.0	0	1.0
5. σ_i	4.0%	4.0%	4.0%
6. σ_j	3.0%	3.0%	3.0%
Portfolio variance [(1 + 2) + (3 × 4 × 5 × 6)]	0.00%	5.88%	11.76%
Portfolio standard deviation $(\sigma_p^2)^{1/2}$	0.00%	2.42%	3.43%

Factoring Equation 6-8 and solving for the standard deviation by taking square roots gives

$$\sigma_p^2 = (W_i\sigma_i - W_j\sigma_j)^2 \qquad (6\text{-}9)$$

$$\sigma_p = W_i\sigma_i - W_j\sigma_j \qquad (6\text{-}9a)$$

The negative sign in Equation 6-9a means that with the appropriate choice of investment proportions, the variance (or standard deviation) of the portfolio can be zero. The investment weights used in Table 6-2, (W_i, W_j), were determined by setting Equation 6-9a equal to zero and substituting $(1 - W_j)$ for W_i. That is:

$$\sigma_p = (1 - W_j)\sigma_i - W_j\sigma_j = 0$$
$$\Rightarrow W_j = \sigma_i/(\sigma_i + \sigma_j)$$
$$= 4.0\%/(4.0\% + 3.0\%) = .5714$$
$$W_i = (1 - W_j) = (1 - .5714) = .4286$$

Obviously, if different investment proportions were chosen, the risk of the portfolio would be different from zero. Figure 6-2 presents a plot of the portfolio expected return and portfolio risk for different investment proportions. At point i, $W_i = 100\%$ and $W_j = 0\%$; at the Y-axis $W_i = 42.86\%$ and $W_j = 57.14\%$. Each point between the Y-axis and point i represents an increase in the proportion invested in security i and a decrease in the proportion invested in security j. Each point between the Y-axis and point j represents an increase in the proportion invested in security j and a decrease in the proportion invested in security i.

Note that every point between the Y-axis and point i is superior to every point between the Y-axis and point j. That is, an investor will always receive a higher return for a given level of risk by investing at least 42.86% in security i.

Zero Correlation In the second case, shown in column 2 of Table 6-2, where the correlation is zero, Equation 6-8 reduces to

$$\sigma_p^2 = W_i^2\sigma_i^2 + W_j^2\sigma_j^2 \qquad (6\text{-}10)$$

From Equation 6-10, it might appear that diversification would not reduce the risk, but an examination of Table 6-2 shows that the portfolio variance is 5.88%, which is less than either of the variances of the individual stocks. Thus, diversification has helped. The reason this has occurred is that the weighting terms, (W_i, W_j), which are both less than one, are squared in Equation 6-10. This, of course, reduces the weights to relatively small values.

If there are many securities with uncorrelated returns, Equation 6-10 becomes

$$\sigma_p^2 = W_1^2\sigma_1^2 + W_2^2\sigma_2^2 + \ldots + W_n^2\sigma_n^2 \qquad (6\text{-}11)$$

|||| **FIGURE 6-2**

Risk and Return Relationship When Correlation Equals −1.0

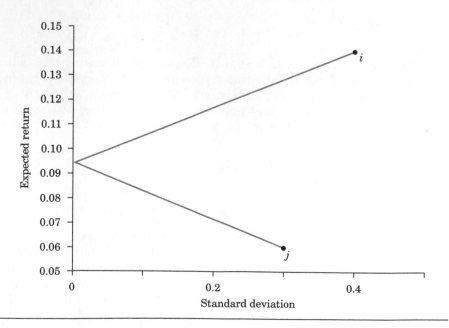

where

W_i = the proportions invested in security i, $i = 1, 2 \ldots n$

σ_i^2 = the variance of the returns of security i

n = the number of securities.

If we assume that an equal amount is invested in each of the n securities, Equation 6-11 becomes

$$\sigma_p^2 = (1/n)^2(\sigma_1^2 + \sigma_2^2 + \ldots + \sigma_n^2) \qquad (6\text{-}12)$$

If we rearrange the terms in Equation 6-12 slightly, it becomes

$$\sigma_p^2 = (1/n)[(1/n)(\sigma_1^2 + \sigma_2^2 + \ldots + \sigma_n^2)] \qquad (6\text{-}12a)$$

Note that the terms in the square brackets in Equation 6-12a equal the sum of n numbers divided by n, that is, an average. Therefore,

$$\sigma_p^2 = \overline{\sigma}^2/n \qquad (6\text{-}12b)$$

Given the mean of the variances, as the number of securities gets larger, the variance of the portfolio decreases. This relationship is the basis for risk pooling or insurance.

Substantial risk reduction can occur when large numbers of uncorrelated securities are formed into portfolios. This is one reason why insurance companies attempt to write large numbers of policies. They are attempting to spread the risks over a great number of customers. It also explains why one of the major exclusions in life insurance policies is the event of war. In this case, deaths become highly correlated.

Perfect Positive Correlation When security returns are perfectly positively correlated, as shown in the last column of Table 6-2, Equation 6-8 becomes

$$\sigma_p^2 = W_i^2\sigma_i^2 + W_j^2\sigma_j^2 + 2W_iW_j\sigma_i\sigma_j \qquad (6\text{-}13)$$

Factoring Equation 6-15 results in

$$\sigma_p^2 = (W_i\sigma_i + W_j\sigma_j)^2 \qquad (6\text{-}13a)$$

$$\sigma_p = W_i\sigma_i + W_j\sigma_j \qquad (6\text{-}13b)$$

In this case, since the weighted risks are additive, diversification does not reduce the risk below the weighted average. The lowest possible risk is obtained by purchasing only the lowest risk security. In our example, this means investing 100% in security j.

Figure 6-3 presents a graph of the expected return and risk for each of the limiting cases described above ($\rho = -1.0, 0, 1.0$). Each point on the respective curves represents a different proportion invested in each security. Note that for the case of zero correlation, the plot is a parabola between security i and security j. The parabola shape graphically demonstrates that risk reduction is possible. If the correlation were negative, but greater than -1.0, the parabola would be to the left of the zero-correlation parabola. If the correlation were positive, the parabola would

|||| **FIGURE 6-3**

Risk and Return Relationship When $\rho = -1.0, 0,$ and $+1.0$

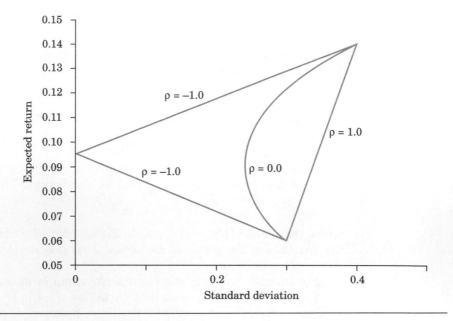

be to the right of the current position. The implication of defining a parabola, even though returns are positively correlated and less than $+1.0$, is that risk reduction is possible.

Portfolio Risk with Positive Correlation Less Than One

When any two common stocks, whose correlation of returns is less than 1.0, are combined in a portfolio, the standard deviation of the portfolio return is smaller than the weighted average of the individual standard deviations. The smaller the correlation, the smaller the standard deviation of the portfolio return relative to the weighted average standard deviation. To illustrate this, we will assume that the stocks of Hewlett–Packard and Kimberly Clark were combined in a two-stock portfolio for a period of 18 quarters from January 1985 through June 1989. Table 6-3 shows the quarterly returns and calculations of the covariance and correlation.

In 12 of the 18 quarters, the returns for the two stocks were on the same side of their mean return, and their prices usually moved in the same direction during periods of big change, as in the first quarter of 1987. This contributed to the positive correlation of .58. We would expect their returns to be positively correlated in the future, since most stocks are affected in a similar way by such market-wide influences as changes in interest rates and changes in the outlook for the economy.

|||| **TABLE 6-3**
Covariance and Correlation for Hewlett–Packard and Kimberly
Clark Quarterly Returns, 1985 through June 1989

| | Quarterly Returns | | Covariance Calculations | | |
| | (1) Hewlett–Packard R_h | (2) Kimberly Clark R_k | (3) $R_h - \bar{R}_h$ | (4) $R_k - \bar{R}_k$ | (5) (3) × (4) |
Year–Quarter					
1985–1	3.60	3.32	−0.20	−3.67	0.75
1985–2	−15.19	22.79	−18.99	15.80	−299.98
1985–3	19.46	4.58	15.66	−2.41	−37.82
1985–4	−19.99	10.33	−23.79	3.34	−79.54
1986–1	30.35	29.28	26.54	22.29	591.68
1986–2	15.06	7.26	11.26	0.27	3.03
1986–3	−12.86	−10.51	−16.67	−17.50	291.70
1986–4	−0.81	−1.08	−4.62	−8.07	37.28
1987–1	28.67	42.06	24.86	35.07	871.90
1987–2	11.83	−2.02	8.03	−9.01	−72.34
1987–3	9.25	6.12	5.45	−0.87	−4.73
1987–4	−17.89	−12.98	−21.69	−19.98	433.38
1988–1	13.35	8.30	9.54	1.31	12.48
1988–2	7.82	16.09	4.02	9.10	36.58
1988–3	−17.28	−6.81	−21.08	−13.81	291.04
1988–4	0.17	2.22	−3.64	−4.77	17.34
1989–1	14.52	5.84	10.72	−1.15	−12.38
1989–2	−1.58	1.07	−5.39	−5.93	31.94
Total					2,112.32
Mean	3.80	6.99			
Variance	246.70	187.87			
Standard deviation	15.71	13.71			
Covariance (2,112.32/17)					124.25
Correlation [(124.25)/(15.71 × 13.71)]					0.58

With a 35% investment in Hewlett–Packard and a 65% investment in Kimberly Clark, the portfolio standard deviation, calculated on the basis of the correlation of .58 and the variances and standard deviations shown in Table 6-3, was 10.4% as shown below:

$$\sigma_p^2 = (.35)^2(246.7) + (.65)^2(187.7) + (2)(.35)(.65)(.58)(15.7)(13.7)$$
$$= 166.3$$
$$\sigma_p = (166.3)^{1/2}$$
$$= 12.9$$

The security risk and return relationship for various investment proportions in Hewlett–Packard and Kimberly Clark is shown in Figure 6-4. The parabola shape indicates the possibility of risk reduction. Note that the minimum risk combination of Hewlett Packard and Kimberly Clark occurs approximately at a risk level of 12.9% and return of 5.87%. As indicated in Figure 6-4 this portfolio level of return and risk will occur when 35% of available funds are invested in Hewlett–Packard and 65% in Kimberly Clark. The rational investor in this two-security world will always invest along the positive slope of the curve from the minimum variance point. That is, the rational investor will always invest 65% or more of his or her portfolio in Kimberly Clark, if the historical risks and returns are accepted as accurate forecasts of future risks and returns.

General Formula for Portfolio Variance

The general formula for calculating the variance of a portfolio containing any number of securities can be expressed in various ways. Perhaps the easiest to understand is Equation 6-14:

$$V_p = \sum_{i=1}^{N} W_i^2 \sigma_i^2 + \sum_{\substack{i=1 \\ i \neq j}}^{N} \sum_{j=1}^{N} W_i W_j \rho_{ij} \sigma_i \sigma_j \qquad (6\text{-}14)$$

The first expression $(\Sigma\ W_i^2\sigma_i^2)$ represents a weighted average of the variances, and the second expression $(\Sigma\ \Sigma\ W_i W_j \rho_{ij}\sigma_i\sigma_i)$ represents a weighted average of the covariances $(\text{Cov}_{ij} = \rho_{ij}\sigma_i\sigma_j)$. For example, the variance of a portfolio containing three securities is

$$V_p = W_1^2\sigma_1^2 + W_2^2\sigma_2^2 + W_3^2\sigma_3^2 + 2W_1W_2\rho_{12}\sigma_1\sigma_2$$
$$+ 2W_1W_3\rho_{13}\sigma_1\sigma_3 + W_2W_3\rho_{23}\sigma_2\sigma_3 \quad (6\text{-}14a)$$

With N securities in the portfolio, there are N variance terms $(W_i\sigma_i^2)$ and $[(N^2 - N)/2]$ covariance terms $(W_iW_j\text{Cov}_{ij})$. The weighted average of

||| **FIGURE 6-4**

Risk and Return Relationship for Various Investment Proportions in Hewlett–Packard and Kimberly Clark

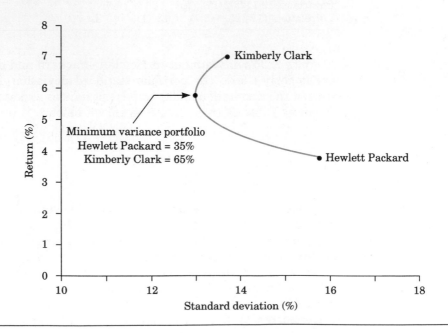

|||| **TABLE 6-4**

Influence of Correlations on Portfolio Variance

Portfolio	A	B	C
A. N	20	20	20
B. σ_i^2	0.36	0.36	0.36
C. σ_i	0.60	0.60	0.60
D. $W_i = (1/20)$	0.05	0.05	0.05
E. $\sum_{i=1}^{20} W_i^2 = (20 \times .0025)$	0.05	0.05	0.05
F. $\sum_{i=1}^{20} W_i^2\sigma_i^2 = (E \times B)$	0.018	0.018	0.018
G. $2\sum_{i=1}^{20}\sum_{j=1}^{20} W_iW_j = (2)[(20^2 - 20)/2](.05)(.05)$	0.95	0.95	0.95
H. ρ_{ij}	0	0.50	1.00
I. $\text{Cov}_{ij} = (\rho_{ij} \times \sigma_i \times \sigma_j) = (H \times C \times C)$	0	0.18	0.36
J. $2\sum_{i=1}^{20}\sum_{j=1}^{20} W_iW_j\text{Cov}_{ij} = (G \times I)$ $i \neq j$	0	0.171	0.342
K. $\sigma_P^2 = (F + J)$	0.018	0.189	0.360
L. σ_P (portfolio standard deviation)	0.134	0.435	0.600

the covariances is multiplied by two. The double summation means that the covariance is calculated for the return of each security with every other security. Each covariance is then multiplied by the product of the weights for the two securities. For example, if a portfolio contains four stocks, there are six covariances $[(4^2 - 4)/2]$ and six pairs of weights, one pair for each covariance. If the portfolio contains 20 securities, there are 20 variance terms and 190 $[(20^2 - 20)/2]$ covariance terms.

For portfolios containing a number of securities, the risk depends largely upon the correlations between the returns of the individual securities. With a large number of securities, the weighted average of the variances is small because the weights, which are squared, are small. Even with a large number of securities, however, the weighted average of the covariances can be large if the correlations between the returns are large.

The example in Table 6-4 illustrates the importance of the correlations between the returns. The variances and standard deviations are calculated for three portfolios of 20 common stocks, with each stock having the same market value, a variance of 0.36, and a standard deviation of 0.60, or 60%. In portfolio A, the correlations are all zero; in B, they are 0.50; and in C they are 1.0. In terms of the standard deviation of the return, the portfolio with correlations of 0.50 is more than three times as risky as the portfolio with correlations of 0.00 (.435/.134), and the portfolio with correlations of 1.00 is 38% riskier than a portfolio with correlations of 0.50 [(.600 − .435)/.435].

|||| **EFFICIENT PORTFOLIOS**

The Markowitz theory of portfolio selection assumes that only two characteristics of a portfolio are relevant: the expected return and the risk. As we have just seen in the two-security case with less than perfect correlation, the combination of the securities traces a parabola in the risk-return space. We have also indicated that the rational investor will always invest on the upper portion of the parabola to achieve the maximum return for a given amount of risk.

In the real world, the correlation coefficients of a majority of stocks are positive, and investors hold more than two stocks. When securities are combined together, the locus of all the possible minimum variance sets will form a parabola-shaped curve, as in the two-security case. Minimum variance sets provide the lowest portfolio variances for a given return with the securities under consideration by an investor.

A minimum variance set or investment opportunity set for N risky securities is depicted in Figure 6-5. All of the securities depicted in Figure 6-5, as well as any combination of the securities, are feasible portfolios. However, only those on the boundary above point *MVP* (the minimum variance portfolio) are preferred portfolios. That is, all portfolios on the boundary dominate all other possible portfolios since they provide the maximum return for a given amount of risk. These maximum return, minimum variance portfolios define the efficient set or efficient frontier of risky securities.

|||| **FIGURE 6-5**
Markowitz Efficient Frontier

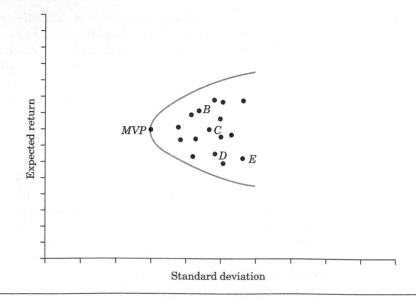

EXTENSION OF THE MARKOWITZ THEORY

Sharpe and Tobin extended the Markowitz theory to include portfolios containing risk-free assets and portfolios purchased in part with borrowed funds. If we combine the risk-free asset with a portfolio (designated as M) on the efficient frontier, the return and risk functions for the resulting portfolio are

$$E(R_p) = W_{rf}(R_f) + W_M E(R_M) \qquad (6\text{-}15)$$
$$\sigma_p = (W_{Rf}^2 \sigma_{Rf}^2 + W_M^2 \sigma_M^2 + 2W_{Rf} W_M \rho_{Rf,M} \sigma_{Rf} \sigma_M)^{1/2} \qquad (6\text{-}16)$$

or, since the risk-free asset has zero risk ($\sigma_{Rf}^2 = \sigma_{Rf} = 0$):

$$\sigma_p = W_M \sigma_M$$

These risk and return relationships are linear in the expected return and standard deviation space as shown in Figure 6-6.[7] With the possibility of lending funds at the risk-free rate of interest, the line from R_f to M replaces the curved line from the minimum variance portfolio A to M as a portion of the efficient frontier. When it is further assumed that an investor can borrow at the risk-free rate (sell the risk-free asset short) to

[7]The linear equation may be derived from Equations 6-15 and 6-16. Note that

$$E(R_p) = (1 - W_M)R_f + W_M E(R_M) \quad \text{and} \quad \sigma_p = W_M \sigma_M$$

Solving both equations for W_m and equating the results provides

$$E(R_p) = R_f + \{[E(R_M) - R_f]/\sigma_M\}\sigma_p$$

|||| **FIGURE 6-6**

Efficient Frontier with Lending and Borrowing at the Risk-Free Rate (Capital Market Line)

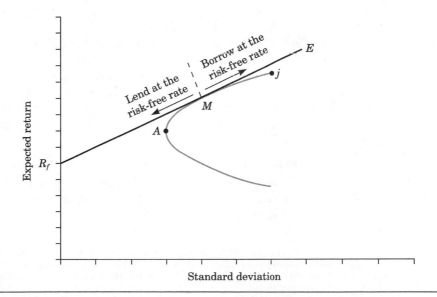

increase the investment in risky assets, the line from M to E replaces M to j as the rest of the efficient frontier. It should be clear that the risk-free asset can be combined with any portfolio on the efficient frontier. However, the portfolio providing the best combination of risk and return is at the tangent point for a line extending from the return for the risk-free asset.

The opportunity to borrow or lend at the risk-free rate creates a linear efficient frontier and defines an optimal risky portfolio for all investors. That is, no other risky investment or combination of investments provides a higher return for a given amount of risk. The implication of these observations is that all investors should hold the same mix of risky securities (portfolio M in Figure 6-6) and use borrowing or lending of the risk-free asset to attain their preferred risk/return level.

THE CAPITAL ASSET PRICING MODEL

It would be difficult to overstate the impact that the capital asset pricing model (CAPM) has had on both theory and practice in the field of finance. It was the first theory to explain in a rigorous manner the relationship between risk and expected return, and it was the first to partition total risk into its systematic and unsystematic components. The distinction between systematic and unsystematic risk is of great importance under the CAPM because expected returns vary with the amount of systematic risk but are completely independent of unsystematic risk.

In the remainder of this chapter, we will be discussing the CAPM in its original form. The development of the model will rely on "intuitive mathematics." Those interested in a more rigorous development of the model are referred to the appendix to the chapter. Important modifications of the theory will be examined in Chapter 7.

CAPM ASSUMPTIONS

The CAPM builds on the portfolio theory of Markowitz and assumes, as did Markowitz, that investors (1) are concerned with only two aspects of an investment, the risk and the return, and (2) seek to hold portfolios that are efficient, that is, portfolios that offer the highest expected return for a given amount of total risk, as measured by the variance or standard deviation of the return. The following additional assumptions are peculiar to the CAPM:

1. Investors can lend and borrow any amount at the risk-free rate.
2. All investors have the same information, use it in the same way, and arrive at the same expectations about the future risk and return of each security.[8]

[8]Although the CAPM applies to the pricing of all risky assets, including tangibles as well as intangibles, it is usually analyzed and tested as though it applies only to the pricing of securities. Our discussion of the model will therefore be in terms of stocks, bonds, and other securities.

3. Securities can be bought and sold without transaction costs, and assets are completely divisible and liquid.

4. Taxes have no impact on investment policies.

5. All investors are price takers,[9] and all asset quantities are fixed.

These extreme assumptions make it possible for the model to focus on risk and return and arrive at certain powerful conclusions that have considerable validity in spite of the unrealistic assumptions. Note that the test of a theory is not in the realism of its assumptions but in whether it can be used to make reasonably reliable predictions.

THE CAPITAL MARKET LINE

In the world of the CAPM, where everyone has the same information and the same expectations about every risky asset, everyone seeks the same set of risky assets. The only way that all investors can hold the same risky assets is for every investor to have a portfolio containing proportionate amounts of all risky assets. This portfolio, with each risky asset represented in proportion to its aggregate market value, is called the market portfolio.

In Figure 6-6 portfolios between R_f and M are composed of a combination of portfolio M (the market portfolio) and a risk-free asset, such as U.S. Treasury bills. Portfolios between M and E, with higher expected returns and greater risk than portfolio M, are the market portfolio financed in part with borrowed funds. Depending on the investor's attitude toward risk, the optimal portfolio may consist of R_f alone, M alone, M combined with a risk-free asset, or M financed in part with borrowed funds.[10] Those who want a safer portfolio than M and are willing to accept a lower expected return can invest a portion (perhaps all) of their funds in a risk-free asset. Those who are willing to accept more risk for the possibility of a higher rate of return can leverage their investment in M by borrowing.

With every investor holding the same set of risky assets, the risk preferences of investors are reflected in the amount that is loaned or borrowed at the risk-free rate. Portfolio M dominates all other portfolios of risky assets when borrowing and lending at the risk-free rate are possible. The definition of a single optimal risky portfolio is in sharp contrast to the original Markowitz theory, where the optimal combination of risky assets was determined by each individual investor's risk preferences.

The linear efficient frontier of Figure 6-6 is called the capital market line (CML). All inefficient portfolios, including portfolios composed of a

---

[9]In a perfectly competitive market, no individual can influence the market price of a security through buy and sell decisions.

[10]The fact that the choice of an optimal portfolio is independent of, or separate from, the choice of the optimal combination of risky assets, which is the same for all investors, is called the separation theorem. The separation theorem is one of the building blocks of the CAPM.

single risky asset, lie below the line. The formula for the capital market line is stated as follows:

$$E(R_p) = R_f + [(E(R_m) - R_f)/\sigma_m]\sigma_p \qquad (6\text{-}17)$$

where

$E(R_p)$ = expected portfolio return

R_f = risk-free rate

σ_p = standard deviation of the portfolio return

$E(R_m)$ = expected return on market portfolio

$E(R_m - R_f)$ = expected market risk premium

σ_m = standard deviation of the market return

Figure 6-6 shows, and Equation 6-17 states, that the expected return for an efficient portfolio is a linear function of its risk, as measured by the standard deviation of the return. The expression $[E(R_m) - R_f)/\sigma_m]$ is the slope of the capital market line. It is also the price, or premium, per unit of risk. Thus, the capital market line states that in equilibrium investors expect to receive the risk-free rate plus a risk premium for each unit of risk in the portfolio (σ_p).

In Figure 6-7 the risk-free rate of interest is 7%, the expected return on the market portfolio is 12%, and the estimated standard deviation of the market return is 20%. The slope of the line is $(12 - 7)/20$, or .25.

|||| **FIGURE 6-7**

Capital Market Line

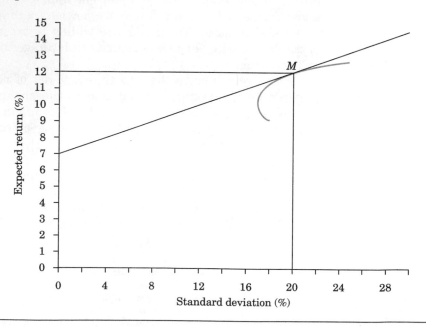

Thus, the reward for each additional percentage point of standard deviation is 0.25% of additional expected return.

Portfolio Choice: Indifference Curves

All points on any one of an investor's indifference curves represent combinations of risk and return that are equally attractive. Figure 6-8 shows a map of indifference curves for a rational investor. Each curved line represents an indifference curve, where all portfolios located on the line are equally desirable to the investor. Thus, for the investor represented in Figure 6-8, portfolios D and F are equally desirable.

Indifference curves are created under the assumption that investors act rationally. The assumed ability of an investor to compare return and risk opportunities of various portfolios and assign preferences is the first principle used to define economically rational behavior.

With return on the vertical axis and risk on the horizontal axis, the higher the level of the curve, the greater the degree of satisfaction (or utility) for the investor. It is assumed that investors want those combinations of risk and return that will place them on the highest indifference curve possible. In Figure 6-8 this second principle of rational choice notes that an investor prefers portfolio A to B and portfolio B to C. In short, an investor will always prefer a portfolio that lies on the most "northwesterly" curve.

A third principle underlying indifference curves is that investors always prefer more return if no additional risk is involved. This principle

‖‖‖ **FIGURE 6-8**

Indifference Curves

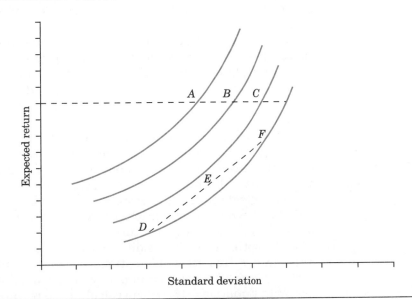

|||| **FIGURE 6-9**
Intersecting Indifference Curves

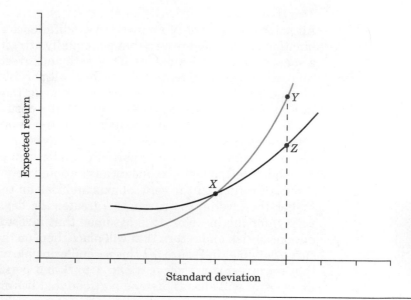

means that indifference curves cannot intersect. Consider the two curves shown in Figure 6-9. At the point of intersection is portfolio X. An investor should be indifferent between portfolios X and Y and should also be indifferent between portfolios X and Z. Note, however, that this means that the investor should also be indifferent between Y and Z. Since Y provides a higher return for the same amount of risk as Z, a contradiction exists. This contradiction can be resolved only if the curves do not intersect.

If an investor combines two portfolios lying on the same indifference curve, the resulting portfolio should be preferred to the originals. This principle is shown in Figure 6-8 with portfolios D, E, and F. Portfolio E represents a linear combination of portfolios D and F. This last principle of rational choice causes the indifference curves to be concave from above.

The available investment opportunities determine which of an investor's indifference curves is relevant. An investor's optimal portfolio is at the point of tangency between one of his or her indifference curves and the capital market line. For investor A in Figure 6-10, the optimal portfolio has an expected return of 9.5% and a standard deviation of 10%. For investor B, whose tolerance for risk is much greater than A's, the optimal portfolio has an expected return of 14.5% and a standard deviation of 30%. A's optimal portfolio is divided equally between the market portfolio and the risk-free asset. B's optimal portfolio contains only the market portfolio, and it is financed in part with borrowed funds.

With Equation 6-18, we can calculate the required amount of leverage for investor B as a percentage of the total investment:

|||| **FIGURE 6-10**

Optimal Portfolios for Two Investors

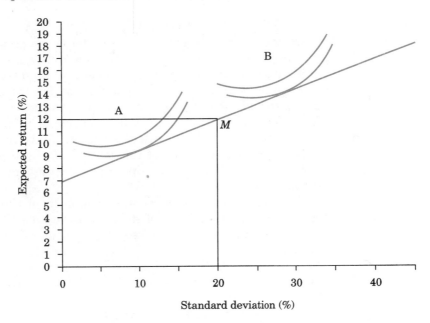

$$R_L = [R_m - (R_f \times d)]/(1 - d) \qquad (6\text{-}18)$$

where

R_L = leveraged rate of return

R_m = rate of return on market portfolio

R_f = risk-free rate of interest

d = percentage of investment financed with borrowed funds

For example, if an investor requires a return (R_L) of 14.5% and the return on the risk-free asset and the market are 7.0% and 12.0%, respectively, the percentage of the investment financed with borrowed funds (d) can be determined by

$$14.5 = [12 - (7 \times d)]/(1 - d)$$
$$d = \tfrac{1}{3}$$

With one-third borrowed, the leveraged return would be 14.5%, as illustrated below.

$$\text{total investment} = \$100.00$$
$$\text{amount borrowed} = 100.00 \times \tfrac{1}{3} = 33.33$$
$$\text{investor's equity} = 100.00 - 33.33 = 66.67$$
$$\text{total income} = .12 \times 100.00 = 12.00$$
$$\text{interest expense} = .07 \times 33.33 = 2.33$$

$$R_L \text{ (return on equity)} = (12.00 - 2.33)/66.67$$
$$= 14.50\%$$

THE MARKET MODEL

As we demonstrated earlier in the chapter, when portfolios are assembled from a large universe of stocks, the Markowitz method of selection requires an enormous number of estimates of correlations or covariances. If N is the total number of stocks from which the selections are being made, the number of correlations or covariances to be estimated is $(N^2 - N)/2$. If, for example, N is 200, the number of correlations is 19,900, and the total number of estimates required, including 200 variances, is 20,100. The impracticality of this method of selecting portfolios was the motivation for Sharpe's development of the diagonal model, now known as the market model.[11]

The market model, which was examined in Chapter 5, is a formal expression of the tendency of stocks to move up and down together. It is widely used in estimating the sensitivity of stocks to market-wide influences such as changes in interest rates and changes in the outlook for the economy. It is also used as a vehicle for partitioning the total risk of a stock or portfolio into systematic risk and unsystematic risk.

Systematic and Unsystematic Risk

Systematic risk (also called market risk) is that portion of the total variability of the return associated with movements of the market as a whole. Unsystematic risk (also called residual risk) is all of the remaining variability. The variance (or its square root, the standard deviation) is the measure of total risk for an individual security or portfolio of securities. The variance of the return of stock i can be stated:

$$\sigma_i^2 = \beta_i^2 \sigma_m^2 + \sigma^2(\epsilon_{it}) \tag{6-19}$$

$$\frac{\text{total}}{\text{risk}} = \frac{\text{systematic}}{\text{risk}} + \frac{\text{unsystematic}}{\text{risk}}$$

As Equation 6-19 makes clear, beta is an index of relative systematic risk rather than a measure of total systematic risk. The higher the beta, the higher the systematic risk of the security relative to the risk of other securities. Total systematic risk depends on the market variance as well as beta. Since the variance of the market is the same for all securities, however, differences in systematic risk are due entirely to differences in beta, which is a security's measure of sensitivity to the market.

The total risk of a *diversified portfolio* can be partitioned into systematic and unsystematic risk with a procedure similar to that used for individual securities. Equation 6-20 shows the end result:[12]

$$\sigma_p^2 = \beta_{pm}^2 \sigma_m^2 + \sigma^2(\epsilon_{pt}) \tag{6-20}$$

---

[11]William F. Sharpe, "A Simplified Model for Portfolio Analysis," *Management Science* 9 (January 1963):277–93.

[12]For convenience we have assumed that the security returns are unrelated so that we can ignore the covariance terms in this portfolio variance equation.

where

$$\beta_{pm} = \sum_{i=1}^{N} W_i \beta_i = \text{weighted average of the security betas}$$

$$\sigma^2(\epsilon_p) = \sum_{i=1}^{N} W_i^2 \sigma^2(\epsilon_{it})$$

The systematic risk of a portfolio is the product of the portfolio's beta squared and the variance of the market return, just as the systematic risk of an individual security is the product of the security's beta-squared and the variance of the market return. However, the unsystematic risk of a portfolio, unlike that of a single security, is weighted by the factor (W_i^2). Each W_i is the value of the security as a percentage of the value of the portfolio. When a diversified portfolio contains a number of stocks, the unsystematic risk is very small. If, for example, an investor invests an equal amount in each of N securities, the systematic risk term becomes

$$\sigma^2(\epsilon_p) = \sum_{i=1}^{N} W_i^2 \sigma^2(\epsilon_i)$$

$$= (1/N)[(1/N)(\sigma^2 \epsilon_1 + \sigma^2 \epsilon_2 + \ldots + \sigma^2 \epsilon_N]$$

$$(6\text{-}21)$$

The term in the square brackets [ ] is the average of the unsystematic risk components of the individual securities in the portfolio. Since this average is divided by N to obtain the portfolio unsystematic risk, the larger the number of securities, the smaller the portfolio unsystematic risk. Therefore since

$$\lim_{n \to \infty} \sigma^2(\epsilon_{pt}) = 0$$

When N is large, Equation 6-21 can be written as

$$\sigma^2(R_p) = \beta_{pm}^2 \sigma^2(R_m)$$

and

$$\sigma(R_p) = \beta_{pm} \sigma(R_m) \qquad (6\text{-}22)$$

Thus, if investors are rational, they will diversify their security holdings to eliminate unsystematic risk, since the market does not, on the whole, reward investors who accept unsystematic risk. This observation will be used in our development of the equilibrium model of asset pricing.

THE SECURITY MARKET LINE

Recall that the capital market line, when it is assumed that all investors have the same expectations about risk and return, is defined as

$$E(R_p) = R_f + [(E(R_m) - R_f)/\sigma_m]\sigma_p \qquad (6\text{-}23)$$

Equation 6-23 shows that the expected return on an efficient portfolio is the risk-free rate of return plus a risk premium. In the previous section and in Chapter 5, we showed that, for a diversified portfolio, systematic risk is the relevant measure of risk since unsystematic risk tends to zero as the portfolio size increases.

It has also been demonstrated that under the assumption of homogeneous expectations and unlimited riskless lending and borrowing all investors will hold the market portfolio. Since the market portfolio is a well-diversified portfolio, investors should be concerned with expected return and systematic risk. Therefore, Equation 6-22 can be substituted into Equation 6-23, with the following result

$$E(R_p) = R_f + [(E(R_m) - R_f)/\sigma_m](\beta_p \sigma_m) \qquad (6\text{-}24)$$

Equation 6-24 defines the relationship between the expected return and risk for a portfolio of securities under conditions of market equilibrium. The expected return of a portfolio and the beta of a portfolio are the weighted averages of the individual security returns and betas, i.e.:

$$E(R_p) = \sum_{i=1}^{N} W_i R_i$$

$$\beta_p = \sum_{i=1}^{N} W_i \beta_i$$

Therefore Equation 6-24 is valid for individual securities contained in the market portfolio, as indicated by Equation 6-25, which defines the security market line.

$$E(R_{it}) = R_f + [E(R_{mt}) - R_f]\beta_i \qquad (6\text{-}25)$$

where

$$E(R_{it}) = \text{expected return on asset } i \text{ in period } t$$
$$R_f = \text{risk-free rate}$$
$$\beta_i = \text{beta coefficient for asset } i, \text{ or the index of systematic risk for asset } i$$
$$E(R_{mt}) = \text{expected market return in period } t$$
$$[E(R_{mt}) - R_f] = \text{expected market risk premium, or price for risk, in period } t$$
$$\beta_i[E(R_{mt}) - R_f] = \text{expected risk premium for asset } i \text{ in period } t$$

The equation states that the expected return for a risky asset is a linear function of its beta coefficient. Since the risk-free rate and the market return are the same for all assets, differences in expected returns are due entirely to differences in beta, the index of systematic risk. According to the original CAPM, beta is the only risk measure that is priced in the market. Investors do not require, or expect, higher rates of return for accepting greater amounts of unsystematic risk because they know that unsystematic risk can be avoided through diversification. Thus, investors should expect to receive at least the risk-free rate plus *the* risk premium adjusted for the level of systematic risk, as measured by beta.

The linear risk-return relationship described by the security market line will be true for all assets contained in the market portfolio when the market is in equilibrium. That is, there is a linear relationship between betas and expected returns if the betas are determined with respect to the market portfolio.[13]

The expected market rate of return (R_m), as illustrated in Figure 6-11, is the rate associated with the market beta of 1.0, and the expected market risk premium $(R_m - R_f)/1.0$ is the slope of the security market line. With an increase in beta from zero to 1.0, the expected return increases from the risk-free rate of 8% to the expected market return of 14%. Investors purchasing a security or portfolio with a beta of 1.0 should expect to receive the risk-free rate of 8% and the risk premium of 6% (14% − 8%). For anyone willing to accept 20% more risk (beta = 1.20), the expected risk premium would be 20% higher (1.20 × 6%). For anyone wanting 20% less risk (beta = 0.80), the expected risk premium would be 20% lower (0.80 × 6%).

[13] While this concept was recognized by Sharpe in 1964, its implications for the tests of the model were not realized until Roll's 1977 critique of the test of the CAPM and performance measures based on the CAPM.

|||| **FIGURE 6-11**

Security Market Line

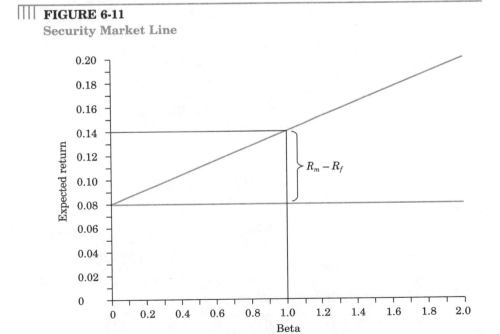

THE SECURITY MARKET LINE AND THE CAPITAL MARKET LINE

It is sometimes said that the capital market line (CML) shows the relationship between expected returns and total risk for efficient portfolios, which is true, and that the security market line (SML) shows the relationship between expected returns and beta (as an index of systematic risk) only for individual securities, which is not strictly true. The SML shows the expected return as a function of beta for any and all portfolios as well as for individual assets. Why are inefficient portfolios on the SML but not on the CML? They are on the SML because unsystematic risk, which makes inefficient portfolios inefficient, is ignored by the SML. If two portfolios have the same systematic risk, as indicated by their identical betas, their expected returns will be the same even though one has considerably more total risk than the other. Both will be at the same point on the SML. However, the inefficient portfolio, with the greater total risk, will not be on the CML because it offers the same expected return as the efficient portfolio but at a higher level of total risk. The horizontal axis of the CML, as shown earlier in Figures 6-6 and 6-7, is total risk, which is measured by either the variance or standard deviation of the return.

ASSET PRICING WITH THE CAPM

The capital asset pricing model does not explain fully how assets are priced; it explains, or attempts to explain, only how investors determine required rates of return. The required return is very important, but it is only one of the two inputs needed to estimate asset values with the models described in Chapter 9. Also required is an estimate of the expected future cash flows. For example, if the only expected cash flow from an investment (C_1) is to be received at the end of one year, and the required annual return is k, the valuation model is

$$P_0 = C_1/(1 + k)$$

Application of the formula is illustrated with the following:
  Given these estimates

$$E(R_m) = 10\%$$
$$R_f = 6\%$$
$$B_{im} = 1.30$$
$$C_1 = \$50$$

The required return, according to the CAPM, is

$$R_1 = 6\% + 1.30\,(10\% - 6\%)$$
$$= 11.2\%$$

And the estimated value is

$$P_0 = \$50/1 + .112)$$
$$= \$44.96$$

THE ZERO-BETA CAPM

A model similar to the SML has been developed that substitutes the return on a zero-beta portfolio for the risk-free return.[14] Figure 6-12a depicts the situation in the return and standard deviation space.[15]

We have observed previously that since the M portfolio is on the efficient set, there is a linear relationship between the beta factors of individual portfolios or securities (determined with respect to portfolio M) and their returns. This relationship, shown in Figure 6-12b, intersects the expected-return axis at the expected return of the zero-correlated portfolio, $E(R_z)$.[16] If a security or portfolio is uncorrelated with the market portfolio, then its beta relative to the market portfolio must be zero. The equation of the zero-beta SML is

[14]F. Black, "Capital Market Equilibrium with Restricted Borrowing," *Journal of Business* 45 (July 1972):444–55.

[15]Note that since all the assumptions of the CAPM hold except for the risk free asset assumption then all investors perceive this efficient set in the same way. However, without the risk free asset it cannot be assumed that all investors will invest in the same risky portfolio, i.e., the market portfolio.

[16]It is possible to construct a zero-beta capital market line, describing the tangent connecting portfolio M and the expected return of the zero-correlated portfolio. Note, however, that such a line is a mathematical construct that does not have any economic meaning. Recall that we assumed there is no risk-free asset. Therefore a linear combination of a nonexistent asset and the market cannot exist in standard deviation space. The only relationship that will have economic meaning will exist in the beta space.

|||| **FIGURE 6-12**
Zero-Beta CAPM

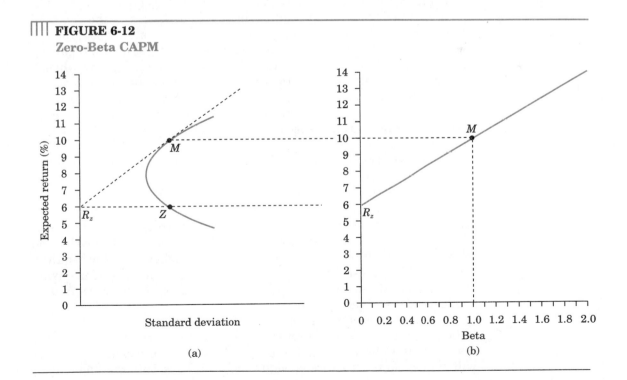

(a)

(b)

$$E(R_i) = E(R_z) + \beta_i[E(R_M) - E(R_z)] \qquad (6\text{-}26)$$

The primary contribution of the zero-beta model comes from the observation that Equation 6-26 is nonunique. If a different efficient portfolio and its corresponding zero-beta portfolio were chosen, a similar SML relationship would occur. However, the betas would be determined with respect to the new portfolio, and the return on the new zero-beta portfolio would replace the risk-free return. The implications of this observation have had a profound effect upon the tests of the validity of the CAPM as well as on the definition of performance measurement. We will cover these issues in more detail in the next chapter and in Chapter 21.

EMPIRICAL SECURITY MARKET LINES

The intercept and slope of the SML are estimated by regressing expected returns for a number of stocks on their estimated betas. In regression form, the equation can be stated:

$$R_{it} = Y_0 + \beta_i Y_1 + \epsilon_{it} \qquad (6\text{-}27)$$

where

Y_0 = the intercept (expected to equal R_f, the risk-free rate)

Y_1 = the market risk premium (expected to equal $R_m - R_f$)

For large investment organizations, the resulting equation represents an estimate of the average relationship between beta and the expected return for as many as several hundred common stocks. Any point on the SML represents an estimate of the rate of return investors are requiring at a certain level of beta. The price of a stock is in equilibrium when it is on the SML, indicating that the expected return is equal to the required return. The required return is sometimes referred to as the required expected return to emphasize the fact that the required return at a specified value of beta is the expected return investors are requiring at that level of risk.

If analysts believe that the price of a stock is not at the equilibrium level, as in the case of stocks X and Y in Figure 6-11, the expected return will not be on the SML. Stock X is below the line, indicating that the expected return is lower than the required return. If marginal buyers and sellers of the stock believe the expected return is too low, the price of the stock will decline until the expected return rises to the level of the required return. The expected return for Y is higher than the required return. If this represents the opinion of those who are interested in buying or selling the stock, the price will rise until the expected return falls to the level of the required return.

In a perfectly efficient market, all stocks would plot on the SML, indicating that all expected returns are equal to the returns required by investors. If a stock moves off the line, the actions of buyers and sellers will raise or lower its price enough to move it back onto the line.

|||| SIDELIGHT

An Alpha-Beta Man

Louis G. Navellier has a system that [considers] risk as well as reward.

Navellier is an earnest 28-year-old who wears glasses, loves computers, and took a crash course through college . . . because he couldn't wait to get to work. . . .

Navellier's $150-a-year *OTC Insight* letter, published monthly out of El Cerrito, California, has been racking up a remarkable record. His fledgling money management business, with a reported $22 million already under its wing, is increasing its minimum account to $250,000 on October 1. And he's doing it all with modern portfolio theory (MPT), the rigorously quantitative, academically approved investment technique that scared Wall Street when it burst out of the business schools in the 1970s but more recently has been greeted with resounding yawns.

OTC Insight's performance is a matter of public record, because since 1985 it has been one of about 100 such advisory services monitored by the Washington D.C.–based *Hulbert Financial Digest,* arbiter of the investment letter industry. "Navellier's nine model portfolios appreciated an average of 144.3% from January 1985 through the end of August 1986," says HFD editor Mark Hulbert. That's over twice the Dow's gain in the same period, assuming that all dividends were reinvested, and two and a half times that of the NASDAQ OTC Composite Index. . . .

Navellier concentrates on relatively obscure over-the-counter stocks. "His showing is particularly impressive," says Hulbert, "in that he's been able to select the right stocks even when the secondary sector has been weak. . . ."

The operating assumption of the *OTC Insight* system is that the stock market is not completely efficient—it does not discount information so quickly that it cannot be outguessed. Diversified portfolios can be designed to achieve returns that are not canceled out by the accompanying level of risk. The market can be beaten with a disciplined approach that assesses the odds carefully, particularly with stocks that are traded in the less liquid over-the-counter market rather than on an exchange.

Every month Navellier's computer begins by inspecting a database containing 1,000 over-the-counter stocks. For each one, it crunches out a "beta" and an "alpha." "Beta" in MPT-speak is the extent to which a stock's fluctuation is related to the movement of the market. A beta of 2 would mean that a stock goes up (or down) twice as much as the average. "Alpha" represents the stock's propensity to move independently of the market. . . .

Navellier's computer has been told to calculate betas and alphas over a 12-month period; this has proved more sensitive to market movements than the five years usually favored in academe. The computer works out each stock's mean monthly rate of return—which, since OTC stocks pay minimal dividends, generally turns out to be the mean monthly capital appreciation. Additionally, it computes the variance from the mean monthly return, a statistical measure that tells you how likely the return is to occur.

(continued on next page)

|||| SIDELIGHT
An Alpha-Beta Man (continued)

Got that? Now, the crucial step: The computer divides each stock's alpha by its monthly variance of return. This gives a reward/risk ratio—the market-independent gain per unit of volatility. The computer then lists the top 98 stocks in order of reward/risk. This constitutes the *OTC Insight Buy List*—those stocks for which the reward potential is highest relative to the risk involved.

For the *OTC Insight* model portfolio, Navellier uses only the top 20 or so Buy List stocks. At this stage, he doesn't hesitate to contaminate the process by inserting his own eyeball: "I like stocks with strong earnings growth, in low-risk industries, preferably dominating their market niches," he says. . . .

Navellier keeps *OTC Insight* fully invested at all times. He says he just can't figure out any objective way to time the market. . . .

Navellier and his partner are now investigating the extension of his system to listed stocks. "But to be very frank with you," says Navellier, "the stock market is much more efficient in the listed stocks. There's no way we are going to get the same returns."

SOURCE: Adapted from Peter Brimelow, "An Alpha-Beta Man," *Forbes,* October 6, 1986, pp. 62, 64. Reprinted by permission of Forbes, © Forbes, Inc., 1986. All rights reserved.

A number of investment organizations periodically construct SMLs on the basis of estimated betas and expected rates of return for large numbers of stocks. Discounted cash flow models are used to estimate the rates of return. The three SMLs in Figure 6-13 were estimated by Wells Fargo Investment Advisors, and the two more recent SMLs in Figure 6-14 were derived from estimates of beta and required returns published by Merrill Lynch.[17]

Rarely is the market risk premium $(R_m - R_f)$ as low as the 0.5% of June 1972. Investors had an extremely optimistic outlook on the economy and an unusually sanguine feeling about future corporate profits. Price/earnings ratios were at or near an all-time high of nearly 20 on the S&P 500, dividend yields were at or near an all-time low of less than 3% on the S&P 500, and investor aversion to risk was apparently at or near an all-time low, as indicated by the slope of the Wells Fargo SML.

The market risk premiums on the other SMLs in Figures 6-13 and 6-14 range from 2.0% in June 1975 to 4.8% in January 1985. None are as high as the average risk premium of 6.4% reported by Ibbotson Associates for large common stocks for the years 1926 through 1990.

---

[17]William L. Fouse, "Risk and Liquidity: The Keys to Stock Price Behavior," *Financial Analysts Journal* 32 (May/June 1976):35–45. Merrill Lynch, "Quantitative Analysis," (January/September 1985).

|||| **FIGURE 6-13**
Empirical Security Market Lines

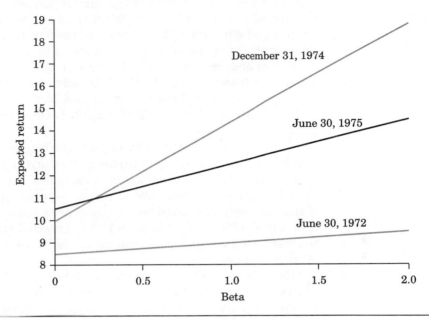

SOURCE: William L. Fouse, "Risk and Liquidity Revisited," *Financial Analysts Journal* 33 (January/February 1977):35–45.

|||| **FIGURE 6-14**
Empirical Security Market Lines

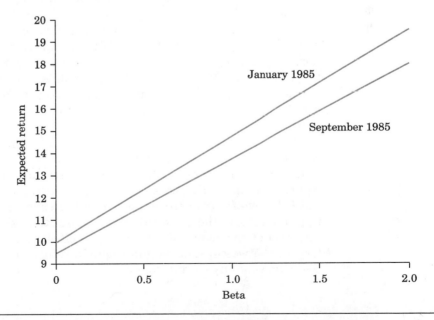

SOURCE: Merrill Lynch, "Quantitative Analysis," (January/September 1985).

|||| **SUMMARY**

This first chapter on portfolio and capital market theory has focused on the portfolio selection theory of Markowitz and the original capital asset pricing model (CAPM). Markowitz was the first to define risk in terms of the variability of the return, as measured by the variance or standard deviation, and he explained that the risk of a portfolio depends on the correlation between the returns of the individual assets as well as on the standard deviations of the returns themselves. When the returns of any two assets are less than perfectly positively correlated, their fluctuations partly offset one another.

The Markowitz portfolio theory and the original CAPM both assume that investors consider only the expected return and risk in making portfolio choices. Rational investors hold portfolios that offer the highest expected return at a given level of risk or, equivalently, the least amount of risk for a given expected return; these are known as efficient portfolios. A plot of all efficient portfolios, with the expected return on one axis and the variance or standard deviation of the return on the other, is the efficient frontier.

Under the Markowitz theory, portfolios are composed only of risky assets, and the efficient frontier is a curved line that does not touch the Y-axis. When the investment possibilities are expanded to include a risk-free asset and to permit borrowing at the risk-free rate of interest, the efficient frontier becomes an upward-sloping straight line that originates at the risk-free rate. Investors who have little tolerance for risk will commit most of their funds to the risk-free asset and the remainder to the market portfolio. Investors with little aversion to risk may invest all of their funds in the market portfolio and leverage their investment by borrowing.

The CAPM makes use of the concepts of systematic and unsystematic risk. The central thesis of the CAPM is stated in the equation for the security market line. Expected returns are related positively and linearly to expected systematic risk and are completely independent of unsystematic risk. The expected return includes no premium for unsystematic risk because unsystematic risk can be avoided by holding a diversified portfolio.

If the market price of a security is in equilibrium, the expected return will be on the security market line, indicating it is equal to the return required by investors at that level of systematic risk. If the expected return is temporarily above the required return, the price will be bid up until the two returns are equal, and if the expected return is below the required return, the price will decline until the expected return rises to the level of the required return. In an efficient market, significant differences between expected and required returns are soon eliminated by the actions of buyers and sellers.

DERIVATION OF THE CAPITAL ASSET PRICING MODEL

The security market line is a market equilibrium relationship between the returns and risk for individual securities or portfolios. Consider the situation depicted in Figure 6A-1. Security i does not reside on the efficient frontier, but like any security, it may be combined with the market portfolio. If the security is not perfectly correlated with the market portfolio, the risk-return relationship between i and M will be the line segment iM.

To develop the relationship between the risk and return of any asset, we will first note that the slopes of the CML, the efficient frontier, and the iM parabola are identical at point M. The slope of the CML is the derivation of the CML with respect to σ_p as shown below:

$$\partial E(R_p)/\partial\sigma_p = [E(R_M) - R_f]/\sigma_M \tag{6A-1}$$

FIGURE 6A-1
Security Market Line Derivation

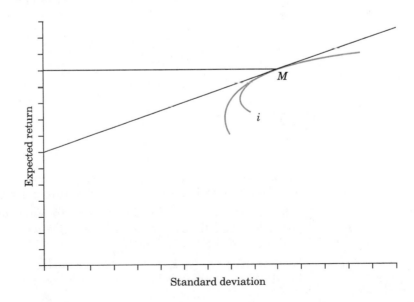

The slope of the parabolas (efficient frontier or iM) at M may be determined by recalling that the expected return for a two-security portfolio consisting of i and M is

$$E(R_p) = W_i E(R_i) + (1 - W_i)E(R_M) \tag{6A-2}$$

and the risk is

$$\sigma_p^2 = [W_i \sigma_i^2 + (1 - W_i)\sigma_M^2 + 2W_i(1 - W_i)\text{Cov}(R_i, R_M)]^{1/2} \tag{6A-3}$$

The slope of the parabola and the efficient frontier may be obtained from these two relations by using the chain rule for differentiation:

$$\partial E(R_p)/\partial \sigma_p = [\partial E(R_p)/\partial W_i](\partial W_i/\partial \sigma_p) \tag{6A-4}$$

The derivatives of the return and risk equations are

$$\partial E(R_p)/\partial W_i = E(R_i) - E(R_M) \tag{6A-5}$$

$$\partial W_i/\partial \sigma_p = \frac{1}{2}[W_i \sigma_i^2 + (1 - W_i)\sigma_M^2 + 2W_i(1 - W_i)\text{Cov}(R_i, R_M)]^{1/2}$$
$$\times [2W_i \sigma_i^2 - 2\sigma_M^2 + 2W_i \sigma_M^2 + 2\text{Cov}(R_i, R_M) - 4W_i\text{Cov}(R_i, R_M)] \tag{6A-6}$$

Recall that in a two-security portfolio, the end points of the investment parabola represent an investment of 100% in one of the securities. At point M the investment is 100% in portfolio M and therefore $W_i = 0$. Substituting Equations 6A-5 and 6A-6 into 6A-4 and evaluating the resulting expression at $W_i = 0$ results in

$$\partial E(R_p)/\partial \sigma_p = \{[E(R_i) - E(R_M)]\sigma_M\}/[\text{Cov}(R_i, R_M) - \sigma_M^2] \tag{6A-7}$$

Since the slope of the CML (Equation 6A-1) is equal to the slope of the parabolas (Equation 6A-7) at point M, we can write the following:

$$[E(R_M) - R_f]/\sigma_M = \{[E(R_i) - E(R_M)]\sigma_M\}/[\text{Cov}(R_i, R_M) - \sigma_M^2]$$

Solving this equation for $E(R_i)$ results in the equation for the security market line:

$$E(R_i = R_f + [\text{Cov}(R_i, R_M)/\sigma_M^2] \times [E(R_M) - R_f]$$
$$= R_f + \beta_i[E(R_M) - R_f] \tag{6A-8}$$

|||| # QUESTIONS

1. Explain why the standard deviation of the rate of return is considered a good measure of risk.

2. Explain how the future standard deviation of a security's return can be estimated with a subjective probability distribution.

3. Why is the variance of the return of an equal-weighted two-stock portfolio virtually always smaller than a weighted average of the variances of the two stocks?

4. Explain how the covariance and the correlation coefficient are related. Why is the correlation coefficient easier to interpret?

5. What is the Markowitz efficient frontier?

6. Comment on the factors that determine how the total risk of a common stock portfolio will be affected by the addition of one more stock.

7. How do investors express their risk preferences when the efficient frontier is an upward-sloping straight line that originates at the risk-free rate?

8. Explain the equation for the capital market line:

$$E(R_p) = R_f + [E(R_m - R_f)/\sigma_m]\sigma_p$$

Why does it not hold for inefficient portfolios?

9. Explain why the coefficient of determination (R^2) is larger in a regression of the return for a diversified common stock portfolio on the market return than in a regression of the return of a single stock on the market return.

10. Express systematic risk in terms of beta and the variance of the market return.

11. Explain the following equation:

$$\beta_i = \rho_{im} \times \sigma_i/\sigma_m$$

12. Why do most common stocks have a positive covariance with other stocks?

13. What determines the optimum portfolio for an investor? Can it be a single asset?

14. Explain why a stock can have a low beta even if the standard deviation of its return is higher than the standard deviation of the market return.

15. Demonstrate how total risk can be decomposed into systematic and unsystematic risk with the market model.

16. According to the CAPM, why is the systematic risk of a stock relevant and the unsystematic risk irrelevant?

17. Explain the differences between the CML and the SML.

18. What does the SML say about the relationship between the expected return and beta?

19. What is the relationship between the required return and the expected return?

20. What causes the slope of the SML to change? Why is a small slope associated with a high market P/E ratio and a low average dividend yield?

21. Why are inefficient portfolios on the SML but not on the CML?

22. Explain why investors should not expect to earn higher rates of return by assuming greater amounts of unsystematic risk.

|||| PROBLEMS

1. Using the following data, calculate the expected return, variance, and standard deviation for a security. (*Hint:* you may have to refer back to Chapter 5.)

Probabilities	Possible Returns
.10	+.40
.20	+.30
.50	+.20
.15	−.20
.05	−.40

2. Using the following data, calculate the portfolio variance for a two-stock portfolio:

Proportion invested in each stock: $A = 40\%$ $B = 60\%$
Variance of the returns: $A = .16$ $B = .09$
Correlation of the returns: .40

3. A portfolio contains two assets with the following characteristics:

$$E(R_a) = .18 \quad E(\sigma_a) = .30 \quad W_a = .50$$
$$E(R_b) = .14 \quad E(\sigma_b) = .10 \quad W_b = .50$$

Calculate the portfolio's expected return and the standard deviation of the return under two different assumptions as to the correlation between the returns: $\rho_{ab} = .60$ and $\rho_{ab} = -.50$.

4. Security A has a variance of return of .16, and security B has a variance of return of .09. If the correlation between the two securities is -1.0, determine the investment proportions that will cause the portfolio risk to be zero.

5. If the correlation between the securities in Problem 4 is zero, show that diversification can still reduce the risk.

6. Using the following quarterly rates of return for stocks X and Y, calculate the covariance between the returns and the correlation coefficient.

Quarter	Quarterly Returns	
	X	Y
1	2%	4%
2	5	6
3	2	7
4	−3	1
5	6	6

| | Quarterly Returns | |
Quarter	X	Y
6	3	5
7	7	8
8	2	−1

7. With the data provided in Problem 6, is it possible to construct a portfolio with less risk than the risk of investing in security X or Y? Show the calculations to prove your answer.

8. Given the following information:

$$\sigma_1^2 = .16 \qquad \rho_{1,2} = .20 \qquad W_1 = \tfrac{1}{3}$$
$$\sigma_2^2 = .09 \qquad \rho_{1,3} = .40 \qquad W_2 = \tfrac{1}{3}$$
$$\sigma_3^2 = .12 \qquad \rho_{2,3} = .30 \qquad W_3 = \tfrac{1}{3}$$

determine the variance of a portfolio of securities 1, 2, and 3.

9. Given the variance and correlation data in Problem 8, how many other variances and correlation coefficients would be necessary to calculate the variance of a 5-security portfolio?

10. How many variances and correlation coefficients are needed to calculate the variance of a 30-security portfolio?

11. Given the following data:

$$R_f = .06 \qquad W_{Rf} = .20$$
$$\sigma_p = .20 \qquad W_p = .80$$

determine the risk of a portfolio made up of the risk-free asset and a risky portfolio on the efficient frontier.

12. Calculate the rate of return on nonborrowed funds (the leveraged rate of return), given the following facts and assuming the investor can borrow at the risk-free rate:

$$R_m = 14\%$$
$$R_f = 10\%$$
$$d = 40\%$$

13. The betas for 15 securities are 1.00, 1.30, 2.00, .80, .90, .95, 1.35, 1.24, 1.13, 1.53, 1.65, 1.15, .98, .75, 1.90. If the risk-free asset provides a return of 8.0% and the return on a market proxy portfolio is 18%, what is the expected return of a portfolio of these 15 securities?

14. If the risk of the market (σ_m^2) is .25, what is the risk of the portfolio in Problem 13?

15. With a graph, explain the zero-beta CAPM.

|||| **REFERENCES**

Alexander, Gordon J., and Norman L. Chervany. "On the Estimation and Stability of Beta." *Journal of Financial and Quantitative Analysis* 15 (March 1980): 123–37.

Black, Fisher. "Capital Market Equilibrium with Restricted Borrowing." *Journal of Business* 45 (July 1972): 444–55.

Blume, Marshall E. "On the Assessment of Risk." *The Journal of Finance* 26 (March 1971): 1–10.

Cooley, Philip L., Rodney L. Roenfeldt, and Naval K. Modani. "Interdependence of Market Risk Measures." *Journal of Business* 50 (January 1977): 356–63.

Fouse, William L. "Risk and Liquidity Revisited." *Financial Analysts Journal* 33 (January/February 1977): 40–45.

Ibbotson, Roger G., and Rex A. Sinquefield. *Stocks, Bonds, Bills and Inflation: The Past and the Future* (Charlottesville, Va.: The Financial Analysts Research Foundation, 1982).

Markowitz, Harry M. "Portfolio Selection." *The Journal of Finance* 7 (March 1952): 77–91.

———. *Portfolio Selection—Efficient Diversification of Investments* (New Haven: Yale University Press, 1959).

Roll, Richard. "A Critique of the Asset Pricing Theory's Tests: Part I: On Past and Potential Testability of the Theory." *Journal of Financial Economics* 4 (March 1977): 129–76.

Sharpe, William F. "Capital Asset Prices: Theory of Market Equilibrium under Conditions of Risk." *The Journal of Finance* 19 (September 1964): 425–42.

———. "A Simplified Model for Portfolio Analysis." *Management Science* 9 (January 1963): 227–93.

7 CAPM TESTS AND THE ARBITRAGE PRICING THEORY

The capital asset pricing model (CAPM) has been tested many times and in many different ways over the past 15 to 20 years, and the testing will no doubt continue. There is still much to be learned about the possibilities for improving the model.

One of the principal difficulties in testing the CAPM arises from the fact that the model is stated in terms of expected returns. It is, of course, impossible to determine the rates of return investors have been expecting. Sometimes analysts' forecasts are used as proxies for expected returns, but more often the tests are based on actual returns. The assumption is made that over long periods of time the expected and actual returns are approximately the same.[1]

TESTING THE CAPM

CRITERIA FOR TESTING THE CAPM

Modigliani and Pogue have stated that the CAPM is valid if empirical tests show the following:[2]

1. On the average, and over long periods of time, securities with higher systematic risk provide higher rates of return.

2. On the average, there is a linear relationship between systematic risk (measured by beta) and the rate of return.

3. The slope of the relationship between beta and the rate of return is equal to the market risk premium $(R_m - R_f)$.

4. In the risk premium form of the equation for the security market line (Equation 7-1), the intercept is zero.

---

[1]Richard Roll believes it is impossible to test the model because it is based on the concept of a market rate of return, which is literally a weighted average of the returns on all risky assets. This portfolio cannot be determined. However, others have been williing to assume that returns on broad-based indexes of the stock market are reasonable proxies for the market return. We will discuss Roll's criticisms of the tests of the CAPM later in the chapter. R. Roll, "A Critique of the Asset Pricing Theory's Tests: Part I: On Past and Potential Testability of the Theory," *Journal of Financial Economics* 4 (March 1977): 129–76.

[2]Franco Modigliani, and Gerald A Pogue, "An Introduction to Risk and Return: Concepts and Evidence," *Financial Analysts Journal* 30 (May/June 1974): 69–86.

5. Unsystematic risk does not play a significant role in explaining differences in security returns.

The equation for the security market line, in risk premium form, is

$$R_{it} - R_{ft} = \beta_i(R_{mt} - R_{ft}) + \epsilon_{it} \tag{7-1}$$

With the addition of an intercept, Equation 7-1 becomes a regression equation:

$$R_{it} - R_{ft} = \alpha'_i + \beta_i(R_{mt} - R_{ft}) + \epsilon_{it} \tag{7-2}$$

It can be stated more briefly as

$$r_{it} = \gamma_0 + \gamma_1\beta_i + \epsilon_{it} \tag{7-3}$$

where

$r_{it} = R_{it} - R_{ft}$

γ_0 = intercept (expected value is zero)

β_i = beta for stock i

$\gamma_1 = R_{mt} - R_{ft}$ (slope of regression line)

ϵ_{it} = error term

The model assumes that ϵ_{it} is uncorrelated with beta and has an average value of zero.

The α' term in Equation 7-2 is often referred to as the risk-adjusted excess return. The reason for this description can be seen by observing that

$$\alpha'_i = \alpha_i - R_f(1 - \beta_i) \tag{7-4}$$

where

α_i = the intercept term of the regression of R_i against R_m, i.e., it is the intercept term of the normal characteristic line equation

The second term on the right-hand side of Equation 7-4 is the same as the intercept term of the SML written in the following form:

$$R_i = R_f(1 - \beta_i) + R_m\beta_i$$

According to the risk premium form of the market model, α' may be greater than, less than, or equal to zero. The CAPM, on the other hand, asserts that if R_i from the market model is to equal that of the SML then α' must be equal to zero.[3] Therefore if α' is observed to be greater than zero, there is excess return above what is expected on the basis of the CAPM, i.e., $R_f(1 - \beta_i)$.[4]

---

[3]Note that the same argument can be made for portfolios since the α'_p is simply the weighted average of the security alpha primes.

[4]The use of α' as a performance measure will be discussed in a later chapter.

FACTORS OF IMPORTANCE TO INVESTORS

According to the original (traditional) CAPM, differences in expected returns among risky assets are due solely to differences in systematic risk, as reflected in the beta coefficient. Research has shown that this is not an accurate description of reality. Systematic risk and the expected return are not the only factors of importance to investors. Studies indicate, for example, that differences in expected returns may be due to differences in income taxes, asset liquidity, and the costs of collecting information.

Before we turn to studies dealing with the effects of income taxes, investment liquidity, and other factors, two early studies that explored the relationship between beta and the rate of return should be examined.

A Study by Black, Jensen, and Scholes

In conducting their analysis of the traditional CAPM, Black, Jensen, and Scholes based their findings on the monthly returns of nearly all New York Stock Exchange stocks for the years 1931 through 1965.[5] The monthly returns for each stock were regressed on the market return over a period of years to estimate the historic betas for each year from 1931 through 1965. The proxy for the market return was the return on a portfolio consisting of an equal investment in every stock listed on the New York Stock Exchange at the beginning of each month. The proxy for the risk-free rate was the return on 30-day U.S. Treasury bills.

To test the validity of the CAPM, the stocks were grouped according to their historic betas into 10 portfolios containing equal numbers of stocks.[6] The portfolios were adjusted annually to reflect the new betas and any changes in the listed stocks. Each of the 10 portfolios can be thought of as a mutual fund with a policy of investing in stocks with betas of a specified level relative to the betas of other stocks. For example, portfolio 1 was always composed of stocks with the highest betas, and portfolio 10 always contained stocks with the lowest betas.

The authors used both time series and cross-section regressions to evaluate the CAPM. In the time series analysis, each portfolio was analyzed separately with time series regressions covering various periods of time. One set of regressions (with separate calculations for each of the 10 portfolios) was for the entire period of 420 months from 1931 through 1965. For each of the 10 portfolios, the 420 excess returns (portfolio return minus the risk-free rate) were regressed on the 420 excess returns for the market to arrive at estimates for the parameters α_k, the intercept, and β_k, beta, ($k = 1 \ldots 10$) for the full period of 35 years.

---

[5] Fischer Black, Michael C. Jensen, and Myron Scholes, "The Capital Asset Pricing Model: Some Empirical Tests," in *Studies on the Theory of Capital Markets,* Michael C. Jensen, ed. (New York: Praeger, 1972), pp. 79–121.

[6] By testing portfolios instead of individual stocks, the authors avoided the problem known as "errors in the variables bias." Estimates of portfolio betas, as we have seen, are much more stable and predictable than betas of individual stocks. With the stocks grouped into portfolios, the study can focus on the relationship between portfolio betas and portfolio returns.

The estimated parameters for the 35-year time series regressions, along with the t values of the intercepts, the average monthly excess return (total return minus risk-free rate) for each portfolio, and the standard deviation of the excess returns, are reported in Table 7-1. The pattern of the average monthly excess returns supports the traditional form of the CAPM. Without exception, the higher the portfolio beta, the higher the portfolio excess return. Also, as one would expect, the higher the beta, the larger the standard deviation of the portfolio excess return. Highly volatile stocks tend to have high betas. However, contrary to the CAPM's prediction of a zero intercept, the intercepts for the high-beta portfolios were negative, and the intercepts for the low-beta portfolios were positive.[7] Although the high-risk stocks earned higher returns than the low-risk stocks, the returns for the high-risk stocks (with negative intercepts) were lower than the model would predict, and the returns for the low-risk stocks (with positive intercepts) were higher than the model would predict. Note, however, that only three of the t values (those close to 2.0 or larger) were large enough to be statistically significant.

The same portfolio betas that were used in the time series analysis were used in the cross-sectional tests. The cross-sectional parameters (γ_0 and γ_1) of Equation 7-3 were estimated by regressing, for a given time period, the actual mean excess return for each of the 10 portfolios on the portfolio betas. The results for the 35-year period and four subperiods are reported in Table 7-2.

[7]Since the intercepts were estimated with regressions of monthly excess returns, their absolute values were considerably smaller than if the regressions had been based on annual returns.

|||| **TABLE 7-1**

Summary Statistics for Time Series Tests, 1931–1965: Sample Size for Each Regression = 420

Portfolio	β_k	α_k	$t(\alpha_k)$	r_k	σ_k
1	1.56	−0.083%	0.43	2.13	14.45
2	1.38	−0.194	−1.99	1.77	12.48
3	1.25	−0.065	−0.76	1.71	11.26
4	1.16	−0.017	−0.25	1.63	10.45
5	1.06	−0.054	−0.89	1.45	9.50
6	0.92	0.059	0.79	1.37	8.36
7	0.85	0.046	0.71	1.26	7.72
8	0.75	0.081	1.18	1.15	6.85
9	0.63	0.197	2.31	1.09	5.86
10	0.50	0.201	1.87	0.91	4.95
Market	1.00			1.42	8.91

β_k = portfolio beta
α_k = portfolio intercept
$t(\alpha_k)$ = t value of the intercept
r_k = portfolio monthly excess return $(R_k - R_f)$
σ_k = standard deviation of portfolio monthly excess return

||| **TABLE 7-2**
Statistics for Cross-Sectional Tests

Period	γ_0	γ_1	$R_m - R_f$	$t(\gamma_0)$
35 years	0.36%	1.08%	1.42%	6.52
1/31–9/39	−0.80	3.04	2.20	−4.45
10/39–6/48	0.44	1.07	1.49	3.20
7/48–3/57	0.78	0.33	1.12	7.40
4/57–12/65	1.02	−0.12	0.88	18.89

The regression lines for the four subperiods of 105 months each, based on the values of γ_0 and γ_1 in Table 7-2, are plotted in Figures 7-1 through 7-4. Not only are the intercepts quite different from the CAPM predicted value of zero, but the slopes in the two later subperiods (0.33 and −0.12) are far below the actual market risk premium $(R_m - R_f)$. During those two periods of nearly nine years each, average returns on high-beta stocks were about the same as the returns on low-beta stocks.

The Fama and MacBeth Study

In a study based on data similar to those used by Black, Jensen, and Scholes, Fama and MacBeth set out to answer four questions:[8]

1. Do the data support the hypothesis of the original CAPM that the expected value of the intercept (γ_0) is equal to the risk-free rate? (The authors assume that the equation is stated in terms of returns rather than excess returns; that is, $R_{pt} = \gamma_{0t} + \gamma_{1t}\beta_p + \epsilon_{it}$, where R_{pt} is the portfolio return in period t.)

2. Is there a positive relationship between the expected return and systematic risk?

3. Is the relationship between the expected return and systematic risk linear?

4. Does nonbeta (unsystematic) risk have a systematic effect on the expected return?

The authors found that if the actual returns over long periods of time are assumed to be the same as the expected returns, the last three questions can all be answered affirmatively. There was a positive linear relationship between beta and the returns, and unsystematic risk did not have a systematic effect on the returns. However, they also found (as did Black, Jensen, and Scholes) that the answer to the first question is negative. The intercepts were substantially different from the risk-free rate. Over the full 34-year period of the study, the average value of γ_0 on a monthly basis was 0.61%, compared to an actual risk-free rate of only 0.13%. The study provided further evidence that the so-called two-factor,

[8]Eugene F. Fama and James D. MacBeth, "Risk, Return, and Equilibrium: Empirical Tests," *Journal of Political Economy* 71 (May/June 1973): 607–636.

FIGURE 7-1
Regression Line for Subperiod 1/31 to 9/39 (Black, Jensen, and
Scholes)

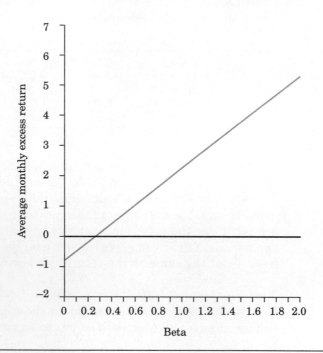

FIGURE 7-2
Regression Line for Subperiod 10/39 to 6/48 (Black, Jensen, and
Scholes)

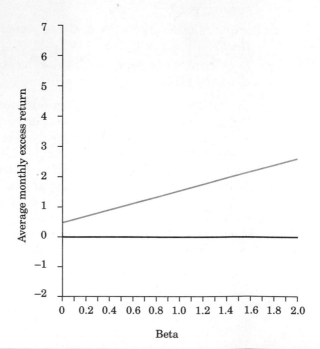

FIGURE 7-3
Regression Line for Subperiod 7/48 to 3/57 (Black, Jensen, and Scholes)

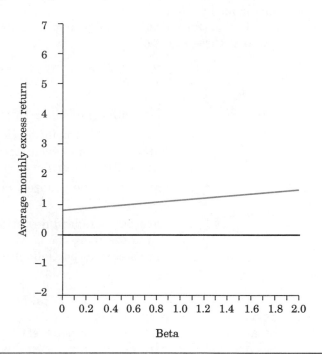

FIGURE 7-4
Regression Line for Subperiod 4/57 to 12/65 (Black, Jensen, and Scholes)

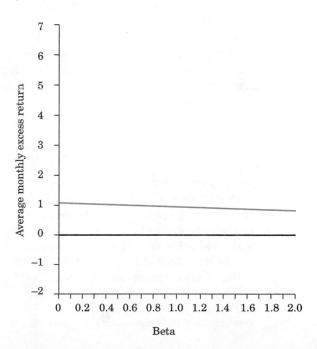

or zero-beta, version of the CAPM may be superior to the original single-factor model.[9]

The authors used the following equation in arriving at answers to the last three questions:

$$R_{pt} = \gamma_{0t} + \gamma_{1t}\beta_{p,t-1} + \gamma_{2t}\beta_{p,t-1}^2 + \gamma_{3t}\sigma_{p,t-1}(\epsilon_i) + \epsilon_{pt} \qquad (7\text{-}5)$$

where

R_{pt} = return for portfolio p in month t, $p = 1, \ldots, 20$

$\beta_{p,t-1}$ = average of betas for stocks in portfolio p based on regression of each stock's monthly return on the market return over the previous five years

$\beta_{p,t-1}^2$ = average of the squared values of the individual betas

$\sigma_{p,t-1}(\epsilon_i)$ = average standard deviation of the residuals from the regressions with which the betas of the stocks in portfolio p were estimated

ϵ_{pt} = error term

The explanatory variables are beta, beta-squared, and the standard deviation of the residuals from the regressions with which the individual betas were estimated. The parameter estimates for month t are γ_{0t}, γ_{1t}, γ_{2t}, and γ_{3t}. The parameters were estimated for each month from the beginning of 1935 to the end of 1968 by regressing the monthly return for each of the 20 portfolios on the values of the explanatory variables for the portfolios.

The study provided strong evidence of a positive relationship between systematic risk and the rate of return. γ_1 was large and positive for the 34-year period as a whole and for all but one of nine subperiods. The linear nature of the relationship between risk and return was evidenced by a very small value for γ_2 for the 34-year period as a whole and for most of the subperiods. A large value for γ_2 would have meant that β_p^2 was important, indicating a nonlinear relationship between systematic risk and the return. And, finally, the coefficient γ_3 was small, and the signs were randomly positive and negative, which means that unsystematic risk did not have a systematic influence on the rate of return.

Taxes and the CAPM

The original CAPM assumes that investors choose portfolios that are mean-variance efficient (offer the highest expected return at a given level of risk) in terms of the before-tax rate of return. This is a realistic assumption for investors such as pension funds and college endowment funds that are exempt from income taxes, but certainly inappropriate for most individual investors and for taxable corporate investors. These two classes of investors can be expected to choose portfolios that are efficient in terms of after-tax rates of return.

---

[9]See Chapter 6 for a discussion of the zero-beta model.

Because historically individuals have paid higher taxes on dividend income than on long-term capital gains, it was assumed that individual investors required higher expected before-tax returns on high-yield stocks with small expected capital gains than on low-yield stocks with large capital gains.[10] Taxable corporate investors, on the other hand, paid lower taxes on dividends received than on capital gains. Thus, it was expected that they would require lower returns on high-yield stocks than on low-yield stocks. Yet Black and Scholes found it impossible to demonstrate that the before-tax expected returns on high-yield stocks were different from the expected returns for low-yield stocks.[11] In more recent studies, however, others have found that the dividend yield does affect common stock prices and expected rates of return.[12] Here we will examine the findings of Vandell and Stevens relating to this question.

These authors set out to determine whether the original CAPM can be improved by adding a variable to account for the difference in tax treatment of dividends and long-term capital gains. Their study was one of very few that have been based on ex ante data (analysts' estimates of returns and betas) rather than historical information. Since the CAPM is formulated in terms of expected risk and the expected return, it would seem best to test it with analysts' estimates of future returns and future betas, assuming that these estimates are good proxies for the expectations of investors generally.

Data for the study, which was supplied by a major bank, included monthly estimates of long-term expected returns and betas for 205 stocks for the 60 months from 1974 through 1978. The bank's analysts used a sophisticated dividend discount model, which allowed for changing rates of growth, to maintain up-to-date forecasts of the total rate of return for each stock. The estimated return was the rate that equated the forecasted stream of dividends with the market price of the stock. Using the data on expected returns and estimated betas, the authors first ran a cross-section regression for each month in the five-year period to estimate a total of 60 security market lines, called empirical SMLs. The parameters were estimated with the following regression equation:

$$R_{it} = \gamma_{0t} + \gamma_{1t}\beta_{it} + \epsilon_{it} \tag{7-6}$$

where

R_{it} = expected total return for stock i in month t

γ_{0t} = intercept for month t, which, according to the CAPM, is equal to the risk-free rate

---

[10] Current tax law makes no distinction between capital gains and ordinary or dividend income.

[11] Fischer Black and Myron Scholes, "The Effects of Dividend Yield and Dividend Policy on Common Stock Prices and Returns," *Journal of Financial Economics* 1 (1974): 1–22.

[12] Robert H. Litzenberger and Krishna Ramaswamy, "The Effect of Personal Taxes and Dividends on Capital Asset Prices," *Journal of Financial Economics* 7 (June 1979): 163–95; Robert F. Vandell and Jerry L. Stevens, "Personal Taxes and Equity Security Pricing," *Financial Management* 11 (Spring 1982): 31–40.

γ_{1t} = slope of the security market line, which, according to
the CAPM, is equal to the market risk premium
$(R_{mt} - R_{ft})$

ϵ_{it} = error term

The 60 empirical SMLs were compared with theoretical SMLs with
intercepts of R_{ft} (the rate on 90-day U.S. Treasury bills) and slopes equal
to estimates of the market risk premium $(R_{mt} - R_{ft})$, as prepared by the
bank's analysts.

	Intercept	Slope
Empirical SML (estimated with regression analysis, using analysts' estimates of individual betas and expected returns)	γ_{0t}	γ_{1t}
Theoretical SML (based on analysts' forecasts of R_{mt} and R_{ft})	R_{ft}	$R_{mt} - R_{ft}$

Figure 7-5 compares a typical empirical SML, developed by regressing
analysts' estimates of the expected returns on the estimated betas for 205
stocks, with a theoretical SML, which was based on analysts' forecasts
of R_{ft} and R_{mt}.

|||| **FIGURE 7-5**

Theoretical and Empirical SMLs

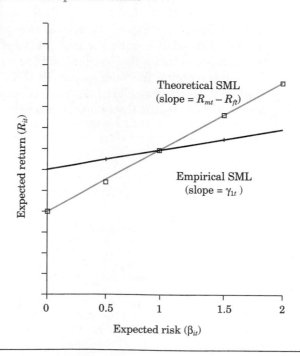

Vandell and Stevens found, as have a number of other investigators, that the average intercept of the empirical SMLs was higher than predicted by the CAPM (i.e., higher than R_{ft}), and the average slope was smaller than predicted by the CAPM, i.e., smaller than $R_{mt} - R_{ft}$. In fact, 55 of the 60 calculated intercepts were greater than the risk-free rate of interest, and most of the slopes were smaller than the estimated market risk premium. Seven of the slopes were negative. Moreover, the average R^2 for the 60 cross-section regressions was only 0.06, indicating that only 6% of the differences in expected returns among the 205 stocks were attributable to their betas. It was clear that something besides differences in systematic risk, as measured by beta, was needed to explain the differences in before-tax expected returns.

After finding a positive correlation between the dividend yield and expected return, the authors decided to test the following model, which contains both beta and the dividend yield as explanatory variables:

$$R_{it} = \gamma_0 + \gamma_1 \beta_{it} + \gamma_2 \text{Yld}_{it} + \epsilon_{it} \qquad (7\text{-}7)$$

where

R_{it} = expected return on stock i in period t

γ_0 = the intercept

γ_1 = slope coefficient for beta

β_{it} = estimated beta for stock i as of period t

γ_2 = slope coefficient for the dividend yield

Yld_{it} = dividend yield for stock i in period t

ϵ_{it} = error term

With two independent variables, Equation 7-7 represents a security market plane, as illustrated in Figure 7-6. The security market plane is steeply upward sloping with respect to the dividend yield and only moderately upward sloping with respect to beta. Thus, if the plane represented conditions actually prevailing in the market at a certain time, the expected return for a stock with a beta of 1.5 and a dividend yield of 4% (stock A) would be slightly less than 15%, while the expected return for a stock with a beta of 1.0 and a dividend yield of 10% (stock B) would be approximately 19%.

In Equation 7-7, yield is a proxy for the taxability of the returns. The higher the dividend yield (and, by implication, the lower the expected capital gain), the higher the effective tax rate on the income and the higher the expected before-tax rate of return.

The inclusion of dividend yield as an explanatory variable increased the average R^2 for the 60 regressions from 0.06 to 0.27. It also caused the slope coefficient for beta to become much larger and closer to the theoretical value of $(R_{mt} - R_{ft})$, as well as more stable over time. The increased importance of beta, when dividend yield was included as a proxy for taxability of the income, indicates that beta was more closely associated with expected after-tax returns than with returns on a before-tax basis.

|||| **FIGURE 7-6**
Security Market Plane

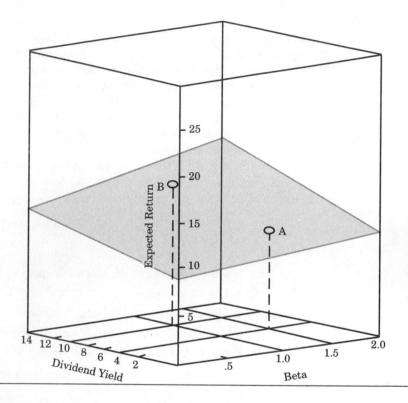

Vandell and Stevens have provided evidence that the expected before-tax returns on common stocks vary directly with the dividend yield. However, it is important to keep in mind that these same procedures might have produced quite different results if applied to data developed by a different set of analysts or data for a different period of time. The authors carefully pointed out that the forecasts prepared by the analysts of a major bank may or may not be representative of the market as a whole. Nevertheless, their findings are quite consistent with the conclusions drawn by Litzenberger and Ramaswamy on the basis of historical data for large numbers of common stocks over a total period of 42 years.[13]

Liquidity and the CAPM

Analysts have observed that the expected returns of highly liquid stocks tend to lie below the security market line, while the expected returns of relatively illiquid stocks lie above the line.[14] The willingness of investors

---

[13]Ibid.

[14]William L. Fouse, "Risk and Liquidity Revisited," *Financial Analysts Journal* 33 (January/February 1977): 40–45.

to accept lower expected returns on highly liquid stocks is expressed in Equation 7-8:

$$R_{it} = \gamma_0 + \gamma_1\beta_i - \gamma_2L_i \qquad (7\text{-}8)$$

where

γ_0 = risk-free rate

γ_1 = market risk premium (slope coefficient for beta)

β_i = beta coefficient for stock i

γ_2 = slope coefficient for liquidity index

L_i = liquidity index for stock i

A stock's *liquidity index,* as calculated with Equation 7-9, represents the dollar volume of trading for each change of 1% in its price:

$$\text{liquidity index} = \frac{\Sigma\, P_iV_i}{\Sigma\, |\, (P_i - P_{i-1})/P_{i-1}\, |} \qquad (7\text{-}9)$$

where

P_i = daily closing price of stock i

V_i = daily share volume of stock i

The higher the ratio, the greater the liquidity of the stock. Table 7-3 illustrates the calculation.

The influence of liquidity on expected returns can be estimated by segregating stocks into several liquidity classes and constructing a separate security market line (referred to as a liquidity market line) for each class. Figures 7-7 and 7-8 are liquidity market lines constructed by Wells Fargo Investment Advisors as of December 31, 1974, when the market was near a cyclical low, and June 30, 1975, after the market had risen steeply for several months.

From the end of 1974 to mid-1975, risk premiums and liquidity premiums both declined substantially, as shown by the decrease in the slope

---

|||| **TABLE 7-3**
Calculation of Stock Liquidity

Day	Shares Traded (Thousands)	Closing Price	Dollar Volume Traded (Thousands)	Percentage Price Change
0		$50		
1	10	48	$ 480	4.00%
2	8	50	400	4.17
3	7	47	329	6.00
4	12	48	612	2.13
5	6	49	318	2.08
Total			2,139	18.38

Liquidity index = 2,139/18.38
  = 116.4

FIGURE 7-7
Liquidity Market Lines, December 31, 1974

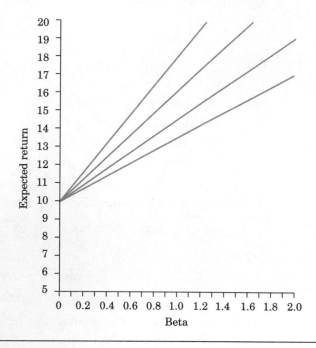

FIGURE 7-8
Liquidity Market Lines, June 30, 1975

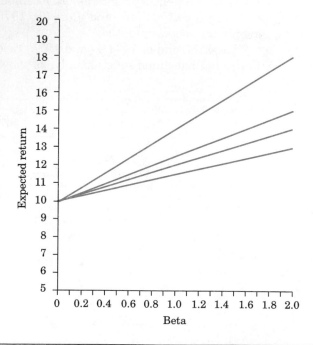

of the liquidity market lines and the decrease in the spread between the lines. At a beta of one, the spread between the expected returns for the first and fourth liquidity classes narrowed from 440 basis points on December 31, 1974, to 230 basis points on June 30, 1975. Risk premiums and liquidity premiums both tend to be high when the market is depressed, and both become smaller as the market rises.

ANOMALIES

During the past 15 to 20 years, academics and practitioners have discovered a number of *anomalies* in the stock market that are difficult to explain. Certain types of stocks have seemed to outperform the market over extended periods of time, even after adjusting the returns for differences in systematic risk as measured by historical betas. The super-performers include stocks selling at low price/earnings ratios, stocks with small total market capitalization, and so-called neglected stocks that are followed by few analysts and held by few, if any, institutional investors. The purpose of the present discussion is to consider whether these anomalies are the result of inefficiencies in the market or deficiencies in the capital asset pricing model or, perhaps, both.

According to the traditional CAPM, differences in risk premiums and expected returns among stocks are directly proportional to differences in betas. For example, if the risk-free rate is 7% and the expected market return is 13% the market risk premium is 6%, and a difference of 0.1 between the betas of two stocks makes a difference of 0.6% between their risk premiums as well as their expected returns. This is illustrated in Table 7-4.

Under the traditional CAPM, the difference between the expected returns for any two stocks is the product of the market risk premium and the difference between their beta coefficients as shown below:

$$R_i - R_k = \{[R_f + \beta_i(R_m - R_f)] - [R_f + \beta_k(R_m - R_f)]\}$$
$$R_i - R_k = (\beta_i - \beta_k)(R_m - R_f)$$

For example, the difference between the expected returns for stocks with betas of 0.9 and 1.2 in Table 7-4 is 1.8 percentage points [(14.2 − 12.4)

|||| **TABLE 7-4**

Changes in Risk Premiums and Expected Returns Related to Changes in Beta

Beta	R_f	R_m	$R_m - R_f$	$\beta(R_m - R_f)$	$R_f + \beta(R_m - R_f)$	Change in Risk Premium and Expected Return
0.9	7%	13%	6%	5.4%	12.4%	
1.0	7	13	6	6.0	13.0	0.6%
1.1	7	13	6	6.6	13.6	0.6
1.2	7	13	6	7.2	14.2	0.6
Total						1.8

$= (1.2 - .9) (13 - 7)]$. However, if the stock with a beta of 0.9 is the stock of a large company or is a stock selling at an average or above-average price/earnings ratio, while the stock with a beta of 1.2 is the stock of a small company or a stock selling at a below-average price/earnings ratio, the difference between the expected returns of the two stocks may be substantially greater than indicated by these calculations.

Neglected Stocks

To illustrate the above-average returns on certain types of stocks, we will review the findings of Arbel, Carvell, and Strebel relating to neglected firms.[15] The authors examined the relationship between *abnormal returns* [i.e., returns greater than $R_f + \beta(R_m - R_f)$] and the number of institutions holding the stock. Their study was based on annual returns over the 10-year period from 1971 through 1980 for 510 stocks randomly selected in equal numbers from issues traded on the New York Stock Exchange, the American Stock Exchange, and the over-the-counter market. The stocks were divided into three groups on the basis of the number of institutional holdings. The overall results are reported in Table 7-5.

Some portion of the abnormal return of 5.6% for the stocks in group 3 may reflect high transactions costs (higher commissions and wider bid-asked spreads) on stocks that are not heavily traded. However, differences in transactions costs could hardly account for differences in returns as large as seen here. Either the markets are inefficient or the traditional CAPM leaves out one or more factors, such as the liquidity of the investment or the greater uncertainty associated with investing in the stocks of small companies, that are important to investors.

Estimation Risk

If the returns for two stocks have been equally volatile and equally correlated with the market return, their historical betas would be the same, and the traditional CAPM would treat them as being equally risky, even

[15]Avner Arbell, Steven Garvell, and Paul Strebel, "Giraffes, Institutions and Neglected Firms," *Financial Analysts Journal* 39 (May/June 1983): 57–63.

|||| **TABLE 7-5**

Abnormal Returns Related to the Number of Institutions Holding the Stocks, 1971–1980

Group	Number of Institutions Holding the Stock	Average Annual Abnormal Return
1	More than 12	−5.8%
2	2 to 12	1.1
3	1 or none	5.6

SOURCE: Avner Arbel, Steven Carvell, and Paul Strebel, "Giraffes, Institutions and Neglected Firms," *Financial Analysts Journal* 39 (May/June 1983): 57–63.

though one might be the stock of IBM (which is followed by many analysts and held by 1,700 institutional investors) and the other, the stock of a small, relatively obscure company. Investors, however, might view the stock of the small firm as being riskier than IBM because of greater uncertainty about its future earnings. Many analysts forecast the earnings of IBM, and the dispersion of the forecasts is apt to be quite small. On the other hand, few analysts forecast the earnings of the small firm, and the dispersion of the forecasts may be quite large. The greater the variation among the forecasts, the greater the uncertainty about the future prospects of the firm. This uncertainty is known as *estimation risk*.

The CAPM ignores estimation risk, although investors seem to feel it is quite important. Malkiel found, for example, that the coefficient of variation of analysts' forecasts of earnings per share was much more closely correlated with expected returns, with a correlation coefficient of 0.37, than was the historical beta, with a correlation coefficient of 0.25.[16] Using a different sample, Arbel found a simple correlation of 0.68 between the coefficient of variation of analysts' forecasts and the actual returns on common stocks.[17]

A modified CAPM could include the coefficient of variation of earnings per share as a proxy for estimation risk. In regression form, the model would look like Equation 7-10.

$$R_{it} = \gamma_0 + \gamma_1\beta_i + \gamma_2 CV_i + \epsilon_{it} \qquad (7\text{-}10)$$

where

γ_2 = slope coefficient for the coefficient of variation of earnings forecasts

CV_i = coefficient of variation of earnings forecasts

If the coefficient of variation of earnings forecasts is a good proxy for estimation risk, and if estimation risk is important to investors, this model should explain differences in returns among stocks more fully than the original, single-factor CAPM.

MATHEMATICAL LIMITATIONS OF TESTS OF THE CAPM

Chapter 6 presented the development of the two-factor or zero-beta CAPM. In this model, the risk-free rate of return of the CAPM was replaced by the return on an efficient portfolio that had zero correlation and therefore a zero beta with the market portfolio. The equation of the zero-beta model is

$$E(R_i) = E(R_z) + \beta_{im}[E(R_m) - E(R_z)] \qquad (7\text{-}11)$$

---

[16]Burton G. Malkiel, "Risk and Return: A New Look," National Bureau of Economic Research, Reprint no. 291 (July 1982).

[17]Avner Arbel, "Generic Stocks: The Key to Market Anomalies," *Journal of Portfolio Management* 11 (Summer 1985): 4–13.

Roll noted that this model is not unique.[18] That is, Equation 7-11 will hold when any portfolio in the efficient set is substituted for the market portfolio since there is always a linear relationship between beta determined with respect to an efficient portfolio and the return. If the portfolio used to create beta is not efficient, the return will be not a linear function of beta. This concept is shown in Figure 7-9. The SML-like equation for the T portfolio is

$$E(R_i) = E(R_z') + \beta_{iT}[E(R_T) - E(R_z')]. \tag{7-12}$$

In this case the beta of the security is determined relative to the T portfolio.[19]

The implication of having an infinite number of SML-like equations is that any ex post two-factor form of the CAPM (Equation 7-3) must hold if the proxy chosen to represent the market portfolio is efficient. Therefore, tests using Equation 7-3 are really tests of whether the market proxy portfolio is efficient, not tests of the CAPM. A true test of the CAPM would require the identification of the true market portfolio.

[18]R. Roll, "A Critique of the Asset Pricing Theory's Tests: Part I: On Past and Potential Testability of the Theory," *Journal of Financial Economics* 4 (March 1977):129–76.

[19]Note that there will be as many betas for a security as there are efficient portfolios.

|||| **FIGURE 7-9**
Zero-Beta CAPM

(a)   (b)

If a researcher chooses an ex post portfolio that is not efficient, it is possible to reject the conclusions of the CAPM. For example, recall that the tests of Black, Jensen, and Scholes did not fully support the CAPM. Roll demonstrated, however, that there was a mean-variance efficient market proxy that would perfectly support the CAPM. Thus, Roll concludes:

> Unfortunately, it [the capital asset pricing model] has never been subjected to an unambiguous empirical test. There is considerable doubt, moreover, at least by me, that it ever will.

|||| THE ARBITRAGE PRICING THEORY

The *arbitrage pricing theory (APT)* is an alternative to the capital asset pricing model.[20] The name of the theory is derived from the notion that assets that are close substitutes for one another must sell at the same price, thereby offering the same expected return. If the same asset does sell for different prices, investors will purchase the less expensive asset and sell or short the expensive asset. The excess demand for the less expensive asset will drive its price up, while the excess supply of the expensive asset will cause its price to fall. This simultaneous purchase and sale of the asset is known as *arbitraging*. The actions of arbitragers prevent the prices from being much different for very long.

Several similar ideas underlie both the APT and the CAPM. Both theories assume that investors are rational and risk averse; that systematic risk is the only relevant risk; that actions of buyers and sellers maintain the prices of assets at levels where the expected returns are the same for assets with the same systematic risk; and that expected returns are linearly related to systematic risk. A crucial difference between the two theories is in the definition and measurement of systematic risk.

According to the original, single-factor CAPM, the expected return for an asset, given the expected market rate of return and the risk-free rate, is a linear function of only one variable, the beta coefficient, which is a measure of relative systematic risk. Assets with betas greater than 1.0 have above-average systematic risk and above-average expected returns, while assets with betas less than 1.0 have below-average systematic risk and below-average expected returns. The amount of risk premium incorporated in the expected return is simply the product of the beta coefficient and the market risk premium.

The APT concept of systematic risk is a little more complicated. An asset's total systematic risk depends on its sensitivity to each of several market-wide (common) factors, and the compensation for bearing this risk is comprised of several risk premiums rather than just one. The amount of premium for each risk factor depends on the market price of

[20]Stephen A. Ross "The Arbitrage Theory of Capital Asset Pricing," *Journal of Economic Theory* (December 1976): 341–60.

the risk and the sensitivity of the asset's return to changes in the factor, as measured by a beta coefficient. Each asset has a set of beta coefficients, one for each of the common risk factors. The expected return is the risk-free rate plus the sum of the products of the betas and the prices of risk for all of the factors.[21] The compensation for each element of systematic risk is calculated separately, and the sum of the several compensations is the total risk premium.

From a theoretical viewpoint, the APT is much more flexible than the CAPM. The APT can be used to obtain an expected return-beta relationship that is identical to the CAPM without the requirement that the benchmark portfolio on the security market line be the "true" market portfolio. This result allows portfolio theorists to sidestep the thorny issues raised by Roll's critique. It also means that the central conclusion of the CAPM—that is, the return-beta relationship—is likely to be approximately valid even in the face of the restrictive assumptions imposed by the CAPM.

The cornerstone of the APT is that the relationship between the security returns and the factors is linear, as follows:

$$(7\text{-}13)$$
$$E(R_i) = R_f + (E_1 - R_f)(\beta_{i1}) + (E_2 - R_f)(\beta_{i2}) + \ldots + (E_k - R_f)(\beta_{ik})$$

where

$$E(R_i) = \text{expected return for asset } i$$
$$R_f = \text{risk-free rate}$$
$$\beta_{ik} = \text{beta coefficient for asset } i, \text{ common factor } k$$
$$\text{(amount of change in asset } i\text{'s expected return}$$
$$\text{for a change of one unit in the risk premium}$$
$$\text{for factor } k)$$
$$(E_k - R_f) = \text{market price of risk for common factor } k$$

The quantity $(E_k - R_f)$ is analogous to $(R_m - R_f)$ in the original CAPM. The term $(R_m - R_f)$ is the market price of total systematic risk while $(E_k - R_f)$ is the market price of systematic risk for factor k. The price of risk for any factor is the difference between the riskless rate and the expected return for that factor at a beta of 1.0 when the betas for all other factors are zero.

For example, suppose that two independent economic factors, (F_1, F_2), have been identified for an economy. These factors may be the inflation rate and the growth in the GNP. For two well-diversified portfolios, the following data have been determined:

Portfolio	Expected Return	Beta for F_1	Beta for F_2
A	20	1.2	1.8
B	10	.5	−.5

[21] Alternatively, the risk-free asset may be replaced by the return on a portfolio whose betas for each factor in the model equal zero. This is analogous to the zero-beta CAPM.

The return-beta relationship may be determined by using Equation 7-13:

$$E(R_p) = R_f + (E_1 - R_f)(\beta_{p1}) + (E_2 - R_f)(\beta_{p2}) \qquad (7\text{-}13a)$$

In this equation the unknown quantities are the market price of risk, $(E_i - R_f)$, for the two factors. If the risk-free rate is 8.0% and $(E_i - R_f)$ is defined as λ_i, then the following two equations with two unknowns can be solved:

$$.20 = .08 + 1.2\lambda_1 + 1.8\lambda_2$$
$$.10 = .08 + .5\lambda_1 - .5\lambda_2$$
$$\lambda_1 = .064 \quad \text{and} \quad \lambda_2 = .024$$

Given the price of risk for each of the two factors, the expected return–beta relationship is

$$E(R_p) = .08 + .064\beta_{p1} + .024\beta_{p2}$$

THE COMMON FACTORS

The initial selection of factors is usually made with the statistical procedure known as factor analysis, and the only data used in the procedure are the historical returns for a group of stocks or other assets. The variables that explain most of the variation among the returns are determined simultaneously with the coefficients of the variables. These variables are called factors, and their coefficients are called factor scores. Each factor score or beta is a measure of how the return for the stock responds to changes in the associated factor.

After determining the factor scores for a number of consecutive periods, the cross-sectional returns for a set of stocks are regressed on the scores to estimate the size and statistical significance of the market price of the individual factors. The following example illustrates how the expected return is calculated when three systematic risk factors are involved, assuming a risk-free rate of 5%.

	Factor		
	1	2	3
Price of risk	0.120	0.050	0.020
Beta	0.400	0.600	1.200
Beta × risk	0.048	0.030	0.024

$$\text{Expected return} = R_f + \beta_1 PR_1 + \beta_1 PR_2 + \beta_3 PR_3$$
$$\text{Expected return} = .05 + 0.48 + .030 + .024 = .152$$

One problem with the APT is its failure to specify how many *common factors* there are or what they are. There is no way that factor analysis can identify the "true" variables associated with the security returns. Instead, it simply analyzes the correlations among the returns and is therefore blind to any economic considerations. Thus, spurious factors, i.e., those with no economic meaning, may appear important to the return-generating process. The implication of this observation is that tests of the APT are actually joint tests of the APT and the methodology used to determine the factors.

What Are the Common Risk Factors?

There is lack of agreement as to which economic factors have an important systematic influence on asset returns. Roll and Ross say that empirical research has found the following four economic factors to be relevant:[22]

1. Rate of inflation
2. Rate of industrial production
3. Risk premium (measured by the spread between the yields on low-grade and high-grade bonds)
4. Slope of the term structure of interest rates

The risk premium factor reflects investor attitudes toward risk bearing and investor perceptions about the general level of uncertainty. Changes in the term structure of interest rates are important because most assets have cash flows over a period of years, and a change in the slope of the yield curve changes the discount rates that apply to the various flows.

In commenting on the systematic risk factors, Roll and Ross had this to say:

> Every asset's value changes when one of these variables changes in an unanticipated way. Thus investors who hold portfolios that are more exposed to such changes, i.e., that contain assets whose β's are higher on the average, will find that their portfolios' market values fluctuate with greater amplitude over time. They will be compensated by a higher total return in the long run.[23]

In a test of the APT that involved factor analysis of the returns of firms in 30 different industries, Pari and Chen suggested that three common risk factors are probably important: an index of the general market (or, alternatively, an indicator of overall economic activity), the price volatility of energy, and a measure of interest rate risk.[24] They omitted two factors that are on Roll and Ross's list of important market-wide influences (rate of inflation and risk premium), but included one factor (volatility of energy prices) that Roll and Ross left out.

Measuring the Influence of Company Attributes

Sharpe attempted to measure the importance of certain firm-specific factors by analyzing the returns of virtually all New York Stock Exchange stocks for the years 1931 through 1979.[25] For each of the 588 months in

---

[22]Richard Roll and Stephen A. Ross, "The Arbitrage Pricing Theory Approach to Strategic Portfolio Planning," *Financial Analysts Journal* 40 (May/June 1984): 14–26.

[23]Ibid, p. 19.

[24]Robert A. Pari and Son-Nan Chen, "An Empirical Test of the Arbitrage Pricing Theory," *Journal of Financial Research* 8 (Summer 1984): 121–30.

[25]William F. Sharpe, "Factors in New York Stock Exchange Security Returns, 1931–1979," *Journal of Portfolio Management* 8 (Summer 1982): 5–19.

this period, he fitted a security market hyperplane (another way of saying that he fitted a multiple regression equation) to the returns of the stocks and a number of explanatory variables, including beta, the dividend yield, and the total market value of the company's stock, along with the bond beta, the stock's alpha, and the firm's industry.

The average R-squared for Sharpe's 588 regressions was only 0.104. Beta, the dividend yield, and company size explained between 5 and 10% of the variance among the returns for the different stocks. While this was very low, the average amount of variation in an individual return associated with variations in each of these three variables was quite impressive. For example, on average, the annual return for a stock with a beta of 1.5 exceeded the return of a stock with a beta of 0.5 by 5.36%; the return for a stock with a dividend yield of 6% exceeded the return for a stock with a dividend yield of 2% by 0.95%; and the return for a stock with an aggregate market value of $100 million exceeded the return of a stock with an aggregate market value of $1 billion by 5.56%. These findings are consistent with other studies that have concluded that common stock returns are correlated positively with beta and the dividend yield and negatively with the size of the firm.

THE APT AND THE CAPM

From an analyst's or investor's point of view, the most important difference between the APT and the CAPM may be in their methods of dealing with systematic risk. With the CAPM, the combined influence of all macroeconomic and psychological factors on the market as a whole is reflected in the risk-free rate and the market risk premium. The degree to which the market factor has a greater or smaller effect on an individual security is reflected in the security's beta coefficient, which together with the market risk premium, determines the risk premium for the individual security.

The APT weighs separately the influence that each important macroeconomic and psychological factor has on asset returns, and it also measures separately the sensitivity of an individual asset's return to changes in each of these factors. The APT seems to deal with systematic risk in a more discriminating manner than the CAPM since it recognizes that individual assets have different sensitivities to different sources of systematic risk. On the other hand, the APT does not include certain company-specific explanatory variables, such as the dividend yield and company size, which can be included in expanded versions of the CAPM.

Several tests comparing the explanatory power of the APT with that of the original, single-factor CAPM have been favorable to the APT. For example, a study dealing with public utility stocks found that the APT explained a larger share of return variation among the securities and provided better forecasts of returns than the CAPM.[26] For another example, in their analysis of the returns of 2,090 stocks for the years 1975

---

[26]Dorothy H. Bower, Richard S. Bower, and Dennis E. Logue, "Arbitrage Pricing Theory and Utility Stock Returns," *The Journal of Finance* 39 (September 1984): 1041–54.

through 1980, Pari and Chen found that a three-index APT model accounted for much more of the variation among the returns (40.3% versus 28.5%) than the single-index CAPM.[27] On the other hand, Reinganum found that the APT was no more effective than the single-factor CAPM in dealing with the size effect.[28] The higher returns on the stocks of small companies were still there after adjusting for differences in systematic risk with a five-factor APT model, just as they were still present after adjusting for differences in risk with a single-factor CAPM.

Studies in which the APT has been found superior to the CAPM were based on the original, single-factor CAPM and historical betas. It is not known what the results would have been if the researchers had used an extended version of the CAPM or if the betas had been fundamental rather than historical. The CAPM can be improved by adding additional explanatory variables, such as the coefficient of variation of earnings forecasts. Also, beta estimates can be improved by using fundamental analysis instead of relying completely on the average past relationship between a stock's return and the return on a market index.

|||| SUMMARY

Elaborate tests of the original, single-factor capital asset pricing model indicate that over long periods of time common stock returns have been positively and linearly related to systematic risk, as asserted by the model. However, the average relationship between beta and the rate of return has sometimes been negative for periods as long as 5 or 10 years. Also, tests have usually found the intercept to be considerably larger or smaller than predicted by the CAPM.

Recent studies indicate that a two-factor CAPM, with beta and the coefficient of variation of earnings forecasts as the two independent variables, may explain differences in returns among stocks more fully than the original, single-factor CAPM. In the two-factor model, the coefficient of variation of earnings forecasts is a proxy for estimation risk.

For some investors, the liquidity of stocks is an important consideration. Evidence indicates that expected returns are higher on stocks of low liquidity than on highly liquid stocks. It has also been found that when the market is at or near a cyclical low, the spread between the expected returns for stocks of high and low liquidity tends to be much greater than when the market is at or near a cyclical high. Investors seem to value liquidity more highly in a bear market than in a bull market.

Several classes of stocks have provided abnormally high returns over long periods of time according to studies based upon the CAPM. These include low P/E stocks, stocks of small companies, low-priced stocks, and stocks of firms that are followed by few analysts or held by few institu-

---

[27]Pari and Chen, "An Empirical Test," p. 128.

[28]Marc R. Reinganum, "Discussion: What the Anomalies Mean," *The Journal of Finance* 39 (July 1984): 837–40.

tions. Differences in systematic risk, as measured by differences in historical betas, do not account for the extraordinary returns such stocks have often provided. However, the return differences may be at least partially explained by differences in estimation risk, which is the risk associated with uncertainty about a firm's future earnings. The dispersion of analysts' forecasts of earnings may be a good proxy for this risk. Expected returns seem to be more closely correlated with the coefficient of variation of earnings forecasts than with historical betas.

The arbitrage pricing theory (or model) has been proposed as an alternative to the CAPM. While the APT and the CAPM share a number of assumptions, there are important differences between the two models. First, the APT does not require the assumption that all investors hold the market portfolio. Second, it weighs separately the influence of several systematic factors on the expected return. However, it does not identify these systematic factors.

Some investigators have found the APT superior to the CAPM in explaining differences in returns. Others have found it no more effective than the single-factor CAPM in eliminating the influence of company size on the rate of return. Whether the APT is superior to various multifactor versions of the CAPM, or even to the original CAPM when betas are estimated with fundamental analysis, remains to be seen.

|||| QUESTIONS

1. What test results tend to support the validity of the CAPM?
2. Why is the intercept assumed to be zero in the risk premium version of the CAPM?
3. What is the slope of the SML?
4. What assumptions are made about the error term in the regression equation for the SML?
5. Why did Fischer, Jensen, and Scholes group the New York Stock Exchange stocks into portfolios in testing the CAPM?
6. What is the difference between a time series regression of portfolio returns on the market return and a cross-section regression?
7. What parameters were estimated by Fischer, Jensen, and Scholes in the regression of portfolio excess returns on the market excess return?
8. Why does a negative intercept for a high-beta portfolio mean that the portfolio return was lower than the CAPM would predict? Illustrate with an example.
9. Under the CAPM, what is the assumed relationship between unsystematic risk and the expected return?
10. How did Fischer, Jensen, and Scholes suggest that the CAPM be modified because of the nonzero intercept?

11. How did Fama and MacBeth determine whether unsystematic risk had a systematic effect on the expected return?

12. What is the difference between an empirical SML and a theoretical SML?

13. What evidence did Vandell and Stevens develop that indicates that the traditional CAPM is not valid?

14. Explain why dividend yield was at one time probably a good proxy for the taxability of common stock returns.

15. Why did Vandell and Stevens conclude that beta is more closely associated with after-tax returns than with before-tax returns?

16. What is a liquidity market line?

17. Compare the spread between liquidity market lines when the market is at or near a peak with the spread when the market is at or near a trough. Explain.

18. What is a stock market anomaly? What is an abnormal return?

19. What is estimation risk? What evidence indicates that estimation risk is important to investors?

20. What assumptions are shared by the CAPM and the APT?

21. How does the APT deal with systematic risk? Explain in detail.

22. What economic and psychological phenomena have been suggested as common factors?

23. Expanded versions of the CAPM include certain variables that are not explicitly included in the APT. What are they?

24. On what grounds can it be argued that the APT deals with systematic risk in a more refined (precise) manner than does the CAPM?

25. What is known about the relative abilities of the CAPM and the APT to explain differences in expected returns?

26. What did Sharpe's 1982 study reveal as to the importance of dividend yield and company size in explaining cross-sectional differences between common stock returns?

|||| SELECTED REFERENCES

Ang, James S., and David R. Peterson. "Return Risk and Yield: Evidence from Ex Ante Data." *The Journal of Finance* 40 (June 1985):537–48.

Arbel, Avner. "Generic Stocks: The Key to Market Anomalies." *Journal of Portfolio Management* 11 (Summer 1985):4–13.

Arbel, Avner, Steven Carvell, and Paul Strebel. "Giraffes, Institutions and Neglected Firms." *Financial Analysts Journal* 39 (May/June 1983):57–63.

Beaver, William H., Roger Clarke, and William F. Wright. "The Association between Unsystematic Security Returns and the Magnitude of

Earnings Forecast Errors." *Journal of Accounting Research* 17 (Autumn 1979):316–40.

Beaver, William H., and James Manegold. "The Association between Market-Determined and Accounting-Determined Measures of Systematic Risk: Some Further Evidence." *Journal of Financial and Quantitative Analysis* 10 (June 1975):231–66.

Black, Fischer, and Myron Scholes. "The Effects of Dividend Yield and Dividend Policy on Common Stock Prices and Returns." *Journal of Financial Economics* 1 (May 1974):1–22.

Black, Fischer, Michael C. Jensen, and Myron Scholes. "The Capital Asset Pricing Model: Some Empirical Tests." In Michael C. Jensen, ed., *Studies in the Theory of Capital Markets*. New York: Praeger, 1972.

Blume, Marshall E. "Betas and Their Regression Tendencies." *The Journal of Finance* 30 (June 1975):785–95.

Blume, Marshall E., and Irwin Friend. "Risk Investment Strategy and Long-Run Rate of Return." *The Review of Economics and Statistics* 41 (August 1974):259–69.

Bower, Dorothy H., Richard S. Bower, and Dennis E. Logue. "Arbitrage Pricing Theory and Utility Stock Returns." *The Journal of Finance* 39 (September 1984):1041–54.

Chen, Nai-Fu. "Some Empirical Tests of the Theory of Arbitrage Pricing." *The Journal of Finance* 38 (December 1983):1393–1414.

Chen, Son-Nan. "An Examination of Risk-Return Relationships in Bull and Bear Markets Using Time-Varying Betas." *Journal of Financial and Quantitative Analysis* 17 (June 1982):265–86.

Dhrymes, Phoebus J., Irwin Friend, Mustafa N. Gultekin, and N. Bulent Gultekin. "New Tests of the APT and Their Implications." *The Journal of Finance* 40 (July 1985):659–74.

Dhrymes, Phoebus J., Irwin Friend, and N. Bulent Gultekin. "A Critical Reexamination of the Empirical Evidence on the Arbitrage Pricing Theory." *The Journal of Finance* 39 (June 1984):323–46.

Dybvig, Philip H., and Stephen A. Ross. "Yes, the APT Is Testable." *The Journal of Finance* 40 (September 1985):1173–88.

Elgers, Pieter, and Joanne Hill. "Research Design for Systematic Risk Prediction." *Journal of Portfolio Management* 8 (Spring 1982):43–52.

Estep, Tony, Nick Hanson, and Cal Johnson. "Sources of Value and Risk in Common Stocks." *Journal of Portfolio Management* 9 (Summer 1983):5–13.

Evans, John L., and Stephen H. Archer. "Diversification and the Reduction of Dispersion: An Empirical Analysis." *The Journal of Finance* 23 (December 1968):761–67.

Fabozzi, Frank J. "Mutual Fund Systematic Risk for Bull and Bear Markets: An Empirical Examination." *The Journal of Finance* 34 (December 1979):1243–50.

Fabozzi, Frank J., and Jack Clark Francis. "Stability Tests for Alphas and Betas over Bull and Bear Market Conditions." *The Journal of Finance* 32 (September 1977):1093–99.

Fama, Eugene F., and James D. MacBeth. "Risk, Return, and Equilibrium: Empirical Tests." *Journal of Political Economy* 71 (May/June 1973):607–636.

Fouse, William L. "Risk and Liquidity Revisited." *Financial Analysts Journal* 33 (January/February 1977):40–45.

————. Risk and Liquidity: The Keys to Stock Price Behavior." *Financial Analysts Journal* 32 (May/June 1976):35–45.

Francis, Jack Clark, and Frank J. Fabozzi. "The Effects of Changing Macroeconomic Conditions on the Parameters of the Single Index Market Model." *Journal of Financial and Quantitative Analysis* 14 (June 1979):351–60.

Frankfurter, George M., and Herbert E. Phillips. "Alpha-Beta Theory: A Word of Caution." *Journal of Portfolio Management* 6 (Summer 1977):35–40.

Gahlon, James M., and James A. Gentry. "On the Relationship between Systematic Risk and the Degree of Operating and Financial Leverage." *Financial Management* 11 (Summer 1982):15–23.

Harrington, Diana R. "Whose Beta Is Best?" *Financial Analysts Journal* 39 (July/August 1983):67–72.

Haugen, Robert A., and Dean W. Wichern. "The Intricate Relationship between Financial Leverage and the Stability of Stock Prices." *The Journal of Finance* 30 (December 1975):1283–92.

Hawawini, Gabriel. "Why Beta Shifts as the Return Interval Changes." *Financial Analysts Journal* 39 (May/June 1983):73–77.

Hill, Ned C., and Bernell K. Stone. "Accounting Betas, Systematic Risk, and Financial Leverage: A Risk-Composition Approach to the Determinants of Systematic Risk." *Journal of Financial and Quantitative Analysis* 15 (September 1980):595–637.

Johnson, Dana J., and Richard F. Deckro. "The Role of Economic Variables in Relating Changes in a Firm's Earnings to Changes in the Price of Its Common Stock." *Review of Business and Economic Research* (Fall 1981):27–39.

Kim, Moon K., and Kenton Zumwalt. "An Analysis of Risk in Bull and Bear Markets." *Journal of Financial and Quantitative Analysis* 14 (December 1979):1015–25.

Klemkosky, Robert C. "The Adjustment of Beta Forecasts." *The Journal of Finance* 30 (September 1975):1123–28.

Klemkosky, Robert C., and John D. Martin. "The Effect of Market Risk on Portfolio Diversification." *The Journal of Finance* 30 (March 1975):147–54.

Kwan, Clarence C. Y. "On Testing the Arbitrage Pricing Theory: Inter-Battery Factor Analysis." *The Journal of Finance* 39 (December 1984):1485–1502.

Lakonishok, Josef, and Alan C. Shapiro. "Stock Returns, Beta, Variance and Size: An Empirical Analysis." *Financial Analysts Journal* 40 (July/August 1984):36–41.

Levy, Haim. "Measuring Risk and Performance over Alternative Investment Horizons." *Financial Analysts Journal* 40 (March/April 1984):61–67.

Litzenberger, Robert H., and Krishna Ramaswamy. "The Effect of Personal Taxes and Dividends on Capital Asset Prices: Theory and Empirical Evidence." *Journal of Financial Economics* 7 (June 1979):163–95.

Malkiel, Burton G. "Risk and Return: A New Look." National Bureau of Economic Research, Reprint no. 291 (July 1982).

Martin, John D., and Arthur Keown. "A Misleading Feature of Beta for Risk Measurement." *Journal of Portfolio Management* 3 (Summer 1977):31–34.

McDonald, John G., and Richard E. Stehle. "How Do Institutional Investors Perceive Risk?" *Journal of Portfolio Management* 2 (Fall 1975):11–16.

McEnally, Richard W., and David E. Upton. "A Reexamination of the Ex Post Risk-Return Tradeoff on Common Stocks." *Journal of Financial and Quantitative Analysis* 14 (June 1979):395–419.

Modigliani, Franco, and Gerald A. Pogue. "An Introduction to Risk and Return: Concepts and Evidence." *Financial Analysts Journal* 30 (May/June 1974):69–86.

Muller, Frederick L., Bruce D. Fielitz, and Myron T. Greene. "S&P Quality Rankings: Risk and Return." *Journal of Portfolio Management* 10 (Summer 1983):39–42.

Olsen, Robert A. "The Association between Common Stock Ratings and Market Measures of Risk." *Review of Business and Economic Research* 14 (Spring 1979):61–69.

Pari, Robert A., and Son-Nan Chen. "An Empirical Test of the Arbitrage Pricing Theory." *Journal of Financial Research* 7 (Summer 1984):121–30.

Poterba, James M., and Lawrence H. Summers. "New Evidence That Taxes Affect the Valuation of Dividends." *The Journal of Finance* 39 (December 1984):1397–1415.

Reilly, Frank K., and Eugene F. Drzycimski. "Alternative Industry Performance and Risk." *Journal of Financial and Quantitative Analysis* 9 (June 1974): 423–46.

Reinganum, Marc R. "The Arbitrage Pricing Theory: Some Empirical Results." *The Journal of Finance* 36 (May 1981):313–21.

————. "Discussion: What the Anomalies Mean." *The Journal of Finance* 39 (July 1984):837–40.

Robichek, Alexander A., and Richard A Cohn. "The Economic Determinants of Systematic Risk." *The Journal of Finance* 29 (May 1974):439–47.

Roll, Richard. "A Critique of the Asset Pricing Theory's Tests: Part I: On Past and Potential Testability of the Theory." *Journal of Financial Economics* 4 (March 1977):129–76.

————. "Vas Ist Das?" *The Journal of Portfolio Management* 9 (Winter 1983):18–28.

Roll, Richard, and Stephen A. Ross. "The Arbitrage Pricing Theory Approach to Strategic Portfolio Planning." *Financial Analysts Journal* 40 (May/June 1984):14–26.

————. "A Critical Reexamination of the Empirical Evidence on the Arbitrage Pricing Theory: A Reply." *The Journal of Finance* 39 (June 1984):347–50.

————. "Regulation, the Capital Asset Pricing Model and the Arbitrage Pricing Theory." *Public Utilities Fortnightly* (May 26, 1983): 22–28.

————. "An Empirical Investigation of the Arbitrage Pricing Theory." *The Journal of Finance* 35 (December 1980):1073–1101.

Rosenberg, Barr. "The Capital Asset Pricing Model and the Market Model." *Journal of Portfolio Management* 7 (Winter 1981):5–16.

Rosenberg, Barr, and James Guy. "Prediction of Beta from Investment Fundamentals (Part 1)." *Financial Analysts Journal* 32 (May/June 1976):60–72.

————. "Prediction of Beta from Investment Fundamentals (Part 2)." *Financial Analysts Journal* 32 (July/August 1976):62–70.

Ross, Stephen A. "The Arbitrage Theory of Capital Asset Pricing." *Journal of Economic Theory* (December 1976):341–60.

Schwendiman, Carl J., and George E. Pinches. "An Analysis of Alternative Measures of Investment Risk." *The Journal of Finance* 30 (March 1975):193–200.

Shanken, Jay. "Multi-Beta CAPM or Equilibrium APT?: A Reply." *Journal of Finance* 40 (September 1985):1189–96.

————. "The Arbitrage Pricing Theory: Is It Testable?" *The Journal of Finance* 37 (December 1982):1129–40.

Sharpe, William F. "Factors in New York Stock Exchange Security Returns, 1931–1979." *Journal of Portfolio Management* 8 (Summer 1982):5–19.

Sharpe, William F., and Guy Howard B. Sosin. "Risk, Return and Yield: New York Stock Exchange Common Stocks, 1928–1969." *Financial Analysts Journal* 32 (March/April 1976):33–42.

Sharpe, William F., and Guy M. Cooper. "Risk-Return Classes of New York Stock Exchange Common Stocks, 1928–1967." *Financial Analysts Journal* 28 (March/April 1972):46–54, 81.

Stambaugh, Robert F. "Testing the CAPM with Broader Market Indexes." *Journal of Banking and Finance* 7 (March 1983):5–16.

Thompson, Donald J. "Sources of Systematic Risk in Common Stocks." *Journal of Business* 39 (April 1976):173–88.

Tole, Thomas M. "How to Maximize Stationarity of Beta." *Journal of Portfolio Management* 7 (Winter 1981):45–49.

Vandell, Robert F. "Is Beta a Useful Measure of Security Risk?" *Journal of Portfolio Management* 7 (Winter 1981):23–31.

Vandell, Robert F., and Jerry L. Stevens. "Personal Taxes and Equity Security Pricing." *Financial Management* 11 (Spring 1982):31–40.

Wagner, W. H., and S. C. Lau. "The Effects of Diversification on Risk." *Financial Analysts Journal* 27 (November/December 1971):48–53.

Wallace, Anise. "Is Beta Dead?" *Institutional Investor* (July 1980):23–30.

8   MARKET EFFICIENCY

The constant search for superior stocks is either a rational endeavor requiring careful analysis and vision or a matter of luck in a game of chance.[1] If the market is *micro-efficient* (all information bearing on relative stock values is accurately reflected in current prices), the search for superior stocks is a pure gamble. In a micro-efficient market, no stocks are overpriced relative to others as a result of unfounded enthusiasm, and none are underpriced relative to others due to excessive pessimism. Any attempt to select tomorrow's winners in such a market is, in effect, a bet that completely unpredictable future developments will cause the selected stocks to perform better than the average.

Just as searching among many stocks for the best performers may be either a gamble or a rational endeavor that requires unusual talent, attempts to time the market (shifting funds back and forth between stocks and other securities) may or may not be grounded on logical analysis. If the market is *macro-efficient* (all stocks are priced appropriately relative to other securities), any attempt to earn higher returns by moving funds into and out of stocks is like betting on the spin of a roulette wheel. Thus, the degree to which the market is efficient in a macro sense, as well as in a micro sense, is very important to investors.

THE RANDOM WALK AND MARKET EFFICIENCY

For many years economists and statisticians have had an interest in the behavior of stock prices, and their explorations led eventually to the development of efficient market theory. Beginning with studies of stock price patterns, they wondered, do stock prices follow predictable trends, or does their path resemble a *random walk?*[2] Among the first to address this question empirically was the distinguished British statistician, Maurice Kendall, who examined weekly changes in a number of indexes of

---

[1] In this context, a superior stock is one that is expected to provide an above-average risk-adjusted return.

[2] The term "random walk," as applied to common stocks, refers to price changes that are serially independent and normally distributed. If stock price changes are random, knowing that the price of a stock increased $1.00 yesterday is of no help in predicting whether the price will move up, down, or remain unchanged today.

British industrial common stocks. After reviewing a large number of *serial correlation* coefficients, he wrote:

> The series looks like a wandering one, almost as if once a week the Demon of Chance drew a random number from a symmetrical population of fixed dispersion and added it to the current price to determine next week's price.[3]

A few years later, Harry Roberts used a table of random numbers to simulate the level and changes in the level of the Dow Jones Industrial Average for a period of 52 weeks.[4] The resulting simulation showed a striking similarity to the actual weekly changes in the average. Further evidence of stock price randomness was provided by Fama in a five-year analysis of the daily price changes for the 30 stocks in the Dow Jones Industrial Average.[5] He found small serial correlations, but they were insignificant.

Why should one expect short-term stock price movements to be random? The answer comes from efficient market theory. In an efficient market, prices accurately reflect all relevant information and they change only when market participants receive new information. Since new information comes randomly, stock prices change randomly.

|||| REQUISITES FOR EFFICIENCY

To a large degree, the conditions necessary for efficiency are present in the market for publicly traded stocks. Information bearing on values is widely and rapidly distributed at low cost; many rational, well-informed, profit-seeking investors buy and sell stocks in a highly competitive environment; and trading costs, although not negligible, are low. Yet, some inefficiencies do exist. The stock market is probably best characterized as being highly, but not perfectly, efficient.

|||| LEVELS OF EFFICIENCY

Studies of *market efficiency,* a number of which are examined in the present chapter, have generally tested one or more of the following forms of the *efficient market hypothesis (EMH):*

1. *Weak efficiency:* Prices accurately reflect all information contained in previous price changes and volumes of trading.

---

[3]Maurice B. Kendall, "The Analysis of Economic Time-Series, Part I: Prices," *Journal of the Royal Statistical Society* 96 (1953):11–25.

[4]Harry V. Roberts, "Stock Market Patterns and Financial Analysis: Methodological Suggestions," *The Journal of Finance* 14 (March 1959):1–10.

[5]Eugene F. Fama, "The Behavior of Stock Market Prices," *Journal of Business* 38 (January 1965):34–105.

2. *Semistrong efficiency:* Prices accurately reflect *all public information,* including previous price changes and volumes of trading.

3. *Strong efficiency:* Prices accurately reflect *all information,* including information known only to insiders and private information developed by professionals from public information.

On the whole, studies addressing weak efficiency have found that stock price changes are random. Nothing can be gained by studying past price changes and trading volumes, since they are already reflected in current prices. To the extent that this is true, the price charts of technical analysts are of no value in selecting stocks.

Semistrong efficiency depends heavily upon the quality of the work done by professional and amateur security analysts who evaluate stocks on the basis of fundamental factors such as interest rates, risk premiums, and forecasts of earnings and dividends. To the extent that these evaluations are correct and reflected in stock prices, the market is efficient.

Studies provide considerable support for semistrong efficiency, at least in a micro sense. Generally, stock prices reflect public information quickly and accurately enough that stocks are correctly priced relative to one another. However, certain possible exceptions have been found. Sometimes prices have adjusted slowly to new information; sometimes risk-adjusted returns for stocks of certain types (e.g., those with small aggregate market value) have been well above average for a number of years; and sometimes price performance has varied systematically with the day of the week or the time of the year.

Evidence of strong efficiency is less convincing than the evidence supporting weak and semistrong efficiency. Validity of strong efficiency is tested by evaluating the performance of (1) stocks bought and sold by insiders, (2) portfolios managed by professionals, and (3) stocks recommended by professional analysts.

In the following pages, micro-efficiency is discussed first, starting with the weak form of the EMH. After examining the three levels of micro-efficiency, the chapter deals with the efficiency of the market in a macro sense; that is, with the degree to which stocks are priced correctly relative to other investments. If prices reflect all relevant information, the market is macro-efficient as well as micro-efficient. Finally, the chapter discusses the relevance of market efficiency to security analysis and portfolio management.

|||| **WEAK EFFICIENCY**

Technical analysts have criticized the correlation studies of Fama and others on the grounds that statistical tests cannot capture the complex relationships among price changes that a technical trader might use. To meet this objection, economists and others have tried many trading strategies based on past price changes to see if any could have produced greater profits than a strategy of buying and holding.

Trading strategies based on price changes usually involve the use of *filter rules*. With a filter strategy, a specified percentage change in the price of a stock serves as a buy or sell signal. The underlying assumption is that once the price has changed by more than the amount of the filter, say, 5%, it will move substantially farther in the same direction. Filters can be of any size, and the filters for buying and selling can be different percentages. If the filters are small, the gains and losses on individual transactions will also be small, and there will be many transactions and heavy transactions costs. If the filters are large, there will be relatively few transactions, and the trader will often miss a substantial part of the potential gain when the price is trending upward and will sustain large losses when the price is declining. Filter systems have been tried over various periods of time with filters ranging from 0.5% to 50%. None have worked with enough consistency to merit their use.[6]

Recent Opposing Evidence

A recent study by Fama and French indicates that stock price changes are not always random.[7] They found significant negative serial correlations in stock returns when the intervals between the returns were more than a year. Portfolios of stocks that performed poorly during one period of years tended to perform well in a subsequent period of years, and portfolios that performed well in one period tended to perform poorly in the next.

Similarly, De Bondt and Thaler found that the poorest performing stocks over periods ranging from two to five years often became very good performers over succeeding periods of the same length, while the best performing stocks in the earlier period became poor performers in the succeeding period.[8] They concluded that this was the result of investor overreaction to particularly favorable or unfavorable earnings reports. Overreaction causes the prices of stocks with unfavorable earnings reports to fall below their true value and causes the prices of stocks with especially favorable earnings reports to rise above their true value. When it later turns out that things were better or worse than they seemed, prices of the stocks move to more appropriate levels. De Bondt and Thaler observed that individuals are inclined to overreact to new information, and they cited several authorities to buttress their position.

In a psychological study, Kahneman and Tversky found that individuals have a tendency to place too much weight on recent information and

[6]Eugene F. Fama and M. E. Blume, "Filter Rules and Stock Market Trading," *Journal of Business* 39 (January 1966):226–41.

[7]Eugene F. Fama and Kenneth R. French, "Permanent and Temporary Components of Stock Prices," *Journal of Political Economy* 96 (1988):246–73.

[8]Werner F. M. De Bondt and Richard Thaler, "Does the Stock Market Overreact?" *The Journal of Finance* 40 (July 1985):793–805; and "Further Evidence on Investor Overreaction and Stock Market Seasonality," *The Journal of Finance* 42 (July 1987):557–81.

too little on prior knowledge.[9] Three renowned economists have made similar observations relating specifically to investors. According to John Maynard Keynes, " . . . day-to-day fluctuations in the profits of existing investments, which are obviously of an ephemeral and nonsignificant character, tend to have an altogether excessive, and even absurd, influence on the market." John Burr Williams, the father of modern valuation theory, noted that "prices have been based too much on current earning power and too little on long-term dividend paying power." And Nobel Laureate Kenneth Arrow made the following comment about the work of Kahneman and Tversky: "It typifies very precisely the character of all the securities and futures markets."[10]

De Bondt and Thaler wondered whether the changed performance of the winners and losers could have resulted from changes in their systematic risk over the years. A substantial increase in the systematic risk of the losers and a decrease in the systematic risk of the winners might explain why their performance differed so widely from one period to the next. This possibility was explored, and the authors found that changes in systematic risk were not large enough to account for the dramatic changes in the performance of the stocks.[11]

|||| ## SEMISTRONG EFFICIENCY

Most semistrong studies fit into one of the following categories:

1. *Event studies:* How quickly and accurately do prices of stocks respond to events (such as a merger announcement) affecting their fundamental values? Are prices sometimes affected by events that have no bearing on the values of the stocks?

2. *Stock-characteristic studies:* Do stocks with certain characteristics (such as a low price/earnings ratio or small aggregate market value) provide abnormal returns?

3. *Time-of-the-trade studies:* Do purchases and sales at certain times of the week, month, or year provide abnormal returns?

The efficiency of the market is tested by attempting to determine whether abnormal returns could have been earned (1) by purchasing

---

[9]D. Kahneman and A. Tversky, "Intuitive Prediction Biases and Corrective Procedures," in D. Kahneman, P. Slovic, and A. Tversky, eds., *Judgment under Uncertainty: Heuristics and Biases* (London: Cambridge University Press, 1982).

[10]J. M. Keynes, *The General Theory of Employment, Interest and Money* (London: Harcourt Brace Jovanovich, 1964 reprint of 1936 edition); J. B. Williams, *The Theory of Investment Value* (Amsterdam: North-Holland, 1956 reprint of 1938 edition); K. J. Arrow, "Risk Perception in Psychology and Economics," *Economic Inquiry* 20 (January 1982):1–9.

[11]De Bondt and Thaler's findings were criticized in a study by Zarowin that argued that the long-run overreaction phenomenon is simply a manifestation of the January effect and the size effect (discussed later in this chapter in connection with the semistrong hypothesis). Paul Zarowin, "Does the Stock Market Overreact to Corporate Earnings Information?" *The Journal of Finance* 44 (December 1989):1385–99.

stocks immediately after the release of new information; (2) by purchasing stocks with certain characteristics; or (3) by purchasing and selling stocks at certain predetermined times. An abnormal return is the amount by which the actual return is higher or lower than expected, given the market return and the usual relationship of the stock's return to the market return. The relationship of a stock's return to the market return is expressed in regression form with Equation 5-15, the market model:

$$R_{it} = \alpha_i + \beta_{im}R_{mt} + \epsilon_{it}$$

The return for stock i in period t is a fixed amount (α_i), plus a percentage of the market return ($\beta_{im}R_{mt}$), plus a firm-specific component (ϵ_{it}). The quantity ϵ_{it}, the abnormal return, is that portion of the total return for stock i in period t that is not explained by the market return.

Rearranging Equation 5-15 and designating ϵ_{it} as AR_{it}, it becomes

$$AR_{it} = R_{it} - (\alpha_i + \beta_{im}R_{mt}) \tag{8-1}$$

The *abnormal return* for stock i in period t is the actual return minus the return one would expect, given the market return and the estimated relationship of the stock's return to the market return as expressed in α_i and β_{im}. Abnormal returns indicate the presence of a market inefficiency. Market efficiency studies focus on average abnormal returns for a large number of stocks.

It is apparent that alpha (α_i) and beta (β_{im}) are very important quantities that must be estimated individually for each stock. This is usually done by regressing the returns for a stock against the returns for the market for a number of periods. Such estimates are necessarily crude because the relationship of a stock's return to the market return changes over time as a result of developments peculiar to the individual stock.

EVENT STUDIES

In *event studies*, which examine the relationship of unusual returns to important or unimportant events, the abnormal return is usually calculated for each stock for each day of a period preceding, including, and following the event. Daily average abnormal returns *(AARs)* for all stocks under review are then calculated for each day. Finally, the cumulative effect of the event over a specified number of days is determined by calculating *cumulative average abnormal returns,* or *CAARs*. For example, if t is any day covered by the study, $t = 0$ is the day of the event, and the study covers each day from $t - 30$ to $t + 50$, the *CAAR* for day $t + 20$ would be

$$CAAR_{t+20} = \sum_{d=-30}^{+20} AAR_d$$

The *CAAR* for any day is the sum of the daily average abnormal returns through that day. Z-statistics are calculated to determine the statistical significance of the daily and cumulative average abnormal returns.

One way to evaluate semistrong efficiency is to determine whether stock prices are influenced by the announcement of company decisions that affect fundamental values but not by decisions that lack real substance. Examples of superficial, nonsubstantive decisions include stock splits and accounting changes, such as a switch from accelerated to straight-line depreciation for reporting to shareholders, that have no effect on cash flows. Announcements of such decisions are properly viewed as "noise" rather than information. Can investors tell the difference between real information and company-produced noise?

Another kind of event that may affect the price of a stock are quarterly announcements of earnings and dividends. If the announcement brings new information in the form of a surprising increase or decrease in either earnings or dividends, it should, according to the semistrong EMH, be fully and immediately reflected in the price of the stock.

Stock Splits

Many corporations issue new shares to existing shareholders from time to time without requiring any payment. If the number of shares issued is 25% or more of the number already outstanding, the transaction is called a *stock split*. Smaller issues are classified as *stock dividends*. Clearly, a stock dividend or split does nothing to increase the value of a corporation. It neither increases its prospective earnings nor decreases its risk, and it is not at all likely to increase the liquidity of the stock. The ownership is simply divided into a larger number of shares, with each stockholder retaining the same percentage of the outstanding shares as before. Therefore, a split should have no effect on the aggregate market value of the stock and should reduce the per-share price in proportion to the size of the split. A two-for-one split would be expected to cut the per-share price in half. If the price per share was $100 before a two-for-one split, the price should be $50 after the split, assuming no change in the level of the market and no unexpected developments relating to the company.

It is difficult to justify stock splits since they do not change the company in any fundamental way, and splitting involves costs. Attempts to rationalize stock splits are usually based on the notion that a split reduces the price of the stock to a more popular trading range, which makes it attractive to a greater number of investors, thereby increasing its liquidity. Some argue that since commissions on *round lots* (100 or more shares) are lower than on *odd lots,* more investors are interested in lower-priced stocks, which are easier for small investors to purchase in round lots. The weakness in this argument is that the amount of odd-lot trading is small. Prices are largely determined by the actions of large individual and institutional investors.

If the market is efficient, a stock split should not, by itself, affect the price of a stock, and that is what studies have found. Figure 8-1, which is based on 219 stock splits between 1945 and 1965, shows abnormally high returns during much of the 30-month period preceding the split but

|||| **FIGURE 8-1**

Cumulative Abnormal Returns Before and After a Stock Split

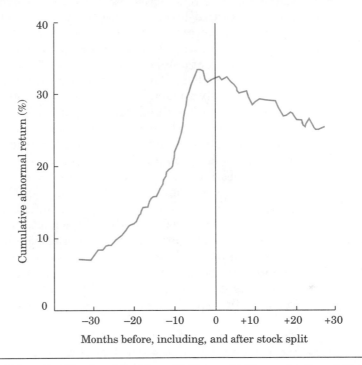

SOURCE: Sasson Bar-Yosef and Lawrence D. Brown, "A Reexamination of Stock Splits Using Moving Betas," *The Journal of Finance* 32 (September 1977): 1069–80.

below-normal returns after the split.[12] While the positive abnormal returns during the presplit period could have been due to anticipation of the split, that seems most unlikely. Even if investors had been expecting a split, why would they have looked favorably upon the prospect—unless, by chance, they expected it to be accompanied by a greater than previously expected increase in dividends? It appears most likely that the price of the stock increased for other reasons before the split, and that the split was due to the increase in price.

The negative abnormal returns after the split may have been due to disappointment with the size of the cash dividend at the time of the split. An earlier study found that stock splits accompanied by a decrease in the aggregate cash dividend did, on average, lead to negative abnormal returns.[13]

[12]Sasson Bar-Yosef and Lawrence D. Brown, "A Reexamination of Stock Splits Using Moving Betas," *The Journal of Finance* 32 (September 1977):1069–80.

[13]Eugene F. Fama, Lawrence Fisher, Michael C. Jensen, and Richard Roll, "The Adjustment of Stock Prices to New Information," *International Economic Review* 10 (February 1969):1–21.

Accounting Changes

An accounting change should have a positive effect on the price of a stock only if it is likely to increase the firm's cash flows. A change from accelerated to straight-line depreciation for reporting to shareholders produces higher reported earnings but has no effect on cash flows. Many firms have made this change for the apparent purpose of improving the performance of their stock, but studies indicate that investors have not been deceived, at least not for long. Any abnormally high returns following the change have lasted only a short time and were soon offset by lower returns. The results are consistent with the semistrong form of the EMH.[14]

News of a switch from the *FIFO* to *LIFO* method of accounting for inventories is important information. In periods of inflation, which for many years has been all of the time, the switch to LIFO almost always reduces reported earnings but increases cash flows because it generally results in lower taxes. Surprisingly, one study found that investors reacted either negatively or not at all to the adoption of LIFO, indicating that they failed to recognize the probable positive impact on cash flows.[15] However, another, more convincing study found that investor reactions to a switch to LIFO were not only positive but varied directly with the amount cash flows increased due to the decrease in taxes.[16] Thus, while the results of the FIFO-LIFO studies are mixed, the weight of the evidence in accounting studies favors semistrong efficiency.

Earnings Surprises

Stock investors pay a great deal of attention to earnings forecasts and quarterly and annual earnings reports. In spite of the fact that a firm's reported earnings are affected by its methods of accounting and are apt to be based on estimates of various kinds, they are usually a good indicator of how successfully the firm is being operated. Also, changes in earnings provide one basis for estimating future earnings. Knowing this, it is not surprising that investors often respond to earnings reports that are substantially better or worse than expected.[17] Stock prices reflect investors' expectations about future earnings, and when actual results or revised forecasts are better or worse than investors have expected, prices change. The principal inquiry in earnings surprise studies is how quickly prices change in response to a surprise. In a perfectly efficient market, prices

---

[14]T. Ross Archibald, "Stock Market Reactions to the Depreciation Switch-Back," *Accounting Review* 47 (January 1972):22–30; R. Ball, "Changes in Accounting Techniques and Stock Prices," *Journal of Accounting Research* Supplement 10 (1972):1–38; Robert S. Kaplan and Richard Roll, "Investor Evaluation of Accounting Information: Some Empirical Evidence," *Journal of Business* 45 (April 1972):225–57.

[15]William E. Ricks, "The Market's Response to the 1974 LIFO Adoptions," *Journal of Accounting Research* 20 (Autumn 1982):367–87.

[16]Gary C. Biddle and Frederick W. Lindahl, "Stock Price Reactions to LIFO Adoptions: The Association between Excess Returns and LIFO Tax Savings," *Journal of Accounting Research* 20 (Autumn 1982):551–87.

[17]Earnings surprises do not always have an appreciable effect on the price of a stock. For example, it may be apparent that reported earnings reflect nonrecurring items or are extraordinary for some other reason.

adjust immediately. In a market that is less than perfectly efficient, the adjustment takes longer.

A number of studies have examined the impact of earnings surprises. Almost without exception, they have found that the surprise has been reflected in the stock price gradually. Surprises are identified by comparing actual earnings with expected earnings. Sometimes it is assumed that expected earnings are equal to the consensus forecast of earnings; and sometimes expected earnings are approximated with a model like the following:

$$E_{i,t} = E_{i,t-4} + a_i(E_{i,t-1} - E_{i,t-5}) + g \qquad (8\text{-}2)$$

where

$$E_{i,t} = \text{firm } i\text{'s estimated earnings for the current quarter}$$

$$E_{i,t-4} = \text{firm } i\text{'s actual earnings for the fourth preceding quarter}$$

$$a_i = \text{an adjustment factor peculiar to firm } i$$

$$E_{1,t-1} - E_{i,t-5} = \text{growth in earnings from the fifth preceding quarter to the last quarter}$$

$$g = \text{growth factor for firm } i$$

Estimates of a and g for each firm are made with regression analysis.

Using Equation 8-2, Foster, Olsen, and Shevlin (FOS) estimated expected earnings for more than 2,000 firms between 1974 and 1981.[18] To measure surprise, they divided the difference between the actual and expected earnings by the standard deviation of the difference between the two over a number of previous periods. The result is called *standardized unexpected earnings (SUE)*. It is a better measure of surprise than the unadjusted difference between actual and expected earnings because it takes into account the variability of the firm's earnings. If earnings have been highly variable and thus very difficult to predict, the difference between actual and expected earnings would have to be very large to surprise investors.

To measure the effect of earnings surprises on stock prices, FOS calculated the cumulative abnormal returns for each stock for a period beginning 60 days before the earnings announcement and ending 60 days after. Each quarterly observation for each stock was placed in one of 10 deciles based upon the magnitude of the SUE, with the largest positive surprises placed in decile 10. The results are shown in Figure 8-2.

The findings of this study are noteworthy. Overall, the amount of the abnormal return is highly correlated with the degree of surprise. The larger the positive earnings surprise, the larger the positive cumulative abnormal return, and the larger the negative surprise, the larger the negative abnormal return. Note that the abnormal returns began before

[18]George Foster, Chris Olsen, and Terry Shevlin, "Earnings Releases, Anomalies, and the Behavior of Security Returns," *The Accounting Review* 59 (October 1984):574–603.

|||| **FIGURE 8-2**

Cumulative Abnormal Returns Before and After an Earnings
Announcement

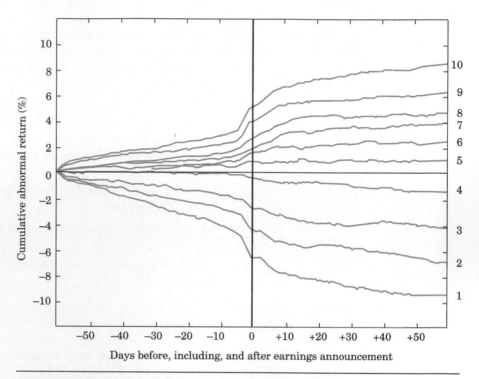

SOURCE: George Foster, Chris Olsen, and Terry Shevlin, "Earnings Releases, Anomalies, and the Behavior of Security Returns," *The Accounting Review* 59 (October 1984):574–603.

the announcement date, indicating that investors began to revise their expectations about the earnings before they were reported. This may have reflected changes in analysts' forecasts.

From an investor's point of view, the results show a possible simple strategy for earning abnormal returns: buy stocks with positive earnings surprises immediately after the earnings are announced. On the average, stocks with a positive earnings surprise continued to earn abnormal returns for some time after the announcement date. Do the results point to an easy way to "beat the market"? Probably not. "Market inefficiencies carry the seeds of their own destruction." If a certain type of inefficiency is exploitable, the larger the number of people who are aware of it, and the sooner they receive the crucial information, the less chance anyone has to take advantage of it. Some money managers have used earnings surprises as an important part of their stock selection strategy for a number of years; and now the *Wall Street Journal* reports quarterly earnings surprises, as explained in the Sidelight. The earnings surprise phenomenon is almost surely less important today than in the past.

STOCK CHARACTERISTICS AND CALENDAR EFFECTS

Possible exceptions to the efficient market hypothesis, such as the earnings surprise effect, are called anomalies. Several of these relate to stock characteristics, such as aggregate market value (the *small-firm effect*), and the time of the week or year (the *calendar effect*).

Historical Performance of Small Stocks

Until 1984 many people believed that small stocks would provide higher returns than large stocks most of the time. During the 20 years ending with 1983, small-stock returns were higher than large-stock returns 85% of the time (in 17 of the 20 years); and for the 20-year period as a whole, the compound annual return on small stocks was 17.6%, compared to 8.3% for large stocks. Then, just as thousands of investors were buying shares in small-stock mutual funds (see the Sidelight on the next page), a drastic change occurred. The returns on small stocks fell below large-stock returns in six of the seven years from 1984 through 1990; and the compound annual return on small stocks for that seven-year period was only 2.6%, compared to 14.4% for large stocks.[19] In spite of recent history, however, small stocks did provide a higher average return than large stocks (11.6% versus 10.1%) over the 65-year period from 1926 through 1990.

[19]*Stocks, Bonds, Bills and Inflation: 1991 Yearbook* (Chicago: Ibbotson Associates, 1991).

||| SIDELIGHT

Small Companies Outperform Large Ones, the Academics
Said—Now if Only the Stock Market Would Cooperate

David Booth and Rex Sinquefield are making a lot of money out of an
academic theory, but the folks who invest with them aren't doing nearly
so well. In 1981 Booth, a former vice president for A. G. Becker, and
Sinquefield, head of the trust department for Chicago's American National Bank & Trust, set up Dimensional Fund Advisors (DFA). The
purpose? To profit from research by their alma mater, the University of
Chicago Graduate School of Business, that bastion of efficient market
theory.

DFA's first product was a mutual fund that exploits an exception to
that theory known as "the small-company effect." The exception to the
theory holds, in essence, that small-company stocks outperform large-
company stocks in the long term.

The money poured in. Assets under management in DFA's six equity
portfolios climbed from $6 million in 1981 to $4.4 billion today. It has
since introduced new funds that invest in small companies in the U.K.
and Japan and also offers several fixed-income products. DFA's clients
include Amoco, W. R. Grace, IBM, Harvard University, and the City of
New York—small investors need not apply. Management fees now produce $11 million in revenues a year. Booth and Sinquefield together own
half the company.

Because they sell theory rather than stock selection, Booth and Sinquefield don't do much stock picking. Their Small Company Portfolio, for
example, is essentially an index fund that buys NYSE, AMEX, or OTC
companies with a market capitalization in the bottom 20% of all NYSE
firms. That works out to a market capitalization of up to $100 million.
Other portfolios buy different but defined segments of the small company
universe. Stocks are sold when price increases push their market capitalization above the target range.

Size, Price/Earnings Ratio, and January Effect

For a number of years, there was considerable confusion about the relative
influence of three variables on stock returns: aggregate market value, or
size; the price/earnings ratio; and the month of the transaction. A study
by Jaffe, Keim, and Westerfield (JKW) has clarified the situation a great
deal. The JKW research covered a much longer period (1951–1986) than
prior studies and measured the independent effects of four variables: size,
P/E ratio, month of the transaction, and stock price.[20]

JKW arranged New York Stock Exchange and American Stock Exchange stocks into 30 portfolios. The stocks were first assigned to six
groups on the basis of P/E ratios. All stocks with negative earnings were
placed in group 0, and the stocks with positive earnings were placed in

---

[20] Jeffrey Jaffe, Donald B. Keim, and Randolph Westerfield, "Earnings Yields, Market
Values, and Stock Returns," *The Journal of Finance* 44 (March 1989):135–48.

Performance? About C+. The Small Company Portfolio has outperformed the S&P 500 during only one and a half years of DFA's five-year history. The average return on the Small Company Portfolio for the five years ending April 30 was 21.6%. That's three points below the S&P 500. The most recent 12 months were particularly grim, with a 9.6% total return for the DFA portfolio versus a whopping 26.5% for the S&P 500. "Every idea has its time in the sun. It hasn't been our time for a while," says Booth.

Is the whole small-stock thing just an academic illusion? Quite possibly. Binkley Shorts, the highly respected portfolio manager for the Over-the-Counter Securities Fund, believes the theory may have been responsible for the bubble in small-company stock prices in the early 1980s that cost investors so dearly. Now, says Shorts, "they've been debunked. By the standards of history their theory has been disproven."

The original work on the small-company effect was done in 1975 by Rolf Banz, then a University of Chicago graduate student and now head of DFA's U.K. operations. Banz studied 54 years of NYSE data and concluded that small companies outperformed large ones by 3% annually. . . .

Sinquefield, who coauthored a major study on the historical performance of financial assets with Roger Ibbotson, believes he has the answer. "Small companies are riskier than large companies," he says. The market recognizes it and provides superior returns.

It sure does for Booth and Sinquefield.

SOURCE: Adapted from Ruth Simon, "Sounds Good . . . ," *Forbes*, July 27, 1987, p. 168. Reprinted by permission of Forbes © Forbes, Inc., 1987. All rights reserved.

groups 1 through 5, with the highest P/E stocks in group 1. The stocks in each of the six groups were then arranged into five subgroups or portfolios on the basis of size, with the smallest stocks in each group assigned to portfolio 1. The resulting 30 portfolios were updated annually over a period of 36 years, from 1951 through 1986. JKW drew the following conclusions:

1. Although size and stock price are substantially correlated (stocks of smaller firms have lower prices), each has an independent effect on the return. However, the effects are limited almost entirely to January. On the average, the smaller the size and/or the lower the price, the higher the January return.

2. The *P/E effect* is small in January but significant in the remainder of the year. On the average, the lower the P/E ratio, the higher the return, especially during the last 11 months of the year.

3. On the average, returns are high for firms of all sizes with negative earnings.

Comments on the Size and January Effects

Why have small stocks often provided higher risk-adjusted returns than large stocks, and why has the superior performance of small stocks occurred mostly in January? The answer to the first part of the question is probably to be found in differences in liquidity. While there is definitely a relationship between size and the return, a joint test of the relationship of the return to three variables (beta, size, and the bid-ask spread) found that the bid-ask spread was highly significant and the influence of size was negligible.[21] Smaller stocks have larger bid-ask spreads, and the bid-ask spread dominates size when their relationship to the return is tested jointly. Size seems to be important only because smaller stocks have higher bid-ask spreads, and therefore have lower liquidity.

Why, on the whole, has the size effect been present only in January? This is perhaps best explained in terms of income tax considerations and the behavior of individual investors.[22] Individuals are large buyers of small stocks, and as the end of the year approaches, they sell stocks that are being held at a loss in order to receive a tax benefit. They reinvest in January, and that pushes the prices of small stocks up. This pattern of trading is evidenced by the low buy/sell ratio for individual investors in late December and the high buy/sell ratio early in the year.

Comments on the P/E Effect

The weight of the evidence seems to favor a separate P/E effect, but why should it exist? One possible explanation is that low P/E stocks tend to be stocks about which investors have become too pessimistic. Then when confidence is restored, abnormal returns are realized.

Another possible reason for the apparent superior performance of low P/E stocks is poor performance by the high P/E stocks of fast-growth companies. Investors often become too enthusiastic about the future growth prospects of such firms, and when the growth turns out to be disappointing, prices of the stocks plummet. Finally, there may be no inefficiency at all. What appears to be an inefficiency may be simply the result of underestimating the risk of low P/E stocks relative to that of high P/E stocks in calculating risk-adjusted returns.

The Neglected Firm Effect

As we observed in Chapter 7, studies have found that stocks of "neglected firms" (those followed by few analysts or held by few institutions) have earned abnormal returns.[23] The results might have been different, how-

[21]Yakov Amihud and Haim Mendelson, "The Effects of Beta, Bid-Ask Spread, Residual Risk, and Size on Stock Returns," *The Journal of Finance* 44 (June 1989):479–86.

[22]Jay R. Ritter, "Buying and Selling Behavior of Individual Investors at the Turn of the Year," *The Journal of Finance* 43 (July 1988):701–17.

[23]Avner Arbel and Paul J. Strebel, "Pay Attention to Neglected Firms," *Journal of Portfolio Management* 9 (Winter 1983): 37–42; Avner Arbel, "Generic Stocks: An Old Product in a New Package," *Journal of Portfolio Management* 11 (Summer 1985): 4–12.

ever, if the investigators had incorporated the bid-ask spread and the month of the transaction into their models.

The Weekend Effect

Why, on the average, have stock returns been negative on Monday and generally positive on every other day of the week, as shown in Table 8-1?[24] The pattern has been very consistent. In every five-year period from 1928 through 1982, Monday returns were negative, and, with only a few exceptions, the returns on the other four days were positive. One study found that half of the negative return actually occurs over the weekend; that is, from the close of the market on Friday to the opening on Monday, while the other half occurs during Monday.[25] Surprisingly, most of Monday's negative return occurs during the first 45 minutes of trading. Efficient market theory suggests that investors, seeing this pattern, would do more selling on Friday and more buying on Monday, leading to higher prices and returns on Monday.

Lakonishok and Maberly have observed that this perplexing anomaly may be related to the fact that individuals tend to trade more on Mondays than on other days, and they do more selling on Monday than buying.[26] Since brokerage firms offer mostly buy recommendations (about six buys to one sell), individuals are largely on their own in deciding what to sell and when to sell it. So, on the weekends, when there is more time to think about personal financial matters, they decide what to sell and become heavy sellers on Monday. For anyone who is unwilling to accept such an hypothesis, the *weekend effect* is still a puzzle.

[24]Donald B. Keim and Robert F. Stambaugh, "A Further Investigation of the Weekend Effect in Stock Returns," *The Journal of Finance* 39 (July 1984): 819–35.

[25]Lawrence Harris, "How to Profit from Intradaily Stock Returns," *Journal of Portfolio Management* 12 (Winter 1986): 61–64; and "A Transaction Data Study of Weekly and Intradaily Patterns in Stock Returns," *Journal of Financial Economics* 16 (May 1986): 99–117.

[26]Josef Lakonishok and Edwin Maberly, "The Weekend Effect: Trading Patterns of Individual and Institutional Investors," *The Journal of Finance* 45 (March 1990): 231–43.

|||| **TABLE 8-1**

Percentage Returns of the Standard & Poor's 500 Index by Day of the Week

	Monday	Tuesday	Wednesday	Thursday	Friday	Saturday	All Days
1928–1982	−.18	.05	.09	.05	.06	.15	.02
1953–1982	−.15	.03	.10	.04	.09		.03
1978–1982	−.10	.07	.13	−.02	.10		.04

Note: The all-days return is not an arithmetic average of the daily returns; the days are not weighted equally.

SOURCE: Donald B. Keim and Robert V. Stambaugh, "A Further Investigation of the Weekend Effect in Stock Returns," *The Journal of Finance* 39 (July 1984): 819–35.

STRONG EFFICIENCY

Tests of the strong-form EMH attempt to determine whether insiders or professionals who develop private information from public information (e.g., security analysts and mutual fund managers) have been able to earn abnormal returns. If prices incorporate all inside and private information, abnormal returns cannot be earned by insiders, professional investment managers, and those who follow recommendations of sercurity analysts.

CORPORATE INSIDERS

As noted in Chapter 3, corporate officers and directors and anyone who owns more than 10% of a company's common stock are deemed to be "insiders" and are required to file a report with the Securities and Exchange Commission (SEC) for any month in which they have changed their holdings. This information is published monthly in the SEC *Official Summary of Transactions,* which makes it possible to determine whether insiders have earned abnormal returns.[27]

Clearly, insiders have an advantage in trading the stocks of their own companies, and a number of studies have found that they often make abnormally large returns on such transactions, contrary to the strong form of the EMH. For example, a study by Seyhun showed that during the period 1975–1981 stocks purchased by insiders earned an average positive abnormal return of 4.3% over the following 14 months, whereas stocks sold by insiders earned an average negative abnormal return of 2.2%. What does this imply for investors generally? Under most circumstances, probably not much, because the lag time between insiders transactions and publication of the SEC report is too great.[28] However, as noted later in the section on macro-efficiency, in extraordinary circumstances, like the market crash of October 1987, investors may be able to earn exceptional returns by purchasing stocks the insiders were buying a couple of months ago, as reported in the *Official Summary of Transactions.*

MUTUAL FUND PERFORMANCE

Test of mutual fund performance support strong-form efficiency. Very few funds have earned positive abnormal returns over a long period of time.

In a leading study of 115 funds, Michael Jensen found that mutual funds were unable to achieve better performance than a policy of buying and holding a well-diversified portfolio of common stocks.[29] Net of expenses, and after adjusting for differences in systematic risk, the annual return for the average fund was 1.1 percentage points lower than the

[27]Information about insider purchases and sales is also published in the *Wall Street Journal* and various investment services.

[28]H. Nejat Seyhun, "Insiders Profits, Costs of Trading, and Market Efficiency," *Journal of Financial Economics* 16 (June 1986): 189–212.

[29]Michael C. Jensen, "The Performance of Mutual Funds in the Period 1945–1964," *The Journal of Finance* 23 (May 1968): 389–416.

return for the Standard & Poor's 500 Index. In a more recent study, Lehmann and Modest measured the performance of 130 common stock funds from 1968 through 1982, using a number of methods of measuring abnormal performance.[30] They found that all methods of measurement indicated widespread negative abnormal performance by common stock funds in two of three five-year periods.

VALUE LINE

Every week Value Lines assigns a timeliness rank to each of the 1,700 or so stocks included in the *Value Line Investment Survey;* the ranking is a prediction of the stock's relative performance over the next 12 months. Stocks in rank 1 are expected to perform the best. The number of stocks in each rank are approximately as follows:

Timeliness Rank	Number of Stocks	Percentage of Total
1	100	6%
2	300	18
3	900	52
4	300	18
5	100	6

The rankings are based on five factors, and each week a number of stocks are moved up or down in rank as a result of changes in their scores under these factors. Three of the five factors are based entirely on the firm's earnings; another is based on the relationship between earnings and the stock price; and the fifth is based on changes in the stock price. More specifically, the factors can be described as follows:

1. Change in relative earnings: Relative earnings for the last 12 months are compared to relative earnings for the past 10 years. Relative earnings are the company's earnings per share divided by average earnings per share for all Value Line companies for the same period. Stocks with the greatest improvement in relative earnings receive the highest rank.

2. Earnings momentum: Earnings for the latest quarter are compared to earnings of the same quarter a year earlier. Stocks with the greatest percentage increase receive the highest score. Value Line analysts can modify the earnings momentum factor if they are confident that earnings per share will change markedly in the next quarter.

3. Earnings surprise: Earnings for the latest quarter are compared to Value Line's estimate for the quarter. Stocks with the greatest improvement over the Value Line estimate receive the highest score.

[30]Bruce N. Lehmann and David M. Modest, "Mutual Fund Performance Evaluation: A Comparison of Benchmarks and Benchmark Comparisons," *The Journal of Finance* 42 (June 1987): 233–65.

4. Earnings rank relative to price rank: Relative earnings rank for the latest 12 months is compared to relative price rank for the same period. The higher the earnings rank relative to the price rank, the higher the score. For example, a stock would receive a high score if its earnings were close to the highest they had been relative to the earnings of other Value Line companies for the past 10 years, and if the price of its stock was close to the lowest it had been relative to the other Value Line stocks in the past 10 years.

5. Price momentum: The ratio of the 10-week average relative price to the 52-week average relative price is calculated. The higher the ratio, the higher the score.

Several studies have tried to determine whether Value Line's timeliness rankings are of any value to investors, and the findings have been mixed. However, one thing is clear: Value Line's mutual funds have not performed well. The returns to investors over recent 5-year and 10-year periods, as reported in *Business Week,* were considerably lower than the returns on the Standard & Poor's 500 Index.[31]

	S&P 500 Index	Value Line Common Stock Fund	Value Line Special Situations Fund
Annual return through 1990:			
Five years	13.2%	11.9%	2.8%
Ten years	13.8	10.1	4.1
Risk	Average	High	Very high

David Peterson examined the performance of several hundred stocks just before and after they were first included in the *Value Line Investment Survey* in the years 1969 through 1982.[32] The returns for stocks initially ranked number 1 for timeliness were abnormally high for each day of a three-day period beginning one day before publication of the rankings and ending two days later. As Figure 8-3 shows, the timeliness rankings seem to have had the most impact on stocks ranked 1 although there is some indication that the rankings also affected stocks in ranks 2 and 4.

In any case, the ranking effects were short-lived. None of the five ranks had statistically significant abnormal returns for any 10-day period in the first 150 days following the initial ranking. The positive abnormal returns for stocks in rank 1 on the day before the ranks were published indicate that either information leaked internally or that some of the reports were delivered to subscribers before the scheduled publication date.

[31]*Business Week,* February 18, 1991.

[32]David R. Peterson, "Security Price Reactions to Initial Reviews of Common Stock by the Value Line Investment Survey," *Journal of Financial and Quantitative Analysis* 22 (December 1987): 483–94.

FIGURE 8-3
Cumulative Abnormal Returns Before and After an Initial Value
Line Report

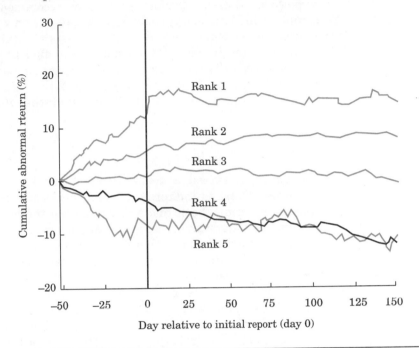

SOURCE: David R. Peterson, "Security Price Reactions to Initial Reviews of Common Stock
by the Value Line Investment Survey," *Journal of Financial and Quantitative Analysis* 22
(December 1987):483-94.

For the 50-day period prior to the publication of the ranks, the returns
were abnormally high for stocks placed in ranks 1 and 2, and abnormally
low for stocks in ranks 4 and 5. Since recent price performance is one of
the factors on which Value Line timeliness rankings are based, it is not
surprising that stocks with rapidly rising prices in the weeks before they
were added to the Value Line service were ranked highly, whereas stocks
with declining prices were placed in ranks 4 and 5.

BROKERS' RECOMMENDATIONS
Do stocks recommended by analysts earn abnormal returns? If so, this
might be evidence against the strong form of the EMH. Elton, Gruber,
and Grossman examined the results of 10,000 recommendations made
over a 33-month period by about 700 analysts in 34 brokerage firms. The
study found that, on the average, broker-recommended stocks outperformed other stocks by a wide margin.[33] The excess returns occurred in

[33]Edwin J. Elton, Martin J. Gruber, and Seth Grossman, "Discrete Expectational Data
and Portfolio Performance," *The Journal of Finance* 41 (July 1986): 699–713.

the month of the recommendation and for two months after, and they were especially large on stocks with improved recommendations. These findings are clearly opposed to the strong form of the efficient market hypothesis. Superior performance of the recommended stocks indicated strong-form inefficiency, whether it resulted from valuable private information developed by the security analysts or from the sales efforts of brokers. If the former, the market was inefficient because it took time before prices rully reflected the analysts' recommendations. If the latter, the market was inefficient because prices of the recommended stocks were bid up on the basis of sales efforts (noise) rather than information.

|||| MACRO-EFFICIENCY

It is generally agreed, at least among academics, that efforts to explain differences in prices and returns among stocks have been fairly successful. Less progress has been made in explaining the behavior of the market as a whole. Large market fluctuations sometimes occur in the absence of any new information affecting fundamental values.

Cutler, Poterba, and Summers took a close look at the 50 largest one-day returns (positive or negative) on the Standard & Poor's Composite Index between 1946 and 1987, along with the *New York Times* account of fundamental factors that affected the prices.[34] The authors were often unable to link major market moves, including the dramatic decline of October 1987, to the release of economic or other information. In the case of several major market moves, the *New York Times* reported that there were no apparent explanations of the market's rise or decline. The authors concluded that using regression analysis, it was difficult to explain as much as half the variance in aggregate stock prices on the basis of publicly available news bearing on fundamental values. They suggested that the difficulty of connecting market moves with new information may result from the fact that price changes are partly the result of investors reexamining existing data.[35]

INSIDERS' TRANSACTIONS DURING THE OCTOBER 1987 CRASH

In the four trading days ending with October 19, 1987, the Dow Jones Industrial Average dropped 30.7%. No one knows why this sharp, sudden decline in market values occurred, but various reasons have been suggested, including a sudden downward revision of expectations for worldwide economic activity, a sudden realization of lower expected returns, and an upward revision of required returns. It has also been suggested that the crash was due not so much to changes in the fundamentals as

---

[34]David M. Cutler, James M. Poterba, and Lawrence H. Summers, "What Moves Market Prices?" *Journal of Portfolio Management* 15 (Spring 1989): 4–12.

[35]Similarly, any delay in investors' reaction to earnings surprises may be, at least in part, due to reexamination of existing information.

to positive feedback investment strategies, possibly abetted by destabilizing speculation.[36]

It is evident that many investors use a *positive feedback strategy,* basing their decisions not on what they think stocks are worth but on what prices have been doing recently. They buy when prices have been going up and sell when prices have been going down. Survey evidence indicates, for example, that most sellers in the wake of the October 1987 crash cited price declines as the reason they sold.[37] Experimental evidence indicates that individuals have a strong tendency to form their expectations about future prices by extrapolating from the latest trend, and they are especially apt to chase the trend after a significant change in the price level.[38]

How does destabilizing rational speculation enter in? For a number of years, it has been widely believed that rational speculators always stabilize prices by purchasing assets when prices fall below fundamental values and selling when prices rise above fundamental values. But rational speculators may not behave this way when they believe that prices are responding to the actions of positive feedback investors. If, for example, prices are moving up, speculators may "jump on the bandwagon" rather than buck the trend. By entering the market as buyers, they hope to stimulate the trend chasers to push prices still farther away from fundamental values. Similar motivation may cause destabilizing speculators to sell when the market has been going down.

Who was buying stocks in October 1987 as prices fell? To a large degree, it was corporate insiders.[39] Insiders were heavy purchasers of stock during the month of the crash, particularly on October 19 and October 20, when prices were lowest. For the month as a whole, insiders purchased an extraordinary 64% more than they sold; and on October 19 and 20, when prices were at or near the low point, insiders purchased more than three times the amount they sold.

Are insiders better judges of fundamental values than other investors? The experience during and after the 1987 crash indicates that they are. A study of insider purchases and sales during 1987 and 1988 found that stocks that were purchased but not sold by insiders during October 1987 (1,074 companies) provided an average return from January 1988 to December 1988 that was 18.6 percentage points higher than the return on stocks of the 246 companies that insiders were selling but not buying. The results indicate that not only did the market fall more than was

[36]J. Bradford De Long, Andrei Shleifer, Lawrence H. Summers, and Robert J. Waldmann, "Positive Feedback Investment Strategies and Destabilizing Rational Speculation," *The Journal of Finance* 45 (June 1990): 379–95.

[37]Robert Shiller, "Portfolio Insurance and Other Investor Fashions as Factors in the 1987 Stock Market Crash," *NBER Macroeconomic Annual 1988,* pp. 287–96.

[38]Paul Andreassen and Stephen Kraus, "Judgmental Prediction by Extrapolation," Mimeograph, Harvard University, 1988.

[39]H. Nejat Seyhun, "Overreaction or Fundamentals: Some Lessons from Insiders' Response to the Market Crash of 1987," *The Journal of Finance* 45 (December 1990): 1363–88.

justified by any changes in the fundamentals, but that insiders were able to see this, and other investors could have profited by buying stocks in December, perhaps even later, that the insiders were buying in October. The market was not macro-efficient during October 1987.

|||| IMPLICATIONS OF EFFICIENCY

In an efficient market, the price charts of technical analysts are worthless because all historic price and volume information is reflected in current prices; and the recommendations of even the best security analysts are worthless to all investors except the first to follow them, because all information (including analysts' recommendations) is very quickly incorporated in prices. However, that does not mean that analysts perform no useful function; without their work, the market could not be efficient.

The only sensible portfolio strategy in an efficient market is a passive one. There is no point in trying to find underpriced stocks, and nothing is to be gained by trying to time the market. Investors should buy and hold diversified portfolios that have the optimal combination of risk and return for their needs. Portfolio adjustments should be made only when the investor needs to change the level of risk.

THE RISK IN MARKET TIMING

Making large moves into and out of stocks on the basis of changes in expectations about the relative returns of stocks and fixed-income securities involves a great deal of risk. Market timers must decide not only when to get out of the market (totally or partially) but when to get back in. A study covering the years 1975 through 1982 demonstrated that the potential decrease in income from completely imperfect timing was nearly twice the potential increase in income from completely perfect timing.[40] Strong uptrends usually last only a short period of time; if the investor is out of the market during much of that time, he or she would be better off staying out of the stock market entirely. Nevertheless, many investors do attempt to time the market, often using a technique called "tactical asset allocation," which is described in the Sidelight box.

|||| SUMMARY

The U.S. stock market is quite efficient, but not perfectly so. Generally, prices are equal to intrinsic, or fundamental, values, and they move up and down in response to new information bearing on values. The conditions required for a high level of efficiency (free flow of information, competition among many rational, profit-seeking investors, and low trans-

[40]Robert H. Jeffrey, "The Folly of Stock Market Timing," *Harvard Business Review* 62 (July/August 1984): 102–10.

||| SIDELIGHT
Market Timing in New Form Gains Adherents

Although many studies have found that shifting funds between stocks and other securities is seldom profitable, a new brand of market timing, called "tactical asset allocation," has become popular among those who rely heavily on computers in making decisions. The process, which is strictly quantitative, compares the expected returns for various securities. When the expected returns become abnormal relative to one another based on past relationships, the fund manager sells the securities that have become relatively overpriced and buys those that have become relatively underpriced.

The process of evaluating the asset mix is a continuous one that may result in putting 100% of a portfolio in one type of security at certain times. Tactical asset allocation has been made available to individual investors through mutual funds. Many market professionals, however, are skeptical about whether the potential gains from such strategies are large enough to outweigh the risks.

SOURCE: Adapted from Barbara Donnelly, "Market Timing in New Form Gains Adherents," *The Wall Street Journal*, July 7, 1988, p. 25. Reprinted by permission of *The Wall Street Journal* © Dow Jones & Company, Inc. (1988). All Rights Reserved Worldwide.

---

actions costs) are generally, but not always, present. Sometimes investors are poorly informed, and sometimes their decisions are based on emotion rather than reason. For example, many investors use a positive feedback strategy, which leads them to buy when prices have been rising and to sell when prices have been going down. This behavior contributes to extreme market fluctuations.

Typically, tests of market efficiency in the weak sense are based on statistical analysis of stock price changes to see if there are any predictable patterns. Tests of semistrong efficiency are usually based on analysis of the performance of portfolios of stocks over a number of periods to see whether abnormal returns are associated with certain events (e.g., announcement of a surprisingly large change in earnings), certain types of stocks (e.g., those with low P/E ratios), or the day of the week or the time of the year. Tests of the strong form look for abnormal performance of stocks acquired or recommended by those who either have inside information or private information developed from public information, including corporate insiders, professional portfolio managers, and security analysts.

Abnormal returns are usually calculated with the market model, which requires an estimate of the relationship between the stock's return and the market return as expressed in alpha (α_I) and beta (β_{im}). An abnormal return is the difference between the actual return and an estimate of the expected return, given the market return and estimates of alpha and beta. Since the calculations are based on estimates, it is always possible that returns that appear to be abnormal are merely the result of poor estimates. It is important to remember that even if an abnormality has existed in some past period, it may not occur under similar circumstances in the future.

Efficient market tests have found the following, partially unexplained contradictions to the semistrong EMH: (1) prices sometimes respond slowly to earnings surprises; (2) small-stock returns are generally higher in January than in any other month; (3) the risk-adjusted returns on stocks with low P/E ratios, when averaged over long periods of time, have been higher than the returns on stocks with high P/E ratios; and (4) average stock returns are negative on Monday and positive on the other four days of the week.

Studies have found significant strong-form inefficiencies. Insiders have shown an ability to earn abnormal returns; and there is some evidence that, on average, analysts have been able to identify superior stocks.

The stock market may be more efficient in a micro sense (that is, in pricing one stock relative to another) than in a macro sense. Psychological factors seem to carry the market to extremes. For example, many investors followed a positive feedback strategy and sold stocks during the crash of October 1987 simply because the market had been going down.

Often, investors try to time the market, selling when they think stocks are too high and buying back in at a later date. To be a successful market timer over a long period of time requires good forecasts of market turning points. Many experienced market observers doubt that anyone is capable of making such forecasts with reasonable consistency.

|||| QUESTIONS

1. Explain why, according to the EMH, changes in stock prices are random.

2. Describe the three forms of the EMH and explain their implications for technical analysis, fundamental analysis, and portfolio management.

3. Explain why positive feedback strategies and investor overreaction may cause price changes to be correlated. Compare the kinds of correlations they are expected to produce.

4. Explain how the market model is used in testing the EMH.

5. Why are tests of the semistrong and strong forms of the EMH joint tests of the EMH and the pricing model?

6. Why would you expect that a stock split, by itself, would not have any impact on the market value of a firm's stock?

7. Compare the stock return effects of a switch from accelerated depreciation to straight-line for reporting to shareholders with a switch

from FIFO to LIFO for inventory accounting. Why are they different? What does this say about market efficiency?

8. Explain how the size effect and the bid-ask spread effect are related. Why do you think the bid-ask spread effect dominates the size effect?

9. What is an abnormal return? What variables must be estimated before calculating abnormal returns? Why are abnormal returns called residuals?

10. Do the results achieved with the Value Line timeliness rankings tend to disprove the strong form of the EMH? Why or why not?

11. Small stocks tend to perform better in January than in any other month. Can you suggest one reason for this?

12. Stock returns are generally negative on Monday. Can you suggest one reason for this?

13. Explain how destabilizing speculation is related to positive feedback investing.

14. Some empirical studies indicate the presence of a P/E effect. Comment on possible reasons for such an effect. For what reason, or reasons, might you be skeptical about it?

15. What are the necessary conditions for an efficient market? Comment on the extent to which those conditions exist in the United States. Do you think the securities markets are becoming more or less efficient? Why?

16. Explain two methods of estimating whether reported earnings are a surprise.

17. Explain why abnormal profits from brokers' recommendations tend to disprove the EMH whether the recommendations are based on superior analysis or not.

18. Explain why it is difficult to reconcile the severe market decline of October 1987 with the EMH, even assuming that program trading had little to do with it. How would you try to explain that the decline was simply an efficient market operating efficiently?

19. Why is it probably more difficult to earn abnormal profits now by following what the insiders have been doing, as indicated in the monthly SEC report, than it was during the first several years the report was issued?

20. What is a passive portfolio strategy? How would you try to convince someone that a passive strategy is the best strategy?

21. Small stocks performed very poorly during much of the 1980s. Can you draw any general inference from that relating to the selection of an active investment strategy?

22. What was learned about the strong-form EMH from the experiences of insiders during and after the crash of October 1987?

|||| # PROBLEMS

1. Calculate stock i's abnormal return for month 1, given the following:

R_{i1}	3.2%
α_i	0.3%
β_i	.90
R_{m1}	2.0%

    Calculate the cumulative abnormal return for month 2 if the abnormal return for month 2 is -4.2%.

2. See if you can find a one-day market rise or decline of more than 2% during the past two years that is not easily explained in terms of that day's news.

3. Calculate the aggregate market capitalization of Ford and General Motors at the present time.

4. Calculate the percentage change in the Standard & Poor's 500 Index from Thursday's close to Friday's close and from Friday's close to Monday's close for each of the past four weeks. Do the results tell you anything?

5. Calculate the percentage change in the Standard & Poor's 500 Index and the percentage change in the NASDAQ Composite Index for last January. Do these figures tell you anything about the January effect and the small-firm effect? Explain why or why not.

6. A regression of IBM monthly stock returns against the returns for the Standard & Poor's 500 Index produced the following estimated equation:

    $$R_{IBM} = -.25\% + .90R_{S\&P}$$

    If the market return for the latest month was 2.5% and the IBM return was 4.8%, what was the IBM abnormal return?

7. Using data reported in the *Federal Reserve Bulletin,* calculate the spreads between the yields on Aaa, Aa, A, and Baa corporate bonds for a recent month. What do these spreads have to do with the efficiency of the market?

8. Find two stocks that have split during the past year and compare the price of the stock the day after the split was announced with the price the day before it was announced. (Be sure to adjust the presplit price for the split.) Some of the percentage change in the price can be attributed to the market effect, that is, to the percentage change in the market during the same day. Remove the market effect from the percentage change in the stock's price. Was an unexpected increase in the aggregate dividend announced at the same time as the split? If so, do you think this had anything to do with the change in the price of the stock? What did you learn?

9. Find two stocks that were being purchased, but not sold, heavily by insiders a year ago. Compare their performance with the market's

performance 1 month, 2 months, 3 months, 6 months and 12 months after the purchases were made. Be sure to make an adjustment based on an estimate of beta. Can you draw any conclusions?

||| SELECTED REFERENCES

Amihud Yakov, and Haim Mendelson. "The Effects of Beta, Bid-Ask Spread, Residual Risk, and Size on Stock Returns." *The Journal of Finance* 44 (June 1989): 479–86.

Arbel, Avner. "Generic Stocks: An Old Product in a New Package." *Journal of Portfolio Management* 11 (Summer 1985): 4–12.

Arbel, Avner, and Paul J. Strebel. "Pay Attention to Neglected Firms." *Journal of Portfolio Management* 9 (Winter 1983): 37–42.

Archibald, T. Ross. "Stock Market Reactions to the Depreciation Switch-Back." *Accounting Review* 47 (January 1972): 22–30.

Ball, R. "Changes in Accounting Techniques and Stock Prices." *Journal of Accounting Research Supplement* 10 (1972): 1–38.

Bar-Yosef, Sasson, and Lawrence D. Brown. "A Reexamination of Stock Splits Using Moving Betas" *The Journal of Finance* 32 (September 1977): 1069–80.

Benesh, Gary A., and Pamela P. Peterson. "On the Relation between Earnings Changes, Analysts' Forecasts and Stock Price Fluctuations." *Financial Analysts Journal* 42 (November/December 1986): 29–39, 55.

Biddle, Gary C., and Frederick W. Lindahl. "Stock Price Reactions to LIFO Adoptions: The Association between Excess Returns and LIFO Tax Savings." *Journal of Accounting Research* 20 (Autumn 1982): 551–87.

Black, Fischer. "Noise." *The Journal of Finance* 41 (July 1986): 529–43.

Brown, Philip, and Ray Ball. "An Empirical Evaluation of Accounting Income Numbers." *Journal of Accounting Research* 6 (Autumn 1968): 159–78.

Cutler, David M., James M. Poterba, and Lawrence H. Summers. "What Moves Stock Prices?" *Journal of Portfolio Management* 15 (Spring 1989): 4–12.

De Bondt, Werner F. M., and Richard H. Thaler. "Does the Stock Market Overreact?" *The Journal of Finance* 40 (July 1985): 793–805.

_____ "Further Evidence on Investor Overreaction and Stock Market Seasonality." *The Journal of Finance* 42 (July 1987): 557–81.

De Long, J. Bradford, Andrei Shleifer, Lawrence H. Summers, and Robert J. Waldmann. "Positive Feedback Investment Strategies and Destabilizing Rational Speculation." *The Journal of Finance* 45 (June 1990): 379–95.

Elton, Edwin J., Martin J. Gruber, and Seth Grossman. "Discrete Expectational Data and Portfolio Performance." *The Journal of Finance* 41 (July 1986): 669–713.

Fama, Eugene F., and M. E. Blume. "Filter Rules and Stock Market Trading." *Journal of Business* 39 (January 1966): 226–41.

Fama, Eugene F. "The Behavior of Stock Market Prices." *Journal of Business* 38 (January 1965): 34–105.

Fama, Eugene F., Lawrence Fisher, Michael C. Jensen, and Richard Roll. "The Adjustment of Stock Prices to New Information." *International Economic Review* 10 (February 1969): 1–21.

Foster, George, Chris Olsen, and Terry Shevlin. "Earnings Releases, Anomalies,and the Behavior of Security Returns." *The Accounting Review* 59 (October 1984): 574–603.

Harris, Lawrence. "How to Profit from Intradaily Stock Returns." *Journal of Portfolio Management* 12 (Winter 1986): 61–64.

——— "A Transaction Data Study of Weekly and Intradaily Patterns in Stock Returns." *Journal of Financial Economics* 16 (May 1986): 99–117.

Hawkins, Eugene H., Stanley C. Chamberlin, and Wayne E. Daniel. "Earnings Expectations and Security Prices." *Financial Analysts Journal* 40 (September/October 1984): 24–38.

Jaffe, Jeffrey F., Donald B. Keim, and Randolph Westerfield. "Earnings Yields, Market Values, and Stock Returns." *The Journal of Finance* 44 (March 1989): 135–48.

Jeffrey, Robert H. "The Folly of Stock Market Timing." *Harvard Business Review* 62 (July/August 1984): 102–10.

Jensen, Michael C. "The Performance of Mutual Funds in the Period 1945–1964." *The Journal of Finance* 23 (May 1968): 389–416.

Jones, Charles P., and O. Maurice Joy. "Should We Believe the Tests of Market Efficiency?" *Journal of Portfolio Management* 12 (Summer 1986): 49–54.

Jones, Charles P., Richard J. Rendleman, Jr., and Henry A. Latane. "Stock Returns and SUEs during the 1970s." *Journal of Portfolio Management* 10 (Winter 1984): 18–22.

Kahneman, D., and A. Tversky. "Intuitive Prediction Biases and Corrective Procedures." In D. Kahneman, P. Slovic, and A. Tversky, eds., *Judgment under Uncertainty: Heuristics and Biases*. (London: Cambridge University Press, 1982.)

Kaplan, Robert S., and Richard Roll. "Investor Evaluation of Accounting Information: Some Empirical Evidence." *Journal of Business* 45 (April 1972): 225–57.

Keim, Donald B. "The CAPM and Equity Return Regularities." *Financial Analysts Journal* 42 (May/June 1986): 19–33.

Keim, Donald B., and Robert V. Stambaugh. "A Further Investigation of the Weekend Effect in Stock Returns." *The Journal of Finance* 39 (July 1984): 819–35.

Lakonishok, Josef, and Edwin Maberly. "The Weekend Effect: Trading Patterns of Individual and Institutional Investors." *The Journal of Finance* 45 (March 1990): 231–43.

Lehmann, Bruce N., and David M. Modest. "Mutual Fund Performance Evaluation: A Comparison of Benchmarks and Benchmark Comparisons." *The Journal of Finance* 42 (June 1987): 233–65.

Modigliani, Franco, and Richard Cohn. "Inflation, Rational Valuation, and the Market." *Financial Analysts Journal* 35 (March/April 1979): 24–44.

Oppenheimer, Henry R., and Gary G. Schlarbaum. "Investing with Ben Graham: An Ex Ante Test of the Efficient Market Hypothesis." *Journal of Financial and Quantitative Analysis* 16 (September 1981): 341–60.

PART **3** ANALYSIS AND SELECTION OF COMMON STOCKS

9 COMMON STOCK VALUATION MODELS

In 1990 the price of Sears' common stock dropped 33%, while the price of Procter & Gamble's stock rose 23%. In early 1991, the prices, price/earnings ratios, and dividend yields of the two stocks were as follows:

	Sears	Procter & Gamble
Price	$33	$83
P/E ratio	13	17
Dividend yield	6.1%	2.4%

Why was the market willing to pay so much more for a dollar of Procter & Gamble's earnings and dividends than for a dollar of the earnings and dividends of Sears? The question is easy to answer in general terms. Sears' earnings had been falling while Procter & Gamble's were rising; Sears' earnings were highly volatile, while Procter & Gamble's were stable and, in recent years, were growing. Sears' long-term growth prospects looked poor, while Procter & Gamble's looked good; shareholders of Procter & Gamble could look forward with some confidence to higher earnings and dividends in the future; shareholders of Sears had reason to be less confident about its future earnings and dividends.[1]

While it is easy to make general comments about the relative values of the stocks of Sears and Procter & Gamble as of early 1991, it is very difficult to explain why the price of Sears was $33 and the price of Procter & Gamble was $83. In fact, it is impossible to determine how investors actually arrived at those figures, but it is possible to determine how they could have done so; and that's what this chapter is all about—how to value common stocks.

FUNDAMENTAL VERSUS TECHNICAL APPROACHES

Methods used in stock valuation depend in part on whether the interested party is a trader looking for short-term gains or an investor looking for income over a longer period of time. Traders are inclined to use technical

---

[1]Nevertheless, it was apparent that buyers of Sears stock were expecting some growth in earnings and dividends or they would not have been willing to acquire and hold it at a dividend yield of 6.1% when U.S. government bonds were yielding 8%.

methods that involve analysis of past price changes and the volume of trading.[2] Traders try to forecast what the price will be in a few minutes, hours, days, or weeks; and they believe that price movements over short periods can be predicted on the basis of recent price and volume patterns.

Longer-term investors usually focus on the fundamental determinants of value, such as earnings, dividends, and risk. Under certain circumstances, they may also consider *book values,* estimated *liquidation values,* and *replacement costs,* particularly if any of those values or costs are higher, or thought to be higher, than the current price of the stock. One of the intriguing things about common stock valuation is the virtual impossibility of determining what models or numbers have been used in arriving at a price.

FUNDAMENTAL VALUATION METHODS

Generally, bond values are estimated in only one way—by calculating the present, or discounted, value of the expected interest payments and maturity value. Common stock values, for various reasons, are estimated in a number of ways, including the following, which are discussed in this chapter:

1. Book values
2. Liquidation and replacement values
3. Discounted cash flow (DCF) models
4. Price/earnings ratio (P/E) models

The discounted cash flow and price/earnings ratio models will be used to show how investors could have arrived at a price of $83 for the stock of Procter & Gamble in early 1991.

BOOK VALUES

The one regularly published measure of a stock's value, other than the market price, is the book value. It has the appearance of authenticity and soundness because it is based on figures (total common equity and the number of shares issued and outstanding) reported in audited financial statements. Nevertheless, despite its apparent soundness, the book value of a stock often has little influence on its market price. For example, in early 1991 Procter & Gamble's stock was priced at close to four times the company's reported common equity per share.

Book values are based largely on historical costs and depend heavily upon when the assets were acquired and the methods used in accounting for fixed assets and inventories, in particular. Book values reveal nothing

[2]Technical methods are the subject of Chapter 12.

Many successful investors say that the best way to find undervalued stocks and possible takeover candidates is to look for stocks that are selling below their book value. Charles Allmon, manager of Growth Stock Outlook Trust, says that the best single criterion for selecting stocks is the ratio of price to book value. The focus is usually on tangible book value, which excludes such things as patents and goodwill.

While buying below book value has often been a successful strategy, the results can be very poor. Some stocks selling below book are simply out of favor, but others are stocks of companies in real trouble. Of the 227 stocks on the New York Stock Exchange recently selling below book, many were priced below $5 a share, and their prospects were poor.

The book value approach worked out very well for steel company stocks in 1986. Bethlehem Steel and Inland Steel seemed to have a dismal future, and their stock prices were way below book value. Analysts couldn't foresee how they could ever become competitive again. But two things happened: their costs were lowered, and the price of imported steel rose due to a decline in the value of the dollar. These stocks now sell for more than book value.

SOURCE: Adapted from Earl C. Gottschalk, Jr., "Picking Stocks by the Book is a Standby Some Swear by," *The Wall Street Journal*, November 3, 1988, p. C1. Reprinted by permission of *The Wall Street Journal*, © Dow Jones & Company, Inc. (1988). All Rights Reserved Worldwide.

||| **TABLE 9-1**

Market Value versus Book Value: Stocks in Four Industries

	Price 7/24/90	Book Value 12/31/89	Price/ Book Value
Commercial banking			
Chase Manhattan	$ 19.75	$36.40	.54
Citicorp	20.63	25.36	.81
First Chicago	26.75	34.82	.77
Morgan, J. P.	36.75	21.78	1.69
Wells Fargo	73.13	48.08	1.52
Drugs			
American Home Products	51.25	9.67	5.30
Bristol-Myers	62.88	6.30	9.98
Lilly (Eli)	83.88	13.48	6.22
Merck	88.50	8.90	9.94
Upjohn	40.75	9.44	4.32
Electrical equipment			
Cooper Industries	44.25	18.21	2.43
Emerson Electric	39.63	13.79	2.87
General Electric	72.88	23.09	3.16
Honeywell	102.88	47.96	2.15
Westinghouse	37.25	15.10	2.47
Paper and forest products			
Boise Cascade	32.13	33.52	.96
Champion International	28.63	41.83	.68
Georgia Pacific	46.75	31.35	1.49
Stone	15.50	22.50	.69
Weyerhaeuser	24.75	18.55	1.33

about the ability of a firm to generate income, and, as a rule, they are a poor indicator of liquidation or replacement values. Nevertheless, as explained in the Sidelight box, it is not unusual for investors to be attracted by stocks that are selling for less than book value.

As Table 9-1 shows, ratios of market value to book value vary widely from company to company, and they are influenced to some degree by the nature of the industry. For a number of years, a large majority of stocks have been priced considerably above book value. Often, this simply indicates that the assets have greater value as a going concern than their depreciated cost. Stated differently, the asset values on a company's balance sheet usually do not include certain important intangibles, such as brand names, customer relationships, and the value of the organization itself. Also, book values for most companies do not reflect amounts by which assets have appreciated in value since they were acquired. Some stocks sell for less than book value, as in the case of three banks in Table 9-1, indicating that investors believe the enterprise is worth less as a going concern than its book net worth.

|||| LIQUIDATION VALUES AND REPLACEMENT COSTS

A company's liquidation value is the amount for which the assets can be sold, either piecemeal or as smaller operating units, less the liabilities and costs of liquidation. The liquidation value of an entire company is often less than its replacement cost, which is the cost of replacing all assets, including the intangibles. When the liquidation value appears to be greater than the market value of the stock, the company may be attractive to parties who are interested in breaking it up and selling the pieces. When the replacement cost appears to be greater than the market value of the stock, the company may be attractive to acquisition-minded corporations as a relatively inexpensive vehicle for expanding their operations.

|||| PRESENT VALUE MODELS

In theory, the best way to value any income-producing asset, including stocks and bonds, is by *discounting* the expected cash flows to their present value. The theory underlying present value models was developed by Irving Fisher, an eminent economist, who wrote in 1906:

> The present worth of any article is what buyers are willing to give for it and sellers are ready to take for it. In order that each man may logically decide what he is willing to give or take, he must have: (1) some idea of the value of the future benefits which that article will yield, and (2) some idea of the rate of interest by which

these future values may be translated into present values by discounting.[3]

Some 30 years later, another distinguished economist, John Burr Williams, developed the first models for calculating the present values of stocks and bonds. In *The Theory of Investment Value*, Williams said:

> Let us define the investment value of a stock as the present worth of all the dividends to be paid upon it. Likewise let us define the investment value of a bond as the present worth of its future coupons and principal.[4]

BASIC COMMON STOCK MODEL

Equation 9-1 is Williams's basic model for valuing common stocks:

$$P_0 = \frac{D_1}{1 + k} + \frac{D_2}{(1 + k)^2} + \frac{D_3}{(1 + k)^3} + \cdots + \frac{D_n}{(1 + k)^n} \qquad (9\text{-}1)$$

or, more simply,

$$P_0 = \sum_{t=1}^{\infty} \frac{D_t}{(1 + k)^t} \qquad (9\text{-}2)$$

where

P_0 = value of stock at present time

D_1 = dividend in year 1

D_t = dividend in year t

k = required rate of return (the discount rate)

PRESENT VALUES AND EXPECTED RETURNS

With present value models (also called dividend discount models or DDMs when adapted to common stocks), the attractiveness of a stock can be assessed either by comparing the present value to the price or, given the price, by comparing the expected return to the required return. This process is illustrated in Figure 9-1, which plots the present values of two securities at discount rates ranging from 0% to 25%. Each security has total expected cash income of $100. It is expected that the income from security A will be received in five successive year-end payments of $20, and the income from B will be received in 50 year-end payments of $2. The market price of A is $84, and the price of B is $16.

The present values, or estimated *equilibrium prices,* of the two investments (based upon required returns of 8% for A and 10% for B) are $80 for A and $20 for B. Security A, priced at $84, appears to be selling

---

[3]Irving Fisher, "The Theory of Interest," in *Reprints of Economics Classics* (New York: Augustus M. Kelley, 1965).

[4]John Burr Williams, *The Theory of Investment Value* (Cambridge: Harvard University Press, 1938).

|||| **FIGURE 9-1**
Present Value, Price, and Expected Return: Securities A and B

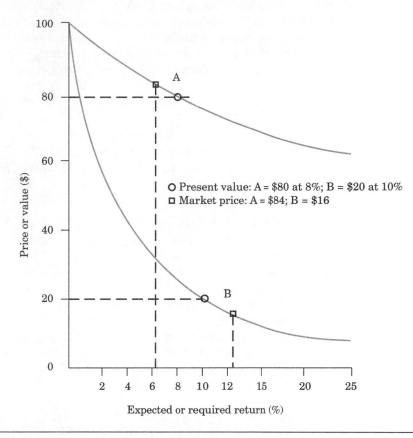

○ Present value: A = $80 at 8%; B = $20 at 10%
□ Market price: A = $84; B = $16

NOTE: Security A is expected to provide 5 year-end payments of $20. Security B is expected to provide 50 year-end payments of $2.

for $4 more than its equilibrium price of $80, and security B, priced at $16, appears to be selling for $4 less than its equilibrium price of $20. If the market is efficient, however, the prices and equilibrium values must be equal, and the differences found here simply indicate that errors were made in estimating the equilibrium prices.

The expected returns of 6.1% for A and 12.5% for B are at the current market prices of $84 and $16, respectively. The relationship between the expected and required returns and the relationship between the present values and market prices lead to the same conclusion: A's estimated present value of $80 is below its price of $84, and its expected return of 6.1% is less than the required return of 8%. B's estimated present value of $20 is greater than its price of $16, and its expected return of 12.5% is greater than the required return of 10%. Thus, B is superior to A under either criterion.

ZERO-GROWTH MODEL

Perpetual bonds, which are a rarity, and many preferred stocks promise the owner equal payments on a monthly, quarterly, semiannual, or annual basis forever. The present values of such assets are simply the expected annual cash inflow multiplied by $1/k$ (the reciprocal of the required rate of return), which is the present value interest factor for a perpetual stream of equal payments. Thus, the *zero-growth model* is

$$P_0 = C \times \frac{1}{k} = \frac{C}{k} \tag{9-3}$$

For example, if the expected annual dividend for an unlimited life preferred stock is $6 and the required return is 12%, the present value is $6/.12, or $50. At a price of $50, the annual income of $6 provides a return of 12% (6/50).

CONSTANT-GROWTH MODEL

If there is no strong reason to expect that a company's earnings will grow either faster or more slowly than the average for other firms, it may be reasonable to assume that its earnings and dividends will grow at a constant rate. This is an attractive assumption because it eliminates the need to forecast earnings and dividends year by year far into the future. When constant growth is assumed, the present value model becomes simple and very useful, especially in evaluating the level of the market as a whole and in studying the relations between the variables that determine stock prices under present value theory. In one form, the *constant-growth model* is expressed as follows:

$$P_0 = \sum_{t=1}^{\infty} \frac{D_0(1 + g)^t}{(1 + k)^t} \tag{9-4}$$

where

D_0 = dividend for the past 12 months

g = expected constant perpetual dividend growth rate

k = required rate of return

Equation 9-4 reduces to

$$P_0 = \frac{D_1}{k - g} \tag{9-5}$$

In general,

$$P_t = \frac{D_{t+1}}{k - g} \tag{9-6}$$

The value of a stock varies directly with the amount of the dividend and the expected dividend growth rate and inversely with the required rate of return. Other things being the same, if interest rates decline, or if investors perceive a decrease in a stock's systematic risk or become less concerned about risk (any one of which would cause a decrease in k), or if they become more optimistic about g (the expected future dividend growth rate), the price of the stock will rise. Under opposite conditions, the price will decline.

Estimating g

Realistic estimates of g and k are essential in evaluating stocks with present value models. This section will explain three methods of estimating g, the expected perpetual growth rate of earnings and dividends. Under the first method, g is the product of return on equity and the percentage of the profits retained in the business. The second method arrives at an estimate of g by assuming that it will be a constant percentage of the predicted constant nominal growth rate of the economy. The third is based on the idea that the expected total return is the sum of the dividend yield and the expected growth rate.

The more profitable the firm in terms of return on common equity *(r)* and the greater the percentage of the earnings retained in the business *(b)*, the higher the earnings growth rate, as shown in Equation 9-7:[5]

$$g = b \times r \qquad (9\text{-}7)$$

At any given level of earnings retention, the higher the return on equity, the faster the dividend growth rate, and at any given level of return on equity, the greater the percentage of earnings retained in the business, the faster the dividend growth rate.

Assume, for example, that a company's common shareholders' equity was $1,000 at the beginning of the year and its income, after payment of preferred dividends, was $160. If the earnings *retention ratio (b)* was 40% (dividend payout 60%), retained earnings would increase by $64 $(.40 \times 160)$, bringing the common equity to $1,064 at year-end. That would make r, the return on average equity, $\dfrac{160}{\dfrac{(1,000 + 1,064)}{2}}$ or 15.5%.

If the company can do this consistently, its earnings growth rate will be $b \times r = 40\% \times 15.5\%$, or 6.2%. An increase in either b or r, with the other remaining unchanged, would increase the growth rate.

Equation 9-7 assumes that the company's earnings on new investments and existing assets are such that r is constant. Table 9-2 illustrates how assets, earnings, and dividends will all grow at a constant rate equal to $b \times r$ if the return on equity and earnings *retention ratio* are constant. It also illustrates how a relatively small change in r can cause a large change in the growth rate.

When the expected long-term growth rate *(g)* is estimated as a percentage of the expected nominal growth rate of the economy, as measured by GNP, it is necessary to estimate the expected real growth rate of GNP

[5]Return on common equity is calculated in various ways. Typically, it is net income (minus preferred dividends, if any) divided by an average of the common shareholders' equity at the beginning and end of the year.

|||| **TABLE 9-2**
Effect of a Small Change in r on the Earnings Growth Rate

	Return on Equity Constant at 15%		Return on Equity Declines to 14.5%	
	Year 1	Year 2	Year 1	Year 2
Balance at first of year:				
Assets	$100.00	$106.00	$100.00	$106.00
Liabilities (40%)	40.00	42.40	40.00	42.40
Shareholders' equity	60.00	63.60	60.00	63.60
Earnings and dividends:				
Earnings (r = 15% or 14.5%)	9.00	9.54	9.00	9.22
Dividends (60%)	5.40	5.72	5.40	5.53
Increase in retained earnings (40% of earnings)	3.60	3.82	3.60	3.69
Calculation of assets at beginning of year 2:				
Balance at beginning of year 1		$100.00		$100.00
Increase (100 × b × r, or 100 × .40 × .15)		6.00		6.00
Total		$106.00		$106.00
Percentage increases:				
From beginning of year 1 to beginning of year 2:				
Assets				
[(106 − 100)/100]		6.0%		6.0%
Shareholders' equity				
[(42.40 − 40.00)/40.00]		6.0%		6.0%
From year 1 to year 2:				
Earnings (and dividends)				
[(9.54 − 9.00)/9.00]		6.0%		
[(9.22 − 9.00)/9.00]				2.4%

Assumptions and calculations:
1. The firm maintains a constant liability/asset ratio; assets, liabilities, and equity grow at the same rate.
2. When r is 15% and b is 40%, the growth rate from year 1 to year 2 is 6%.
3. Return on equity (r) is calculated on beginning equity.

and the expected rate of inflation. If, for example, the expected growth rate of real GNP is 2.5%, and the expected inflation rate is 3.5%, the expected nominal growth rate of GNP will be close to 6%.[6] Then, if a company's sales are expected to grow at the same rate as the economy, and if its profit margin is expected to remain constant, the expected earnings growth rate will be equal to that of nominal GNP, or 6% as well. And, if the *dividend payout ratio* is expected to remain constant, the expected dividend growth rate will also be 6%.

A third way to estimate g is with Equation 9-8, which is derived from Equation 9-5.

$$g = k - \frac{D_1}{P_0} \tag{9-8}$$

[6] With a real growth rate of 2.5% and an inflation rate of 3.5%, the actual nominal growth rate is (1.025 × 1.035) − 1 = 6.1%.

This approach requires an estimate of the expected (or required) return *(k)*, which is discussed in the next section.

Estimating *k*

All present value models require estimation of the required return, or discount rate. In an efficient market (where prices are always in equilibrium), the required return is equal to the expected return. If the price of a stock or other security becomes momentarily too high (causing the expected return to drop below the required return), it will fall until the expected return rises to the level of the required return; and if the price becomes too low (causing the expected return to rise above the required return), it will be bid up until the expected return declines back to the level of the required return. Thus, it is fair to assume that the required return is usually very close to the expected return in a reasonably efficient market.

In Chapter 1 we expressed the expected return as the risk-free rate plus a premium for risk:

$$E(R_{it}) = R_{ft} + RP_{it}$$

The capital asset pricing model specifies that RP_{it} (the risk premium for a security) is the product of the market risk premium ($R_{mt} - R_f$) and the security's beta (β_i), as stated in Equation 6-25:

$$E(R_{it}) = R_f + \beta_i[E(R_{mt}) - R_f]$$

Market Risk Premium

Estimates of the expected return [$E(R_{it})$] are based upon estimates of the risk-free rate, the stock's beta coefficient, and the market risk premium, which is the expected return for the market as a whole (usually represented by the expected return for the Standard & Poor's 500 Index) minus the risk-free rate. The risk-free rate, often estimated as the 30-day Treasury bill rate, depends on the expected real rate of interest and the expected rate of inflation. Forecasts of Treasury bill rates are strongly influenced by expectations about Federal Reserve monetary policy. The historical real rate can be approximated by deducting the actual rate of inflation from the 30-day Treasury bill rate. For the years 1926 through 1990, the average real rate was close to 0.6% (3.7% − 3.1%). Real rates varied greatly from year to year, ranging from a low of −11.5% in 1946 to a high of 6.4% in 1982.

The expected market (or equity) risk premium is the expected compensation for assuming systematic risk. The *expected* premium is always positive (investors always expect higher returns on stocks than on Treasury bills), but the actual premium is often negative. Since 1950, it has ranged from a low of −34% in 1974 to a high of 42% in 1958. Even over long holding periods, the spread between the market return and the risk-free rate varies appreciably, as shown on the next page:

	R_m	R_f	$R_m - R_f$
65 years (1926–1990)	10.3%	3.6%	6.7%
40 years (1951–1990)	11.6	5.4	6.2
20 years (1971–1990)	11.2	7.6	3.6
10 years (1981–1990)	13.9	8.5	5.4

Given this history, it is assumed here that in early 1991 investors were expecting a risk premium of about 5% for investing in common stocks. With the 30-day Treasury bill rate at 5.8% in early 1991, the required market return is estimated at about 10.8% (5.8 + 5.0).

Valuation of Procter & Gamble Stock

If it is reasonable to assume that Procter & Gamble's earning and dividends will grow at a more or less constant rate indefinitely into the future, the constant-growth model can be used to value its stock.[7] The following are initial estimates for the variables of Equation 9-5, the constant-growth model.

$$
\begin{aligned}
D_{1991} &= \text{4 times 1st quarter's dividend} \\
&= 4 \times \$.495 \\
&= \mathbf{\$1.98} \\
R_f &= 5.8\% \\
\beta_{P\&G} &= 1.00 \text{ (per Value Line)} \\
R_m - R_f &= 5.0\% \text{ (as estimated above)} \\
\beta_{P\&G}\,(R_m - R_f) &= 1.0(5.0) = 5.0\% \\
k_{P\&G} &= 5.0\% + 5.8\% \\
&= \mathbf{10.8\%} \\
g &= b \times r \\
&= .49 \times 16.0\% \text{ (based on 5-year} \\
&\quad \text{averages of Value Line figures)} \\
&= \mathbf{7.8\%}
\end{aligned}
$$

As shown below, the price of Procter & Gamble's stock in early 1991 would have been around $66, rather than $83, if those who were buying and selling it had used the constant-growth model and the above estimates of $1.98 for the 1991 dividend, 10.8% for k, and 7.8% for g in arriving at its worth:

$$
\begin{aligned}
P_0 &= \frac{\$1.98}{.108 - .078} \\
&= \$66
\end{aligned}
$$

[7]All estimates for Procter & Gamble in this chapter are made mechanically rather than on the basis of careful analysis of the prospects for the company's products and operations. The objective here is to show how various models could be used to value the company's stock, given the necessary estimates.

Assuming no change in the expected 1991 dividend of $1.98, the estimated value of Procter & Gamble's stock can be raised to $83 from $66 only by decreasing the spread between k and g. It does not take a large reduction in the spread (in absolute terms) to produce a large increase in the estimated value of the stock. For example, if k is reduced to 9.8% or g is increased to 8.8% (reducing the spread from 3% to 2%), the estimated stock value becomes $1.98/.02, or $99.

In this situation, it is probably more reasonable to assume that investors expected a return lower than 10.8% than to assume they expected Procter & Gamble's perpetual dividend growth rate to be higher than 7.8%. One would not expect a firm in Procter & Gamble's lines of business (principally soap, personal care products, and food and beverages) to grow faster than the economy over a long period of time, although it may for the next several years as it continues to expand rapidly in foreign markets. Based on the information available in early 1991, an expected nominal growth rate of 7.8% (assuming a GNP real growth of rate of 3%) would seem to be plenty high.

The required return at which the price would be $83 (rounded) instead of $66, given the expected dividend of $1.98 and the expected growth rate of 7.8%, is 10.20% (rather than 10.8%), calculated with Equation 9-9, a rearranged version of Equation 9-5:[8]

$$k = \frac{D_1}{P_0} + g \qquad (9\text{-}9)$$

$$k = \frac{\$1.98}{\$83} + .078$$

$$= .024 + .078$$

$$= .102, \text{ or } 10.2\%$$

With a required return of 10.2%, the estimated value becomes $82.50, calculated as follows:

$$P_0 = \frac{\$1.98}{.102 - .078}$$

$$= \frac{\$1.98}{.024}$$

$$= \$82.50$$

Analysis of Historical Market Returns

Equations 9-5 and 9-9 assume that the dividend and price grow at the same rate (g), thus maintaining a constant *dividend yield (D/P)*. Equation 9-9 is especially useful in analyzing historical returns for the market as a whole. When used in this way, g is defined not as the expected constant growth rate of earnings, dividends, and the stock price, but

---

[8]Since Procter & Gamble's estimated beta is 1.0, the required market return is also 10.2%.

||| **TABLE 9-3**
Annual Returns for the Standard & Poor's 500 Index, 1981–1990

Year	Total Return	Capital Appreciation	Dividend Yield	Reinvestment Income
1990	−3.2%	−6.6%	3.4%	0.0%
1989	31.5	27.2	3.9	0.4
1988	16.8	12.4	4.2	0.2
1987	5.2	2.0	3.6	−0.4
1986	18.5	14.7	3.4	0.4
1985	32.1	26.3	4.7	1.1
1984	6.3	1.4	4.8	0.1
1983	22.5	17.3	4.5	0.7
1982	21.4	14.7	5.9	0.8
1981	−4.9	−9.7	5.3	−0.5
Geometric mean:				
1981–1990	13.9	9.3	4.4	0.2
1926–1990	10.1	5.1	4.7	0.3

Note: Reinvestment income arises from reinvestment of quarterly dividends in the index itself.

SOURCE: *Stocks, Bonds, Bills and Inflation: 1991 Yearbook* (Chicago: Ibbotson Associates, Inc., 1991).

as the actual rate of appreciation or depreciation in the price of stocks. Thus, the total return for the market as a whole is the dividend yield plus or minus the percentage change in the price of stocks. Table 9-3 shows that from 1981 through 1990 the dividend yield on the Standard & Poor's 500 was fairly stable, ranging from 3.4% to 5.9%. The year-to-year changes in the total return were largely due to changes in stock prices rather than changes in the dividend yield. The capital appreciation varied greatly over the years and provided two-thirds of the total return. Over a much longer period of time (1926 through 1990), capital appreciation and the dividend yield were nearly equal, as shown near the bottom of Table 9-3.

Price Change Required to Maintain Dividend Yield
When g is subtracted from both sides of Equation 9-9, it becomes

$$\frac{D_1}{P_0} = k - g \qquad (9\text{-}10)$$

The dividend yield (or required dividend yield) is the total return (or required total return) minus the expected growth rate. If, for example, the required total return is 10% and the expected growth rate is 6%, the required dividend yield is 4%. Assuming no change in the required return, any change in the expected growth rate will cause the price of the stock to move up or down until the dividend yield is brought to the required level, as illustrated in Example 9-1.

EXAMPLE 9-1   CHANGE IN PRICE REQUIRED TO RESTORE
DIVIDEND YIELD TO ACCEPTABLE LEVEL

Status before decrease in expected growth rate:

Stock price		$40.00
Dividend		$1.60
Dividend yield	(1.60/40.00)	4%
Expected perpetual growth rate		6%
Expected (and required) return		10%

Status after decrease in expected growth rate
to 5%, assuming no change in the dividend:

Required return		10%
Expected growth rate		5%
Required dividend yield (10 − 5)		5%
Stock price	(1.60/.05)	$32.00

||||

Non-Dividend-Paying Stocks

It is difficult to use any present value model for young, fast-growing companies that have not yet started to pay dividends, and it is rarely if ever appropriate to use a constant-growth model for such companies. The difficulty in using a present value model arises from the need to predict not only the size of the dividends but when the company will begin to pay them. The inappropriateness of the constant-growth model is due to the improbability that the dividend will grow at a constant rate.

TWO-STAGE MODELS

Typically, present value models for common stocks, other than the zero-growth and constant-growth versions, assume that earnings growth will be rapid for a time and eventually will level off at a constant rate. Simple *two-stage models* assume a constant, above-average dividend growth factor (g_1) for a specified number of years, followed by an abrupt change to a somewhat lower constant rate (g_2) that will be maintained forever, as shown in Equation 9-11. The estimated value of the stock is the present value of the estimated dividends during the rapid-growth period of n years, plus the present value of the estimated value of the stock $[P_n/(1 + k)^n]$ at the end of that period. P_n can be estimated with the constant-growth model, as assumed here, or by some other method, such as multiplying estimated earnings for the first year of the constant-growth period by a predicted price/earnings ratio.

$$P_0 = \sum_{t=1}^{n} \frac{D_0(1 + g)^t}{(1 + k)^t} + \frac{P_n}{(1 + k)^n} \qquad (9\text{-}11)$$

where

$$P_n = \frac{D_0(1 + g_1)^n(1 + g_2)}{k - g_2} = \frac{D_{n+1}}{k - g_2}$$

|||| **SIDELIGHT**
Bird-in-Hand Theory

Is it possible to assign a "true" value to stocks? Fans of so-called dividend discount investing think they have just such a philosopher's stone. This is their reasoning: People buy a stock to get the dividends. Indeed, so goes the theory, dividends are ultimately the *only* reason to buy a stock. Even growth stocks like Apple and Genentech, with no payouts, are valuable only because of the expectation that their businesses will someday mature and throw off cash to the owners. This theory assumes stocks are not all that much different from bonds, except that the dividend stream is less predictable than the stream of interest payments.

The dividend discount theory has had some success in the real world. "Historically, dividend discount valuation has been the most successful model at figuring which stocks will give an investor the highest rate of return," boasts George Reid, a former mathematics and philosophy professor at St. Louis University, who helped create just such a model for money manager Sanford C. Bernstein & Co. in New York City. An independent evaluation by CDA Investment Technologies puts Bernstein 16th among 129 managers for performance over the past five years.

Wells Fargo Bank has had impressive results attracting pension money with a dividend discount model. Here Wells Fargo is not picking individual stocks but simply using the formula to divine when stocks are cheap relative to bonds.

Ford Investor Services, a small database and newsletter firm in San Diego, publishes stock picks based on a dividend discount model. David Morse, author of the Ford model, is not a purist. Rather than attempting to project dividends into the distant future as Reid does, Morse takes the forecasting out only 10 years. In lieu of summing dividends for years 11 through eternity, he takes a termination stock value for 1997 and discounts that into 1987 dollars.

The shortcomings of [dividend discount models] are obvious. In estimates of earnings growth rates, such factors as competition, technological breakthroughs, and lawsuits can't be fully anticipated, so future earnings are guesses at best. Cautions Barton M. Biggs, chairman of Morgan Stanley Asset Management, which uses the Ford service only to suggest which market sectors are overpriced: "An analyst can make a stock's value come out any way he wants to simply by changing the growth rates." However, the discipline of discounting distant returns forces the analyst to put a low value on profits that won't turn into hard cash for the shareholder until the next century.

SOURCE: Adapted from Michael Ozanian, "Bird-in-Hand Theory," *Forbes,* February 23, 1987, pp. 104, 106. Reprinted by permission of Forbes, Inc. All rights reserved.

Professional money managers have differing views on the merits of dividend discount models such as the one above. The comments in the Sidelight are principally by professionals who have found the models useful.

Valuation of Procter & Gamble Stock

Application of the two-stage model to Procter & Gamble stock as of early 1991 is illustrated in Example 9-2. All estimates are the same as when the company was valued with the constant-growth model, except that dividends are expected to grow at an annual rate of 20% for the years 1992 through 1994 before declining to a constant rate of 7.8%. Notice that increasing the expected growth rate from 7.8% to 20% for just the first three years raises the estimated value of the stock from $82.50 to $112.45, or by more than one-third.

EXAMPLE 9-2   APPLICATION OF A TWO-STAGE MODEL
Symbols and assumptions:

$$D_{1991} = \$1.98 \quad k = 10.2\% \quad g_1 = 20\%$$
$$g_2 = 7.8\% \quad n = 3 \text{ years (starting with 1992)}$$
$$P_{1994} = \text{estimated value of stock at } 12/31/94$$
All dividends are received at year-end

Calculation of present values:

Year	Dividends and P_{1994}	Present Value Interest Factor (10.2%)	Present Value
1991	$1.98	.907	$1.80
1992	2.38	.824	1.96
1993	2.85	.747	2.13
1994	3.42	.678	2.32
Total			8.21
P_{1994}	153.75*	.678	104.24
Estimated value of stock, 1/1/91			112.45

*Calculation of P_{1994}:

$$D_{1995} = D_{1994} \times 1.078 = \$3.42 \times 1.078 = \$3.69$$

$$P_{1994} = \frac{D_{1995}}{.102 - .078} = \frac{\$3.69}{.024} = \$153.75$$

||||

THREE-STAGE MODELS

It is often more realistic to assume that a company's future growth will occur in more than two stages. For this reason, analysts sometimes use *three-stage models* based on the following stages: first, a period of very rapid growth during which all or most of the earnings are retained in the business to help finance growth; second, a transition period during which sales and earnings are still growing faster than the economy but the growth rate is declining as attractive new investment opportunities become fewer; and, third, a final period of perpetual, constant growth. Dividends are forecast year by year for the first two stages. In the first stage, the dividend payout is low, perhaps zero. The payout ratio is increased during the transition period as the rate of growth and the need for internal financing decline.

As with all other present value models, the estimated value of the stock is the sum of the present values of all expected dividends. Dividends for the first two stages are discounted individually, while those for the final, constant-growth stage are first discounted to the beginning of the constant-growth period using the constant-growth model; then, in a separate step, they are discounted to the valuation date.

Forecasts and calculations for a three-stage model are illustrated in Example 9-3. To avoid unnecessary complications, the example assumes a constant earnings growth rate and constant dividend payout ratio during the first stage, which lasts five years. During the second stage, the earnings growth rate declines from 20% to 12%, while the dividend payout ratio increases from 20% to 40%. In the final stage, the growth rate is 8% and the payout ratio is 50%.

EXAMPLE 9-3 APPLICATION OF A THREE-STAGE MODEL
Assumptions:

Current price of stock	$32.00
Required rate of return	12%
Number of years in stage one	5
Number of years in stage two	2
Earnings per share, year 1	$2.00
Earnings growth rates:	
Years 2–5	20%
Years 6–7	16%, 12%
After year 7	8%
Dividend payout ratio:	
Years 1–5	20%
Years 6–7	30%, 40%
After year 7	50%

Forecasted earnings and dividends, years 1–8:

Year	Earnings per Share Growth Rate	Earnings per Share Amount	Payout Percentage	Dividends per Share
1		$2.00	20%	$ .40
2	20%	2.40	20	.48
3	20	2.88	20	.58
4	20	3.46	20	.69
5	20	4.15	20	.83
6	16	4.81	30	1.44
7	12	5.39	40	2.16
8	8	5.82	50	2.91

Estimated price of stock at end of year 7 (P_7), last year of fast-growth period:

$$P_7 = \frac{D_8}{k - g} = \frac{2.91}{.12 - .08} = \$72.75$$

Present values:

Year	Dividends and P_7	Present Value Interest Factor (12%)	Present Value
1	$ .40	.893	$ .36
2	.48	.797	.38
3	.58	.712	.41
4	.69	.636	.44
5	.83	.567	.47
6	1.44	.507	.73
7	2.16	.452	.98
P_7	72.75	.452	32.88
Total value			**36.65**

Internal rate of return at stock price of $32.00 = 14.3%*

*The internal rate of return is the rate that discounts the dividends for the first 7 years and the estimated value of the stock at the end of year 7 to a present value equal to the market price of $32.00.

||||

||| VALUING STOCKS WITH P/E RATIOS

Many who are interested in common stocks make little or no use of dividend discount models because of the difficulty of forecasting dividends far into the future. Popular alternatives to pure dividend discount models often involve the use of price/earnings ratios. Sometimes DDMs and P/E models are combined, as in Equation 9-12, where the estimated value of a stock is the present value of the forecasted dividends (DPS) for n years (during which dividends are expected to grow at a constant rate of g), plus the present value of the predicted value of the stock at the end of the nth year, which is the product of earnings per share (EPS_n) and the predicted P/E ratio as of that time.

$$P_0 = \sum_{t=1}^{n} \frac{DPS_0(1 + g)^t}{(1 + k)^t} + \frac{(EPS_n)(P/E)}{(1 + k)^n} \tag{9-12}$$

P/E ratios have an intuitive appeal because they relate the price of a stock to an important determinant of its value, namely, earnings. Given an appropriate earnings per share figure and an appropriate P/E ratio (both of which may be estimated with considerable difficulty in practical applications), the estimated value of a stock is simply the product of the two:

$$P = E \times P/E \qquad (9\text{-}13)$$

In actual practice, P/E ratios are often used more as a means of comparing stocks than as a device for estimating their absolute values. Instead of trying to determine what each stock is worth, the analyst tries to determine if any are selling at P/E ratios that are too low relative to others. For example, suppose stocks A and B are selling at P/E's of 12 and 10, respectively, based on the latest 12 months' earnings. If an analyst believes that A has much brighter prospects for earnings growth than B, he or she might conclude that A's P/E ratio, although higher than B's, is too low comparatively and that A is therefore underpriced relative to B.

METHODS OF CALCULATING P/E RATIOS

P/E ratios published for individual stocks in the newspapers, called trailing P/E's, are based on earnings for the latest 12 months. They are often less meaningful than leading P/E's, which are based on predicted earnings for some future 12-month period. Stock prices depend on expectations about future earnings and dividends rather than on the earnings and dividends of the past. Value Line publishes a P/E ratio that is part trailing and part leading since it is based on actual earnings for the last six months and forecasted earnings for the next six months.

One problem with using trailing P/E ratios is that they are often distorted by cyclical or other temporary peaks and troughs in earnings. This problem can sometimes be mitigated by basing the ratio on "normalized" earnings rather than reported earnings. Normalized earnings can be loosely defined as an estimate of what the firm would have earned under normal, or mid-cyclical, conditions. One very crude method of estimating normalized earnings for the latest year is to fit a trendline to the firm's annual earnings over a period of 10 or 15 years and then read the latest year's earnings off the trendline.

HISTORICAL P/E RATIOS AND INFLATION

Individual stocks are sometimes valued by multiplying forecasted earnings for some future period by the stock's average P/E ratio over some past period. In many cases this is not a very sensible procedure. An average of the P/E ratios over some past period may not be appropriate for the present for a number of reasons, including changes in inflation, or in the risk characteristics or earnings prospects of the firm.

Inflation often leads to overstatement of profits for two principal reasons: first, ending inventories (except when calculated with the LIFO method) are valued at higher prices than beginning inventories, and this gives rise to meaningless but taxable inventory profits; second, depreciation charges based on historical costs are inadequate to cover the costs of replacement. Because of these distortions in reported profits, an in-

|||| **TABLE 9-4**

Inflation Rate, Commerce Department Profit Adjustments for
Inventory Valuations and Depreciation, and Price/Earnings
Ratios

Year	Inflation Rate[a]	Profit Adjustments[b] (%)	Price/Earnings Ratio[c]
1976	4.8%	−20.5%	11.2
1977	6.8	−17.7	9.3
1978	9.0	−21.1	8.3
1979	13.3	−29.3	7.4
1980	12.4	−32.4	7.9
1981	8.9	−16.9	8.4
1982	3.9	−4.4	8.6
1983	3.8	14.9	12.5
1984	4.0	18.7	10.0
1985	3.8	29.5	12.3
1986	1.1	29.3	16.4

[a]Inflation rates are based on the consumer price index.

[b]Negative profit adjustments indicate the percentage by which the Department of Commerce adjusted profits downward.

[c]Price/earnings ratios are annual averages based on the Standard & Poor's 500 Index.

SOURCES: U.S. Department of Commerce, *Survey of Current Business;* and Superintendent of Documents, *1990 Economic Report of the President.*

crease in the rate of inflation should reduce the amount investors are willing to pay per dollar of profits reported. And, apparently, that is what happened during the late 1970s, as shown in Table 9-4. As the rate of inflation increased, the P/E ratio for the Standard & Poor's 500 Index dropped sharply, and when the inflation rate declined in the early 1980s, the P/E ratio rose back up again. While this does not prove that overstatement of earnings caused P/E ratios to drop, it does appear that the reduced quality of earnings was at least one reason why investors placed a lower value on a dollar of reported earnings in the late 1970s and early 1980s than either immediately before or after those years.[9]

FUNDAMENTAL INFLUENCES ON P/E RATIOS

The constant-growth model provides a good framework for considering the factors that determine P/E ratios. When both sides of Equation 9-5 are divided by E_{t+1} (expected earnings for the next 12 months), the equation becomes

$$\frac{P_0}{E_{t+1}} = \frac{D_{t+1}/E_{t+1}}{k - g} \tag{9-14}$$

The P/E ratio varies directly with the dividend payout ratio *(D/E)* and the expected dividend growth rate *(g)*, and inversely with the required

[9]The impact of inflation on stock prices and returns is discussed in the appendix to this chapter.

rate of return *(k)*. It is important to recognize that to some degree these variables are interdependent. For example, payout ratios are often increased when opportunities for growth have become fewer. Thus, an increase in the percentage of earnings paid out as dividends can have a negative impact on the P/E ratio if it causes investors to lower their growth expectations more than enough to offset the increase in dividends.

Similarly, an increase in financial leverage as a result of borrowing to finance growth can have either a positive or negative effect on the P/E ratio. Expansion of the firm's assets may increase *g*, but the increase in financial leverage might increase *k* by a greater amount. The impact of the borrowing and expansion on *k* depends upon how the increase in risk resulting from greater leverage compares to any decrease in risk that might result if sales and operating profits are expected to become more stable as a result of the expansion.

Year-to-year changes in a company's P/E ratio, as well as differences in P/E ratios among companies, are often due to abnormalities in earnings—something that cannot be seen in Equation 9-14. For example, if company A's stock is selling at a P/E of 14 and B's is selling at a P/E of 10, one might guess that the market is expecting A's earnings to grow faster than B's. But it could be that growth expectations for the two companies are about the same, and A's higher ratio reflects a drop in its earnings last year without a proportionate decrease in the price of the stock. This happens when investors view the earnings decline as something very unusual and expect a quick recovery. Or, it could be that B's P/E ratio of 10 is unusually low because of a sharp increase in its earnings that is viewed as a temporary bulge.[10]

Selecting an Appropriate P/E Ratio

It may seem that using P/E ratios to value stocks relative to one another makes it possible to avoid making long-range predictions, but that is an illusion. Market prices do reflect long-range expectations, and that makes it necessary to determine, as best one can, whether those expectations are reasonable or not.

Weighing the Variables with Regression Analysis

In an effort to discover how the market decides that one stock should sell at a higher P/E ratio than another, and by how much, Malkiel and Cragg analyzed data collected from analysts at 17 investment firms on 178 companies as of the end of each of five years.[11] With this data, the authors regressed normalized P/E ratios (based on analysts' estimates of normalized earnings) on three variables: (1) forecasted long-term earnings growth rate, (2) dividend payout ratio (dividends divided by normalized

---

[10]Another possible reason for the difference in the ratios is a difference in the quality of the reported earnings. Company A's accounting practices may be more conservative than B's, and for this reason, investors consider a dollar of A's earnings more valuable than a dollar of B's.

[11]Burton G. Malkiel and John G. Cragg, "Expectations and the Structure of Share Prices," *American Economic Review* 60 (September 1970):601–17.

|||| **TABLE 9-5**
Malkiel and Cragg's Normalized P/E Regressions

Year	Constant	Forecasted Long-Term Growth Rate	Dividend Payout Ratio	Beta	R^2
1961	3.63	3.29 (17.20)	3.24 (0.73)	0.97 (0.89)	.74
1962	9.79	1.87 (16.88)	2.25 (1.01)	−2.65 (−5.69)	.72
1963	3.47	2.57 (21.38)	7.17 (2.90)	−0.84 (−1.37)	.75
1964	6.16	2.10 (21.40)	5.87 (2.88)	(−1.41) (−2.67)	.76
1965	0.25	2.86 (29.14)	5.01 (2.50)	−0.47 (−0.96)	.86

Note: Numbers in parentheses are *t* values.
SOURCE: Burton G. Malkiel and John G. Cragg, "Expectations and the Structure of Share Prices," *American Economic Review* 60 (September 1970): 601–17.

earnings), and (3) beta.[12] As Table 9-5 shows, the regressions explained from 72% to 86% of the variation in normalized P/E ratios, and long-term earnings growth was by far the most important explanatory variable. Assuming that analysts' forecasts are a good proxy for investor's expectations, Malkiel and Cragg's findings indicate that investors' expectations about long-term earnings growth rates are the most important influence on normalized P/E ratios. However, as they pointed out, it is possible that the influence goes in the other direction: analysts may be guided by P/E ratios in forecasting earnings. Thus, if a stock's P/E ratio rises and analysts believe that the higher price will continue to be justified by investors' expectations about the firm's future earnings, analysts may simply adjust their earnings forecasts upward to justify the new earnings multiple.

Malkiel and Cragg also tried to determine whether a multiple regression model can be useful in identifying securities that will have above-average future returns. If the normalized P/E ratio at which a stock is being traded is lower than one would expect, given the estimated regression coefficients and estimates of the stock's long-term earnings growth rate, dividend payout ratio, and beta, the stock is considered underpriced by the market, and it should be a good performer.

It didn't work out that way. "Overpriced" stocks outperformed "underpriced" stocks more than half the time over periods ranging from one quarter to two years. Three reasons were suggested for the lack of success in forecasting relative stock performance. First, the relative importance of each variable may change over time. A stock that appeared to be cheap on the basis of a valuation model that reflected investors' weightings of the variables last year may have performed poorly because of changes in

[12]Note how closely these variables correspond to the variables of Equation 9-14.

investors' ideas as to the relative importance of the variables. Second, analysts' forecasts may have been poor proxies for investors' expectations. Third, the valuation model may have omitted one or more significant variables. For example, the model indicated that stocks of tobacco companies were consistently underpriced, but the model's measure of risk (beta) failed to reflect the risk of government regulation. Finally, Malkiel and Cragg observed that nothing is gained from knowing what investors' expectations are today, since those expectations are already reflected in market prices. It would be very useful, however, if one could predict what their expectations will be a year from now.

Benjamin Graham's Maximum P/E Ratios

Few teachers or managers of investments have achieved the eminence of Benjamin Graham, author of *The Intelligent Investor* and coauthor of *Security Analysis*.[13] Graham emphasized the importance of P/E ratios. By 1976, near the end of his career, Graham stated that he had lost interest in the details of security analysis and believed that stocks could be selected with a simple P/E criterion.[14] He concluded that no stock should be purchased unless its earnings/price ratio (E/P) was at least twice the yield on AAA corporate bonds. In today's market, that would be an extremely conservative standard. With AAA corporate bond yields at 9%, the minimum E/P ratio would be 18% (2 × 9%), and the maximum P/E ratio would be 1/.18, or 5.6. In the middle and late 1970s, P/E ratios were much lower than now, and many more stocks were trading at P/E ratios of less than 6.

P/E Ratio of Procter & Gamble Stock

At a price of $83 and P/E ratio of 17 in early 1991, was Procter & Gamble stock overpriced, underpriced, or priced correctly relative to other stocks? Was its P/E ratio too high, too low, or about right in comparison to those of stocks with similar risk characteristics and future earnings prospects? The purpose of this discussion is not to answer those questions (which would require a thorough analysis of Procter & Gamble's risk and earnings prospects, as well as comparisons with others), but to see what would be involved in arriving at an answer. For anyone who believes completely in the ability of the market to price closely-followed, widely-traded stocks like Procter & Gamble correctly relative to others (even if it might not price stocks as a whole correctly relative to other investments), the answer comes easily: No analysis is required. However, it will be assumed here that mispricing could have occurred.

At the same time that Procter & Gamble was selling at a P/E ratio of a little over 17, the P/E for the Dow Jones Industrial Average was

---

[13]Benjamin Graham and David Dodd, *Security Analysis: Principles and Techniques*, 3rd ed. (New York: McGraw-Hill, 1951;) Benjamin Graham, *Intelligent Investor*, 4th ed. (New York: Harper & Row, 1973).

[14]Irving Kahn and Robert D. Milne, "Benjamin Graham: The Father of Financial Analysis," *Occasional Paper No. 5* (Charlottesville, Va.: The Financial Analysts Research Foundation, 1976).

16.2, and the P/E for the Standard & Poor's 500 was 16.8. Since Procter & Gamble's estimated beta (according to Value Line) was 1.0, indicating that its systematic risk was about equal to the average, investors possibly viewed the company's earnings outlook as being just a little better than average, as indicated by its slightly higher than average P/E ratio.

To form a judgment as to whether Procter & Gamble's P/E of 17 was too low relative to that of other companies, it is necessary to compare their growth prospects and risk. Of these two variables, prospective earnings growth is often the more important and the more difficult to evaluate. Growth is subject to many influences and follows many patterns. Prediction of earnings growth is the principal topic of Chapter 10.

|||| SUMMARY

Investors value stocks in a number of ways. In theory, the value of a stock (with a few exceptions, such as the stock of a company that may be of special value to another company) is the present value of all future dividends. Present values of common stocks are calculated with dividend discount models, or DDMs. The present value is the equilibrium price, which is also the market price in an efficient market.

Three widely used dividend discount models are the constant-growth model, the two-stage model, and the three-stage model. The constant-growth model is more likely to be appropriate for valuing the market as a whole than for individual stocks. Even the two-stage and three-stage models assume that at some point the company's dividends will begin to grow at a constant rate roughly equal to that of the economy.

With present value techniques, the attractiveness of a stock can be assessed either by comparing the expected return with the required return or by comparing the estimated present value with the market price. If the expected return is above (below) the required return, the present value will be above (below) the market price.

Present value models require a long-range forecast of earnings and dividends and an estimate of the appropriate required rate of return, or discount rate. The required return is the risk-free rate of interest plus a risk premium; and, according to the capital asset pricing model, the risk premium is the product of the required market risk premium and the stock's beta coefficient. In the absence of a survey, there is no way to know how large a risk premium investors are requiring at any time. Therefore, the market risk premium is often estimated as an average of the actual market risk premium over a long period of time.

Many investors prefer to compare stocks on the basis of P/E ratios rather than with estimates of present values. It might seem that this avoids the need for long-range forecasts. However, that is an illusion. Since market prices are based, to a significant degree, on long-range expectations about future earnings, long-term earnings forecasts should be taken into account.

||| # QUESTIONS

1. What assumptions underlie the constant-growth model?

2. Demonstrate that $(k - g)$ in the constant-growth model is the expected (or required) dividend yield. Explain the relationship between g and the dividend yield.

3. Explain how the expected rate of return can be calculated with a three-stage valuation model.

4. In selecting stocks, why would it be more helpful to know what analysts will be forecasting a year from now than to know what they are forecasting today?

5. Why are book values of little help in evaluating stocks, even though cross-section analysis would show a positive correlation between market values and book values?

6. Explain in terms of earnings retention ratios and growth rates why the stocks of fast-growing companies sell at low dividend yields.

7. Why do stocks of slow-growing companies sell at high dividend yields?

8. Using the following data, give two plausible explanations (one in terms of k and the other in terms of g) for the increase in stock A's P/E ratio from time t to time $t + 1$.

	Time t	Time $t + 1$
Stock price	$20	$24
EPS (last 4 quarters)	$2	$2
P/E	10	12
Dividend	$1	$1

9. In the context of a dividend discount model, what is the equilibrium price?

10. Explain why the equation $g = b \times r$ may result in a very poor earnings forecast. Give an example.

11. Explain the equation $g = b \times r$ intuitively.

12. Explain why a change of three percentage points (from 15% down to 12%) in the return on equity can cause a drastic decline in earnings even if the shareholders' equity has increased 10%.

13. Explain two methods of valuing a company's stock as of the end of the rapid-growth period.

14. Why do ratios of stock prices to book values vary widely among companies?

15. Why is the liquidation value usually a poor indicator of a stock's worth?

16. Explain why many investors prefer to use P/E models rather than present value models in valuing stocks.

17. Why isn't the value of a stock the present value of the expected earnings rather than the present value of the expected dividends?
18. What is the market risk premium?
19. Why is it impossible to determine from stock market and U.S. Treasury bill returns what the required market risk premium is?
20. Why doesn't an increase in the dividend payout necessarily increase the price of a stock?
21. Why doesn't an increase in the expected earnings growth rate necessarily increase the price of a stock?
22. Why might a three-stage DDM provide a better estimate of a stock's value than a two-stage model?

||| PROBLEMS

1. Calculate the estimated value of stock X and the expected return, given the following, and using the required return to find P_6:

Required return	10%
Market price of stock	$60
Estimated length of fast-growth period	6 years
EPS in year 0	$3

Year	EPS Growth Rate	Dividend Payout
1	25%	0%
2	25	10
3	25	10
4	20	20
5	15	30
6	10	40
7 and after	5	50

2. By what percentage will earnings decline, assuming a 10% increase in the shareholders' equity, and a decline in the return on equity from 14% to 12%?
3. If a firm's earnings are $2 million, the dividend payment is $1.1 million, and shareholders' equity is $16 million, at what rate will earnings grow if the earnings retention ratio and dividend payout ratio are constant?
4. Assuming a constant return on equity, how much, and by what percentage, will the firm's earnings increase above $5 million in the following year?

Dividend payout ratio	40%
Earnings	$5 million

Assets	$50 million
Liabilities	$20 million
Preferred stock	None

5. If earnings per share are $1, the stock price $10, expected return 16%, earnings retention ratio 40%, and the ratio of stock price to book value 2.5, what is the dividend yield? Assuming that constant growth is expected, what is the expected earnings growth rate?

6. Calculate the earnings growth rate from year t to year $t + 1$, given the following:

	Year t	Year $t + 1$
Assets	$200	
Liabilities	$80	
Equity	$120	$120
r	10%	12%
Earnings	$12	
Dividends	$12	

If the equation $g = b \times r$ were applicable, what growth rate would it indicate? How do you reconcile that with the growth rate you have just calculated?

7. X Corporation is expected to earn 14% on common shareholders' equity forever and retain 40% of its earnings in the business. The required return on stocks of similar risk is 12%. At what rate are its earnings expected to grow? Assuming that the constant-growth model is applicable, what portion of the expected return is capital gain? How much is the dividend yield? What is an appropriate price-earnings multiple for the stock?

8. Suppose an analyst believes that the dividends of X Corporation will grow at a rate of 4% forever, and that the required return on stocks of similar risk is 12%. The dividend for the latest 12 months was $2, and the price of the stock is $24. What growth rate is implied by the price of the stock, assuming it is being priced according to the constant-growth model?

9. Assuming expected constant growth of earnings, dividends, and stock price, find the stock's required P/E ratio, given the following:

Expected market return	12%
Risk-free rate of interest	7%
Beta	1.2
Earnings	$4 million
Dividends	$1.8 million
Assets	$80 million
Liabilities, deferred income taxes, and preferred stock	$32 million

10. Calculate the present value and expected return, given the following, and using the required return to find P_4:

Expected dividends:	
Year 1	$1.50
2	$2.10
3	$2.80
4	$3.50
Required return	11%
Market value of stock	$40
Estimated length of fast-growth period	4 years
Expected constant growth rate after 4th year	6%

||| SELECTED REFERENCES

Beaver, William, and Dale Morse. "What Determines Price-Earnings Ratios?" *Financial Analysts Journal* 34 (July/August 1978): 65–76.

Bower, Dorothy, and Richard S. Bower. "Test of a Stock Variation Model." *The Journal of Finance* 25 (May 1970): 483–92.

Brigham, Eugene F., and James L. Pappas. "Duration of Growth, Changes in Growth Rates, and Corporate Share Prices." *Financial Analysts Journal* 22 (May/June 1966): 157–62.

Craig, Darryl, Glenn Johnson, and Maurice Joy. "Accounting Methods and P/E Ratios." *Financial Analysts Journal* 43 (March/April 1987): 41–45.

Davenport, Martin W. "Is the Stock Market Really Undervalued by 50 Percent?" *Business Economics* 25 (May 1980): 32–38.

Fama, Eugene F., and William Schwert. "Asset Returns and Inflation." *Journal of Financial Economics.*" 5 (November 1977): 115–46.

Farrell, J. L., Jr. *"The Dividend Discount Model: A Primer."* *Financial Analysts Journal* 41 (November/December 1985): 16–19, 22–25.

Feldstein, Martin. "Inflation and the Stock Market." *American Economic Review* 70 (December 1980): 839–47.

_____. "Inflation and the Stock Market: Reply." *American Economic Review* 72 (March 1982): 243–46.

Friend, Irwin, and Joel Hasbrouck. "Inflation and the Stock Market: Comment." *American Economic Review* 72 (March 1982): 237–42.

Graham, Benjamin. *Intelligent Investor*, 4th ed. New York: Harper & Row, 1973).

Graham, Benjamin, and David Dodd. *Security Analysis: Principles and Techniques*, 3d ed. New York: McGraw-Hill, 1951.

Holt, Charles C. "The Influence of Growth Duration on Share Prices." *The Journal of Finance* 27 (September 1962): 465–75.

Kahn, Irving, and Robert D. Milne. "Benjamin Graham: The Father of Financial Analysis." *Occasional Paper No. 5.* Charlottesville, Va.: Financial Analysts Research Foundation, 1976.

Keenan, Michael. "Models of Equity Valuation: The Great SERM Bubble." *The Journal of Finance* 25 (May 1970): 243–73.

Levy, Kenneth N., and Bruce I. Jacobs. "Disentangling Equity Returns: New Insights and Investment Opportunities." *Financial Analysts Journal* 44 (May/June 1988): 18–43.

Lewellen, Wilbur G. "Inflation and Dividends" (comment on Modiglianai and Cohn). *Financial Analysts Journal* 37 (May/June 1981): 61–62.

Malkiel, Burton, and John Cragg. "Expectations and the Structure of Share Prices." *American Economic Review* 60 (September 1970): 601–17.

Michaud, Richard O. "A Scenario-Dependent Dividend Discount Model· Bridging the Gap between Top-Down Investment Information aι. Bottom-Up Forecasts." *Financial Analysts Journal* 41 (November/ December 1985): 49–59.

Modigliani, Franco, and Richard A. Cohn. "Inflation, Rational Valuation, and the Market." *Financial Analysts Journal* 35 (March/April 1979): 24–44.

Sorenson, Eric H., and David A. Williamson. "Some Evidence on the Value of Dividend Discount Models." *Financial Analysts Journal* 41 (November/December 1985): 60–69.

Wilcox, Jarrod W. "The P/B-ROE Valuation Model." *Financial Analysts Journal* 40 (January/February 1984): 58–66.

9a INFLATION AND STOCK RETURNS

NOMINAL AND REAL RETURNS

Investors are more interested in real returns (i.e., returns adjusted to a constant price level) than in nominal returns. For example, if a $100 investment in a common stock grows to $115 at the end of one year (due to an increase in the price, plus dividends and earnings from reinvestment of the dividends), the nominal return is 15% [(115 − 100)/100]. If the inflation rate is 6%, the investor's real return is approximately 9% (15% − 6%). More precisely, it is 8.49% [(1.15/1.06) − 1]. The nominal annual return on the Standard & Poor's 500 Index for the 10 years ending with 1990 was 13.9%, and the inflation rate (based on the *consumer price index*) was 4.5%, making the approximate real return 9.4% (13.9 − 4.5), and the actual real return 9.0% [(1.139/1.045) − 1].

The formula for calculating the exact real return, given the nominal return *(NR)* and the rate of inflation *(I)*, is

$$RR = (1 + NR)/(1 + I) - 1 \qquad \text{(9A-1)}$$

Typically, the rate of inflation is calculated with either the consumer price index or the GNP deflator. With *PIE* as the ending price index and *PIB* the beginning price index, the inflation rate is calculated as follows:

$$I = (PIE/PIB) - 1 \qquad \text{(9A-2)}$$

For example, the consumer price index increased from 126.1 at the end of 1989 to 133.8 at the end of 1990, and the inflation rate was 6.1%, calculated as follows:

$$I = (133.8/126.1) - 1$$
$$= 6.1\%$$

Figure 9A-1 shows that, in nominal terms, $1.00 invested at the beginning of 1926, with all dividends reinvested, grew to $517.50 at the end of 1990, whereas in real terms it grew to only $69.33. The nominal compound annual rate of return was 10.1% ($517.50^{1/65} - 1$), and the real return was 6.7% ($69.33^{1/65} - 1$). Or, given that the inflation rate was 3.14% over this 65-year period, the real return can be calculated with Equation 9A-1: (1.101/1.0314) − 1 = 6.7%.

|||| **FIGURE 9A-1**

Common Stocks: Nominal and Real Return Indexes, 1926–1990

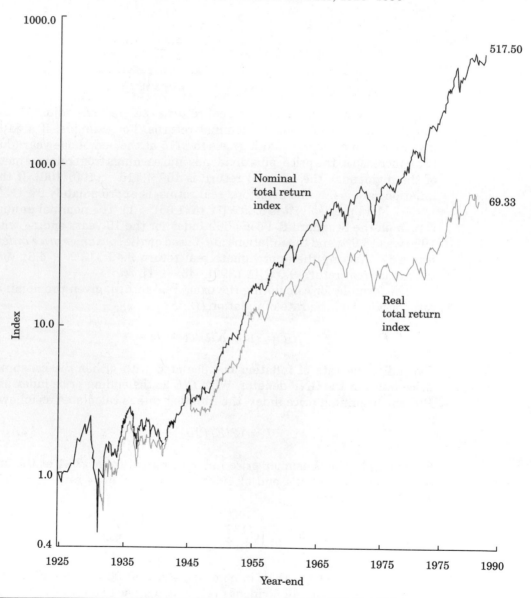

Source: *Stocks, Bonds, Bills and Inflation: 1991 Yearbook* (Chicago: Ibbotson Associates, Inc., 1991). Reprinted by permission of Ibbotson Associates, Inc. All rights reserved.

|||| INFLATION'S IMPACT ON HISTORICAL RETURNS

Assessing the effect of inflation on stock returns involves more than just converting nominal returns to real returns. There is considerable evidence that inflation has a negative impact on stock prices.[15] The reasons are not entirely clear.

Table 9A-1 shows inflation rates and common stock nominal and real returns by five-year periods from 1950 through 1989. Real returns were low in the three periods of highest inflation, stretching from 1970 to 1984. Returns were also low in the years 1965–1969, even though the average inflation rate was not much higher than in the high-return years of 1950 to 1959. The low returns of the 1965–1969 period probably reflected the increase of inflation during those years, which started with a rate of 1.9% in 1965 and ended with 6.1% in 1969.

Stock market performance during the 1985–1989 period, when the average inflation rate was 3.7%, indicates that nominal and real returns can be high in periods of moderate inflation. While stocks have not proved to be a good hedge against high and rising rates of inflation, they may be a good hedge against inflation at rates as high as 3% to 5%.

---

[15]Eugene F. Fama and William Schwert, "Asset Returns and Inflation," *Journal of Financial Economics* 5 (November 1977): 115–46.

|||| **TABLE 9A-1**

Inflation Rates and Nominal and Real Stock Returns for Five-Year Periods, 1950–1989

Years	Annual Inflation Rate[a]	Annual Stock Returns	
		Nominal[b]	Real[c]
1950–1954	2.5%	23.9%	20.9%
1955–1959	1.9	15.0	12.9
1960–1964	1.2	10.7	9.4
1965–1969	3.8	5.0	1.2
1970–1974	6.6	−2.4	−8.4
1975–1979	8.1	14.8	6.2
1980–1984	6.5	14.8	7.8
1985–1989	3.7	31.5	26.8

[a]The inflation rate is based on the consumer price index.

[b]Nominal returns, from *Stocks, Bonds, Bills and Inflation: 1991 Yearbook* (Chicago: Ibbotson Associates, Inc., 1991), are for the Standard & Poor's 500 Index.

[c]Real returns are calculated with Equation 9A-1.

|||| WHY DOES INFLATION AFFECT RETURNS?

In the context of the constant-growth model, the impact of increases in inflation and inflationary expectations on stock prices depends on how they affect D_1 (expected dividend for the coming 12 months), k (the required return), and g (the expected long-term growth rate). While higher inflation is not likely to have much effect on D_1, it is almost sure to have considerable effect on k and g. If higher inflation leads to equal increases in k and g, with no effect on D_1, there will be no immediate effect on stock prices. However, nominal stock prices will grow faster in the future due to the increased growth rate of earnings and dividends, as illustrated in Table 9A-2.

The increase in the growth rate of the stock price from 5% to 9.2% as a result of an increase in the inflation rate from zero to 4% (assuming no change in k or real g) can be explained either with a modified version of Equation 9-7 ($g = b \times r$) or in terms of the P/E ratio. When modified for inflation, the growth equation becomes

$$g = (1 + br)(1 + I) - 1 \qquad (9A\text{-}3)$$

For example, assuming the growth rate of 5% with no inflation is based on an earnings retention ratio *(b)* of 41.7% and a return on equity *(r)* of 12%, an inflation rate of 4% raises the nominal growth rate to 9.2%:

$$[1 + (.417 \times .12)](1 + .04) - 1 = (1.05)(1.04) - 1 = 9.2\%$$

The P/E ratio of 10 in Table 9A-2 is kept at the same level with 4% inflation as with zero inflation on the assumption that the company's reported earnings are not distorted by inflation but are simply increased in proportion to the increase in the rate of inflation. It is assumed that investors are willing to pay as much (in inflated dollars) for a dollar of inflated earnings as for a dollar of zero-inflated earnings.[16] With the

---

[16]If reported earnings were increased by more than the inflation rate due to FIFO inventory accounting or understatement of depreciation expense, the P/E ratio would almost surely decline.

|||| **TABLE 9A-2**

Growth of Nominal Stock Prices with Zero and 4% Inflation

	Zero Inflation			Steady 4% Inflation		
	Year 1	Year 2	Year 3	Year 1	Year 2	Year 3
Sales	$100.00	$105.00	$110.25	$100.00	$109.20	$119.25
Profit margin	5%	5%	5%	5%	5%	5%
Earnings	$5.00	$5.25	$5.51	$5.00	$5.46	$5.96
P/E ratio	10	10	10	10	10	10
Stock price	$50.00	$52.50	$55.10	$50.00	$54.60	$59.60
Stock price growth rate		5%	5%		9.2%	9.2%

P/E ratio held constant, the increase in the growth rate of the stock price as a result of inflation is the same as the increase in the growth rate of earnings and dividends.

Various reasons have been suggested as to why increases in inflation and inflationary expectations are likely to increase the required return more than the expected growth rate and thereby depress stock prices. One is the suggestion that when the rate of inflation increases, investors realize that taxable profits will be overstated and taxes increased as a result of inventory profits and inadequate depreciation. It has also been suggested that an increase in inflation often leads to less optimism about the real growth of before-tax earnings because of the fear that costs will rise faster than revenues. A third view is that higher inflation causes greater uncertainty about future profits, which results in a higher market risk premium.

|||| APPENDIX QUESTIONS

1. Explain why distortion of earnings during inflationary periods has probably been a cause of the decline in the P/E ratio during such periods.

2. Outline three theories as to why common stocks have performed poorly during periods of high inflation.

3. Explain why you would expect stock prices to rise faster during a period of moderate (3% to 5%) inflation than during a period of no inflation.

4. Explain, in terms of the constant-growth model, why stocks have generally performed poorly during periods of high inflation.

|||| APPENDIX PROBLEMS

1. If the nominal return is 10% and the inflation rate is 6%, what is the exact real return?

2. Calculate the rate of inflation, given the following:

Price index at beginning of year	185
Price index at end of year	192

3. Calculate the real returns and real equity risk premiums for small common stocks for the years 1988 and 1989, given the following:

    Small-stock nominal returns:

1988	22.9%
1989	10.2

Inflation rate:
1988	4.4
1989	4.6

Treasury bill rate (30-day)
1988	6.3
1989	8.4

4. Calculate the present value, expected nominal return, and expected real return, given the following, and using the required return to find P_4:

Expected dividends:	
Year 1	$1.00
2	1.50
3	1.80
4	2.00
Required return	12%
Market value of stock	$30
Estimated length of fast-growth period	4 years
Expected constant growth rate after 4th year	6%
Expected inflation rate	4%

10 FUNDAMENTAL ANALYSIS

Dividend discount models and P/E models like those described in Chapter 9 are based on the plausible premise that expected earnings and dividends are important determinants of common stock prices. Studies have found that this is a valid premise. Stock prices are highly dependent on expected earnings growth rates; and they are sensitive to unexpectedly large increases and decreases in earnings. In light of the importance of expectations about future earnings, it is easy to see why security analysts spend so much time trying to make superior forecasts of earnings.

The principal focus of the present chapter is on earnings forecasts and the analysis of fundamental factors (including the operating margin, asset utilization, and financial leverage) that have an effect on earnings. The chapter begins with a discussion of the effects of different accounting practices on reported earnings. That is followed by a review of certain evidence relating to the importance and predictability of earnings.

Earnings are difficult to predict because they are affected by a number of factors (including, for example, changes in consumer tastes and habits, technological developments, and changes in competitive conditions) that are themselves highly uncertain. Past earnings growth rates are generally a poor indicator of future growth rates.

A logical first step in preparing an earnings forecast is to examine the sources of past growth. One approach is through ratio analysis, which is illustrated with the earnings of Procter and Gamble. The objective is to identify the likely sources of future growth. The chapter concludes with a discussion of cash flows and inflation, both of which should be taken into account in estimating future earnings.

WHAT ARE EARNINGS?

You can be sure that the most carefully examined figures in corporate quarterly and annual reports are total earnings and earnings per share. However, these figures are not always what they seem. Because of differences in accounting practices and in the estimates used in accruing expenses such as depreciation or in amortizing assets such as goodwill, a dollar of earnings reported by one company is often not equivalent to a dollar of earnings reported by another. Similarly, the meaning of a

|||| SIDELIGHT

The Eroding Quality of Corporate Profits

Some analysts believe that the quality of corporate profits has been deteriorating and that the stock market has not reflected the decline. To determine "true" earnings, analysts adjust depreciation to a realistic level and remove the effect of inflation on reported inventory values. They also look for any evidence that expenses have been understated or put off to the future, and they are concerned about deterioration in the quality of earnings due to the rise in corporate debt. Leveraged earnings are worth less to investors because of the increased risk.

The head of one investment research firm stated that corporate operating profits as reported by the Commerce Department fell 16.2% between the first quarter of 1986 and the first quarter of 1989, but the per-share profits reported by the 500 companies in the Standard & Poor's 500 Index rose 71.5% over the same period. The market seems not to have noticed the decline in earnings quality. In the three years ending in March 1989, a time when "true" operating profits were falling, stock prices gained 36.7%. Contrary to previous experience, stock prices during this period were more closely correlated with reported profits than with "true" operating profits.

SOURCE: Adapted from Barbara Donnelly, "Quality of Corporate Profits is Said to Erode, Undetected by the Market," *The Wall Street Journal,* June 29, 1989, p. C1. Reprinted by permission of *The Wall Street Journal,* © Dow Jones & Company, Inc. (1989). All Rights Reserved Worldwide.

dollar of earnings reported by an individual company can change over time with changes in accounting policies or practices. Under Generally Accepted Accounting Principles (GAAP), firms have considerable leeway in reporting the results of their operations. As noted in the Sidelight, some analysts believe there was a serious decline in the quality of corporate profits during the late 1980s.

Difference in earnings growth rates among companies often reflect unusual events or transitory conditions as well as differences in accounting practices. Analysts need to separate the temporary from the permanent in reported earnings. For example, a company's profits may be swollen by gains from the sale of properties or depressed by expenses incurred in starting up a new facility. The estimated impact of such conditions or events must be removed from reported earnings to arrive at a starting point for predicting future earnings.

|||| ## THE IMPORTANCE OF EARNINGS

Even casual observation indicates that corporate earnings are important to shareholders. Empirical studies reveal just how important earnings are.

In an early but still very impressive study, Niederhoffer and Regan found, as have others, a remarkable correspondence between changes in stock prices and changes in earnings.[1] They related price changes to earnings growth for the 50 best-performing and 50 worst-performing stocks on the New York Stock Exchange for the five-year period 1966– 1970.[2] As Figure 10-1 shows, the median five-year price increase for the 50 best-performing stocks was 181.9%—very close to the median earnings increase of 199.4%; and the median five-year price decrease for the 50 worst-performing stocks was 62.3%, which was nearly the same as the earnings decrease of 61.3%. For all 650 stocks in the study, the median annualized price change for the five-year period was a decrease of 1.0% $[(1 - .049)^{1/5} - 1]$, and the median annualized earnings change was an increase of 3.4% $[(1.183)^{1/5} - 1]$. Thus, there was a close correspondence between earnings growth and price change for the 650 stocks as a whole.

|||| THE INFLUENCE OF EARNINGS FORECASTS

One reason for forecasting earnings is to look for stocks that will out-perform the market. This raises two questions: First, do stocks whose earnings are predicted to grow the fastest perform better than the av-

[1]Victor Niederhoffer and Patrick J. Regan, "Earnings Changes, Analysts' Forecasts, and Stock Prices," *Financial Analysts Journal* 28 (May/June 1972): 65–71.

[2]In this context, the expressions "best-performing" and "worst-performing" refer to stocks with the largest percentage price gains and largest percentage price losses. Dividends are ignored, and no adjustment is made for differences in beta.

|||| FIGURE 10-1

Earnings Changes and Stock Price Changes, 1966–1970

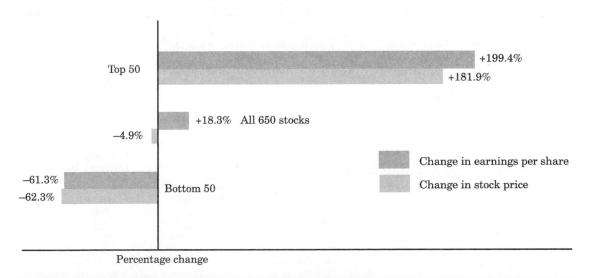

SOURCE: Victor Niederhoffer and Patrick J. Regan, "Earnings Changes, Analysts' Forecasts, and Stock Prices," *Financial Analysts Journal* 28 (May/June 1972): 65–71.

erage? Second, how do the prices of stocks react when earnings are higher or lower than forecasted?

There seems to be virtually no correlation between predicted earnings growth rates and future stock performance (see Table 10-1).[3] Although the average price increase of stocks in portfolio A (for which the fastest earnings growth rates were predicted) was greater than for portfolios B, C, and D, it was smaller than for portfolio E, which contained stocks of companies that were expected to have a decrease in earnings. The rosy earnings predictions for companies with stocks in portfolios A, B, and C were evidently reflected in the stock prices before the year began. These results indicate that one should not expect to earn abnormal returns simply by investing in stocks of companies whose earnings are expected to grow rapidly.

We noted in Chapter 8 that when a company's earnings are higher or lower than predicted, the returns on its stock are likely to be abnormally high or low for a time. Niederhoffer and Regan found that price performance was closely related to the difference between reported earnings and the consensus forecast (see Figure 10-2). The best-performing stocks were the stocks of companies whose earnings were expected to grow only 7.7%, but whose actual earnings growth was 21%. The worst-performing stocks were of companies whose earnings were expected to grow 15.3%, but actually declined 83%.

|||| THE IMPORTANCE OF DIVIDENDS

It might seem that shareholders should be indifferent to dividends because their wealth is the same whether a dividend is paid or not. On the day a stock goes ex-dividend, the price of the stock drops by the amount of the dividend, and so far as anyone knows, it remains permanently lower than if no dividend had been paid. Thus, it may appear that share-

---

[3]Leonard Zacks, "EPS Forecast—Accuracy Is Not Enough," *Financial Analysts Journal* 35 (March/April 1979): 53–55.

|||| **TABLE 10-1**

Stock Price Performance Compared to Forecasted Earnings Growth Rates, 1976

Portfolio	Number of Securities	Range of Consensus Forecasts of EPS Growth Rates	Percentage Increase in Stock Price
A	47	40% to 335%	31.0%
B	36	23% to 40%	20.4
C	68	12% to 23%	25.1
D	82	0 to 12%	27.0
E	27	−44% to 0	38.0

SOURCE: Leonard Zacks, "EPS Forecasts—Accuracy Is Not Enough," *Financial Analysts Journal* 35 (March/April 1979): 53–55.

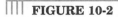

FIGURE 10-2
Earnings Forecast Errors and Stock Price Changes, 1970

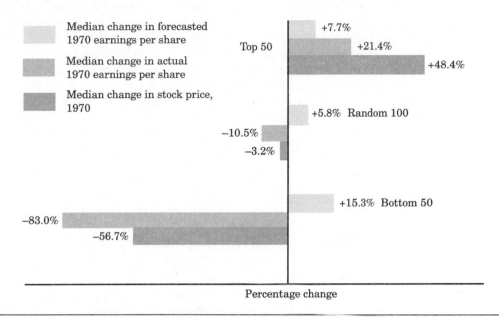

Percentage change

SOURCE: Victor Niederhoffer and Patrick J. Regan, "Earnings Changes, Analysts' Forecasts, and Stock Prices," *Financial Analysts Journal* 28 (May/June 1972): 65–71.

holders gain nothing other than the pleasure of receiving money in the mail. For shareholders who need income, however, receiving dividends is a more convenient way to obtain cash than selling shares. Also, dividends convey information, as well as money, to the shareholders. Through dividend announcements, directors give shareholders and others some notion as to their view of the company's future.

Whatever the merits of cash dividends may be, most companies believe they are important. The popularity of dividends is indicated by the number of companies that choose to pay them. Nearly 80% of the 1,700 common stocks listed on the New York Stock Exchange paid cash dividends in 1989 totaling $102 billion.

DIVIDEND POLICIES
Knowing that investors like stability and growth, companies try to maintain a stable but growing dividend. In periods of high profits, dividend increases are often modest because corporate directors want to minimize the possibility of having to reduce the dividend in later years. Great effort is made to maintain the dividend when profits are low. An example of the reluctance with which companies reduce or discontinue dividend payments is Ford Motor Company's decision to pay dividends in 1980 and 1981, years in which the company sustained heavy losses and had to borrow more than $1 billion.

DIVIDEND ANNOUNCEMENTS AND STOCK PRICES

A number of studies have found that dividend surprises have an effect on stock prices similar to that of earnings surprises.[4] A large, unexpected increase in the dividend has resulted in abnormal stock returns on the announcement date, and generally for a number of days after that. Stock repurchases by companies through tender offers have had a similar effect. One study found that, on average, the tender offer price was 23% higher than the price just before the tender announcement, and that after the offer expired, the price remained substantially above its previous level.[5] Tender offers, like dividends, are a source of information. When a company offers to buy its own stock at a price substantially higher than the current market price, investors have reason to believe that the directors, on the basis of inside information, view the stock as being worth more than its recent price.

|||| THE PREDICTABILITY OF EARNINGS

Anyone who can make superior earnings forecasts with some consistency can earn exceptionally high returns in the stock market by investing in securities of companies for which the consensus earnings forecasts appear to be too low. That is one reason why analysts spend so much of their time forecasting earnings. But how forecastable are the earnings of individual companies? Do analysts make better forecasts than could be made with a *random walk model?*

The predictability of earnings has been tested in at least five ways: (1) by measuring the serial correlations in companies' annual earnings; (2) by examining the lengths of the runs of above-average and below-average earnings growth rates for a number of companies; (3) by comparing the accuracy of forecasts made with sophisticated time series models with the accuracy of forecasts made with the random walk model; (4) by comparing the accuracy of forecasts made with a multiple regression model with forecasts made with the random walk model; and (5) by comparing the accuracy of analysts' forecasts with the accuracy of forecasts based on time series models.

SERIAL CORRELATIONS

Prior to any statistical testing for patterns in earnings growth rates, many in the investment field had assumed it would not be unusual to find strong positive or negative correlations in the annual earnings growth rates of

---

[4]Joseph Aharony and Itzhak Swary, "Quarterly Dividend and Earnings Announcements and Stockholders' Returns: An Empirical Analysis," *The Journal of Finance* 35 (March 1980): 1–12; Gary A. Benesh, Arthur J. Keown, and John M. Pinkerton, "An Examination of Market Reaction to Substantial Shifts in Dividend Policy," *Journal of Financial Economics* 7 (Summer 1984): 131–42; Dennis Proffitt and Alan A. Stephens, "The Market Response to Unexpected Dividend Announcements," *Journal of Applied Business Research* 4 (Fall 1988): 57–65.

[5]T. Vermaelen, "Common Stock Repurchases and Market Signalling," *Journal of Financial Economics* (June 1981): 139–83.

individual firms. Consequently, there was a great deal of surprise when two British studies (titled "Higgledy Piggledy Growth" and "Higgledy Piggledy Growth Again") found that, on the whole, there was virtually no correlation between earnings growth rates of successive periods.[6] The growth rates were described as a random walk. Similar results were obtained in a study of U.S. companies.[7]

RUNS TESTS

Counting the number of runs of each length of above-average and below-average earnings growth rates is similar to measuring serial correlations. A run is a succession of one or more observations of the same kind, such as an above-average rate of growth. If fast or slow growth rates tend to persist, there will be more long runs of above-average or below-average growth than would occur if annual growth rates were independent of one another. Alternatively, if fast growth rates tend to be followed by slow growth rates and slow growth rates tend to be followed by fast rates, there will be more short runs than would occur if there was no negative serial correlation between successive growth rates.

In a study of the annual earnings of 610 industrial companies from 1950 through 1964, Brealey compared the actual number of runs of above-average or below-average earnings growth with the expected number in a random distribution. He found that the year-to-year changes in earnings growth rates were nearly the same as if they had been determined by chance.[8]

TIME SERIES MODELS

The best earnings forecasts are sometimes made with the random walk (or naïve) model, which states that

$$E(EPS_t) = EPS_{t-1} \qquad (10\text{-}1)$$

That is, expected earnings for the current year are the same as actual earnings for last year.

Forecasts have been made with a number of considerably more sophisticated *time series* models to see if any can make better earnings predictions than the simple random walk model. Although the findings have been mixed, it seems fair to conclude that earnings forecasts made

[6]I. M. D. Little, "Higgledy Piggledy Growth," Oxford: Institute of Statistics, November 1962, 24, no. 4; and A. C. Rayner, "Higgledy Piggledy Growth Again," Oxford: Basil Blackwell, 1966.

[7]John Lintner and Robert Glauber, "Higgledy Piggledy Growth in America," unpublished paper presented to the Seminar on the Analysis of Security Prices, May 1967, University of Chicago; reprinted in James Lorie and Richard Brealey, *Modern Developments in Investment Management,* 2d ed. (Hinsdale, Ill.: Dryden Press, 1978), pp. 594–611.

[8]R. A. Brealey, *An Introduction to Risk and Return from Common Stocks,* 2d ed. (Cambridge, Mass.: MIT Press, 1983).

with the random walk model have been as accurate, on the average, as forecasts made with any other time series model.[9]

MULTIPLE REGRESSION MODEL

If a firm's earnings growth is positively correlated with the growth of the economy as well as with the growth of its own industry, forecasts of economic growth and industry growth may be helpful in forecasting the firm's earnings growth. Eckel developed a *multiple regression* model to see if this could be true.[10] He started with the random walk model (earnings this year = earnings last year) and added two variables: a proxy for expected growth of the economy and a forecast of growth for the firm's industry. For the expected growth of the economy, he used the composite diffusion index from *Business Conditions Digest,* which indicates the percentage of the leading economic indicators that have been rising over a certain period. For the industry forecast, he used the predicted percentage change in the value of the industry's shipments, as reported in the *U.S. Industrial Outlook,* an annual publication of the U.S. Department of Commerce.

The Eckel multiple regression model was used to forecast one year's earnings for 31 companies selected at random from all stocks in *Moody's Handbook of Common Stocks* that met certain criteria. The average forecast error was about 15% smaller than for the simple random walk model, indicating that analysts may find GNP forecasts and industry forecasts useful in predicting the earnings of individual companies.

ANALYSTS' FORECASTS VERSUS TIME SERIES MODELS

Analysts' forecasts of earnings one year ahead appear to be superior to extrapolations from past earnings data, no matter how sophisticated the time series model may be.[11] In one study, the mean of analysts' predictions for each of 92 New York Stock Exchange companies for the years 1972 through 1976, as reported in *Standard & Poor's Earnings Forecaster,* was compared with projections made with three time series models. Table 10-2 compares the forecast errors for the analysts and the simple

---

[9]Kenneth S. Lorek, "Predicting Annual Net Earnings with Quarterly Earnings Time Series Models," *Journal of Accounting Research* 17 (Spring 1979): 190–204; Steve W. Albrecht, Larry I. Lookabill, and James C. McKeown, "The Time Series Properties of Annual Earnings," *Journal of Accounting Research* 15 (Autumn 1977): 226–44; Ross I. Watts and Richard W. Leftwich, "The Time Series of Annual Accounting Earnings," *Journal of Accounting Research* 15 (Autumn 1977): 253–71.

[10]Norm Eckel, "An EPS Forecasting Model Utilizing Macroeconomic Performance Expectations," *Financial Analysts Journal* 38 (May/June 1982): 68–77.

[11]Lawrence D. Brown and Michael S. Rozeff, "The Superiority of Analyst Forecasts as Measures of Expectations: Evidence from Earnings," *The Journal of Finance* 33 (March 1978): 1–16; R. Malcolm Richards, James J. Benjamin, and Robert H. Strawser, "An Examination of the Accuracy of Earnings Forecasts," *Financial Management* 6 (Autumn 1978): 78–86.

||| **TABLE 10-2**

Mean Absolute Relative Errors in EPS Forecasts: Analysts versus
Random Walk Model

	1972	1973	1974	1975	1976	Five-Year Average
Random walk model	17.4%	19.0%	62.4%	25.3%	20.4%	28.9%
Analysts	7.8	13.7	59.6	22.5	16.7	24.1
Difference	9.6	5.3	2.8	2.8	3.7	4.8

SOURCE: R. Malcolm Richards, James J. Benjamin, and Robert H. Strawser, "An Examination of the Accuracy of Earnings Forecasts," *Financial Management* 6 (Autumn 1978): 78–86.

||| **TABLE 10-3**

Analysts' Forecast Errors and Earnings Stability

Industry	Forecast Error	Stability Measure*
Banking	4.9%	.94
Building	23.6	.67
Chemical	20.8	.75
Drugs	7.8	.91
Electrical equipment	18.0	.72
Electric utilities	8.9	.88
Office equipment and computers	88.8	.93
Paper	19.6	.69
Petroleum	23.3	.72
Retail stores	46.7	.59

*The measure of earnings stability is the coefficient of determination (R^2) in a regression of aggregate earnings per share for all firms in an industry against time. The higher the R^2, the smaller the deviations of the actual earnings from a fitted trendline.

SOURCE: R. Malcolm Richards, James G. Benjamin, and Robert H. Strawser, "An Examination of the Accuracy of Earnings Forecasts," *Financial Management* 6 (Autumn 1978): 78–86.

random walk model, which was the most accurate of the three time series models.[12]

For the five-year period as a whole, the analysts' average error was about 17% smaller (24.1% versus 28.9%) than the average error for the random walk model. The extremely high errors for the recession year 1974 (59.6% for the analysts and 62.4% for the random walk model) indicate that the analysts were only slightly better at predicting earnings during the recession than was the backward-looking random walk model.

The forecast errors for 10 industries in Table 10-3 show that, with one major exception (office equipment), the errors were closely related to the past stability of the industry's earnings. As one would expect, the

[12]The comparative accuracy of earnings forecasts is evaluated by comparing the mean absolute relative forecast errors. The mean absolute relative error is the average of the absolute values of the relative forecast errors. If n is the number of forecasts, F the forecast, and A the actual, the mean absolute relative forecast error is

$$1/n \sum |(F - A)/A|$$

more stable the earnings, generally the easier they are to predict. However, the degree of stability in the past is not always a good indicator of the amount of stability in the future.

|||| ANALYSIS OF PROFITS AND FINANCIAL CONDITION

Predicting the future earnings of a business firm is somewhat like predicting the future health of an individual. It is a highly chancy undertaking, but the more you know about the previous experience, present condition, and likely future environment and behavior of the business or individual, the better your prediction is likely to be.

Typically, earnings forecasts are made with a top-down approach, which means starting with a forecast of general economic conditions (e.g., GNP and interest rates), which to a large degree determine the environment in which the firm will be operating. Second, given the expected outlook for the economy, assess the prospects for the industry, or industries, in which the firm operates. What is the probable total demand for each of the company's major products, and in view of the expected competitive environment, what is the outlook for prices? In capital-intensive industries, such as pulp and paper, price competition is strongly influenced by the amount of excess production capacity. The third and final step is to predict sales, earnings, number of shares outstanding, and earnings per share for the firm itself. Eckel's multiple regression model was based on the same general idea of tying a company's expected earnings growth rate to the expected growth of the economy and the firm's industry, although his model included no company-specific variable other than the previous year's earnings.

RETURN ON SHAREHOLDERS' EQUITY

Generally, it is both difficult and unwise to predict a firm's earnings per share (EPS) without evaluating its financial condition and examining the sources of its past growth. In the simplest terms, EPS growth depends on sales growth, the margin of profit (net income/sales), and any change in the number of shares outstanding. If sales grow at a rate of 10%, the profit margin remains constant, and the number of outstanding shares does not change, net earnings and EPS will both grow at a rate of 10%. But since profit margins and shares outstanding do change, along with a number of other factors, analyzing EPS growth requires the examination of a number of financial relationships.

In Chapter 9 we noted that if the return on equity is constant, the earnings growth rate (which differs from the EPS growth rate if the number of shares outstanding changes) is the product of the return on equity (r) and the earnings retention ratio (b). The following paragraphs will examine, with financial ratios, the factors that determine r, or ROE, the return on equity.

SYMBOLS, RATIOS, AND EQUATIONS

The following symbols, ratios, and equations are useful in analyzing EPS growth:

1. EBIT = earnings before interest and taxes
2. EBT = earnings before taxes
3. T = income taxes/EBT = effective tax rate
4. 1 − T = percentage of earnings remaining after taxes
5. EAT = earnings after taxes (net income)
6. IE = interest expense
7. NW = common shareholders' equity
8. SO = average number of common shares outstanding
9. EBIT/sales = before-tax operating margin
10. Sales/assets = total asset utilization, or turnover
11. Assets/NW = a measure of financial leverage
12. ROA = return on assets = EAT/assets
13. ROE = r = return on equity or return on net worth = EAT/NW
14. NW/SO = net worth, or book value, per share

The relationships of various key factors to earnings per share are expressed in the following equations:

$$\text{EBIT/assets} = \text{operating profit return on assets} = (\text{EBIT/sales})(\text{sales/assets}) \tag{10-2}$$

$$\text{EBT/assets} = \text{before-tax return on assets} = \text{EBIT/assets} - \text{IE/assets} \tag{10-3}$$

$$\text{EAT/assets} = \text{return on assets} = (\text{EBT/assets})(1 - T) \tag{10-4}$$

$$\text{EAT/NW} = \text{return on equity} = (\text{EAT/assets})(\text{assets/NW}) \tag{10-5}$$

$$\text{EPS} = \text{earnings per share} = (\text{EAT/NW})(\text{NW/SO}) \tag{10-6}$$

OPERATING PROFIT RETURN ON ASSETS

The return on assets, before interest and taxes, is the product of the operating margin (EBIT/sales) and total asset utilization or turnover (sales/assets). Other things being the same, an improvement in either the operating margin or asset turnover will increase the before-tax return on assets. However, any attempt to improve one of these ratios may have an adverse effect on the other. For example, increasing prices to improve the operating margin may result in smaller sales and a lower asset turnover. Alternatively, lowering prices to increase sales and the asset turnover may reduce the profit margin. On the other hand, some improvements, such as better management of accounts receivable and inventories, can increase both the profit margin and asset utilization.

BEFORE-TAX RETURN ON ASSETS

The before-tax return on assets that remains after paying interest is EBIT/assets − IE/assets. Borrowing and investing will enhance a firm's profit if EBIT/assets on the assets acquired is greater than the interest burden (IE/assets) for the funds borrowed. For example, if EBIT/assets on newly acquired, debt-financed assets is 20%, and the interest rate on the borrowed funds is 12%, the new assets will contribute an amount equal to 8% of their book value to before-tax profits. Whether that will increase or decrease the overall before-tax return on assets (EBT/assets) depends on the return for the firm's other assets. For example, if EBT/assets for previously owned assets is 10%, and EBT/assets for newly acquired assets is only 8%, EBT/assets will decline.

RETURN ON ASSETS

Return on assets is the product of the before-tax return on assets (EBT/assets) and the tax retention $(1 − T)$, which is the percentage of profits remaining after taxes. The effective tax rate *(T)* is income tax expense divided by earnings before taxes. Given EBT/assets, the return on assets increases with a decrease in the effective tax rate. Sometimes the most important single reason for a change in the return on assets—and a resulting change in earnings per share—is an increase or decrease in the effective tax rate.

RETURN ON EQUITY OR NET WORTH

Return on equity (ROE) is the product of return on assets (EAT/assets) and financial leverage (assets/NW). The larger a firm's assets in relation to its net worth, the greater the proportion of its assets that are financed with debt. For example, if the asset/NW ratio is 4/3, three-fourths of the assets are financed with equity (the reciprocal of 4/3) and one-fourth with liabilities. If the asset/NW ratio is 4/1, only one-fourth of the assets are financed with equity and three-fourths are financed with liabilities. Given the return on assets, the greater the proportion of assets financed with debt, the higher the return on equity.

Borrowing to finance assets needed for growth always results in more volatile earnings than if growth is financed with retained earnings or by the issuance of stock, and it increases the possibility of a severe cash shortage and bankruptcy. Whether borrowing results in higher earnings per share than would the issuance of stock depends on the operating margin (EBIT/sales), the interest rate on the borrowed funds, and the price at which stock could be issued.[13] The lower the interest rate and the lower the stock price, the better debt financing looks.

Possible outcomes with debt and common stock financing are illustrated in Example 10-1.

---

[13] Whether an increase in the expected earnings growth rate as a result of debt-financed expansion will raise the price of a stock depends on whether the expected increase in earnings is more important to investors than the increase in risk.

EXAMPLE 10-1   EPS WITH DEBT AND EQUITY FINANCING

Assumptions:

1. Before the proposed expansion, the company has no interest-bearing debt. Its assets total $150 and its liabilities are $40.

2. An asset increase of $100 (from $150 to $250) can be financed with either 12% debt or a new stock issue. Stock can be issued at a net price of $33.33, so three shares would have to be issued to raise $100.

3. Sales and EBIT/sales after the expansion will be either $300 and 30%, $250 and 20%, or $200 and 3%, respectively.

4. The effective tax rate is 40%. Tax expense is rounded.

5. The number of outstanding shares before a new stock issue is 10.

	Debt Financing			Equity Financing		
EBIT/sales	30%	20%	3%	30%	20%	3%
Assets	$250	$250	$250	$250	$250	$250
Liabilities	140	140	140	40	40	40
Shareholders' equity	110	110	110	210	210	210
Sales	300	250	200	300	250	200
EBIT	$ 90	$ 50	$ 6	$ 90	$ 50	$ 6
Interest expense	(12)	(12)	(12)	0	0	0
EBT	78	38	(6)	90	50	6
Taxes (40%)	(31)	(15)	2	36	20	2
EAT	47	23	(4)	54	30	4
Shares outstanding	10	10	10	13	13	13
Earnings per share	4.70	2.30	(.40)	4.15	2.31	.31

Observations: Net earnings and earnings per share are considerably more sensitive to changes in sales and the profit margin when the financing is with debt rather than with common stock. With debt, the range of earnings per share is $5.10 (4.70 + .40), compared to $3.84 (4.15 − .31) with stock. Also, with debt, a loss is sustained when the profit margin is low. ||||

EARNINGS PER SHARE

According to Equation 10-6, EPS is the product of return on equity (EAT/NW) and book value per share (NW/SO). This equation is closely related to Equation 9-7, which states that the earnings growth rate is the product of return on equity and the earnings retention ratio ($g = r \times b$). Thus, return on equity and earnings retention affect both EPS and the EPS growth rate. Earnings retention affects EPS through its impact on the book value per share.[14]

---

[14]Book value per share can also be increased by repurchasing the company's stock if the market price is below the book value or by issuing stock if the market price is above the book value.

Growth of earnings and EPS are usually associated with increases in sales, assets, and other measures of the scale of a firm's operations. In Equation 10-6, increases in the scale of operations are reflected through increases in the book value per share (BVPS). The rate of BVPS growth will equal the sales growth rate if $r \times b$ equals the sales growth rate and no shares are issued or repurchased at a price other than book value.

Sustained growth in EPS over a long period of time must come from growth in the scale of the firm's operations rather than from continuous improvement in the return on equity, which is impossible. Competition limits the potential for improvement of the operating margin; competition and physical constraints limit the amount of sales that can be generated with a given amount of assets; and risk considerations limit the amount of financial leverage.

OTHER RATIOS

A number of ratios, including those of Equations 10-2 through 10-6, are used in evaluating a firm's financial condition and the quality of its management. Analysts look for favorable and unfavorable trends in the operating margin, asset utilization, and financial leverage and make comparisons with other firms in the same industry.

Asset Utilization

Management effectiveness is sometimes reflected in the utilization ratios for accounts receivable, inventories, and gross fixed assets. Low utilization for accounts receivable may indicate that the firm is either too liberal in extending credit or too lax in making collections. Low inventory utilization may indicate poor inventory management. On the other hand, it may reflect a policy of carrying high inventories in order to provide superior customer service. High inventories are not undesirable if the additional costs of carrying the higher inventories are more than offset by profit increases from higher sales or better operating margins. Low utilization of fixed assets may indicate that the firm has unused capacity that could be liquidated.

Debt Ratios

Certain debt ratios should be examined. One of the most important is *interest coverage,* or the ratio of EBIT to interest expense. This ratio gives a rough indication of how far profits could drop before the firm would have difficulty making interest payments. Other commonly used debt ratios include total liabilities to total assets and long-term debt to total capital; in the latter, total capital consists of long-term debt plus preferred stock and common equity.

Analysts examine debt ratios and changes in debt ratios not only to assess the risk of financial stress and bankruptcy but to estimate the firm's beta and evaluate its ability to take on additional leverage. For example, an increase in financial leverage is likely to make earnings and the stock price more volatile, thereby increasing beta. On the other hand, the lower the ratio of debt to assets, the greater the capacity of the firm to take on additional leverage for the possible benefit of its shareholders.

Conclusions about Ratios

Ratios are often more useful for the questions they raise than for the answers they provide. If a firm's operating margin has declined or is lower than the margin for other firms in the same industry, the question is, why? If a firm's debt ratios are higher and its interest coverage is lower than for similar companies, two questions should be asked: First, how much additional debt capacity, if any, does the firm have? Second, what is the probability that the firm will have financial difficulties, and how serious might they be? Ratio analysis is a good way to begin an evaluation of a firm's financial condition and profitability; to make a complete evaluation, one must look behind the ratios.

SUSTAINABLE EARNINGS

Typically, financial ratios are calculated with figures from published financial statements, which are sometimes quite misleading. Reported earnings often exceed the firm's true or *sustainable earnings;* that is, the amount it could pay out as dividends without adversely affecting future earnings. If the reported earnings are greater than the sustainable earnings, the quality of the reported earnings is said to be low.

The quality of a firm's reported earnings depends on three things: the tightness or looseness (degree of conservatism or liberality) of the firm's accounting policies; the assumptions underlying expense accruals; and the amount of extraordinary income. Loose accounting practices, inadequate expense accruals, and extraordinary income reduce the quality of reported earnings.

Inventory profits reported during inflationary periods with the FIFO method of accounting are a good example of "phantom profits" that cause reported earnings to exceed sustainable earnings. For example, if reported earnings of $10 million include after-tax inventory profits of $2 million as a result of valuing ending inventories at higher prices than beginning inventories, the firm's sustainable earnings would be $8 million instead of $10 million. The $2 million of inventory profits do nothing for the firm. Payment of $10 million in dividends would shrink the firm's earning capacity.

Example 10-2 illustrates the concept of sustainable earnings by comparing two companies that are identical in every respect except one: company A uses the LIFO method of accounting for inventories, and company B uses the FIFO method. In periods of rising prices, reported earnings are higher with FIFO than with LIFO.

EXAMPLE 10-2   SUSTAINABLE AND UNSUSTAINABLE
EARNINGS

Assumptions:

1. Beginning inventories of company A are lower than the beginning inventories of company B ($20 versus $35) because company A

adopted the LIFO method number of years ago when costs were much lower.

2. Physical quantities in inventory at the end of the year are the same as at the beginning of the year. Thus, company A's ending inventories, valued with LIFO, are the same as the beginning inventories. Company B's ending inventories, valued with FIFO, are higher than the beginning inventories ($40 versus $35) because of increases in costs during the year.

3. Company A's reported earnings are its sustainable earnings. It could pay out all of its earnings as dividends without causing future earnings to decline. (This implies, for example, that the provision for depreciation is equal to the amount that must be invested in fixed assets to maintain the current level of earnings.) Company B's reported earnings would be its sustainable earnings except for the inventory profits, which bring in no cash but are subject to taxation.

4. Neither company had excess cash at the beginning of the year; capital expenditures were equal to depreciation; net working capital did not change; no other assets were acquired or sold; and there was no change in the company's liabilities or capital stock.

	Company A Sustainable (LIFO)		Company B Unsustainable (FIFO)	
Sales		$200		$200
Cost of sales:				
Beginning inventories	$ 20		$ 35	
Cost of goods manufactured	120		120	
Ending inventory	(20)		(40)	
Cost of sales		120		115
Gross profit		80		85
Selling and administrative expenses		60		60
Earnings before taxes		20		25
Income taxes (40%)		8		10
Net earnings		12		15
Cash flows:				
Net earnings		12		15
Depreciation		8		8
FIFO inventory profit		—		(5)
Cash flow from operations		20		18
Capital expenditures		8		8
Cash available for dividends		12		10

Observations: Company B's reported earnings of $15 are $3 higher than A's because they include $5 of before-tax profit that resulted from valuing the ending inventories at higher prices than the beginning inventories. After allowing for the $2 tax on this illusory profit of $5, B's sustainable earnings are actually $2 less than A's. Given the assumptions underlying the example, the amount of cash available for dividends is equal to the sustainable earnings, which were $12 for A and $10 for B.

ANALYSIS OF PROCTER & GAMBLE'S PROFITS

Procter & Gamble is one of the largest U.S. industrial corporations, with sales of $24 billion and net earnings of $1.6 billion for the fiscal year 1990. In a recent *Fortune* survey, it was selected as one of America's most admired corporations. Its principal products include soap, detergents and other laundry products, cosmetics and other personal care products, and beverages.

The following analysis of Procter & Gamble is largely limited to things that can be learned from the figures and other information contained in the company's annual report for the fiscal year ended June 30, 1990. No comparisons are made with other companies. The principal objectives here are to illustrate certain useful analytical techniques and to indicate the kinds of information that are, and are not, provided in a typical corporate annual report.

RATIO ANALYSIS: INTRODUCTION

In its 1990 annual report, the company reported an increase of $.93 (26%) in earnings per share. The present analysis will explain, to the extent possible with information contained in the annual report, the sources of this increase. The data have been derived principally from the company's financial statements, including the accompanying notes. The ratios in Table 10-6 were calculated with the income statement and balance sheet data appearing in Tables 10-4 and 10-5. Table 10-7 summarizes the sources of the $.93 increase in EPS, which were as follows:

	Changes in EPS from 1989 to 1990
Increase in operating margin (EBIT/sales)	$.40
Decrease in effective tax rate (T)	.23
Increase in book value per share	.42
Increase in preferred dividend	(.08)
Other	(.04)
Total	.93

INCREASE IN OPERATING MARGIN

The improvement in the firm's operating margin (from 10.89% to 11.89%) accounted for $.40 of the $.93 increase in EPS. The annual report does not provide the information needed to determine how much, if any, of the improvement resulted from changes in the product mix or lower fixed

|||| **TABLE 10-4**

Procter & Gamble Sales and Profit Information: Fiscal Years 1986–1990

	1990	1989	1988	1987	1986
Sales*	$24,081	$21,398	$19,336	$17,000	$15,439
EBIT*	2,863	2,330	1,951	970	1,432
Interest expense*	442	391	321	353	257
EBT*	2,421	1,939	1,630	617	1,175
Income taxes*	819	733	610	290	466
EAT*	1,602	1,206	1,020	327	709
Preferred dividends	47	16	11	11	5
EAT on common*	1,555	1,190	1,009	316[b]	704
Average number of shares outstanding*	346.3	334.4	338.6	337.2	335.6
EPS	$4.49	$3.56	$2.98	$ .94[b]	$2.10
EPS (Value Line)	$4.13[a]	$3.56	$2.98	$2.30	$2.10
Dividend	$1.75	$1.50	$1.38	$1.35	$1.31

*In millions.
[a] EPS reported by Value Line for 1990 excludes recovery of $125 million ($.36 a share) in settlement of litigation.
[b] EAT on common and EPS for 1987 would have been $775 million and $2.30, respectively, if the company had not absorbed an after-tax charge of $459 million ($1.36 a share) for restructuring.

costs per dollar of sales. However, an examination of the notes to the financial statements reveals that a significant part of the improvement came from sources that are unlikely to provide future increases.

Extraordinary Charges and Credits

Three important contributors to the improved operating margin were the recovery of $125 million in settlement of a lawsuit, a gain of $141 million from the sale of a soft drink business, and a saving of $104 million in profit sharing expense compared to what the expense would have been if it had continued at the same rate of operating income (before profit sharing) as in 1989. These gains were partly offset by an increase of $146 million in the provision for consolidation of manufacturing facilities. The impact on EBIT and EBIT/sales can be summarized as follows:

Extraordinary increases in EBIT:	
Lawsuit recovery	$125
Gain on sale of soft drink business	141
Saving on profit sharing	104
Total	370
Less increase in provision for consolidation of manufacturing facilities	146
Net extraordinary increase in EBIT	224
Adjusted EBIT (2,863 − 224)	$2,639
EBIT/sales (before adjustment)	11.89%
EBIT/sales (after adjustment, 2,639/24,081)	10.96%

Without these extraordinary items, EBIT/sales would have been only .07 percentage points higher (10.96 − 10.89) in 1990 than in 1989, and the

|||| **TABLE 10-5**

Procter & Gamble Balance Sheet Information: Fiscal Years
1986–1990 (amounts in millions)

	1990	1989	1988	1987	1986
Total assets	$18,487	$16,351	$14,820	$13,715	$13,005
Average assets	17,419	15,586	14,268	13,385	11,369
Total common equity	8,481	7,215	6,337	5,990	5,554
Average common equity	7,848	6,776	6,163	5,772	5,413

|||| **TABLE 10-6**

Procter & Gamble Profit Analysis: Fiscal Years 1986–1990

	1990	1989	1988	1987	1986
EBIT/assets					
EBIT/sales $\times$	.1189	.1089	.1009	.0571	.0928
Sales/assets =	1.3825	1.3738	1.3555	1.2701	1.3586
EBIT/assets	.1644	.1496	.1368	.0725	.1260
EBT/assets:					
EBIT/assets −					
Interest expense/assets =	.0254	.0251	.0255	.0264	.0226
EBT/assets	.1390	.1245	.1113	.0461	.1034
EAT/assets:					
EBT/assets $\times$					
$(1 - T)$ =	.6617	.6220	.6258	.5300	.6034
EAT/assets	.0920	.0774	.0697	.0244	.0624
EAT/NW:					
EAT/assets $\times$					
Assets/NW =	2.2195	2.3002	2.3735	2.3190	2.1003
EAT/NW	.2042	.1780	.1654	.0566	.1311
EAT on common/NW					
EAT/NW −					
Preferred dividends/NW =	.0060	.0024	.0018	.0019	.0009
EAT on common/NW	.1982	.1756	.1636	.0547	.1302
EPS					
EAT on common/NW $\times$					
NW/SO	22.66	20.26	18.20	17.12	16.13
EPS	4.49	3.56	2.98	.94	2.10

increase in EPS due to the increase in EBIT/sales would have been only
$.03 instead of $.40.

Inventory Profits and Depreciation

Two common sources of year-to-year changes in earnings are changes in
inventory profits and changes in depreciation and amortization. The inventory profits were probably somewhat higher in 1990 than in 1989
because of a significant increase in non-LIFO inventories, but the amount
cannot be determined from information in the annual report. Depreciation

|||| **TABLE 10-7**

Procter & Gamble: Factors Contributing to an Increase of $.93 in
EPS from 1989 to 1990

	1989 EPS Adjusted to 1990 Ratios					
	EBIT/ Sales	1 − T	Preferred Dividends	NW/SO	Other	Total
EBIT/assets:						
EBIT/sales ×	.1189*	.1089	.1089	.1089		
Sales/assets =	1.3738	1.3738	1.3738	1.3738		
EBIT/assets	.1633	.1496	.1496	.1496		
EBT/assets:						
EBIT/assets −						
Interest expense/assets =	.0251	.0251	.0251	.0251		
EBT/assets	.1382	.1245	.1245	.1245		
EAT/assets:						
EBT/assets ×						
(1 − T) =	.6220	.6617*	.6220	.6220		
EAT/assets	.0860	.0824	.0774	.0774		
EAT/NW:						
EAT/assets ×						
Assets/NW =	2.3002	2.3002	2.3002	2.3002		
EAT/NW	.1978	.1895	.1780	.1780		
EAT on common/NW						
EAT/NW −						
Preferred dividends/NW =	.0024	.0024	.0060*	.0024		
EAT on common/NW	.1954	.1871	.1720	.1756		
EPS						
EAT on common/NW ×						
NW/SO	$20.26	$20.26	$20.26	$22.66*		
EPS (1989 adjusted)	3.96	3.79	3.48	3.98		
EPS (1989 actual)	3.56	3.56	3.56	3.56		
Increase (decrease) attributable to change in 1990	.40	.23	(.08)	.42	(.04)	.93
Increase in reported EPS from 1989 to 1990 (4.49 − 3.56) =						.93

*A 1990 figure substituted into 1989 to determine how EPS would have been affected if this had been the only change from 1989 to 1990.

and amortization expense was virtually the same percentage of sales in 1990 as in 1989, indicating the absence of any profit boost from this source.

INCREASE IN BOOK VALUE PER SHARE

Of the $.93 increase in EPS, $.42 was associated with the increase of 11.8% in BVPS. The percentage increase in book value was only slightly less than the 12.5% increase in sales, and thus served as a fairly good measure of the increase in the scale of the firm's operations.

One way to predict the future growth of BVPS is with Equation 9-7 $(g = r \times b)$. For the 10 years ending with the fiscal year 1990, Procter & Gamble's return on equity was 16.3% and its average retention ratio was 47.5%. If those percentages were to hold each year in the future, and if the number of shares outstanding did not change, earnings, NW, and BVPS would all grow at a rate of 7.7%.

DECREASE IN EFFECTIVE TAX RATE

Procter & Gamble's effective income tax rate (income taxes/earnings before taxes) declined from 37.8% in 1989 to 33.8% in 1990. Further significant decreases in the effective rate seem unlikely. As Table 10-7 shows, this factor alone contributed $.23 to the EPS increase in 1990.

INCREASE IN PREFERRED DIVIDENDS AND OTHER

An increase of $31 million in preferred dividends, net of taxes, in 1990 had a negative impact of $.08 on EPS. Other factors, principally a small decrease in financial leverage, had a negative impact of $.04.

SUMMARY OF PROCTER & GAMBLE'S CHANGE IN EPS

Of the reported increase of $.93 (26%) in EPS in the fiscal year 1990, about $.52 is attributable to items that appear to be nonrecurring.

Extraordinary items affecting EBIT/sales (.40 − .03) =	$.37
Decrease in the effective tax rate	.23
Increase in preferred dividends	(.08)
Total	.52

Without these items, the increase in EPS would have been about $.41 ($.93 − $.52), or 11.5%.

QUALITY OF REPORTED EARNINGS

The notes to Procter & Gamble's financial statements give some indication of the quality of its reported profits, particularly with respect to inventory valuation and retirement expenses. At June 30, 1990, the company valued $1.6 billion of its inventories with methods that could result in inventory profits. If, on average, these inventories were valued at prices 5% higher than the prices of the beginning inventories, the company's before-tax earnings would include about $80 million of inventory profits, which would be about $53 million after taxes, or $.15 a share. From the annual report alone, it is impossible to determine whether this is a reasonable estimate.

In 1990, the company's retirement expenses were $213 million (8.1% of earnings before taxes and retirement expenses), compared to $285 million (12.8% of earnings before taxes and retirement expenses) in 1989. Most of Procter & Gamble's employees in the United States are covered by company-funded, *defined contribution* profit sharing plans that provide retirement benefits. Generally, employees outside the United States are covered by *defined benefit* retirement plans. In addition, many retirees are provided health care and life insurance benefits. The 1990 and 1989 retirement costs, in millions, were as follows:

	1990	1989
Profit sharing	$140	$204
Other pensions	54	60
Post-retirement health care and life insurance	19	21
Total	213	285

Profit sharing expense declined from 9.5% of earnings before profit sharing and taxes in 1989 to 5.5% in 1990. Presumably, the 1990 expense was properly accrued, but the annual report provides no reason for believing that it will remain at this level in the future.

The company has not been accruing the costs of post-retirement health care and life insurance during the working years of its employees. Instead, it recognizes the expense as the claims and premiums are paid. Earnings reported by the company in the future will be affected adversely if it begins to accrue the cost of these benefits as they are earned. Depreciation and amortization expense is a very important item that cannot be evaluated with information contained in the annual report. A difference of just one percentage point in the average rate of depreciation would make a difference of about $110 million in depreciation expense, and a difference of 1% in the amortization rate would make a difference of about $26 million in amortization expense, but there is no way to tell from the annual report whether the rates used are liberal, conservative, or somewhere in between. Notes to the financial statements indicate only that depreciation is calculated on a straight-line basis over the estimated useful lives of the properties, and amortization of intangible assets is on a straight-line basis over periods not exceeding 40 years.

It is probably safe to assume that the provisions for depreciation and amortization are not unreasonable since they have been approved by the firm's public accountants. However, depreciation is calculated on the basis of historical costs and may therefore be inadequate to cover the costs of replacement. Also, the provision for depreciation in the report to shareholders was considerably lower than the amount deducted for tax purposes, as indicated by an increase of $67 million in deferred income taxes due to differences in depreciation. If deferred taxes were calculated at the company's average tax rate of 33.8%, this would indicate that depreciation in the shareholder's report was about $198 million (67/.338) less than the amount deducted on the company's tax return.

|||| PROFIT EXPECTATIONS

In January 1991, Value Line was forecasting an EPS increase of 15.8% for Procter & Gamble for the fiscal year ending June 30, 1991. Reported earnings for the first six months of the fiscal year were 14.0% above the same period of the previous year. If the company could be expected to continue to earn 20% on equity capital, which was the rate it reported for the year 1990, and if it were to continue to retain about 60% of its earnings in the business, the expected earnings growth rate would be about 12%. But, if the expected return on equity is close to the 16.3% average for the years 1981 through 1990, as reported in Value Line, and if the expected earnings retention ratio is close to the 10-year average of 50%, the expected earnings growth rate would be about 8%.

Procter & Gamble's earnings will grow faster than the economy on a continuing basis only if its sales grow faster than GNP, or if the margin of profit continues to increase. Since a continuing increase in the profit margin seems highly unlikely, above-average earnings growth will have to come from above-average sales growth.

All in all, the prospects look good for an above-average earnings growth rate for Procter & Gamble for the next several years, primarily as a result of foreign expansion and the introduction of new products. Beyond that, growth comparable to the GNP growth rate seems more likely.

|||| ANALYSIS OF CASH FLOWS

The success of a business depends in large measure on the wisdom with which it acquires and uses cash. For that reason, it is important to analyze the sources and uses of cash in the annual statement of cash flows, which provides useful information about a company's financial policies. Some of the data in the cash flow statement are derived directly from the income statement and balance sheet, but much of the data appear only in the statement of cash flows.

PROCTER & GAMBLE'S CASH FLOWS

Table 10-8 is a statement of cash flows for Procter & Gamble for the years 1989 and 1990. The first of the three sections in the statement, called "cash provided by (used for) operations," shows the amount of cash generated through operations, after providing for the increase in net working capital. The second section, "cash provided by (used for) financing activities," shows the amount of cash obtained from and paid to lenders, as well as the amount of dividends paid and the amount used to repurchase the company's stock. The third section, "cash provided by (used for) investment activities," consists principally of cash payments for capital assets (property, plant, and equipment) and corporate acquisitions.

Procter & Gamble's statement of cash flows shows that it required less than $200 million of additional borrowings in 1990. At the same time, the company's capital expenditures exceeded depreciation and amortization by more than $400 million, and it invested nearly $500 million in acquisitions, as well as $300 million in additional net working capital and nearly $200 million in its own stock. The company found it possible to make these large expenditures with little increase in debt because net earnings exceeded dividends by nearly $1.0 billion, and it obtained more than $250 million from the sale of assets.

|||| **TABLE 10-8**

Procter & Gamble Statement of Cash Flows: Fiscal Years
1989–1990 (amounts in millions)

	1990	1989
Cash provided by (used for) operations		
Net earnings	$1,602	$1,206
Depreciation, depletion, and amortization	859	767
Deferred income taxes	(129)	(16)
Total	2,332	1,957
Cash provided by (used for) working capital		
Receivables	(387)	(331)
Inventories	(312)	(103)
Accounts payable and accrued liabilities	236	779
Other	137	193
Total	(326)	538
Cash provided by operations	2,006	2,495
Cash provided by (used for) financing activities		
Repayments of long-term debt	(786)	(369)
Additions to long-term debt	734	532
Changes in short-term debt	205	(385)
Issuance of preferred shares	—	1,000
Purchase of treasury shares	(179)	(794)
Cash dividends paid	(639)	(520)
Cash provided by (used for) financing activities	(665)	(536)
Cash provided by (used for) investment activities		
Capital expenditures	(1,300)	(1,029)
Proceeds from asset sales	263	98
Acquisitions	(484)	(506)
Cash (used for) investment activities	(1,521)	(1,437)
Increase (decrease) in cash and cash equivalents	(180)	522

In the years 1989 and 1990, the company invested close to $1 billion
in its own stock, acquiring 19.7 million shares at an average cost of about
$50. These stock purchases supplied about 80% of the shares needed
during those two years for the acquisition of Noxell Corporation and for
the company's stock option and stock remuneration plans.

FREE CASH FLOW

Analysts attempt to estimate the amount of cash available to a company
for discretionary spending, which is called "free cash flow." It is the
amount generated by a firm in excess of certain "basic requirements."
Views differ as to what should be classified as basic requirements. Increases in net working capital are always considered a basic requirement,
as are capital expenditures needed to maintain the current level of operations. Some analysts also consider dividends a basic requirement because of the extreme reluctance of corporations to reduce or omit dividend
payments. Debt payments are generally not treated as a basic requirement because principal payments are often made with new borrowings.

Calculation of free cash flow begins with cash provided by operations,
which is net income, plus noncash charges, less any increase (or plus any

decrease) in net working capital. Cash is not free until increases in working capital have been provided for.

The calculation of free cash flow can look something like this:

Cash provided by operations	$5,000
Necessary capital expenditures	(3,000)
Dividends	(500)
Free cash flow	1,500

Why is free cash flow so important? It is the amount of cash available (without issuing stock or increasing the company's debt) to finance growth through capital spending and cash acquisitions of other corporations. It can also be used to repurchase the company's own stock. In a word, cash is needed for the financial flexibility that enables a company to meet its obligations and respond to new needs and opportunities.

|||| INFLATION AND REPORTED EARNINGS

Finally, in analyzing a company's profitability, it is important to take inflation into account. For security analysts, one of the most troubling things about inflation is the distortion it causes in reported earnings. Three items require special attention: inventories, depreciation expense, and interest expense. As already noted, for the many firms that use FIFO inventory accounting, rising prices result in inventory profits that come from valuing ending inventories at higher prices than beginning inventories. For the even greater number of firms that use straight-line depreciation for reporting to shareholders, and for some that use accelerated depreciation, the amounts charged to depreciation expense are often far below the cost of necessary replacements. Both of these items result in phantom profits, which distort reported earnings.

Partly offsetting the upward-biasing effects of FIFO inventory accounting and understated depreciation is the overstatement of interest expense caused by inflation. If the rate of inflation rises above the rate that was expected when a fixed-rate debt was incurred, the debtor benefits at the expense of the creditor. The real value of the debt to the lender and the real cost of the debt to the borrower decline continuously as the value of money decreases. This inflation-produced benefit for borrowers is not reflected in reported earnings.

Inflationary profit distortions resulting from FIFO inventory accounting and inadequate depreciation allowances must be given special attention in predicting dividends because they make reported earnings a poor indicator of the amount of cash available for financing growth and paying dividends. With FIFO accounting, part of the reported earnings are nothing more than increases in inventory values, which do not represent cash income. When the provision for depreciation is too small, part of the reported earnings will be needed for replacement of fixed assets. For these and other reasons, careful analysis of past and prospective cash flows is an important part of security analysis.

SUMMARY

Financial analysts provide portfolio managers with estimates of risk and return and attempt to find mispriced securities. In valuing stocks, much of their attention is on forecasting earnings, cash flows, and dividends because these variables, along with risk, are of primary interest to investors. Since prices of individual stocks often react favorably when actual earnings turn out to be higher than the consensus forecast, superior earnings forecasts can lead to superior returns on stocks.

Analysis of sources of past earnings growth can be helpful in predicting future growth. In analyzing growth, attention is focused on anything that can affect the return on the shareholder's equity. Thus, changes in the operating margin (EBIT/sales), the asset turnover (sales/assets), the percentage of earnings left after taxes $(1 - T)$, or the amount of financial leverage (assets/NW) are important. An increase in any one of these, if not offset by decreases in others, will increase the return on equity. However, competitive and other constraints prevent these ratios from increasing indefinitely. Over a long period of time, earnings growth is tied closely to the growth of book value per share, which depends upon the rate of return on equity and the percentage of earnings retained in the business.

Reported earnings often exceed sustainable earnings, the amount the firm could pay out as dividends without affecting its future rate of growth. The extent to which reported earnings exceed sustainable earnings depends on the quality of the reported earnings.

Cash flow analysis is useful in assessing a firm's financial condition and growth potential. Operating cash flows are earnings plus noncash charges, less any increase (or plus any decrease) in net working capital, exclusive of cash and borrowings. All other cash flows are categorized as either financial transactions or investments. Free cash flow is the amount of cash generated in excess of certain basic requirements, including increases in net working capital, the amount of capital expenditures needed to maintain the current level of operations, and possibly dividends.

In analyzing a firm's profits, it is important to take inflation into account because it often causes reported earnings to exceed sustainable earnings.

QUESTIONS

*1. Which of the following methods can be used to inflate current reported earnings?

*Note: All questions and problems preceded by an asterisk are from Chartered Financial Analysts (CFA) examinations.

   I.   Charge depreciation and amortization at the highest permitted rates.
   II. Capitalize intermediate-term expenses.
   III. Accrue pension expenses at the lowest possible rate.
   IV. Recognize sales only when payment has been received.
      a. II and IV only
      b. II and III only
      c. II, III, and IV only
      d. I, II, III, and IV

*2. In an inflationary period, which of the following will be more realistic if FIFO rather than LIFO is used?
   a. Balance sheet
   b. Income statement
   c. Cash flow statement
   d. None of the above

*3. Which of the following best explains a ratio of "net sales to net fixed assets" that exceeds the industry average?
   a. The firm expanded its plant and equipment in the past few years.
   b. The firm makes less efficient use of its assets than other firms.
   c. The firm has a lot of old plant and equipment.
   d. The firm uses straight-line depreciation.

*4. Why might a firm's ratio of "long-term debt to long-term capital" be lower than the industry average, but its ratio of "income before interest and taxes to interest charges" be lower than the industry average?
   a. The firm has higher profitability than average.
   b. The firm has more short-term debt than average.
   c. The firm has a high ratio of "current assets to current liabilities."
   d. The firm has a high ratio of "total cash flow to total long-term debt."

*5. Which of the following statements is true?
   a. During inflation, LIFO makes the income statement less representative than if FIFO were used.
   b. During inflation, FIFO makes the balance sheet less representative than if LIFO were used.
   c. After inflation ends, distortion due to LIFO will disappear as inventory is sold.
   d. None of the above.

6. Explain the concept of sustainable earnings. Why is it important?

7. Explain how to calculate free cash flow.

8. Discuss how free cash flow can affect a company's future earnings and financial condition.

9. A member of the stock selection committee of Potomac Associates maintains that quantitative valuation methodologies are worthless.

He believes that the way to select the best-performing stocks is to "just get there first with the best earnings forecast. If you are a good analyst, the stock will take care of itself." Briefly discuss and support his approach.

10. Explain how common stock prices are affected by earnings forecasts.

11. Explain why companies often have a lower dividend payout ratio in years of substantial earnings increases.

12. Describe a random walk model. What assumption underlies the use of a random walk model to forecast a company's earnings?

13. Explain Eckel's forecasting model. What is the composite diffusion index, and why was it included as an independent variable?

14. Explain why cash flows are an important consideration in evaluating a common stock.

15. Explain how the choice between the FIFO and LIFO methods of accounting for inventories affects the funds provided from operations.

16. Why does the FIFO method of accounting produce illusory earnings during inflationary periods? In what sense are illusory earnings not real?

17. Explain why reported earnings may be higher but the cash flows lower with the FIFO method than with LIFO.

18. In what sense are earnings likely to be of higher quality with the LIFO method and fast depreciation than with the FIFO method and slower depreciation?

19. Explain why industry segment information in a company's annual report can be useful in forecasting the firm's earnings.

20. What is the principal source of growth in book value per share? Why is it the principal source?

21. Explain why increases in EBIT/sales, sales/assets, and assets/NW cannot be continuing sources of earnings growth.

22. Explain how the assets/NW ratio is related to the proportion of assets financed with debt.

23. Explain how earnings quality and sustainable earnings are related.

24. Explain why financial analysts have to take inflation into account.

PROBLEMS

*1. Using the financial data in Tables 1 through 3, prepare a statement of cash flows for Philip Morris Companies. *Important note:* The acquisition of Kraft by Philip Morris requires that you remove the assets acquired and liabilities incurred as a result of that acquisition

TABLE 1

Philip Morris Companies, Inc.
Balance Sheet
As of December 31
(Millions)

	1988	1987
Assets		
Cash and cash equivalents	$ 168	$ 90
Accounts receivable	2,222	2,065
Inventories	5,384	4,154
Current assets	$ 7,774	$ 6,309
Property, plant, & equipment (net)	8,648	6,582
Goodwill (net)	15,071	4,052
Investments	3,260	3,665
Total assets	$34,753	$20,608
Liabilities & stockholders' equity		
Short-term debt	$ 1,259	$ 1,440
Accounts payable	1,777	791
Accrued liabilities	3,848	2,277
Income taxes payable	1,089	727
Dividends payable	260	213
Current liabilities	$ 8,233	$ 5,448
Long-term debt	17,122	6,293
Deferred income taxes	1,719	2,044
Stockholders' equity	7,679	6,823
Total liabilities & stockholders' equity	$34,753	$20,608

TABLE 2

Philip Morris Companies, Inc.
Income Statement
For the Year Ending December 31, 1988
(Millions)

Sales	$31,742
Cost of goods sold	(12,156)
Selling & administrative expenses	(14,410)
Depreciation expense	(654)
Goodwill amortization	(125)
Interest expense	(670)
Before-tax income	3,727
Income tax expense	(1,390)
Net income	$2,337

Dividends declared: $941 million

TABLE 3
Philip Morris Purchase of Kraft
Allocation of Purchase Price
(Millions)

Accounts receivable	$ 758
Inventories	1,232
Property, plant, & equipment	1,740
Goodwill	10,361
Short-term debt	(700)
Accounts payable	(578)
Accrued liabilities	(530)
Long-term debt	(900)
Purchase price (net of cash acquired)	$11,383

from the balance sheet changes used to prepare the statement of
cash flows. Philip Morris paid $11.383 billion for Kraft, net of cash
acquired.

*2.   Discuss the internal sources of earnings growth for Thomson News-
papers, Ltd., and Southam, Inc., explaining the trend in return on
equity (see Table 4). You have identified five key return on equity
components: operating profit margin, interest expense, income taxes,
asset utilization, and financial leverage.
a.   Calculate the return on equity for 1988 for both companies, using
equations 10-2 through 10-5. Show calculations.
b.   Discuss how the 10-year trend in each of the five components
has affected return on equity for each company.

TABLE 4

Thomson Newspapers, Ltd.

Year	Earnings per Share	Annual Percentage Change	Dividend per Share	Annual Percentage Change	Dividend Payout
1988	$1.72	10.3%	$0.72	16.1%	41.9%
1987	1.56	14.7	0.62	14.8	39.7
1986	1.36	14.3	0.54	17.4	39.7
1985	1.19	14.4	0.46	17.9	38.7
1984	1.04	22.4	0.39	14.7	37.5
1983	0.85	26.9	0.34	17.2	40.0
1982	0.67	3.1	0.29	16.0	43.3
1981	0.65	27.5	0.25	19.0	38.5
1980	0.51	15.9	0.21	16.7	41.1
1979	0.44	15.8	0.18	50.0	40.9
1978	0.38	19.8	0.12	13.4	31.6

TABLE 4 (continued)

Southam, Inc.

Year	Earnings per Share	Annual Percentage Change	Dividend per Share	Annual Percentage Change	Dividend Payout
1988	$1.23	−6.8%	$0.62	19.2%	50.4%
1987	1.32	8.2	0.52	13.0	39.4
1986	1.22	32.6	0.46	15.0	37.7
1985	0.92	4.5	0.40	0.0	43.5
1984	0.88	10.0	0.40	14.3	45.5
1983	0.80	110.5	0.35	−2.8	43.8
1982	0.38	−56.8	0.36	−10.0	94.7
1981	0.88	23.9	0.40	0.0	45.5
1980	0.71	9.2	0.40	33.3	56.3
1979	0.65	3.2	0.30	3.4	46.2
1978	0.63	23.5	0.29	31.8	46.0

Thomson Newspapers, Ltd.

Year	Total Assets/ Common Equity	Profit Margin	Income Tax Rate	Revenues/ Total Assets	EBIT/ Revenues	Interest/ Total Assets	Return on Average Equity
1988	1.53	21.2%	28.0%	0.61	32.2%	1.9%	—
1987	1.31	21.0	38.1	0.77	33.5	0.5	20.5%
1986	1.32	19.5	43.8	0.86	35.4	0.6	22.1
1985	1.41	19.0	41.6	0.80	34.2	1.5	21.2
1984	1.41	18.9	43.0	0.84	34.4	1.0	22.3
1983	1.45	17.9	44.3	0.86	33.2	1.0	22.2
1982	1.60	14.9	42.9	0.98	28.4	2.2	23.5
1981	1.67	15.0	45.7	0.91	30.8	3.2	22.6
1980	1.48	14.5	48.5	0.95	30.9	3.0	20.0
1979	1.37	19.4	46.9	0.81	38.1	1.3	21.4
1978	1.34	18.5	48.0	0.81	37.0	1.4	19.9

Southam, Inc.

Year	Total Assets/ Common Equity	Profit Margin	Income Tax Rate	Revenues/ Total Assets	EBIT/ Revenues	Interest/ Total Assets	Return on Average Equity
1988	2.39	4.6%	43.0%	1.29	7.3%	2.7%	—
1987	2.22	5.4	44.7	1.38	8.9	3.1	11.3%
1986	2.20	5.6	42.7	1.37	9.4	3.1	12.4
1985	2.47	4.2	42.7	1.46	8.9	3.6	13.3
1984	2.82	4.1	46.4	1.61	9.9	4.3	17.6
1983	2.70	4.5	46.7	1.57	10.2	3.3	18.2
1982	2.65	2.3	46.0	1.54	7.9	5.8	9.1
1981	2.73	5.4	46.1	1.62	13.5	6.2	23.2
1980	2.39	6.1	45.9	1.54	12.9	4.1	20.4
1979	2.03	7.0	44.3	1.62	13.0	2.5	21.1
1978	1.85	8.2	41.1	1.64	12.2	1.1	20.6

*3.   Use equations 10-2 through 10-5 to explain the change that occurred in Tennant's return on equity from 1981 to 1987 (see Table 5). Work with the five factors listed below.
   I.   EBIT margin
   II.   Asset turnover
   III.   Interest burden
   IV.   Financial leverage
   V.   Tax retention rate
      a.   Compute the 1981 and 1987 values of each of these factors.
      b.   Identify the individual component that had the greatest influence on the change in return on equity from 1981 to 1987. Briefly explain the possible reasons for the changes in the value of this component between the two years.

TABLE 5

Tennant Company
Selected Historic Operating and Balance Sheet Data
(000 Omitted)

	1981	1987
Net sales	$109,333	$166,914
Cost of goods sold	62,373	95,005
Gross profit	46,960	71,909
Selling, general, & administrative expenses	29,649	54,151
Earnings before interest and taxes	17,311	17,758
Interest on long-term debt	53	248
Before-tax income	17,258	17,510
Income taxes	7,655	7,692
After-tax income	9,603	9,818
Total assets	$ 63,555	$106,098
Common stockholders' equity	46,593	69,516
Long-term debt	532	2,480
Common shares outstanding	5,402	5,320
Earnings per share	$1.78	$1.85
Dividends per share	.72	.96
Book value per share	8.63	13.07

---

*4.   MAC Corporation had net income of $500,000 for 1986. Contained in the notes to the annual report was the following statement: "Inventory is valued using LIFO. If the FIFO method of inventory accounting had been used to value all inventories, they would have been $100,000 higher than reported ($75,000 higher at previous year-end)." Assuming a tax rate of 40%, how much would net income have been if FIFO had been used?
   a. $455,000
   b. $515,000
   c. $560,000
   d.   None of the above

*5. Calculate earnings per share for the Seattle Manufacturing Company, given the following (in millions):

	1986	1985
Common stock, $10 par value; 4,000,000 shares authorized; 3,000,000 and 2,680,000 outstanding, respectively	$30.0	$26.8
Cumulative preferred stock, series A 8%, $25 par value; 1,000,000 authorized; 600,000 outstanding	15.0	15.0
Income before taxes	64.8	89.2
Income taxes	10.4	19.2
Net income	54.4	70.0

6. Using the formula

EPS = [(EBIT/sales × sales/assets) − interest expense/assets] × (1 − T)(assets/NW)(NW/SO)

analyze the increase in EPS from year t to year $t + 1$ with the figures given below. (Calculations that involve balance sheet figures can be made with either the year-end figures or the average of the beginning and ending figures.)

Income statement:

	Year t	Year $t + 1$
Sales	$8,123	$8,659
EBIT	960	903
Interest expense	170	118
Income taxes	340	272
Net earnings	450	513
Average shares outstanding	210	210

Balance sheet figures:

	End of Year		
	t	$t + 1$	$t + 2$
Assets	$6,546	$6,718	$6,874
Shareholders' equity	4,710	4,824	5,068

7. Using the following data, calculate the funds provided by operations:

Net income	$5,450
Depreciation	940
Current assets:	
Beginning	1,248
Ending	1,425
Cash and marketable securities:	
Beginning	526
Ending	372

Short-term loans:
Beginning   124
Ending   289
Current liabilities (including short-term
loans):
Beginning   760
Ending   645

8. Given the following, calculate earnings per share:

Interest expense	$ 400	Sales	$5,000
Shareholders' equity	$2,000	T	38%
Total liabilities	$1,000	EBIT/sales	18%
Number of shares outstanding	500		

9. Given the following, calculate sustainable earnings:

Reported earnings (based on FIFO method)	$800
Inventories:	
If valued with LIFO:	
Beginning	$220
Ending	240
If valued with FIFO:	
Beginning	280
Ending	330
Goodwill:	
Beginning balance	200
Amortization	12
Estimated number of years (from beginning of year) during which it will have value	10

10. Given the following, calculate free cash flow:

Net income	$300
Depreciation	48
Patent amortization	6
Increase in net working capital, excluding cash	12
Dividends	140
Necessary capital expenditures	72
Payment on bank loan	15

|||| # SELECTED REFERENCES

Aharony, Joseph, and Itzhak Swary. "Quarterly Dividend and Earnings Announcements and Stockholders' Returns: An Empirical Analysis." *The Journal of Finance* 35 (March 1980): 1–12.

Albrecht, Steve W., Larry I. Lookabill and James C. McKeown. "The Time Series Properties of Annual Earnings." *Journal of Accounting Research* 15 (Autumn 1977): 226–44.

Benesh, Gary A., Arthur J. Keown, and John M. Pinkerton. "An Examination of Market Reaction to Substantial Shifts in Dividend Policy." *Journal of Financial Economics* 7 (Summer 1984): 131–42.

Brealey R. A. *An Introduction to Risk and Return from Common Stocks,* 2d ed. Cambridge, Mass.: MIT Press, 1983.

Brown, Lawrence D., and Michael S. Rozeff. "The Superiority of Analyst Forecasts as Measures of Expectations: Evidence from Earnings." *The Journal of Finance* 33 (March 1978): 1–16.

Eckel, Norm. "An EPS Forecasting Model Utilizing Macroeconomic Performance Expectations." *Financial Analysts Journal* 38 (May/June 1982): 68–77.

Lintner, John, and Robert Glauber. "Higgledy Piggledy Growth in America." Unpublished paper presented to the Seminar on the Analysis of Security Prices, May 1967, University of Chicago; reprinted in James Lorie and Richard Brealey, *Modern Developments in Investment Management,* 2d ed. Hinsdale, Ill.: Dryden Press, 1978. Pp. 594–611.

Little, I. M. D. "Higgledy Piggledy Growth." Oxford: Institute of Statistics, November 1962, 24, no. 4.

Little, I. M. D., and A. C. Rayner. "Higgledy Piggledy Growth Again." Oxford: Basil Blackwell, 1966.

Lorek, Kenneth S. "Predicting Annual Net Earnings with Quarterly Earnings Time Series Models." *Journal of Accounting Research* 17 (Spring 1979): 190–204.

Niederhoffer, Victor, and Patrick J. Regan. "Earnings Changes, Analysts' Forecasts, and Stock Prices." *Financial Analysts Journal* 28 (May/June 1972): 65–71.

Proffitt, Dennis, and Alan A. Stephens. "The Market Response to Unexpected Dividend Announcements." *Journal of Applied Business Research* 4 (Fall 1988): 57–65.

Richards, R. Malcolm, James J. Benjamin, and Robert H. Strawser. "An Examination of the Accuracy of Earnings Forecasts." *Financial Management* 6 (Autumn 1978): 78–86.

Vermaelen, T. "Common Stock Repurchases and Market Signalling." *Journal of Financial Economics* (June 1981): 139–83.

Watts, Ross I., and Richard W. Leftwich. "The Time Series of Annual Accounting Earnings." *Journal of Accounting Research* 15 (Autumn 1977): 253–71.

Zacks, Leonard. "EPS Forecasts—Accuracy Is Not Enough." *Financial Analysts Journal* 35 (March/April 1979): 53–55.

11 STOCK SELECTION

Discovering the kinds of stocks that have performed best over some past period is easy. Predicting with a high degree of accuracy the kinds of stocks that will perform best over a specified future period is extremely difficult. The challenge is to find stocks of companies that investors view with too little optimism.

The lure of large profits in the stock market has led to the publishing of many books that purport to offer unique and reliable methods of beating the market. If the market were perfectly efficient, none of these books would be worth anything. As it is, a few may have some value for some readers. One of the best is a book by Peter Lynch, the highly successful former manager of the Fidelity Magellan Fund.[1] Although it is very difficult for anyone to explain how to select stocks that are likely to perform better than the average, Lynch's book has probably helped some investors make better decisions and thereby has increased the efficiency of the market. The material in the first part of this chapter relating to various types of stocks reflects some of Lynch's ideas.

Stocks are viewed here as long-term investments that should be held until they no longer have suitable risk-return characteristics for the investor's portfolio. Stock characteristics do change over time. Electric utilities were once fast-growth stocks, as were IBM and Xerox.

Anyone who buys and holds only a small number of stocks has the chance of selecting superior performers through luck. Achieving consistent superior performance as the manager of a portfolio containing a large number of stocks requires either remarkable luck or an exceptional ability to discern and calculate the odds relating to the future profitability of business firms. The aggressive investment manager's task is to assess the odds that certain young businesses will become highly successful, that certain older firms will maintain fast earnings growth rates, and that certain troubled firms will make successful comebacks.

METHODS OF SELECTING STOCKS

Stocks are selected in many different ways. Technicians look primarily at price patterns and the volume of trading. Others use methods ranging from simple rules of thumb to techniques that require a considerable

---

[1]Peter Lynch, *One Up on Wall Street,* (New York: Simon and Schuster, 1989).

amount of judgment. For example, one rule of thumb is to buy stocks only if the price is below the book value. This makes little sense because it eliminates stocks of virtually all companies that are expected to earn an above-average return on the shareholders' equity, and it concentrates on stocks with poor growth prospects. Other rules of thumb have similar shortcomings.

The present chapter deals with two basic approaches to *stock selection,* neither of which necessarily requires explicit long-term forecasts of earnings and dividends, although both require that future profitability be taken into account. The first approach begins by classifying stocks into five or six groups according to certain fundamental characteristics, such as fast earnings growth or cyclical sales and earnings. Within these groups, stocks are selected with methods that require judgments about asset values and future earnings prospects, as discussed in Chapters 9 and 10. The second approach, called *attribute screening,* involves sorting through large numbers of stocks to find those with a single attribute (such as a low P/E ratio or high return on equity) or set of attributes the investor considers desirable. A variety of methods, including, for example, random choice or analysis of financial condition and profitability, can then be used to select individual stocks from those passing the screen.

|||| STOCK CLASSIFICATIONS

Stocks are classified for two reasons: first, to eliminate types that are of no interest to the investor, and, second, to form groups in which the stocks are roughly homogeneous with respect to expected performance and the kinds of analysis required. Peter Lynch classifies all stocks into the following six categories: (1) slow-growth; (2) stalwarts; (3) fast-growth; (4) cyclical; (5) asset plays; and (6) turnarounds. Some fit into more than one category. For example, Ford and Chrysler are cyclical as well as turnaround stocks when the companies are losing money. IBM was once a fast-growth stock, later became a stalwart, and is now looking more like a cyclical.

SLOW-GROWTH STOCKS

A *slow-growth stock* is the stock of a company whose earnings are expected to grow no faster than the economy. The company earns a low return on the shareholders' equity and consequently cannot grow very fast. Since earnings growth is slow, growth of the stock price is also slow, and the dividend yield has to be high. Most public utilities are in this category.

STALWARTS

A stalwart is the stock of a company whose earnings are expected to grow at an annual rate of more than 5% but not much more than 10%, assuming a moderate rate of inflation. Stalwarts are largely consumer-goods stocks, such as companies like Bristol-Myers, Coca-Cola, Hershey Foods, Procter & Gamble, and Ralston Purina.

FAST-GROWTH STOCKS

Fast-growth stocks are the stocks of companies whose earnings are expected to grow at a rate of more than 10% for at least several years. The group includes fast-growing large companies as well as small companies. Fast-growing large companies can be either in a fast-growing industry, such as waste disposal, or in a slow-growing industry in which they are achieving a larger and larger share of the market, such as Wal-Mart in retailing, Marriott in hotels, and Anheuser-Busch in beer.

Table 11-1 provides a crude comparison of slow-growth, fast-growth, and stalwarts, showing return on equity for the year 1989 and average annual return to shareholders for the years 1987–1989.

CYCLICALS

Cyclicals are the stocks of companies whose earnings fluctuate widely with changes in economic conditions. The cyclical group includes stocks in industries such as airlines, automobiles, chemicals, forest products, and steel. Prices of cyclical stocks fluctuate widely along with the earnings.

ASSET PLAYS

An asset play is a stock with a price lower than the estimated realizable value of its assets. Penn Central became an asset play after going through bankruptcy. Its tax-loss carryforward, plus its extensive property holdings and other assets, turned out to be worth considerably more than the stock market initially believed.

TURNAROUNDS

Turnarounds are the stocks of companies that have come on hard times and are expected to recover, such as Halliburton in the oil services industry in the mid-1980s.

|||| TAKING A REALISTIC VIEW OF SALES PROSPECTS

Never buy a stock unless you have a clear idea how the company is going to achieve the predicted growth in earnings. This simple rule will steer you away from the overpriced stocks of companies whose earnings have been growing rapidly but cannot be reasonably expected to grow as fast in the future. Classic examples are Brunswick Corporation and Avon Products of 20 to 25 years ago.

|||| **TABLE 11-1**

Return on Equity and Return to Shareholders: Selected
Companies

	Return on Shareholders' Equity, 1989*	Annual Return to Shareholders, 1987–1989*
Fast-growth companies:		
Anheuser-Busch	24.7%	29.4%
Marriott	28.2	26.0
Wal-Mart	27.1	46.1
Waste Management	20.5	36.1
Stalwarts:		
Bristol-Myers Squibb	14.7	23.9
Coca-Cola	49.5	26.8
Colgate-Palmolive	24.9	22.1
Procter & Gamble	19.4	19.0
Slow-growth companies		
Alcoa	17.9	15.0
Commonwealth Edison	8.6	18.9
Houston Industries	11.2	17.2
Pacific Gas & Electric	10.4	18.2

*Fortune, April 23, 1990.

Brunswick is an excellent example of a stock whose price, at a certain point, is based on blind faith in fanciful forecasts; in this case, forecasts of very high long-term growth rates for the sales of automatic pinsetters. In 1956, when the company entered the burgeoning automatic pinsetter business, its stock became a "glamorous growth issue" almost overnight. Brunswick and American Machine and Foundry Company were the only companies in the business and, to some, the market must have seemed unlimited. Earnings doubled from 1956 to 1957, doubled again in 1958 and 1959, and continued to grow rapidly through 1961. Meanwhile, the price of the stock quadrupled, reaching a high of $75 in 1961 and a P/E ratio of 33. The total market value of the company was greater than that of Weyerhaeuser—but not for long.

In 1961–62 the price of Brunswick stock dropped more than 80% in a period of less than 12 months. By then the two competing companies had installed 120,000 automatic pinsetters in the country's estimated 125,000 bowling lanes. Pinsetter sales dropped dramatically, and Brunswick was soon losing money. It seems clear that many who bought Brunswick stock during those early years were overly impressed with the company's recent earnings growth and did not pay enough attention to its future prospects. Some, no doubt, were looking only at the spectacular growth of the stock's price.

For a number of years, Avon was one of the country's leading fast-growth companies, and in 1972 its stock was selling at a P/E ratio of 64. It was by then a very large company, with cosmetics sales of over $1 billion. Anyone who thought carefully about its future earnings prospects would have realized that it was virtually impossible for the company to grow fast enough long enough to justify the price of its stock, which fell from a high of $140 in 1972 to a low of less than $20 in 1974.

|||| ANALYSIS OF VARIOUS KINDS OF STOCKS

Before buying a stock, you should know how the company plans to do what it says it is going to do. Peter Lynch pointed out that there are just five basic ways a company can increase its profits: reduce costs; raise prices; expand into new markets; increase market share in existing markets; and revitalize, sell, or close losing operations. Which of these does the company plan to do? Are its plans realistic? What do present and prospective customers think of the company's products or services?

If the company's plan seems attainable and its potential is not yet recognized by the market, you may decide to buy the stock. Then, knowing how the company plans to achieve its growth objective, you can monitor its actions and the quarterly results to see if the plan is being carried out.

SLOW-GROWTH STOCKS

The dividend yields on slow-growth stocks are high because the potential for price appreciation is low. Slow-growths are generally unattractive to investors who are seeking high returns. Their appeal is somewhat like that of a bond, although the expected return is higher than many bond yields because of greater uncertainty. Investors are interested in how generously the dividend is covered by earnings, as well as the potential for growth.

STALWARTS

Stocks with above-average but not spectacular earnings growth rates are largely consumer-goods stocks that are relatively insensitive to changes in economic conditions. Don't expect them to make spectacular gains, but they do seem to become underpriced at times, which makes it possible to earn abnormal returns—if purchases and sales are well timed. How do you pick the right times? Principally through watching the price/earnings ratio. An unusually low ratio in comparison to the stock's average P/E ratio for past periods may indicate that the stock is bargain priced.

FAST-GROWTH STOCKS

Fast-growth stocks are an area where day-to-day observation and common sense are especially important. If you observe that a highly profitable company such as Wal-Mart Stores is offering essentially the same products or services as others but at lower prices, and if the opportunity for expansion looks good, you may have found a fast-growth stock. Of course, fast growth seldom lasts very long; by the time you read this, competition may have converted Wal-Mart into a cyclical operation.

Trying to pick the winners from the large numbers of new companies that have not yet earned a profit is an especially risky undertaking. Smaller but more certain gains can be earned by selecting small fast-growth stocks soon after they have become profitable. Peter Lynch recommends looking for winners in the stocks that have uninteresting names and sell dull products or services, such as bottle caps or the cleaning of greasy tools. They will be followed by few analysts and purchased by few large investors. The claimed superior performance of such stocks is sometimes referred to as the "neglected firm effect." Lynch does not advise looking for winners among the high-tech stocks that you have no hope of understanding but are followed by many analysts and purchased by large investors. (If enough people take his advice, bottle cap stocks will soon be overpriced, and high-tech stocks underpriced.)

CYCLICAL STOCKS

The potential gains and losses on cyclicals are great. Earnings and stock prices of cyclical companies fluctuate widely. Timing of purchases and sales is the key, and it is not easy. The time to buy is when everything looks bad and the price of the stock has dropped at least 25% to 30% from its high. Prices of cyclicals often fall considerably more than that. P/E ratios of cyclicals tend to be low when profits are high because investors recognize that the big increase is only temporary, and the P/E's tend to be high when profits are low because investors look for early and substantial profit improvement.

Cyclicals should be sold when signs of trouble begin to appear. Inventories often build up before profits turn down. Other signs of a pending downturn are new competition entering the field and the cutting of prices.

TURNAROUNDS

To purchase turnaround stocks takes a lot of daring. Here's where luck— or an exceptional ability to weigh the odds in a highly risky situation— becomes very important. Those who bet on Chrysler when it was nearly bankrupt made huge profits, but only after assuming substantial risk. The risk, however, may not have been as great as many thought it to be.

In a turnaround situation, the cash and debt position of the company are highly important. The greater the cash and the smaller the debt, the more time the company has to succeed. After Chrysler received the $1.4 billion government loan guarantee, its position was good in both of these areas. It had $1 billion in cash and loan terms that provided considerable flexibility. Also, by this time the company had made considerable progress toward cost reduction.

ASSET PLAYS

An asset play tends to be safer than a turnaround. The price paid for the stock is less than the estimated market value of the firm's assets. These are the companies that attract corporate raiders. Sometimes a stock is an asset play as well as a cyclical, turnaround, or slow-growth security.

In 1988, Ford stock, at $38 a share, seemed fully priced to many observers, but a close look at the value of certain of its assets indicated that relative to other stocks it was not. Cash alone, after deducting all debts, amounted to $16.30 a share, and its finance subsidiaries (assuming a price/earnings ratio of 10) were worth another $16.60 a share. Thus, one could say that at a price of $38, investors were paying only $5.10 for all other assets of the company. However, this method of analysis does have an important flaw. Since there was virtually no chance that Ford would be either liquidated or taken over by another company, and very little chance that a major portion of the cash would be paid out as a dividend, the value of the stock depended more on the expected earnings from the aggregate assets of the company than on the estimated worth individual assets would have if disposed of separately.

|||| SCREENING FOR ATTRIBUTES

One way to search for undervalued stocks is by screening a large number of stocks to find those with certain attributes thought to be desirable. Often, the purpose of screening is to identify securities that seem worthy of further analysis. The underlying assumption is that, on the whole, stocks that pass the screen have a better than average chance of outperforming the market.

Typically, attribute screens (other than screens based on past price changes) come under one of the following headings:

1. Excellent companies
2. Low price relative to sales, earnings, dividends, book value, or net working capital
3. Earnings surprise
4. High-risk stocks
5. Multiple attributes

EXCELLENT COMPANIES

At first glance, it would seem reasonable that the best stocks to own (the ones that will provide the highest risk-adjusted returns) are the stocks of the best-managed companies. To believe this, however, is to believe that such stocks can be purchased at prices that are low relative to the rest of the market. This idea was tested a few years ago by measuring the performance of 29 stocks from the group of 43 companies selected in

1981 as "America's best-run corporations."[2] Common characteristics of the excellent companies included a bias toward action; innovativeness; close relations with customers; encouragement of entrepreneurship; productivity through people; willingness to limit activities to fields of special competence; and maintenance of a lean staff.

In the original list of 43 excellent firms, there were 36 publicly traded companies, of which 29 were still in existence as publicly traded companies on December 31, 1985. The performance of those 29 stocks was measured over a five-year period ending with 1985. The average annual risk-adjusted return was slightly (1.1 percentage points) higher than the return on the Standard & Poor's 500 Index, but almost two-thirds of the stocks (18 of 29) provided a lower return than the S&P 500.

Ironically, the average return for the stocks of the 29 excellent companies over the five-year period was far below that of the stocks of 39 "mediocre companies" in Standard & Poor's 500 Index that were the slowest growing and least profitable during the years 1976 through 1980. Growth rates, measures of profitability, and the ratio of stock price to book value for the excellent and mediocre companies are shown in Table 11-2.

Although the overall profitability of the mediocre companies declined from the earlier five-year period to the later period, their stock prices increased substantially. Not only did the average ratio of stock price to book value increase from 0.6 to 1.0, but more than 60% of the mediocre companies' stocks provided higher returns than the S&P 500. An equally weighted portfolio of the mediocre companies' stocks, with a beta no higher than that of the excellent companies, outperformed the S&P 500 by 12.4% per annum.

[2]Michelle Clayman, "In Search of Excellence: The Investor's Viewpoint," *Financial Analysts Journal* 43 (May/June 1987): 54–63; Thomas A. Peters and Robert H. Waterman, Jr., *In Search of Excellence: Lessons from America's Best-Run Corporations* (New York: Harper & Row, 1981).

|||| **TABLE 11-2**

Average Performance and Ratio of Stock Price to Book Value of Excellent and Mediocre Companies, 1976–1980 and 1981–1985

	Excellent Companies		**Mediocre Companies**	
	1976–1980	1981–1985	1976–1980	1981–1985
Annual asset growth rate	21.8%	10.7%	5.9%	4.7%
Annual equity growth rate	18.4	9.4	3.8	3.9
Average annual return on sales	8.6	6.4	2.5	1.4
Average return on equity	19.1	12.9	7.1	−15.0
Average ratio of stock price to book value	2.5	2.1	0.6	1.0

NOTE: Return on equity for the 39 mediocre companies for the years 1981–1985 is distorted by the extremely large negative figures of one company. When that company is removed, return on equity for the mediocre companies changes from −15.0% to +4.3%.

SOURCE: Michelle Clayman, "In Search of Excellence: The Investor's Viewpoint," *Financial Analysts Journal* 43 (May/June 1987): 54–63.

The results of the "excellent-mediocre study" demonstrate that stocks of the best companies are not necessarily the best-performing stocks. The study also illustrates the tendency of highly profitable companies to become less profitable over a period of time due to competition. The results do not mean that the stocks of mediocre companies will perform better than the stocks of excellent companies over any specific period in the future.

LOW RELATIVE PRICE

With dividend discount models, the price of a stock is compared to the estimated present value of expected future dividends. Many investors believe it is better to relate the price to something that does not have to be estimated, such as recent sales, earnings, book value, or the current annual dividend. Each of these variables can have a bearing on what a stock is worth. A low ratio of price to earnings or price to book value is sometimes viewed as prima facie evidence that the stock is undervalued.

Low Price/Earnings Ratio

Low relative prices are especially favored by investors known as *contrarians,* who believe that popular opinions about stock values are often wrong. More specifically, contrarians believe that high P/E stocks of fast-growing companies are often overvalued, and that low P/E stocks of less exciting companies tend to be undervalued. As we noted in Chapter 8, there is conflicting evidence as to whether contrarians have, on the whole, been right about low P/E stocks. In any case, they have not been right all the time, as indicated in the Sidelight.

Low Price/Dividend Ratio

A low price/dividend ratio means a high dividend/price ratio, or high dividend yield. A high dividend yield indicates a low expected earnings growth rate. Companies with few opportunities for expansion retain only a small percentage of earnings to finance future growth. When little earnings growth and slow price appreciation are expected, the dividend yield must be high in order to provide an acceptable total return.

Do the expected returns for stocks with high dividend yields differ from the expected returns for stocks with low dividend yields? Before the Tax Reform Act of 1986 eliminated preferential tax treatment of long-term capital gains, investors seemed to require higher before-tax returns on stocks with high dividend yields because capital gains were valued more highly than dividends. Now that dividends and long-term capital gains are generally taxed at the same rate, investors may or may not require higher before-tax returns on higher-yielding stocks. High dividends have the disadvantage of being taxed currently rather than when the stock is sold, but they have the advantage of being subject to less uncertainty than future capital appreciation.

|||| SIDELIGHT
Value Investing Isn't a Guaranteed Winner

Buying out-of-favor stocks that look underpriced on the basis of price/ earnings ratios and dividend yields is known as value investing. This classic investment strategy has generally worked well in the past, but not since 1984. The year 1989 was especially bad. One professional said, "It left us value managers wanting to jump out the window." Some believe that after five years of underperformance, stocks purchased on the basis of value are sure to go up. Others believe that until the economy hits the skids, steady-growth stocks—rather than value stocks—will perform best.

Value-oriented mutual funds with excellent long-term records—like Lindner Fund, Mutual Shares, and Vanguard Group's Windsor Fund— earned only 10% to 20% last year, compared to the 31.7% rise in Standard & Poor's 500 Index.

One reason for the mediocre results with the value strategy in recent years is that it led to the purchase of stocks in industry groups—such as banks, airlines, and office equipment—that were cut down by a number of unlucky surprises. In any case, value investors should avoid stocks that appear to be bargains but have weak balance sheets and unstable earnings.

SOURCE: Adapted from Barbara Donnelly, "Value Investing Isn't Guaranteed Winner," *The Wall Street Journal*, January 11, 1990, p. C1. Reprinted by permission of *The Wall Street Journal*, © Dow Jones & Company, Inc. (1990). All Rights Reserved Worldwide.

Low Price/Book Value Ratio

When a company's growth prospects look poor, its stock is likely to sell at a low price/book value ratio as well as a low P/E ratio since both ratios depend on the price. The price/book ratio is the product of the P/E ratio and the return on equity, as shown in Equation 11-1, where BVPS is book value per share, and EPS/BVPS is return on equity:

$$\text{price/BVPS} = \text{price/EPS} \times \text{EPS/BVPS} \qquad (11\text{-}1)$$

Given the return on equity, the higher the P/E ratio, the higher the ratio of price to book value.

Assuming that low P/E ratios indicate a strong likelihood of abnormally high future returns, one might expect low price/book ratios to identify better performing stocks as well. In the Clayman study of excellent and mediocre companies, the mediocre companies' stocks had low price/book ratios and provided the highest returns. However, we do not know how the stocks of the mediocre companies performed either before or after the five-year period of the study. At least one recent study found that the P/E ratio was much more closely related to stock returns than the price/book ratio.[3] This is not surprising, since dividends depend on earnings rather than book values.

Low Price/Sales Ratio

It is sometimes suggested that the price/sales (P/S) ratio might be a better indicator of relative values among stocks than the P/E ratio. Such ideas stem from the problems involved in using P/E ratios: P/E's cannot be calculated for companies with losses; and if a low P/E is the selection criterion, high P/E stocks will be rejected even where the reason for the high P/E is a temporary decline in earnings. Nevertheless, one would expect investors to pay more attention to P/E ratios than to P/S ratios because earnings are more important than sales.

A study that compared the performance of stocks relative to their P/E ratios with the performance relative to their P/S ratios found that the average return for stocks with the lowest P/S ratio was about the same as for stocks with the lowest P/E ratio.[4] However, the stocks with low P/S ratios were much riskier than the stocks with low P/E ratios in terms of both the standard deviation of the return and beta.

Low Price/Net Current Assets

In *The Intelligent Investor*, Benjamin Graham stated that:

> It always seemed, and still seems, ridiculously simple to say that if one can acquire a diversified group of common stocks at a price less than the applicable net current assets alone—after deducting all prior claims, and counting as zero the fixed and other assets—the results should be quite satisfactory.[5]

He defined net current assets as current assets minus all liabilities and preferred stock.

One investigator tested Graham's *net asset value (NAV)* criterion with New York Stock Exchange, American Stock Exchange, and over-the-counter stocks for the years 1971 through 1983.[6] The stocks were selected at the end of each year and held for a period of 30 months. The number of stocks in each 30-month portfolio ranged from 18 to 89. The study found that while the NAV criterion did not work well for New York Stock Exchange stocks, it produced abnormally high returns for 30-month holding periods for American Stock Exchange and OTC stocks for a majority of the years from 1971 through 1983 and for the period as a whole. Also, tests showed that the abnormal returns were not attributable to the size effect.

[3]Bruce I. Jacobs and Kenneth N. Levy, "Disentangling Equity Return Regularities: New Insights and Investment Opportunities," *Financial Analysts Journal* 44 (May/June 1988): 18–43.

[4]A. J. Senchack, Jr., and John D. Martin, "The Relative Performance of the PSR and PER Investment Strategies," *Financial Analysts Journal* 43 (March/April 1987): 46–56.

[5]Benjamin Graham, *The Intelligent Investor*, 5th ed. (New York: Harper & Row, 1973).

[6]Henry R. Oppenheimer, "Ben Graham's Net Current Asset Values: A Performance Update," *Financial Analysts Journal* 42 (November/December 1986): 40–47.

Does the NAV criterion promise success? One shouldn't count on it. The next time it may work well for New York Stock Exchange stocks and not for the others. Or, it may work well for a 12-month holding period and not for shorter or longer periods of time.

EARNINGS SURPRISE

As we pointed out in Chapter 8, studies have found that stocks of companies whose latest quarterly earnings were higher or lower than expected have, on the average, provided abnormally high or low returns for a number of weeks after the earnings were announced. The market, it seems, has reacted gradually to both favorable and unfavorable earnings reports. Some investors use positive earnings surprise as a principal stock selection criterion.

HIGH-RISK STOCKS

If an investor decides to seek higher long-term returns by holding riskier stocks, he or she must do two things: (1) select the risk measure that will be positively correlated with returns in the future, and (2) predict the risk of individual stocks with that measure. Among numerous plausible candidates for measuring risk are beta, the standard deviation of the returns, and the debt/equity ratio.

Beta, the cornerstone of the capital asset pricing model, has been highly unreliable as an aid in predicting differences in returns, either for individual stocks or for portfolios of stocks. Beta's correlation with the return is usually low and sometimes negative. A study based on monthly returns of a large number of New York and American Stock Exchange stocks for the years 1974 through 1985 found that differences between the returns for individual stocks were much more closely related to differences in the standard deviations of the returns than to differences in betas.[7] In one of the three four-year periods being studied, however, the returns were negatively related to both the standard deviation and beta. In that period, the riskier the stock, the lower the return.

In another risk-return study, Bhandari compared the relationships of the debt/equity ratio, beta, and market capitalization to the rate of return.[8] Calculations were based on the returns of individual New York Stock Exchange stocks for 16 two-year periods. Because of the still-perplexing January effect (discussed in Chapter 8), calculations were made both with and without returns for the month of January. The final results showed the relationship of each variable (individually and in combination with the other variables) to the rate of return, both including and excluding the January return.

---

[7]Russell J. Fuller and G. Wenchi Wong, "Traditional versus Theoretical Risk Measures," *Financial Analysts Journal* 44 (March/April 1988): 52–57, 67.

[8]Laxmi Chand Bhandari, "Debt/Equity Ratio and Expected Common Stock Returns: Empirical Evidence," *The Journal of Finance* 43 (June 1988): 507–28.

Bhandari found a significant simple correlation between each of the three variables (beta, debt/equity ratio, and market capitalization) and the rate of return for the entire year, but virtually no correlation when January was left out. However, with beta and market capitalization held constant, there was a strong relationship between the debt/equity ratio and the return, even in months other than January. In 14 of the 16 two-year periods, the return on manufacturing company stocks varied directly with the debt/equity ratio when beta and market capitalization were neutralized. These findings suggest the possibility of earning higher returns over a long period of time by holding stocks of companies with high debt/equity ratios, but only if these stocks have appropriate, but as yet undetermined, combinations of market capitalization and beta. The study was not designed to determine which combinations of debt/equity ratio, market capitalization, and beta were associated with higher returns.

COMBINATIONS OF ATTRIBUTES

Stocks can be screened for any number of combinations of attributes in an effort to find superior investments. One approach is to combine attributes that have been associated individually with higher gross returns. The following procedure, which Dowen and Bauman used in selecting a portfolio each year from 1969 through 1983, is an example of this approach:[9]

[9]Richard J. Dowen and W. Scott Bauman, "A Fundamental Multifactor Asset Pricing Model," *Financial Analysts Journal* 42 (July/August 1986): 45–51.

|||| **TABLE 11-3**

Returns of "Special Effects" Portfolios Compared to Returns of Entire Sample, 1969–1983

	Special Effects Portfolios	Portfolios Selected with One Attribute	Entire Sample
Average characteristics:			
Market capitalization (millions)	$31		$671
Number of institutional owners	2		79
P/E ratio	5.8		10.5
Annual return:			
Arithmetic mean:			
Special effects portfolio	25.3%		
Small capitalization		18.1%	
Small number of institutional owners		17.7%	
Low P/E ratio		17.8%	
Geometric mean	19.5%		4.3%
Standard deviation	31.8%		14.8%

SOURCE: Richard J. Dowen and W. Scott Bauman, "A Fundamental Multifactor Asset Pricing Model," *Financial Analysts Journal* 42 (July/August 1986): 45–51.

1. With the stocks arranged by market capitalization, select the lowest one-third.
2. From those stocks, select the one-third with the smallest number of institutional owners.
3. From those stocks, select the one-third with the lowest P/E ratios.

As Table 11-3 shows, the resulting annual "special effects" portfolios of 18 to 25 stocks earned a much higher average return than the large collections of stocks (referred to as the "sample") from which the special effects portfolios were selected. Also, the arithmetic mean annual return of the special effects portfolio, at 25.3%, was seven to eight percentage points higher than the mean returns of portfolios selected with any one of the three criteria (small market capitalization, small number of institutional owners, and low P/E) alone. On the other hand, the standard deviation of the return of the special effects portfolios was also much higher than the average.

|||| # THE NEW WAVE THEORY

Some observers believe that investment managers will be placing more emphasis on factor timing in the future, which means selecting stocks with different attributes at different times.[10] The so-called *new wave theory* holds that new factors, such as the ratio of price to book value, are continually emerging in the stock market. A factor may be very important for a time but becomes less important as its popularity increases and prices of stocks with that attribute are bid up. In time, according to the new wave theory, stocks become efficiently priced with respect to any factor. The challenge is to find factors that will be dominant in the period immediately ahead.

|||| # SELECTING INDUSTRIES

The performance of individual stocks is often closely associated with the performance of other stocks in the same industry because they are sensitive to similar macroeconomic developments as well as to developments in the industry.

ARBITRAGE PRICING THEORY RISK FACTORS

Aggressive stock investors often shift their holdings from one industry, or group of industries, to another, depending on changes in expected relative performance. This is known as *sector rotation*. One motivation for such shifts is a change in expectations about general economic con-

[10]Lawrence S. Speidell, "The New Wave Theory," *Financial Analysts Journal* 44 (July/August 1987): 9–12.

ditions. For example, if the probability of a recession increases, funds may be shifted out of stocks that are highly sensitive to cyclical changes (i.e., stocks with high systematic risk) and into stocks that are expected to offer more stability.

Differences in systematic risk can be evaluated in the context of the arbitrage pricing theory (APT), as explained in Chapter 7.[11] One form of the APT is shown in Equation 11-2, which states that the difference between the actual and expected return on stock i is due to unexpected macroeconomic changes (f_1 to f_4), changes in the level of the market as a whole that are not explained by the first four factors (f_5), and unexpected developments that are peculiar to the individual firm (e_1):

$$R_i - E(R_i) = \beta_{i1} \times f_1 + \beta_{i2} \times f_2 + \beta_{i3} \times f_3 + \beta_{i4} \times f_4 + \beta_{i5} \times f_5 + e_i \qquad (11\text{-}2)$$

The coefficients (β_{i1} to β_{i4}) are measures of the sensitivity of the stock to four types of unexpected economic changes:

1. Default risk premium: This is measured by the spread between the returns on long-term government bonds and long-term corporate bonds. An increase in the *default premium* causes an increase in the required return and a decrease in stock prices.

2. Spread between long-term and short-term interest rates: An increase in this factor means an increase in the slope of the yield curve; it has a positive impact on stock prices.

3. Expected rate of inflation minus actual rate of inflation: If the actual rate of inflation is below the expected rate, this factor is positive and has a positive impact on most stock prices.

4. Expected long-run growth rate of corporate profits at the beginning of the period minus expected long-run growth rate of corporate profits at the end of the period: If expected profits are lower at the end of the period than at the beginning of the period, this factor has a negative impact on stock prices.

The industries in Table 11-4 are either highly sensitive (building materials and computers) or quite insensitive (brewers and food packagers) to unexpected changes in the economy. Thus, on the whole, it would be advantageous to hold stocks in industries like building materials and computers when it seems that investors will soon become less concerned about risk; similarly, it would be better to hold stocks in industries like breweries and food packaging when investors are expected to become more averse to risk and less optimistic about the future. The problem is how to predict these changes in attitude. It is apparent that with this model, as with any other, successful prediction of the future relative performance of any stock or group of stocks requires forecasts

[11]Michael A. Berry, Edwin Burmeister, and Marjorie B. McElroy, "Sorting out Risks Using Known APT Factors," *Financial Analysts Journal* 44 (March/April 1988): 29–42.

|||| **TABLE 11-4**
Sensitivities to Systematic Risk, 1972–1982

Industry	Sensitivities to Unexpected Macroeconomic Changes				
	Increase in Default Risk Premium	Increase in Premium for Longer Maturities	Actual Minus Expected Inflation Rate	Decrease in Expected Corporate Profits	Residual Market Risk
Beverages, brewers	−1.10	0.41	1.09	−0.86	0.77
Building materials	−2.22	0.65	6.29	−0.88	1.57
Electronics, computers, etc.	−2.49	0.35	3.47	−1.17	1.63
Food, packaged	−1.30	0.69	2.76	−0.40	0.69

SOURCE: Michael A. Berry, Edwin Burmeister, and Marjorie B. McElroy, "Sorting out Risks Using Known APT Factors," *Financial Analysts Journal* 44 (March/April 1988): 29–42.

|||| **SIDELIGHT**
Picking Stocks by Broad Industry Groups May Be Alluring But It Seldom Pays Off

Few strategies for beating the stock market are as enticing—or as hazardous—as sector rotation, which is a market timing strategy. The investor selects stocks in certain industry groups, such as capital goods, consumer durables, and consumer nondurables, and switches among them on the basis of which look most attractive at the time.

A vice president of Fidelity Investments, which manages $2.4 billion in nearly three dozen sector funds, states that most of their investors who have tried sector rotation have not been very successful. Even if you are able to make superior economic forecasts, you may not be able to predict which sectors will perform best, because economic cycles do not affect each sector the same way every time.

Robert Jones of Goldman Sachs has tried a number of models for picking "attractive" stocks and has found none of them a reliable guide. He believes that intuition, luck, and insightful macroeconomic analysis are important. Price momentum is one of the worst sector indicators, but that's what many individuals use. Money tends to flow into sector funds that have performed best recently.

Sector rotation is a high-risk strategy because it involves concentration in a few industry groups rather than broad diversification.

SOURCE: Adapted from Barbara Donnelly, "Picking Stocks by Broad Industry Groups may be Alluring, but it Seldom Pays Off," *The Wall Street Journal,* September 20, 1988, p. 41. Reprinted by permission of *The Wall Street Journal,* © Dow Jones & Company, Inc. (1988). All Rights Reserved Worldwide.

---

that are better than the consensus, because the consensus forecasts are already reflected in stock prices. The information in the Sidelight indicates that, on the whole, investors have not been very successful in predicting which industry groups will perform best in the stock market in the near future.

|||| **SUMMARY**

This chapter has dealt with certain methods by which investors attempt to select stocks that will outperform the market. Although no one is sure whether anyone can consistently select portfolios that will provide superior risk-adjusted returns, except through luck, it appears that the extraordinary success of a few investment managers must have resulted, at least in part, from special talent.

One approach to stock selection begins by classifying stocks into five or six groups, such as slow-growth, stalwart, fast-growth, cyclical, asset play, and turnaround. Stocks are classified for two reasons: first, because risk and expected return characteristics differ among the groups, and, second, because the investor may want to stay away from certain groups. Stocks within each group are then analyzed with techniques that are appropriate for stocks of that kind.

In any case it is important to know how the company plans to achieve its stated profit goals and to determine whether the plans are realistic. After a stock has been purchased, the investor should monitor the company's progress, not just by looking at sales and earnings but by observing its actions in pursuit of the plan. A sound financial condition is always important, particularly for turnaround companies because of their lack of profits.

It may be easier to make abnormal profits with stocks in companies that do not have broad appeal and are largely ignored by analysts and institutions. The probability that the stock of a bottle cap manufacturer is undervalued may be greater than the probability of a computer stock being priced too low.

Countless schemes have been developed in attempts to find one or more easily measured characteristics (such as strong financial condition and profitability, low P/E ratio, or low price/book value ratio) to identify stocks that will outperform the market. It is always possible to find characteristics that identify the superior performers of the past. One can never be sure that those same characteristics will identify the superior performers of next year, the next 5 years, or the next 10 years.

Capital market theory holds that expected returns vary directly with systematic risk. Historical evidence indicates, however, that over long periods of time actual returns have been more closely associated with total risk (measured by the standard deviation of the return) than with systematic risk, measured by beta. This suggests that if an investor can predict which stocks will have the most variable returns, he or she may be able to identify stocks that will provide the highest long-term geometric mean rates of return.

Some common stock investors try to earn superior returns by shifting funds from one industry group, or sector, to another on the basis of changes in the outlook for the economy. Successful execution of such a strategy requires more than good economic forecasts. Since stock prices move in response to changes in investors' attitudes and expectations, successful sector switching requires good forecasts of such things as changes in investor expectations about corporate profits.

|||| QUESTIONS

1. Outline briefly the characteristics of slow-growth, stalwart, fast-growth, cyclical, asset play, and turnaround stocks.
2. Why are dividend yields high on slow-growth stocks?
3. Explain how classifying stocks can be helpful.
4. What are the five sources of earnings growth identified by Lynch?
5. Why is it important to know how the company expects to achieve a specified earnings growth rate?
6. Why are P/E ratios thought to be especially helpful in timing purchases and sales of stalwarts?
7. Why is a firm's cash and debt position so important, especially in the case of a turnaround?
8. By what signs can you tell that a cyclical stock may be about to turn downward?
9. Why might it have been easier to earn abnormal returns in the past with the stock of a bottle cap manufacturer than with the stock of a computer manufacturer?
10. At what stage of development is it probably best to buy the stock of a young company? Why?
11. Should anyone expect to earn abnormal returns by reading and understanding Peter Lynch's good book? Why or why not?
12. Explain why you would, or would not, expect the stocks of the best-managed companies in the most profitable industries to provide the highest risk-adjusted returns.
13. Explain why the expected return on stocks with high dividend yields might differ from the expected return on stocks with low dividend yields.
14. Explain why contrarians do not necessarily expect above-average returns on stocks trading at low P/E ratios.
15. Explain how the price/book value ratio is related to the return on equity.
16. Why are P/E ratios more widely used than price/sales ratios?
17. On the basis of the Fuller-Wong study, compare the historical relationship of beta and the standard deviation to the rate of return.
18. On the basis of the Bhandari study, compare the historical relationship of beta and the debt/equity ratio to the rate of return.
19. How is the price/dividend ratio related to the dividend yield?

20. The Dowen-Bauman study found that stocks with small market capitalization, small institutional ownership, and low P/E ratios provided much higher returns than stocks with only one of these three characteristics. Does this mean that investors have a better chance of finding undervalued stocks if they use more than one selection criterion? Explain.

21. The risk factors of the arbitrage pricing theory can provide a basis for predicting the performance of the stocks in a given industry relative to the performance of the market as a whole. However, to make such predictions, one must first forecast the values of four macroeconomic variables. What are they?

|||| PROBLEMS

1. Suppose you have screened all stocks on the New York and American Stock Exchanges and a number of NASDAQ stocks to find those that meet the following criteria:

Assets	less than	$200 million
P/E ratio	less than	12
Equity/assets	greater than	60%

What more would you want to know about the stocks meeting these criteria before making any selections?

2. Select a random sample of 15 stocks ranked number one for timeliness and another 15 ranked number five for timeliness by Value Line at the beginning of a recent year.
    a. Calculate the average beta for each group of 15 stocks as of the beginning of that year.
    b. Calculate the total return for each stock for that year. Total return is the dividend yield (dividend for the year divided by the average of the price at the beginning and at end of the year) plus the percentage change in the price of the stock from the beginning to the end of the year.
    c. Calculate the average return for each group of 15 stocks. Compare these returns with one another and with the total return for the Standard & Poor's 500 Index.
    d. Calculate and compare the reward/variability (R/V) ratios for these two groups of stocks and the Standard & Poor's 500.

$$R/V = (\text{return} - \text{risk-free rate})/\text{beta}$$

The numerator of the fraction is referred to as the excess return. The following information is needed to calculate the R/V ratios:
    (1) The average beta for each group of stocks, as determined under part (a). The average beta for the S&P 500 is assumed to be one.

(2)   The average total return for each group of stocks, as determined under part (b), and for the S&P 500.

(3)   The risk-free rate. For this purpose, the rate on three-month Treasury bills, as reported in the *Economic Report of the President,* is satisfactory.

3.   Perform an exercise like that of Problem 2, but use 30 stocks selected randomly from the Standard & Poor's 500. Divide the 30 stocks into two groups on the basis of either the price/earnings ratio, price/sales ratio, price/book value ratio, or dividend yield and calculate the return for each group for the year following the time of the ratio. Remember that except for the dividend yield, the ratio cannot be calculated until the earnings per share, sales, or book value for the year is known, which is February or March for most calendar year companies.

|||| **SELECTED REFERENCES**

Berry, Michael A., Edwin Burmeister, and Marjorie B. McElroy. "Sorting out Risks Using Known APT Factors," *Financial Analysts Journal* 44 (March/April 1988): 29–42.

Bhandari, Laxmi Chand. "Debt/Equity Ratio and Expected Common Stock Returns: Empirical Evidence," *The Journal of Finance* 43 (June 1988): 507–528.

Clayman, Michelle. "In Search of Excellence: The Investor's Viewpoint," *Financial Analysts Journal* 43 (May/June 1987): 54–63.

Dowen, Richard J. and W. Scott Bauman. "A Fundamental Multifactor Asset Pricing Model," *Financial Analysts Journal* 42 (July/August 1986): 45–51.

Fuller, Russell J. and G. Wenchi Wong. "Traditional versus Theoretical Risk Measures," *Financial Analysts Journal* 44 (March/April 1988): 52–57, 67.

Graham, Benjamin. *The Intelligent Investor,* 5th ed. (New York: Harper & Row, 1973).

Jacobs, Bruce I. and Kenneth N. Levy. "Disentangling Equity Return Regularities: New Insights and Investment Opportunities," *Financial Analsysts Journal* 44 (May/June 1988): 18–43.

Lynch, Peter. *One Up on Wall Street* (New York: Simon and Schuster, 1989).

Oppenheimer, Henry R. "Ben Graham's Net Current Asset Values: A Performance Update," *Financial Analysts Journal* 42 (November/December 1986): 40–47.

Peters, Thomas A. and Robert H. Waterman, Jr. *In Search of Excellence: Lessons from America's Best-Run Corporations,* (New York: Harper & Row, 1981).

Senchack, A.J., Jr. and John D. Martin. "The Relative Performance of the PSR and PER Investment Strategies," *Financial Analysts Journal* 43 (March/April 1987): 46–56.

Speidell, Lawrence S. "The New Wave Theory," *Financial Analysts Journal* 44 (July/August 1987): 9–12.

12 TECHNICAL ANALYSIS

The phrase *technical analysis* covers a variety of practices and procedures used by analysts in forecasting the level of the stock market and the prices of individual stocks. Technical analysis ignores fundamental factors such as corporate earnings and dividends. Some technical analysts (also called technicians) base their predictions solely on past prices, or on past prices and the volume of trading. Others consider a wide variety of technical indicators. Some analysts consider both technical and fundamental factors in forecasting the market.

Although most technical traders recognize that fundamental factors affect prices of securities, they argue that fundamental data are not useful. As with any statistical data, fundamental information contains significant statistical and interpretation errors. In addition, a combination of market forces may cause price movements that appear contradictory to specific fundamental information. Finally, new information often appears with amazing speed. Thus by the time a trader learns of, or reacts to, new information, prices have already responded.

Because of these limitations, technical analysts argue that prices are the best indicators of trading opportunities. Therefore, based on the assumption that consecutive price changes are related, technicians believe that plots of historical price patterns contain information that can be used to predict future price changes.

In the present chapter, various tools used by technicians in predicting the prices of individual stocks will be examined; these include relative strength analysis, bar charts, and point-and-figure charts. Several technical indicators that analysts use to forecast the market will also be discussed. Though there is little evidence to indicate that technical approaches have been fruitful, a large segment of the market follows technical systems, and the jargon of technical traders is widely used by market participants. Thus, the student of investments should have at least a nodding acquaintance with technical systems. Students who want more detail on the systems outlined here should refer to the list of references at the end of the chapter.

The reader should note that many of the examples in this chapter deal with the securities of the futures markets. Although technical analysis was born as a stock market evaluation technique, it has found a strong following in the futures markets.

||| SIDELIGHT
Technical Analysis in an Uncertain Market

A growing number of Wall Street professionals believe that technicians, or technical analysts, can provide useful insights. Most brokerage houses have at least one technician.

Some practitioners believe that technical indicators provide a means of getting a feel for the market as a whole. Robert Nurock, editor of the *Astute Investor,* believes that the best investment decisions are made when technical and fundamental factors are in agreement.

Some market analysts and many, if not most, academicians believe that only fundamental factors—such as the ratio of the stock price to earnings, the health of the economy, and interest rates—are important. In any case, technical analysts Martin Zweig and Stan Weinstein are gloomy these days. Some technicians believe it is like 1972, just before the severe bear market of 1973–1974.

SOURCE: Adapted from Earl C. Gottschalk, Jr., "Technical Analysis Gains in Uncertain Market," *The Wall Street Journal,* December 12, 1988, p. C1. Reprinted by permission of *The Wall Street Journal,* © Dow Jones & Company, Inc. (1988). All Rights Reserved Worldwide.

|||| THE RATIONALE FOR TECHNICAL ANALYSIS

The assumptions and beliefs that underlie technical analysis were well stated by Robert Levy a number of years ago.[1] His summary contained five points:

1. Market value is determined solely by the interaction of supply and demand.

2. Supply and demand are governed by numerous factors, both rational and irrational. These factors include those that fundamentalists rely on, as well as opinions, moods, guesses, and blind necessities. The market weighs all of these factors continually and automatically.

3. Disregarding minor fluctuations in the market, stock prices tend to move in trends that persist for an appreciable length of time.

4. Changes in trend are caused by shifts in supply and demand relationships. Regardless of why these shifts occur, they can be detected sooner or later in the action of the market itself.

5. History tends to repeat itself, so past patterns of market behavior will recur in the future and can thus be used for predictive purposes.

It is easy to accept much of what Levy outlined as technical theory. Yes, in a free market, prices are determined by supply and demand, and,

---

[1]Robert A. Levy, "Conceptual Foundations of Technical Analysis," *Financial Analysts Journal* 2 (July/August 1966): 83–89.

yes, supply and demand are governed by numerous factors. Also, the market does tend to move in trends that sometimes persist for an appreciable length of time. Bull markets tend to last for at least a few years, while bear markets are usually of shorter duration. And, it seems clear that changes in trends are associated with shifts in supply and demand relationships that can be detected sooner or later in the action of the market itself. But technical theory is inconsistent with the idea of an informationally efficient market. In such a market, price changes are the result of rational actions taken by profit-seeking investors in response to new information. Moods and sentiments play no part. Price changes do not follow any predictable patterns because new information comes to light randomly. Any tendency for price patterns to recur, for whatever reason, is soon recognized by market participants and eliminated by their efforts to take advantage of it.

|||| MARKET ANALYSIS: THE DOW THEORY

Any discussion of technical analysis would be incomplete without some comment on the *Dow theory,* the oldest approach to stock market forecasting. Although it is largely discredited in the eyes of many analysts, the theory is still used by some technicians as one of many predictive tools. Portions of the theory were originated by Charles Dow, who, with Edward Jones, founded Dow Jones and Company and began to publish the *Wall Street Journal* in 1889. The rudiments of the Dow theory were set out by Dow in a series of editorials in the *Wall Street Journal* between 1899 and 1901.

Dow observed that stock price movements are of three types: short-term fluctuations, which last no more than a few days; intermediate trends, which may last for several months; and long-term trends, which last at least four years. He believed that stock prices are affected by three forces: sentiment, manipulation, and facts. Of these, he said, sentiment is the most powerful and is the basis for major trends. He believed that the market reflects changes in sentiment long before those changes are widely known.[2]

Dow himself did not attempt to use his theory of market movements to forecast stock prices. In fact, he had little confidence that anyone could predict changes in trends or identify new major trends in their early stages. In May 1902 he wrote, "The first thing that is necessary to note is that in dealing with the stock market there is no way of telling when the top of an advance or the bottom of a decline has been reached until sometime after such top or bottom has been made."[3] However, around 1910, William Hamilton, another editor of the *Journal,* used Dow's ideas in developing a technique for predicting the market.

---

[2]Technicians still place great emphasis on the sentiments of various market participants, and, as we shall see, they have a number of ways of measuring these sentiments.

[3]Robert Sobel, *Inside Wall Street* (New York: W. W. Norton & Company, 1977), p. 120.

Hamilton suggested that bull and bear markets are both characterized by three phases. A bull market begins with a reaction against the
panic selling at the end of a bear market. The second phase is a long,
persistent rise in response to expected and actual increases in corporate
profits. The third phase is marked by wild speculation and emotional
buying as the uninformed public joins the parade. In a bear market, the
whole process is reversed.

Hamilton suggested certain rules for determining whether there has
been a change in the trend. According to the Dow theory, as stated by
Hamilton, a major uptrend begins only when the Dow Jones Industrial
Average and the Dow Jones Rail Average (now the transportation average) have both reached important new highs, and a major downtrend
begins only when both averages have dropped to important new lows.
Opinions differ, of course, as to how one can tell whether a new high or
low is important.

According to the Dow theory, when the market is in a long-term
upward trend, there will be secondary reactions that may last for a few
months. If it is a true bull market, however, the low after each secondary
reaction is higher than the previous low, and each new peak is higher
than the previous peak. In a bear market, each new low is lower than
the previous low, and in each temporary recovery, the peak is lower than
the previous peak. The full cycle is illustrated in Figure 12-1.

|||| **FIGURE 12-1**
Bull and Bear Markets

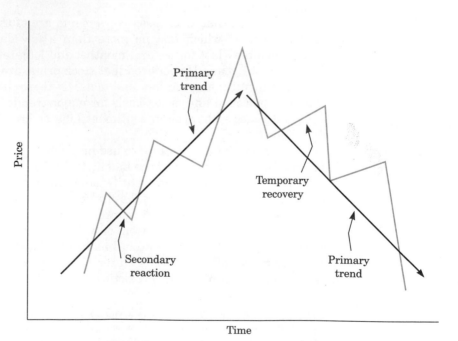

Hamilton applied the Dow theory during the 1920s with mixed results. In early 1926 he predicted a bear market, but the market rose nearly 100% during the next 3½ years. However, he achieved considerable fame a few years later by predicting on October 25, 1929, just four days before the beginning of the great stock market crash, that a bear market was coming.

Most observers believe that the Dow theory is more useful in describing what has happened in the past than in predicting what will happen in the future. A trend provides no information that is helpful in predicting how long the trend will continue. To say that the market will continue to rise because it has been rising over a considerable period is like saying the next toss of a fair coin will produce a head because all of the previous six tosses yielded heads.

|||| CHART READING

Analysts who use technical methods to select stocks spend much of their time studying charts: bar charts, point-and-figure charts, and simple line graphs.[4] Chart readers fall into two major camps: the purists, who believe that price charts, perhaps supplemented by graphs of the trading volume, tell everything of importance about the prospects for a stock, and the nonpurists, who use charts primarily for finding interesting situations that seem to merit further investigation. Purists can be further subdivided into those who favor bar charts and those who prefer point-and-figure charts. The task of the purist, in either case, is to discern the nature of the price patterns and what they indicate about future trends.

Chartists, like Dow theorists (which a chartist may be), believe that a price trend continues until there is a signal indicating that a new trend has been established. Since a trend is expected to continue until there is a clear reversal, chartists are inclined to prefer stocks or other securities whose prices have been rising over those that have been trending downward.

BAR CHARTS AND POINT-AND-FIGURE CHARTS

Bar charts are the most widely used type of chart. The vertical axis of a bar chart represents the price of the security. The horizontal axis represents time. For each day a vertical line (bar) is drawn connecting the high price for the day with the low price of the day. A short horizontal line is drawn through the vertical bar to indicate the closing price for the day. Price information for each day is plotted along the horizontal axis.[5] Figure 12-2 show a typical bar chart for March 1988 soybean futures during June and July of 1987. Other examples of bar charts can be found

[4]Some of the material in this section was taken from *Commodity Trading Manual* (The Chicago Board of Trade, 1985).
[5]The unit of time does not have to be a day; both shorter and longer periods are used.

|||| **FIGURE 12-2**

Bar Chart for Soybean Futures, March 1988

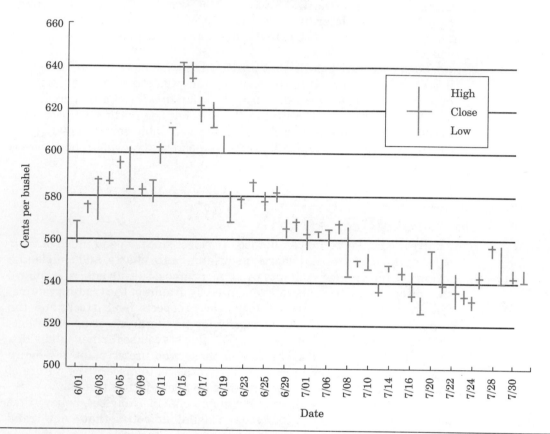

in the *Wall Street Journal,* which prints charts every day showing the patterns of the Dow Jones Indexes.

Unlike bar charts, which show daily high, low, and closing prices, entries are made on *point-and-figure charts* only when there is a significant change in the price of the stock. A change of $1 may be considered significant for a stock selling at or about $20 a share, while a change of $5 would be significant for a stock priced at or about $100 a share. All entries are made in the same column, with an X or an O, until there is a significant reversal in the price. A significant reversal could be $1 for a $20 stock and $5 for a $100 stock. Entries are made with X's when the price of the stock is rising and with O's when the price is falling.

Point-and-figure charts have no time dimension. The more unstable the price of the stock, the greater the number of entries, and the faster they will move across the page. The entries in Figure 12-3 could represent the price changes for a period as short as two or three weeks or as long as many months, depending on the volatility of the price of the stock.

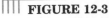

FIGURE 12-3
Point-and-Figure Chart

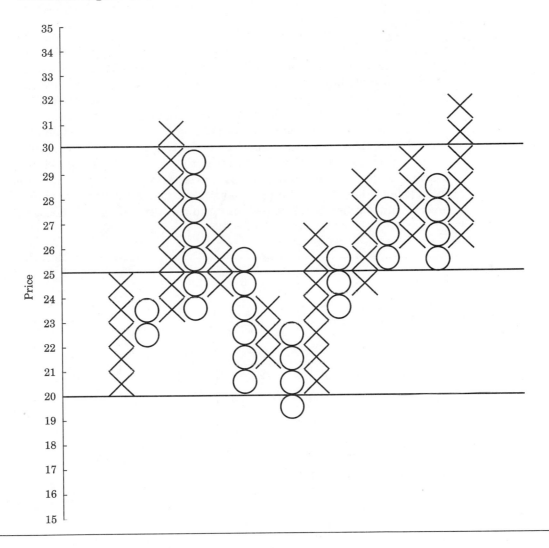

Figure 12-3 was prepared on the assumption that the smallest significant price change or reversal is $1. The five X's in the first column indicate that over some period (which could have been as short as a day or as long as many months) the price of the stock rose from approximately $20 a share to as high as $24 but not as high as $25. After reaching the $24 level, the price declined to $23, as indicated by the O recorded in the second column. The price fell to $22, or perhaps a little lower, but did not go down to $21. Eventually, the price turned up again, as indicated by the X's in the third column. The price rose from $23 to $30 before changing direction again.

Support and Resistance Levels

Whether chartists use point-and-figure charts or bar charts, their objective is to identify patterns that lead them to buy or sell decisions. Chartists look for support and resistance levels.

A *support level* is a price, or price range, lower than the current price at which a technician expects many buyers to enter the market; that is, it is a price from which price rallies may take place. Thus, if a security (stock or commodity) rallies, then falls back to the previous price area, and then rallies and falls to the same price area again, a support level is defined. The chartist believes that the demand for the stock at the support level will be strong enough to prevent any further erosion of the price. Figure 12-4 shows a support level for a hypothetical commodity.

If a declining stock breaks through the support level, the chartist usually locates another, lower support price and predicts that the stock will not fall below this new support level. Sometimes stocks break through several support levels before beginning to recover—if they do recover.

|||| **FIGURE 12-4**
Support Levels

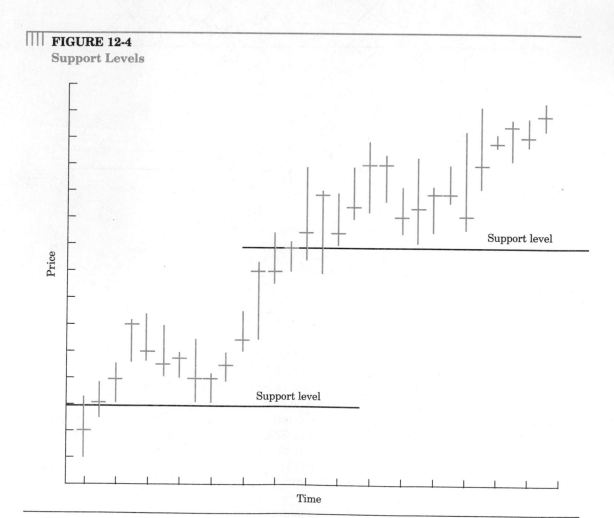

If the market rallies to a particular price and then falls back, a *resistance level* is defined. A resistance level is a price, or price range, above the current price at which the technician expects many holders of the stock to sell. He or she believes it will be difficult for the stock to break through this level. As with support levels, stocks often break through resistance levels, and the technician then looks for a new, higher resistance level. Figure 12-5 shows the resistance level for a hypothetical security.

The concepts of support and resistance levels are dependent on each other. For example, if a stock's price drops and breaks through a support level, this level becomes a resistance level. The reason for this is that traders who purchase at the support level and hold their positions during a market drop will likely sell when the market rallies toward their purchase price. The converse is true when a resistance level is broken by increasing prices.

|||| **FIGURE 12-5**

Resistance Levels

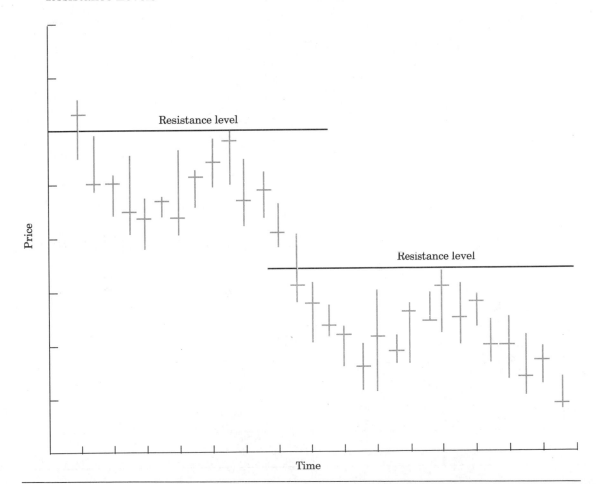

Trends, Tops, and Bottoms

The price formations that technicians observe in their charts are very important to the chartist's trading strategy. For example, a trend line is established when two or more of the daily lows fall on a roughly 45-degree line. Concurrently, when a line connecting the daily highs is parallel to this line, a channel is said to exist. Channels indicate either a major uptrend or a downtrend. Figure 12-6 shows a hypothetical uptrend and downtrend chart.

Once a major market trend is identified, the next job of the technical analyst is to determine when the trend either tops or bottoms out. Certain chart patterns are recognized as predictors that a trend is ending. The most common of these patterns is called a head and shoulders formation. This formation portends a major market reversal. There are four stages

|||| **FIGURE 12-6**

Uptrends, Downtrends, and Channels

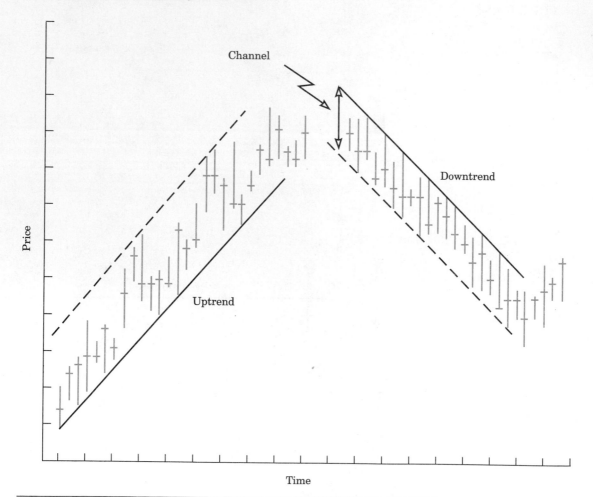

to the head and shoulders formation: first, the formation of the left shoulder; next, the head; then, the right shoulder; and finally, the penetration of the neckline. Thus, after the head and shoulders formation is complete, i.e., after the right shoulder is complete, the price must fall to a point lower than when the neckline was formed. The head and shoulders formation occurs in a bull market but indicates that the market will soon fall.

Conversely, an inverted head and shoulder formation occurs in a falling market and indicates that the market will soon be on the rise. In this case, the neckline penetration must be higher than when the neckline was formed. Figure 12-7 shows a head and shoulders and an inverted head and shoulders chart.

Other formations used to signal market moves are the double tops or double bottoms and the rounded tops or rounded bottoms. Figures 12-8 and 12-9 illustrate these configurations. Again these formations signal the end of a major market move.

Technical traders also use a variety of other formations in their analysis of the market. These include symmetrical triangles, ascending triangles, descending triangles, and trading gaps, to name just a few. For the interested reader, many books are available that more fully describe the patterns and rules followed by technical traders. Some of these books are referenced at the end of the chapter.

LINE GRAPHS

Besides the standard charts, technicians also make wide use of line graphs. These charts are plotted with time on the horizontal axis and the variable of interest on the vertical axis. Very often bar charts are plotted simultaneously with the line graph.

Moving Average

One of the simplest and most widely used line graphs is a plot of the moving average of past prices. Obviously, the intent of the moving average system is to smooth out volatile short-term movements in security prices so that only the important trends are left. Our discussion will focus on two of the many variations of the moving average system.

The moving average at any time t is simply the average of the closing prices over the past n days. A five-day moving average would be calculated as follows:

$$MA_t(5) = \tfrac{1}{5} \sum_{i=1}^{5} P_{t-i+1} = \tfrac{1}{5}(P_t + P_{t-1} + P_{t-2} + P_{t-3} + P_{t-4}) \quad (12\text{-}1)$$

In the next period, the price five days earlier is dropped, and the current price is added to the moving average. Figure 12-10 shows the moving averages for 5 and 15 days for June 1988 Treasury bonds between March and June of 1987. The trading rule for this simple moving average system is to buy when increasing prices move above the moving average and sell when decreasing prices move below the moving average.

|||| **FIGURE 12-7**
Head and Shoulders Formation

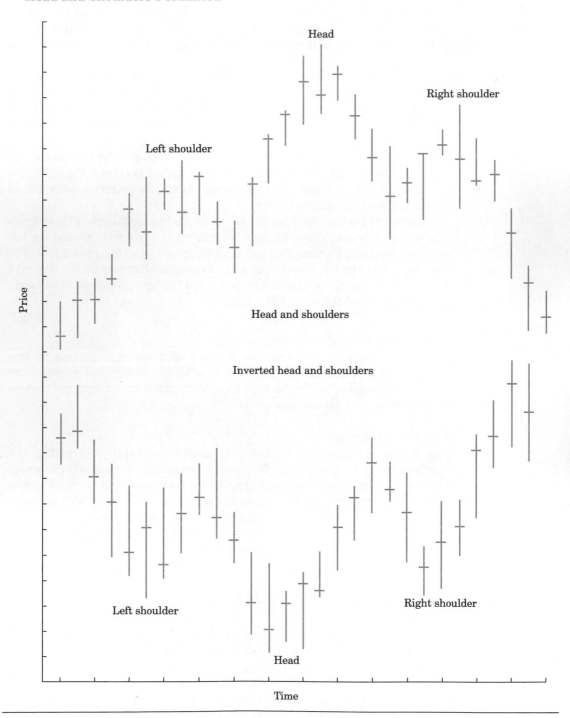

||| **FIGURE 12-8**
Double Tops and Bottoms

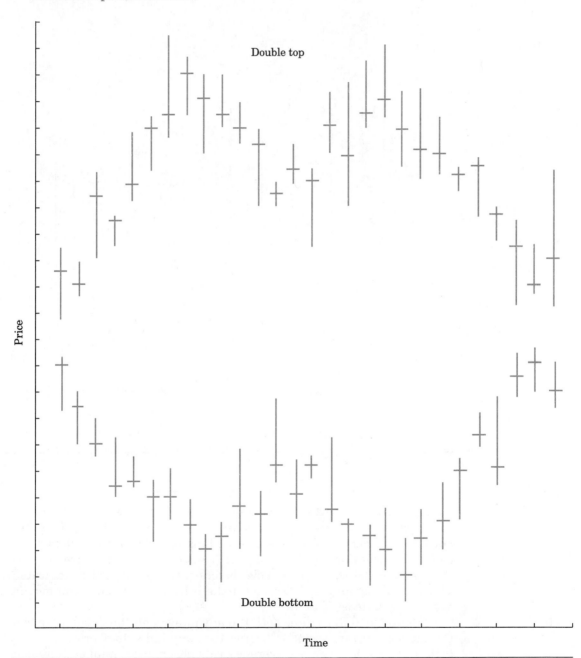

Double top

Price

Double bottom

Time

|||| **FIGURE 12-9**
Rounded Top and Bottom

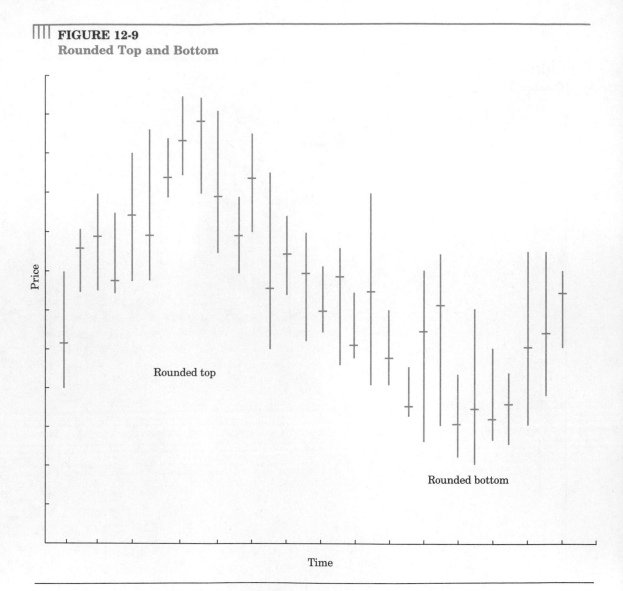

As indicated above, the moving average system is a trend identification system and thus may do well in trending markets. In a flat market, however, it tends to give excessive trading signals that result in small losses. One solution to this problem is to define how much above or below the average the price must move before a trading signal is indicated. Thus, a buy signal might be: buy if the price crosses above the moving average by at least X units.

Figure 12-10 illustrates both the advantage and the disadvantage of the moving average graph. Observe that any individual price has very little effect on the moving average. This observation implies that non-directional volatile price movements (called whipsawing) will be smoothed out in a moving average system. This means that only consistent and significant price movements will impact the average. Note also that the longer the average, the smaller the impact of individual security price changes and the more pronounced the market moves must be to affect the average. The disadvantage of the system is that the longer the average, the slower the response time to market movement. This feature may result in repeated losses when the market is not trending. The key to a moving average system is to set the right sensitivity for the system, i.e., the number of days in the average. Short moving averages will increase the sensitivity of the system to trends, while long moving averages will prevent trading action on insignificant trends.

A variation of the simple moving average system is to trade with two moving averages, one short and the other long. The long-term average is used to identify major trends, and the short-term average is used to time market transactions. Short-term averages are generally calculated between 5 and 25 days, while long-term averages range from 25 to several hundred days.

The trading rules for two moving averages are similar to those for the simple moving average. A buy signal is indicated when the short moving average crosses above the long-term average, and a sell or short sale signal is indicated when the short average crosses below the long-term average. Figure 12-11 shows 5- and 20-day moving averages for September 1987 12-year Treasury notes.

|||| FIGURE 12-10
Moving Averages for Treasury Bonds

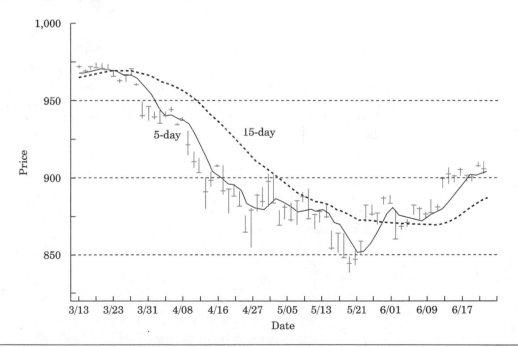

|||| **FIGURE 12-11**

Two Moving Averages Trading System for Treasury Notes

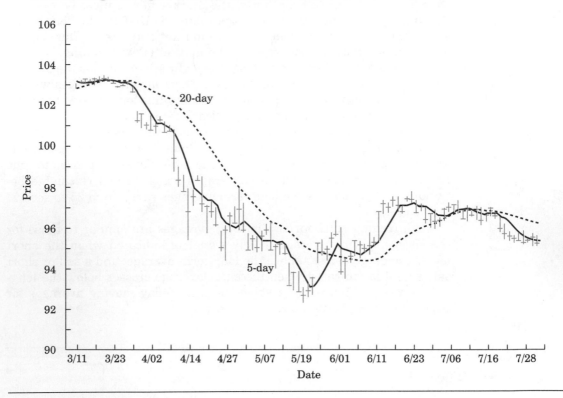

Relative Strength

Another line graph system is the plot of the *relative strength* of an individual security or group of securities. Not only is this a popular technical analysis tool, but its effectiveness has been the subject of several tests.

A relative strength graph shows how an individual stock or group of stocks has been performing relative to a market index. Past relative strength is often used as one means of predicting future performance.

The relative strength approach to stock selection is based on the notion that stocks that have outperformed the market recently have a better than 50–50 chance of outperforming the market in the future. Relative strength is calculated in various ways. Perhaps the most common method is to divide the price of the stock by a market index:

$$\text{RSI}_t = P_{at}/P_{mt} \qquad (12\text{-}2)$$

where

RSI_t = relative strength index at time t

P_{st} = price of a security at time t

P_{mt} = market index at time t

For example, if the price of Hewlett-Packard stock has risen from $40 six months ago to $50 today, and the S&P 500 Index has moved from 220 to 240 during the same period, the relative strength of Hewlett-Packard stock has increased as shown below:

	(A) Price of Hewlett- Packard	**(B)** S&P 500 Index	**(C)** Relative Strength (A/B)
Six months ago	$40	220	.182
Today	50	240	.208

Relative strength figures are usually graphed so investors can easily see what has been happening to a stock's (or industry's) relative strength over some period of time.

Another common method of calculating relative strength involves three steps. First, the latest price of the stock is divided by its price at an earlier date, or by its average price over some time interval. Second, the latest level of a market index is divided by the value of the index at an earlier date, or by its average value over some time interval. Third, the relative strength is computed by dividing the result of the first calculation by the result of the second. Again these calculations are shown for Hewlett-Packard and the S&P 500 Index:

	(A) Price of Hewlett-Packard	**(B)** S&P 500 Index
Six months ago	$40	220
Today	50	240
Ratio (P_1/P_0)	1.25	1.09
Relative strength (1.25/1.09) = 1.15		

Trendline and Value Line relative strength charts are calculated with the three-step method. Value Line relates the current price of the stock and the current level of the index (in this case, the Value Line Composite Index) to the price of the stock and the value of the index one month earlier. Trendline relates the latest stock price and index level to their 30-week moving averages. Their respective formulas are as follows:

$$VLRSI_t = \frac{P_{s,t}/P_{s,t-1}}{VLI_t/VLI_{t-1}} \qquad (12\text{-}3)$$

$$TLRSI_t = \frac{P_{s,t}/MA_{s,t}}{TLI_t/MA_{TLI,t}} \qquad (12\text{-}4)$$

where

$VLRSI_t$ = Value line relative strength index at time t

$P_{s,t}$ = price of the stock at time t

$$VLI_t = \text{Value Line Index at time } t$$

$$TLRSI_t = \text{Trendline relative strength index at time } t$$

$$TLI_t = \text{Trendline Index at time } t$$

$$MA_{s,t} = \text{moving average of the security price at time } t$$

$$= \frac{1}{30} \sum_{i=1}^{30} P_{s,t-i+1}$$

$$MA_{TLI,t} = \text{moving average of the Trendline Index}$$

$$= \frac{1}{30} \sum_{i=1}^{30} TLI_{t-i+1}$$

Thus, each relative strength figure indicates how the increase or decrease in the price of the stock compares to the increase or decrease in the market index. Suppose, for example, that the latest price of Hewlett-Packard stock is $50, and the 30-week moving average is $42, while the latest level of the S&P 500 Index is 250, compared to a 30-week moving average of 220. The relative strength of the Hewlett-Packard stock, based on the Trendline method, would be 1.048, calculated as follows:

		Price of Stock	Value of Index	Relative Strength
(A)	Current value	$50	250	
(B)	30-week average	$42	220	
(C)	A/B	1.190	1.136	
(D)	Relative strength (1.190/1.136)			1.048

Figure 12-12 presents the Value Line relative strength index for Hewlett-Packard.

|||| **FIGURE 12-12**
Value Line's Relative Strength Index

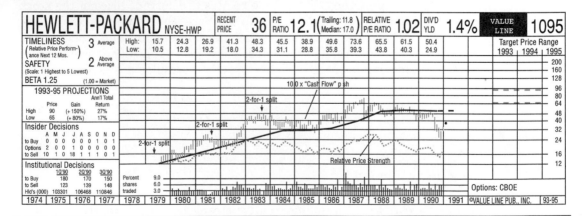

SOURCE: Value Line.

Relative Strength Strategies: Levy's Analysis

There is considerable lack of agreement concerning the value of relative strength analysis. In an early attempt to test its usefulness, Robert Levy tried 68 different trading rules (or strategies) based on relative strength figures. He concluded, erroneously, that his results proved the usefulness of relative strength analysis and refuted the efficient market theory of security pricing.[6]

Levy's method of testing relative strength was to try many different trading rules based on relative strength to see if any would outperform a buy-and-hold strategy. Thus, he was on a searching expedition in which he could as well have been looking for correlations between changes in stock prices and football scores or between changes in stock prices and the number of rainy days in October. It is not very difficult to find several quantitative factors with which stock price performance has been positively correlated in the past. Levy looked at 68 different sets of factors (his trading rules) and found a few that were positively related to the returns on the stocks in his sample, unadjusted for any differences in risk. From Levy's study, one could not tell whether those same rules would have produced above-average returns over different time intervals, with different groups of stocks, or on a risk-adjusted basis.

Jensen and Bennington found several deficiencies in Levy's analysis when they applied his trading rules to different stocks over different time intervals. They observed returns that were lower than the returns with a buy-and-hold strategy.[7] They also found that Levy's strategies tended to select portfolios of above-average risk when stock prices were rising. Thus, after adjusting the returns for differences in systematic risk, Levy's strategies were even more unattractive.

Relative Strength: Recent Studies

If the market is perfectly efficient, historical price trends do not contain any useful information for predicting future prices. This means that the past performance of individual stocks or groups of stocks should not be considered in estimating what their future performance will be.[8] Three studies indicate, however, that when the recent performance of a group of stocks has been exceptionally strong, the group tends to provide higher-than-average risk-adjusted returns for some time in the future.[9]

[6]Robert A. Levy, "Random Walks: Reality or Myth," *Financial Analysts Journal* 23 (November/December 1967); "Relative Strength as a Criterion for Investment Selection," *The Journal of Finance* 22 (November/December 1967): 595–610.

[7]Michael C. Jensen and George A. Benington, "Random Walks and Technical Theories: Some Additional Evidence," *The Journal of Finance* 25 (May 1970): 469–82. A buy-and-hold strategy is one where a diversified portfolio of stocks is selected and held continuously.

[8]For a discussion of the efficient market, see Chapter 8.

[9]Charles A. Ackerman and Werner E. Keller, "Relative Strength does Persist," *Journal of Portfolio Management* 4 (Fall 1977): 38–45; James Bohan, "Relative Strength: Further Positive Evidence," *Journal of Portfolio Management* 8 (Fall 1981): 36–39; John S. Brush and Keith E. Boles, "The Predictive Power in Relative Strength & CAPM," *Journal of Portfolio Management* 5 (Summer 1983): 20–23.

The 1981 study by Bohan illustrates a historical tendency for stocks with extremely high or low relative strength to remain in those categories. Bohan investigated the persistence of relative performance for Standard & Poor's industry groups from 1969 through 1980. His basic data consisted of the annual percentage increases or decreases for all of Standard & Poor's industry indexes. On the basis of these data, the industry groups were ranked at the beginning of each year from best to worst. The groups were then sorted annually into quartiles on the basis of their relative performance during the latest year. Each quartile of approximately 100 stocks, or 20 industry groups, was treated as an individual portfolio.

The portfolios were re-formed at the beginning of each year on the basis of the performance of each industry group in the latest year, and an equal amount was then invested in each portfolio. Portfolio 1 always contained the stock groups whose prices had increased by the greatest percentage in the latest year. An industry group might be in portfolio 1 in one year and in portfolio 2, 3, 4, or 5 the following year.

The author found a definite tendency for the best-performing industry groups in one year to be the best in the next year and for the worst groups to remain in portfolio 5. Industry groups in portfolio 1 in a given year remained in portfolio 1 the following year 29% of the time, and industry groups in portfolio 5 remained in portfolio 5 the following year 32% of the time.[10] In addition, the average annual percentage gain of 13.4% for portfolio 1, net of estimated annual commissions of 2%, was much higher than the 5.3% gain for the S&P 500, as well as much higher than the gains for the other four portfolios.

Portfolio 1 outperformed portfolio 5 in 7 of the 11 years and outperformed the S&P 500 in every year but one. The average beta of portfolio 1 was 1.0, and the standard deviation of the returns for portfolio 1 was lower than for all portfolios except 2, which had a slightly lower standard deviation than portfolio 1. Thus, the extraordinary performance of portfolio 1 was achieved without incurring above-average risk.

Care should be taken not to infer too much from Bohan's findings. His study showed that for one 11-year period industry groups that performed best one year tended to perform best the following year. It is not clear what his findings would have been over a different period or with different stocks. Nor is it clear what the results would have been if the portfolios had been re-formed either more or less frequently than once a year. Most important of all, it is not certain that his findings will apply to any specific future period.

The author of a fourth study found an overall negative correlation between past and future relative performance, but suggested that his findings were not necessarily inconsistent with studies that indicate that exceptionally high and low relative strength tends to persist.[11] Stocks at

---

[10]These percentages are to be compared with the 20% that would remain in the same portfolio from one year to the next if the performance of a group in one period provided no indication as to what its performance would be in the next period.

[11]Robert D Arnott, "Relative Strength Revisited," *Journal of Portfolio Management* 5 (Spring 1979): 19–23.

the extreme in relative strength may have a tendency to stay at the extreme even though there is an overall tendency for strong performance to be followed by weak performance, and vice versa. And, of course, any correlation at all between past and future relative performance, whether positive or negative, can be helpful to investors if it is strong enough and persistent.[12]

|||| MERRILL LYNCH TECHNICAL INDICATORS

Robert Farrell, a highly regarded technician and chief market analyst at Merrill Lynch, predicts the market on the basis of both fundamental and technical factors. For example, in May 1985 he predicted (correctly, as it turned out) that the secular bull market in common stocks would continue through 1985 and into 1986.[13] The principal basis for his forecast was an expectation that the rate of inflation and interest rates would continue to decline, giving stock prices a further boost. He noted that the Federal Reserve Board had recently reduced the discount rate, and he expected further easing of monetary policy because of the sluggish economy. He also noted that previous cuts of the discount rate had been followed by rising stock prices 80% of the time.

Stock market forecasts by the Merrill Lynch Market Analysis Department are based in part on 30 technical factors that are classified into four categories: (1) *momentum indicators,* (2) *sentiment* (or psychological) *indicators,* (3) *speculative indicators,* and (4) *monetary and stock market credit indicators.* Each of these categories is assigned a score ranging from +10 to −10. To arrive at a composite score, the indicators are arranged into three groups by combining the third and fourth. Thus, the total score could range from +30 to −30. However, the market analysts believe that the composite score will rarely go above +20 or below −20.

A composite score of +20 would be very bullish (strong evidence that a bear market will soon end or that a bull market will be sustained), and a score of −20 would be very bearish. A small positive score is not necessarily bullish, nor is a small negative score necessarily bearish. For example, in March 1986, when the composite score was −7, the Market Analysis Department expected stocks to continue their long-term upward trend, with no more than a 5% to 10% correction, or decline, sometime during the year.

---

[12]When stocks are selected on the basis of their recent relative strength, the investor's portfolio will turn over quite rapidly as poor-performing stocks are replaced by stocks that have performed well in recent months. Transactions costs will be much higher than with a buy-and-hold strategy. Because of the higher transactions costs, a fairly strong correlation between past and future performance is required to make a relative strength strategy more profitable than a policy of buying and holding.

[13]*Barron's,* May 27, 1985, p. 13.

KEY TECHNICAL INDICATORS

Of the 30 technical indicators used by Merrill Lynch to calculate a composite score, 12 receive the most attention from the firm's chief market analyst in his weekly "Market Analysis Comment." These 12 indicators are shown in Table 12-1.

Momentum Indicators

Technicians believe that if a high percentage of all stocks are participating in a bull market and the rate of advance is not extraordinarily high, the uptrend is likely to continue. However, an unusually steep advance is a sign that the market will soon peak and turn downward. The S&P 500 annual rate of change is a measure of the rate of advance, and the other three momentum indicators are measures of the breadth of the advance.

Rate of Change of the S&P 500 The annual rate of change of the S&P 500 is the rate of increase or decrease for the latest month on an annualized basis. A positive rate of more than 30% is unusually high, and a rate of less than −15% is unusually low. The historical record indicates that high positive rates are followed by bear markets and large negative rates by bull markets. However, this information by itself is not very helpful to investors who are trying to anticipate a reversal of the trend. While a high positive rate may indicate that a bear market is coming, the downtrend may not actually begin for many months, and before it begins, stock prices may rise considerably higher. Similarly, a large negative rate may indicate that a bull market is coming, but prices may continue to fall for several months before the market reaches bottom and turns upward.

|||| **TABLE 12-1**

Merrill Lynch's Key Technical Indicators

Momentum indicators:
  S&P 500 annual rate of change
  Five-week advance-decline diffusion index
  Percentage of stocks above the 200-day moving average
  Weekly new highs minus weekly new lows
Sentiment indicators:
  CBOE put/call ratio
  Percentage of investment services that are bearish and bullish
  Consensus of speculators on stock index futures
Speculative activity measures:
  OTC volume/NYSE volume ratio
Stock market credit and interest rates:
  Margin debt (billions)
  New equity financing (billions)
  Consensus of speculators on Treasury bond futures
  Yield on three-month Treasury bills versus yield on Moody's Aaa bonds

Advance-Decline Line and Advance-Decline Diffusion Index In the 1920s and earlier, when the Dow Jones averages were the only readily available measures of the stock market's performance, a daily calculation of the number of advances and declines on the New York Stock Exchange was a useful check on what was happening to all stocks. Technicians still relate the number of advances to the number of declines to measure the breadth of a trend.

Market breadth can be measured either by the cumulative difference between the number of stocks that have advanced each day and the number that have declined, or by an index that reflects the proportion of the stocks that have advanced. A graph of the cumulative difference between the number of stocks that have advanced and the number that have declined is called an advance-decline line. An index that reflects the percentage relationship of the number of stocks that have advanced plus one-half of the number that are unchanged to the total number of issues traded is called a diffusion index. It is calculated as follows:

$$ADDI_t = [(A_t + U_t/2)/VOL_t] \times 100$$

where

$ADDI_t$ = advance-decline diffusion index at time t

A_t = number of stocks that advanced at time t

U_t = number of stocks that were unchanged at time t

VOL_t = number of issues traded at time t

For example, if on a day when 1,600 issues were traded on the New York Stock Exchange, 800 advanced, 600 declined, and 200 were unchanged, the index for that day would be

$$ADDI = [(800 + 200/2)/1,600] \times 100 = 56.25\%$$

A five-week moving average of the advance-decline diffusion index, along with the Dow Jones Industrial Average (DJIA), is plotted in Figure 12-13. When the five-week moving average reaches an unusually high or low level, it may foreshadow a change in the trend of the market. Technicians look for divergences between the advance-decline line and the DJIA. If the DJIA has been moving upward and the advance-decline line downward for a few months, a technician might conclude that the market is about to establish a new downtrend. Sometimes the technician would be right. For example, in early 1985, the 5-week advance-decline ratio reached a high of nearly 60, well above any reading since late 1983. This reading followed the two-year period when the DJIA was meandering between 1000 and 1200 points. Such a reading would indicate a major bull market, as happened between 1985 and 1987.

The five-week advance-decline ratio reached a low of nearly 40 after the market crash of 1987, indicating the major trend was turning down. The market, however, surged upward until well into 1990. As with the many other market indicators, the signals given by the advance-decline

|||| **FIGURE 12-13**

Advance-Decline Diffusion Index

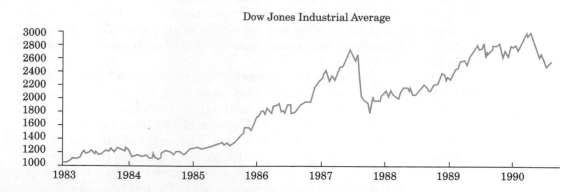

Dow Jones Industrial Average

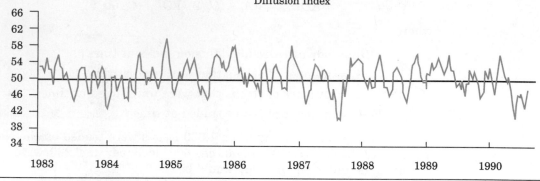

5-Week Advance-Decline
Diffusion Index

SOURCE: Merrill Lynch, "Where the Indicators Stand," (November 1990).

ratio are sometimes misleading and rarely sharp and clear. There is no evidence to indicate that the advance-decline line or the advance-decline index has been a reliable indicator of a change in the market's major trend.

Percentage of Stocks above the 200-Day Moving Average In predicting the future trend of the market, some technicians find it helpful to relate the current prices of many stocks to their 200-day moving averages. As an example, if the prices of 80% or more of all New York Stock Exchange stocks are above their 200-day moving average, the market may be considered overbought. Prices are too high, and the market is expected to decline. Or, if 20% or fewer of the stocks are above their 200-day moving average, the market may be considered oversold, and the indexes may soon begin to rise.

Figure 12-14 shows the percentage of New York Stock Exchange stocks above their 200-day moving average for the years 1972 through mid-1990. Figure 12-15 shows the level of the market from 1972 through mid-1990 as measured by the DJIA. For a crude test of the results

|||| **FIGURE 12-14**

Market Overbought (Prices High) or Oversold (Prices Low)

Percentage of NYSE common stock above their 200-day moving average

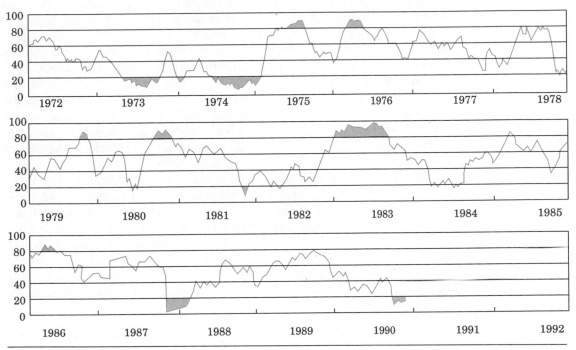

SOURCE: Merrill Lynch, "Where the Indicators Stand," (November 1990).

|||| **FIGURE 12-15**

Dow Jones Industrial Average

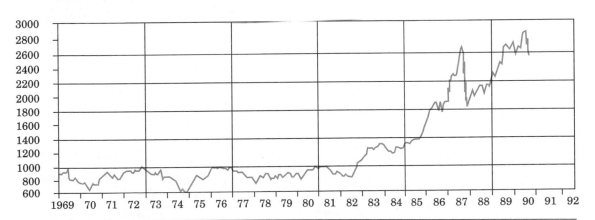

SOURCE: Merrill Lynch, "Where the Indicators Stand," (November 1990).

of buying when the market is oversold (20% or fewer of New York Stock Exchange stocks above their 200-day moving average) and selling when the market is overbought (80% or more of New York Stock Exchange stocks above their 200-day moving average), assume that an investor purchased the DJIA immediately after seeing the market was oversold and sold the average immediately after the market became overbought.[14] Table 12-2 shows the approximate results of following such a strategy, ignoring transactions costs, dividends on the stocks, and any income the investor could have earned by investing the proceeds of the stock sales in other assets. The investor would have held stocks for only about 5 of the 14½ years from 1972 to mid-1986. The investor's total gain on the DJIA stocks would have been approximately 450 points, compared to a gain of around 975 points with a buy-and-hold strategy. It is assumed that with both strategies the investor first purchased stocks in the second quarter of 1973 when the DJIA was about 900.

With a buy-and-hold policy, if the investor had purchased the DJIA at 900 in the second quarter of 1973 and held the stocks to mid-1986, when the average was about 1900, her gain would have been about 1,000 points. Even at the high interest rates available during much of this 13-year period, it is unlikely that any investor would have earned enough on short-term investments when she was not holding stocks to cover the loss of dividends, plus the additional transactions costs, plus the loss of 600 points (1,000 minus 400) from not following a buy-and-hold strategy.

[14]Note that although the market was oversold in both 1973 and 1974, the investor acquired a portfolio of stocks in 1973 and had no additional funds to invest in stocks in 1974. Also, although the market was overbought in both 1975 and 1976, the investor sold the portfolio of stocks in 1975 and had nothing left to sell in 1976.

|||| **TABLE 12-2**

Approximate Gain from Buying When the Market Is Oversold and Selling When the Market Is Overbought, 1972 to Mid-1986

Date of Transaction		Approximate DJIA		Gain (Loss)
Quarter	Year	Buy	Sell	
2nd	1973	900		
1st	1975		800	(100)
4th	1978	800		
3rd	1979		850	50
2nd	1980	850		
3rd	1980		950	100
3rd	1981	850		
4th	1982		1050	200
2nd	1984	1150		
1st	1985		1300	150
Net gain				400

Weekly New Highs Minus Weekly New Lows Another indication of market momentum is a three-week moving average of the number of New York Stock Exchange stocks that have reached a new high relative to their price over the previous 52 weeks minus the number that have reached a new low. This indicator is based on the notion that when the market is approaching a top, investors are buying stocks that have lagged the market. Thus, when the market is close to a top, few new lows are being registered. Similarly, when the market is approaching a bottom, many stocks will be establishing new lows and few will be rising to new highs.

Sentiment Indicators

Most sentiment indicators, other than the specialist short-sale ratio and the insiders sell/buy ratio, are contrary indicators. When contrary indicators are bullish, technicians expect a bear market, and when contrary indicators are bearish, technicians expect a bull market. For example, one closely watched contrary sentiment indicator is the percentage of investment services giving bearish predictions. When most investment services are bearish, technicians expect stock prices to rise, and when most investment services are bullish, technicians expect stock prices to fall.

Technicians are inclined to believe that a bull market is likely to last as long as many investors still have a pessimistic outlook. It is only after most investors have become optimistic and committed most of their funds to the market that few buyers remain and stock prices begin to fall. Then, as prices decline, more and more investors become pessimistic and are heavy sellers of stock. Finally, after most of the anxious sellers have sold, the demand for stocks becomes greater than the supply, and the market turns up once again.

The *specialist short-sale ratio* and the insiders sell/buy ratio are straightforward indicators. If specialists and insiders are optimistic, technicians are inclined to be optimistic, and if they are pessimistic, technicians are inclined to be pessimistic. Technicians believe that people in these two groups are likely to be right about the future trend of the market. Thus, the outlook for the market is thought to be bearish if short selling by specialists is unusually heavy, or if selling by insiders is far greater than the amount they are buying.

CBOE Put/Call Ratio Owning a call option is analogous to going long or buying a security. Owning a put option is like selling a security short. The put/call sentiment indicator is a five-day average of the ratio of the number of put options sold on the Chicago Board Options Exchange (CBOE) to the number of call options sold. A high ratio indicates that many investors (speculators) have become pessimistic about the market and are purchasing put options either as a speculation or as a hedge against a decline in the values of the stocks they hold.

The ratio of puts to calls is nearly always less than 1.0. A ratio of more than .80 is unusually high, and a ratio of less than .35 is unusually low. Technicians believe that a ratio lower than, say, .40 in a bull market indicates the kind of widespread optimism that usually prevails before a market top. In a bear market, the put/call ratio is likely to be high, reflecting a high level of pessimism. Investors are often most pessimistic shortly before the market begins to recover.

Number of Investment Services That Are Bearish and Bullish Technicians are inclined to believe that publishers of investment advisory services are trend followers rather than trend leaders. In a bull market, the optimism of investment advisers tends to increase along with the prices of stocks. As the market moves up, more and more advisers recommend heavy investment in common stocks. The number of optimistic advisers is likely to become very high as the market approaches a major top. Then, as prices decline, more and more advisory services become pessimistic. By the time the market reaches a major bottom, few optimists remain. Pessimism continues to reign until the market has moved substantially above its low point for the cycle.

The percentages of bullish and bearish investment services are tabulated weekly by *Investors Intelligence*. Their figures show that as the market declined in 1981 and early 1982, the percentage of bearish investment services increased from roughly 40% in the late fall of 1981 to between 50% and 60% in the spring and summer of 1982. Bearish sentiment was widespread shortly before the beginning of the great bull market in August 1982. Then, as the market approached a peak in late 1983, nearly 60% of the investment services were bullish, and only about 20% were making bearish recommendations.

Merrill Lynch has found that the bearish percentages are more reliable than the bullish percentages as predictors of major reversals. In the spring of 1986, Merrill Lynch assumed that a bull market would be close to the top if 15% or fewer of the investment services were bearish, and a bear market would be close to the bottom if 60% or more of the services were making bearish recommendations.

Percentage of Speculators Who Are Bullish on Stock Index Futures Technicians have observed that the sentiments of speculators in *stock index futures* tend to move in cycles similar to those of professional investment advisers. The figures compiled by Market Vane indicate that few speculators are pessimistic when the market is near a major high and many are pessimistic when it is near a major low. According to Merrill Lynch in June 1986, the outlook for stocks is bearish if more than 70% of the speculators are bullish, and the outlook is bullish if fewer than 30% of the speculators are bullish.

SPECULATIVE ACTIVITY MEASURE

Ratio of OTC Volume to NYSE Volume

Over-the-counter stocks are predominantly the issues of smaller companies, and they tend to be lower priced than stocks that are traded on the New York Stock Exchange. Technicians are inclined to believe that unusually heavy activity in a rising OTC market indicates that individuals are becoming highly optimistic about future stock prices. As of June 1986, Merrill Lynch considered speculative activity high if the ratio of OTC volume to NYSE volume exceeded 80%. In general, the higher the level of speculation, the higher the probability of an early downturn in the market.

STOCK MARKET CREDIT AND INTEREST RATES

Margin Debt and the Amount of New Equity Financing

The level of margin debt and the amount of new equity financing can be viewed as indicators of investor sentiment as well as of the amount of speculative activity. Large increases in margin debt and *initial public offerings (IPOs)* during a bull market indicate that investors are becoming very bullish, and this may indicate that a downturn is imminent.

Consensus of Speculators on Treasury Bond Futures

Market Vane provides weekly figures on the percentage of speculators who are bullish on Treasury bond futures. A three-week moving average of these figures serves as a contrary technical indicator. If a high percentage of speculators are bullish about Treasury bond futures (indicating an expectation of declining interest rates), this is a bad omen for stocks because interest rates are likely to go up rather than down. On the other hand, if relatively few speculators on bond futures are bullish (indicating that few expect interest rates to decline), this is a positive indicator for stocks because interest rates are likely to fall, contrary to the expectations of the speculators.

   Merrill Lynch believes that if more than 75% of the speculators are bullish on Treasury bond futures (more than 75% expect interest rates to decline), this is a bearish sign for stocks; and if fewer than 35% are bullish on the futures, this is a positive sign for stocks. There is no evidence as to how useful this information may be.

Rate on Moody's Aaa Bonds Minus Rate on Three-Month Treasury Bills

Because of the strong influence of interest rates on stock prices, technicians use several indicators concerning interest rate expectations and Federal Reserve monetary policy. Changes in monetary policy and the degree of tightness or looseness in the money and capital markets can be measured in various ways. One method is to calculate the spread between the yield on Moody's Aaa corporate bonds and the yield on three-month Treasury bills. Generally, there is a positive spread between the bond rate and the rate on Treasury bills. However, a tight monetary policy can narrow the spread and even cause Treasury bill rates to rise above the rates on high-grade corporate bonds. A tightening of monetary policy tends to raise interest rates and depress stock prices, while a loosening of monetary policy usually leads to lower interest rates for a time, which tends to raise stock prices. For example, the sharp decline in interest rates that began in 1982 was a major force behind the bull market in stocks that started on August 12 of that year.

|||| OTHER TECHNICAL INDICATORS

SHORT SELLING

Technical analysts use two kinds of statistics about short sales: (1) the amount of short selling by various types of market participants and (2) the total amount of short interest. The short interest is the number of shares previously sold short that have not yet been purchased by the short sellers for return to the lenders. The New York and American Stock Exchanges report the total short interest in their stocks four business days after the 15th of each month, and these figures are published in the *Wall Street Journal* immediately thereafter.

SHORT-INTEREST RATIO

Using the short-interest figures reported by the exchanges, *Barron's* calculates for each exchange the ratio of the short interest to the average daily volume of trading for a month. For example, the May 26, 1986 issue of *Barron's* reported that the *short-interest ratio* for the New York Stock Exchange as of May 15 rose to a record high of 2.34 from 2.02 for the previous month.

In the past, many technicians have considered the short-interest ratio a good indicator of future market direction. The conventional wisdom among technicians was that a high short-interest ratio and a rising trend in the ratio were bullish because the greater the short interest, the more buying the short sellers would have to do in the future to cover their short positions. This buying was expected to raise the prices of stocks. It has been found, however, that short-interest figures for individual stocks are of no value in predicting the prices of those stocks.[15]

Are aggregate short-interest figures of any greater use than the figures for individual stocks? There is no evidence to support such a conclusion. This is in spite of the fact that from 1952 to 1969 there was a strong correlation between declining short-interest ratios and rising stock

---

[15]Barton M. Biggs, "The Short Interest—A False Proverb," *Financial Analysts Journal* 22 (July/August 1966): 111–16; Randall D. Smith, "Short Interest and Stock Market Prices," *Financial Analysts Journal* 24 (November/December 1968): 151–54.

prices.[16] The reason the short-interest ratio declined as stock prices rose, however, was not a decrease in the short interest but an increase in the trading volume. Thus, what observers were seeing was an increase in the price of stocks associated with an increase in the trading volume. Similarly, decreases in stock prices were associated with decreases in the volume of trading, which resulted in increases in the short-interest ratio.

At one time, an increase or decrease in the aggregate short interest indicated an increase or decrease in the bearish sentiment of speculators. However, since much of the short selling in recent years has been by arbitragers rather than speculators, a change in the aggregate short interest may no longer convey any information about market sentiment. For example, if company A is proposing to acquire company B and is offering stock that is worth more than the current market value of B, arbitragers will purchase shares of B and sell short the shares of A that they expect to receive for their shares of B when the merger is consummated. The shares of A are sold short to "lock in" the profit that will result from the disparity between the market price of B and the price A is paying for B in the merger. Thus, the short sale is a *hedge* rather than a speculation.

Short sale figures may be more useful in the future. Recently, Advest, Inc., of Hartford, Connecticut, has begun to issue revised short sale ratios (called "at-risk ratios") that are based upon all short sales except those made in arbitrage transactions. The at-risk ratio increased dramatically from 1.21 in May 1986 to 1.85 in June. Advest interpreted this to be a very bullish sign.

SPECIALIST SHORT-SALE RATIO

The *specialist short-sale ratio* is a good example of a market indicator that was once thought to be a good predictor of future trends but has been found wanting in recent years because of changes in the market.[17] The ratio is calculated by dividing the number of shares New York Stock Exchange specialists sold short during the week by the total number of shares sold short on the Exchange during the same week. Technicians have assumed that specialists are better than average forecasters of market trends and that heavy short selling by specialists indicates that prices will be trending downward. When a specialist expects the price of a stock to fall or to continue a downward trend that has already begun, he is likely to sell more stock short than his responsibility as a market maker requires him to do.[18] Thus, heavy short selling by specialists as compared to total short selling has been treated as a bearish signal. However, as

---

[16]Thomas J. Kerrigan, "The Short Interest Ratio and Its Component Parts," *Financial Analysts Journal* 30 (November/December 1974): 45–49.

[17]Frank K. Reilly and David T. Whitford, "A Test of the Specialists' Short Sale Ratio," *Journal of Portfolio Management* 8 (Winter 1982): 12–18.

[18]If there are too few buyers in a declining market to keep the price changes on successive transactions small, the specialist is required to supply additional stock to the market even if he must sell short to do so.

noted earlier, total short sales have ballooned in recent years due to the large amount of short selling in arbitrage transactions, where the short sale is used to hedge a long position in stocks or options. The impact of short selling by arbitragers on the specialist short-sale ratio has seriously reduced its usefulness as a market indicator, unless it is adjusted by removing arbitrage transactions from total short sales as Advest has done in calculating the short-interest ratio. The specialist short-sale ratio is still in the Merrill Lynch list of 30 market indicators.

MUTUAL FUND CASH/ASSET RATIO

If common stock mutual funds were good market timers, they would be fully invested (have minimum cash balances) at the beginning of a bull market and have large cash balances and relatively small holdings of common stocks at the beginning of a bear market.[19] However, as Figure 12-16 shows, the cash positions of mutual funds, as measured by the ratio of cash to net assets, are just the opposite of what is expected. *Mutual*

[19]The "cash balances" of mutual funds include short-term securities, such as Treasury bills, as well as cash.

|||| **FIGURE 12-16**

Mutual Fund Cash

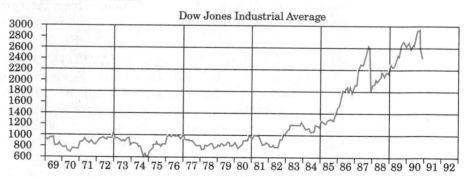

Dow Jones Industrial Average

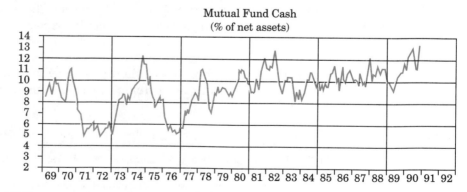

Mutual Fund Cash
(% of net assets)

SOURCE: Merrill Lynch, "Where the Indicators Stand," (November 1990).

fund cash/asset ratios are high when the market is down, as in 1974 and early 1982, and are low when the market is at or near a cyclical peak, as in 1972 and 1976. Some observers explain this negative relationship in terms of the impact of mutual fund buying and selling on the prices of stocks.

Those who believe that the actions of mutual funds have a significant impact on stock prices argue that the supply of stocks is essentially fixed. Therefore, an increase in stock purchases by mutual funds tends to push prices up, and net selling by mutual funds tends to drive prices down. Thus, when mutual fund cash/asset ratios are high (and stock prices are down), stock prices can be expected to rise as mutual funds commit more funds to the market. And, when mutual fund cash/asset ratios are low (and stock prices are high), the market can be expected to decline because mutual funds no longer have excess cash that can be used to purchase stocks. As the market declines, mutual funds sell stocks and build up their cash balances.

If the previous analysis is an accurate description of the relationship between mutual fund cash positions and the prices of stocks, then one should be able to forecast market reversals (from a bull market to a bear market or vice versa) on the basis of the mutual fund cash/asset ratio. Unfortunately, the analysis overlooks the fact that cash/asset ratios are affected by changes in total assets as well as by changes in cash. Thus, often the principal reason the mutual fund cash/asset ratio has declined during a rising market is not because mutual funds were reducing their cash balances and investing more heavily in common stocks but simply because the denominator of the ratio (mutual fund net assets) was increasing due to the increase in stock prices.[20] Similarly, the reason the mutual fund cash/asset ratio has increased when stock prices were declining is not because the institutions were selling stocks and building up their cash balances but simply because declining stock prices caused the total value of their assets to become smaller. Accordingly, an investor using the mutual fund cash/asset ratio to forecast major turning points for the stock market may really be forecasting market turning points on the basis of the level of stock prices. A simple example will illustrate the point.

	Time A	Time B
Market index	100	60
Mutual fund net assets	1,000	600
Mutual fund cash assets	6	6
Cash/net assets	6%	10%

At time B, an investor might judge that the market was ready to start moving up because the mutual fund ratio of cash to net assets was at or near a peak. However, the investor would really be deciding that the

[20]R. David Ranson and William G. Shipman, "Institutional Buying Power and the Stock Market," *Financial Analysts Journal* 37 (September/October 1981): 62–68.

market was ready to start moving up because it had declined 40% from time A. It was the market decline of 40% that caused the mutual fund cash/asset ratio to rise from 6% to 10%.[21]

BARRON'S CONFIDENCE INDEX

When investors are especially worried about the economic outlook, they require larger risk premiums on medium- and lower-grade bonds. The average yield spread between Baa corporate bonds and Aaa bonds increased from 8.2% of the yield on AAA bonds in the prosperous year 1978 to 16.8% in 1982, a year in which the economy was struggling through a deep recession. *Barron's confidence index* is a measure of the spread between the yields on medium- and high-grade bonds. A narrow spread indicates a high degree of confidence in the future profitability of corporations.

The bond yields in Barron's confidence index are based on two bond indexes that are maintained by *Barron's:* an index of best-grade bonds, which is composed of the yields on 10 bonds with an average Standard & Poor's rating of AA+, and an index of medium-grade bonds, which is composed of the yields on 10 bonds with an average rating of BBB+. The confidence index is simply the ratio of the average yield on the best-grade bonds to the average yield on the medium-grade bonds. Since the yields on high-grade bonds are always lower than the yields on medium-grade bonds, the confidence index is always less than 1.0. The greater the confidence of investors in the future of the economy, the closer the yields on medium-grade bonds will be to the yields on high-grade bonds, and the higher the confidence index. A high, or rising, confidence index is supposed to be bullish for stocks on the theory that as investors become more optimistic about the economy and less concerned about the risk of medium-grade bonds, they will also become more optimistic about common stocks and less concerned about the risks they entail.

The record of the confidence index as a leading indicator for stock prices has been mixed.[22] One reason for its uneven performance is that yield spreads are affected by the supplies of various grades of bonds as well as the demand. If unusually large quantities of medium-grade bonds and relatively small quantities of high-grade bonds are being issued, the yield spread between medium- and high-grade bonds will tend to widen. This will lower the confidence index even though investors may be highly optimistic about the future of the economy. Some observers believe that the confidence index is especially useful in predicting major downturns in the stock market. A substantial drop in the index is seen as a red flag.

The yield spread between U.S. Treasury bonds and speculative Ba corporate bonds, which is published by Salomon Brothers and reported

[21]We should note that the mutual fund cash/asset ratio does not always decline as stock prices move higher. For example, from June 20, 1985, to June 20, 1986, the mutual fund cash/asset ratio for equity funds and balanced funds increased from 9.3% to 10.8% while the S&P 500 was increasing 30.6%.

[22]*Barron's,* April 1, 1985, p. 30.

weekly in *Barron's,* is another measure of investor sentiment. The confidence index and the spread between U.S. Treasury and Ba corporate yields both indicated a small decrease in investor confidence from early June 1985 to early June 1986, as shown below:

	Barron's Confidence Index	Yield Spread: U.S. Treasuries and Ba Corporates
Early June		
1986	93.3	−2.43%
1985	93.9	−1.59

|||| **SUMMARY**

This chapter has provided a brief look at stock market forecasting and stock selection by technical methods. The chapter began with the rationale for technical analysis and explained how it is inconsistent with the idea of market efficiency.

The oldest approach to market forecasting, the Dow theory, was created by Charles Dow mainly as a description of market patterns. It was later refined, polished, and adopted by William Hamilton as a technique for forecasting the market. It is now regarded as being more useful for describing what has happened than for predicting what will happen.

Technicians make extensive use of bar charts, line charts, and point-and-figure charts in predicting individual stock prices and the trend of the market. The chapter described certain simple technical trading systems that are based on the use of price charts.

Technicians also use a number of technical indicators, particularly in forecasting the market. With these, they attempt to determine such things as: (1) the amount of momentum behind the current trend of the market; (2) the psychology, or sentiment, of investors and others as revealed in the statements or actions of market letter writers, option traders, stock exchange specialists, and bond investors; and (3) the potential future demand for stocks by short sellers, managers of mutual funds, and others.

|||| **QUESTIONS**

1. Two assumptions underlying technical analysis are inconsistent with the idea that capital markets are efficient. What are these assumptions?

2. Explain the Dow theory.

3. What are support and resistance levels?

4. What is a point-and-figure chart?

5. How is a moving average chart created?

6. Explain an investment strategy that uses moving averages.

7. Explain the meaning of relative strength.

8. Show, with a numerical example, how Trendline calculates relative strength.

9. Under what conditions might relative strength analysis be helpful in forecasting the price trend for a group of stocks?

10. What was wrong with Levy's analysis of the usefulness of relative strength analysis?

11. Comment on the studies that investigated the persistence of relative strength for stocks in the same industry group.

12. Why should an investor be cautious in drawing any conclusions about future stock performance on the basis of recent findings that under certain circumstances relative strength has a tendency to persist?

13. What is meant by "breadth of the market"? How can it be measured?

14. What is an advance-decline diffusion index? How is it calculated?

15. Explain how technicians try to determine whether the market is overbought (too high) or oversold (too low) on the basis of the number of stocks above their 200-day moving average.

16. Two sentiment indicators are positive rather than contrary. What are they? Why do technicians believe they are positive indicators?

17. Why do technicians believe that a bull market is about over when most investors and investment advisers have an optimistic outlook?

18. Why is the put/call ratio a contrary indicator? Explain.

19. Explain why the percentage of investment services with a bearish outlook is a contrary indicator.

20. Explain how technicians forecast market trends on the basis of the amount of margin debt and the amount of new equity financing.

21. Explain how the spread between the rate on Moody's Aaa corporate bonds and the rate on three-month Treasury bills is used in judging the tightness or looseness of Federal Reserve monetary policy. Why does a loosening of the policy tend to have a positive impact on stock prices?

22. Why is the short-interest ratio (that is, the ratio of the total short interest to the volume of trading) thought to be less useful than it once was?

23. Historically, the stock market has tended to rise with a decline in the short-interest ratio. Comment on the possible reasons for this tendency.

24. Why do technicians think that the specialist short-sale ratio may be a good market indicator?

25. Explain why forecasting the market on the basis of the mutual fund cash/asset ratio may amount to forecasting the market on the basis of the level of stock prices.

26. Explain the Barron's confidence index. Give one good reason why it is not a very reliable indicator of the future trend of the market.

|||| PROJECT
Technical Analysis

The data disk provided with this book has a Lotus file containing a daily record of the following:

1. Trading date (YYMMDD)
2. Daily price of Hewlett-Packard Corporation
3. The daily S&P 500 Composite Index

ASSIGNMENT

1. Assume you purchased shares in a mutual fund that replicated the S&P 500 in May of 1986. Prepare a single moving average graph (you choose the period of the average) of the S&P 500 Index data. Had you used your analysis, would you have been out of the market prior to the October 1987 market crash?

2. Prepare the same analysis for Hewlett-Packard Corporation (HP). Had you used the technical program, would you have sold HP before the market crash?

3. Assume you purchased HP on the first trading day of January 1987 and sold and purchased HP as your technical chart indicates. What profit, excluding commissions, would you have achieved?

4. Using a double moving average system, repeat the above analysis for the S&P 500 and for HP.

5. Create the two relative strength indexes shown in the chapter for HP. Devise a trading rule based on relative strength, and test the performance of the rule during 1987. Your trading rule may be something like the following: If the relative strength increases by $X\%$, buy; and if it decreases by $X\%$, sell.

6. After completing the preceding five problems, prepare a position paper explaining your views on the efficient market hypothesis discussed in Chapter 6. Citations to papers or books that influence your beliefs are an important part of this analysis. Note that this assignment does not ask you to repeat what you think your instructor believes. Any position is viable as long as it is defended.

|||| SELECTED REFERENCES

Akermann, Charles A., and Werner E. Keller. "Relative Strength Does Persist." *Journal of Portfolio Management* 4 (Fall 1977): 38–45.

Arnott, Robert D. "Relative Strength Revisited." *Journal of Portfolio Management* 5 (Spring 1979): 19–23.

Bohan, James. "Relative Strength: Further Positive Evidence." *Journal of Portfolio Management* 8 (Fall 1981): 36–39.

Bookstaber, Richard. *The Complete Investment Book: Trading Stocks, Bonds, and Options with Computer Applications*. Glenview, Ill: Scott, Foresman and Company, 1985.

Besant, Lloyd, ed. *Commodity Trading Manual* Chicago, Ill.: Chicago Board of Trade, 1985.

Branch, Ben. "The Predictive Power of Stock Market Indicators." *Journal of Financial and Quantitative Analysis* 11 (June 1976): 269–85.

Brush, John S., and Keith E. Boles. "The Predictive Power in Relative Strength & CAPM." *Journal of Portfolio Management* 5 (Summer 1983): 20–23.

Glickstein, David A., and Rolf E. Wubbels. "Dow Theory Is Alive and Well." *Journal of Portfolio Management* 5 (Spring 1983): 28–32.

Harrington, Diana R., Frank J. Fabozzi, and H. Russell Fogler. *The New Stock Market*. Chicago, Ill.: Probus Publishing Company, 1990.

Jensen, Michael C., and George A. Benington. "Random Walks and Technical Theories: Some Additional Evidence." *The Journal of Finance* 25 (May 1970): 469–82.

Kerrigan, Thomas J. "The Short Interest Ratio and Its Component Parts." *Financial Analysts Journal* 30 (November/December 1974): 45–49.

Levy, Robert A. "Conceptual Foundations of Technical Analysis." *Financial Analysts Journal* 2 (July/August 1966): 83–89.

Massey, Paul H. "The Mutual Fund Liquidity Ratio: A Trap for the Unwary." *Journal of Portfolio Management* 5 (Winter 1979): 18–21.

Merrill Lynch. "Where the Indicators Stand." (various issues).

Pinches, George E. "The Random Walk Hypothesis and Technical Analysis." *Financial Analysts Journal* 26 (March/April 1970): 104–10.

Reilly, Frank K., and David T. Whitford. "A Test of the Specialists' Short Sale Ratio." *Journal of Portfolio Management* 8 (Winter 1982): 12–18.

Seneca, Joseph J. "Short Interest: Bearish or Bullish?" *The Journal of Finance* 22 (March 1967): 67–70.

4 ANALYSIS OF FIXED-INCOME INVESTMENTS

13 FIXED-INCOME INVESTMENTS

This is the first of three chapters on fixed-income investments. These chapters emphasize bond investments, but also cover a variety of other debt-type securities as well as preferred stock.

To make informed choices among the many kinds of fixed-income investments, one must be aware of their principal features. The more a person knows about the potential risks and rewards, the better the chance of selecting investments that are well suited to the investor's specific needs. Fixed-income investments usually have a number of features that require evaluation. The main purposes of this chapter are to explain the principal features of a wide variety of fixed-income securities and the process of rating bonds.

Some fixed-income investments are considerably more complicated, and therefore require more extensive analysis, than others. For example, corporate bonds usually have a number of features such as call provisions, sinking fund requirements, protective covenants, and credit risk that generally do not apply to U.S. Treasury bonds.

CLASSIFICATION OF FIXED-INCOME INVESTMENTS

Fixed-income investments can be divided into seven categories: (1) money market securities, (2) U.S. Treasury notes and bonds, (3) corporate notes and bonds, (4) municipal bonds, (5) federal agency notes and bonds, (6) mortgage-backed securities, and (7) preferred stocks. Within these categories are a number of interesting securities with special features or distinctive characteristics, including zero-coupon bonds, floating rate notes and bonds, bonds with a "put" provision, extendable notes, insured bonds, and junk bonds. Some of these securities (including money market securities, U.S. Treasury notes and bonds, and federal agency issues) are explained in Chapter 2 and are mentioned only briefly here.

MONEY MARKET INVESTMENTS

Money market securities are short-term, low-risk IOUs that investors can sell in a secondary market if they decide to convert them to cash before maturity. The principal issuers are the U.S. Treasury Department (Treasury bills), corporations of all types (commercial paper), commercial banks and bank holding companies (negotiable certificates of deposit, Eurodollar deposits, bankers' acceptances, and commercial paper), and thrift institutions (negotiable certificates of deposit). Other issuers include federal agencies and state and local governments.

The principal investors in money market securities include Federal Reserve Banks, foreign and domestic banks, thrift institutions, money market mutual funds, insurance companies, other financial institutions, corporations of all kinds, pension funds, and individuals. Individuals invest in money market securities either directly, primarily through the purchase of Treasury securities, or indirectly by purchasing shares in money market mutual funds.

Table 13-1 indicates the relative importance of the four most important types of money market securities. The Treasury bills of $414 billion at the end of 1988 represented about 30% of the U.S. Treasury's total outstanding marketable securities.

U.S. Government Notes and Bonds

About 70% of the interest-bearing debt of the U.S. government is marketable (consisting of Treasury bills, notes, and bonds), and 30%, including U.S. savings bonds, is nonmarketable. Table 13-2 shows the amount in each category on December 31, 1988.

Owners of the government debt include a variety of private institutions as well as the U.S. government itself (in various trust funds under the control of the Secretary of the Treasury), government-sponsored agencies, the Federal Reserve Banks, state and local governments, foreign official institutions (principally central banks), other foreign investors, and individual investors (see Table 13-3). As Table 13-3 shows, individuals invest large amounts in marketable U.S. government securities as well as in U.S. savings bonds.

|||| **TABLE 13-1**

Principal Money Market Securities and Large Nonnegotiable Certificates of Deposit, December 31, 1988 (Billions)

U.S. Treasury bills	$414
Large (over $100,000) certificates of deposit:*	
Issued by commercial banks	365
Issued by thrift institutions	174
Commercial paper	455
Bankers' acceptances	67
Total	$1,475

*Certificates of deposit do not include amounts held by money market mutual funds, depository institutions, and foreign banks and official institutions. An undetermined portion of the total certificates of deposit are nonnegotiable.

SOURCE: *Federal Reserve Bulletin.*

|||| **TABLE 13-2**

Interest-Bearing Debt of the U.S. Government, December 31, 1988
(Billions)

Marketable:	
Bills	$414
Notes	1,084
Bonds	309
Other	15
Total	1,822
Nonmarketable	842*
Total	2,664

*Includes U.S. savings bonds of $108 billion.

SOURCE: *Treasury Bulletin* (Spring 1989).

|||| **TABLE 13-3**

Estimated Ownership of U.S. Government Debt, December 31,
1988 (Billions)

U.S. government accounts		$588
Foreign and international		348
Commercial banks		194
State and local governments		287
Federal Reserve Banks		238
Individuals:		
Savings bonds	109	
Other	78	
		187
Insurance companies		135
Corporations		86
Money market funds		19
Other investors		581
Total		2,663

SOURCE: *Treasury Bulletin* (Spring 1989).

CORPORATE BONDS

Corporate bonds, with over $1,200 billion outstanding at the end of 1988, are an important form of investment for individuals and institutional investors. The total includes a number of long-term notes that are essentially the same as bonds. For example, it includes the notes of Citicorp (owner of Citibank), which has a number of long-term note issues outstanding, including some with maturities of more than 20 years, but no outstanding bonds.

Bond Indentures

The terms of a bond issue are stated in the *indenture,* which is an elaborate, detailed contract between the issuer and the bondholders. In addition to covering such simple, but essential details as the par value, coupon rate, maturity date, and interest payment dates, the indenture contains covenants for the protection of the bondholders and may contain additional provisions such as the following:

1.   Terms under which the bonds are callable prior to maturity at the discretion of the issuer.
2.   Amounts and due dates of required sinking fund payments.
3.   Description of the collateral, if any.
4.   Degree of seniority or subordination to other debt.

When bonds are issued to the general public instead of being placed privately with institutional investors, a trustee (usually a commercial bank) is appointed to look out for the interests of the bondholders. Most large public issues are subject to the Trust Indenture Act of 1939, which requires the trustee to be free of any conflict of interest and to take appropriate action if the issuer should default by failing to comply with the terms of the contract.

Examples of Corporate Bond Issues

The corporate bonds listed in Table 13-4 were selected to illustrate various types of bonds and certain important features, including call provisions, sinking fund requirements, and the degree of seniority or subordination. All of these issues are in *registered* form, and all pay interest twice a year, as do most corporate bonds.

Several of the companies in Table 13-4 have a number of bond issues outstanding. For example, Baltimore Gas and Electric has 25 first *mortgage bonds,* five pollution control and industrial development bond issues, and two sinking fund *debentures.* This is not unusual for a utility company. For another example, J. C. Penney's bonds and notes include four sinking fund debentures, one debenture without a sinking fund, two zero-coupon notes, and two coupon notes.

Call Provisions

Corporate bonds typically contain a deferred *call provision,* which means that the bonds are *callable* by the issuer after a specified number of years. Of the 11 bonds in Table 13-4, 8 contain deferred call provisions, and 3 are noncallable.

Call provisions usually require the issuer to pay a premium if the bonds are called a number of years before maturity. Almost invariably, the premium declines from year to year and reaches zero a few years before the bond reaches maturity.

Sinking Fund Provisions

All bond issues in Table 13-4 except the AT&T debentures and the National Rural Utilities Cooperative Finance Corporation's *collateral trust bonds* have required sinking fund payments that, in a majority of the cases, are deferred for eight or more years. *Sinking funds* spread the repayment of principal over a number of years. They are designed to reduce the possibility of a cash flow crisis within the firm.

||| **TABLE 13-4**

Examples of Corporate Bonds

Company	Type	Coupon Rate	Date of Issue	Original Maturity (Years)	Size of Issue (Millions)
Abbott Labs.	S.F. debs.	9.20	10/15/74	25	$100
AT&T	Debentures	7.00	2/15/71	30	500
Baltimore G&E	1st mtge.	8.38	8/15/76	30	75
Burl. Northern	Eq. trust	9.25	12/1/78	15	15
Florida P&L	1st mtge.	7.50	1/1/73	30	70
General Elec.	S.F. debs.	8.50	5/1/74	30	300
Goodrich	Sub. debs.	7.00	8/15/72	25	75
IBM	S.F. debs.	10.50	7/15/85	30	500
NRUCFC[a]	Coll. trst.	10.50	7/15/85	10	100
Penney	S.F. debs.	11.50	6/15/80	30	200
Union Tank Car	Eq. trust	14.00	1/15/81	20	75

Company	Rating	Years until Callable	Initial Call Price	Years until Sinking Fund Payments Begin	Percentage Retired before Maturity
Abbott Labs.	Aa1	10	105.06	10	93.75%
AT&T	Aa1	12	103.50	No payments	None
Baltimore G&E	Aa2	7	106.86	2	—[b]
Burl. Northern	Aaa	NC	—	1	93.33
Florida P&L	Aa3	10	105.87	—[c]	—[c]
General Elec.	Aaa	10	105.44	11	75.00
Goodrich	Ba2	10	103.85	8	92.00
IBM	Aaa	10[d]	109.85	11[e]	95.00
NRUCFC	Aa2	NC	—	No payments	None
Penney	A1	4	109.35	11	80.87
Union Tank Car	A3	NC	—	4	96.00

[a]NRUCFC is the National Rural Utilities Cooperative Finance Corporation. The security for the company's collateral trust bonds consists of notes receivable from member cooperatives.

[b]A single sinking fund is established for all 25 of the company's first mortgage bond issues. The indenture does not require that a specified amount be in the fund for any one issue when it reaches maturity.

[c]Payments must be made to the trustee if amounts expended on maintenance and replacement of property are below a specified level.

[d]Nonrefundable prior to 7/15/95 with lower interest cost debt. Otherwise callable, in whole or in part, at any time.

[e]Company can make optional payments of $37.5 million annually in addition to the annual sinking fund payments of $25 million from 7/15/96.

SOURCE: *Moody's Manuals.*

Typically, the issuer has the option of making the sinking fund payments either in cash or in debentures purchased by the company for this purpose. When the payment is made in cash, the indenture trustee is usually required to randomly call bonds for redemption. In most cases, the *call price* for sinking fund purposes is equal to the par value of the bonds. Thus, when investors hold bonds that are selling at a premium, they face the risk that the bonds will either be called or that the trustee will select the bonds for redemption under the sinking fund provisions.

Degree of Seniority

Many companies have bonds outstanding with different degrees of seniority. As noted earlier, the Baltimore Gas and Electric Company has
25 separate issues of first mortgage bonds and two issues of sinking fund
debentures. The mortgage securing the first mortgage bonds is open-
ended, which means that the company may issue additional mortgage
bonds. Each new issue acquires a lien on the company's property along
with all of the existing issues. The mortgage applies to all properties
owned by the company now or in the future. In the event of bankruptcy,
if the properties were liquidated, the debenture holders would receive
none of the proceeds from sale of the mortgaged properties until holders
of the first mortgage bonds were paid in full. The two *equipment trust
certificates* in Table 13-4 are collateralized by large numbers of designated
railroad cars.

Most corporations other than public utilities, railroads, airlines, and
other transportation companies do not issue collateralized securities like
mortgage bonds and equipment trust certificates. The senior bond issue
for an industrial company is likely to be a debenture. As with Abbott
Laboratories, General Electric, and other industrial companies listed in
Table 13-4, many companies have more than one debenture issue with
the same level of seniority, and some, like Goodrich, have debentures that
are subordinated to their other bonds.

The bond indenture often contains provisions that prohibit the issuer
from mortgaging any of its properties to other creditors, present or future.
Alternatively, indentures may state that if the company incurs any debt
secured by a lien on any of its properties, the debentures shall be provided
with equal security. Such restrictions may not be imposed if the aggregate
amount of the new debt is less than a small, specified percentage of the
company's tangible assets. To establish and protect the position of debenture holders vis-à-vis other unsecured creditors of the company, bond
indentures often provide that the debentures rank *pari passu* (on an equal
basis) with all other unsecured and unsubordinated indebtedness of the
company.

The claims of *subordinated debenture* holders are, of course, inferior
to those of other bondholders in the event of bankruptcy. A company's
subordinated debentures are usually assigned a lower quality rating
than its other bonds. For example, if a firm's senior debentures are rated
A2 by Moody's its subordinated debentures will probably be rated A3
or even Baa1. Many subordinated debentures are convertible into common stock.

MUNICIPAL BONDS

Bonds and notes issued by state and local governments and their various
agencies, districts, and authorities are known as *municipals,* or munis,
or *tax-exempts*. The interest payments on municipals are exempt from
federal income taxes as well as from state and local income taxes in the
state where they were issued, which makes them attractive to investors

with high marginal tax rates.[1] A substantial portion of all municipal bonds are owned by individuals, either directly or through municipal bond funds or unit investment trusts.

Municipal Yields versus Corporate Yields

The yields at which municipal bonds are issued and traded relative to the yields on taxable securities depend to a large extent upon the supply of municipal bonds and the tax rates at various levels of taxable income. If the supply of municipals were small enough that all could be easily held by investors with high marginal tax rates—that is, by investors to whom the tax-free status of the income would mean the most—the yields on municipals would be quite low relative to the yields on taxable securities. However, when the supply of municipals is so large that investors in the highest tax brackets are either unable or unwilling to hold the entire supply, the yields must be high enough to attract investors with lower marginal tax rates.

Figure 13-1 shows the average annual yields on Aaa municipals as a percentage of the yields on Aaa corporate bonds for the years 1974 through 1988. (A graph of Baa municipal yields against Baa corporate yields would show a similar picture.) The increase in the yields on municipal bonds relative to the yields on corporate bonds in the early 1980s reflects the large supply of municipals and the decrease in federal income tax rates during that period. With large offerings of municipal bonds and lower income tax rates, the yields on municipals had to increase relative to the yields on taxable bonds to attract more investors to the municipal bond market.

General Obligation and Revenue Bonds

Municipal bonds are classified broadly into two categories: *general obligation (GO) bonds* and *revenue bonds*. General obligation bonds, also known as full faith and credit bonds, are backed by the full taxing power of the issuing unit of government. Revenue bonds, on the other hand, are backed only by the revenues from the facilities that are financed by the bonds. In recent years, close to three-fourths of all new municipal bond issues have been revenue bonds, and a high percentage of the revenue bonds have been issued by special districts and authorities. These quasi-governmental entities are created by state and local governments for activities such as hospitals, public power facilities, turnpikes, toll bridges, public transportation facilities, and public housing.

Denominations

The usual minimum denomination for municipal bonds is $5,000, compared to $1,000 for most corporate bonds and U.S. government bonds. However, some cities, including Boston, have issued bonds in much smaller denominations with considerable success. Boston has sold bonds

---

[1] Methods of comparing the yields of taxable and tax-exempt investments are explained in Chapter 2.

|||| **FIGURE 13-1**

Yields on Aaa Municipal Bonds as a Percentage of the Yields on Aaa Corporate
Bonds, 1974–1988

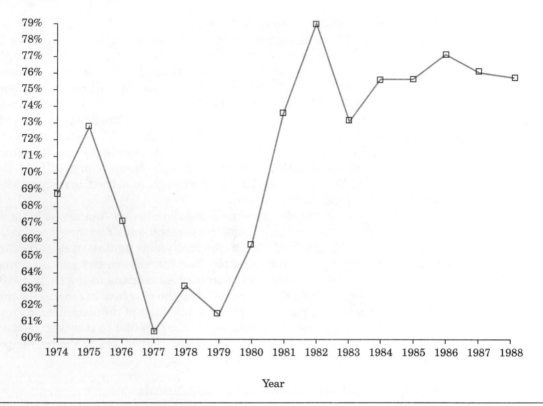

SOURCE: Data from Federal Reserve Bulletin.

through the city treasurer's office, without the aid of an investment firm,
with denominations as low as $100.

For many individuals, the best way to invest in a portfolio of municipal
securities is to buy shares in a municipal bond mutual fund or units in
a municipal bond unit investment trust. The minimum initial investment
in municipal bond mutual funds ranges from $1,000 to $3,000, and the
price of one unit in a unit investment trust is usually $1,000. After the
initial investment in a mutual fund, subsequent investments can be as
small as $100 to $300.

Serial versus Term Bonds

Municipal bonds are usually issued in *serial* form, which means that a
single issue consists of a number of sets of bonds, with each set maturing
on a different date. For example, a $100 million serial bond issue dated
September 1, 1992, might be composed of 20 sets of bonds, the first set
maturing on September 1, 1993, the second on September 1, 1994, and
the twentieth on September 1, 2012. Serial bonds are an alternative

to term bonds with a sinking fund provision. A *term bond* issue has a single, final maturity date. With a serial bond issue, certain specific bonds mature each year. Some serial bonds are callable by the issuer prior to maturity.

All of the bonds in a serial bond issue are under the same indenture and are covered by the same security if the bonds are collateralized. Also, failure to pay interest or principal on any of the bonds constitutes a default for the entire issue. Except for these features, which tie serial bonds together in certain respects, the 20 or so sets of bonds in a typical serial bond issue are like 20 separate bond issues. Investors in a new issue have a choice between short-, intermediate-, and long-term bonds.

Except for the possibility of default, if serial bonds are not callable, investors can count on holding them to the maturity date. This eliminates one of the risks associated with sinking fund bonds—the risk that the bonds will be called for the sinking fund at a time when interest rates are much lower than the coupon rate.

In recent years, a number of governmental units and agencies have made combination issues consisting of both serial bonds and term bonds. For example, in mid-1985 the Ohio Housing Finance Agency's $346 million bond issue to supply financing for single-family residences consisted of $135 million of serial bonds, with maturities ranging from 1987 to the year 2000, and $211 million of term bonds with longer maturities.

Other Municipal Bond Features

High and volatile interest rates have led to various new features in municipal bonds, as well as corporate bonds, to reduce the interest rate risk for investors. These include variable-rate provisions, "put" provisions (which give investors the right to sell the bonds back to the issuer at par value at one or more specified times), and zero-coupon bonds. Since these features are used with corporate bonds as well as municipal, we will discuss them in more detail later in the chapter.

MORTGAGE-BACKED SECURITIES

At year-end 1988, total residential mortgage debt in the United States exceeded $3.2 trillion, and in recent years the annual increases have been roughly $200 billion. To accomplish this amount of financing, mortgage lenders have had to tap the vast resources of the nation's capital markets. They have been doing this primarily by issuing *mortgage-backed securities,* which represent an undivided interest in a pool of mortgages. The process of pooling mortgage loans and issuing securities against the pool is referred to as "securitizing mortgages." Many individual and institutional investors who would be unwilling to invest in individual mortgages are happy to invest in securities backed by pools of mortgages. The reasons are apparent. Most mortgage-backed securities offer relatively attractive yields, involve little or no credit risk, and can be easily sold.

Government National Mortgage Association

The securitizing of mortgage debt began in 1970 when Congress authorized the Government National Mortgage Association (GNMA or Ginnie Mae) to guarantee securities backed by Federal Housing Administration (FHA), Veterans Administration (VA), and Farmers Home Administration (FmHA) guaranteed loans. This led to the creation of Ginnie Mae pass-through certificates, also known as *Ginnie Mae pass-throughs*. Each certificate represents a share in a pool of mortgages, all with the same interest rate and similar term to maturity. Each month the security holder receives a pro rata share of the principal and interest payments accruing to the underlying mortgages in the pool.

Ginnie Mae pass-throughs were the first, and are still the most important, of the several types of mortgage-backed securities. They are the only mortgage-backed securities that are also backed by the "full faith and credit" of the U.S. Treasury. Ginnie Mae pass-throughs are sometimes referred to as "modified pass-throughs" because the issuers of the certificates are required to make the scheduled principal and interest payments to the certificate holders whether the mortgagors make their payments or not.

The average interest rate on the mortgages underlying a Ginnie Mae pass-through is 50 basis points higher than the coupon rate of the pass-through certificate. The mortgage holder (creator of the mortgage pool and issuer of the securities) retains 44 basis points for servicing the mortgages and pays 6 basis points to the GNMA as a fee for the guarantee. The fee is higher than mortgage servicers usually receive because the servicer must make the scheduled principal and interest payments to the pass-through holders whether the mortgage payments are received in a timely manner or not.

From the standpoint of credit risk, GNMA pass-throughs are as safe as U.S. Treasury securities, and they have certain distinct advantages over a direct investment in FHA and VA guaranteed mortgages. Perhaps the most important is their high degree of marketability. A number of dealers make a market in Ginnie Mae pass-throughs, and the volume of trading is large. A second advantage is the ease with which the income from pass-throughs can be accounted for. The investor never has to deal with delinquent payments, and for large investors, the number of payments to be processed is much smaller. Reinvesting funds in pass-throughs is also easier than reinvesting in individual mortgages.

The yields on GNMA pass-throughs are a little higher (about 70 basis points) than the yields on U.S. Treasury securities with similar maturity dates. However, it is difficult to compare the expected yields on pass-throughs with the expected yields on other securities because of the uncertainty as to what the maturity of a pass-through will be. Mortgages are often paid off long before their final maturity. If a pass-through is selling at either a premium or a discount, and if the underlying mortgages are paid off either more slowly or more quickly than expected, the actual yield will not be the same as the expected yield. For example, if a pass-through certificate is selling at a premium and investors are expecting the underlying mortgages to be paid off at the end of 12 years, the actual yield will be lower than the expected yield if the mortgages are paid off in less than 12 years.[2] The reason for the lower yield is that the premium must be amortized over fewer years.

FHLMC and FNMA Pass-Throughs

The Federal Home Loan Mortgage Corporation (Freddie Mac) and the Federal National Mortgage Association (Fanny Mae) guarantee mortgage-backed pass-throughs that are almost as safe and marketable as Ginnie Maes. However, they differ from Ginnie Maes in certain respects. First, the underlying mortgages are conventional loans rather than mortgages insured or guaranteed by the FHA, VA, or FmHA. Second, the pass-throughs themselves, while guaranteed by the FHLMC or FNMA, are not backed by the full faith and credit of the U.S. government. Third, the FHLMC and FNMA issue the *pass-through securities* themselves against mortgages that they have previously purchased, whereas Ginnie Mae guarantees pass-through securities issued by others.

Private Issues of Mortgage-Backed Bonds and Pass-Throughs

Some mortgage lenders issue mortgage-backed bonds, as well as pass-through certificates, without a GNMA guarantee. Except for the fact that they are collateralized by a pool of mortgages, the terms of mortgage-backed bonds are similar to those of U.S. Treasury bonds. The interest and principal payments are fixed, and there is a definite maturity. The principal difference between a mortgage-backed bond and a pass-through is that the timing of the cash flows from the bond is independent of the cash flows from the mortgage loans.

Some mortgage-backed bonds are rated by Standard & Poor's and Moody's. Most of the publicly issued bonds are assigned a triple-A rating, and their yields are close to the yields on the highest-grade corporate bonds.

Private issue pass-through certificates, like other pass-throughs, give the holder a pro rata interest in the underlying pool of mortgages. Although the certificates themselves are not guaranteed by a government agency, the underlying mortgages, or some of them, may be covered by insurance policies written by commercial insurance companies.[3] Securities firms make a market for some of the larger issues.

Collateralized Mortgage Obligations

Collateralized mortgage obligations (CMOs) are mortgage-backed bonds with more predictable maturities than pass-through certificates or the ordinary mortgage-backed bonds. With CMOs, each issue is structured into three or four classes of bonds, with each class bearing a different

---

[2] The opposite is true if the security is selling at a discount. In this case, the yield increases if the mortgages are paid off sooner than expected.

[3] The insurance policies are normally structured as surety-type policies.

stated maturity. For example, on one recent issue the class A bonds have a stated final maturity in 1996; the class B in 1999; the class C in 2002; and the class D in 2015. Each class of bonds receives interest payments at a specified rate, but all of the principal payments on the underlying mortgages are first applied to the class A bonds until they have been paid off, then to the class B bonds, and so on until all four class of bonds have been redeemed. The principal and interest payments are semiannual.

A weighted average maturity is calculated for each class of CMO bonds on the basis of the historic pattern of loan payoffs. Thus, investors in each class of bonds have a fairly good indication as to the period of time over which their principal payments will be received. From the issuer's point of view, CMOs make it possible to sell mortgage-backed bonds with different final maturities and to price them accordingly.

The sequential payment scheme of CMOs is attractive to investors because it makes the term of the investment more definite than with pass-through securities or ordinary mortgage-backed bonds. Investors wanting a relatively short-term investment will buy bonds of the first class, those wanting intermediate-term investments will buy bonds of the second and third classes, and those wanting longer-term investments will buy bonds of the fourth class. Typically, the interest rates are significantly higher for the classes with longer maturities.

CMOs were introduced in June 1983 with a $1 billion issue by the FHLMC. The three classes of bonds in that issue were collateralized by conventional loans and FHLMC pass-throughs. The bond yields were less than 100 basis points higher than the yields on Treasury securities with comparable maturities. A majority of the early CMO issues have been backed by GNMA pass-throughs. The issuers include large mortgage banking firms, New York securities firms, insurance companies, home-builders, and so-called conduit companies that have been set up for the sole purpose of issuing CMOs.

ZERO-COUPON AND LOW-COUPON BONDS

Zero-coupon bonds are debt securities issued at a discount and redeemed for par value at maturity. Low-coupon bonds pay periodic interest but at a rate significantly below the prevailing market rate for bonds of like quality and similar maturities. They, too, are issued at a discount and redeemed for par value at maturity. This section will emphasize zero-coupon bonds, but the reader should note that low-coupon bonds lie somewhere between zero-coupon bonds and higher coupon bonds with respect to interest rate sensitivity and after-tax yields.

Some bonds are issued as zero-coupon bonds while other zeros are created by "stripping" the interest payments from U.S. Treasury bonds and selling each of the interest payments and the maturity value as separate zero-coupon securities. Zero-coupon bonds have also been issued by industrial corporations, bank holding companies, and state and local governments.

Zeros Created by Stripping U.S. Treasury Bonds

In the early 1980s, four major investment firms began to create zero-coupon bonds by stripping the coupons from U.S. Treasury bonds and selling the interest payments and the maturity value at their discounted present values. They purchased large blocks of Treasury bonds, placed them in trust with commercial banks, and arranged with the banks to issue certificates against each of the coupon payments as well as against the final maturity value. For example, a certificate might entitle the holder to receive $1,000 from the coupon payment at the end of 15 years. This certificate would be a 15-year zero-coupon bond, and its price would be the present value of $1,000 discounted for 15 years at the going rate for such an investment. If the going rate was 11%, the price of the $1,000 zero-coupon bond would be $209 ($1000/[1.11]^{15}).

If the Treasury bonds from which zeros are derived have a final maturity of 20 years, zeros will be issued with maturities ranging from six months to 20 years. If the total par value of the bonds being stripped is $100 million and the semiannual interest payments are $6 million, zero-coupon bonds with a total face value of $6 million would be issued against each of the first 39 interest payments, and zeros with a total face value of $106 million would be issued against the maturity value and final interest payment.

By early 1985, investors had purchased an estimated $15 to $20 billion of zero-coupon bonds that investment firms had derived from U.S. Treasury securities. Zeros created in this way have been assigned various names, including Treasury Investment Growth Receipts (the TIGRs of Merrill Lynch), Certificates of Accrual on Treasury Securities (the CATs of Salomon Brothers), Lehman Investment Opportunity Notes (the LIONs of Lehman Brothers), and Treasury Receipts (the TRs of First Boston). Securities dealers and traders have referred to these securities as "animals."

As explained in Chapter 2, the U.S. Treasury simplified the process of carving zeros out of Treasury bonds in 1985 when it introduced "separate trading of registered interest and principal of securities" or "*STRIPS*." Each semiannual interest payment and the maturity value are registered separately through the Federal Reserve book-entry system. Each payment can then be sold by the bank or securities firm as a set of zero-coupon bonds maturing on the same date. Since these securities are direct obligations of the U.S. government, no credit risk is involved. Their prices are published in daily newspapers along with the quotations for other U.S. Treasury securities.

Zeros Issued by Corporations and State and Local Governments

In periods of unusually high interest rates, corporations and governments are sometimes able to issue zero-coupon bonds and low coupon bonds at yields lower than would be required on bonds that pay periodic interest at the going rate. If investors expect interest rates to decline, they might prefer a zero-coupon bond that promises a return of 9% over a coupon bond with a promised yield to maturity of 9.5%. With a zero-coupon bond, the investor avoids *reinvestment rate risk*.[4] If rates decline, the 9% zeros might provide a higher total realized yield than the 9.5% coupon bonds. With zeros there are no periodic interest payments to reinvest, so falling rates do not reduce the effective yield.

Another advantage of some zero-coupon bonds from an investor's point of view is better *call protection*. Some zeros have a call price equal to the par value of the bond. Since the bonds are issued at a deep discount, they are highly unlikely to be called at par very long before the final maturity date.

After-Tax Yields on Zeros and Coupon Bonds

With zeros that are subject to federal income taxes, a portion of the *original issue discount (OID)* must be reported as taxable income each year unless the bond is held by a tax-exempt investor or is in a tax-deferred IRA or Keogh account. For example, if a 10-year zero with a maturity value of $1,000 is purchased at a yield to maturity of 10%, which makes the price $385.54, the original issue discount of $614.46 must be reported as income over a period of 10 years. The investor can elect to report the income ratably (that is, by allocating the same amount of income to each day of the 10-year period) or by using the constant interest rate method, which allocates smaller amounts of income to the early years and larger amounts to the later years.

To illustrate the ratable and constant interest rate methods of calculating taxes on zero-coupon bonds, Example 13-1 assumes that a 10-year bond priced at $385.54 is purchased at the beginning of the year.

EXAMPLE 13-1   RATABLE AND CONSTANT INTEREST RATE
              METHODS

Assumptions:

Maturity value	$1,000
Yield to maturity	10.0%
Issue price	$385.54 $(1,000/[1.10]^{10})$

	Ratable Method	Constant Interest Rate Method
Annual interest		
Ratable method:		
$(1,000 - 385.54)/10 = \$614.46/10$	$61.45	
Constant interest rate method:		
Year 1 $(385.54 \times .10)$		$38.55

[4] Reinvestment rate risk is the risk of investing the coupon payments at a rate lower than the coupon rate of the bond. Reinvestment rate risk will be discussed at length in the next chapter.

$$\text{Year 2 } (385.54 + 38.55) \times .10$$
$$= (424.10 \times .10) \qquad\qquad \$42.41$$

$$\cdot$$
$$\cdot$$
$$\cdot$$

$$\text{Year 10 } (909.09 \times .10) \qquad\qquad \underline{\$90.01}$$
$$\text{Sum} \qquad\qquad \$614.46$$

When the ratable method of allocating bond discount is used, the after-tax yield on a zero is significantly lower than the after-tax yield on a coupon bond selling at the same before-tax yield. Generally, the longer the maturity and the higher the investor's marginal tax rate, the greater the difference between the yields, as shown in Table 13-5. The calculations for the coupon bonds are based upon the assumption that the bonds are selling at par value, so no capital gains or losses are involved.

The results are quite different if the investor uses the constant interest rate method of allocating the discount. In fact, if a coupon bond and a zero-coupon bond are selling at the same before-tax yield to maturity, the after-tax yield to maturity will be the same for the two bonds if the constant interest rate method is used for allocating the discount on the zero. Thus, an investor who expects interest rates to be lower in the future (which would mean lower returns on reinvested interest from a coupon bond) will be inclined to invest in zero-coupon bonds rather than coupon bonds offering the same before-tax yield to maturity. This assumes that the before-tax yield for the coupon bonds does not include a significant amount of long-term capital gains.

Table 13-6 compares the annual and cumulative cash flows for a zero-coupon bond and a coupon bond where both have the same maturity value

---

|||| **TABLE 13-5**
After-Tax Yield to Maturity: 10% Coupon Bond and 10% Zero-Coupon Bond (Equal Amount of Original Issue Discount Allocated to Each Year)

	10-Year Bonds		20-Year Bonds	
	Coupon Bond	Zero-Coupon Bond	Coupon Bond	Zero-Coupon Bond
Marginal tax rate:				
20%	8.00%	7.89%	8.00%	7.50%
30%	7.00	6.84	7.00	6.37
40%	6.00	5.82	6.00	5.31
50%	5.00	4.81	5.00	4.31

To solve for the after-tax yield on the 10-year coupon bond, use the following equation:

$$1{,}000 = 100(1 - t) \times \text{PVIFA}_{i\%,10} + 1{,}000 \times \text{PVIF}_{i\%,10}$$

To solve for the after-tax yield on the 10-year zero-coupon bond, use the following equation:

$$385.54 = -61.45(t) \times \text{PVIFA}_{i\%,10} + 1{,}000 \times \text{PVIF}_{i\%,10}$$

Note: t = marginal tax rate.

|||| **TABLE 13-6**

Cash Flows: Five-Year, 10% Zero-Coupon Bond and Five-Year, 10% Coupon Bond (Face Value of Both Bonds $1,000; Tax Rate 40%; Interest on Zero-Coupon Bond Allocated with Constant Interest Rate Method)

	Zero-Coupon		Annual Flows			
Year	Accumulated Value	Taxable Income	(A) Zero-Coupon Bond	(B) Coupon Bond	(C) Diff. (A − B)	Cumulative Advantage (Disadvantage of Zero)
0	$620.90[a]		− $620.90	− $1,000.00	$379.10	$379.10
1	682.99	62.09	− 24.84[b]	60.00	− 84.84	294.26
2	751.29	68.30	− 27.32	60.00	− 87.32	206.94
3	826.42	75.13	− 30.05	60.00	− 90.05	116.89
4	909.06	82.64	− 33.06	60.00	− 93.06	23.83
5	1,000.00	90.94	963.62[c]	1,060.00	− 96.38	− 72.55
Total		379.10				

[a]$620.90 is the present value of $1,000.00 discounted for five years at 10%.
[b]$24.84 is the tax liability for the zero in the first year (.40 × $62.09).
[c]The cash flow of $963.64 for the zero in the fifth year is the face value of $1,000.00 minus income taxes of $36.36 on the fifth year interest of $90.91.

of $1,000, both are selling at a yield to maturity of 10%, and the price of the coupon bond is equal to its maturity value. The cash flows for the zero are based upon the constant interest rate method of reporting interest income. You will note that the cumulative cash flows in the right-hand column are favorable to the zero-coupon bond until the final year.

The investment of $620.90 in the zero is $379.10 smaller than the investment in the coupon bond, which gives the zero a substantial cash advantage in the early years. This advantage is gradually reduced, and finally eliminated, by the after-tax interest income from the coupon bond and the tax payments on the income from the zero. Of course, no interest is actually received on the zero until it matures.

Ignoring interest that could be earned by investing the amount of cash "saved" with the zero-coupon bond in the first four years, the coupon bond shows a net cash advantage of $72.55 over the full five-year period. This is the amount by which the interest on the coupon bond exceeds the interest on the zero ($120.90 = $500.00 − $379.10) multiplied by one minus the tax rate of 40%. In this example, the after-tax yield to maturity is 6% for both bonds.

Taxable zeros are especially attractive for IRA and Keogh accounts because the tax is deferred on the original issue discount. Table 13-7 shows the after-tax yields on zeros held in a tax-deferred account, assuming that tax is paid on the entire amount of the discount in the year the bond matures. Of course, in many cases the tax will be deferred much longer than that.

|||| **TABLE 13-7**

After-Tax Yields on 10% Zero-Coupon Bonds under Two Different
Assumptions: Discount Reported Annually with the Constant
Interest Rate Method or Entire Discount Reported When the
Bond Matures

	10-Year Bonds		20-Year Bonds	
	Constant Interest Rate Method	Tax Deferred to Final Year	Constant Interest Rate Method	Tax Deferred to Final Year
Marginal tax rate:				
30%	7.00%	7.78%	7.00%	8.39%
40%	6.00	6.94	6.00	7.73

FLOATING RATE BONDS, PUT BONDS, AND EXTENDABLE NOTES

Approximately 30% of all corporate bonds issued in 1984 contained provisions to protect the investors in the event of a rise in interest rates.[5] Protection against rising rates and falling bond prices is provided with three types of securities: floating rate notes or bonds; *put bonds,* which give the bondholder the right to put (i.e., sell) the bonds back to the issuer at par value at certain specified times, and extendable notes.

Floating Rate Notes and Bonds

The interest rates on floating rate notes and bonds are often tied either to the 13-week or 26-week Treasury bill rate. For example, on the Citicorp notes maturing in 1992, the rate was adjusted weekly to a level one percentage point above the rate on 13-week Treasury bills. The rates on some issues, particularly dollar-denominated notes issued in Europe, are tied to the *London Interbank Offered Rate (LIBOR)* for Eurodollar deposits of a specified maturity. LIBOR rates for various maturities are the rates paid on short-term interbank deposits among the largest and most creditworthy banks in London. LIBOR rates are also used as the base rate in bank loans to large multinational corporations.[6]

Sometimes floating rates are tied to the highest of two or three different indexes. For example, on a recent pollution control bond issue by Prince George's County, Maryland, which matures in 2010, the rate is adjusted weekly to the higher of 66% of the 13-week Treasury bill yield or 72% of the 30-year Treasury bond rate. It is not unusual for floating rate provisions to provide for a floor and a ceiling. The ceiling is referred

---

[5]*Business Week,* January 28, 1985, p. 93.

[6]The use of floating rates has encouraged some borrowers to issue bonds with longer maturities. For example, the Royal Bank of Canada recently issued floating rate bonds with a maturity of 99 years. The interest rate on those bonds is tied to the rate on bankers' acceptances.

to as a "cap." The rates on capped longer-term notes and bonds are usually from one-eighth to one-quarter of a percentage point higher than on non-capped issues. Borrowers are willing to pay a price for the cap.

Floating rate provisions do not give complete protection against interest rate risk. There are two reasons for this. First, if the rate is capped and market rates rise above the cap, the price of the bond will fall until the yield becomes competitive with the yields on similar issues. Second, if the variable rate provision calls for infrequent changes in the rate, and if interest rates rise several months before a rate adjustment is due, the price of the bond will fall because the rate has failed to keep up with the market.

Put Bonds

Put provisions come in many different forms. One example is a 10-year noncallable bond that gives the holder the right to sell the bond back to the issuer at face value at the end of five years. If interest rates rise during the first five years, the price of the bond will fall, but not as much as if there were no put provision. If interest rates remain high, the price of the bond will move toward its par value as the end of the five-year period approaches, unless there is some doubt about the ability of the issuer to pay the bond off.

The greater the number of designated times at which bondholders can sell their bonds back to the issuer at par value, the greater the protection against interest rate risk and also the lower the yield on the bond. Most bonds that can be "put" by the holder are also callable by the issuer. If a 10-year bond can be called by the issuer or sold back to the issuer at face value at the end of any year, both parties are protected against a change in interest rates. The issuer is protected against a decline in rates, and the investor is protected against an increase. If there is a substantial drop in rates, the issuer will call the bonds, and if rates increase, investors will elect to sell the bonds back to the issuer at par. The bonds will behave as though they were one-year securities.

Extendable Notes

Recently, a number of corporations have issued so-called *extendable notes* with maturities of 10 to 15 years. These notes give the issuer the right to change the rate from time to time and give the investors the right to redeem the notes at par value whenever the rate is changed. For example, notes of the Burroughs Corporation that mature July 1, 1995, had an initial rate of 9.25%. This rate applied for the first two years, at the end of which the company could set a new rate that would apply until a specified future date, called the election date. The note holders were given the right to sell their notes back to the corporation at par value at the end of two years or on any subsequent election date. With this arrangement, the notes would be extended beyond the first two years only if the issuer wanted to do so and offered the note holders a rate and extension period that was acceptable to them.

JUNK BONDS VERSUS INSURED AND GUARANTEED BONDS

Junk Bonds

Junk bonds, sometimes called "high-yield bonds," are usually defined as having low investment quality (bonds rated double-B or lower). Bonds with such ratings are considered highly speculative with respect to the ability of the issuer to make the principal and interest payments.

For many years, the junk bond market was composed mainly of former investment-grade issues known as "fallen angels"; that is, issues rated BBB or better that had been downgraded for one reason or another. But since the late 1970s, huge quantities of new junk bonds (called original-issue junk bonds) have been floated. During a period of about five years ending in early 1985, a total of 350 new junk bonds were floated for a total of $30 billion, and by the end of 1989, the junk bond market had ballooned to $200 billion. These original-issue junk bonds are largely the securities of highly leveraged companies, some of which have been in business only a short while.

Over certain past periods, junk bonds have outperformed other bonds. A recent Wharton study states that the realized yield for all junk bonds issued in 1977 and 1978 is 8.51%, compared to 7.6% for intermediate Treasuries, 8.08% for long-term Treasuries, and 8.43% for high-grade corporate bonds. However, contrary to security industry reports that cited default rates of less than 2.1% over the 1970–1985 period, the Wharton study and a concurrent Harvard study suggest that the default rate between 1977 and 1978 was between 32% and 34%. In addition, the future may not be so bright. The Wharton study also suggests that the realized yield from junk bonds issued in 1977 and 1978 was 2.61% less than the "promised yield" because of defaults, early redemptions, and exchanges of near-default junk bonds for other securities. Professor Marshall Blume, one of the authors of the Wharton study, suggests that ". . . some investors who purchased high-yield bond funds were not aware of the risk of their investments."[7]

Many observers believe that the favorable performance of junk bonds through the year 1988 provides no assurance that bonds of this kind will perform well in the future. The first trembling in the junk market occurred in 1984 when junk bonds underperformed other bonds by a wide margin. By 1988 a major junk bond "shakeout" was underway as most junk bonds significantly underperformed "investment-grade" securities. Analysts, however, were quick to point out that many of the bonds in trouble were bad at the time of issuance.

Indeed, many of the junk bonds now outstanding were issued during the economic expansion that began in 1982, and in many cases the issuers are so laden with debt that the probability of default is very high. Some of the low-grade bonds were issued by young companies that have not

[7]*Wall Street Journal,* September 11, 1989.

yet achieved a good earnings record. Some are the bonds of older companies that have fallen on hard times. A number of others have been issued by raiders to finance corporate takeovers. For example, ACF Industries issued $350 million of debentures, which increased its debt/capital ratio from 50% to 90%, immediately after the corporate raider Carl Icahn took over. The prospectus explained that the company would probably not be able to service the bonds. More specifically, it pointed out that during the preceding six months the company's operations had fallen more than $18 million short of covering its new level of fixed charges.[8]

There have been at least a few recent disasters in the junk bond market. A $25 million issue of senior subordinated exchangeable variable-rate notes by Oxoco, Inc., a Texas oil and natural gas company, in late 1984 fell into default shortly after the second quarterly payment was made. Another example is the $230 million issue of low-grade bonds by Oak Industries, a cable television operator, in 1981. Due to large operating losses in 1984, the company was compelled to seek relief from its heavy debt burden. Bondholders were given the option of trading their original bonds for new ones on which the interest payments will be in the form of Oak Industries' common stock rather than cash. Nearly 80% of the bondholders accepted the company's offer, concluding, no doubt, that interest payments in the form of highly speculative common stock may be better than no interest at all.

In 1988, Southland Corporation, the owner of 7–11 Stores, watched its bond prices drop $25.50 in one month. Conventional wisdom held that the dependable business of convenience stores could support large debts. The target of a leveraged buyout (LBO), Southland faced a $448 million interest bill and a $258 million bank payment that its 1989 cash flow could not cover. Campeau Corporation faced a similar growing cash crunch. Two of its units, Allied Stores and Federated Department Stores, saw their bond prices drop 70 points in less than nine months.

The capstone of the junk bond market's problems occurred on February 13, 1990, when Drexel Burnham Lambert announced that it was filing for Chapter 11 bankruptcy. Drexel, with its guiding light Michael Milken, sold managers on using leverage as a corporate takeover tool. The LBO bubble was financed by huge issues of junk bonds, many of them controlled by Drexel. At the time of its demise, an estimated 70% of Drexel's revenues came from LBO deals and junk bonds.

The prosecution and conviction of Milken for violation of the securities laws, along with the problems of several LBO firms and the collapse of the junk bond market were enough to eliminate Drexel as a player in the securities markets. Drexel's experience shows that if investors want to reach for the higher yields promised by junk bonds, they should diversify widely. One way to do this is by purchasing shares in a junk bond mutual fund and combining these investments with investments in other types of securities.

---

[8]John Train, "Beware Of Junk," *Harvard Magazine*, May/June 1985, pp. 14–18.

Insured and Guaranteed Bonds

While some investors are eagerly investing in junk bonds, others are seeking to minimize credit risk by investing in bonds that are *insured* by one or more insurance companies or guaranteed by commercial banks through the issuance of irrevocable letters of credit. Until recently, bond insurance and bond guarantees have been issued almost exclusively for municipal bonds. Roughly 20% of all recent issues of municipal bonds are insured against default. It is estimated that from 1970, when municipal bond insurance was first offered, to 1985 insurers of municipal bonds collected $750 million to $1 billion in premiums and paid out only about $5 million to cover losses.[9] Since the companies insure only investment-grade bonds, it is not surprising that the loss record has been good. The obvious reason why many municipal bonds are insured is that issuers can save more in interest expense by upgrading their bonds than they pay for the insurance. The credit rating assigned to an insured bond is based upon the strength of the insurance companies. Most insured municipal's are rated AAA.

Recently, a number of large commercial banks have begun to compete with the insurance companies for the business of guaranteeing municipal bonds and other debt securities. Bank guarantees take the form of irrevocable letters of credit. In one recent case, 25 banks from 11 different countries issued irrevocable letters of credit to guarantee a $625 million municipal bond issue by the Northern California Power Agency.

If the credit rating of a bond guarantor is lowered, the credit ratings on the bonds it has guaranteed will also be reduced. For example, in 1982, Standard & Poor's reduced the credit ratings on all long-term municipal bonds guaranteed by the Crocker National Bank because of the bank's reduced profitability.

In 1985 seven large companies formed the first insurance company to specialize in insuring corporate bonds.[10] Prior to that time, only a small number of corporate issues had been insured. Backers of the new company expect the business to grow rapidly as issuers find that the interest savings are significantly greater than the cost of the insurance.

|||| BOND RATINGS

Bond rating agencies assign quality ratings to thousands of corporate and municipal bonds, as well as to numerous issues of preferred stock and commercial paper. The two preeminent rating firms are Standard & Poor's

[9]*American Banker,* June 24, 1985. The largest insurer of municipal bonds, by far, is the Municipal Bond Insurance Association (MBIA), a consortium of five of the country's largest multiline insurance companies, Aetna Casualty and Insurance Company, Fireman's Fund, The Travelers, Aetna Insurance Company, and Continental Insurance. Each company pledges its entire resources to cover its share of each MBIA guarantee.

[10]The seven companies are Canadian Imperial Bank of Commerce, Equitable Life Assurance Society of the United States, Ford Motor Credit Company, John Hancock Mutual Life Insurance Company, New England Mutual Life Insurance Company, Transamerica Corporation, and Westpac Banking Corporation.

and Moody's, both of which rate the bonds of more than 2,000 companies and about 8,000 tax-exempt issuers.[11] A *bond rating* represents the rating agency's judgment as to the investment quality of the security and serves as a measure of its relative default risk.

The bond rating business was started in 1907 by John Moody. Standard Statistics, a forerunner of Standard & Poor's, entered the business in 1923. Rating activities were limited to corporate bonds until the 1940s, when the firms began to rate municipal bonds as well. In the late 1960s the coverage was extended to commercial paper.

Figure 13-2 provides details on the ratings assigned by Standard & Poor's and Moody's. Bonds in the four highest categories are commonly referred to as *investment-grade securities,* while bonds rated below BBB or Baa are referred to as *speculative.* Many institutional investors are precluded by law, regulation, or policy from acquiring any bonds that are not rated as investment grade.

Bond ratings have been refined recently by establishing three levels within each of the ratings from AA (or Aa) through B. For example, Standard & Poor's has ratings of AA+, AA, AA−, A+, A, and A−, and so on, while Moody's system includes ratings like Aa1, Aa2, Aa3, A1, A2, and A3.

It is common practice for bond mutual funds to formulate their policies in terms of the ratings they will buy. For example, the Vanguard Investment Grade Bond Fund will not invest in any bonds rated lower than BBB, whereas the Fidelity High Income Fund will invest in no bonds rated higher than BBB.

It is important to understand that a bond rating is a rating of a specific bond issue, not a rating of the issuer. Many companies have more than one issue outstanding, and if these include senior as well as subordinated bonds, the senior issues will probably be rated higher than the subordinated bonds. For example, Crane Company's 6½% sinking fund debentures maturing in 1992 were rated BBB by Standard & Poor's, while the company's 7% subordinated sinking fund debentures maturing in 1993 were rated BBB−.

RATING INDUSTRIAL BONDS

The process by which bonds and preferred stock are rated will be explained in terms of the methods used by Standard & Poor's in rating the securities of industrial corporations and the long-term bonds of state and local governments.[12] Standard & Poor's points out that "The key distinction between rating the debt of a municipal entity and a corporate debt issue is the latter's vulnerability to competitive forces. This is especially

[11]Other, smaller, rating agencies include Fitch Investors Service (Fitch rates the bonds of more than 500 companies as well as 300 municipalities, hospitals and other tax-exempt issuers), Duff & Phelps, and McCarthy, Crisanti and Maffei.

[12]The discussion of rating methodologies draws heavily upon three Standard & Poor's publications: *Credit Overview: Industrial Ratings; Credit Overview: Corporate and International Ratings;* and *Credit Overview: Municipal Ratings.*

||||| **FIGURE 13-2**
Rating Definitions—Standard & Poor's and Moody's

S&P	Moody's	

High Grade Bonds

S&P	Moody's	
AAA	Aaa	Highest quality. Extremely strong capacity to pay interest and repay principal. Sometimes referred to as "gilt edge."
AA	Aa	Very strong capacity to pay interest and repay principal. Risks appear to be slightly larger than in highest quality securities, often because margins of protection are not as large or income fluctuations are greater.

Medium Grade Bonds

S&P	Moody's	
A	A	Upper medium grade. Strong capacity to pay interest and repay principal. Somewhat more susceptible to adverse effects of changes in circumstances and economic conditions than high grade bonds.
BBB	Baa	Medium grade. Adequate capacity to pay interest and repay principal. Normally exhibits adequate protection parameters, but adverse conditions are more likely to lead to weakened capacity to pay. Have some speculative characteristics.

Speculative Grade Bonds

S&P	Moody's	
BB	Ba	Often the protection of principal and interest payments may be very moderate. Faces major ongoing uncertainties or exposure to adverse business, financial, or economic conditions that could lead to inadequate capacity to meet timely interest and principal payments.
B	B	Presently has the capacity to make interest payments and principal repayments, but adverse business, economic, or financial conditions would likely impair the capacity or willingness to make payments.
CCC	Caa	In the event of adverse business, economic, or financial conditions, the issuer is not likely to have the capacity to pay interest and repay principal.
CC	Ca	Typically applies to debt subordinated to senior debt rated CCC. Speculative in a high degree.
C	C	Typically applies to debt subordinated to senior debt rated CCC−. Or, it may indicate imminent default.
D	D	Issue is in payment default or the obligor has filed for bankruptcy.

Rating Modifiers

Standard & Poor's ratings from AA to CCC may be modified by the addition of a plus (+) or minus (−) sign to show relative standing within a major rating category. For example, an upper medium grade bond could be rated A+, A, or A−.

All Moody's ratings from Aa through B include a numerical modifier, 1, 2, or 3. The modifier 1 indicates that the security ranks in the higher end of its rating category; the modifier 2 indicates a mid-range ranking; and the modifier 3 indicates that the issue ranks in the lower end of its category.

Investment and Speculative Grades
(Standard & Poor's)

The term "investment grade" was originally used by various regulatory bodies to connote obligations eligible for investment by institutions such as banks, insurance companies and savings and loan associations. Over time, this term gained widespread usage throughout the investment community. Issues rated in the four highest categories (AAA, AA, A, and BBB) generally are recognized as investment grade. Debt rated BB or below generally is referred to as speculative grade. The term "junk bond" is merely a more irreverent expression for this category of more risky debt. Neither term indicates which securities S&P deems worthy of investment, as an investor with a particular risk preference may appropriately invest in securities that are not investment grade.

Ratings continue as a factor in many regulations. For example, the SEC requires investment-grade status in order to register debt via shelf registration. The Federal Reserve Board allows members of the Federal Reserve System to invest in securities rated in the four highest categories. In similar fashion, California regulates investments of municipalities and county treasurers, Illinois limits collateral acceptable for public deposits, and Vermont restricts investments of insurers and banks.

SOURCE: *Moody's Bond Record,* March 1991; *Standard & Poor's Corporate Finance Criteria 1991.*

true with respect to that broad category of corporate issues called 'industrials.'" The purpose of the rating agency's analysis is to determine the capacity of the issuer to make timely interest and principal payments.

In rating the bonds of an industrial corporation, Standard & Poor's considers the following nine types of criteria:

1. Industry risk (stability and growth of sales and earnings; amount and nature of competition).

2. Issuer's market position in its industry or industries (the company's present position and future plans in each of its major fields).

3. Issuer's relative operating efficiency (level and trend of the company's operating margin; prospects for future costs of labor, materials, and energy).

4. Quality of management (degree of success in achieving past objectives; corporate strategies and financial policies).

5. Quality of accounting (method of accounting for inventories; rates used in amortizing intangibles and depreciating fixed assets; assumptions used in accruing pension costs; degree to which financial ratios overstate or understate the financial performance and condition of the firm relative to its competitors).

6. Earnings protection (operating income as a percentage of sales; before-tax return on average invested capital).

7. Leverage and asset protection (leverage ratios; extent to which any of the firm's assets, such as LIFO inventories or natural resources,

---

|||| SIDELIGHT
Credit-Rating Services Are Slow in Changing Ratings

Since changes in credit ratings often lag behind actual events, it is not a good idea to simply instruct your broker to buy anything that has a rating of A or above. Even officials of the rating services say that investors should look at more than the rating. Ratings don't deal with market price risk, and the rating agencies cannot predict market psychology, court rulings, or political developments. One investment officer observed that "by the time a rating has been lowered on a given credit, you've already lost the bulk of your money."

Rating services are likely to be of more value to smaller investors than to firms that have their own research staffs.

Bond analysts outside the rating agencies sometimes see problems before the ratings are lowered. This occurred in 1981 when analysts spotted problems at the Washington Public Power Supply System (WPPSS). Sometime later the company's bond ratings were lowered, and it defaulted on $2.25 billion of bonds in the summer of 1983.

SOURCE: Adapted from Tom Herman, "Credit-Rating Services' Lag Rates Investor Skepticism," *The Wall Street Journal,* June 23, 1989, p. C1. Reprinted by permission of *The Wall Street Journal,* © Dow Jones & Company, Inc. (1989). All Rights Reserved Worldwide.

are significantly undervalued, or assets such as intangibles, obsolete inventories, and uncollectible receivables are overvalued).

8. Adequacy of cash flows (cash flow as a percentage of long-term debt and as a percentage of total debt; relationship between expected cash flows and projected requirements).

9. Financial flexibility (ability of firm to accomplish its financing program under adverse conditions, taking into account variability of cash flows, flexibility of spending programs, and amount of short-term debt).

The first four types of rating criteria relate to business analysis, and the last five to financial analysis. Obviously, the rating agencies look at more than historical financial data in making their decisions, even though such information is given considerable weight.

Standard & Poor's examines a number of financial ratios in evaluating the financial condition and profitability of a firm. Table 13-8 shows that bond ratings, overall, are highly correlated with certain ratios. Thus, the rating assigned to any bond issue is likely to depend heavily upon certain key financial ratios.

RATING MUNICIPAL BONDS

Municipal bonds include general obligation bonds of state, county, and city governments as well as many types of revenue bonds, including water and sewer bonds, airport bonds, parking revenue bonds, toll roads bonds, health care facility bonds, and college and university financing of various types. As noted earlier, general obligation bonds are backed by the full taxing power of the issuing state or local government. Some state courts have held, however, that this does not mean that the bondholders must be paid according to schedule regardless of the impact on the ability of the city to provide necessary services to its residents. Consequently, the

|||| **TABLE 13-8**
Median Key Financial Ratios of Industrial Companies by Rating Category 1987–1989

	AAA	AA	A	BBB	BB	B	CCC
Before-tax interest coverage (×)	12.0	9.1	5.5	3.6	2.3	1.0	0.8
Before-tax fixed charge coverage, including rents (×)	4.8	5.0	3.3	2.2	1.8	1.0	0.7
Before-tax funds flow interest coverage (×)	14.9	11.4	7.7	5.3	3.4	1.7	1.7
Free operating cash flow/total debt (%)	26	17	9	4	(2)	(3)	(3)
Before-tax return on permanent capital (%)	26	21	18	15	13	9	5
Operating income/sales (%)	21	16	13	12	13	10	10
Long-term debt/total capitalization (%)	16	19	30	37	53	77	75
Total debt/capitalization, including short-term debt (%)	23	28	35	41	55	78	78

SOURCE: *Standard & Poor's Corporate Finance Criteria,* 1991.

rating factors for general obligation bonds are of some interest and will be briefly examined in the following paragraphs.

Economic Health of the Community

Standard & Poor's considers the community's economic base to be the most critical factor in determining a municipal bond rating. The ability of the community to raise tax revenues and the demands on the community for welfare payments both depend upon the condition of the local economy. Indications of a strong economy include the following: income per capita and per household is high compared to other communities and growing; employment is not heavily concentrated in one or a few declining industries; the unemployment rate is low; and total employment is growing. The economic health of the leading employers, the age of their facilities, their expansion plans, and their commitment to the area are all important. Other measures of economic health include the amount of building activity, the age of the housing stock, and the growth rates of retail sales and bank deposits.

Financial Condition of the Issuer

Factors that are viewed positively in evaluating the financial condition of a community include the following: (1) more than one principal source of tax revenue; (2) little dependence upon the state and federal governments for revenues; (3) a budget that is growing more slowly than the population and the tax base; (4) actual expenditures not greater than the budgeted amounts; (5) little use of short-term financing; (6) pension fund assets accumulating at least as fast as the benefits that are being earned; (7) small amount of debt currently outstanding; (8) debt not used to finance operating expenditures and deficits; (9) debt maturities no longer than the useful lives of the facilities being financed; and (10) realistic amount of projected borrowing to finance planned capital improvements.

Quality of Management

The ratings agencies place substantial importance upon the quality of the local government's management. Management is evaluated by considering such things as budgeting techniques and ability to hold expenditures to the budgeted amounts; the quality of management controls; the quality of long-range planning; labor relations; and the range and level of services provided in relation to the community's financial ability to pay for such services.

Financial Ratios

Three ratios are considered especially important in evaluating a community's financial health.

1. Debt service requirements (i.e., principal and interest payments) as a percentage of the total budget. The debt burden is viewed as being high if principal and interest payments exceed 20% of the annual operating expenditures plus debt service.

2. Debt as a percentage of estimated market values of assessed properties. This relates the amount of the debt to a rough indicator of the community's tangible wealth.

3. Debt per capita as a percentage of the per-capita personal income. This ratio relates the debt to a crude measure of the ability of the community to pay.

RATING CHANGES

Bond ratings are under constant surveillance by the rating agencies, and ratings are changed quite frequently. The agencies must perform a careful balancing act, changing any ratings that need to be changed, but not changing them so often that the public will lose confidence in the quality of their work. Changes in ratings can have important consequences for the issuer as well as investors. For example, if a rating is lowered, it may mean higher future financing costs for the issuer as well as a decline in the market value of the downgraded securities for investors.

In recent years, the agencies have started giving advance notice of possible changes in ratings through a report that Standard & Poor's calls "Credit Watch." When a rating agency analyst becomes aware of a development that may warrant a change in a rating sometime in the future but does not call for an immediate change, the securities of the issuer are listed in "Credit Watch," with an indication as to the direction of the possible change and the reasons. These facts are then reported in the *Wall Street Journal*. Investors should understand that a listing in "Credit Watch" does not always lead to a rating change, and rating changes are not always preceded by a listing in "Credit Watch."

The number of rating changes for the bonds of industrial corporations increased significantly in the 1980s, as shown in Table 13-9. In 1983 only 143 changes were made, with roughly 66% of the changes being downgrades. In 1990 a record 398 changes were made, of which 75% were downgrades.

Rating changes are sometimes made in response to a favorable or unfavorable development that affects most of the firms in an industry. For example, in 1983 the federal government tightened its policy for reimbursing hospitals under the Medicare program, and many hospitals experienced a significant decline in inpatient days and total revenues.

||| **TABLE 13-9**
Number of Rating Changes Bonds of Industrial Corporations

| | **Years Ended December 31** | | | | | | | |
	1983	1984	1985	1986	1987	1988	1989	1990
Upgrades	49	54	49	53	109	129	141	99
Downgrades	94	98	187	221	141	182	159	299
Total	143	152	236	274	250	311	300	398

SOURCE: *Standard & Poor's Corporate Finance Criteria 1991.*

This was no doubt a major reason why Standard & Poor's downgraded 83 hospital bond ratings in 1983 and 1984, compared to the upgrading of only 25 hospital issues. The general deterioration of hospital bonds led some brokers to recommend that such bonds be purchased only if they were insured or backed by a bank letter of credit.

|||| PREFERRED STOCK

Preferred stock can be defined as shares that rank ahead of common stock in regard to dividends and on liquidation, but do not have general voting rights. Legally, preferred stock is an *equity security,* which means that it is subordinate to all debt and that dividends are paid at the discretion of the directors, usually with two conditions: (1) that no dividends may be paid on the company's common stock until the preferred dividends have been paid, and (2) that preferred dividends are *cumulative.* The cumulative feature means that if any preferred dividends are skipped, they are carried over to future years and must be paid in full before any common dividends can be paid.

Preferred shareholders rarely have general voting rights, but most issues give the preferred shareholders some voting power if a dividend is missed.

Most preferred shares have a fixed dividend rate, but a number of firms have recently issued preferred stock with adjustable dividends. Some, but not many, preferred shares are participating. This means that if common shareholders are paid a dividend that exceeds the dividend for the preferred stock on a per-share basis, the dividend on the preferred shall be increased until it equals the dividend on the common stock.

It is often said that preferred stock is like common stock in not having any final repayment date. This is not always true. Some preferred stock has a mandatory sinking fund that is designed to retire all of the shares within a specified period.

Many recent issues of preferred stock are callable, usually at a premium in the early years and at face value in later years. The call price tends to set a ceiling on the market price of the stock. Not only that, it exposes investors to the risk that their stock will be called at a time when preferred dividend yields and interest rates are down.

For individual investors, the most important fact about preferred stock is that the dividend yields are almost invariably lower than the rates of return offered by other investments of comparable risk. This is true for one reason: Federal tax law provides that up to 70% of intercorporate dividends received are excluded from taxable income. With this exclusion, corporations can invest in the preferred stock of other companies and pay tax on only 30% of the dividends received. If a corporation's marginal tax rate is, say, 40%, its effective tax rate on dividends received from other corporations is only 12% (.40 × .30). As a result of the low tax on intercorporate dividends, corporate investors bid up the prices of preferred stock to a point where the dividend yields are unattractive to individual investors. A before-tax yield of 10% on preferred stock provides an after-tax return of 8.8% to a corporate investor with a marginal tax rate of 40% but an after-tax return of only 7% to an individual investor with a marginal tax rate of 30%.

The unsatisfactory level of preferred dividends for individual investors compared to the yields on bonds is illustrated by the terms of an issue of adjustable-rate cumulative preferred stock by the Houston Lighting and Power Company in August 1985. The stock offered a dividend yield of 9.10% for the first quarter, at a time when the yields on intermediate- and long-term U.S. government bonds ranged from 9½% to 10½%. For periods after the first quarter, the dividend rate was set at 1.85 percentage points below the highest of the following three rates: three-month U.S. Treasury bill rate, U.S. Treasury bond 10-year constant maturity rate, and U.S. Treasury bond 20-year constant maturity rate. The stock was attractive to many corporate investors but quite unattractive to individual investors.[13]

A significant percentage of all preferred issues are convertible into common stock. Some convertible preferreds may be attractive to individual investors even though straight preferred stock is not.

|||| SUMMARY

Fixed-income investments can be classified into seven categories: money market securities; U.S. Treasury notes and bonds; corporate notes and bonds; municipal bonds; federal agency notes and bonds; mortgage-backed securities; and preferred stocks.

Money market securities are short-term, generally low-risk IOUs that are traded regularly in the secondary market. They include Treasury bills, commercial paper, negotiable certificates of deposit, Eurodollar deposits, and bankers' acceptances. Treasury bills, free of default risk and traded in very large quantities, are considered the safest and most liquid type of marketable investment. U.S. Treasury notes and bonds differ from Treasury bills in two principal respects: the maturities are longer, and they are issued on an interest-bearing basis rather than a discount basis.

Corporate bonds are issued by many types of business firms and have many different features and characteristics. Variables relating to corporate bonds include the coupon rate, maturity, call provisions, default risk, sinking fund requirements, degree of seniority, taxability, convertibility, and nature of the collateral, if any. The terms of the issue, including covenants for the protection of investors, are incorporated into the bond indenture.

[13]An issue of adjustable-rate money market preferred stock by Citicorp in June 1985 provided an interesting method for adjusting the rate. The terms of the issue provided that the dividend is subject to change every 49 days by means of a Dutch auction. At the auction, bidding is in terms of the dividend yield, and after the auction, the dividend is set at the lowest rate that includes enough bids to cover the entire issue.

Municipal bonds can be broadly classified as either general obligation bonds or revenue bonds. General obligation bonds are backed by the full taxing power of the issuer. Revenue bonds are backed only by the revenues from the facilities financed with the bonds. The interest on municipal bonds is, with certain exceptions, exempt from federal income tax. Therefore, in comparing yields on municipals with the yields on taxable bonds, it is helpful to calculate the fully taxable equivalent yield of the municipals based on the investor's marginal tax rate.

Securities backed by pools of mortgages (mortgage-backed securities) have become one of the most important types of fixed-income investments. Of these, the most widely held are Ginnie Mae pass-throughs, which are guaranteed by the Government national Mortgage Association, and thus by the U.S. government. They offer yields a little higher than U.S. Treasury securities of comparable maturities, largely because of considerable uncertainty as to the time over which the payments will be received.

For investors wanting protection against having to reinvest interest payments at rates lower than the coupon rate, zero-coupon bonds can be very attractive. Zeros are issued at a discount and redeemed at face value at maturity. Unless the zero is a municipal bond or is held by a tax-exempt organization or is in a tax-deferred account, taxes must be paid on the income as it is accrued. Therefore, in comparing a zero-coupon bond with a coupon bond, it is important to examine the timing of the after-tax cash flows.

In recent years, corporations have issued large amounts of bonds rated double-B or lower, which are known as high-yield or junk bonds. The promised yields, or coupon rates, of junk bonds are, of course, much higher than for bonds with little risk of default. In some periods, they have also provided higher realized yields. In recent years, however, the number of defaults has increased materially, which has greatly reduced the average realized yield.

Many municipal bonds and some corporates are guaranteed by insurance companies or commercial banks. Such guarantees reduce the risk of loss but also make it possible for the bonds to be issued at lower yields.

Most large bond issues, except private placements with institutional investors, are rated by one or more bond rating agencies. A bond rating indicates the agency's evaluation of its relative risk of default. In arriving at their ratings, the agencies try to consider all factors that might affect the ability of the issuer to make the principal and interest payments as scheduled.

Preferred stocks are similar to bonds in some respects and to common stocks in others. The promised dividends are generally, but not always, fixed, as are the interest payments on most bonds. But payment of the dividend is nevertheless largely in the discretion of the board of directors. Generally, preferred stock, unless convertible into common, is not attractive to individual investors because the partial tax-exemption of intercorporate dividends makes such stocks attractive to corporate investors at yields that are lower than the yields on other investments of comparable risk.

QUESTIONS

1. What is a bond indenture?
2. Describe a typical bond sinking fund provision.
3. Describe, generally, the terms under which most of the bonds in Table 13-4 are callable.
4. To what extent is the income from a municipal bond nontaxable?
5. Explain the difference between a serial bond issue and an issue of term bonds.
6. Why might an investor prefer serial bonds to term bonds?
7. Explain, in terms of investors' marginal tax rates, why the yields on municipals tend to rise relative to taxable yields when the supply of municipals is unusually large.
8. Describe a Ginnie Mae pass-through certificate. How does it originate? What part does Ginnie Mae play? What does the investor receive? How does the pass-through differ from an ordinary coupon bond? Why is it difficult to know what the yield will be if the pass-through is selling at a premium or a discount? Why is it sometimes called a modified pass-through?
9. How do the pass-throughs of Fannie Mae and Freddie Mac (FNMA and FHLMC) differ from Ginnie Mae pass-throughs?
10. Describe collateralized mortgage obligations (CMOs). Why were they developed? With what are they collateralized?
11. Explain the difference between a zero-coupon bond derived from a U.S. Treasury bond and an original-issue zero-coupon bond.
12. Explain the pros and cons of zero-coupon bonds from an investor's point of view.
13. Explain how the U.S. Treasury has facilitated the creation of zero-coupon bonds from U.S. Treasury bonds.
14. Explain why tax-exempt zeros as well as taxable zeros may be especially attractive investments for IRA and Keogh accounts.
15. Explain the difference between the ratable method and the constant interest rate method of allocating the original issue discount for a zero-coupon bond. Why is the constant interest rate method preferable?
16. How does the after-tax yield to maturity for a zero-coupon bond compare to the after-tax yield to maturity for a coupon bond if both bonds are selling at a yield to maturity equal to the coupon rate of the coupon bond, and the ratable method of allocating the original discount is used? If the constant instant rate method is used?
17. Describe the patterns of the annual cash flows for a zero-coupon bond and a coupon bond.
18. What is a "put" bond?

19. What factors determine the extent to which a floating interest rate provision protects the investor against interest rate risk?

20. What is an extendable note?

21. What is a junk bond? How do original-issue junk bonds differ from other junk bonds?

22. How do commercial banks guarantee bonds? What determines the quality rating of a guaranteed bond?

23. Why is preferred stock usually unattractive to individual investors?

24. What is a Dutch auction? Explain how Dutch auctions are used to change the dividend rate on adjustable-rate money market preferred stocks.

25. Most preferred stocks are cumulative. What does that mean?

26. What profitability and cash flow ratios does Standard & Poor's seem to emphasize in rating the bonds of industrial corporations?

27. Comment on the factors other than financial ratios that are considered in rating the bonds of industrial corporations.

|||| **SELECTED REFERENCES**

American Banker, June 24, 1985.

Business Week, January 28, 1985, p. 93.

Credit Overview. Standard and Poor's Corporation.

Credit Overview: Corporate and International Ratings. Standard and Poor's Corporation.

Credit Overview: Municipal Ratings. Standard and Poor's Corporation.

Fabozzi, Frank J., and Irving M. Pollack, eds. *The Handbook of Fixed Income Securities,* 2d ed. Homewood, Ill.: Dow Jones-Irwin, 1987.

Industrial Ratings. Standard and Poor's Corporation.

Train, John. "Beware of Junk." *Harvard Magazine,* May/June 1985, pp. 14–18.

Wall Street Journal, September 11, 1989.

14 FIXED-INCOME INVESTMENTS: CONCEPTS AND THEORIES

For many years bond investment was considered a rather staid investment opportunity. This perception changed in the 1970s and early 1980s when the volatility and level of interest rates radically altered the fixed-income markets.

This chapter explains a number of important concepts and theories relating to fixed-income investments. To the basic concept of bond yields are added many principles of bond investment that are not obvious to the average investor. The axioms developed in this chapter allow the development of sophisticated bond investment strategies, some of which will be discussed in the next chapter.

BOND YIELDS

Several bond yield definitions are used in the marketplace. The five principal types of yield are the coupon rate, current yield, yield to maturity, yield to call, and total realized yield.[1] Although these methods of measuring bond returns often produce widely differing results, each can provide useful information.

The current price of a bond represents the present value of the promised coupon (interest) and principal payments. In the present chapter, we will show that the discount rate used in calculating the present value is either the yield to maturity or yield to call. It is important to understand how the yield to maturity and the yield to call relate to the current yield and the total realized yield.

CURRENT YIELD

The *current yield* of a note or bond is simply the total annual interest divided by the market price of the security:

$$CY = C/P \qquad (14\text{-}1)$$

where

$$C = \text{annual interest or coupon payment}$$
$$P = \text{current market price of the security}$$

[1]As explained later in the chapter, the total realized yield for a bond is like the annual geometric mean rate of return for any investment.

417

For example, if the coupon rate on a $1,000 bond is 10%, making the coupon payment $100, and the price of the bond is $800, the current yield is 100/800, or 12.5%. The current yield is often a poor measure of the actual return an investor will receive because it does not reflect potential capital gains or losses, and it makes no provision for compounding.[2]

YIELD TO MATURITY

The promised *yield to maturity* is the rate of return that will discount the promised cash flows to a present value equal to the market price of the security. Yield to maturity is mathematically identical to the *internal rate of return* for a proposed capital investment. The yield to maturity for a bond may also be considered the market rate of interest for all bonds of similar characteristics.

Assuming annual interest payments, yield to maturity is calculated with Equation 14-2:[3]

$$P = \sum_{t=1}^{n} C/(1 + i)^t + M/(1 + i)^n$$

$$= C\left[\frac{1 - (1 + i)^{-n}}{i}\right] + \frac{M}{(1 + i)^n} \qquad (14\text{-}2)$$

$$= C \cdot \text{PVIFA}_{i,n} + M \cdot \text{PVIF}_{i,n}$$

where

P = market price of the bond

C = annual coupon payment

i = yield to maturity with annual compounding

n = number of years to maturity

M = maturity value (also called par value or face value) of the bond

---

[2]The *Wall Street Journal* and other newspapers report only the current yield for corporate bonds and only the yield to maturity for the notes and bonds of the U.S. Treasury and federal agencies.

[3]Sometimes only an approximate yield is needed. The following formula may provide a satisfactory answer if the price of the bond is within 10% or 15% of the face value:

$$Y = \frac{I + (M - P)/n}{(P + M)/2}$$

where

Y = approximate yield to maturity

I = annual interest

M = face value

P = purchase price

n = number of years to maturity

For any given maturity, the closer the market value of the bond is to the face value, the smaller the difference between the approximate yield to maturity and the actual yield to maturity.

$\text{PVIF}_{i,n}$ = Present value interest factor for $i\%$ and n years

$\qquad = 1/(1 + i)^n$

$\text{PVIFA}_{i,n}$ = Present value interest factor of an annuity for $i\%$ and n years

$\qquad\quad = [(1 - (1 + i)^{-n})/i]$

With semiannual interest payments, the semiannual yield to maturity is calculated as follows:

$$P = \sum_{t=1}^{2n} (C/2)/(1 + r)^t + M/(1 + r)^{2n}$$

$$= \frac{C}{2}\left[\frac{1 - (1 + r)^{-2n}}{r}\right] + \frac{M}{(1 + r)^{2n}} \qquad (14\text{-}3)$$

$$= (C/2)\text{PVIFA}_{r,2n} + M \cdot \text{PVIF}_{r,2n}$$

where

$C/2$ = semiannual interest payment

$2n$ = number of semiannual periods to maturity

$r = i/2$ = semiannual yield to maturity

Equations 14-2 and 14-3 show that the yield to maturity is a function of three variables: the market price, the coupon rate, and the number of years to maturity. Given these values, any financial calculator will easily produce the yield to maturity.[4] With more difficulty, a trial and error approach using present value tables will also produce the yield to maturity. With either method the objective is to find the value of i or r that will make the present value of the cash inflows equal to the market price of the bond.

The annual yield to maturity with semiannual compounding is the semiannual yield times two. Example 14-1 shows the semiannual yield to maturity and the annual yield to maturity with semiannual compounding for a heavily discounted bond.

EXAMPLE 14-1   SEMIANNUAL AND ANNUAL YIELD TO MATURITY

Face value of bond	$1,000
Market price	$600
Coupon rate	6%
Number of years to maturity	20
Semiannual yield to maturity *(r)*	5.49%
$\quad(600 = 30 \cdot \text{PVIFA}_{i,40} + 1{,}000 \cdot \text{PVIF}_{i,40})$	
Annual yield to maturity *(i)* with semiannual compounding	10.98%
$\quad(2 \cdot 5.49)$	

||||

---

[4]Before the advent of inexpensive financial calculators, bond yield tables provided the prices and yields to maturity for bonds with various coupon rates. Although bond tables are still used, calculators are often more convenient.

The Reinvestment Assumption

Equations 14-2 and 14-3 assume that all interest payments will be invested at a rate equal to the yield to maturity. This assumption makes the yield to maturity similar to the effective annual rate of return on a savings account or savings certificate. If an investor deposits $1,000 in a savings account paying 9% compounded semiannually, his account balance in 20 years would be $5,816 ($1,000 $\times$ $FVIF_{4.5\%,40}$). Implicit in this sort of investment is the assumption of the reinvestment of interest, i.e., the investor makes no withdrawals from his account.

EXAMPLE 14-2   IMPORTANCE OF REINVESTMENT
OF INTEREST

Consider a bond with the following characteristics:

Face value	$1,000
Market price	$1,000
Coupon rate	9%
Number of annual periods to maturity	20
Semiannual interest payment	$45
Yield to maturity: semiannual rate	4.50%
Annual yield with semiannual compounding (2 · 4.50)	9.00%

If the semiannual interest payments are reinvested to earn interest at a rate equal to the yield to maturity (4.50% semiannual), the accumulated value at the end of 20 years will be $5,816:

Face value of bond	$1,000
40 interest payments of $45 (40 · $45)	1,800
Interest earned on reinvested interest at semiannual rate of 4.50%:	
(45 · $FVIFA_{4.5\%,40}$ − 1,800)	3,016
Total	5,816

In terms of value relatives, the annual yield to maturity with semiannual interest payments and semiannual compounding is calculated as follows:

$$[(5,816/1,000)^{1/40} - 1][2]$$
$$= [(5.816)^{1/40} - 1][2]$$
$$= (.0450)(2)$$
$$= .0900, \text{ or } 9.00\%$$

Observe that if the investor did not reinvest the coupon payments, his total accumulation of wealth in 20 years would be $2,800 ($1,000 + $1,800). The actual or realized yield over the 20-year investment horizon, without reinvestment, would be only 5.28% ($1,000 \times FVIF_{i,20} = 2,800 \rightarrow i = 5.28\%$). ||||

The impact of the reinvestment assumption for a long-term bond held to maturity can be seen in Figure 14-1. This figure demonstrates the increasing importance of interest on interest as the investment horizon

|||| **FIGURE 14–1**
Interest on Reinvested Interest: 20-Year, 9% Bond with Semiannual Reinvestment at Semiannual Rate of 4.5%

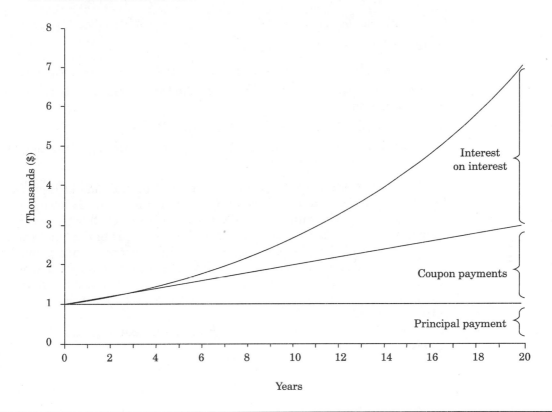

approaches the maturity of the bond. Clearly, if the interest payments on the bond were reinvested at any rate other than a semiannual rate of 4.5%, the accumulated amount for the bond investment would be larger or smaller than the ending balance in the savings account. In that case, the total realized yield on the bond would be higher or lower than the yield to maturity of 4.5% semiannual or 9.20% annual. The yield to maturity is a good measure of the yield that will be realized only if the reinvestment rate is equal to the yield to maturity.

Yield Equations on Non-Interest Dates

Equations 14-2 and 14-3 are accurate yield equations if a bond investor purchases or sells bonds on the date that interest is due. The bond valuation formula for noninterest date bonds purchases is a logical extension of Equation 14-3. When purchasing a bond on a non-interest date, the bond investor is faced with the problem of discounting the bond payments to the *settlement date,* the date the investor takes ownership of the bond.

The equation for a non-interest date bond is

$$P = \frac{\sum_{t=1}^{2n} \dfrac{C/2}{(1+r)^t} + \dfrac{M}{(1+r)^{2n}}}{(1+r)^{(sc/cp)}} + \frac{\dfrac{C}{2}}{(1+r)^{(sc/cp)}} - \frac{Ca}{2cp} \qquad (14\text{-}4)$$

where

n = the number of annual periods to maturity from the next coupon date

$sc = cp - a$ = the number of days from the settlement date to the next coupon date

cp = the number of days in the coupon period[5]

a = accrued days, the number of days from the beginning of the coupon period to the settlement date

The numerator of the first term on the right-hand side of Equation 14-4 is the present value of a bond as of the coupon date following the settlement date. The numerator of the second term ($C/2$) is the coupon payment on the next interest date (since it is not a part of the bond value in the first term). The denominator in both the first and second terms is the present value function that discounts the bond value and the next coupon payment to the settlement date. The last term on the right in Equation 14-4 is the accrued interest from the last coupon date to the settlement date.

When the bond matures on the next coupon date, Equation 14-4 becomes

$$P = \frac{M + C/2}{(1+r)^{[(cp-a)/cp]}} - \frac{Ca}{2cp}$$

As an application of Equation 14-4 consider the following example.

EXAMPLE 14-3   PRICE OF A NON-INTEREST DATE BOND

Assume an investor wishes to determine the actual price of a corporate 10% bond maturing on December 31, 1997, that is selling to yield 8%. If the bond is purchased on March 15, 1988, and the next coupon date is June 30, 1988, the selling price will be

$$P = \frac{\sum_{t=1}^{19} \dfrac{100/2}{(1.04)^t} + \dfrac{1,000}{(1.04)^{19}}}{(1.04)^{(105/180)}} + \frac{\dfrac{100}{2}}{(1.04)^{(105/180)}} - \frac{100 \times 75}{2 \times 180}$$

$$= \$1,105.75 + 48.87 - 20.83 = \$1,133.79$$

The investor would pay $1,133.79 for the bond, plus $20.83 for the accrued interest, or a total of $1,154.62. ||||

---

[5]Municipal, state, and corporate bonds issued in the United States typically assume a 30-day month, 360-day year, regardless of the actual number of days. Treasury securities use the 365-day calendar and the actual days in a month. For a corporate bond paying interest semiannually, the coupon period, cp, is 180 days.

Yield to Maturity Compared to Current Yield

In comparing different bonds or in comparing bonds with other investments, the yield to maturity is superior to the current yield.[6] The yield to maturity not only reflects the capital gain or loss for a bond held to maturity, but it also includes the compounding of interest. The yield to maturity is greater than the current yield when the market price of a bond is below the face value and is less than the current yield when the market price is above the face value. However, as Table 14-1 illustrates, the longer the maturity, the smaller the difference between the two kinds of yields.

YIELD TO CALL

Bond indentures often give the issuer the right to call the bonds for redemption long before the scheduled maturity date. Issuers are especially anxious to have this right when they expect interest rates to be lower in the future. If bonds are callable and interest rates decline substantially, the issuer can redeem the bonds with the proceeds of a new issue bearing a lower coupon rate. To obtain this privilege, issuers are willing to offer, and investors are sure to require, higher coupon rates than for noncallable bonds. The evaluation of callable bonds requires investors to estimate both the probability of a bond call and when the call might occur. It is often impossible to make such estimates with confidence because of the difficulty of forecasting interest rates.

A bond called before maturity will almost certainly cause the bondholder's yield to be different from the yield if held to maturity. When the indenture provides for a deferred call, which means that the issuer must wait a specified number of years before calling the bonds, a bondholder is often wise to assume that the call will take place at the earliest possible date. The yield calculated to the earliest permitted call date under the indenture, is the "yield to first call." The *yield to call* with annual compounding is calculated with Equation 14-5:

[6]The yield to maturity can be misleading if the bond is callable or if the interest payments are likely to be reinvested at a rate significantly higher or lower than the yield to maturity.

|||| **TABLE 14-1**

Yield to Maturity Compared to Current Yield (Face Value, $1,000; Coupon, 10%)

Years to Maturity	8% Current Yield		10% Current Yield		12% Current Yield	
	Current Price	Yield to Maturity	Current Price	Yield to Maturity	Current Price	Yield to Maturity
5	$1,250	4.38%	$1,000	10.00%	$833.33	14.84%
10	1,250	6.55	1,000	10.00	833.33	13.03
20	1,250	7.56	1,000	10.00	833.33	12.25
30	1,250	7.83	1,000	10.00	833.33	12.07

$$P = \sum_{t=1}^{nc} C/(1 + i)^t + (M + CP)/(1 + i)^{nc}$$

$$= C\left[\frac{1 - (1 + i)^{-nc}}{i}\right] + \frac{M + CP}{(1 + i)^{nc}} \qquad (14\text{-}5)$$

$$= C \cdot \text{PVIFA}_{i,nc} + (M + CP)\text{PVIF}_{i,nc}$$

where

P = market price of the bond

C = annual coupon payment

i = yield to call with annual compounding

nc = number of years to call

M = maturity value (also called par value or face value) of the bond

CP = call premium, if any

Note that this formula is the same as Equation 14-2 with the substitution of the years to call for the years to maturity and the addition of a call premium, if any. Obviously, the semiannual yield to call formula will be similar to Equation 14-3 after the appropriate adjustments for the call date and the call premium. Just as yield to maturity calculations assume that interest will be reinvested at rate equal to the yield to maturity, yield to call calculations assume that interest payments will be reinvested at a rate equal to the yield to call.

When the price paid for a bond is less than the face value, the yield to call will be greater than the yield to maturity because the capital gain accrues over a shorter time period. Consider the following example:

EXAMPLE 14-4   YIELD TO CALL VERSUS YIELD TO MATURITY

	Yield to Call	Yield to Maturity
Coupon rate	10%	10%
Purchase price	$900	$900
Call price and maturity value	$1,000	$1,000
Years to call or maturity	10	20
Yield to call or maturity, assuming interest is paid:		
Annually	11.75%	11.28%
Semiannually (i^*)	12.07%	11.59%

In this case, yield to maturity may be more relevant than yield to call. It is unlikely that these bonds will be called unless long-term interest rates drop enough that similar new bonds can be issued at a yield considerably lower than 10%.||||

If a bond is selling at a premium (price higher than face value), the yield to call may be either higher or lower than the yield to maturity. In this case, the relationship between the two yields depends upon the purchase price, the relationship between the call price and the face value, the expected number of years until the call, and the number of years to maturity. If the call price is higher than the face value of the bonds but lower than the purchase price, as in Example 14-5, the capital loss will be less if the bonds are called. However, since the loss is sustained over a shorter time period, the yield to call may be lower than the yield to maturity.

EXAMPLE 14-5   CALL PRICE HIGHER THAN FACE VALUE BUT
              LOWER THAN PURCHASE PRICE

	Yield to Call	Yield to Maturity
Coupon rate	10%	10%
Purchase price	$1,200	$1,200
Call price or maturity value	$1,100	$1,000
Years to call or maturity	10	20
Yield to call or maturity, assuming annual interest payments	7.77%	7.98% ||||

TOTAL REALIZED YIELD

Total realized yield, yield to maturity, and yield to call have one important characteristic in common: all are compound, or geometric mean, rates of return. Total realized yield differs from the other two measures of return in the way the reinvestment rate is handled. While yield to maturity calculations are based upon the assumption that interest payments will be reinvested at a rate equal to the yield to maturity, and yield to call assumes that the reinvestment rate will be equal to the yield to call, *total realized yield* is based upon the expected actual reinvestment rate or, if the yield is being calculated for prior periods, upon the actual reinvestment rate. While it is possible to use more than one reinvestment rate, with each rate covering a specified period of time, the difficulty of forecasting interest rates far into the future is a reason for using a single rate for all periods. Total realized yield can be defined as the rate that will discount the accumulated value of an investment at the end of the holding period to a present value equal to its value at the beginning of the holding period. It can be used to measure either past actual returns or expected future returns.

Before examining the procedure for calculating total realized yield, recall briefly three concepts that were introduced earlier in the text: value relative, holding period return, and geometric mean rate of return. It is necessary to understand how these three quantities are related to one another.

A value relative *(VR)* is the ratio of the accumulated value of an investment at the end of a holding period to the value at the beginning of the period. Thus, if V_0 represents the value at the beginning of the period and V_n the accumulated value at the end of the period, the value relative is

$$VR = V_n/V_0 = 1 + r$$

The accumulated value at the end of the holding period includes the market value at that time plus all income received during the holding period. When the objective is to calculate the total realized yield, the accumulated value also includes earnings on reinvested earnings. If the total holding period is more than one year, the compound annual, or geometric mean, rate of return is the geometric mean of the annual value relatives minus one. For example, if the total holding period is three years, the three annual value relatives are

$$V_3/V_2, \ V_2/V_1, \ \text{and} \ V_1/V_0$$

The product of these three annual value relatives is the value relative for the three-year period:

$$V_3/V_0$$

The geometric mean of the three annual value relatives can be expressed either as

$$[(V_3/V_2) \times (V_2/V_1) \times (V_1/V_0)]^{1/3}$$

or as

$$(V_3/V_0)^{1/3}$$

And the geometric mean annual rate of return, or compound annual rate of return, is

$$(V_3/V_0)^{1/3} - 1$$

Table 14-2 illustrates the calculation of annual value relatives, annual holding period returns, and the total realized yield, or compound annual rate of return, based upon estimated actual interest on reinvested interest. The investment is a \$1,000 bond purchased at par at the beginning of an estimated holding period of three years. The total realized yield (geometric mean annual rate of return) of 11.55% is 24 basis points lower than the arithmetic mean return of 11.79%. The geometric mean of a set of numbers is always lower than the arithmetic mean unless all of the numbers (in this case, all of the value relatives) are the same. The total realized yield of 11.55% will discount the accumulated value of \$1,388 at the end of three years to a present value equal to the initial value of the investment $[1,388/(1.1155)^3 = \$1,000]$.

Yield to Maturity versus Total Realized Yield

Yield to maturity is a convenient measure for comparing bonds with different prices, coupon rates, and maturities. Given the price, it is a function of just two variables, the coupon rate and time to maturity, both of which are easy to ascertain. The total realized yield is somewhat more complicated in that it requires an estimate of the reinvestment rate or rates. Nevertheless, if it seems likely that the reinvestment rate will be significantly higher or lower than the yield to maturity, it is important

|||| **TABLE 14-2**
Calculation of the Total Realized Yield on a $1,000, 10% Bond

	Face value (V_0)	$1,000
	Coupon rate	10%
	Annual interest	$ 100
	Years to maturity	5

Year	Estimated Market Interest Rates	Estimated Interest on Interest	Estimated Market Value of Bond
1	8%	$ 2.00	$1,067.33[a]
2	11	14.28	975.02
3	7	17.01	1,055.10

Calculation of accumulated values:

	Year 1	Year 2	Year 3
Coupon for current year	$ 100	$ 100	$ 100
Coupon for prior years		$ 100	$ 200
Interest on interest:			
Current year[b]	$ 2	$ 14	$ 17
Prior years		$ 2	$ 16
Bond value at year-end	$1,067	$ 975	$1,055
Accumulated value	$1,169	$1,191	$1,388
Value relatives:			
$V_1/V_0 = 1,169/1,000$	1.1693		
$V_2/V_1 = 1,191/1,169$		1.0188	
$V_3/V_2 = 1,388/1,191$			1.1656
Annual holding period returns	16.93%	1.88%	16.56%
Average annual holding period return			
$(16.93 + 1.88 + 16.56)/3 =$			11.79%
$V_3/V_0 = 1388/1000$			1.388
Total realized yield (geometric mean annual rate of return)			
$(1.388)^{1/3} - 1 =$			11.55%

[a]$PV = 50 \cdot PVIFA_{8\%,8} + 1,000 \cdot PVIF_{8\%,8} = \$1,067.33$.

[b]The interest in year 1 is the interest on the first $50 coupon for six months ($50 \cdot .04 = \$2$). The interest in the second year is the interest on $102 for the first six months ($102 \cdot .055 = 5.61$) plus the interest on $157.61 for the second six months ($157.61 \cdot .055 = 8.67$).

to calculate total realized yield rather than making a decision on the basis of the yield to maturity. As demonstrated previously, two bonds with the same yield to maturity but with different coupon rates or maturities may have widely different total realized yields if the reinvestment rate is not equal to the yield to maturity.

|||| **DETERMINANTS OF BOND YIELDS**

The prices at which bonds are bought and sold, or the yields at which they are being traded, are determined by the characteristics of the individual bond issues and the general level of interest rates. Relevant bond characteristics include (1) time to maturity; (2) coupon rate; (3) marketability; (4) call provisions; (5) default risk (which depends, in part, upon provisions of the bond indenture); (6) convertibility; and (7) taxability. All of these bond attributes except taxability affect the riskiness of bonds and therefore the prices and yields at which they are traded.[7]

In Chapter 7, we saw that the market risk-free rate of interest (R) is the sum of the expected real rate of interest (r) and a premium (p) to compensate investors for the expected rate of inflation (i.e., $R = r + p$). When this equation is expanded to allow for default and other risks, R becomes the promised return, which is the nominal return the investor will receive if all payments are received on schedule.

$$R = r + p + RP + DP \qquad (14\text{-}6)$$

where

$$RP = \text{risk premium}$$
$$DP = \text{default premium}$$

Even with U.S. Treasury securities, RP is positive because of interest rate risk. The default premium is to cover expected losses due to default. Thus, when there is no default risk, the expected nominal return is the expected real return plus the expected inflation rate and the premium for other risks, as shown in Equation 14-7.

$$E(R) = r + p + RP \qquad (14\text{-}7)$$

The amount of the risk and default premiums depends upon the riskiness of the specific investment.[8] The various types of risk that apply to fixed-income investments can be classified as follows:

1. Interest rate risk
   a. Price risk
   b. Reinvestment rate risk
2. Risk of default
3. Marketability, or liquidity, risk
4. Call risk
5. Purchasing power, or inflation, risk

Interest rate risk arises from changes in the general level of interest rates, which affect bond returns in two ways: through their impact on bond prices (price risk) and their effect on reinvestment income. For bonds of high quality, *price risk* or the risk that bond prices will fall due to

[7]The extent to which the income from a bond is taxable affects the before-tax yield at which it is traded because investment decisions are based upon expected after-tax rates of return. Most high-quality municipal bonds, for example, are traded at yields lower than the before-tax yields on U.S. Treasury bonds because the interest on municipal bonds is generally exempt from federal income taxes.

[8]According to the capital asset pricing model, the risk premium is only large enough to compensate investors for any systematic risk associated with the investment. Since betas for most bonds are low, risk premiums for most bonds should also be low.

rising interest rates is of much greater concern than the risk of default or of poor marketability. Reinvestment risk arises from the possibility that interest rates will decline after bonds have been purchased, causing the amount of interest earned on reinvested interest to be less than expected. Falling interest rates are both good news and bad news for bond investors. The good news is that lower rates mean higher bond prices; the bad news is that lower rates mean lower returns on any new investments that are made. The desire of investors to avoid reinvestment risk and to "lock in" attractive yields for an extended period of time accounts for the remarkable popularity of zero-coupon bonds in recent years.

Interest rate risk has become much greater since the Federal Reserve made a fundamental change in its operating strategy on October 6, 1979. On that date the Federal Reserve Open Market Committee abandoned its long-standing practice of attempting to control short-term interest rates and focused, instead, on the growth rate of the money supply. One result has been a significant increase in the volatility of interest rates and greater fluctuations in bond prices. Both the pricing and reinvestment aspects of interest rate risk will be explored in greater detail later in the chapter.

Default risk is the risk that the promised payments, or some of them, will be delayed or not made at all. There is no default risk with U.S. Treasury securities or securities guaranteed by the U.S. government. The relative amount of default risk for other large issues of notes and bonds, except for private placements, is indicated (not always accurately) by the quality ratings assigned by Standard & Poor's, Moody's, and other bond rating agencies. The terms of bond indentures have an important bearing on the risk of default. A recent study has demonstrated that bonds with seniority or security covenants sell at lower yields (higher prices) than bonds of the same company that are similar in other essential terms to the senior or secured bonds except that they are subordinated or unsecured.[9] Investors believe that the default risk is lower on senior bonds and secured bonds and are willing to pay a price for the added safety.

Marketability or liquidity risk relates to the amount of difficulty an investor might have in selling a security in the secondary market. Since the volume of trading in many bonds and notes is very light, marketability risk is often an important consideration for fixed-income investors. Selling bonds in a thin market is apt to require discounting of the price.

Call risk is present when the issuer has the right to call bonds for redemption prior to maturity. The usual reason for calling bonds is to reduce interest expense by replacing high-coupon bonds with a new, lower-coupon issue. This is often done after a general decline in interest rates. Call provisions are a valuable right for bond issuers but a detriment for bond investors. From an investor's point of view, a call provision creates the risk that the call price will act as a ceiling on the price of the bonds. When interest rates decline, the price of a callable bond will not

[9]Gordon S. Roberts and Jerry A. Viscione, "The Impact of Seniority and Security Covenants on Bond Yields: A Note," *The Journal of Finance* 39 (December 1984): 1597–1602.

rise much above the call price if investors believe there is a strong pos-sibility the bond will be called in the near future.

The sections that follow deal with interest rate risk (including the relevance of bond duration), default risk, theories relating to the term structure of interest rates, yield spreads, and factors that affect market interest rates.

INTEREST RATE RISK

Price Risk

In May 1973, the U.S. Treasury issued 7% bonds maturing in May 1998; and in February 1982, the Treasury issued 14⅝% notes maturing in February 1992. As of mid-1988, the 7% bonds were selling at a yield to maturity of 8.09% and at a price that was 7% below face value. At the same time, the 14⅝% notes were selling at a yield to maturity of 7.56% and at a price 15% above face value. The rise in market interest rates between 1973 and 1988 caused a 7% decline in the price of the 7% bonds, and the drop in interest rates between early 1982 and mid-1988 caused a 15% increase in the price of the 14⅝% notes.

Rising interest rates mean falling bond prices, and falling interest rates mean rising bond prices. The bond market is "strong" when interest rates are declining, and the market is "weak" when interest rates are moving up. The reason for the inverse relationship between bond prices and yields is to be found in the constant bond payments. With the interest and principal payments being fixed in amount, the only way the yield on the 7% bonds could become 8.09% was for the price of the bonds to become much lower; and the only way the yield on the 14⅝% notes could decrease to 7.56% was for the price of the notes to become much higher. Investors were willing to buy the 7% bonds only at a substantial discount, but they were willing to pay a large premium for the 14⅝% notes.

Another way to view the inverse relationship between bond prices and yields is in terms of present value theory. An increase in market interest rates means that investors are requiring higher rates of return. The higher the required return, with no change in the expected income, the lower the present value of the investment. Or, a decrease in market interest rates means lower required returns and higher present values.

Following are three useful generalizations about the sensitivity of bond prices to changes in interest rates:

1. **The longer the maturity of a bond, given the coupon rate, the more sensitive the price of the bond to changes in interest rates.** This is illustrated in Table 14-3. With an increase or decrease in interest rates, the present values of the overall more remote cash flows of longer-term bonds are affected more than the present values of the cash flows from shorter-term bonds. The prices of all three 10% bonds in Table 14-4 fall when the required yield increases to 12%, but the price of the 20-year bond falls 14.94% compared to 11.30% for the 10-year bond and only 1.78% for the one-year bond.

|||| **TABLE 14-3**

Sensitivity of the Price of 10% Bonds to an Increase in the
Required Yield to Maturity

	1-Year Bond	10-Year Bond	20-Year Bond
Face value	$1,000	$1,000	$1,000
Coupon rate	10%	10%	10%
Market value at required yield of 10%	$1,000	$1,000	$1,000
Market value at required yield of 12%	$982.19	$887.02	$850.64
Percentage decrease in price due to increase in required yield	1.78%	11.30%	14.94%

2. **The sensitivity of the price of a bond to changes in required yields, given the coupon rate, increases with maturity but at a decreasing rate.** This is illustrated by the decreasing slope of the two curves for the 10% coupon bond in Figure 14-2 as well as by the price changes in Table 14-3. The difference between the percentage change in the price of the one-year bond and the 10-year bond, with a given change in yield, is much greater than the difference between the percentage change in the price of the 10-year bond and the 20-year bond with the same change in yield. This means, for example, that if an investor replaces a one-year bond with a 10-year bond, the increase in interest rate risk is much greater than if a 10-year bond is replaced with a 20-year bond.

3. **The lower the coupon rate, given the maturity, the more sensitive the price of a bond to a given change in interest rates.** This is illustrated in Table 14-4 and Figure 14-2, both of which are based upon the assumption that the bonds were selling at a yield to maturity of 10% before the required yield increased to 12% or decreased to 8%. Zero-coupon bonds and low-coupon bonds are considerably more sensitive to changes in interest rates than are bonds with high coupons. For example, an increase in the required yield from 10% to 12% decreases the price of a 20-year zero-coupon bond 30.3% compared to a decrease of 15% for a 10% coupon bond.

The greater sensitivity of zero-coupon bonds and low-coupon bonds to changes in interest rates is due to the longer average amount of time over which the cash flows are received.[10]

Reinvestment Rate Risk

Table 14-5 and Figure 14-3 show that the impact of an increase or decrease in the reinvestment rate depends upon the length of the holding period. For example, if the planned holding period for a 30-year, 10% bond is only five years, a reduction in the semiannual reinvestment rate from 5%

---

[10]As explained later in the chapter, a measure of the average amount of time over which the cash flows are received is called duration. Duration is a function of the bond's coupon rate and maturity.

|||| **FIGURE 14–2**

Percentage Change in Price if Yield to Maturity Decreases from 10% to 8% or Increases from 10% to 12% for 10% Coupon Bond and Zero-Coupon Bond

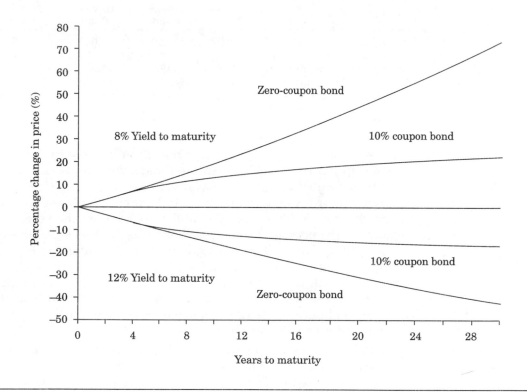

|||| **TABLE 14-4**

Percentage Change in Price of 10% Coupon Bonds and Zero-Coupon Bonds with a Change in Required Yield

| | Percentage Change in Price | | | |
| | Coupon Bond | | Zero-Coupon Bond | |
	5-Year Maturity	20-Year Maturity	5-Year Maturity	20-Year Maturity
Yield changes from 10% to				
8%	+8.1%	+19.8%	+9.6%	+44.3%
12%	−7.4	−15.0	−8.6	−30.3

to 4% reduces the accumulated value by less than 2% (29/1,629) and the realized yield by only 40 basis points (10.25% − 9.85%). But if the planned holding period is 30 years, this same reduction in the reinvestment rate lowers the accumulated value by nearly 31% (5,779/18,679) and the realized yield by 136 basis points (10.25% − 8.89%).

The higher the coupon rate, the greater the influence of the reinvestment rate on the total realized yield because there is a greater amount

|||| **TABLE 14-5**

Accumulated Values and Realized Yields: 30-Year, 10% Bond
(Semiannual Reinvestment Rates, 5% and 4%; Bond Is Sold or
Redeemed at Face Value)

Holding Period (Years)	5% Reinvestment Rate			4% Reinvestment Rate		
		Realized Yield			Realized Yield	
	Accumulated Value	Semi-annual	Annual	Accumulated Value	Semi-annual	Annual
5	$ 1,629^a	5.00%^{c}	10.25%	$ 1,600^b	4.81%	9.85%
10	2,653	5.00	10.25	2,489	4.67	9.56
15	4,322	5.00	10.25	3,804	4.55	9.31
20	7,040	5.00	10.25	5,751	4.47	9.14
25	11,467	5.00	10.25	8,653	4.41	9.01
30	18,679	5.00	10.25	12,900	4.35	8.89

^{a}\$50 · FVIFA$_{5\%,10}$ + \$1,000.
^{b}\$50 · FVIFA$_{4\%,10}$ + \$1,000.
^{c}\$1,000 = \$1,629 · PVIF$_{i\%,10}$ → i = 5.0%.

|||| **FIGURE 14–3**

Accumulated Values: 30-Year, 10% Bond (Semiannual Reinvestment Rates, 5%, 4%, and 0%)

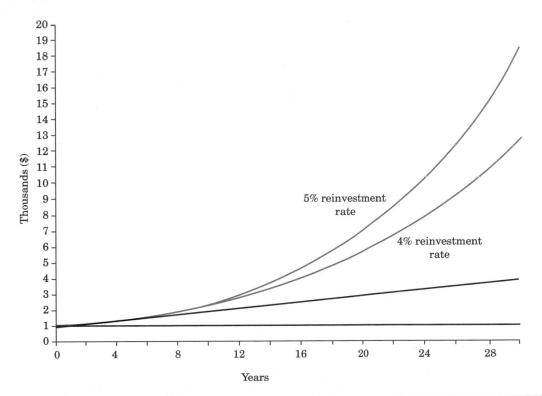

of interest to reinvest. If two bonds with different coupon rates are selling at the same yield to maturity, the bond with the higher coupon rate will earn a smaller total realized yield if the reinvestment rate is low, but a higher total realized yield if the reinvestment rate is high. This is illustrated in Tables 14-6 and 14-7 as well as in Figure 14-4. The bonds in Tables 14-6 and 14-7 are both selling at a yield to maturity of 10.00%. with semiannual compounding. The bond in Table 14-6, with a coupon rate of 10%, is selling at face value, and the bond in Table 14-7, with a coupon rate of only 4%, is priced at $485.18. Figure 14-4 plots realized yields against reinvestment rates for the bonds of Tables 14-6 and 14-7.

Bond Duration

The *duration* of an investment is a measure of the amount of time over which the payments are expected to be received. More specifically, the duration of a bond is a weighted average of the years over which the interest and principal payments are expected to be received, with the present values of the payments serving as the weights. Duration is a better measure of a bond's sensitivity to changes in market interest rates than the number of years to final maturity because it reflects the amount and timing of all the cash flows, not just the number of years until the final payment. Duration is particularly significant because of its usefulness in managing interest rate risk. As explained in Chapter 15, for investors who want to avoid taking undue interest rate risk, it is sensible to match the duration, rather than the maturity, of their bond holdings to their planned holding period.

Duration is a function of the two factors—maturity and coupon rate—that determine the sensitivity of a bond's price to changes in market interest rates. The lower the coupon rate, given the maturity, the longer the duration and the more sensitive the price of the bond to interest rate changes. For zero-coupon bonds, the duration is the same as the number

|||| **TABLE 14-6**

Realized Yield with Semiannual Compounding at Various Reinvestment Rates: 20-Year, 10%, Noncallable Bond Purchased for $1,000 and Held to Maturity (Yield to Maturity 10.00% with Semiannual Compounding)

| Reinvestment Rate | Face Value | Coupon Income | Interest on Interest | | Total Cash Inflow | Total Realized Yield |
			Amount	Percentage of Total Income		
0%	$1,000	$2,000	$ 0	0%	$ 3,000	5.65%
4	1,000	2,000	1,020	25	4,020	7.20
6	1,000	2,000	1,770	37	4,770	8.13
8	1,000	2,000	2,751	48	5,751	9.14
10	1,000	2,000	4,040	57	7,040	10.25
12	1,000	2,000	5,738	66	8,738	11.45
14	1,000	2,000	7,982	73	10,982	12.73
16	1,000	2,000	10,953	78	13,953	14.09

|||| **TABLE 14-7**

Realized Yield with Semiannual Compounding at Various
Reinvestment Rates: 20-Year, 4%, Noncallable Bond Purchased
for $485.18 and Held to Maturity (Yield to Maturity 10.25% with
Semiannual Compounding)

| Reinvest-ment Rate | Face Value | Coupon Income | Interest on Interest | | Total Cash Inflow | Total Realized Yield |
			Amount	Percentage of Total Income		
0%	$1,000	$800	$ 0	0%	$1,800	6.77%
4	1,000	800	408	18	2,208	7.87
6	1,000	800	708	28	2,508	8.56
8	1,000	800	1,101	38	2,901	9.35
10	1,000	800	1,616	47	3,416	10.25
12	1,000	800	2,295	56	4,095	11.25
14	1,000	800	3,193	64	4,993	12.36
16	1,000	800	4,381	71	6,181	13.57

|||| **FIGURE 14–4**

Total Realized Yields at Various Reinvestment Rates: 20-Year, 10%, Noncallable
Bond Purchased for $1000 and Held to Maturity, and 20-Year, 4%, Noncallable Bond
Purchased for $485.18 and Held to Maturity (Semiannual Compounding)

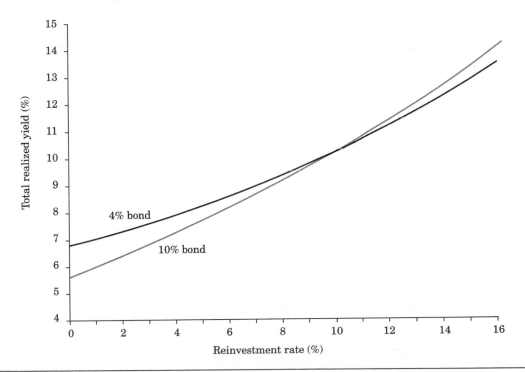

of years to maturity because no payments are received prior to maturity. For all other bonds, the duration is shorter than the maturity because some of the payments are received before the bond matures.

Duration is calculated with Equation 14-8:

$$D = \frac{\sum_{t=1}^{n} \frac{C_t}{(1 + i)^t} t}{\sum_{t=1}^{n} \frac{C_t}{(1 + i)^t}} \tag{14-8}$$

where

n = number of years to maturity

C_t = cash payment received in year t

i = yield to maturity (required rate of return)

Table 14-8 calculates the duration of a bond with the following characteristics:

Face value	$1,000
Coupon rate	8%
Annual interest (received at year-end)	$80
Yield to maturity	10%
Years to maturity	4
Market price	$936.58

Observe that the numerator of Equation 14-8 is the sum of the products of the present values of the cash flows and the number of years until the cash flows are received. For example, in year 2 in Table 14-8 the present value of the cash flow is $66.11, which is multiplied by 2, the year number of the cash flow. The denominator in Equation 14-8 is the present value of all the cash flows, which is the market value of the bond.

The difference between duration and maturity tends to be much larger for bonds of longer maturities. For example, the duration of a 20-year, 12% bond selling at a yield to maturity of 10% is only 9.09 years. The duration of a 10-year, 12% bond selling at a yield to maturity of 10% is

---

|||| **TABLE 14-8**
Calculation of Bond Duration

(1) Year	(2) Cash Flow (C_t)	(3) Present Value Factor $(1/1 + r)^t$	(4) Present Value (2×3)	(5) Year $\times$ Present Value (1×4)
1	$ 80	.9091	$ 72.73	$ 72.73
2	80	.8264	66.11	132.22
3	80	.7513	60.10	180.30
4	1,080	.6830	737.64	2,950.56
Total			936.58	3,335.81

Duration = 3,335.81/936.58 = 3.56 years

|||| **FIGURE 14–5**

Bond Durations versus Maturities: 6% Bond and 12% Bond Selling at Yield to
Maturity of 10%

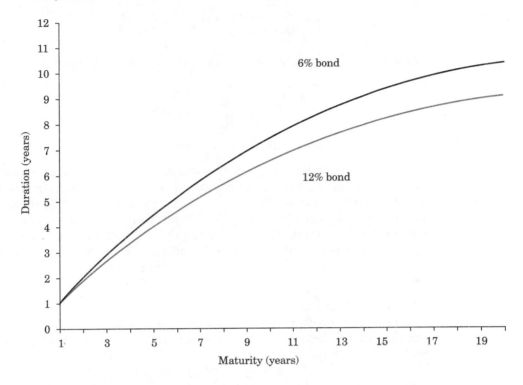

6.54 years. For the 10-year bond, the term to maturity and duration are
much closer than for the 20-year bond. Figure 14-5 shows the durations
of 6% bonds and 12% bonds maturing between 1 and 20 years and selling
at a yield to maturity of 10%.

For small changes in the level of interest rates, duration may be used
as an approximate measure of the interest rate elasticity of a bond's price.
The formula to measure the percentage change is

$$\frac{P_t - P_{t\text{-}1}}{P_{t-1}} = -D \frac{i_t - i_{t-1}}{(1 + i_{t-1)}} \tag{14-9}$$

where

P_t = price of the bond at time t

D = duration of the bond at the current interest rate

i_t = interest rate at time t

EXAMPLE 14-6   PERCENTAGE CHANGE IN A BOND'S PRICE
Consider a bond with the following characteristics:

Face value	$1,000.00
Market value	$960.07
Coupon	7%
Maturity	5 years
Yield to maturity	8%
Duration	4.37 years

If the yield increases to 9%, the approximate price change for the bond will be

$$-4.37 \times \frac{.09 - .08}{(1.08)} = -.0405 = -4.05\%$$

This figure compares with the actual change of -3.95%. ||||

Note that duration is an appropriate measure of price elasticity only for small changes in the level of interest rates. An examination of the duration formula shows that a rise in the yield shortens the duration. Therefore, duration is a relatively accurate measure of price sensitivity only for small shifts in the yield. In Example 14-6, the actual percentage change in the price was .10 percentage points (4.05 − 3.95) less than the change calculated on the basis of the duration.

DEFAULT RISK

The *promised yields to maturity* on corporate bonds are always greater than the promised yields on U.S. Treasury bonds of the same coupon rate and maturity because of the risk of default. In a monumental, though old, study of the relationships among corporate bond quality ratings, default rates, promised yields, and actual yields, W. Braddock Hickman found that of the $71.5 billion par value of straight corporate bonds issued in the years 1900 through 1943, $14.6 billion, or 20.4%, defaulted during that period.[11] Losses on defaulted issues ranged from very small to very substantial.

In the years since 1943, the economy has been much more stable than during the period of Hickman's study, and the default rate on corporate bonds has been much lower. Atkinson and Simpson found, for example, that during the 22 years from 1944 through 1965 the par value of the corporate bonds that defaulted was $496 million, or about 3.4% of the amount that defaulted from 1900 through 1943.

Figure 14-6 shows the par amount of new defaults of straight bonds from 1900 through 1965. During the period of Hickman's study, the volume of defaults reached peaks during or right after low points in the business cycle, but from 1944 through 1965 the economic recessions were not severe enough to produce a strong pattern.

As Table 14-9 shows, Hickman found a strong association between bond quality ratings (a composite of ratings by Standard & Poor's,

---

[11]W. Braddock Hickman, *Corporate Bond Quality and Investor Experience* (Princeton, N.J.: Princeton University Press, 1958).

|||| **FIGURE 14–6**
Bond Defaults, 1960–1965

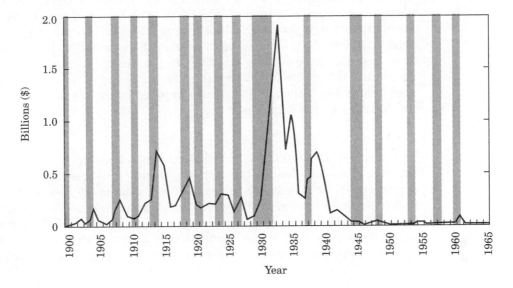

Shaded areas represent business contractions.

SOURCE: Thomas R. Atkinson and Elizabeth T. Simpson, *Trends in Corporate Bond Quality* (New York: National Bureau of Economic Research, 1967).

|||| **TABLE 14-9**
Default Rates, Promised Yields, and Actual Yields: Corporate Bonds Classified by Rating at Time of Offering, 1900–1943

Composite Rating	Comparable Standard & Poor's Rating	Percentage Defaulting Prior to Maturity	Promised Yield to Maturity	Actual Yield
I	AAA	5.9%	4.5%	5.1%
II	AA	6.0	4.6	5.0
III	A	13.4	4.9	5.0
IV	BBB	19.1	5.4	5.7
V–IX	Below BBB	42.4	9.5	8.6

SOURCE: W. Braddock Hickman, *Corporate Bond Quality and Investor Experience* (Princeton, N.J.: Princeton University Press, 1958).

Moody's, and Fitch's) and default rates, promised yields, and actual yields. However, the actual yields in his study are misleading in that many of the bonds were called before maturity at a premium, and Hickman's actual yields include these call premiums. That is the reason why most of the actual yields were greater than the promised yields, and it is also the reason why the actual yields were so high for the low-grade bonds.

In a later analysis of Hickman's data, Fraine and Mills set out to determine what the actual yields would have been without the call premiums. Their findings, which relate only to investment-grade (BBB and better) bonds, are shown in Table 14-10. The modified actual yields to maturity in the right-hand column were calculated by substituting the promised yield for the actual yield whenever the actual yield was larger. This had the effect of removing the call premiums. As modified by this procedure, the actual yields became the same for all four levels of investment-grade bonds, and they also dropped below the promised yields in all cases, as one would expect.

Bond Ratings and Yields: 1950–1966

The period from 1950 through 1966 was one of low, but generally rising interest rates and falling bond prices. During this period, the annual average yield on Aaa bonds (as calculated by Moody's) rose from 2.62% to 5.13%, for an increase of 96%, and the average yield on Baa bonds rose from 3.24% to 5.67%, for an increase of 75%. In a carefully prepared study, Soldofsky and Miller found that because of the declining bond prices, bond yields for this 17-year period were very low, as shown in Table 14-11.

IIII **TABLE 14-10**

Promised and Modified Actual Yields: All Large Corporate Issues of Investment-Grade Bonds, 1900–1943

Composite Rating	Comparable Standard & Poor's Rating	Promised Yield to Maturity	Actual Yield	Modified Actual Yield
I	AAA	4.5%	5.1%	4.3%
II	AA	4.5	5.1	4.3
III	A	4.9	5.0	4.3
IV	BBB	5.4	5.8	4.3

SOURCE: Harold G. Fraine and Robert H. Mills, "The Effects of Defaults and Credit Deterioration on Yields of Corporate Bonds," *The Journal of Finance* 16 (September 1961): 433.

IIII **TABLE 14-11**

Corporate Bond Yields: Annual Geometric Mean Returns, 1950–1966

Aaa	1.31%
Aa	1.45
A	2.15
Baa	1.30
Ba	4.51

SOURCE: Robert M. Soldofsky and Roger L. Miller, "Risk-Premium Curves for Different Classes of Long-Term Securities, 1950–1966," *The Journal of Finance* 24 (June 1969): 429–45.

Bond Ratings and Yields: Mutual Funds

A convenient way to compare actual yields on bonds of different risk classes is to compare the performance of bond mutual funds that have different investment policies. Three mutual fund management companies—Vanguard Group, Kemper Group, and Putnam Group—offer bond funds with clearly different investment policies. Each has one fund that invests in bonds rated BBB or higher and another that invests in bonds rated BBB or lower. In addition, each of the bond funds was ranked in the top 10 funds for its category over the 10 years from 1979 to 1989. Table 14-12 compares the performance of lower-quality, high-yield bonds with the performance of higher-quality bonds. Over the last five years, two of the three high-quality (investment-grade) bonds outperformed the lower-quality, high-yield bonds. Over 10 years, however, all three lower-quality bonds outperformed the high-quality bonds.

MATURITY AND THE TERM STRUCTURE OF INTEREST RATES

When two bonds are alike, or nearly so, in all respects except time to maturity, they usually sell at different yields because of the difference in their maturities. The relationship between yields and maturities is known as the *term structure of interest rates*. A plot of this relationship is called a *yield curve*. Each monthly issue of the *Treasury Bulletin* contains a yield curve showing the relationship between the yields and maturities for U.S. Treasury securities. The *Wall Street Journal* also regularly provides yield curve graphs. Economists and investment managers are interested in yield curves for a number of reasons, including what they may reveal about investor expectations relating to future interest rates and the relative attractiveness of bonds with different maturities.

|||| **TABLE 14-12**

Geometric Mean Returns and Betas: Six Corporate Bond Funds, as of July 31, 1989

	Bond Rating	5-Year Geometric Average	10-Year Geometric Average
Vanguard Group:			
High Yield Fund	BBB and lower	14.44	11.84
Investment Grade Bonds	BBB and higher	14.78	11.12
Kemper Group:			
High Yield	BBB and lower	16.17	13.46
Income & Capital Preservation	BBB and higher	13.76	10.76
Putnam Group:			
High Yield Trust	BBB and lower	13.82	12.22
Income Fund	BBB and higher	14.21	11.14

SOURCE: *Standard and Poor's/Lipper Mutual Fund Profile* (August 1989).

Ideally, yield curves would be plotted for securities that are identical in all respects except time to maturity so that other influences on the promised yields, such as default risk, call risk, and taxability, would not be reflected. U.S. Treasury securities come close to meeting this ideal, although they do have widely differing coupon rates, which affects their taxability.

The three yield curves in Figures 14-7, 14-8, and 14-9 illustrate three common shapes—upward-sloping, downward-sloping, and humped. Why did the term structure on December 31, 1987 (Figure 14-7) differ from that on December 31, 1980 (Figure 14-8), and why was the structure at the end of 1980 so different from that on November 30, 1978 (Figure 14-9)? Three main theories have been developed in an effort to answer questions of this kind: the expectations theory, the liquidity preference theory, and the market segmentation theory.

|||| **FIGURE 14–7**

Yield Curve, December 31, 1984

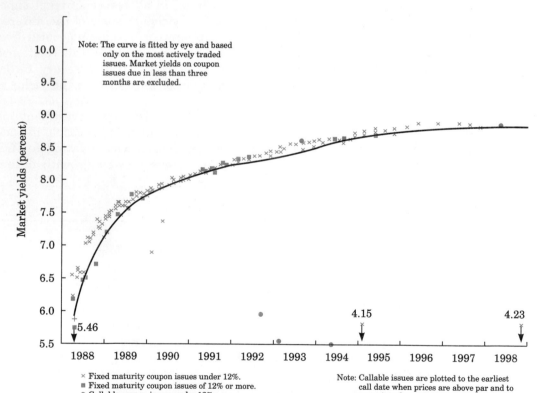

Note: The curve is fitted by eye and based only on the most actively traded issues. Market yields on coupon issues due in less than three months are excluded.

× Fixed maturity coupon issues under 12%.
■ Fixed maturity coupon issues of 12% or more.
● Callable coupon issues under 12%.
+ Bills. Coupon equivalent yield of the latest 13-week, 26-week, and 52-week bills.

Note: Callable issues are plotted to the earliest call date when prices are above par and to maturity when prices are at par or below.

SOURCE: *Treasury Bulletin.*

|||| **FIGURE 14–8**

Yield Curve, December 31, 1980

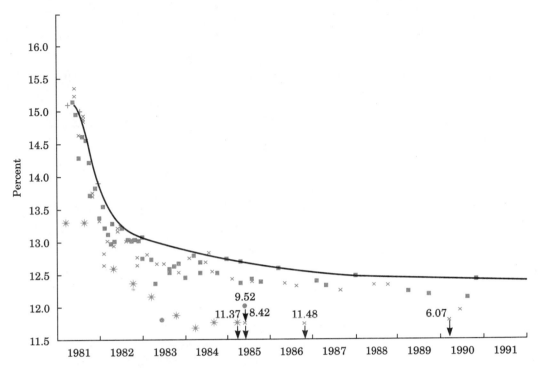

× Fixed coupon issues.
■ High coupon issues; 9% and higher fixed maturity issues.
● Callable issues. ▲ High coupon callable issues; plotted
   to earliest call date when prices are above par and
   to maturity date when prices are at par or below.
✳ 1¹/₂% exchange notes.
+ Bills; coupon equivalent of 3mo., 6mo., and 1yr. bills.

SOURCE: *Treasury Bulletin.*

Expectations Theory

The *expectations theory* assumes that the yield on a long-term bond is an average of the short-term yields that are expected to prevail over the life of the long-term bond. Its validity rests on the further assumption that investors and borrowers have no reason to prefer one maturity over another except for differences in the expected yields or costs. In other words, investors are indifferent to any variation in risk associated with different maturities. They consider long-term and short-term bonds to be perfect substitutes for one another, and therefore move freely from one maturity to another, always looking for the highest expected return.

With investors and borrowers both moving freely from one maturity to another, the yields on long-term securities are kept in line with the returns expected to prevail on short-term securities over the lives of the

|||| **FIGURE 14–9**

Yield Curve, November 30, 1978

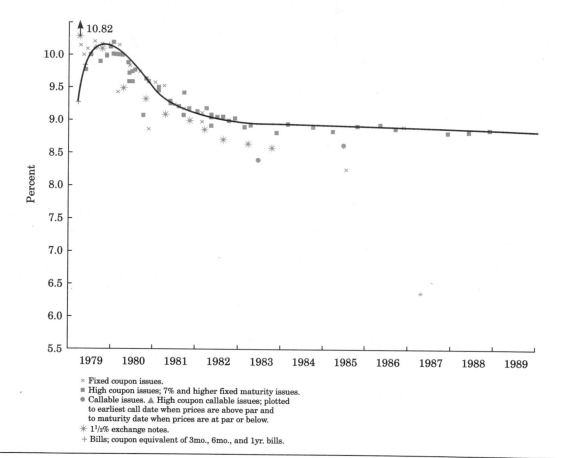

× Fixed coupon issues.
■ High coupon issues; 7% and higher fixed maturity issues.
● Callable issues. ▲ High coupon callable issues; plotted
   to earliest call date when prices are above par and
   to maturity date when prices are at par or below.
✳ 1½% exchange notes.
+ Bills; coupon equivalent of 3mo., 6mo., and 1yr. bills.

SOURCE: *Treasury Bulletin.*

long-term securities. If investors believe, for example, that the yields on bonds maturing in two years are lower than would be earned by investing in a series of two one-year bonds, they will sell two-year bonds and buy one-year bonds. This will depress the yields on one-year bonds and raise the yields on two-year bonds until the two-year yields are no longer lower than the yields that are expected to prevail on one-year bonds over the two-year period.

Arbitraging operations, like those just described, assume the indifference of borrowers and investors to differences in maturities and imply the following relationship:

$$(1 + {_0}R_T)^T = (1 + {_0}R_1)[1 + E({_1}R_1)][1 + E({_2}R_1)]$$
$$\ldots [1 + E({_{T-1}}R_1)]$$

(14-10)

where

$$_0R_T = \text{current yield on a bond having } T \text{ years to maturity}$$
$$_0R_1 = \text{current yield on a one-year bond}^{12}$$
$$E(_1R_1) = \text{expected one-year rate one year hence}$$
$$E(_2R_1) = \text{expected one-year rate two years hence}^{13}$$

Solving Equation 14-10 for the current rate on a T maturity bond results in

$$_0R_T = \{(1 + {}_0R_1)[1 + E(_1R_1)][1 + E(_2R_1)] \\ \dots [1 + E(_{T-1}R_1)]\}^{1/T} - 1.0 \qquad (14\text{-}11)$$

Equation 14-11 states that the current, or *spot,* rate on a T maturity bond is equal to the geometric mean of the current one-year rate and expected future or forward one-year rates.

As an application of Equations 14-10 and 14-11, the following shows how to calculate the yield at which a two-year Treasury note or bond should be trading if the current one-year rate is 7% and the expected one-year rate for Treasury securities one year ahead is 9%.

$$(1 + {}_0R_2)^2 = (1 + {}_0R_1)[1 + E(_1R_1)]$$
$$= (1 + .07)(1 + .09)$$
$$_0R_2 = \{(1 + {}_0R_1)[1 + E(_1R_1)]\}^{1/2} - 1.0$$
$$= [(1 + .07)(1 + .09)]^{1/2} - 1.0$$
$$= .07995 \text{ or } 8.0\%$$

The expectations hypothesis can be used to an unbiased estimate of future spot rates using data observable today. The one-period rate $T - 1$ years into the future, $E(_{T-1}R_1)$, may be determined by rearranging Equation 14-10:

$$E(_{T-1}R_1) = \frac{(1 + {}_0R_T)^T}{(1 + {}_0R_1)[1 + E(_1R_1)][1 + E(_2R_1)] \dots [1 + E(_{T-2}R_1)]} - 1.0$$
$$(14\text{-}12)$$

Since

$$(1 + {}_0R_1)[1 + E(_1R_1)][1 + E(_2R_1)] \dots [1 + E(_{T-2}R_1)] = (1 + {}_0R_{T-1})^{T-1}$$

Equation 14-12 becomes

$$E(_{T-1}R_1) = \frac{(1 + {}_0R_T)^T}{(1 + {}_0R_{T-1})^{T-1}} - 1.0 \qquad (14\text{-}13)$$

---

[12]Current yields on bonds having T years to maturity, $_0R_1, {}_0R_2, \dots, {}_0R_T$, are commonly called spot rates.

[13]The expected one-year rates T periods into the future, $E(_1R_1), E(_2R_1), \dots,$ are called forward rates.

With Equation 14-13, expected future rates can be determined with information available today in the form of yields on longer-term bonds.

For example, an investor in January 1981 would have observed eight-year government bond yields of 12.47% and seven-year bond yields of 12.43%. Using Equation 14-13, the investor's expected one-year rate seven years ahead would have been

$$E(_7R_1) = \frac{(1 + .1247)^8}{(1 + .1243)^7} - 1.0 = .1275$$

In January 1988, one-year interest rates were approximately one-half the rate predicted above. Does this imply that prediction based on the expectations hypothesis is worthless? No, the procedure shown here provides an unbiased estimate of a future rate based on the information available at the time the estimate was made. Market conditions and expectations change over time. In fact, yield curves can change dramatically based on new information available to the market.

According to the expectations hypothesis the shape of the yield curve is a function of aggregate investor expectations about future spot rates. Thus, if investors expect future short-term rates to be the same as the current spot rate, Equation 14-10 implies that long-term rates will also be equal to the current short-term rate, and the yield curve will be flat. When the yield curve is upward-sloping, as in Figure 14-7, the expectations hypothesis would indicate that future short-term rates are expected to be higher than the current short-term rate, and Equation 14-10 implies that long-maturity bonds will have higher rates than short-maturity bonds. Downward-sloping yield curves like Figure 14-8 imply that investors expect short-term rates to fall and are therefore willing to buy long-maturity bonds at lower yields than short-maturity bonds.

Liquidity Preference Theory

According to the *liquidity preference theory,* investors prefer short-term securities over long-term securities unless the yields on the longer-term securities are high enough to compensate for the greater interest rate risk. Borrowers, in turn, are willing to pay a premium for longer-term loans so they can avoid the risks of borrowing on a short-term basis. Bonds with different maturities are not perfect substitutes for one another, as is assumed by the expectations hypothesis.

The liquidity preference theory assumes that because of the liquidity preferences of investors and borrowers, yield curves will tend to be upward-sloping but can be downward-sloping when expected future short-term rates are low enough to more than offset the *liquidity premium.*

The relationship describing the liquidity preference hypothesis is very similar to Equation 14-11:

$$R_T = \{(1 + _0R_1)[1 + E(_1R_1) + _1L_1][1 + E(_2R_1) + _2L_1] \\ \dots [1 + E(_{T-1}R_1) + _{T-1}L_1]\}^{1/T} - 1.0 \tag{14-14}$$

where

$_jL_1$ = liquidity premium demanded by investors. $j = 1$ to $T - 1$.

The liquidity preference theory assumes that liquidity premiums increase with maturity, but at a decreasing rate. The underlying reason for this, as demonstrated earlier, is that interest rate risk increases with maturity but at a decreasing rate.

There are three reasons for believing that liquidity premiums are not very large. First, while it is true that longer-term investments are subject to greater interest rate risk, short-term investments have greater reinvestment rate risk. With short-term investments, the proceeds have to be reinvested frequently and possibly at a lower rate of return. Second, transactions costs are greater with short-term investments. Third, many investors in long-term securities are able to hedge against interest rate risk by matching the maturities of their assets with the maturities of their liabilities.[14]

Market Segmentation Theory

According to the *market segmentation theory* (also called the segmented markets theory or the hedging theory), interest rates for various maturities are determined by demand and supply conditions in the various segments of the market. Investors and borrowers have their "preferred habitats" and do not move readily from one maturity to another. Investors are not indifferent to differences in maturities. Instead, they have definite maturity preferences, which are based largely on the nature of their business.

In contrast to the liquidity preference theory, the market segmentation theory does not assume that all investors prefer short-term securities and that all borrowers prefer long-term loans if the interest rates are the same. Instead, investors have preferred holding periods, which are related to the maturities of their liabilities. The market segmentation theory assumes, for example, that commercial banks, with mostly short-term liabilities, prefer to invest in short-term loans and securities, while life insurance companies, with mostly long-term liabilities, prefer long-term investments. The term structure is thus determined by equilibrium rates set in several investor-specific markets.

Changes in the Yield Curve

Early in a period of economic expansion, when the outlook is for rising interest rates, all three theories would predict an upward-sloping yield curve. With the expectations theory, long-term rates are higher than short-term rates because short-term rates are expected to be higher in the future. The liquidity preference theory would predict an even greater upward slope than the expectations theory because of the liquidity premium. And, according to the market segmentation theory, short-term

---

[14]This immunization against interest rate risk is based on the concept of duration discussed earlier in the chapter.

rates are low in the early part of an expansion because the Federal Reserve System supplies banks and thrift institutions with ample reserves to stimulate business activity. Since banks, in particular, are major suppliers of short-term funds, there is downward pressure on short-term interest rates. At the same time, the demand for long-term funds to finance the expansion of production facilities is high, putting upward pressure on long-term rates.

In the later stages of an expansionary period, as the economy approaches a peak, the outlook is for declining growth rates and lower interest rates. Anticipating lower rates in the future, investors move funds out of short-term securities and into longer-term securities. This has the effect of raising short-term yields relative to long-term yields, and the result is a downward-sloping yield curve. Even under the liquidity preference theory, the yield curve will slope downward at such times if the expected decline in short-term rates is more than enough to offset the liquidity premium. The market segmentation theory explains the downward-slope in terms of conditions in the money and capital markets. With business still growing rapidly, the demand for short-term funds to finance working capital is heavy, and the Federal Reserve is tightening up on bank reserves to discourage inflation. The result is higher short-term rates. But business firms, having made heavy capital expenditures for several years and seeing a weaker economy ahead, cut back on their capital expenditures. Long-term rates become soft, and the yield curve slopes downward.

Empirical Evidence on the Term Structure

There is some merit in each of the three term structure theories. Elaborate studies have found considerable evidence in support of the expectations theory. There is also some evidence that liquidity premiums exist. For example, over a period of many years, there have been more upward-sloping yield curves than downward-sloping. Also, at cyclical peaks, when long-term rates are lower than short-term rates, the difference between the two is less than at cyclical troughs, when long-term rates are higher than short-term rates. The market segmentation theory is primarily useful in explaining temporary increases and decreases in the rates for certain maturities as a result of large new issues of securities or retirements of old issues. In summary, it seems that all three theories are useful in explaining the relationship between interest rates and maturities.

YIELD SPREADS

A *yield spread* is the difference between the promised yields on any two bond issues or classes of bonds. For example, it can be the difference between the promised yields on long-term U.S. Treasury bonds and Aaa-rated corporate bonds, or between Aaa-rated corporate bonds and Baa-rated corporate bonds, or between one-year Treasury securities and ten-year Treasury securities.

Yield spreads—other than spreads between different maturities—are caused primarily by differences in risk and taxability, but they are also influenced by anything that affects the supply of and demand for various kinds of bonds. For example, when borrowing by state and local governments is extraordinarily high, the promised yields on municipals tend to rise relative to the yields on taxable bonds, and the spreads narrow. Or, when investors begin to expect a decline in corporate profits, they may become more concerned about the riskiness of medium- and lower-grade corporate bonds, causing the yields on bonds rated Baa or lower to rise relative to the yields on higher-grade bonds.

Figure 14-10 is a graph of long-term bond yields for the years 1926 through 1984. As one would expect, it shows that the yields on Baa-rated corporate bonds have always been higher than the yields on Aaa-rated corporate bonds; that the yields on Aaa-rated corporate bonds have almost always been higher than the yields on long-term U.S. Treasury bonds; and that the yields on all three of these taxable bonds have generally been higher than the yields on Aaa-rated tax-exempt municipal bonds.

Figures 14-11 and 14-12 provide a closer look at the spread between the yields on Aaa-rated and Baa-rated corporate bonds for the years 1960

|||| **FIGURE 14–10**
Long-Term Bond Yields, 1926–1984

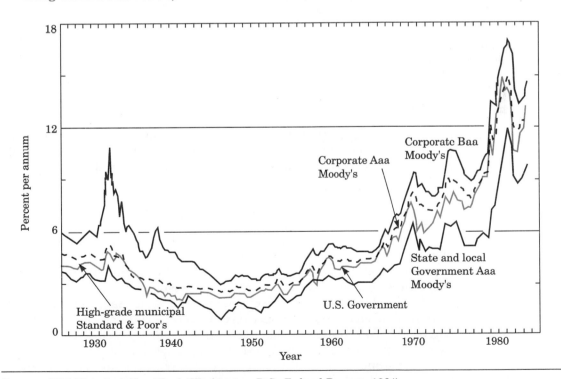

SOURCE: *1984 Historical Chart Book* (Washington, D.C.: Federal Reserve, 1984).

|||| **FIGURE 14–11**

Yield Spread: Baa Corporates versus Aaa Corporates

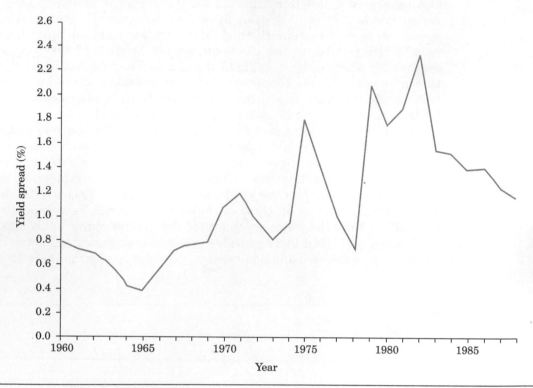

SOURCE: *Federal Reserve Bulletin.*

through 1988 on the basis of average annual promised yields. Two things are evident: the yield spreads changed substantially from time to time, and the trend over the 28-year period, along with the trend of interest rates, was upward. However, as shown in Figure 14-12, where an adjustment has been made for the change in scale by dividing the spread by the Aaa rate, there was no upward trend in the ratio of the yield spread to the promised yields on Aaa bonds.

FACTORS AFFECTING MARKET INTEREST RATES

There are, of course, many interest rates in the market, and they do not always move in the same direction or by the same amount at the same time. Therefore it is sometimes useful to select one rate to represent the short-term market. The rate on 90-day Treasury bills is often used for this purpose because it is relatively pure, in the sense that it is not affected by individual characteristics such as coupon rate, call risk, marketability, and default risk. Rates on longer-term U.S. Treasury securities are often used to represent the market for longer-term securities.

It is commonly believed that four factors are dominant in determining interest rate levels. These are the state of the economy, Federal Reserve

‖‖‖ **FIGURE 14–12**

Yield Spread: Baa Corporates versus Aaa Corporates, as a Percentage of Aaa
Corporate Yields

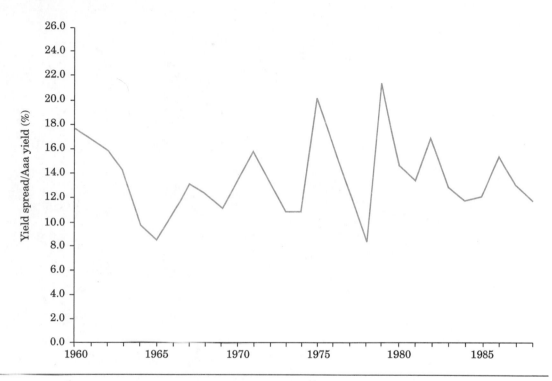

monetary policies, inflation expectations, and the federal budget. Three
additional factors that can be important are the rate of saving by individuals and corporations, international capital flows, and the amount of
premium required by investors to compensate for interest rate risk. The
first four factors (economic conditions, monetary policies, inflation expectations, and the federal budget) along with the risk premium for interest rate risk are considered below.

Economic Conditions

Interest rates have a tendency to move up and down with changes in the
volume of business activity. In periods of rapid economic growth, business
firms require large amounts of outside capital to finance increases in
working capital and fixed assets. The heavy business demand for borrowed funds, combined with increases in consumer borrowing, puts upward pressure on interest rates. Then, typically, after several years of
prosperity, business firms, consumers, or both cut back on their rate of
spending, the demand for borrowed funds decreases, and interest rates
decline as the economy falls into a recession.

Empirical evidence provides some support for the pattern just outlined. For example, Figure 14-13 shows a substantial decline in the yield

|||| **FIGURE 14–13**

Nominal and Real 10-Year Interest Rates

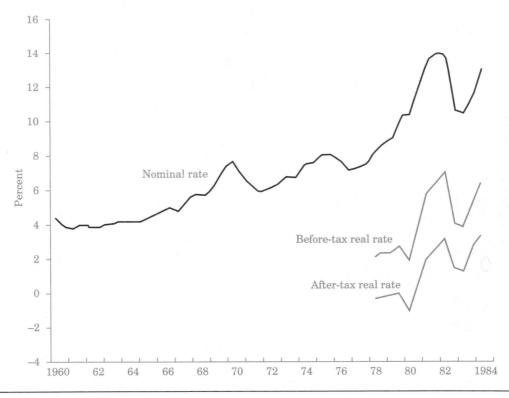

SOURCE: A. Stephen Holland, "Real Interest Rates: What Accounts for Their Recent Rise?"
Federal Reserve Bank of St. Louis, Review, 66 (December 1984): 18–29.

on 10-year U.S. Treasury securities in the recessions of 1970 and 1982, although rates did not decline in the recession of 1974 or the short recession of 1980. The correlation between changes in interest rates and changes in business activity is obviously far from perfect. Sometimes other factors, notably changes in the expected rate of inflation, have more impact than an increase or decrease in the demand for borrowed funds.

Monetary Policy

One of the primary objectives of the Federal Reserve System is to achieve stable economic growth at a low rate of inflation. The usual method of pursuing this objective is by controlling the growth rate of legal reserves in the banking system. Generally, the faster legal reserves are allowed to grow, the greater the volume of lending and the faster the growth rate of the money supply. The short-term effects of monetary policy on interest rates are a subject of considerable controversy. It is generally agreed, however, that if the supply of money grows faster than the economy for a considerable period of time, nominal interest rates will rise due to an increase in the rate of inflation.

Expected Rate of Inflation

Purchasing power risk arises from unanticipated inflation. More specifically, it is the risk that the rate of inflation will be greater than the investor expected when the investment was made, causing the real rate of return to be lower than expected. Because of this risk, market interest rates and other required returns include an inflation premium.

As shown in Equation 14-15, the market rate of interest on a risk-free security can be separated into two elements: the real rate and an inflation premium.

$$R_f = r + p \qquad (14\text{-}15)$$

where

$$R_f = \text{nominal, or market, rate of interest}$$
$$r = \text{expected real rate}$$
$$p = \text{inflation premium}$$

Ignoring any tax effect, the inflation premium is equal to the expected rate of inflation during the life of the investment.[15]

The only variable in Equation 14-15 that can be observed directly is the market rate of interest. The expected real rate is estimated by deducting an estimate of the expected inflation rate from the market rate. Thus, if the rate on a 90-day Treasury bill is 9% and the expected annualized rate of inflation for the next 90 days is thought to be 6%, the estimated before-tax real rate is 3%. Changes in market interest rates are caused by changes in expectations about inflation rates as well as by anything that might cause a change in the expected real rate, such as a large increase in the demand for borrowed funds.

The plot of nominal rates and estimated real rates on 10-year U.S. Treasury securities in Figure 14-13 indicates an increase in real rates during the early 1980s.[16] The higher real rates are believed to have been due, at least in part, to greater fluctuations in the growth rate of the money supply, which made future interest rates more uncertain and bonds riskier. Investors reacted by requiring higher real rates of return.

Government Deficits

Increases in government borrowing, unless offset by decreases in other borrowing, mean an increase in the total demand for loanable funds. Still, there is rarely a positive correlation between the amount of government

---

[15]For investors who pay income taxes, the inflation premium must be greater than the expected rate of inflation because taxes are paid on total interest, including the inflation premium. Suppose, for example, that the before-tax real rate would normally be 3%, making the after-tax rate 2% for an investor with a marginal federal and state tax rate of 33⅓%. If the expected inflation rate is 6%, Equation 14-15 implies that the market rate would be 9% (3% plus 6%). But this would leave an investor who pays a marginal tax rate of 33⅓% with a nominal after-tax return of 6% (9% minus one-third of 9%) and a real after-tax return of zero.

[16]The before-tax real rates were estimated by subtracting the average 10-year inflation expectations of a large number of institutional portfolio managers from the nominal rates. A. Steven Holland, "Real Interest Rates: What Accounts for Their Recent Rise?" *Federal Reserve Bank of St. Louis Review* 66 (December 1984): 18–29.

borrowing and the level of interest rates. This lack of correlation between government deficits and interest rates may be traced to the historical fiscal policy of the government. Until recently, deficits and government borrowing tended to increase during recessions, when the borrowing needs of business were relatively low, and to decrease during periods of economic expansion, when business borrowing tended to be high.

|||| **SUMMARY**

Three common measures of the promised returns on bonds and other fixed-income securities are the current yield, yield to maturity, and yield to call. All three are useful, but each has its shortcomings. The current yield ignores potential capital gains and losses and makes no provision for compounding. Yield to maturity is based upon the often unrealistic assumption that all interest payments will be reinvested at a rate of return equal to the yield to maturity, and yield to call assumes that the reinvestment rate will be equal to the yield to call.

If it appears that the reinvestment rate is likely to be higher or lower than the yield to maturity, or yield to call, the promised yield should be calculated with the formula for the total realized yield, which is based upon an estimate of the actual reinvestment rate. Total realized yield can be calculated to the earliest call date or to the maturity date. It is similar to yield to maturity and yield to call in one important respect: all three are geometric mean (or compound) annual rates of return.

Bond price movements are related inversely to changes in yields. Higher interest rates mean lower bond prices, and lower interest rates mean higher bond prices. If the coupon rate is fixed, which is true of most bonds, the only way the yield can change is for the price to change.

The promised yield at which a bond is traded depends upon the level of interest rates and the characteristics of the bond itself. Promised yields are a function of four factors: the real rate of interest, the expected rate of inflation, the risk premium, and the default premium. The risk premium is to compensate investors for risks other than default risk, while the default premium is to cover expected actual losses due to default. The expected yield is the promised yield minus the default premium.

The risks associated with fixed-income investments can be classified into five categories: (1) interest rate risk; (2) default risk; (3) marketability, or liquidity, risk; (4) call risk; and (5) inflation risk. Interest rate risk has become especially important as a result of the increased volatility of interest rates. Bonds with low coupons and long maturities (thus, with long durations) are the most sensitive to changes in interest rates.

The relative default risk of thousands of corporate and municipal bonds, as well as many issues of commercial paper, is evaluated by bond rating agencies. Generally, the assigned ratings have been a good measure of relative default risk and have been highly correlated with promised returns. The lower (poorer) the rating, the higher the promised return. The relationship between bond ratings and actual realized returns is uncertain.

The relationship between bond yields and maturities is known as the term structure of interest rates, and a graph of this relationship is a yield curve. Three principal theories have been developed to explain the shapes of yield curves, which may be upward-sloping, downward-sloping, humped in the middle, or nearly horizontal. The expectations theory is based upon the assumption that long-term rates are an average of present and expected future short-term rates. The liquidity preference theory assumes that yield curves tend to be upward-sloping because long-term loans are better for a borrower's liquidity and short-term loans are better for the liquidity of a lender. Thus, lenders demand, and borrowers are willing to pay, higher rates for longer-term loans. The market segmentation theory is based upon the notion that different types of investors (e.g., commercial banks and life insurance companies) have different maturity preferences, and the shape of the yield curve depends upon how their supplies of loanable funds compare to the demand. Evidence indicates that all three term structure theories have something to offer in explaining the relationship between yields and maturities.

The difference between the promised yields for any two bonds or any two classes of bonds is called a yield spread. One example is the spread between the yields on Aaa and Baa corporate bonds; another is the spread between the yields on U.S. Treasury bonds and high-grade municipal bonds. Unusually large or small spreads sometimes offer unusual investment opportunities.

|||| QUESTIONS

1. Explain how to calculate current yield. What are its shortcomings? Under what circumstances is current yield an accurate measure of the promised return?

2. Define yield to maturity. If a bond is purchased at a yield to maturity of, say, 12% and held to maturity, with all payments being made on time, what can cause the actual yield to be larger or smaller than the yield to maturity at which the bond was purchased?

3. If r is the semiannual rate that discounts the cash flows from a bond to a present value equal to the market price, what is the yield to maturity?

4. Why does the approximate formula for yield to maturity produce an answer that is only approximately correct?

5. If a bond is purchased for less than the call price and is called at a premium prior to maturity, why is the yield to call greater than the yield to maturity?

6. Explain how to calculate total realized yield.

7. Explain the inverse relationship between bond prices and yields, intuitively and in terms of the present value model.

8. If a high-coupon bond and a low-coupon bond are trading for the same yield to maturity, why does a low reinvestment rate make the total realized yield for the high-coupon bond lower than for the low-coupon bond, while a high reinvestment rate makes the total realized yield for the high-coupon bond higher than for the low-coupon bond?

9. Why are longer-term bonds subject to more interest rate risk than shorter-term bonds with the same coupon rate? Explain in terms of present value interest factors.

10. Define bond duration. Why is duration the same as the maturity for zero-coupon bonds but shorter than the maturity for bonds that pay periodic interest?

11. Write out the bond duration formula. Explain what the numerator and the denominator represent.

12. What combination of bond characteristics produces the greatest interest rate risk?

13. In terms of duration, explain why a 20-year bond is not twice as interest-sensitive as a 10-year bond.

14. Why do high-coupon bonds have shorter durations than low-coupon bonds?

15. What is meant by the term structure of interest rates?

16. Explain the expectations theory. What are the underlying assumptions?

17. Explain the liquidity preference theory, including the reasons why the yield curve is ordinarily expected to be upward-sloping. Under what circumstances is the yield curve expected to be downward-sloping?

18. Why is the liquidity premium thought to be not very large?

19. Explain the market segmentation theory.

20. Explain why an upward-sloping yield curve in the early part of a business expansion is consistent with all three theories.

21. Explain what is meant by the "real rate" of interest. How is the real rate estimated?

22. Comment on the factors that influence market rates of interest.

23. Explain the meanings of risk premium and default premium. Explain why the difference between the promised return and the expected return is the amount of the default premium.

24. Why are long-term U.S. Treasury bonds quite risky?

25. Explain why interest rate risk varies directly with the maturity and inversely with the coupon rate.

26. What is reinvestment risk?

27. Explain why purchasing power risk is not simply the risk that there will be inflation, causing payments received in the future to have less real value, or even the risk that the rate of inflation will increase.

28. Explain what happened to the spread between the yields of Aaa and Baa corporate bonds during the period from 1960 through 1984.

|||| PROBLEMS

1. Calculate the yield to maturity of the following bond:

Par value	$1,000
Market price	$800
Years to maturity	6
Coupon rate	12%
Interest payments	Semiannual

2. Using the approximate formula, calculate the approximate yield to maturity for the following bond:

Par value	$1,000
Market price	$900
Years to maturity	10
Coupon rate	11%

   Compare your approximate answer with the correct answer, to two decimal places.

3. Consider the following bond:

Coupon	10% (semiannual payments)
Par value	$1,000
Maturity	5 years
Current price	$1,124
Call price	$1,100 (effective in 1 year)

   Determine the appropriate yield measure.

4. The following is a bond quotation from the *Wall Street Journal:*

XYZ	9.2s09	9.2	26	100	+1

   Determine the amount of interest on interest an investor could earn if all of the interest payments are reinvested at 9% over the remaining life of the bond. Use today's date as the purchase date and assume that the bond will be due on the same month and day in the year 2009.

5. Calculate total realized yield for the following bond:

Par value	$1,000	Semiannual interest	$50
Purchase price	$900	Years to maturity	10
Coupon rate	10%	Assumed reinvestment rate	8%

6. Calculate the annual value relatives, annual holding period returns, value relative for the five-year period, and total realized yield, with annual compounding, given the following information:

	Year				
	1	2	3	4	5
Cost of bond at beginning of five-year period (V_0)	$800				
Annual interest	90	$ 90	$ 90	$ 90	$ 90
Interest for prior years		90	180	270	360
Interest on interest:					
Current year		8	17	27	38
Prior years			8	25	52
Value of bond at year-end	850	900	880	950	1,000

7. Calculate the duration of the following bond:

Par value	$1,000
Coupon rate	12%
Years to maturity	4
Interest payments	Semiannual
Yield to maturity	8%

8. Given that the current one-year yield on Treasury securities is 7.0%, and investors expect the one-year rate to be 7.5% next year and 9.0% the year after, determine the approximate current yield to maturity on a three-year Treasury security.

9. In March 1988, the following Treasury yield information was available:

Maturity	Yield
Mar 88	5.17%
Mar 89	6.82
Mar 90	7.21
Mar 91	7.43
Mar 92	7.57

Estimate the expected one-year rate for the 12 months beginning March 1989.

10. Given the following, what are the promised return and the expected return?

Risk premium	1.0%
Real rate	3.0
Default premium	0.5
Expected inflation rate	4.0

Problems 11 and 12 assume that the date is 12/07/1988 and that all bonds mature on 12/07 in the year indicated.

11. Determine the required rate of return for the class of bonds that includes the following:

    IBM 7s 1998 that is selling at a price to provide a current yield of 10%. Assume the coupon is paid annually. (*Hint:* Recall that the current yield is one of the numbers provided in the *Wall Street Journal* bond quotation.)

12. Determine the value of the following bond that belongs to the risk class that requires a return of 12%:

    IBM 16s 1998, call date 1993 at a call premium of 1070 (assume semiannual payment of interest).

13. Determine the percentage of total income earned from interest on interest on the IBM 12s 2014, assuming they are purchased for $1,200 on December 31, 1993 and mature December 31, 2014.

14. An investor wishes to determine the duration of the following bond and make an estimate, based on its duration, of the percentage the price of the bond would change if the yield were to increase 150 basis points immediately. With present value calculations, determine the exact percentage by which the price of the bond would change.

Par value	$1,000
Coupon rate	10%
Years to maturity	6
Market price	$ 917.75

|||| SELECTED REFERENCES

Atkinson, Thomas R., and Elizabeth T. Simpson. *Trends in Corporate Bond Quality* New York: National Bureau of Economic Research, 1967.

Bierwag, G. O., George Kaufman, and Alden L. Toeves. "Single Factor Duration Models in a Discrete General Equilibrium Framework." *The Journal of Finance* 37 (May 1982): 325–38.

Branch, Ben. "Testing the Unbiased Expectations Theory of Interest Rates." *Financial Review* 13 (Fall 1978): 51–66.

Cagan, Phillip, and Jack M. Guttentag. *Essays on Interest Rates,* vols. 1 and 2. New York: National Bureau of Economic Research, 1969 and 1971.

Cox, John C., Jonathan E. Ingersoll, Jr., and Stephen A. Ross. "A Reexamination of Traditional Hypotheses about the Term Structure of Interest Rates." *The Journal of Finance* 36 (September 1981): 769–99.

Cramer, Robert H., and James A. Seifert. "Measuring the Impact of Maturity on Expected Return and Risk." *Journal of Bank Research* (Autumn 1976): 229–35.

Darst, David M. *The Handbook of the Bond and Money Markets.* New York: McGraw-Hill, 1981.

Fisher, Lawrence. "Determinants of Risk Premiums on Corporate Bonds." *Journal of Political Economy* 67 (June 1959): 217–37.

Fraine, Harold G., and Robert H. Miller. "Effect of Defaults and Credit Deterioration on Yields of Corporate Bonds." *The Journal of Finance* 16 (September 1961): 423–34.

Farrell, James L., Jr. *Guide to Portfolio Management.* New York: McGraw-Hill, 1983.

Haugen, Robert A., and Dean W. Wichern. "The Elasticity of Financial Assets." *The Journal of Finance* 29 (September 1974): 1229–40.

Hawawini, Gabriel A., and Ashok Vora. "Yield Approximations: A Historical Perspective." *The Journal of Finance* 37 (March 1982): 145–56.

Hickman, W. Braddock. *Corporate Bond Quality and Investor Experience.* Princeton, N.J.: Princeton University Press, 1958.

Homer, Sidney, and Martin L. Leibowitz. *Inside the Yield Book.* Englewood Cliffs, N.J.: Prentice-Hall, 1972.

Hopewell, M. H., and G. C. Kaufman. "Bond-Price Volatility and Term to Maturity: A Generalized Respecification." *American Economic Review* (September 1973): 749–53.

Kane, Edward J. "The Term Structure of Interest Rates: An Attempt to Reconcile Teaching with Practice." *The Journal of Finance* 25 (May 1970): 361–74.

Kessel, Reuben A. *The Cyclical Behavior of the Term Structure of Interest Rates.* New York: National Bureau of Economic Research, 1965.

Kolb, Robert W. *Interest Rate Futures,* pp. 42–58. Richmond, Va.: Richard F. Dame, 1982.

Livingston, Miles, and Suresh Jain. "Flattening of Bond Yield Curves for Long Maturities." *The Journal of Finance* 37 (March 1982): 157–67.

Malkiel, Burton G. *The Term Structure of Interest Rates.* Princeton, N.J.: Princeton University Press, 1966.

Meiselman, David. *The Term Structure of Interest Rates.* Englewood Cliffs, N.J.: Prentice-Hall, 1962.

Nelson, Charles R. *The Term Structure of Interest Rates.* New York: Basic Books, 1972).

Perritt, Gerald W., and L. Kay Shannon. *The Individual Investor's Guide to No-Load Mutual Funds.* Chicago, Ill.: Investment Information Services Press, 1985.

Roberts, Gordon S., and Jerry A. Viscione. "The Impact of Seniority and Security Covenants on Bond Yield: A Note." *The Journal of Finance* 39 (December 1984): 1597–1602.

Roley, V. Vance. "The Determinants of the Treasury Security Yield Curve." *The Journal of Finance* 36 (December 1981): 1103–26.

Sinkey, Joseph F., Jr. "The Term Structure of Interest Rates: A Time-Series Test of the Kane Expected-Change Model of Interest-Rate Forecasting." *Journal of Money, Credit and Banking* (February 1973): 193–200.

Soldofsky, Robert M., and Roger L. Miller. "Risk Premium Curves for Different Classes of Long-Term Securities, 1950–1966." *The Journal of Finance* 24 (June 1969): 429–45.

Tinic, Seha M., and Richard R. West. *Investing in Securities: An Efficient Markets Approach.* Reading, Mass.: Addison-Wesley, 1979.

Van Horne, James C. *Financial Market Rates and Flows.* Englewood Cliffs, N.J.: Prentice-Hall, 1978.

Yawitz, Jess B., George H. Hempel, and William J. Marshall. "The Use of Average Maturity as a Risk Proxy in Investment Portfolios." *The Journal of Finance* 30 (May 1975): 325–33.

15 FIXED-INCOME INVESTMENT STRATEGIES

The development of a bond investment strategy requires decisions on such things as the kinds of bonds to hold, the maturity structure of the portfolio, and the circumstances under which portfolio changes will be made. For strategic purposes, bonds can be classified broadly with respect to quality, maturity, coupon rate, call features, and taxability. The first four attributes all have a bearing on the riskiness and the expected rate of return. The fifth attribute, taxability, determines the portion of the return that will remain after taxes.

If an investor is highly averse to risk, but is willing to commit a certain amount of funds to fixed-income securities for a certain period of time, a logical choice would be zero-coupon bonds derived from U.S. Treasury securities.[1] These bonds are completely free of default risk, reinvestment rate risk, and call risk. Also, price risk is of no concern if the investor knows that the funds will not be needed before the bonds mature. But even with default-free zero-coupon bonds, the investor is still subject to the risk that the investment is being made at a poor time, which is called "timing risk." Timing risk can be defined as the risk that bonds are being purchased when interest rates are at or near a cyclical low point. This risk can be reduced by diversifying over time, which involves investing more or less equal amounts at regular intervals of not more than six months or a year.

Since most bonds are coupon bonds, reinvestment rate risk is important to many bond investors. One way to reduce, and possibly eliminate, reinvestment rate risk is by adopting a strategy known as portfolio immunization. This method of dealing with reinvestment rate risk will be discussed after considering several portfolio management techniques that involve changes in the composition of the portfolio with a view to achieving superior performance.

MANAGING FOR HIGHER YIELDS

Generally, if bond investors want to earn higher yields than are available on bonds of the highest quality, they must be willing to accept greater risk and possibly manage their portfolios more actively.[2] For example,

---

[1]Investors with relatively high marginal tax rates who are willing to accept a small amount of default risk might find it more profitable to invest in a diversified portfolio of high-quality (possibly insured) zero-coupon municipal bonds with appropriate maturities.

some investors seek higher returns by investing in a portfolio of medium- or lower-grade corporate bonds that entail significant credit risk. Another approach is through aggressive management rather than following a buy-and-hold strategy.

Aggressive management of a bond portfolio usually involves rather frequent changes in the composition of the portfolio by making various kinds of *bond swaps,* or exchanges. Another strategy explained in this chapter is known as *riding the yield curve.* Yield curve riders try to earn higher returns by buying and selling when there is an upward-sloping yield curve.

BOND SWAPS

Changes are made in actively managed fixed-income portfolios whenever the manager sees an opportunity to improve the portfolio's performance. These changes often involve selling some of the portfolio's current holdings and replacing them with others, which is known as bond swapping. The following paragraphs examine five types of widely used bond swaps.

Pure Yield Pickup Swap

It is not uncommon for two bonds that are nearly the same in all important respects to be trading at slightly different yields. For example on September 15, 1985, two U.S. Treasury bonds were quoted as follows:[3]

Coupon	Maturity	Bid	Ask	Yield to Maturity	Current Yield
10⅜	May 1995	99.24	100.00	10.37%	10.38%
11¼	May 1995	104.04	104.08	10.54	10.79

An investor holding the 10⅜s of May 1995 might be able to earn a higher yield by switching to the 11¼s of May 1995.

EXAMPLE 15-1   PURE YIELD PICKUP SWAP

To illustrate the *pure yield pickup swap,* assume that a large investor owns $1 million of the 10⅜% Treasury bonds that were purchased a few years earlier at 99.24 (i.e., 99²⁴/₃₂), the same price at which they could have been sold on the day of these quotations. To estimate how much the

---

[2]Sometimes market conditions make it possible to earn higher after-tax returns without taking greater risks. For example, when the supply of municipal bonds is so large that financial institutions and individual investors with high marginal tax rates do not want to hold the entire supply, the yields must be high enough to attract investors with lower marginal tax rates. As a result, many individuals are able to earn higher after-tax returns on high-grade municipal bonds than are available on taxable securities of comparable quality.

[3]These quotations, from the *Wall Street Journal,* are representative midafternoon quotations supplied by the Federal Reserve Bank of New York, based on transactions of $1 million or more. We cannot be sure that the difference in yields we are seeing here actually existed at any one time, and if the difference did exist, it was no doubt soon eliminated by the arbitraging activities of government securities dealers or other large traders. We are using these quotations because they provide a convenient example.

investor might gain by selling the 10⅜'s at no gain or loss and buying the 11¼'s with the proceeds, the accumulated values at maturity are compared with the total realized yields for the two bonds at two different assumed semiannual reinvestment rates, 5% and 4%.

The total realized yields in Table 15-1 are the annual yields with semiannual compounding. The total realized yield, as defined here, is the annual rate at which the accumulated value of the investment has grown, or is expected to grow. An investment of $1,032,083 in the old 10⅜% bonds will grow to $2,715,299 in 10 years if the semiannual reinvestment rate is 5%. The compound annual growth rate, or realized yield, is $(2,715,299/1,032,083)^{1/9.67} - 1.0$, or 10.52%. The investment in the 11¼% bonds will grow slightly faster, providing a yield 9 basis points higher (10.61% − 10.52%) than the yield on the 10⅜% bonds. Both are higher than the yield to maturity quotations in the *Wall Street Journal,* which are the semiannual yield multiplied by two and assume a reinvestment rate equal to the yield to maturity.

Table 15-2 shows that with an assumed reinvestment rate of 4%, the projected yield for the 11¼% bonds is only 5 basis points (9.84% − 9.79%) higher than the yield for the other issue. A decrease in the reinvestment rate reduces the yield for the 11¼% bonds more than it reduces the yield of the 10⅜% bonds. The higher the coupon rate the greater the amount of income to reinvest, thus the greater the decrease in the yield due to a reduction in the reinvestment rate. ||||

Substitution Swap

A *substitution swap* resembles a pure yield pickup swap in that both involve the sale and purchase of bonds that are very similar in terms of quality, coupon, maturity, and other important characteristics. The two swaps differ in two ways. First, the yield pickup swap always involves trading for a bond that offers a higher yield, whereas the substitution swap may involve swapping for a bond that offers a lower yield based upon current prices but is expected to offer a higher yield over the next several months or years as a result of an increase in its price relative to the price of the bond that is being sold. Second, a substitution swap is often made with the intention of holding the newly acquired bond only until its price has moved to a "normal" level relative to the prices of other bonds. The period during which this is expected to happen is called the workout period. Thus, in using a substitution swap, a bond manager is trading on a perceived aberration in the yield spread.

Even though a pure yield pickup swap or substitution swap might be more likely to involve corporate bonds, where the market is apt to be less efficient than with U.S. Treasury securities, we will illustrate the substitution swap with the same two U.S. Treasury bonds that were used to illustrate the yield pickup swap. In this case, assume the investor expects that within a year the yield on the 11¼% bonds will drop and the price will rise relative to the price for the 10⅜% bonds.

TABLE 15-1

Pure Yield Pickup Swap: Accumulated Values and Total Realized Yields at 5% Semiannual Reinvestment Rate

Calculations

Proceeds from sale of 10⅜% bonds at bid price of 99²⁴/₃₂, or 99.75% of face value:

Principal amount (.9975 × $1,000,000)	$ 997,500
Four months' interest (May to September) at 10⅜% (.10375 × $1,000,000 × $\frac{4}{12}$)	34,583
Total proceeds	$1,032,083

Cost of 11¼% bonds per $100 of face value, including four months' accrued interest:

Asked price (104⁸/₃₂)	$104.25
Four months' interest ($11.25 × 4/12)	3.75
Cost of new bonds per $100 of face value	$108.00

(The cost of the bonds can also be expressed as 108% of the face value, or as a decimal, 1.08.)

Amount of 11¼% bonds purchased with proceeds from the old bonds ($1,032,083/1.08)	$955,632

Semiannual interest:

Old bonds (.10375 × $1,000,000 × 0.5)	$51,875
New bonds (.1125 × $955,632 × 0.5)	$53,755
Amount of investment for purpose of calculating total realized yields	$1,032,083

(This is the amount of the investment for both the old and new bonds since it is the amount that will be received from the old and invested in the new.)

	Old Bonds		New Bonds	
Accumulated value on May 15, 1995				
Par value	(33.066 × $51,875)	$1,000,000	($1,032,083/1.08)	$ 955,632
Future value of 20 semiannual interest payments at the semiannual rate of 5% (FVIVA₅%,₂₀ × payment)		1,715,299	(33.066 × $53,755)	1,777,463
Total accumulated value		$2,715,299		$2,733,095
Value relative				
Ending value/beginning value	(2,715,299/1,032,083)	2.6308	(2,733,095/1,032,083)	2.6481
Semiannual realized yield	$[(2.6308)^{1/19.33} - 1.0]$	5.13%	$[(2.6481)^{1/19.33} - 1.0]$	5.17%
Total realized yield	$(2.6308)^{1/9.667} - 1.0$	10.52%	$(2.6481)^{1/9.667} - 1.0$	10.60%

|||| **TABLE 15-2**

Pure Yield Pickup Swap with 5% and 4% Reinvestment Rates: Summary Data

	Summary at 5% Semiannual Reinvestment Rate		
	Total Accumulated Value	Total Realized Yield	Reported Yield to Maturity
11¼% bonds	$2,733,095	10.60%	10.54%
10⅜% bonds	2,715,299	10.52	10.37
Difference	17,796	0.08	0.17

	Summary at 4% Semiannual Reinvestment Rate		
	Total Accumulated Value	Total Realized Yield	Reported Yield to Maturity
11¼% bonds	$2,556,348	9.84%	10.54%
10⅜% bonds	2,544,734	9.79	10.37
Difference	11,614	0.05	0.17

EXAMPLE 15-2 SUBSTITUTION SWAP

To analyze the substitution swap, consider the sale of one 10⅜% bond for 99²⁴/₃₂, or 99.75% of face value, and the purchase of one 11¼% bond for 104⁸/₃₂, or 104.25% of face value. The swap is based upon the following facts and assumptions:

1. Interest rates will neither rise nor fall appreciably over the next 12 months, and the asked price for the 10⅜% bonds will remain at 100.

2. The yield to maturity of the 11¼% bonds (based upon the asked price) will drop from 10.54% to 10.37%, which is the yield on the 10⅜% bonds.

3. On September 15, 1986 (one year from the date of the quotations), both bonds, which mature May 15, 1995, will be 8⅔ years, or 17⅓ semiannual periods, from maturity.

4. The asked price for the 11¼% bonds on September 15, 1986, will be based upon a yield to maturity of 10.37%, or a semiannual discount rate of 5.185% (10.37/2).

5. The bonds will be sold at the bid price at the end of one year, which will be ⁸/₃₂ below the asked price.

6. The first semiannual interest payment will be reinvested at a semiannual rate of 5%.

Before analyzing the results of the swap based upon the above assumptions, let us recall that reported yields to maturity are based upon asked prices.

Table 15-3 presents the calculations for the substitution swap. Note that the predicted advantage of the swap is .81% (11.47% − 10.66%). ||||

Sector or Intramarket Swap

With a *sector* or *intramarket swap,* the investor tries to take advantage of changing yield spreads between bonds in different sectors of the market. Sectors are based upon variables such as bond quality, coupon rate, type of issue, and type of issuer. For example, as noted in Chapter 14, from 1960 through 1988 the yields on Baa corporate bonds ranged from about 8% to 21% higher than the yields on Aaa-rated bonds. On the basis of this evidence, an investor might shift funds from Aaa bonds to Baa bonds when the spread (as a percentage of the Aaa yields) is close to 20% and shift from Baa bonds to Aaa bonds when the spread is less than 10%.

Sometimes the yield on a particular type of security rises to extraordinary heights relative to other yields because of an abnormal decline in the demand for the security. This happened, for example, in the fall of 1973 when the yields on GNMA pass-through securities rose to unprecedented levels relative to the yields on corporate bonds because most savings and loan associations and mutual savings banks, which had been major buyers of Ginnie Maes, had virtually no new funds to invest. Investors who bought Ginnie Maes in the fall of 1973 realized substantial gains over the next several months as the spreads relative to corporate bonds narrowed by more than 75 basis points.

⦀⦀ **TABLE 15-3**

Substitution Swap Using 10⅜% and 11¼% Treasury Issues

	Swap Is Not Made: 10⅜% Bond		Swap Is Made: 11¼% Bond	
Accumulated value in one year				
Present value of par (par × PVIF$_{5.1875\%,17.33}$)	($1,000 × .41625)	$ 416.25	($1,000 × .41625)	$ 416.25
Present value of interest payments (PMT × PVIFA$_{5.1875\%,17.33}$)	($51.875 × 11.253)	583.75	($56.25 × 11.253)	632.98
Ask price of the bond		$1,000.00		$1,049.23
− spread between bid and ask	(8/32)	(2.50)	(8/32)	(2.50)
Bid price		$ 997.50		$1,046.73
Two semiannual interest payments	(2 × $51.875)	103.75	(2 × $56.25)	112.50
Interest on first interest payment @ 5% semiannually	(.05 × $51.875)	2.59	(.05 × $56.25)	2.81
Total accumulated value		$1,103.84		$1,162.04
Value relative				
Ending value/beginning value	(1,103.84/997.5)	1.1066	(1,162.04/1,042.5)	1.1147
Total realized yield	(1.1066 − 1.0)	10.66%	(1.1147 − 1.0)	11.47%

EXAMPLE 15-3   INTRAMARKET SWAP

As an illustration of the intramarket swap, let us again assume that the bond to be sold is the 10⅜% Treasury bond maturing May 15, 1995, and selling at 100 to yield 10.37%. The bond to be purchased is an A-rated utility bond also maturing May 15, 1995.* This bond has a 12⅜% coupon and is selling at $993.10 to yield 12.5%. If the investment horizon is one year and the anticipated yields for the two bonds in one year are 10.37% for the Treasury and 12% for the utility, the expected advantage of the swap is as shown in Table 15-4.

Of critical importance in the sector swap is the reliability of the bond rating on the newly acquired bond. If the bond issue defaults, or if the yield spread between the swapped issues widens, this strategy can backfire. ||||

Rate Anticipation Swap

Rate anticipation swaps are designed to benefit from changes in market interest rates. Thus, the swap is based upon interest rate forecasts and tends to be very risky. If the investor's forecast is reasonably accurate, large gains can be made, but if the forecast is inaccurate, the losses can

*Identical maturity dates are not a requirement of this swap, but are used here to simplify the calculations.

|||| **TABLE 15-4**

Sector Swap between a Treasury Bond and an A-Rated Utility Bond

	Swap Is Not Made: 10⅜% Bond		Swap Is Made: 12⅜% A-Rated Bond	
Accumulated value in one year				
Present value of par (par × PVIF$_{5.1875\%,17.33}$)	($1,000 × .41625)	$ 416.25	($1,000 × .36429)	$ 364.29
Present value of interest payments (PMT × PVIFA$_{5.1875\%,17.33}$)	($51.875 × 11.253)	583.75	($61.875 × 10.595)	655.57
Ask price of the bond		$1,000.00		$1,019.86
− spread between bid and ask	(8/32)	(2.50)	(0)	0.00
Bid price		$ 997.50		$1,019.86
Two semiannual interest payments	(2 × $51.875)	103.75	(2 × $61.875)	123.75
Interest on first interest payment @ 5% semiannually	(.05 × $51.875)	2.59	(.05 × $61.875)	3.09
Total accumulated value		$1,103.84		$1,146.70
Value relative				
Ending value/beginning value	(1,103.84/997.5)	1.1066	(1,146.70/993.10)	1.1547
Total realized yield	(1.1066 − 1.0)	10.66%	(1.1547 − 1.0)	15.47%

be substantial. An aggressive investor who expects rates to decline will swap bonds with short maturities and high coupon rates for bonds with long maturities and low coupon rates. The longer the maturity and the lower the coupon rate, the longer the duration and the greater the gain from the drop in rates. An investor who expects interest rates to rise will, of course, adopt just the opposite strategy, swapping bonds with long maturities and low coupon rates for bonds with short maturities and high coupon rates.

When interest rates are unusually high, the yield curve is likely to be downward sloping, reflecting a general expectation that rates will be lower in the future. During such periods, there is a strong temptation to take advantage of the high short-term rates by investing heavily in short-term securities. Some investors overlook the fact that a relatively small decline in long-term rates can lift bond prices enough to make the total yield on long-term bonds higher than the yields on short-term securities.

EXAMPLE 15-4   RATE ANTICIPATION SWAP

Consider the example in Table 15-5 where it is assumed that the short-term rate will drop from 15% to 10% and that the long-term rate will drop from 12% to 11% at the end of a 12-month period.

The table shows that even though the yield curve shifts from a negative slope to a positive slope, the most important factor in this swap is the gain from the overall decline in interest rates.||||

Tax Swap

In periods of high interest rates, many investors hold bonds with market values far below their cost. This creates an opportunity to gain a tax benefit if the investor is willing to sell the bonds at a loss. The tax benefits from losses on securities can be especially valuable to commercial banks and other corporations that are permitted to deduct such losses against ordinary income. However, publicly owned corporations are often reluctant to take losses because of their negative impact on the company's reported earnings.

In a *tax swap,* the investor sells securities at a loss and replaces them with securities that are sufficiently different from the securities that have been sold that the loss will be allowed for tax purposes. (If the new securities are virtually identical to the old, the sale will be considered a *"wash sale"* and the loss disallowed.)

EXAMPLE 15-5   TAX SWAP

Our illustration of a tax swap assumes that the investor is a commercial bank with a marginal tax rate of 50%, federal and state income taxes combined.

In mid-September 1985, the bank was thinking about selling a block of 8% U.S. Treasury bonds at a loss and replacing them with 13⅜% Treasury bonds that mature on the same date. The 8% bonds were purchased at par value for $1 million a number of years earlier; and the bid price on September 15, 1985, was 79. The bank wanted to know how much

|||| **TABLE 15-5**

Rate Anticipation Swap with Downward-Sloping Yield Curve

Income for One Year on an Investment of $1,000,000		
Treasury bill	$(.15 \times 1,000,000)$	$150,000
Treasury bond		
Price of 6%, 20-year bond selling at yield of 12%		
Present value of par (par $\times$ PVIF$_{6\%,40}$)	($1,000 $\times$ .0972)	$ 97.22
Present value of interest payments (PMT $\times$ PVIFA$_{6\%,40}$)	($30 $\times$ 15.0463)	451.39
Price of the bond		$ 548.61
Price as a percentage of face value		54.86%
Par amount of 6% bonds purchased with $1,000,000	($1,000,000/.5486)	$1,822,822
Interest income		
Two semiannual interest payments	(2 $\times$ .03 $\times$ $1,822,822)	$ 109,369
Interest on first interest payment @ 5% semiannually	(.05 $\times$ $54,685)	2,734
Total interest income		$112,103
Capital gain on bonds due to interest rate decline		
Value of bond in one year		
Present value of par (par $\times$ PVIF$_{5.5\%,38}$)	($1,822,822 $\times$ .1307)	$ 238,314
Present value of interest payments (PMT $\times$ PVIFA$_{5.5\%,38}$)	($54,685 $\times$ 15.8047)	864,282
Price of the bond		$1,102,596
Beginning value		1,000,000
Capital gain		$102,596
Total income from 6% bond		$214,699
Income from bond minus income from treasury bill		$ 64,699

this swap would increase the after-tax yield to maturity on this portion of its portfolio and how much it would increase the value of the bank, assuming an after-tax annual discount rate of 5%, or semiannual rate of 2.5%. Following are the quotations for the two bonds:

	Coupon	Maturity	Bid	Ask	Yield
Sell	8	Aug. 1996–01	79.00	79.16	10.16%
Buy	13⅜	Aug. 2001	117.00	117.10	11.26

The time to maturity is 15 years and 11 months, or 31.834 semiannual periods. Table 15-6 presents the annual cash flows for the new and old bonds.

For the purpose of calculating the after-tax yields on the two sets of bonds, the amount of the investment is $895,000 in both cases. That is the cost of the new bonds and the value of the old bonds to the bank after taking the tax savings into account. The semiannual after-tax yields for the two bonds, then, are the rates of return that will discount the semiannual cash flows for 30.834 semiannual periods, plus the cash flow at

|||| **TABLE 15-6**
Tax Swap: Annual Cash Income Net of Taxes

Proceeds from sale of 8% bonds:		
Sale price (.79 × $1,000,000)		$790,000
Tax benefit from loss (.50)($1,000,000 − $790,000)		105,000
Total		$895,000
Purchase price of 13⅜% bonds as a percentage of par value		117.3125%
Face value of 13⅜% bonds purchased with proceeds from sale of old bonds		$762,920
($895,000/1.173125)		
Annual cash income net of taxes:		
New bonds:		
Interest (.13375 × $762,920)	$102,041	
Less amortization of premium [($895,000 − $762,920)/15.917 years]	8,298	
Taxable income	$93,743	
Income tax (.50 × $93,743)	46,872	
Annual cash income ($102,041 − $46,872)		$55,169
Semiannual cash income ($55,169/2)		$27,585
Old bonds:		
Interest (.08 × 1,000,000)	$80,000	
Less taxes (.50 × 80,000)	40,000	
Annual cash income (80,000 − 40,000)		$40,000
Semiannual cash income (40,000/2)		$20,000
Proceeds at maturity:		
New bonds		$762,920
Old bonds		$1,000,000%

maturity (including the final interest payment net of taxes) to a present value of $895,000. Table 15-7 presents the after-tax yields and the increase in the bank value following the proposed swap.||||

RIDING THE YIELD CURVE

An upward-sloping yield curve often gives investors an opportunity to augment their yields by riding the curve. If a one-year security is purchased at a yield of 9% and sold six months later at a yield of 8%, the annualized yield will be 10% before transaction costs. To ride a yield curve is to purchase a fixed-income security with the hope and intention of selling it before maturity at a yield lower than the yield at which it was purchased, thereby earning a yield higher than the yield at which it was purchased. This requires an upward-sloping yield curve and, for the best results, stable or declining interest rates. Even if interest rates increase after the security has been purchased, however, the investor may have a successful ride if the increase is not too great.

The yield expected, or actually realized, by the yield curve rider can be calculated with Equation 15-1:

$$Y_P = W_1 X + W_2 Y_S \qquad (15\text{-}1)$$

where

Y_P = yield at which the security is purchased

W_1 = percentage of time the security is held by
     the rider

|||| **TABLE 15-7**
Tax Swap: After-Tax Yields and Increase in Bank Value

After-Tax Yields		
New bonds:		
Amount of investment	$895,000	
Annual cash flows for 30.834 periods	27,585	
Cash flow at maturity ($27,585 + $762,920)	790,505	
Semiannual after-tax yield to maturity		2.79%
Annual after-tax yield to maturity (2 × 2.79)		5.58%
Old bonds:		
Amount of investment	$895,000	
Annual cash flows for 30.834 periods	20,000	
Cash flow at maturity ($1,000,000 + $20,000)	1,020,000	
Semiannual after-tax yield to maturity		2.48%
Annual after-tax yield to maturity (2 × 2.48)		4.96%

Increase in Bank Value (After-Tax Cash Flows Discounted at Semiannual Rate of 2.5%)

New bonds:	
Present value of cash flows of $27,585 ($PVIFA_{2.5\%,30.834} \times \$27,585$)	$588,085
Present value of final payment of $790,505 ($PVIF_{2.5\%,31.834} \times 790,505$)	360,182
Total	$948,267
Old bonds:	
Present value of cash flows of $20,000 ($PVIFA_{2.5\%,30.834} \times 20,000$)	$426,380
Present value of final payment of $1,020,000 ($PVIF_{2.5\%,31.834} \times \$1,020,000$)	464,748
Total	$891,128
Estimated increase in value of bank	$57,139

X = yield earned by the rider

W_2 = percentage of time the security is held by others after sale by the rider

Y_S = yield at which the rider sells the security

The equation states that the yield at which the rider purchases the security is a weighted average of the yield he or she actually earns and the yield at which the security is sold. The weights are the percentages of the total time to maturity that the rider and all subsequent owners hold the security.

EXAMPLE 15-6   RIDING THE YIELD CURVE
Recently, the following quotations were published for U.S. Treasury notes maturing in approximately one and two years:

Coupon	Maturity	Bid	Ask	Yield
11⅞	One year	103.12	103.16	8.33%
11⅛	Two years	103.22	103.26	9.05

Suppose that an investor who is interested in riding the yield curve believes that interest rates will not change appreciably during the next 12 months. The investor therefore buys two-year notes at a yield of 9.05%

||| **SIDELIGHT**
Yield Curve Arbitrage

Yield curve arbitragers try to anticipate changes in the slope of the yield curve rather than predict whether interest rates are headed up or down. They pay a great deal of attention to Federal Reserve policy, since actions of the Fed can have a major impact on short-term rates.

When interest rates were rising in the fall of 1988, Bear Stearns (one of the principal yield-curve arbitragers) sold short $5 billion of short-term interest rate futures and purchased a total of $635 million of 10-year Treasury notes and 30-year Treasury bonds. They were expecting short-term rates to rise relative to long-term rates, which would tend to flatten the curve. And that is what happened over the next several months; short-term rates moved up considerably more than long-term rates. The large increase in short-term rates and decrease in Treasury bill prices enabled Bear Stearns to buy back the contracts it was short at prices substantially lower than the prices at which they had been sold. The firm's profit on these contracts was $20 million more than its losses on the long-term notes and bonds.

Yield curve arbitrage first became highly profitable in 1979, when the Federal Reserve switched from a policy of controlling interest rates to one of focusing on monetary growth. The new policy resulted in much more volatile interest rates.

SOURCE: Adapted from Craig Torres, "Yield-Curve Arbitrage Rewards the Skillful," *The Wall Street Journal,* July 27, 1989, p. C1. Reprinted by permission of *The Wall Street Journal,* © Dow Jones & Company, Inc. (1989). All Rights Reserved Worldwide.

and hopes to sell them a year later at a yield close to 8.33%. If the investor is able to do that, the effective yield on the investment will be 9.77%, calculated as follows:

$$9.05\% = \tfrac{1}{2}X + (\tfrac{1}{2})(8.33\%)$$
$$18.10\% = X + 8.33\%$$
$$X = 9.77\%$$

Selling the notes at any yield lower than 9.05% will raise the yield curve rider's rate of return above 9.05%, while selling them at any yield above 9.05% will lower the return. For example, if he or she were to sell the notes at a yield of 9.20%, the rate of return would be 8.90%. That would still be 57 basis points (8.90 − 8.33) higher than the return if one-year notes had been purchased. The investor will have earned a lower yield than he or she had hoped to earn, but perhaps a better return than would have been earned under any plausible alternative involving a comparable amount of risk. To earn this higher rate of return, the investor takes the risk that a large increase in one-year rates will reduce the rate of return below what would have been earned by simply investing in one-year notes at a yield of 8.33%. ||||

|||| AVOIDING REINVESTMENT RATE RISK

As noted before, one of the principal risks associated with long-term coupon bonds is the risk of lower rates of return on reinvested interest payments. Investors have three methods of avoiding, or attempting to avoid, this risk. Simplest of all is by investing in zero-coupon bonds. However, except for bonds created by stripping the coupons from U.S. Treasury securities, the supply of zero-coupon issues is quite limited. A second approach is by hedging with interest rate futures, as discussed in Chapter 16. If futures are purchased and interest rates decline, the increase in the value of the futures will offset, at least in part, the reduced earnings on reinvested interest payments. A third method is through bond immunization.

BOND PORTFOLIO IMMUNIZATION

The idea and the term *immunization* were introduced by F. M. Redington, a British actuary, who proposed it as a method by which life insurance companies could reduce the effects of interest rate changes on their net worth. The strategy is designed especially for investors like life insurance companies that use the proceeds of their bond investments to pay liabilities that become due at a fixed or predictable time in the future. It is also used by investors who are accumulating funds for other purposes and would like to lock in the yields on their bond investments over some specific period of time.

The essence of an immunization strategy is to set the average duration of a bond portfolio, rather than the average maturity, equal to the period of time that the proceeds will be needed. If the bonds are to be liquidated to pay liabilities, the average duration of the portfolio is set equal to the duration of the liabilities. If the bonds are to be liquidated to make other investments, the average duration is set equal to the period until the proceeds will be needed for making those investments. If the immunization is completely effective, any reduction in reinvestment income due to a decline in interest rates will be offset by an increase in the value of the bond portfolio. Similarly, any decrease in the value of the portfolio due to an increase in interest rates will be offset by an increase in reinvestment income. Immunization is a hedging strategy, and as with all other hedging strategies, the investor gives up opportunities for extraordinary profits in order to reduce the amount of risk.

What makes immunization possible, although not always realizable, is the fact that changes in interest rates have opposite effects on reinvestment income and bond values. To immunize a portfolio is to structure it so that the two risks will offset one another.

Duration is the essential building block for an immunization strategy. A portfolio is assumed to be immunized from interest rate risk if the duration of the portfolio is equal to the desired investment horizon. The investment horizon is the planned holding period. When a bond portfolio is immunized effectively, the yield to the investment horizon will be equal to the weighted average yield to maturity at which the bonds were purchased. Decreases in the reinvestment rate below the yield to maturity will be offset by capital gains on the bonds, and increases in the reinvestment rate above the yield to maturity will be offset by capital losses on the bonds. With perfect immunization, the portfolio's realized yield is the same as the investor would have earned if all interest payments were reinvested at a rate equal to the yield to maturity and there were no gains or losses on liquidation of the bonds. Or, it can be said that immunization is completely effective if the value of the portfolio at the end of the holding period is at least as large as it would have been if interest rates had remained constant.

A simplified example will illustrate the difference between a duration strategy, which attempts to eliminate interest rate risk by setting the duration of a portfolio equal to the investment horizon, and a maturity strategy, which calls for a portfolio with an average maturity equal to the investment horizon. If an investor uses a duration strategy and the reinvestment rate turns out to be lower than expected, the reduction in reinvestment income tends to be offset by capital gains on the securities. The example illustrates this point even though it is highly unrealistic in two respects. First, it assumes that the reinvestment rate is constant throughout the holding period. Second, it makes no provision for restructuring the portfolio periodically to keep the duration equal to the investment horizon. In the real world, where interest rates change every day, the immunization strategy will not work unless the average duration of the portfolio is kept approximately equal to the investment horizon.

EXAMPLE 15-7 DURATION STRATEGY VERSUS MATURITY STRATEGY

Let us suppose that an investor wants to accumulate a total of $1,629,000 in a five-year period by investing $1 million in U.S. Treasury bonds with a coupon rate of 10%. The bonds mature in five years and are selling at par value.

The semiannual interest payments on the $1 million investment will be $50,000, and the total interest payments over the five-year period will be $500,000. Thus, if the interest were not reinvested, the accumulated amount at the end of five years would be the principal of $1 million plus interest of $500,000, or a total of $1,500,000. However, if the interest can be reinvested to earn 5% semiannually (the same as the bond's coupon rate), the total accumulated amount at the end of five years will be $1,628,850:

Principal	$1,000,000
Coupon interest (5 × 100,000)	500,000
Interest on interest [(FVIFA$_{5\%,10}$ × 50,000) − 500,000]	128,895
Total	$1,628,895

But suppose the reinvestment rate should turn out to be 3% semiannually instead of 5%. The accumulated amount will be $1,573,150, or almost $56,000 less than at a reinvestment rate of 5%:

Principal	$1,000,000
Coupon interest	500,000
Interest on interest [(FVIFA$_{3\%,10}$ × 50,000) − 500,000]	73,194
Total	$1,573,194

The investor has matched the average maturity of the portfolio with an investment horizon of five years. Because of the low reinvestment rate, the accumulated amount is about $56,000 short of the goal, and the realized rate of return is 4.64% semiannually instead of 5%.

With a duration strategy, the investor would buy $1 million of 10% bonds with a duration of five years, which would require the average maturity to be about 6.5 years. If no changes are made in the portfolio, at the end of five years the investor would be holding bonds that mature in 1.5 years. If the yield to maturity at that time is the same as the reinvestment rate (3% semiannual), the value of the bonds will be $1,056,530:

PV of interest payments (PVIFA$_{3\%,3}$ × 50,000)	$141,300
PV of principal amount (PVIF$_{3\%,3}$ × 1,000,000)	915,142
Value of the bonds	$1,056,442

The gain of $56,442 on the bonds is a little more than the decrease in reinvestment income due to the lower reinvestment rate. ||||

Attempts to immunize portfolios of coupon bonds are not always successful. The best results seem to be achieved when the spread of the maturities among the bonds is narrow. Since duration is an average, an infinite number of maturity combinations are consistent with a specific value of duration. If the bonds in a portfolio have a narrow range of maturities, their price movements will be more nearly alike than if the maturity range is wide. This occurs for two reasons: First, if the maturities fall within a narrow range, the yield changes for all the bonds in the portfolio are likely to be about the same when interest rates move up or down. This will be true even when there are substantial changes in the shape of the yield curve. Second, when the maturities are all about the same, a given amount of change in the yield will have about the same effect upon the prices of all the bonds in the portfolio. If there is wide variation among the maturities, the price changes will also vary widely for a given amount of shift in the yield curve.

Effective immunization requires that the portfolio be restructured at least once a year to keep the estimated duration equal to the remaining length of the planning period. This cannot be done with great precision. Frequent restructuring would result in excessive transactions costs, yet the duration of a portfolio may change significantly over a short period of time. Also, it is impossible to measure duration precisely because of uncertainty about such things as the possibility of bonds being called before they mature.[4]

|||| SUMMARY

Bond portfolio management strategies range from largely passive (buy and hold) to highly active. Active management strategies include various bond swapping techniques such as the pure yield pickup swap, substitution swap, sector swap, rate anticipation swap, and tax swap. Generally, the least risky of these are the pure yield pickup and tax swaps. In fact, they are virtually risk-free. Rate anticipation swaps—moving from short maturities to long maturities when rates are expected to decline and from long to short when rates are expected to rise—can be highly risky if major portfolio shifts are made in anticipation of changes in rates.

Another active management strategy is known as riding the yield curve. When the yield curve is upward sloping, an investor buys bonds, notes, or bills with the intention of selling them at a lower yield before they mature. If this goal is achieved, the investor's yield will be higher than the yield at which he or she purchased the securities. The investor's yield will be further enhanced if the yield curve shifts downward before the investor sells the securities; the yield will be impaired if interest rates move up. If the increase in rates is very large, the investor may end up earning a lower return than if he or she had invested in shorter-term securities and held them to maturity.

The bond immunization strategy is intended to reduce reinvestment rate risk and lock in the yield on a bond portfolio for the period of its duration. A portfolio is immunized by making the duration equal to the investment horizon and then keeping it close to the investment horizon by periodic rebalancing. Immunization is possible because changes in interest rates have opposite effects on the reinvestment rate and the market value of the bonds in a portfolio. To achieve effective immunization, the maturities of the bonds in the portfolio should fall within a narrow range, and the portfolio should be rebalanced at least once a year to keep the average duration close to the investment horizon.

|||| QUESTIONS

*1. Active bond management, as contrasted with a passive buy-and-hold strategy, has gained increased acceptance as investors have attempted to maximize the total return on bond portfolios. The fol-

---

[4]A more detailed discussion of bond immunization may be found in F. J. Fabozzi and I. M. Pollack, *The Handbook of Fixed Income Securities* (Homewood, Ill.: Dow Jones–Irwin, 1987), pp. 676–703.

Note: All questions and problems preceded by an asterisk are from Chartered Financial Analyst (CFA) examinations.

lowing bond swaps could have been made in recent years as investors attempted to increase the total return on their portfolios. From the information presented below, identify the reason, or reasons, investors may have made each swap.

		Call Price	Market Price	Yield to Maturity
a.	Sell Baal Ga. Pwr 11⅝%, 2000	108.24	75⅝	15.71%
	Buy Baal Ga. Pwr 7⅜%, 2001	105.20	51⅛	15.39
b.	Sell Aaa AT&T 13¼%, 1991	101.50	96⅛	14.02
	Buy U.S. Treas. 14¼%, 1991	NC	102.15	13.83
c.	Sell Aa1 Chase Man. Zeros, 1992	NC	25¼	14.37
	Buy Aa1 Chase Float Rate notes, 2009	103.90	90¼	—
d.	Sell A1 Texas Oil & Gas 8¼, 1997	105.75	60	15.09
	Buy U.S. Treas. 8¼%, 2005	NC	65.60	12.98
e.	Sell A1 K-mart Conv. Deb. 6%, 1999	103.90	62¾	10.83
	Buy A2 Lucky Strs. Deb. 11¾, 2005	109.86	73	16.26

*2. Assume the following yields to maturity on various classes of bonds in March 1984:

Short treasuries	9.50%
Long treasuries	12.00
Short municipals	6.50
Long municipals	9.25
Short corporates	10.00
Long corporates	12.80
Long Aa corporates	12.50
Long Baa corporates	13.00

Also assume the following "normal" yield spreads:

Long treasuries minus short treasuries	150 basis points
Long municipals minus short municipals	100
Long corporates minus long treasuries	125
Long corporates minus short corporates	175
Long Baa corporates minus long Aa corporates	150

Based upon the March 1984 yields to maturity and the "normal" yield spreads, select the bond that would be preferable in each of the five comparisons (e.g., short treasuries or long treasuries), and briefly state the reason for each of your selections.

*3. The ability to immunize a bond portfolio is very desirable for bond portfolio managers in most instances.
   a. Explain the meanings of interest rate risk (or price risk) and reinvestment risk. (Sometimes interest rate risk is defined as including both price risk and reinvestment risk.)
   b. Define immunization and discuss why a bond manager would immunize his or her portfolio.
   c. Explain why a duration-matching strategy is superior to a maturity-matching strategy for the minimization of the combined impact of price risk and reinvestment risk.
   d. Explain in specific terms how you would use a zero-coupon bond to immunize a bond portfolio. Discuss why a zero-coupon bond is an ideal instrument in this regard.

4. Explain why rate anticipation swaps tend to involve a high degree of risk.

5. Explain what is meant by "riding the yield curve." Explain why yield curve riding may be considered successful even if the security is sold at a yield higher than the yield at which it was purchased.

6. Explain what is meant by bond immunization. What fact makes immunization possible? Explain why immunization is a hedging strategy. What conditions are necessary for effective immunization?

|||| PROBLEMS

*1. As the portfolio manager for a large pension fund, you are offered the following bonds:

	Coupon	Maturity	Price	Call Price	Yield to Maturity
Edgar Corp. (new issue)	14.00%	2002	101¾	114	13.75%
Edgar Corp. (new issue)	6.00	2002	48⅛	103	13.60
Edgar Corp. (1972 issue)	6.00	2002	48⅞	103	13.40

Assuming you expect a decline in interest rates over the next three years, which of these bonds would you select? Justify your selection.

2. As of February 15, 1987, calculate the total realized yield for bond A, which is held by the investor, and bond B, which is being considered for a pure yield pickup swap. Use semiannual compounding and a reinvestment rate of 4.5%. Assume there is no gain or loss on the sale of bond A. The total proceeds from bond A, including accrued interest, will be invested in bond B. Both bonds are Aa-rated corporates.

Bond	Coupon	Maturity	Bid	Asked	Yield to Maturity
A	11⅛	2/15/98	100⅜	100⅝	11.02%
B	11¾	5/15/98	102¼	102½	11.33

3. Compare the expected before-tax difference in income and yield for the next 12 months for the following two investments:
   a. Treasury bill yielding 12%, bond equivalent method.
   b. 20-year Treasury bond with a coupon rate of 5% that is selling at a yield to maturity of 11% at the beginning of the 12-month period and is expected to sell at a yield of 10% at the end of the period.

4. A commercial bank purchased Treasury bond A a number of years ago at par value. The bank is considering selling bond A and purchasing Treasury bond B in a tax swap as of May 15, 1988. Calculate the after-tax yield to maturity and the present value of the cash flows for the two bonds at a semiannual after-tax discount rate of 5%. The bank's marginal tax rate is 40%, and any loss on the sale of bond A is deductible against ordinary income. Assume that the amount invested in bond B will include the tax benefits from the sale of A.

Bond	Coupon	Maturity	Bid	Asked	Yield
A	8%	6/15/04	80.0	80.8	10.59%
B	9½	6/15/04	90.16	90.24	10.72

5. On the basis of the following facts, calculate the annualized yield earned by a yield curve rider:

Maturity at time of purchase	18 months
Yield at time of purchase	10%
Maturity at time of sale	10 months
Yield at time of sale	9.4%

6. As explained in the chapter, it is not uncommon for two bonds nearly the same in all important respects to be trading at slightly different yields. Examine today's Student Loan Marketing Association (SMLA) bond quotations in the *Wall Street Journal*. Find two SLMA bonds that might be candidates for a pure yield pickup swap. Assume you hold a quantity of the lower-yield bonds (principal value = $250,000) and you swap these for the higher-yield bonds. Use semiannual compounding and assume an annual reinvestment rate that is the rate on the most recent auction of six-month T-bills. (See the "Money Rates" box in Section C of the *Wall Street Journal*.) Use the format of Table 15-1 in your calculations, and indicate the gains or losses possible with the swap you select.

7. In February 1991, the *Wall Street Journal* listed the following quotations for bonds of the Federal Farm Credit Bank:

Coupon Rate	Maturity	Bid	Asked
7.70	3/96	99.24	99.28
11.90	10/97	118.26	119.06

Assume you have $1 million invested in bonds with the March 1996 maturity, and you're interested in swapping them for the bonds with the October 1997 maturity. Also, assume each bond pays semiannual interest, and the assumed reinvestment rate is 6.5% per year. What would be the gains (if any) from a pure yield pickup swap?

8. In February 1991, an investor notices the following FNMA bond quotations in the *Wall Street Journal:*

Coupon Rate	Maturity	Bid	Asked	Yield
9.15	10/00	103.20	103.28	8.59
8.25	12/00	100.05	100.13	8.22

The investor believes that any difference in yields is transitory and will be eliminated within a year. Furthermore, the investor believes that both the bonds will sell for a yield of 8.22% at the end of the workout period. Assume you hold $1 million of the 8.25s of December 2000, and the reinvestment rate is 3.5% per semiannual period. Calculate the gains or losses from a substitution swap, using the format of Table 15-3.

9. Assume the following quotes for K-mart bonds:

Bonds	Current Yield	Close
K-mart 8⅛s 97	8.1	100⅜
K-mart 8¾s 17	9.4	89

Assume you expect the yield to maturity for both bonds will fall 1.5 percentage points over the next 12 months. You currently own $200,000 of the 8⅛s of '97. What gains are possible from a rate anticipation swap? (*Note:* The above quotations were observed in February 1991.)

10. It is June of 1992, and you have $500,000 of excess liquidity to invest for your employer for a period of six months. You have the following opportunities in Treasury securities:

Coupon Rate	Maturity	Bid	Asked	Yield
8¾	6 months	101.03	101.05	6.18
8½	12 months	101.26	101.28	6.54

Assume you ride the yield curve by purchasing securities with the 12-month maturity and sell them on the secondary market six months from the date of purchase. What would your total returns be assuming the securities are sold to yield:

a.   5.68%?
b.   6.18%?
c.   6.68%?

|||| SELECTED REFERENCES

Fabozzi, Frank J., and Irving M. Pollack. *The Handbook of Fixed Income Securities*. Homewood, Ill.: Dow Jones–Irwin, 1987.

PART 5 SPECULATIVE INVESTMENTS AND HEDGING

16 FUTURES

Futures contracts stipulate that investors will buy (or sell) a given quantity of a specified asset on a specified *future* date at a specific price. Both the delivery of the asset and the payment occur on a future date. Futures contracts are offered for a wide variety of items, including agricultural commodities, precious metals such as gold and silver, fixed-income instruments such as U.S. Treasury bonds and Eurodollars, and foreign currencies.

The sizes of futures contracts are standardized, such as 5,000 bushels of hard red winter wheat or $100,000 of U.S. Treasury bonds. Thus, a trade involving 50,000 bushels of wheat is for 10 contracts, and a trade involving $2 million of U.S. Treasury bonds is for 20 contracts.

One significant difference between a futures contract and an ordinary contract to buy or sell a commodity is the time specified for delivery. The cash market deals with contracts for current delivery, while the futures market specifies a delivery time of up to one year in advance. The volume of outstanding futures contracts has literally exploded in the past few years. Trading volume on the nation's futures exchanges was more than 241 million contracts in 1988, up 13% from the year before. The 1988 volume of *financial futures,* the most popular type of futures contract, exceeded the entire volume of all futures trading on U.S. exchanges as recently as 1983.[1] Substantial volume increases have been posted at most futures exchanges.

A SHORT HISTORY OF FUTURES TRADING

Futures markets were established in the United States in response to commercial demand. Prior to 1848, when the Chicago Board of Trade was organized, farmers delivered much of their grain to market immediately after the harvest. Naturally, prices plunged around harvest time and skyrocketed a few months later when supplies grew short again. Price swings in the commodities markets caused huge fluctuations in the prices of finished goods. Many products disappeared from the markets entirely during certain periods of the year. There were no standard grades and

---

[1] U.S. Commodity Futures Trading Association, *Annual Report* (1990).

quantities for the various commodities, and the lack of standardized contract sizes fostered unfair practices in weighing and measuring. Deceit and mistrust were so prevalent that physical fighting sometimes erupted between the buyers and sellers of commodities.

The establishment of the Chicago Board of Trade (CBOT) by the city of Chicago in 1848 went a long way toward resolving these problems. One of the first things accomplished by the CBOT was the standardization of contract terms. The exchange established standard quantities for each contract and set up a grading system for commodities to ensure quality. The exchange acted as a *clearinghouse* that brought buyers and sellers together on a continuous basis, smoothing the fluctuations in supply and in price. Grain inspectors were hired to examine incoming shipments to ensure they met CBOT contract specifications. These inspectors were the precursor of federal inspectors for agricultural commodities.

The changes initiated by the CBOT enabled the commodities markets to function in a smooth, orderly manner. This, in turn, has enabled futures contracts to grow into the sophisticated risk-reduction instruments they are today.

|||| TRADING PROCEDURES

In the futures market, the buyer of a contract is said to have taken a long position, while the seller has taken a short position. Long positions generate profits when prices of the underlying commodity rise because holders of long positions can buy the commodity for a fixed price. If the market price of the commodity rises before the contract matures, holders of long positions wind up purchasing the commodity for a below-market price.

In contrast, those holding short positions profit from a price decline because the short position fixes the selling price of the commodity. If the *spot market* price drops before the futures contract matures, the holder of a short position can sell the commodity for an above-market price.

Usually, before the contract matures, both parties will execute *reversing trades* that cancel their initial position.[2] If the initial position was long, a reversing trade is executed by going short in *exactly* the same contract. All facets of the original transaction must be matched, including the delivery month, commodity, grade, and number of contracts. When this is done, the trader's long and short positions in the contract cancel each other, and the trader has no remaining obligation in that contract.

The buyers and sellers of futures contracts do not deal directly with one another; instead, their transactions are all made through a clearing corporation. Each of the futures exchanges has set up a clearing corpo-

---

[2]The exact timing of a reversing trade is up to the investor. It is not necessary to execute a reversing trade with the same person who was party to the original transaction. Futures contracts, like other securities, are traded anonymously through brokers.

ration, whose principal responsibilities are to (1) insulate futures market participants against the risk of contract default by acting as the opposite party in all transactions and (2) monitor changes in the profits and losses of market participants as prices change on a daily basis.

The clearing corporation acts as the opposite party in all transactions, buying futures contracts from all sellers and selling contracts to all buyers. Since the clearing corporation both buys and sells the same contract with each transaction that is processed through the exchange, it always maintains a net zero position in each contract. Its risk of loss through price fluctuations is therefore hedged away. In fact, the only risk assumed by the clearing corporation is the risk of contract default. In the event a seller does not deliver the commodity in accordance with contract specifications, or a buyer cannot pay for the commodity upon delivery, the clearing corporation takes action. In its role as the guarantor of all contracts, the clearing corporation fulfills the contract provisions. In the meantime, it takes action against the defaulting party, initiating a lawsuit if necessary.

MARGIN AND MARGIN CALLS

Recall that investors may purchase or sell equities on margin, and that the amount of margin involved in such a transaction represents the customer's down payment on the total value of the position. Margin has an entirely different meaning when associated with futures trading. Here, *margin* is a security deposit placed by the trader with his or her commodities broker, representing a good faith commitment to carry out the provisions of the futures contract. When the position is liquidated, the margin deposit is returned.

There are two types of margin requirements in futures trading: the initial margin and the maintenance margin. The only payment required to open a futures market position is the *initial margin*. It is usually from 5% to 10% of the value of the contract. For example, there are 5,000 bushels of soybeans in a soybean futures contract. If the price of soybeans is $5 per bushel, and the initial margin required on soybean futures is 10% of the contract value, then the initial margin on soybean futures would be $2,500 ($5 per bushel × 5,000 bushels × 0.10 = $2,500). Margin requirements are set by the exchange, and they vary over time and from contract to contract. Since initial margin is like a performance bond guaranteeing that the trader will not default, commodity brokers often require their customers to supply more than the minimum legal initial margin in order to obtain greater assurance against default.

Margin requirements are met by depositing cash, a letter of credit, or low-risk debt securities with the broker handling the transaction. The broker, in turn, is required to place a margin deposit with the clearing corporation of the exchange. A deposit of securities is the most common form of meeting margin requirements since customers retain title to the securities and any interest they earn while on deposit is the property of the customer.

At the end of the day's trading, the clearing corporation calculates paper losses and gains on each contract and settles with its members, collecting additional margin from those with losses and crediting the margin account of those with gains. In this way, each contract is *marked to market* on a daily basis. Member firms then credit the margin accounts of their customers for any profits earned and charge the margin accounts for any losses incurred. If the value of the margin falls below minimum allowable levels (called the *maintenance margin*), the investor is subject to a *margin call,* which is simply a request from the broker for additional funds or securities to be placed in the customer's margin account. If margin calls are not met on a timely basis, the broker will liquidate the investor's position and return any amount remaining (after brokerage commissions and other charges) to the investor.

TYPES OF ORDERS

Futures are usually bought and sold with a market order, a limit order, or a stop order. Because of the volatility of futures prices, the type of order used can have a large impact on profits and losses. A *market order* is simply an order to buy or sell a futures contract at the current market price. A variation of the standard market order, called a market-on-close order, tells the broker to sell at the market price at the close of daily trading for the exchange. This order is important in program trading. *Limit orders* are designed to establish an advantageous price for the investor. With a long position, a limit order specifies the maximum futures price to be paid, and with a short position, a limit order specifies the minimum price to be accepted. The customer is assured of getting at least the price specified if the order can be executed, but there is a risk that the floor broker will not be able to fill the order at all.

Stop orders instruct the broker to buy or sell a commodity at the market price, once a specific price level (called the *stop price*) is reached. A buy-stop order instructs the broker to execute the order when the price rises to a specified level, while a sell-stop order instructs the broker to sell when the price falls to a specified level. The broker is then obligated to execute the order at the best price available, which may be the stop price or may be above or below the stop price. Buy-stop orders can be used in conjunction with short positions to protect a profit or to limit a loss.

Many experienced traders advise that *all* speculative positions be protected with stop orders.

EXAMPLE 16-1   STOP ORDERS

Suppose a speculator buys one silver contract (5,000 ounces) at a price of $8.50 per ounce and simultaneously places a stop-sell order at $8.25. The purpose of this stop-sell order is to limit potential losses to approximately 25 cents per ounce. If the price drops to $8.25, the stop order is activated and becomes a market order to sell at the best price available. If the price drops and the speculator is able to sell at $8.25, losses before commissions will be $1,250 ($.25 × 5,000 ounces = $1,250). Even with a stop order at $8.25, the speculator will often suffer additional price declines before the contract can be sold.||||

TRADING PROCEDURES: AN EXAMPLE

As an illustration of the concepts discussed thus far, consider a speculator who purchases one gold futures contract for April delivery. This transaction is summarized in Table 16-1. The speculator's position is thus "long one April gold." The current contract value is $45,440, which is obtained by multiplying the price per ounce by the contract size of 100 ounces. Notice the effect of the high leverage. With an initial margin of only $4,500, the speculator controls $45,400 worth of gold. The high degree of risk is obvious—a price decline of 10% would completely wipe out the investment. The appealing thing, though, is that a 10% price increase would double the speculator's initial investment.

Suppose next that within three months after the long position is established, the price of April gold futures rises to $470, an increase of $15.60. If gold is not expected to rise any further, the position can be

|||| **TABLE 16-1**
Trading Gold Futures

Gold futures contract characteristics:		
Contract size		100 troy ounces
Initial margin requirement		$4,500 per contract
Maintenance margin requirement		$3,500 per contract
Opening price of gold futures		$454.40 per ounce
Initial contract value (100 ounces × $454.40)		$45,400
Gold rises to $470 per ounce in three months:		
Profit, assuming an initial long position:		
Closing contract value (100 ounces × $470)		$47,000
Minus initial amount paid		−45,440
Profit		$ 1,560
Rate of return on margin deposit ($1,560/$4,500)		34.67%
Annualized return [34.67% × (12/3)]		139%
Status of margin account:		
Initial margin	$4,500	
Profit	+1,560	
New margin balance	$6,060	
Loss, assuming an initial short position:		
Initial contract value		$45,440
Minus closing value of position		−47,000
Loss		$ 1,560
Return on initial margin deposit		−34.67%
Annualized return		−139%
Status of margin account:		
Initial margin deposit	$4,500	
Loss	−1,560	
New margin balance	$2,940	
Minimum maintenance margin	−3,500	
Margin deficiency	$ 560	

reversed by selling one April gold futures contract. The result is a profit of $1,560 ($15.60 per ounce × 100 ounces) before transaction costs. This increase represents a 34.67% return on the initial margin investment over the three-month period ($1,560/$4,500 = 34.67%), which is an annualized rate of approximately 139% (34.67% × 12/3 = 139%). No wonder so many people are excited about trading futures!

But if the speculator had been on the other side of the transaction— selling instead of buying—losses of 139% would have been generated. In futures trading, one person's profit is another's loss. If there were no transactions costs, futures trading would be a zero-sum game. However, when commissions are taken into account, the total return to all traders is slightly negative, since both buyers and sellers pay brokerage commissions. Thus, while the potential profits are large, potential losses are even greater.

To illustrate maintenance margin and margin calls, suppose the speculator initially went short one April gold futures contract and placed the initial $4,500 margin deposit with a broker. Six weeks later when the price rose to $470 per ounce, the speculator suffered losses of $15.60 per ounce, or $1,560. These losses were charged to the speculator's margin account, reducing its balance to $2,940 ($4,500 − $1,560 = $2,940). Since this is less than the required level of maintenance margin ($3,500), a margin call results. An additional margin deposit of $560 in cash or securities is required.

The maximum price change per contract unit that can be sustained before the investor receives a margin call is calculated as follows:

$$\frac{\text{initial margin} - \text{maintenance margin}}{\text{contract size (units)}} = \begin{array}{l}\text{maximum price} \\ \text{change without} \\ \text{margin call}\end{array} \quad (16\text{-}1)$$

Price decreases of the size specified in Equation 16-1 result in margin calls for long positions. Price increases of this size result in margin calls for short positions. Thus, our gold speculator would receive a margin call when the price changed by $10:

$$\frac{\$4,500 - \$3,500}{100} = \$10$$

Since the speculator was short, the price could rise by $10 (to $464.40 per ounce) before a margin call would be received.

|||| FUTURES EXCHANGES

Futures trading is done in hexagonal-shaped "pits" located at various positions on the exchange trading floor. Usually, futures contracts on only one commodity are traded in each pit, and the size of the pit is a function of the level of interest in trading that particular contract. Where a trader stands in the pit is determined by the length of time to maturity in the particular futures contract he or she desires to trade.

Futures trading is conducted by open outcry as opposed to executing orders through specialists. Open outcry means that the traders literally shout their offers to buy and sell to one another. This gives everyone in the pit an equal chance to participate in all offers. Since the noise level generated with such a system can be very high, an offer to buy or sell is backed by a sophisticated system of hand signals that simultaneously communicate the price, number of contracts, and maturity month of the contract. Most traders are assisted by "runners" who confirm the trades and by personnel monitoring telephones and/or microcomputers who search for profit opportunities by running sophisticated valuation programs and hedging schemes.

In such an environment, errors (called outtakes) do occur, causing buyers and sellers to disagree on some aspect of the trade. The exchange regulates these outtakes and often prohibits the traders involved from any further activity on the trading floor until the dispute is resolved.

The principal function performed by the exchange is contract standardization. Each futures contract traded on an exchange must conform to standard terms, which include (1) a specified delivery month, (2) standard contract size, (3) a uniform, well-defined commodity grade, (4) an established location for delivery of the commodity upon contract maturity, and (5) uniform margin requirements. Liquidity is enhanced by contract standardization. Without liquidity, futures contracts would be far less useful as risk-reduction instruments. Their importance in financial affairs would be greatly reduced.

TYPES OF EXCHANGE MEMBERSHIPS

Only members of a commodities exchange can trade contracts on the floor of the exchange. Memberships, called seats, must be purchased. The price of a seat varies over time and from exchange to exchange. Recent prices of exchange memberships have varied from a low of approximately $1,000 on the New York Futures Exchange to a high of over $300,000 for a seat on the Chicago Board of Trade. Traders with very limited initial capital can often lease a seat from another individual for a limited period of time.

Three types of traders operate on the floor of the exchange. The first, called a *floor broker,* executes orders for others for a small fee—usually a few dollars per transaction. Floor brokers usually have very little of their own capital invested in any position.

A second type of trader is called a *floor trader,* or position trader. They speculate for their own account, but may also serve as brokers for others. As traders, they provide liquidity for the market.

Scalpers, or day traders, speculate for their own account and attempt to take advantage of very small price changes that occur during the day, often executing many trades within a few hours. Like floor traders, they provide liquidity for the market, but in contrast to the floor traders, they do not carry a position over to the next trading session and usually deal in a smaller number of contracts. The presence of large numbers of floor traders and day traders ensures a continuous market for futures contracts, which in turn means that orders can be placed without necessarily causing wide price fluctuations.

REGULATION OF FUTURES MARKETS

Futures market regulation occurs at three levels. At the primary level, the National Futures Association (NFA) is a self-regulating body whose powers are limited to enforcement of trading ethics for members. Since only NFA members can trade commodities, expulsion from the NFA for malfeasance or illegal practices can keep an individual or firm from trading.

The second level of regulation occurs at the exchanges themselves. Assisted by its own clearing corporation, each futures exchange constantly oversees the trading activity, watching for evidence of fraudulent practices such as off-floor trading or withholding orders for the benefit of brokers or other members. Clearing corporations also regulate outtakes and other disputes that arise between exchange members. Although enforcement practices vary somewhat from exchange to exchange, violations of trading rules are usually referred to a committee composed of exchange members. Self-regulation of trading activity is in the best interests of all members, since member livelihood depends upon public trust and a reputation of fairness toward all market participants.

At the highest level, the Commodity Futures Trading Commission (CFTC) has supervisory authority over all regulatory aspects of the futures markets. The CFTC establishes trading rules for existing contracts, approves new contract proposals, and has the authority to intervene when it feels that markets are subject to manipulation or other unfair practices. The CFTC determines the maximum number of contracts that a speculator may hold in a specified commodity. It also establishes rules for the handling of customer funds and is responsible for ensuring minimum competency standards for commodities brokers. Despite the dual surveillance by the CFTC and the exchanges, reports of fraudulent practices and violations of trading rules still appear in the financial press.

|||| BASIS AND HEDGING

Commodity futures contracts have the image of high-risk, fast-paced investments, in which fabulous sums of money may be gained or lost in a very short period of time. This may be the case for speculators, but the futures markets were not designed for speculation. Intead, they were designed to be used for risk management through hedging. Hedging gives the futures markets their fundamental economic purpose.

Hedging means taking opposite positions in the cash market and the futures market. Hedges are undertaken to reduce the risk of adverse price movements. Although hedging reduces risk, it does not completely eliminate risk, since a type of risk known as *basis risk* cannot be hedged away. Basis and hedging are examined more fully in the paragraphs that follow.

BASIS

Basis is equal to the spot price per unit minus the futures price per unit. *Spot price* is the cash price, or the price of a commodity for immediate delivery.

Since the futures price varies by contract maturity, basis varies also. However, the most common expression of basis uses the futures contract with the earliest maturity date to represent the futures price. Basis can be normal or inverted. Normal basis occurs when the basis gets smaller as the contract approaches maturity. Inverted basis occurs when the basis gets larger as the contract approaches maturity. An examination of the reasons for the existence of basis can help explain why basis follows the particular patterns it does.

The total basis for a commodity can be divided into two parts, the cost of carry and location basis. Of the two, the cost of carry is the more important. The *cost of carry* is the amount paid by the owner of a commodity for the costs of rent, insurance, finance charges, spoilage, and obsolescence while the commodity is in storage. Commodity owners who choose to sell in the futures market rather than the cash market want to be compensated for the cost of carry until the futures contract matures. Thus, if the cost of carry for soybeans is $0.05 per bushel per month, then the maximum expected price difference between contracts maturing one month apart is $0.05 per bushel. Under such a scenario, the price of soybean futures in August might exhibit the following pattern:

Contract Maturity	Price per Bushel
September	$8.07
November	8.17
January	8.27
March	8.37

The second part of basis is called location basis. *Location basis* represents the costs of shipping the commodity from its current location to the storage facility specified in the futures contract. Recall that specific delivery points (usually grain elevators or warehouses in the geographic region of the commodities exchange) are specified for all contracts. Depending where the commodity is grown, the cost of shipping to the delivery point specified may be considerable. Thus, just as cash market prices vary from location to location around the country, the basis of a particular contract also varies from location to location, depending upon which cash market price is used to quote basis. Usually, the differences in location basis can be explained by differences in shipping costs to the specific delivery point called for in the futures contract.

Figure 16-1 shows the relationship between location basis, the cost of carry, and the local spot market price for a commodity. Since location

|||| **FIGURE 16-1**

Components of Normal Basis

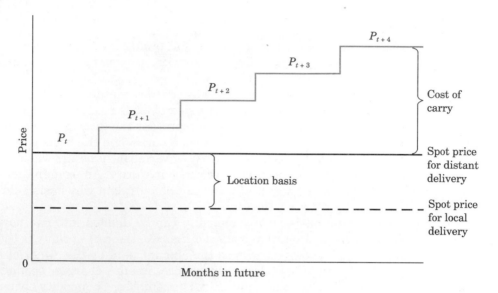

P_t = futures price at delivery month *(t)*

basis is not a function of the length of time until contract maturity, it is shown as a constant. The decline in the futures price as the contract gets closer to maturity is called convergence. Any remaining basis at contract maturity is location basis and is due solely to shipping costs. A narrowing of basis as the contract approaches maturity is the typical pattern for most futures.

As mentioned earlier, not all futures contracts exhibit normal basis, and the basis of some contracts actually grows as the contract gets closer to maturity. Usually, this is due to an especially strong cash market for the commodity that has temporarily driven up spot prices. The drought that occurred during the summer of 1988 created this type of market, and many agricultural commodities had an inverted basis at that time.

SEASONAL PATTERNS IN FUTURES PRICING

Seasonal patterns in commodity prices have an impact on basis. Most commodities, especially agricultural products, exhibit a seasonal pattern in their price levels.[3] For example, prices often fall around harvest time, as the supply of the commodity peaks, and then slowly rise over the

[3]There is some evidence that even financial futures have a seasonal price pattern. See, for example, G. M. Constantinides, "Optimal Trading with Personal Taxes: Implications for Prices and the Abnormal January Returns," *Journal of Financial Economics* (March 1984): 65–89; and Eric Sharp, "Trading Seasonal Patterns in Interest Rate Markets," *Futures* (February 1990): 28–30.

remainder of the year until the next harvest. In this respect, it is important to know the "commodity year" for perishable commodities, i.e., the period between one harvest and the next. Without some understanding of seasonal price patterns, the movement of commodity prices over time will make very little sense. Also, a good knowledge of seasonal patterns can be helpful in generating profits, as the Sidelight describes.

Volume and open interest, two other important statistics, also exhibit a seasonal pattern. Most newspapers report these statistics on a daily basis in their financial section. Volume is the number of contracts traded over a given time period. *Open interest* refers to contract positions (either long or short) that have been opened and not yet reversed. When volume statistics are reported, only one side of the transaction is counted. Thus, when a contract is bought and sold on the exchange, the volume for that day only goes up by one. The change in open interest, however, is a function of the number of new positions created with the transaction. This change could range in value from $+2$ to -2 as a result of a single trade, depending on the situation. For example, if both parties involved in the trade were opening initial positions on the contract, open interest would increase by two. If the trade was executed between two investors who were both closing out an already existing position, open interest would decline by two. Combinations between these two extremes are also possible.

Products whose price is influenced by seasonal factors usually have a seasonal component in volume and open interest statistics. Open interest typically follows price patterns, peaking during the months after harvest, when the commodity is plentiful and the volume in storage is high, and declining gradually over the year until immediately before harvest time, when open interest is at its lowest. The seasonal pattern

---

||| SIDELIGHT
Iowa Trader Compiles Enviable Record

Steve DeCook has been a highly successful manager of commodity money for a number of years, earning an annual compound return of 37.8% from January 1975 through June 1988. He likes to make seasonal trades, which are based on the notion that seasonal price changes of certain commodities are predictable. For example, he likes to sell cattle on July 1st and cover his position three weeks later. But he doesn't always do that. He doesn't bet on the usual seasonal pattern if he has good reason to believe it will not occur.

DeCook observed that some of the trades that worked in the 1970s and early 1980s don't work today, probably because too many traders have already anticipated them.

SOURCE: Adapted from Stanley W. Angrist, "Iowa Trader Compiles Enviable Record Shunning Computers, Sticking to Basics," *The Wall Street Journal,* August 22, 1988, p. 22. Reprinted by permission of *The Wall Street Journal,* © Dow Jones & Company, Inc. (1988). All Rights Reserved Worldwide.

in volume is weak and unpredictable, although there is some tendency for volume to rise as the supply of the commodity rises during harvest.

Profiting from seasonal patterns in the futures market is difficult, but unless a commodity speculator understands the seasonal price patterns that exist for a given futures contract, he or she could suffer tremendous losses. In addition, it is difficult to obtain an insight into the daily drift of commodities prices without understanding seasonal price patterns.

LONG AND SHORT HEDGES

To hedge means to take opposite positions in the cash market and the futures market. Since two positions can be taken with regard to any commodity (long and short), there are two types of hedges, a long hedge and a short hedge. Both are named after the position taken in the futures market. A *short hedge* is formed when a long position in the cash (or spot) market is hedged by going short in the futures market. A *long hedge* is formed when a short position in the cash market is hedged by going long in the futures market.

EXAMPLE 16-2   A "PERFECT" SHORT HEDGE

Suppose it is spring, and a midwestern wheat farmer has planted 1,000 acres of wheat (see Table 16-2 for a summary of this example). He expects an average yield of 40 bushels per acre. The farmer anticipates a long position in the cash market (the market for the crop) of 40,000 bushels (1,000 acres × 40 bushels/acre = 40,000 bushels). The position is long because the commodity exists and has not yet been sold.

|||| **TABLE 16-2**

A "Perfect" Short Hedge

Cash Market	Futures Market

April:
  Open long position by planting wheat: anticipated harvest is 40,000 bushels
  Spot price of wheat: $3.67 per bushel
  Value of cash market position: $3.67 × 40,000 = $146,800
September:
  Close long position in cash market by harvesting 40,000 bushels of wheat; receive $3.52 per bushel, a decline of $0.15 per bushel from April
  Value of closing trade: $3.52 × 40,000 = $140,800
  Loss based upon April price: $140,800 − $146,800 = $6,000
Net loss = $0
	April:
	  Open short position by selling 8 futures contracts (40,000 bushels) with November maturity for $3.86 per bushel
	  Value of futures position: $3.86 × 40,000 = $154,400
	September:
	  Close short position by purchasing 8 futures contracts at $3.71 per bushel, a decline of $0.15 per bushel
	
	  Value of closing trade: $3.71 × 40,000 = $148,400
	  Profit from futures trading: $154,400 − $148,400 = $6,000

Harvest is anticipated in September, but in the meantime, the farmer needs financing for seed, fertilizer, pesticides, and the other expenses associated with growing the crop. Since the wheat is not yet sold, and therefore no income has been realized from the crop, the farmer will usually want to borrow funds to cover these expenses. The crop itself could serve as collateral for the loan, but its value at harvest is not yet known, since the price of wheat fluctuates on a daily basis. Banks prefer collateral with a known value.

The crop's value can be established before harvest by hedging the long cash market position with a short position in the futures market. The bank is unwilling to use the current spot price of wheat ($3.67 per bushel) to establish the crop's value, since the wheat will not be harvested until September, and it will have to be sold at September's price. However, by hedging with wheat futures, the farmer can establish a price for his crop now, even though it will not be harvested for several months into the future.

The hedge is formed when eight wheat futures contracts with a November maturity are sold. Assume the price per bushel on the futures market is $3.86, which is higher than the current spot price. Since each wheat futures contract is written for 5,000 bushels, the sale represents a short position in the futures market of 40,000 bushels (8 contracts × 5,000 bushels per contract = 40,000 bushels). This offsets perfectly the expected crop (long position) of 40,000 bushels.

To see why this position is hedged, let's assume the spot price of wheat falls by $0.15 (from $3.67 to $3.52) before the crop matures in September. Without the hedge, losses (relative to the April price) would be $6,000 (40,000 bushels × $0.15 per bushel = $6,000).

Note that the April sale of wheat in the futures market requires a reversing trade shortly before the futures contracts mature or else the wheat will have to be delivered to a grain storage facility in the Chicago area. High transportation costs from wheat-producing regions in the Great Plains to Chicago make delivery impractical. Assume that, in September, the price of wheat futures contract falls by $0.15 to $3.71 per bushel, just like prices in the cash market. Thus, eight futures contracts (40,000 bushels) can be purchased for only $3.71 per bushel, which covers the eight contracts sold in April at $3.86 per bushel. Profits on this transaction were $6,000 (40,000 bushels × $0.15 per bushel), and the opportunity losses in the cash market are exactly offset by profits in the futures market. ||||

The following example demonstrates a long hedge.

EXAMPLE 16-3   A "PERFECT" LONG HEDGE

Assume that a major grain processor wants to bid on a contract to export soybeans to the Soviet Union. If its bid is successful, the processor will need 100,000 bushels in December. However, before submitting its bid, the firm needs to know the price of the soybeans. It can use a long hedge with soybean futures for this purpose.

Assume it is now June. Since the processor needs soybeans and does not have a current supply, the processor is short 100,000 bushels in the cash market. To offset this short position, the processor should go long 100,000 bushels (or 20 contracts) for January delivery. Assume that the June spot price of soybeans is $6.00 per bushel and that the December futures are selling for $6.40 per bushel.

By December, the demand for soybeans is stronger than anticipated. The spot price advances to $6.50, a gain of $0.50 over June's price. The futures price (December maturity) is $6.90. How would the long hedger have fared? The profits and losses from this hedge are summarized in Table 16-3. Note that the $50,000 loss in the cash market was perfectly offset by a $50,000 profit on the futures side of the hedge. ||||

Example 16-3 has illustrated a "perfect" long hedge. Perfect long hedges result when (1) basis does not change over the life of the hedge, and (2) the cash market position and the futures market position are identical in size. Perfect hedges are usually impossible to attain in practice.

In Example 16-2 (the short hedge), the basis started out as $0.19 ($3.86 − $3.67) and was still $0.19 ($3.71 − $3.52) at the conclusion of the hedge. What would have happened if the basis had changed? Table 16-4 illustrates just this event. Here, basis starts out as $0.19 per bushel and narrows before the hedge matures, to $0.14 per bushel. Because of this, profits from the futures side of the hedge do not exactly offset losses from the cash market side. In this example, the hedge produces a net profit, but it is important to realize that, if the basis had widened instead of narrowed, a net loss would have resulted. Thus, the movement of basis

---

|||| **TABLE 16-3**

A "Perfect" Long Hedge

Cash Market	Futures Market
June:	June:
Grain processor bids on an order to be shipped in December that will require 100,000 bushels of soybeans; thus, the processor is short 100,000 bushels in the cash market.	Processor opens long position in futures by buying 20 soybean contracts with a January maturity at $6.40 per bushel: each contract represents 5,000 bushels of soybeans.
Value of short position: $6.00 per bushel × 100,000 bushels = $600,000	Value of long position: $6.40 per bushel × 100,000 bushels = $640,000
December:	December:
Close short position in cash market by purchasing 100,000 bushels at $6.50 per bushel	Close futures position by selling 20 January contracts at $6.90 per bushel
Value of closing trade: $6.50 × 100,000 = $650,000	Value of closing trade: $6.90 × 100,000 = $690,000
Loss based upon June price: $650,000 − $600,000 = $50,000	Profit based on June price: $690,000 − $640,000 = $50,000

|||| **TABLE 16-4**

An Imperfect Short Hedge: A Change in Basis

Cash Market	Futures Market
April:	April:
Open long position by planting 40,000 bushels of wheat	Open short position by selling 8 futures contracts (40,000 bushels) with November maturity for $3.86 per bushel
Spot price of wheat: $3.67 per bushel	
Value of cash market position: $3.67 × 40,000 = $146,800	Value of futures position: $3.86 × 40,000 = $154,400
September:	September:
Close long position in cash market by harvesting 40,000 bushels; receive $3.52 per bushel, a decline of $0.15 per bushel from the April price	Close short futures position by purchasing 8 futures contracts with November maturity for $3.66 per bushel, a decline of $0.20 per bushel from the April price
Value of closing transaction: $3.52 × 40,000 = $140,800	Value of closing transaction: $3.66 × 40,000 = $146,400
Loss on cash market side, based on April prices: $140,800 − $146,800 = $6,000	Profit on futures side, based on April prices: $154,400 − $146,400 = $8,000
	Net profit = $2,000

|||| **TABLE 16-5**

An Imperfect Short Hedge: Unequal Opening Positions

Cash Market	Futures Market
April:	April:
Open long position by planting 42,000 bushels of wheat at $3.67 per bushel	Open short position by selling 8 futures contracts (40,000 bushels) with November maturity for $3.86 per bushel
Value of position: $3.67 × 42,000 = $154,140	Value of position: $3.86 × 40,000 = $154,400
September:	September:
Close long position in cash market by harvesting 42,000 bushels; receive $3.52 per bushel, a decline of $0.15 per bushel from the April price	Close short futures position by purchasing 8 futures contracts (40,000 bushels) with November maturity for $3.71 per bushel, a decline of $0.15 per bushel from April's price
Value of closing transaction: $3.52 × 42,000 = $147,840	Value of closing transaction: $3.71 × 40,000 = $148,400
Loss based on April price: $154,140 − $147,840 = $6,300	Profit based on April price: $154,400 − $148,400 = $6,000
Net loss = $300	

during the life of the hedge represents risk to the hedger, since it introduces uncertainty that cannot be controlled.

Unequal opening positions also introduce risk to a hedged position. Examine Table 16-5, which depicts an initial position of 42,000 bushels in the cash market and 40,000 bushels (eight contracts) in the futures market. Here, a net loss of $300 results, even though the basis does not change throughout the life of the hedge. Take a moment to examine both Table 16-4 and Table 16-5, and make sure that you understand the full sequence of events in both examples.

INTEREST RATE FUTURES

Since their introduction in 1975, *interest rate futures* have been among the most successful of all futures contracts. Interest rate futures are contracts that call for the purchase (or sale) of debt securities with fixed principal on a specified date at a specified price. Interest rate futures contracts are offered on a variety of securities, but the most popular are the Treasury bond contract traded at the Chicago Board of Trade, the 10-year Treasury note contract also traded at the CBOT, and the Eurodollar contract traded at the International Monetary Market at the Chicago Mercantile Exchange.

The prices of interest rate futures rise and fall with the expected future prices of the underlying securities. The expected future prices of these securities, in turn, move inversely to changes in expected future interest rates.

TREASURY BILL FUTURES

Treasury bills are among the most important of all financial securities. They dominate the U.S. money market in terms of volume and have considerable influence on other short-term interest rates. Treasury bill futures do not play quite as significant a role in the futures markets, although they are an important futures contract.

Treasury bill futures began trading in January 1976 at the International Monetary Market (IMM), which is part of the Chicago Mercantile Exchange. The contracts call for delivery of $1 million of Treasury bills maturing from 90 to 92 days after the specified delivery date. Prices are quoted in terms of percentages of face value. The quoted price is 100% less the annualized discount yield.

The amount the buyer pays upon the maturity of a T-bill futures contract is calculated as follows:

$$pi = \$1,000,000 - (\$1,000,000 \times dy \times \text{days}/360) \qquad (16\text{-}2)$$

where

$$
\begin{aligned}
pi &= \text{principal invoice, or the amount billed from the} \\
&\quad \text{seller to the buyer} \\
\$1,000,000 &= \text{size of contracts traded on the IMM} \\
dy &= \text{discount yield, in decimal form, obtained from} \\
&\quad \text{the quotations} \\
\text{days} &= \text{number of days left until maturity of the bills} \\
&\quad \text{delivered against the futures contract}
\end{aligned}
$$

For example, if the buyer paid 92.76 for the futures, based on a discount yield of 7.24%, and the seller delivered T-bills with 90 days remaining until their maturity, the principal invoice amount would be

$$pi = \$1,000,000 - (\$1,000,000 \times .0724 \times 90/360)$$
$$pi = \$981,900$$

The minimum price change (or "tic") for T-bill futures contracts is 1/100 of 1%, called a basis point, which amounts to a price change of $25 per contract ($1,000,000 × .0001 × 90/360). At this time, exchanges limit the daily price changes to 50 basis points ($1,250 per contract) above or below the previous day's settlement price.

As with other futures contracts, most buyers and sellers offset their positions before the contracts mature. Deliveries are made on fewer than 1% of all contracts.

EURODOLLAR FUTURES

If success is measured by trading volume, Eurodollar futures are the most successful of all financial futures contracts. The large number of contract maturities is possible only because the market supports each of them with sufficient volume.

Eurodollars are large, dollar-denominated deposits placed with overseas banks. Originally, the market was headquartered in London (thus the name "Eurodollars"), but in the past few years, this market has grown immensely and the term "Eurodollar" now refers to a dollar deposit placed in any overseas bank.

Initially, Eurodollar market participants were driven by a desire to circumvent reserve requirements and Regulation Q interest rate ceilings. Today, however, the market has a life of its own. Eurodollar loans often carry lower interest rates than domestic loans, and the Eurodollar savings rate is often higher than the rate offered domestically. The Eurodollar market offers simultaneous rate advantages to both borrowers and savers because the market is extremely efficient. On the savings side, the market enjoys low overhead costs since most deposits are denominated in amounts well into seven figures. On the lending side, the market is relatively safe because Eurodollar participants are large, multinational firms that often possess considerable financial strength.

The underlying security for a Eurodollar futures contract is a Eurodollar time deposit with a 3-month maturity. Eurodollar futures are cash settlement contracts. Cash settlement contracts do not require the underlying security to be delivered at maturity. An equivalent amount of cash is delivered instead.

The Eurodollar market is based upon LIBOR, the London Interbank Offered Rate. LIBOR is the rate at which participating Eurodollar banks are willing to loan excess funds to one another. The federal funds rate might be considered a close domestic parallel. Eurodollar deposits are usually accepted at a small discount from LIBOR, and Eurodollar loans are made at a small premium to LIBOR.

Eurodollar futures are traded domestically on the International Monetary Market of the Chicago Mercantile Exchange. A similar contract is traded in London on the London International Financial Futures Exchange (LIFFE). The contract size on both markets is $1 million. Price quotations for Eurodollar futures are computed by subtracting the annualized add-on yield from 100%. Thus, a quotation of 91.87 for the settlement price of a contract is equivalent to a yield of 8.13% (100 − 91.87 = 8.13).

The IMM requires cash settlement at the maturity of the futures contract. The amount of the settlement is

$$pi = (100\% - \text{average LIBOR})(\$1,000,000) \qquad (16\text{-}3)$$

where

$$pi = \text{principal invoice, or amount the seller is}$$
$$\text{billed upon contract maturity}$$

The average LIBOR is measured with a painstaking process designed to ensure that no single Eurodollar bank can exert undue influence on the futures settlement price. The LIBOR is measured both at closing time on the maturity date of the contract and at another time selected at random within 90 minutes of closing. The average of these two rates is used to establish the LIBOR settlement rate.

To arrive at the average LIBOR, the IMM samples at least 12 major Eurodollar banks from a prepublished list of 20 maintained by the exchange. Quotations as of the closing time and a randomly selected time within 90 minutes of closing are obtained by telephone. The two highest and two lowest quotations for each time are discarded, and the remaining 8 are averaged. The average of those two averages (one for each of the two times) becomes the LIBOR settlement rate.

TREASURY BOND FUTURES

Treasury bond futures are contracts that call for the purchase or sale of 8% U.S. Treasury bonds with face value of $100,000. The bonds must have a maturity of at least 15 years, and if they are callable, they must not be subject to call within the same 15-year time period. Initial margin for T-bond futures is $2,500 per contract, and the maintenance margin is $2,000 per contract.

The Chicago Board of Trade (CBOT) contracts are written for $100,000 of Treasury bonds, while the Mid-America Commodity Exchange contracts are written for only $50,000 of bonds. Prices of both contracts are quoted in percentages of face value, with the unit of measure being $\frac{1}{32}$ of 1%. Thus, a settlement price of 88–24 for the CBOT contract with a September maturity means it closed at 88.75% of its face value, or $88,750 ($88\frac{24}{32}\% \times \$100,000 = \$88,750$). Compare this price to the initial margin requirement of only $2,500, and you can see that there is a great deal of leverage in T-bond futures.

The minimum price change from trade to trade is $\frac{1}{32}$ of 1% of the contract face value, which is $31.25 ($100,000 $\times$ $\frac{1}{32}$ $\times$ $\frac{1}{100}$ = $31.25). The maximum allowable price change, or price limit, is two percentage points (or $2,000) above or below the previous day's settlement price. On days after a limit move is reached, the limit increases to three points, or $3,000.

Since there are almost never any Treasury bonds that meet the exact requirements for delivery, the futures exchange, recognizing this, incorporates a conversion factor that adjusts the value of the bonds actually delivered against a futures contract to a hypothetical bond with an 8% yield and a 15-year maturity. If a Treasury bond existed with a coupon rate of 8% and a maturity of exactly 15 years, it would have a conversion factor of 1.0. Bonds with less than an 8% coupon rate have conversion factors of less than 1.0, and bonds with coupon rates greater than 8% have conversion factors of greater than 1.0. Equation 16-4 shows how conversion factors are used to calculate the amount the buyer is invoiced upon delivery of a T-bond futures contract:

$$pi = P_s \times 1,000 \times cv \qquad (16\text{-}4)$$

where

pi = principal invoice, or the current market value of bonds delivered against the futures contract; the amount the buyer must pay upon contract maturity

P_s = settlement price of the futures contract upon maturity

cv = conversion factor for bonds of the coupon rate and maturity selected by the seller for delivery

EXAMPLE 16-4 CALCULATING THE PRINCIPAL INVOICE FOR TREASURY BONDS

Assume that bonds with a 14% coupon and a term of 21 years, 5 months are delivered against a futures contract. The conversion factor for these bonds is 1.6080. This means that these bonds are worth approximately 161% of the value of 15-year, 8% coupon bonds. Assume that T-bond futures closed at 84–01, indicating that buyers are willing to pay $84,031.25 for 15-year, 8% bonds. If bonds with a 14% yield and a 21-year, 5-month life are delivered, however, the principal invoice is

$$84\tfrac{1}{32} \times 1,000 \times 1.6080 = \$135,122.25$$

This means that the buyer has to pay more than the futures price for the bonds ($135,122.25 versus $84,031.25), because the seller delivered bonds of greater value than called for in the contract. The buyer did not "lose" this money, nor did the seller necessarily profit. Securities with greater value than those called for in the contract were delivered, so the invoice price was adjusted accordingly.

Now let's look at a situation where the seller delivers bonds with a coupon rate of less than 8%. The conversion factor for 7⅝% bonds with 17 years, one month until maturity is 0.9660. This means that the bonds are worth about 96.6% of the value of an 8%, 15-year bond. Assuming the same settlement price (84¹⁄₃₂) as above, the buyer is invoiced

$$84^1/_{32} \times 1{,}000 \times 0.9660 = \$81{,}174.1875$$

In other words, the buyer promised to pay $84,031.25 (indicated by the futures settlement price) for bonds with an 8% coupon and 15 years until maturity. Since the seller delivered bonds that had only a 7⅝% coupon, the invoice price was not quite as great. ||||

Conversion factors for any bond delivered against T-bond futures can be approximated by discounting a bond with $1 of principal by 4% per semiannual period. (Don't forget that Treasury bonds pay coupons semiannually, and that the assumed coupon rate in T-bond futures contracts is 8% per year.) For example, suppose a Treasury bond has 17 years remaining in its life and has a 10% annual coupon. Assuming this bond has a principal of $1, its semiannual coupon payment would be $0.05 for the next 34 periods. With a financial calculator, verify the fact that the present value of its remaining cash flows, when discounted at 4% per semiannual period, is 1.1841, which is also the conversion factor for this bond.[4] The bond is worth approximately 118% of an 8%, 15-year bond, primarily because of its high coupon rate.

Sellers of T-bond futures can select from a variety of bonds to make delivery. Due to nuances in the calculation of conversion factors, different Treasury bonds have slightly different costs when delivered against futures. The bond that results in the greatest profits (at delivery) to the holder of a short futures position is known as "cheapest to deliver."

The profits *(p)* upon delivery of a particular Treasury bond are calculated as

$$p = pi - \text{bond price} \times 1{,}000$$

where

p = profits at delivery

pi = principal invoice (futures price × conversion factor × 1,000)

bond price = market price of T-bond on delivery date

As mentioned earlier, the objective of the holder of a short futures position is to find the one bond that meets the requirements of the T-bond futures contract and that maximizes profits upon delivery. Treasury bond futures are usually priced against the single bond in the cash market that is "cheapest to deliver." This bond varies from time to time. Changes

---

[4]Using your calculator, enter 34 = N, 0.05 = PMT, 4 = i, and 1.00 = FV. A value of 1.1841 is found for PV.

in T-bond futures prices correlate most closely to changes in the cash market price of this bond.

HEDGING WITH INTEREST RATE FUTURES

As with commodity futures, both long and short hedges are possible with interest rate futures. For example, a long hedge involving T-bill futures may be used to lock in current high levels of interest rates on money market securities. Assume that, in 60 days, a corporate treasurer anticipates investing $1 million of excess liquidity for a term of 90 days. He wants to lock in today's rate of interest, which is considered attractive at 8.59%. The actions that are necessary in both the futures market and with cash are summarized in Table 16-6.

Note that the profit from the futures side of the hedge was exactly offset by the opportunity loss on the cash side of the hedge. The hedge described is a "perfect hedge" since the size of the initial position taken in the futures market exactly matches the investment principal anticipated in the cash market, and the basis did not change over the life of the hedge. Thus, the treasurer effectively "locked in" the rate of interest available when the hedge was opened. Of course, had rates moved upward, the treasurer would not have benefited so long as the hedged position was maintained.

Short hedges involving interest rate futures are also relatively common. For example, suppose a large real estate developer plans to initiate a commercial project in six months. The developer will need to borrow a substantial sum of money at that time and would like to lock in today's rate of interest on the loan. This can be done with a short hedge involving the initial sale of interest rate futures on instruments with principal and maturity similar to the anticipated mortgage loan. Depending on the term

|||| **TABLE 16-6**

Long Hedge with T-Bill Futures

Cash Market	Futures Market
Initial position:	Initial position:
If $1 million were invested at this time, the interest earned would be $21,475:	Go long one T-bill futures contract:
$1M × .0859 × (90/360) = $21,475	$pi = \$1M - (\$1M \times .0859 \times 90)/360$ = $978,525
60 days later:	60 days later:
By waiting until this time to invest, the treasurer earns only $18,750:	Cover initial position by selling one T-bill futures contract priced at a rate of 7.5%:
$1M × .075 × (90/360) = $18,750	$pi = \$1M - (\$1M \times .075 \times 90)/360$ = $981,250
Loss on cash: $21,475 − $18,750 = $2,725	Profit on futures: $981,250 − $978,525 = $2,725

of the anticipated mortgage, possible candidates include futures on Treasury bonds and Treasury notes. Futures on mortgage-backed securities, which were once common, are no longer traded in significant volume. A reversing trade would be made on the same day the mortgage was signed. If the basis does not change, and the principal of the futures contracts exactly matches that of the mortgage, a perfect hedge will result, and the interest rate existing on the day the hedge was opened will be the effective rate of the mortgage.

|||| # STOCK INDEX FUTURES

Stock index futures were introduced after interest rate futures and began trading in significant volume only as recently as the mid-1980s. Significant trading volume occurs on four market indexes: (1) the S&P 500 Index, (2) the Value Line Composite Index, (3) the Major Market Index, and (4) the NYSE Composite Index. Certain characteristics of futures contracts on these stock indexes are listed in Table 16-7. The S&P 500 Index and the NYSE Composite Index were discussed in some detail in Chapter 2. The Major Market Index and the Value Line Composite Index, which are used mainly in futures trading, are described here.

The original objective in constructing the Major Market Index (MMI) was to replicate the Dow Jones Industrial Average (DJIA). Legal action by Dow Jones prevented this, so the MMI was developed with 20 stocks, selected so that movements in the MMI correspond as closely as possible to movements in the Dow Jones Industrials. Table 16-8 lists the stocks in the MMI and the DJIA. Note the large number of firms that are listed in both.

The Value Line Composite Index is the broadest of all the stock indexes upon which futures are traded on an active basis. It is composed of approximately 1,700 stocks, listed on all major exchanges and on the over-the-counter market. The index is calculated as a geometric average of the product of each stock's price relative times the index value for the prior day:

|||| **TABLE 16-7**

Stock Index Futures Contracts

Contract	Index Composition	Initial Margin

Est vol 2,200; vol Fri 5,641; open int 6,196, −532.
The index: High 93.36; Low 92.47; Close 92.72 −.16

SOURCE: *The Wall Street Journal,* May 21, 1991. Reprinted by permission of *The Wall Street Journal* © Dow Jones & Co. Inc. (1991). All Rights Reserved Worldwide.

|||| **TABLE 16-8**

Composition of the Major Market Index and the Dow Jones
Industrial Average (May, 1991)

Dow Jones Industrial Average	Major Market Index
Allied Signal	American Express
Alcoa	AT&T
American Express	Chevron
AT&T	Coca Cola
Bethlehem Steel	Dow Chemical
Boeing	DuPont
Caterpillar	Eastman Kodak
Chevron	Exxon
Coca Cola	General Electric
Disney	General Motors
DuPont	IBM
Eastman Kodak	International Paper
Exxon	Johnson & Johnson
General Electric	McDonalds
General Motors	Merck & Co.
Goodyear	Minnesota Mining & Manuf.
IBM	Mobil
International Paper	Philip Morris
McDonalds	Procter and Gamble
Merck & Co.	Sears
Minnesota Mining & Manuf.	
J.P. Morgan	
Philip Morris	
Procter and Gamble	
Sears	
Texaco	
Union Carbide	
United Technologies	
Westinghouse	
Woolworth	

SOURCE: Chicago Board of Trade and *The Wall Street Journal.*

$$VLI_t = \sum_{i=1}^{n} (P_{i,t}/P_{i,t-1})^{1/n}(VLI_{t-1}) \qquad (16\text{-}5)$$

where

VLI_t = Value Line Index value on day t

P_t = stock price on day t

n = number of firms in the index

The changes in value of all four stock indexes are highly correlated
with one another. The MMI, however, is the most volatile. This should
not be too surprising since it is the least diversified, containing only 20
securities.

CHARACTERISTICS OF INDEX FUTURES

Stock index futures are cash settlement contracts. Since it is impossible to deliver an intangible like a stock index, the seller delivers an amount of cash that is determined by the value of the stock index upon contract maturity. The specific amount of cash to be delivered is determined as follows:

$$pi = i_t \times \text{multiplier} \qquad (16\text{-}6)$$

where

$$pi = \text{principal invoice, or the amount of cash due from the seller at contract maturity}$$
$$i_t = \text{index value at contract maturity}$$
$$\text{multiplier} = \text{250 for MMI futures, 500 for NYSE, Value Line, and S\&P 500 futures}$$

PRICING INDEX FUTURES: AN ANOMALY

Two fundamental pressures act upon futures prices.[5] The first pressure tends to equate the current futures price to the spot price expected when the futures contract matures. Without this equality, speculators would have tremendous opportunity to profit from correctly anticipating future spot prices. The second pressure tends to equate futures prices to the current spot price plus the cost of carry. Without this equality, arbitrage opportunities would exist for futures traders who could take positions in the futures markets and hold them to delivery.

If futures markets worked in an orderly manner, these two pressures would act in a consistent fashion to form consensus price levels of futures contracts. As we will see, this is not always the case, especially with stock index futures. In fact, with index futures, it is difficult for the two pressures ever to act together to form a single price.

To illustrate, assume that a market index is truly representative of equity prices, so that changes in the market are fully reflected in changes in the index value. Also, assume that dividends on market index stocks are known in advance and paid at the end of the period. (Recall that dividend announcements usually precede dividend payments by several weeks.)

As a matter of notation, assume that there are only two time periods, now and the future, indicated by the subscripts (0) and (1), respectively. The market return (R_m) is calculated as

$$(I_1 - I_0)/I_0 + D_m = R_m \qquad (16\text{-}7)$$

where

$$D_m = \text{aggregate yield on the market index stocks}$$

[5]The discussion in this section is based upon Robert W. Kolb, *Understanding Futures Markets,* 2d ed. (Glenview, Ill.: 1987), Scott Foresman and Company, Chapter 8.

I_1 = market index value at the end of the future time period

If there is pressure for the current futures price (F_0) to equate to the expected *(E)* future cash market price, so that

$$F_0 = E(I_1) \qquad (16\text{-}8)$$

Equation 16-7, the expected return on the market, can be redefined as

$$E(R_m) = (E(I_1) - I_0)/I_0 + D_m \qquad (16\text{-}9)$$

Substituting the definition of F_0 from Equation 16-8 into Equation 16-9 results in

$$E(R_m) = (F_0 - I_0)/I_0 + D_m \qquad (16\text{-}10)$$

Solving for F_0 and rearranging gives the following result:

$$F_0 = I_0[1 + E(R_m) - D_m] \qquad (16\text{-}11)$$

Equation 16-11 simply states that the current futures price equals the current index value plus the expected appreciation on the index. The expected appreciation on the index is the expected market return less the dividend yield. This equation represents the fundamental result from the assumption that the current futures price must equal the expected future spot price. We will use this result again later.

Recall that the second basic force acting upon futures prices tends to equate futures prices to the sum of the current spot price plus the cost of carry for the contract. Letting R_c be the percentage cost of carry for one period, and assuming this is equal to the financing rate, then the cost of carry acts upon futures prices in the following manner:[6]

$$F_0 = (1 + R_c)I_0 - D_m I_0 \qquad (16\text{-}12)$$

Equation 6-12 simply states that the futures price must equal the current spot price plus the cost of carry to delivery. The cost of carry is reduced by the dollar amount of dividends received over the period.

Factoring Equation 16-12 for the term I_0 yields

$$F_0 = I_0(1 + R_c - D_m) \qquad (16\text{-}13)$$

Substituting the definition of F_0 found in Equation 16-11 into Equation 16-13, we obtain

$$I_0[1 + E(R_m) - D_m] = I_0(1 + R_c - D_m) \qquad (16\text{-}14)$$

Factoring for common terms gives us

$$E(R_m) = R_c \qquad (16\text{-}15)$$

---

[6]The cost of carry for a cash settlement contract like stock index futures equals the cost of short-term financing. No storage, insurance, deterioration, or shrinkage to cash is involved.

Equation 16-15 says that the expected market return equals the cost of carry, a condition that we know will not hold and does not even make sense! The cost of carry is a short-term interest rate, which is aligned very closely to the prime interest rate or other short-term interest rates. The expected return on the market index represents a return on a portfolio of risky assets and should be much higher. The fact that this analysis reduces to Equation 16-15, which cannot hold, indicates that either the expected future spot price assumption or the cost of carry assumption that we discussed earlier (or maybe both!) does not always hold. Consequently, there are profit opportunities in stock index futures for speculators, arbitragers, or both.

|||| HEDGING WITH INDEX FUTURES: PROGRAM TRADING AND INDEX ARBITRAGE

Roughly 10% of the total volume of trading on the New York Stock Exchange can be characterized as program trading, and this proportion is expected to grow in the years to come.[7] The Exchange defines *program trading* as "the purchase or sale of a basket of 15 or more stocks."[8] *Index arbitrage* accounts for about one-half of all program trading. In this strategy, a trader takes opposing positions in stock index futures and a large block of the underlying stocks in an attempt to take advantage of slight price differences between the two. By doing so, the trader hopes to lock in a short-term return over and above the return available from money market securities. Since the trader's position is hedged, this activity involves very little risk.

Arbitrage activities tend to narrow the difference between cash and futures prices. Since stock index futures are cash settlement contracts, the basis of index futures should reflect only the cost of short-term financing. With the predictability of basis, it is not hard for arbitragers to profit from a hedged position when basis climbs outside its normal range.

SOURCES OF PROFITS

Index arbitrage is done with futures on stock indexes and "baskets" of stocks that replicate the indexes that the futures are based upon.

Due to the cost of carry, futures contracts normally sell at a small premium relative to the index value. With financial futures, the cost of carry is calculated assuming the securities underlying the futures contract are purchased and paid for with borrowed funds, and held until the maturity of the futures contract. For example, if a stock index futures contract had 60 days to maturity, and the short-term interest rate was

---

[7]William Power, "Program Traders Back in Gear; Fasten Safety Belts," *Wall Street Journal,* April 19, 1989, p. C1.

[8]Ibid.

8%, the cost of carry would be approximately 1.33% of the contract value (8% × 60/360 = 1.33%). The opportune time for program traders occurs when the futures price moves out of equilibrium relative to the prices of the underlying stocks.

Assume, for example, that the S&P 500 Index is at 250, and that the futures on the S&P Index are selling at 260. Assume also that the futures expire in 60 days. An index arbitrager would go long in the cash market (purchase the stocks that underlie the S&P 500 Index) and take a short position in the futures market by selling a like amount of futures contracts. At this point, the arbitrager is hedged, and the profits to be made from a decrease in the spread between the futures and the underlying stocks are locked in. Index arbitraging is normally done in amounts well into seven figures ($10 million or more is not uncommon) so a large position in futures is necessary to provide a hedge.

No matter what happens to the value of the stocks, the arbitragers should make money. If the stocks fall in value, say, to an index value of 240, arbitrage will force the futures down also, and if the futures prices fall more than the stock index, the losses in the cash market from holding stocks will be more than offset by profits in the futures market when the short sale is covered. If the stocks go up, say, to 260, futures will rise also. When this happens, the stocks may rise in value more than the rise in the underlying futures contracts, and if they do, the losses in the futures market will be more than offset by gains in the cash market.

EXECUTING PROGRAM TRADES

Program trading in the form of index arbitrage is relatively new, having been initiated in the mid-1980s. Prior to the advent of stock index futures in the early 1980s, along with the computer hardware and software necessary to monitor prices in several markets simultaneously, arbitraging was simply not possible.

At first, most arbitraging was done against the S&P 500 Index futures contract. Since August 1985, however, when the MMI futures contract was increased in size by a factor of 1.5, arbitraging with MMI futures has gained in popularity.

MMI futures offer arbitragers several advantages. First, since the index contains only 20 stocks, a smaller number of shares can be purchased and still have the futures position completely offset in the cash market. *Business Week* estimates that only about $2.5 million is required to participate profitably in arbitraging against the MMI, as opposed to twice that amount with S&P 500 Index futures.[9] Also, the MMI is a share-weighted index, as opposed to the value-weighted S&P 500. This means that, with the MMI, arbitragers can simply purchase an equal number of shares in each of the 20 MMI firms. With the S&P 500, the stock

[9]"What's Making the Market Swing So Wildly," *Business Week,* February 9, 1987, pp. 72–73.

portfolio proportions must be constantly adjusted because the S&P 500 is a value-weighted index and the weights of the target portfolio change as the market prices of the stocks change.

Arbitrage positions can be reversed any time that prices in the cash and futures market reflect only normal basis. Normal convergence between futures prices and cash market prices has usually been sufficient for arbitragers to close out their positions well before contract maturity and still generate a handsome profit. Positions are normally reversed with a market-on-close sell order, which instructs the broker to sell the futures contracts at the day's closing market price. Selling or buying the futures contract and the underlying stocks at the closing price ensures

SIDELIGHT

A Real-Life Strategy for Making 14% Risk-Free

On February 26, Jeffrey Miller of the New York brokerage firm Miller Tabak Hirsch & Co. bought 2,000 shares of each of the 20 stocks that make up the Major Market Index (MMI). He paid $2,749,000, putting down half in cash and borrowing the rest at 8.5%. Simultaneously, he sold short 35 futures contracts on the MMI expiring on March 21. Each futures contract was priced at 313.55, while the MMI itself stood at 311.74. The idea was to profit from the spread—in this case, 1.81—between the futures and the index. The value of each futures contract is the price multiplied by $250. So Miller's books were credited for $78,387.50 per contract (313.55 × $250) for a total of $2,743,563.

The 20 Stocks in the Major Market Index	Price Paid on February 26	Price at Closing on March 21	Dividends Paid between Dates
American Express	64	65⅝	
AT&T	22½	22⅞	
Chevron	37⅞	37⅜	
Coca-Cola	92	103⅜	$0.78
Dow Chemical	48¾	52⅜	
Du Pont	70½	72½	
Eastman Kodak	55	59¾	
Exxon	54⅞	54¾	
General Electric	75½	75¾	0.58
General Motors	78¼	83¼	
IBM	158⅛	148½	
International Paper	57	60	
Johnson & Johnson	48⅜	54	
Merck	150¾	161¼	0.90
3M	97¼	104	
Mobil Oil	30⅛	29½	
Philip Morris	101⅛	119¼	1.15
Procter & Gamble	67	73½	
Sears	42⅞	46⅛	
U.S. Steel	22⅝	22¾	
Major Market Index	311.74	328.07	
Futures on MMI	313.55	328.07	

that the prices for the futures contracts and stocks will both be at the settlement price of the contract.

Sidelight 16-2 describes an arbitrage transaction executed by a brokerage firm during the months of February and March 1986. The position was held for slightly less than one month, yet it generated an annualized return in excess of 14%. (This compares quite favorably with the Treasury bill rate of 6.8% during this period.) Examine the table in Sidelight 16-2 to make sure you understand (1) how the initial position was hedged, (2) how the cash market position was selected, and (3) how the returns were calculated. The computer program provided with this text calculates the profits that can be earned from arbitraging against the MMI. Inputs

Miller had no idea which way the market would move, but he knew he couldn't lose. That's because at 4 P.M. on March 21, the futures on the MMI and the index itself would have to be equal. Miller didn't care if the stocks fell, because the futures, which were priced above the index, would fall farther. So the loss on his stocks would be more than offset by the profit from the short sale of the futures.

As things worked out, the opposite happened. Stocks moved up sharply, and so did the futures—but not as much, because the spread disappears at expiration. In this case, Miller's profit from the stocks exceeded his loss from the short sale of the futures.

As the market closed on March 21, Miller sold all his stocks and allowed his futures contracts to expire. The table shows how Miller fared.

Income		
Profit on stocks		
Amount received on March 21	$2,893,000	
Amount paid on February 26	2,749,000	$144,000
Dividends		$6,820
Costs		
Interest on $1,374,500		−8,438
Loss on futures		
Amount credited on February 26	2,743,563	
Amount debited on expiration	2,870,613	−127,050
Miller's transactions fees		−1,100
Net profit		$14,232
Original investment		$1,374,500
Annualized return on investment		14.34%
Treasury bill rate		6.80
Bonus risk-free return		7.54

SOURCE: "Those Big Swings on Wall Street," *Business Week,* April 7, 1986, p. 34.

needed include the cash market prices of the 20 stocks comprising the MMI, the futures index prices, the amount of margin on the share purchases (as well as the borrowing rate), and the length of the holding period.

THE CONTROVERSY SURROUNDING PROGRAM TRADING

Program trading is highly controversial. Long before the stock market crash of October 1987, Wall Street analysts were warning that program trading had the potential to trigger a market meltdown.[10] In addition, many market observers believe that program trading has contributed to increased market volatility in recent years. (Other observers dispute this.) The financial press has coined the phrase "triple witching hour" for days when stock index futures and options mature. These days—usually the third Friday of every third month—have often been accompanied by large movements in the popular stock market averages.

High transactions costs make it difficult for most investors, including many institutions, to benefit from program trading. According to *Business Week,* "it's an insider's game—and the brokerage houses themselves get first crack."[11] Many investors view program trading as an activity that introduces wild market volatility on certain trading days, yet one from which they are excluded. This may cause the stock market as an institution to lose its credibility with the general public.

There is also concern that program trading concentrates tremendous economic power in the hands of a few large, institutional investors. *Business Week* quoted an unnamed Goldman Sachs executive who estimated that from 10% to 15% of all NYSE volume was generated by program trading.[12] Nobody knows for sure, but it is estimated that program trading is done by no more than two dozen major firms.[13] While most of these firms trade for both their clients and their own accounts, *Financial World* estimates that only 30% (approximately) of all program trading is done for clients.[14] This caused John Jensen, of Massachusetts Financial Services, Inc., to comment that "People in the investment advisory business are beginning to feel that the major brokerage houses are their adversaries."[15]

---

[10]A Morgan Stanley executive warned of this possibility in "Those Big Swings on Wall Street," *Business Week,* April 7, 1986, p. 33. John Phelan, the chairman of the New York Stock Exchange, also warned of an "uncontrollable financial meltdown, where the stock market could sink 150, 200, or more points in a single day." "Big Board's Crusade against Program Trading," *Business Week,* March 27, 1987, pp. 134–8. Note that both these warnings came before the stock market crash of October 1987.

[11]"Those Big Swings on Wall Street," p. 35.

[12]Ibid., pp. 32–36.

[13]"Big Board's Crusade against Program Trading," p. 134.

[14]Delia Lachenauer, "Program Trading: Demystifying a Complex Game," *Financial World,* June 24, 1986, pp. 54–59.

[15]Ibid., p. 58.

Another criticism of program trading comes from small investors who invest for the long haul. The bulk purchase and sale of entire portfolios of stocks cause price fluctuations that make the work of traditional investment analysts "a joke" according to an unidentified executive for a major Wall Street firm.[16] According to the management of IBM,

> Program trading has introduced into the marketplace an element of volatility unrelated to economic conditions or to a company's financial performance. Over the long term, we are concerned that investors will lose confidence in the market, because stock prices are being driven by an increasing number of factors that have little to do with business fundamentals.[17]

No doubt, the frustration reflected in this statement has been exacerbated by the opinions of some people in the investment business. Joseph Gahtan, vice president of options and futures trading at Salomon Brothers, says that:

> It's (program trading) a product that's here to stay, and it would behoove the public and institutional customers to learn the mechanics by which these instruments move. By doing that, they'll step forward into the 20th century.[18]

|||| CURRENCY FUTURES

Currency futures call for a specified quantity of foreign currency to be exchanged for dollars at a specified *exchange rate*. Both importers and exporters find currency futures an excellent way to reduce the exchange risk that normally accompanies transactions denominated in a foreign currency.

CONTRACT PROVISIONS

Most of the important features of currency futures contracts are illustrated in the price quotations for these contracts. Table 16-9 contains a sample of currency futures quotations taken from the *Wall Street Journal*.

Since these contracts are traded in the United States, the prices given are denominated in dollars per foreign currency unit.[19] Thus, they represent exchange rates. Note the various contract sizes, which range from 12.5 million Japanese yen downward to 62,500 British pounds. Although the contract sizes are widely divergent when expressed in foreign currency

---

[16]"Those Big Swings on Wall Street," p. 35.

[17]Lachenauer, "Program Trading," pp. 54–55.

[18]Ibid., p. 56.

[19]The one exception is the Japanese yen. The yen futures contracts are priced in hundredths of one cent, as indicated in the price quotations.

|||| **TABLE 16-9**
Currency Futures Quotations

	Open	High	Low	Settle	Change	Lifetime High	Low	Open Interest
JAPAN YEN (IMM)—12.5 million yen; $ per yen (.00)								
June	.7212	.7232	.7205	.7210	−.0012	.8010	.6645	46,858
Sept	.7182	.7205	.7178	.7184	−.0013	.7995	.7032	3,043
Dec	....	....		.7167	−.0014	.7770	.7038	1,605
Mr92	....	....		.7165	−.0014	.7540	.7095	2,237
June	....	....		.7165	−.0015	.7199	.7185	210
Est vol 16,429; vol Fri 30,423; open int 53,953, −176.								
DEUTSCHEMARK (IMM)—125,000 marks; $ per mark								
June	.5734	.5786	.5718	.5762	+.0016	.6870	.5601	73,719
Sept	.5697	.5744	.5679	.5720	+.0016	.6810	.5561	7,650
Dec	.5654	.5700	.5654	.5681	+.0017	.6670	.5538	405
Est vol 43,376; vol Fri 73,140; open int 81,778, +3,653.								
CANADIAN DOLLAR (IMM)—100,000 dlrs.; $ per Can $								
June	.8677	.8684	.8677	.8682	+.0005	.8686	.7995	26,000
Sept	.8620	.8623	.8620	.8622	+.0005	.8627	.7985	2,596
Dec	.8561	.8561	.8561	.8570	+.0005	.8576	.8175	407
Mr92	....	....		.8526	+.0005	.8519	.8253	1,004
June	....	....		.8485	+.0005	.8500	.8330	175
Est vol 669; vol Fri 1,711; open int 30,183, −49.								
BRITISH POUND (IMM)—62,500 pds.; $ per pound								
June	1.7032	1.7146	1.6982	1.7098	+.0070	1.9610	1.6550	28,174
Sept	1.6810	1.6940	1.6760	1.6886	+.0070	1.9360	1.6346	1,554
Dec	....	....	....	1.6716	+.0070	1.7900	1.6200	635
Est vol 14,944; vol Fri 22,322; open int 30,363, −624.								
SWISS FRANC (IMM)—125,000 francs; $ per franc								
June	.6790	.6860	.6767	.6829	+.0039	.8084	.6666	39,705
Sept	.6751	.6824	.6730	.6792	+.0040	.8055	.6632	1,962
Dec		....		.6765	+.0040	.8090	.6620	159
Est vol 27,239; vol Fri 34,040; open int 41,892, +1,662.								
AUSTRALIAN DOLLAR (IMM)—100,000 dlrs.; $ per A.$								
June	.7786	.7801	.7775	.7800	+.0003	.7815	.7551	1,865
Sept	.7705	.7705	.7700	.7720	+.0006	.7725	.7520	160
Est vol 345; vol Fri 192; open int 2,025, −75.								
U.S. DOLLAR INDEX (FINEX)—500 times USDX								
June	93.35	93.58	92.73	93.05	− .20	95.19	81.45	4,956
Sept	94.30	94.49	93.81	94.05	− .15	96.02	83.17	1,030
Dec	94.79	94.82	94.79	94.81	− .19	96.62	67.20	210
Est vol 2,200; vol Fri 5,641; open int 6,196, −532.								
The index: High 93.36; Low 92.47; Close 92.72 −.16								

SOURCE: *The Wall Street Journal,* May 21, 1991. Reprinted by permission of *The Wall Street Journal* © Dow Jones & Co. Inc. (1991). All Rights Reserved Worldwide.

units, they are all of comparable size (approximately $100,000) when converted to dollar values.

HEDGING WITH CURRENCY FUTURES
Currency futures contracts were devised for businesses that wish to transfer the risk of exchange rate fluctuations.

EXAMPLE 16-5 CURRENCY FUTURES

Assume an importer has signed a contract to pay a British supplier £500,000 in November. It is now August, and the importer wishes to fix the price of the contract in dollars, so that it can develop a clear estimate of the costs of the merchandise. Currency futures can be used for this purpose.

The importer is short British pounds, so in order to hedge, it should buy futures contracts on pounds. A futures contract must be selected that matures *after* the date the British pounds are going to be paid, so that the importer can maintain the hedge until the pounds are acquired. Therefore, it selects a December maturity.

Noting, from Table 16-9, that one contract is for £62,500, the importer calculates that eight contracts are required to hedge the November purchase. It arrived at this number as follows:

$$\text{futures position} = \text{cash market position/futures contract size}$$

$$8 = \text{£500,000/£62,500 per contract}$$

In this example, the number of contracts worked out exactly even. Normally, a firm would have to round to the nearest whole number when determining the size of its futures position.

These actions, along with the transactions needed in November to cancel the futures market position and to obtain the required number of British pounds in the spot market, are summarized in Table 16-10. ‖‖‖

Note that, for this hedge, with the exchange rates assumed, the losses in the cash market are offset by gains in the futures market. As we discussed earlier in this chapter, this will occur any time the basis of the

‖‖‖ **TABLE 16-10**

Hedging with Foreign Currency Futures

Cash Market	Futures Market
August:	August:
Sign contract obligating firm to pay £500,000 to a London supplier in November	Buy 8 British pound futures contracts with December maturity
Spot exchange rate: $1.7080/£1	Price = $1.6890/£1
November:	November:
Purchase £500,000 in spot at spot rate of $1.75/£1	Cancel initial futures market position through sale of 8 December contracts Price = $1.7310
Calculation of profit or loss:	Calculation of profit or loss:
Anticipated cost: £500,000 × $1.7080 = $854,000	Cost of futures: $1.6890 × £500,000 = $844,500
Actual cost: £500,000 × $1.7500 = $875,000	Proceeds from futures sale: $1.7310 × £500,000 = $865,500
Loss on cash transaction: $854,000 − $875,000 = −$21,000	Profit on futures: $865,500 − $844,500 = $21,000

futures contract remains constant over the period of the hedge, and the cash and futures positions are exactly the same size. You should be able to verify, from the data in Table 16-10, that the basis in both August and November was $0.019. Basis risk, or the risk that the basis of the futures contract will change over the period of the hedge, is the only risk assumed in a perfect hedge. When the basis remains constant, as in this example, no profits or losses will be sustained.

CURRENCY FUTURES AND THE FORWARD MARKET

Currency futures contracts are the only futures contracts that are actively traded with the simultaneous presence of a forward market. The forward market for currencies is handled through commercial banks. Participating banks contract individually with large corporate customers to exchange currencies at a specified exchange rate on a future date. The forward market is solely an interbank market in which currency trades are arranged over the telephone and funds are moved by wire. There is no organized forward market exchange, and no brokers or traders exist outside the banks' foreign exchange departments.

Forward market transactions are large, with most being in the tens of millions of dollars. Each transaction is negotiated separately with the bank's customer, with the date of the exchange and the amount to be

---

||| SIDELIGHT
What Does It Take to Invest in Futures?

It is possible to make huge profits trading currency futures or options, but the odds against making money are said to be 9 to 1.

For any kind of futures trading, you should have at least $10,000 of pure risk capital—money you don't need and wouldn't mind seeing go down the drain. In addition, brokerage firms have certain requirements. First, customers must meet a brokerage house's suitability requirements. (At one firm, the minimum requirements are annual income of $35,000, net worth of $100,000, and liquid net worth of $25,000.) Second, customers must establish a commodity trading account, putting up an initial deposit of $5,000 to $20,000. Third, customers must put up margin (a good faith deposit) for each trade, which can come out of the initial margin.

Trading currency options is somewhat safer than trading currency futures because the loss is limited to 100%, but the probability of a loss is very high. One market observer believes that 75% to 80% of all currency options expire worthless.

SOURCE: Adapted from John R. Dorfman, "MORE INVESTORS RISK A BATH IN CURrencies," *The Wall Street Journal,* May 30, 1989, p. C1. Reprinted by permission of *The Wall Street Journal,* © Dow Jones & Company, Inc. (1989). All Rights Reserved Worldwide.

exchanged tailored to meet the needs of the individual customer. This feature of forward markets is quite different from the futures exchanges, where all trading is in standardized contracts with limited maturity dates and fixed contract sizes. Futures contract standardization fosters contract liquidity and allows futures market participants to execute reversing trades at any time with very little delay. Forward market transactions are not reversed. They represent commitments on the part of both the bank and the company to fulfill the transaction called for in the contract.

|||| SUMMARY

Futures contracts are agreements in which a specified quantity of a particular asset is bought and sold at a specified price for delivery at a specified future time. Futures exchanges determine the items offered for sale, the maturity dates of the contracts, and the contract size. The actions of futures traders determine the contract price. Almost all futures market transactions are reversed before delivery can occur. The clearing corporation of each futures exchange keeps track of the market positions held by each exchange member, as well as maintains margin account balances and ensures against contract default.

Futures market positions provide a large amount of leverage, since the required margin deposit is small relative to the size of the futures contract. The impact of leverage is felt when a small percentage change in the price of the underlying asset results in a large percentage gain or loss for the futures trader.

Futures market gains or losses are marked to market on a daily basis. Gains are credited to the margin account, while losses are charged to this account. If the margin account balance falls below the minimum maintenance margin level, the futures trader must meet margin calls from his or her broker. If these calls are ignored, the futures market position can be liquidated.

Many individuals and firms use futures contracts as a means of hedging against risks. For example, an individual who is long in a commodity can sell futures to hedge against a decline in the commodity's price. Others use futures to speculate, as they provide a low-cost way to place large bets on the future direction of prices or interest rates.

Commodity futures, interest rate futures, and stock index futures are designed primarily as risk-transfer instruments. The growth and popularity of futures instruments in recent years are due to their risk-reduction potential in hedging applications.

|||| QUESTIONS

1. What is a futures contract? Define and explain the following concepts: long position; short position; open interest.

2. Commodity futures are a convenient instrument for traders and speculators to make high profits. Do you agree? Why or why not?

3. What are the functions of a futures exchange? Of a clearing corporation?

4. Why are all contracts "marked to market" on a daily basis instead of, say, on a weekly basis? Why aren't profits and losses simply calculated when a contract matures or a position is liquidated? Explain.

5. An investment in commodity futures is said to be highly leveraged. Explain what this means. What are the advantages and disadvantages of leverage?

6. What are the disadvantages of a limit order? A market order? A market-on-close order?

7. If you had a short position in silver, what kind of order would you place to limit any possible loss?

8. Hedging is said to replace price risk with basis risk. Explain. Illustrate with an example.

9. Why do cash prices and futures prices for the same commodity tend to move in parallel fashion? Why are cash prices usually lower than futures prices?

10. What are the basic differences between a T-bill futures contract and a T-bond contract?

11. A speculator sells a T-bond futures contract. What interest rate expectations are implied? Explain.

12. How does hedging with foreign currencies facilitate planning and budgeting, as well as product pricing, for a large multinational corporation? Give examples.

13. You expect the U.S. dollar to weaken against the German mark. Should you buy or sell a mark futures contract? Explain.

14. You are fairly confident that stocks are going to be moving up in the near future. Would you be better off buying a portfolio of common stocks or stock index futures? Discuss the advantages and disadvantages of both.

|||| **PROBLEMS**

1. Expecting a smaller coffee crop due to sudden cold weather in Brazil, a speculator decides to buy five contracts of coffee at a price of $1.41 per pound. With each contract, he controls 37,500 pounds. The broker requires a margin of 10% and charges a commission of $75 for each contract. How much margin is the speculator required to deposit?

2. Using the information in Problem 1, determine the speculator's profit if the position is offset at a price of $1.50 per pound six weeks later. What is the annualized rate of return on this trade?

3. If the speculator in Problem 1 wants to limit his losses to approximately $15,000, what should he do?

4. Assume the broker in Problem 1 requires customers to maintain a margin of not less than 75% of the initial margin. At what price per pound would the speculator receive a margin call?

5. A farmer expects to harvest about 40,000 bushels of wheat two months from now. Currently, wheat of the equivalent quality sells for $3.38 per bushel in the cash market. The farmer wants to avoid the risk of falling prices and decides to hedge by selling eight wheat contracts (5,000 bushels per contract) at a price of $3.44 per bushel. In order to finance the required 10% margin and the $65 commission per contract, she takes out a loan for which her local bank charges 12% interest (APR). Two months later, the farmer sells her wheat for $3.25, liquidates her futures position at a price of $3.29, and pays back the loan and interest. How much would the farmer have lost due to the decline in the price of wheat over the two-month period if she had not hedged?

6. How much loss did the farmer in Problem 5 avoid (or how much profit did she gain) by hedging?

7. Using the information in Problem 5, determine what happened to the basis between the beginning and end of the two-month period.

8. Determine the risks the farmer in Problem 5 assumed with this hedge.

9. An investor buys one T-bill futures contract maturing in 90 days with a stated discount yield of 11.23%. How much will he have to pay at delivery?

10. Using the computer program supplied with this text, determine the profits or losses to be made from a program trading strategy involving MMI index futures. Assume you have $4 million to invest in the strategy. Assume you entered the program trade 20 days ago and use *Wall Street Journal* price quotations (or others supplied by your instructor) on that date as the prices of your stocks and your MMI index futures. Use current stock and futures prices as liquidation prices to close out the hedge. What returns could have been earned?

11. Using the information developed in Problem 10, calculate the basis between the stocks and the index futures on the date the hedge was initiated. Was this basis sufficient?

12. Using your answers to Problems 10 and 11, what would you estimate is the minimum basis required to generate a profit from this activity?

13. The following table lists the times to maturity of gold futures prices traded on the COMEX as well as the settlement prices for each

maturity. Calculate the implied monthly cost of carry for gold from these price quotations.

Months to Maturity	Futures Settlement Price
1	$415.50
2	418.20
4	423.90
6	429.30
8	434.70
10	440.10

14. Assume you are a corn producer in north-central Illinois. You have an expected harvest of 200,000 bushels, and the harvest date is September 1993. Currently, you are trying to fix your price at harvest, so that you can anticipate the amount of money you will receive when the crop is sold at your local grain elevator. Determine what actions should be taken now, in both the cash and the futures markets, to accomplish this objective. Supply as much detail as possible, including the number of contracts, the current price (use current *Wall Street Journal* quotations), and the price that you lock in with your actions.

15. Continuing with Problem 14, assume it is now September, and the cash market price of corn has changed to $2.20 per bushel, while the futures price of corn has changed to $2.35. Calculate your profits and/or losses in each market.

16. You are a corporate treasurer who anticipates $1.5 million in excess liquidity by this coming November. You feel that current levels of interest in the money market are attractive, and you want to lock in these rates if possible. Design a hedging strategy to accomplish this objective. Using current quotations from the *Wall Street Journal,* specify the following:
    a. Your initial positions in both cash and the futures market.
    b. The size of your initial futures market position, as well as the contract you select, the initial position (long or short), the maturity month selected, and the price paid for the futures.
    c. Assume that interest rates fall 1.5 percentage points by November, and the current basis of your futures contract does not change. Calculate the price of the interest rate futures contract in November, as well as the profit and/or loss on each leg of the hedge.

|||| # SELECTED REFERENCES

Aggarwal, Reena. "Stock Index Futures and Cash Market Volatility." *The Review of Futures Markets* 7 (1988): 290–99.

Bacon, Peter W., and Richard Williams. "Interest Rate Futures Trading:

A New Tool for the Financial Manager." *Financial Management* (Spring 1980): 32–38.

Boyle, Phelim. "The Quality Option and Timing Option in Futures Contracts." *The Journal of Finance* (March 1987): 101–14.

Castelino, Mark G. "Basis Volatility: Implications for Hedging." *The Journal of Financial Research* (Summer 1989): 157–72.

Harris, Lawrence. "The October 1987 S&P 500 Stock Index Futures Basis." *The Journal of Finance* (March 1989): 77–100.

Howard, Charles T., and Louis J. D'Antonio. "Treasury Bill Futures as a Hedging Tool: A Risk-Return Approach." *The Journal of Financial Research* (Spring 1988): 25–40.

Labuszewski, John. "Examining Duration, Hedge Ratio, and Basis Risk." *Futures* (May 1989): 50–51.

Lasser, Dennis J. "Influence of Treasury Bill Futures Trading on the Primary Sale of the Deliverable Treasury Bill." *The Financial Review* (November 1987): 391–402.

Merrick, John J. "Hedging with Mispriced Futures." *Journal of Financial and Quantitative Analysis* (December 1988): 451–64.

Morris, Charles. "Managing Stock Market Risk with Stock Index Futures." *Economic Review* (Federal Reserve Bank of Kansas City) (June 1989): 3–16.

Pierog, Karen, and Jon Stein. "New Contracts: What Makes Them Fly or Fail?" *Futures* (September 1989): 50–54.

Rutz, Roger. "Clearance, Payment, and Settlement Systems in the Futures, Options, and Stock Markets." *The Review of Futures Markets* (1988): 346–70.

Stein, Jon. "Using Currency Cross Rates in Futures Trading." *Futures* (April 1988): 59–63.

17 OPTIONS

On virtually every day of trading, hundreds of thousands of option contracts are bought and sold on the nation's exchanges. Among the most important of these are options on individual common stocks and stock indices, which are the principal topics of the present chapter.

OPTION CONCEPTS AND DEFINITIONS

Options are contracts that give the buyer the right (but not the obligation) to purchase or sell a specified quantity of a given asset at a specified price on or before a specified date. The option seller has the obligation to comply with the provisions of the contract. Note that this definition includes several elements, each of which is discussed in more detail in the following paragraphs:

The right to buy or sell a specified asset

A specified quantity

A specified price

A specified date

Options to buy are known as calls, and options to sell are puts. Calls were the original options traded, and they are still more common than puts.

Option contracts for individual stocks are written for 100 shares. Thus, 20 call options give the holder the right to purchase 2,000 shares. Contract sizes for options on precious metals, foreign currencies, and stock indexes vary with the contract, but can usually be found along with the option price quotations in the daily newspaper.

Option contracts usually mature within nine months from the day they are originated, on the Saturday after the third Friday of the month. If not exercised before maturity, the option expires worthless. The vast majority of all options expire without being exercised.

The two parties to an option contract are the seller (or writer) and the option buyer. In the case of a call option, the buyer acquires the right to purchase the underlying assets at a fixed price. In the case of a put, the option buyer acquires the right to sell the underlying assets at a fixed price. The option writer must stand ready to buy the assets in the case of a put option or to sell the assets in the case of a call.

Each option specifies a price (called the *striking price,* or *exercise price*) at which the underlying asset can be bought or sold. The striking price remains fixed over the life of an option contract.

The price of an option, called the option premium, represents the amount paid by the option buyer to the writer in exchange for the choices embedded in the contract.

The terms discussed so far are illustrated in Table 17-1, which contains price quotations on selected options from the *Los Angeles Times.* Note the Monsanto quotations at the lower right. From left to right, the quotations show (1) the price per share of the underlying asset (Monsanto common stock); (2) the striking price of the option; and (3) the premiums for calls and puts (denoted by *p*) that mature in April, May, and July, respectively.

Premiums are quoted on a per-share basis. Thus, the Monsanto calls with a 55 striking price and April maturity, quoted at 3¾ in the table, would have a total premium of $375.00. (3¾ × 100 shares = $375.00). The writer of the option receives this amount when the contract is originated. If an option is not exercised, the premium is the only cash flow involved. The option writer sells the choice of whether or not to exercise the contract. In return, the option buyer pays a price (premium) for receiving this choice.

TABLE 17-1
Price Quotations on Selected Options for April 5, 1991

Opt/Clos	Price	—Months—			Opt/Clos	Price	—Months—			Opt/Clos	Price	—Months—		
		Apr	May	Jul			Apr	May	Jul			Apr	May	Jul
Alcoa p	.60	a	⅞	a	Elan	.25	9⅞	b	a	MIPS......	15	4⅛	a	5¼
64⅞	65	1¼	a	a	33⅞	30	a	a	6¼	19¾	17½	2⅜	2¾	a
64⅞	p65	1 7/16	a	a	33⅞	35	1	2 1/16	a	19¾	p17½	⅜	13/16	a
64⅞	70	3/16	a	a	33⅞	p35	1 9/16	a	a	19¾	20	13/16	1 13/16	2½
64⅞	p70	a	6⅜	a	33⅞	40	a	a	1⅝	19¾	p20	1⅜	a	3¼
AmGenl	.25	14¾	b	a	33⅞	p40	a	6	a	19¾	22½	b	1 3/16	1 11/16
39⅞	30	10⅛	a	a	Enron	.55	1⅝	a	a	Molex	22½	a	b	10½
39⅞	35	a	5	a	56⅞					32				
39⅞	40	¾	1¼	2	Everex	.5	11/16	b	b	Monsan....	50	7⅜	a	a
39⅞	45	a	a	7/16	5¾	p5	¼	b	b	56⅝	p50	a	a	11/16
39⅞	p45	a	5¼	a	Exxon......	.50	7¼	b	7¾	56⅝	55	3¾	3⅛	4¾
AmStr	.75	16⅛	a	a	57⅛	55	2 9/16	3	3½	56⅝	p55	⅜	1¼	1⅝
90⅝	p80	a	⅝	2 1/16	57⅛	p55	¼	⅝	1¼	56⅝	60	a	1⅜	2⅜
90⅝	85	6¾	8⅜	a	57⅛	60	3/16	9/16	1 3/16	56⅝	p60	3¼	3¾	a
90⅝	90	2⅝	5⅝	a	57⅛	p60	a	a	4	56⅝	65	a	a	1
AT&T......	.30	4¼	5	a	57⅛	65	a	¼	a	Nucorp	75	1¼	2 1/16	a
34	p30	1/16	a	7/16	FedExpp....	.30	a	¼	a	77⅛	80	a	2½	a
34	35	⅜	13/16	1½	34⅞	35	1	1¾	3	77⅛	p80	a	4⅝	6
34	p35	1¼	1½	2	34⅞	p35	a	1⅞	3	77⅛	85	a	15/16	a
34	40	1/16	a	¼	34⅞	40	⅛	⅜	1⅜	OryxEnp ...	30	a	a	1 5/16
34	p40	a	a	6	34⅞	p40	5⅝	a	6⅝	32⅛	p35	2¾	a	a

[a]Not traded.
[b]None offered.

SOURCE: *Los Angeles Times* (April 6, 1991).

|||| COMPONENTS OF OPTION VALUE

An option premium is the sum of two components: the intrinsic value and the time value. The *intrinsic value* is the profit that would accrue to the holder if the option was exercised, and it had cost the holder nothing. Specifically, the intrinsic value of an option depends upon the relationship between the option's striking price *(E)* and the price of the underlying stock *(P_{so})*. It varies with puts and calls as follows:

$$IV_c = \max\{0, P_s - E\} \tag{17-1}$$
$$IV_p = \max\{0, E - P_s\} \tag{17-1a}$$

where

$$IV_c = \text{intrinsic value for calls}$$
$$IV_p = \text{intrinsic value for puts}$$
$$P_s = \text{current price per share of the underlying asset}$$
$$E = \text{striking price (or exercise price) of the option}$$

If the option's premium equals its intrinsic value, an option holder's profits will be the same regardless of whether the option is exercised or sold. In the case of the Monsanto calls maturing in April with a 55 striking price (see Table 17-1), the price of the stock *(P_s)* is 56⅝, the option's striking price *(E)* is 55, and its intrinsic value *(IV_c)* is therefore

$$IV_c = \max\{0, 56\tfrac{5}{8} - 55\}$$
$$IV_c = 1\tfrac{5}{8}$$

An investor who could buy the call for its intrinsic value of $1.625 per share would break even (excluding transactions costs) if the option were exercised immediately upon purchase.

The intrinsic value for Monsanto/April/55 puts is

$$IV_p = \max\{0, 55 - 56\tfrac{5}{8}\}$$
$$IV_p = 0$$

In this case, the put had no intrinsic value, since its striking price was less than the current market price of the stock. This option gives the holder the right to sell Monsanto common stock for $55 per share, when the price on the open market is $56.625. Not surprisingly, the intrinsic value of such a privilege is zero!

Options whose intrinsic values are positive are said to be in the money, and those with zero intrinsic values are out of the money. Basically, *in-the-money options* are options that, if they were to mature in the immediate future, would be exercised rather than allowed to expire. *Out-of-the-money options* under the same circumstances would be allowed to expire. When an option is *at the money,* the striking price and the market price are the same. The specific definitions vary for puts and calls (see Table 17-2).

|||| **TABLE 17-2**

Relationships between the Stock Price and the Striking Price

	Puts	Calls
$P_s < S$	In the money	Out of the money
$P_s = S$	At the money	At the money
$P_s > S$	Out of the money	In the money

The *time value* (or speculative value) of an option is the amount by which the premium exceeds the intrinsic value. It is the amount the option buyer pays to speculate on future favorable price movements in the underlying security. For a call option, the time value can be expressed as follows:

$$TV_c = P_c - IV_c$$

Substituting the definition of intrinsic value from Equation 17-1,

$$TV_c = P_c - \max\{0, P_s - E\} \qquad (17\text{-}2)$$

For in-the-money calls, this reduces to

$$TV_c = P_c - (P_s - E) \qquad (17\text{-}2a)$$

For out-of-the-money calls, with a zero intrinsic value, Equation 17-2 reduces to

$$TV_c = P_c \qquad (17\text{-}2b)$$

The Monsanto/April/55 calls in Table 17-1 have a premium of 3¾ per share. Since they are calls, and the striking price is less than the market price of the stock, the options are in the money, and Equation 17-2a should be used to calculate their time value. The other variables in the equation are

P_c = current option premium
  = 3¾
P_s = current price of underlying stock
  = 56⅝
E = striking price of option
  = 55

The time value of this option can be calculated from Equation 17-2a:

$$TV_c = 3\tfrac{3}{4} - (56\tfrac{5}{8} - 55)$$
$$TV_c = 2\tfrac{1}{8}$$

The option buyer pays $2.125 per share in time value to acquire the option. Note that the intrinsic value of this option is $1.625, and the total premium is the sum of the time value and the intrinsic value, or $3.75. Time value is the amount paid to speculate on further favorable price movements between the date of the price quotations and the expiration of the option. Obviously, the longer this time period, the more the option buyer would be willing to pay for this privilege.

A similar process can be used to derive the time value of a put option. Starting from the definition of time value as the amount by which an option's premium exceeds its intrinsic value, or

$$TV_p = P_p - IV_p$$

Substituting the definition of the intrinsic value of a put into the above expression gives

$$TV_p = P_p - \max\{0, E - P_s\} \qquad (17\text{-}3)$$

For in-the-money puts, Equation 17-3 reduces to

$$TV_p = P_p - (E - P_s) \qquad (17\text{-}3a)$$

For out-of-the-money puts, Equation 17-3 reduces to

$$TV_p = P_p \qquad (17\text{-}3b)$$

The relationship between intrinsic values, time values, and option premiums is important and can be summarized by the following four principles:

1. $P > IV$. Option premiums always equal or exceed the intrinsic value of the option. Arbitrage forces this relationship. If the premium for an option were to fall below its intrinsic value, a quick profit could be made by purchasing and immediately exercising the option.

2. $P = IV$ at option maturity. At expiration, an option's premium equals its intrinsic value. At maturity, the time value of an option is zero, because there is no remaining life over which additional favorable price movements in the underlying asset could occur.

3. For options with the same striking price, the premium increases with the amount of time until expiration. Options are sometimes called "wasting assets." The time value embedded in option premiums declines as the option approaches maturity. Figure 17-1 shows the typical relationship of time value, intrinsic value, and the length of time to maturity.

4. By exercising an option early, an investor gives up any remaining time value. The only instance in which early exercise would make sense, then, is in the case of a dividend-paying stock whose dividend exceeds the remaining time value. Option holders do not receive dividends. Thus, call options are exercised before maturity if exercise allows the investor to receive a dividend payment that exceeds the time value of the option given up through early exercise.

 **FIGURE 17-1**
Time Value Decay in Options

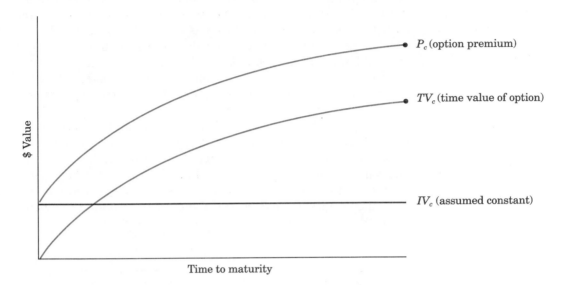

|||| A BRIEF HISTORY OF OPTIONS TRADING

The introduction of *exchange-traded options* on common stocks by the Chicago Board Options Exchange (CBOE) in 1973 was the beginning of a revolution in the option business. Prior to that time, all trading in stock options was over the counter and relatively unimportant. The market was small and obscure, transactions costs were high, and once the options contract had been written, there was no sure way for buyers to dispose of their options or for option writers to liquidate their positions. Few people were interested in either buying or writing options under those conditions. Without a good secondary market, option buyers and writers often had no way out until their contracts expired.

To develop a strong secondary market in options, it was necessary to standardize the contracts and to guarantee performance by an independent agency. That is what the CBOE did. Contracts were standardized with respect to quantities, exercise (or striking) prices, and expiration dates. The Options Clearing Corporation was created to serve as an independent third party, guaranteeing that all options contracts would be fulfilled. The secondary market was further strengthened by the daily publication of option prices in the newspapers. Options soon became attractive to many people, and the volume of trading exploded.

Trading for the first few years was limited to call options on individual stocks. In 1974, the CBOE's first full year of operation, nearly six million call contracts were traded, and from 1974 through 1983, the trading in calls on the CBOE increased tenfold. In 1975 and 1976, four stock exchanges—the American, Philadelphia, Midwest, and Pacific—joined the CBOE in the option business. In 1977 all of the exchanges introduced put options. By 1983, the volume of trading in put options on individual stocks on the CBOE was almost 40% as large as the trading in calls.

In 1983, the volume of put and call options on individual stocks reached a total of 136 million contracts, which is equivalent to 13.6 billion shares of the underlying stock. The dollar volume represented by these contracts was over $50 billion. About 53% of the total trading was on the CBOE.

The CBOE introduced index options in 1983, and other exchanges soon followed. An *index option* is based upon the same principles as a stock option, but the underlying "security" is a stock index rather than a specific common stock. Index options have become extremely popular in a short period of time. It would not be surprising if the volume of trading in index options soon exceeds the total amount of trading of options on individual stocks.

|||| FEATURES OF EXCHANGE-TRADED OPTIONS

One of the main reasons for the development of option exchanges in the early 1970s was to increase liquidity and stimulate trading volume by standardizing the contracts. Contract standardization included the development of uniform policies regarding striking prices and maturities offered in the various contracts.

CONTRACT MATURITIES

When the CBOE first opened, all options were placed in one of three 90-day maturity cycles as follows:

Cycle	Maturities
January cycle	January, April, July, October
February cycle	February, May, August, November
March cycle	March, June, September, December

Only the nearest three months in the cycle were offered at any single time. As a maturity expired, it was replaced with the next month in its cycle.

With the growth of trading volume, the options exchange added additional near-term maturities for each cycle. Now, it is common for options to trade in four maturities at any single time, consisting of the current month, the following month, and the next two months in the regular cycle. IBM, for example, is in the January cycle. On February 1, IBM options maturing in February, March, April, and July will all be offered. Due to the popularity of index options with near-term maturities, some index options trade in cycles consisting simply of the nearest four months.

STRIKING PRICES

Option exchanges have established guidelines for selecting the striking prices that are offered at any particular time. The objective of these guidelines is simply to attract maximum trading volume, and the exchange will modify the policies in pursuit of its goal.

Trading volume has always been concentrated in striking prices that are close to the current price of the stock. Therefore, the exchanges tend to list near-the-money striking prices, and new striking prices are offered as the stock price rises or falls.

In establishing the intervals between the striking prices, the CBOE uses the following rules:

If the Stock Price Is:	Striking Price Intervals Are:
Less than $25	$ 2.50
$25 to $200	5.00
Over $200	10.00

Striking prices are adjusted for stock splits, but not dividends. For example, a stock with a $100 price may have options that trade with $90, $100, and $110 striking prices. If the stock splits two-for-one, the striking prices of these options will automatically adjust to $45, $50, and $55, respectively.

|||| BASIC OPTION STRATEGIES

Options are flexible instruments that are used by both speculators and hedgers. Speculators can buy calls, buy puts, write naked calls, or write naked puts. Hedgers can use options in several ways to manage the risks of their portfolios. These basic option strategies are identified and analyzed in this section.

PURCHASING CALLS AND PUTS

By purchasing a call at a fraction of the cost of the underlying stock, the option buyer acquires a chance to earn a high rate of return if the price of the underlying security rises. The price paid for this chance is the premium for the option. The risk is high because of the strong possibility that the option will lose all or much of its value in a short period of time. (Don't forget that options are wasting assets.)

The potential profits and losses from purchasing calls are graphed in Figure 17-2. The call's value rises as the price of the underlying stock rises, but unless the stock price just before expiration equals or exceeds

||||| **FIGURE 17-2**

Profits and Losses from Purchasing a Call Option versus
Purchasing One Share of the Underlying Stock

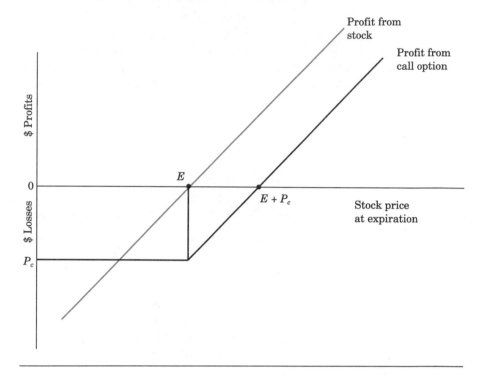

the sum of the call's striking price plus its premium, the call buyer will
lose money.

Figure 17-2 also shows the profit or loss from purchasing shares of
the underlying stock itself, assuming the stock is purchased at the striking
price of the option. As long as the stock price remains above its purchase
price, the per-share profit from the stock exceeds the per-share profit from
a call by the amount of the option premium. Of course, if the price of the
stock falls, the loss from holding the option is limited to the option premium, while the loss from the stock could be as large as the stock's price.
While a loss of 100% is possible with the stock investment, it is unlikely.
Losses of 100% are fairly common with option purchases, since most
options expire unexercised.

Figure 17-3 depicts the profits and losses from purchasing a put. Put
options increase in value when the price of the underlying stock falls;
however, it must fall below the striking price by the amount of the option
premium before the put buyer will break even.

Figure 17-3 also shows the profit or loss generated from selling the
underlying stock short, assuming it is sold at the put's striking price.
Profits from short selling are greater than those from purchasing puts,
but the advantage of puts is that they limit the dollar loss if the price of
the underlying stock rises.

|||| **FIGURE 17-3**

Profits and Losses from Purchasing a Put Option versus Selling
the Underlying Stock Short

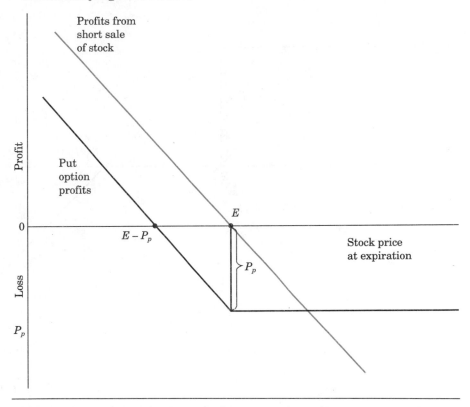

WRITING CALLS AND PUTS

If the option writer owns the underlying stock, a *covered call* is written.
If the underlying stock is not owned at the time the option is written,
it is a *naked call*. As shown in Figure 17-4, the position of a naked
call writer is exactly opposite to that of a call buyer. Potential
profits are limited to the amount of the premium, while losses can be
very large if the price of the underlying stock rises by a great amount.
The bet placed by a naked call writer is similar to that of a short
seller. Both hope the price of the stock will go down. The call writer has the
advantage of receiving a premium, but the disadvantage of a limited
profit.

Writers of naked calls are required to place a margin deposit with
their broker, similar to the margin deposits required of futures market
participants. If the price of the underlying stock moves up, margin calls
may be made.

The writer of a put option receives a premium for agreeing to buy the
optioned stock at the striking price any time before the option expires.
The profit of the put writer is limited to the amount of the option premium.
Figure 17-5 depicts the profits and losses available from writing puts

|||| **FIGURE 17-4**

Writing Naked Calls versus Selling Stock Short

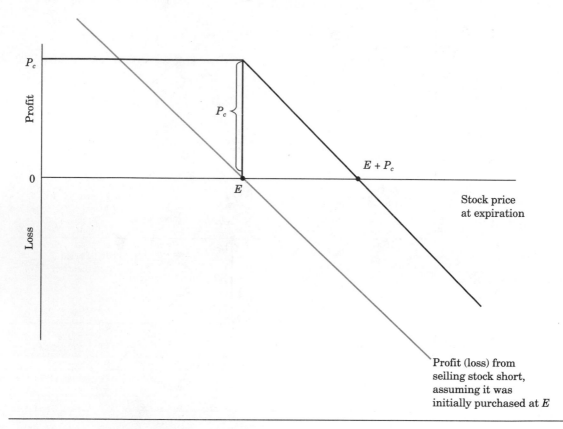

compared to taking a long position in the underlying stock. Losses from writing puts can be very large if the price of the stock declines.

Writing covered call options lowers the risk of holding the underlying stocks, but may reduce the return. Any profit the writer may receive on the stock is limited because all appreciation above the striking price belongs to the holder of the option. However, any loss the writer may sustain due to a decrease in the price of the stock is at least partially offset by the premium collected.

Writers of covered calls assume that the prices of the underlying stocks will not change very much during the option period. If an investor expects the price of a stock to decline substantially, the stock should be sold. As shown in Figure 17-6, the premium from writing covered calls (in this case, $1.48 per share) will not offset large capital losses. And if the price were to increase by a large amount, the option would be exercised to the benefit of the option holder. Figure 17-6 shows that the profit from writing covered calls is limited while the profit from holding the stock is not. The profit limitation *(PL)* in covered call writing can be expressed as

FIGURE 17-5
Profits and Losses from Writing Puts versus Long Positions in the Underlying Stock

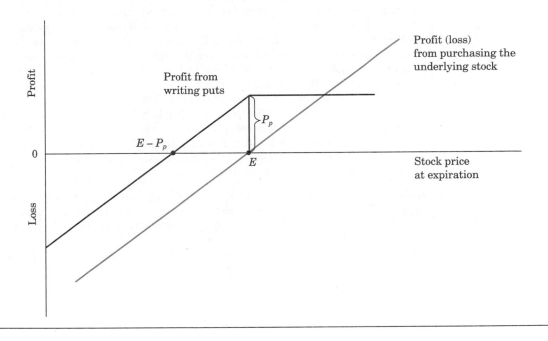

$$PL = 100 \times (E + P_c - P_s) \qquad (17\text{-}4)$$
$$PL = 100 \times (\$50 + \$1.48 - \$40)$$
$$= \$1{,}148$$

with $P_s = \$40$, $E = \$50$, and $P_c = \$1.48$ as in Figure 17-6, the profit is limited to $1,148.

HEDGING WITH CALL OPTIONS

Short sellers purchase calls to hedge against a rise in the price of the stock. If the price of the shorted stock moves up, the profit on the call options may offset any losses on the short position in the stock. A stop-buy order could also be used to protect against losses when selling stock short. Call options have both advantages and disadvantages in such a situation. The obvious disadvantage is that call options are not free and have a maximum life of nine months. If longer-term price protection is desired, a new option must be purchased upon maturity at the cost of an additional premium. However, hedging with calls protects the short seller from the very real possibility that the stop-buy order will not be executed at the stop price.

Table 17-3 illustrates the use of a call option to hedge a short position. Figure 17-7 graphs the resulting profits and losses. As the table shows, the option protects the short seller against a large loss, but due to the

||| **SIDELIGHT**
Why Do Option Buyers Face a Stacked Deck?

The profit on an option can be many times its cost, but such profits are not realized very often. Option buyers are betting that an extraordinary event will cause a substantial change in the price of the underlying stock. The odds are heavily stacked against option buyers for three reasons: (1) options lose value as they approach expiration; (2) about one-third of all option contracts expire worthless; and (3) transactions costs amount to 7% to 10% of the amount invested.

On the whole, option writers have fared better than option buyers, but that doesn't mean that option writing has been profitable. When stock prices rise rapidly, writers of covered calls lose much of the potential capital gain. One study found that over a period of 15 years, the return on a portfolio against which calls had been written was almost the same as if the options had not been written.

SOURCE: Adapted from Stanley W. Angrist, "Why Options Buyers Face Stacked Deck," *The Wall Street Journal*, August 31, 1989, p. C1. Reprinted by permission of *The Wall Street Journal*, © Dow Jones & Company, Inc. (1989). All Rights Reserved Worldwide.

|||| **FIGURE 17-6**

Profits from Writing Covered Calls

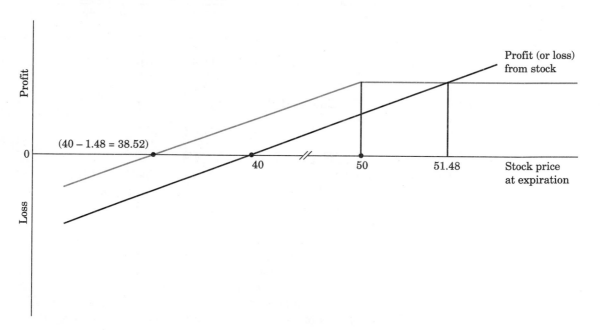

Assumptions: $P_{so} = \$40$; $E = \$50$; $r = 7\%$; $s = 0.30$; $t = 8$ months; no dividends.

NOTE: The assumed option premium of $1.48 was calculated using the Black-Scholes formula and the above assumptions.

|||| **TABLE 17-3**

Short Sale Hedges with a Call Option

Assumptions:
Number of shares sold short	100				
Price of short sale	$40 per share				
Premium of call option	$4 per share, or $400				
Striking price of call	$40				

Results:
Closing stock price	$ 20	$ 30	$ 40	$ 50	$ 60
Profit or (loss) on short sale	2,000	1,000	0	(1,000)	(2,000)
Option profits	0	0	0	1,000	2,000
Cost of option	(400)	(400)	(400)	(400)	(400)
Net gain (loss)	1,600	600	(400)	(400)	(400)

|||| **FIGURE 17-7**

Buying Calls to Hedge a Short Position in Stocks (Based on the Data in Table 17-3)

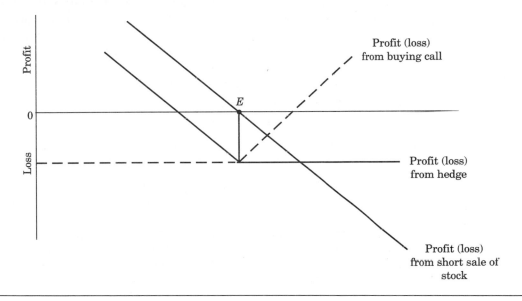

cost of the option, it increases the probability that a loss will occur and reduces the potential profit.

Call options can also be used for price protection by investors intending to purchase stock in the future. If an investor believes that the current price of a stock is unusually attractive, but is unable to buy the stock at the present time, the present price can be "locked in" for the duration of the option contract by purchasing one or more calls. Since option premiums can be quite high, an investor may not want to use calls for this purpose unless a large price increase (larger than the premium paid) is expected within a short period of time.

HEDGING WITH PUT OPTIONS

The reasons for buying put options on common stocks are similar to the reasons for buying calls—to profit from a substantial change in the price of the underlying stock or to gain protection from such a change. With puts, the option buyer is attempting to gain protection from losses due to a decline in stock prices.

Just as a call option can provide a short seller with insurance against an increase in stock prices, a put option can provide a stockholder with protection against a price decline. Generally, it is better to hedge against a decline in stock prices with puts that are at the money rather than deep in the money or deep out of the money. In-the-money puts provide greater price protection because their premiums change more closely with changes in the price of the underlying security. However, the cost of hedging is much higher with in-the-money puts because their premiums are higher. At-the-money puts provide hedgers with a balance between low option premiums and a relatively high level of price protection.

This is demonstrated in Table 17-4 where options A, B, and C are alike in every way but their striking prices. Option A is out of the money, B is at the money, and C is in the money. As you can see, option C provides the best protection against losses on the stock, but its initial cost, which can be thought of as the cost of the "insurance," is also the highest. Option

---

||| SIDELIGHT

Tony Freeland: Pioneering Price Protection with Puts

Tony Freeland trades corn and soybeans—great piles of the stuff—for Demeter, Inc. Freeland's special contribution to his farmer customers has been his creation of option-based hedging.

The advantage of options, he says, is that "farmers can get the protection they ought to have, but options also allow them to hold onto some opportunity."

As helpful as hedging can be, . . . farmers often elect not to use options. According to Freeland, 1988's drought was a perfect case in point. . . . Last summer [1988], farmers had two legitimate concerns. Some were afraid they would have nothing to deliver. Those who had crops didn't like the idea of locking in a price when prices were likely to go much higher.

The option-based hedging approach Freeland developed deals with both concerns. Any option user can choose to exercise the option or let it expire. So the farmer with no crop has a built-in escape clause.

However, Freeland thinks option "sticker shock" drives the farmers for whom options would be the best choice to choose either no protection at all or an inferior futures hedge. At present, option users pay the entire premium up front. Futures users pay only margin fees.

SOURCE: Adapted from Keith Schap, "Tony Freeland: Pioneering Price Protection with Options," *Futures* (August 1989).

|||| **TABLE 17-4**

Hedging against a Decline in Stock Prices by Buying Put Options

	Option A: Out of the Money	Option B: At the Money	Option C: In the Money
Put option purchased:			
Stock price	$40	$40	$40
Striking price	35	40	45
Intrinsic value	0	0	5
Option premium	1.21	2.97	5.69
Time value	1.21	2.97	0.69
Stock price falls to $30:			
Intrinsic value of put	5	10	15
Option premium*	5.01	9.03	13.37
Gain (loss) on option:			
A (5.01 − 1.21) × 100	380		
B (9.03 − 2.97) × 100		606	
C (13.37 − 5.69) × 100			768
Loss on stock	(1,000)	(1,000)	(1,000)
Net loss	(620)	(394)	(212)

*Option premiums were calculated with the Black-Scholes model, using the following assumptions:

Initial time to maturity = 240 days
Time to maturity after stock price decline = 180 days
Volatility = 0.30
Riskless interest rate = 7%

A, with the lowest initial premium, also provides the lowest level of protection against stock price declines.

|||| **INVESTING IN OPTIONS**

The leverage in option contracts and the commission charges have a major impact on investors' profits and losses.

OPTION LEVERAGE

With options, an investor can control a position in stocks worth many times the amount of the premium. Therefore, small changes in the price of a stock can cause large percentage changes in the value of an option. Option leverage magnifies both the profits and the losses.

Some investors mistakenly feel that, because option premiums are relatively small, options represent limited risk investments. Remember, however, that a large proportion of all options expire unexercised, which means their buyers have lost 100% of their investment. Losses of this magnitude are far more common with options than with investments in the underlying common stocks. Thus, while the dollar losses from investing in options may be limited, gains and losses as a percentage of the initial investment are far greater with options than with common stock.

OPTION COMMISSIONS

Table 17-5 offers a sample of typical discount broker commission charges for option trading. Note that the commission charges have a significant fixed component.

Commissions are paid by both option buyers and writers. If a stock option is exercised, additional commissions must be paid to acquire and/or sell the stock. Of course, options that expire unexercised require no commission at expiration.

Options transactions are costly when expressed as a percentage of the option premium—far more costly than common stock commissions. However, when options commissions are expressed as a percentage of the value of the underlying stocks, they are relatively small.

|||| INDEX OPTIONS

For those who want to hedge against a substantial movement in the level of the stock market, or who want to speculate on future market movements, a variety of index options are available, as shown in Table 17-6.

Unlike options on individual stocks, index options call for cash settlement rather than delivery of securities. Calls provide the option buyer with the right to purchase, for a fixed price, an amount of cash equivalent to the index value times the option multiplier. Puts provide the owner with the right to sell, for a fixed price, an amount of cash equivalent to the index value times the option multiplier.

The principal economic function of *stock index options,* as with options on individual stocks, is to provide a vehicle for transferring risk. By purchasing puts on a market index, investors can hedge against market risk. Thus, index options are especially suitable for hedging the risk of widely diversified portfolios, which are largely free of firm-specific risk and industry risk.

INDEX OPTIONS: AN EXAMPLE

Suppose index options mature today, and the S&P 500 Index stands at 261.07 at the close of the day's trading. Index calls with a striking price of 265 allow their holders to receive the following amount of cash:

|||| **TABLE 17-5**

Sample Commission Charges

Option premium	Number of Contracts				
	1	2	5	10	20
½	$30.00	$31.50	$36.00	$ 43.50	$ 58.50
1½	30.00	31.50	36.00	44.00	65.00
3	30.00	31.50	44.00	65.00	95.00
5	30.00	36.00	60.00	85.00	110.00
10	36.00	52.00	85.00	110.00	135.00

TABLE 17-6

Characteristics of Index Options

Index	Exchange	Multiplier
Standard and Poor's:		
S&P 500	Chicago Mercantile	500
S&P 100	Chicago Mercantile	500
OTC	Chicago Mercantile	500
National OTC	Philadelphia Board of Trade	500
Value Line:		
Value Line Index	Kansas City Board of Trade	500
Mini Value Line	Kansas City Board of Trade	100
NYSE Composite Index	New York Futures Exchange	500
CRB Futures Index	New York Futures Exchange	500
Russell 2000	New York Futures Exchange	500
Russell 3000	New York Futures Exchange	500

$$\text{maturity value} = 261.07 \times 100 = \$26,107$$

But for this they would have to pay:

$$\text{purchase price} = \text{striking price} \times 100$$
$$= 265 \times 100 = \$26,500$$

The call option expired out of the money and would not be exercised. A put with the same striking price would be worth $397 (26,500-26,107).

The general formula for calculating the profits from exercise of an index call is

$$\text{profit} = \text{maturity value} - \text{purchase price}$$

For puts, the formula is

$$\text{profit} = \text{selling price} - \text{maturity value}$$

HEDGING WITH INDEX OPTIONS

Stock investors with diversified portfolios can use options to hedge their market risk by purchasing put options on a market index. The protection from writing calls is limited to the amount of the premium. For more complete protection against market risk, an investor should purchase an appropriate number of puts.

The number of put options required to establish a full hedge against market risk depends upon the value of the investor's portfolio and how closely changes in the value are correlated with changes in the market index upon which puts are being purchased. If the investor's portfolio has a beta of approximately 1.0, the value of the puts should be approximately equal to the value of the portfolio. If the portfolio's beta is higher, proportionally more put options will be required. For example, an $80,000 portfolio with a beta of 1.25 would require put options with an approximate face value of $100,000 ($80,000 × 1.25 = $100,000). Assuming these put options were written on an index with a multiplier of 100 and a value of 250, four put options should be purchased for a total of $100,000 (250 × 100 × 4 = $100,000), which is the value of the portfolio to be hedged. Care should be taken that the portfolio's beta is measured against the same market index as the puts are written upon, as beta can vary depending upon the market index used. Also, note that for any portfolio with a beta significantly different from 1.0 the price movements will probably not correlate well with the index, and thus a "dirty hedge" may result.

|||| **OPTION PRICING**

Options premiums are volatile, and the degree of volatility depends on the following variables:

1. The price of the underlying stock (P_s)
2. The striking price of the option (E)
3. The volatility of the underlying stock's price, represented by the standard deviation of returns (s)
4. The length of time until option expiration (t)
5. The continuously compounded riskless rate of interest (r)
6. The dividends paid (if any) during the life of the option (d)

The higher the price of the underlying stock (P_s), the higher the premium for a call option, everything else the same. In the case of a put, the option premium will fall as the price of the underlying security rises.

The value of a call option is inversely related to the option's striking price, all other factors held constant. For puts, the relationship is direct; the higher the striking price, the higher the value of the option.

The greater the volatility of the stock price, the higher the premium for both puts and calls. This relationship between volatility and value is opposite to that normally found in financial markets. Greater volatility improves the chance that the intrinsic value of an option will increase significantly and therefore increases its premium.

The longer the length of time until the option expires, the greater the option's premium. Long time periods provide a greater opportunity for the price of the underlying security to move to a level that will permit favorable option exercise.

An option takes its value from the role that it plays in the formation of a riskless portfolio, and such a portfolio should earn a return no higher than the risk-free rate. The higher this rate, the higher the premium of a call.

Option premiums vary inversely with the level of expected dividends on the stock during the life of the option. The reason for this is that options are not "dividend protected." Striking prices are not adjusted when a dividend is paid, even though, other factors constant, the value of a share of stock declines after dividend payments by the amount of the dividend.

This section describes the Black-Scholes option pricing model, but before turning to this model, we must examine the role of options in a hedged portfolio.

OPTIONS IN A HEDGED PORTFOLIO

As noted earlier, option values have two components: the intrinsic value *(IV)* and the time, or speculative, value *(TV)*. These two components of value are graphed in Figure 17-8. The intrinsic value of the option is the difference between the stock's price and the striking price, as indicated by the straight line in Figure 17-8. The premium, given the level of the price of the underlying stock, is depicted by the curved line. At any given stock price (P_s), the option premium (P_c) is higher than the option's intrinsic value. The difference between the premium and the intrinsic value is the time value of the option.

The slope of the curved line at any given point indicates the sensitivity of the option's price to an incremental change in the price of the underlying stock. For deep out-of-the-money calls, option values are relatively insensitive to changes in the price of the underlying security, while for in-the-money options, changes in the value of the option are more nearly in proportion to changes in the value of the underlying stock.

|||| **FIGURE 17-8**

Behavior of Call Option Prices at Various Stock Prices

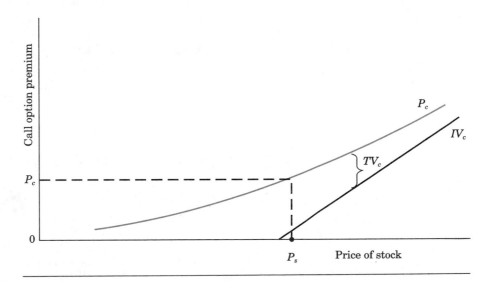

If the slope of the option price line at a given stock price is h, the change in the premium (ΔP_c) can be calculated as follows:

$$(\Delta P_c) = (h)(\Delta P_s) \qquad (17\text{-}5)$$

The slope, h, at any given stock price is the change in the price of a call option on one share of stock for an increase of $1.00 in the price of the stock. Thus, if $h = .60$ at a stock price of $50, an increase of $1.00 in the stock price is expected to increase the option price by $.60. The variable h is called the option's delta, or hedge ratio. It is the number of shares of stock that must be combined with each option written on a share to obtain a hedged portfolio. If an option is written on 1,000 shares of stock for which the hedge ratio is .60, a hedged portfolio will contain 600 shares of the stock. Since delta changes with the price of the stock and options are wasting assets, the hedge must be continually updated in order to remain fully effective.

THE BLACK-SCHOLES OPTION PRICING MODEL

Since its development in 1973, the *Black-Scholes option pricing model* has become the standard for calculating theoretical option premiums.[1] It has been programmed into a variety of financial calculators and into microcomputer software. Portfolio managers and floor traders on options exchanges use it daily. The software diskette accompanying this text includes a program that will calculate option premiums using the Black-Scholes technique.

The Black-Scholes equation was originally developed for European calls (call options that cannot be exercised early) on stocks that pay no dividends. The Black-Scholes formula has been modified for American calls, put options, and options on stocks paying dividends, and these modifications are discussed later in this section. The value of an option is derived from its value in a hedged portfolio assumed to be earning the riskless rate of return.

The basic Black-Scholes pricing equation is

$$P_c = P_s N(d_1) - Ee^{-rt}N(d_2) \qquad (17\text{-}6)$$

where

$$P_c = \text{current option value}$$
$$P_s = \text{current stock price}$$
$$N(d_1) \text{ and } N(d_2) = \text{cumulative normal probabilities of } d_1 \text{ and } d_2,$$
$$\text{respectively}$$
$$d_1 = \{\ln(P_s/E) + [r + (s^2/2)]t\}/[s(t)^{0.5}]$$
$$d_2 = d_1 - s(t)^{0.5}$$

---

[1]This model originally appeared in Fischer Black and Myron Scholes, "The Pricing of Options and Corporate Liabilities," *Journal of Political Economy* (May/June 1973): 637–59.

t = the option's time until expiration, expressed as a fraction of a year

s = the annualized standard deviation of the continuously compounded returns on the underlying stock

When calculating Black-Scholes values by hand, the values of $N(d_1)$ and $N(d_2)$ are found in the table of cumulative normal probabilities in the appendix at the end of this book.

EXAMPLE 17-1 BLACK-SCHOLES FORMULA

Assume we are evaluating IBM/December/120 calls and that the following values apply:

$$P_s = 115$$
$$E = 120$$
$$t = 0.0959 \text{ (35 days/365)}$$
$$r = .08$$
$$\ln(1 + r) = \ln(1.08) = .0770 \text{ (This is the continuously}$$
$$\text{compounded riskless rate of return.)}$$
$$s = 0.25 \text{ (by assumption), so } s^2 = 0.0625$$

Calculating the option's fair market value involves the following steps:

1. Find d_1 and d_2.

$$d_1 = \{\ln(P_s/E) + [\ln(1 + r) + (s^2/2)]t\}/s(t)^{0.5}$$
$$= \{\ln(115/120) + [.0770 + (.0625/2)].0959\}/.25(.0959)^{0.5}$$
$$= -0.42$$
$$d_2 = d_1 - s(t)^{-0.5}$$
$$= (-0.42) - (0.25)(.0959)^{-0.5}$$
$$= -0.50$$

2. Find $N(d_1)$ and $N(d_2)$ from the table of cumulative normal probabilities.

$$N(d_1) = N(-0.42)$$
$$N(-0.42) = 0.3372$$
$$N(d_2) = N(-0.50)$$
$$N(-0.50) = 0.3085$$

3. Input these values into the Black-Scholes formula.

$$P_c = P_s N(d_1) - E e^{-rt} N(d_2)$$
$$= 115(.3372) - 120 e^{-(.0767)(.0959)} (.3085)$$
$$= 1.48$$

If the call sells for less than 1.48, it may be underpriced, and a purchase should be considered. Caution should be used, however, since the estimate of the stock's standard deviation and variance may not be accurate. More is said about estimating the inputs to the Black-Scholes formula later in this section. ||||

RISKLESS HEDGING WITH THE BLACK-SCHOLES MODEL

An optimal hedge is one that combines one call option with $100h$ shares of the underlying common stock in such a way that the value of the portfolio is unaffected by changes in the underlying common stock. The value of the hedged portfolio on which one call has been written is

$$V_{po} = 100hP_s - P_c$$

where

h = the hedge ratio ($N(d_1)$ from the Black-Scholes formula; also called the option's delta)

In the case of the IBM calls in Example 17-1, the value of h is 0.34. This means that 34 shares of IBM common stock should be purchased for every December/120 call written.

With each change in the price of the underlying common stock, the value of $N(d_1)$ will change, and the portfolio must be rebalanced. If $N(d_1)$, the hedge ratio, increases, the hedge is maintained by purchasing additional shares of common. If it decreases, additional shares should be sold.[2] If the portfolio is not updated in this way, it will no longer provide a perfect hedge. Even if the prices do not change, the hedge ratio will change with the passage of time. Recall that the variable t (the time remaining until option expiration) appears in the formula for d_1.

ESTIMATING BLACK-SCHOLES INPUTS

All variables in the Black-Scholes equation but the volatility of the underlying stock are directly observable. Unfortunately, the stock's volatility is difficult to estimate, and the results of the Black-Scholes equation are very sensitive to this estimate. The proper measure of the stock's volatility is the variance of the stock's continuously compounded returns. Two methods are used to obtain this measure: an historical method and an implied volatility method.

To use the historical method, a time series of continuously compounded returns from the underlying stock is needed. This time series could be for several days, several weeks, or several months, but a minimum of 60 observations is usually considered acceptable. The variance must be expressed in annual terms. To do this, the variance must be multiplied by 365 if it was obtained from daily observations, by 52 if it

---

[2]The options position may be adjusted also. In practice, the investor's decision as to whether to modify the position in the stock or in the options would depend upon the transactions cost incurred in each case and upon the availability of additional funds to put into the portfolio.

was obtained from weekly observations, or by 12 if it was obtained from monthly observations.

The Black-Scholes formula calls for an estimate of the stock's future volatility during the life of the option. When the historical method is used to estimate this volatility, the stock's volatility from the recent past is assumed to be the same as the future volatility. This assumption has not been a particularly reliable one, however, as volatility statistics on most securities vary over time. For this reason, many options traders use the implied volatility of the security in their Black-Scholes calculations.

The *implied volatility* of a security is the variance obtained by assuming the security's option is correctly priced and working backward through the Black-Scholes equation to obtain the variance of returns that is associated with that price. Theoretically, all options on a given security with the same maturity date should have the same volatility. It is possible, therefore, to select an option on a given security with a certain striking price and maturity, find its implied volatility, and use that to value an option on the same stock with the same maturity but different striking price.

This technique has a serious shortcoming, however. It assumes that the volatility and the premium are both correct for one striking price; then it attempts to use that volatility to prove that the premium for an option with a different striking price is incorrect. Four variables are present here—the premiums and volatilities of two different options contracts. If they cannot be reconciled, there is no way to tell which of the four estimates are in error. The options analyst should proceed with caution, realizing that no technique offers a foolproof solution.

ADJUSTING THE BLACK-SCHOLES FORMULA FOR DIVIDEND-PAYING STOCKS

As mentioned earlier, the original Black-Scholes formula applies to call options on non-dividend-paying stocks only. The formula can be adjusted for dividends in two ways. The first method applies where the stock pays a known dividend at a discrete future time. This is the case for most options on single stocks. The second method is useful in the case of options on stock indexes, where the dividend yield is more or less continuous.

As an illustration of the discrete method, assume the stock pays a known dividend, d_t, and that day t is the ex-dividend date. Furthermore, day t comes between the present time and the expiration of the option.

Recall that the value of a share of common stock is the present value of the stock's future cash inflows. Upon option expiration, this value (P_{sd}) will be the current value of the stock less the value of the dividend paid during the life of the option, or

$$P_{sd} = P_{so} - d_t e^{-rt} \tag{17-7}$$

where

P_{sd} = the value of the stock ex-dividend, or the present value of the stock after the option's expiration

$$P_s = \text{the present value of all expected future dividends of the stock}$$

The adjustment required in the Black-Scholes formula for this case is straightforward. The value of P_{sd} should be used in the original Black-Scholes formula (Equation 17-6) rather than P_{so}. Other calculations remain the same.

EXAMPLE 17-2   DISCRETE METHOD OF ADJUSTING FOR DIVIDENDS

Assume the IBM/December/120 calls pay a dividend of $1 per share. The next ex-dividend date is 20 days away, before the expiration of the December calls. Using Equation 17-7, the present value of the stock on its next ex-dividend date is

$$P_{sd} = P_{so} - d_t e^{-rt}$$
$$= 115 - 1.00 e^{-(.077)(20/365)}$$
$$= 114$$
$$r = 7.7\%$$

Note that the value of the stock will decline slightly after the next dividend. Now we use the value P_{sd} rather than P_{so} in the Black-Scholes formula.

$$d_1 = \{\ln [114/120] + [.077 + (.0625/2)].0959\}/.25(.0959)^{0.5}$$
$$= -0.53$$
$$d_2 = -0.53 - (.25)(.0959)^{0.5}$$
$$= -0.61$$

Now, from the table of cumulative normal probabilities:

$$N(d_1) = N(-0.53) = 0.2981$$
$$N(d_2) = N(-0.61) = 0.2709$$

Finally, the present value of the call is

$$P_c = 114(.2981) - 120 e^{-(.077)(.0959)} (.2709)$$
$$P_c = 1.23$$

||||

Due to the expected payment of a $1.00 dividend before the option expires, the value of the call is $.25 ($1.48 − $1.23) lower than if no dividend was to be paid. Of course, with the dividend distribution, the likelihood of the stock's price rising above the striking price is diminished, as is the likelihood that the call will ever be exercised.

If there is likely to be more than one dividend before option expiration, the present value of each dividend should be subtracted from the stock's current price in order to arrive at P_{sd} (Equation 17-7). This adjustment works well provided that the underlying stock pays a relatively small number of dividends before option expiration. Since most firms pay dividends quarterly, and options have a life no longer than 270 days, there will rarely be more than two dividends before expiration.

A different adjustment is required for options on stock market indexes. The stocks in these indexes provide a continuous dividend yield. The current index value must therefore be adjusted for the present value of the dividends. The required adjustment is straightforward—simply substitute the term P_{sd} (defined below) for P_{so} in the calculation of the conditional probabilities (d_1 and d_2) and in the option valuation formula itself (Equation 17-6).

EXAMPLE 17-3   ADJUSTING FOR CONTINUOUS DIVIDEND YIELDS

Assume that the market index has a dividend yield of approximately 4% per year ($dy = .04$), that the current value of the underlying stock index (P_{so}) is 250, and that the striking price of the call (E) is 260. Other variables will remain the same as in previous examples. The following modifications are required in the Black-Scholes procedure.

First, calculate P_{sd}, the present value of the underlying index adjusted for dividends, as follows:

$$P_{sd} = P_s e^{-dy(t)} \qquad (17\text{-}8)$$
$$= 250 e^{-(.04)(.0959)}$$
$$= 249.04$$

Next, substituting this value for P_{so}, calculate $N(d_1)$ and $N(d_2)$:

$$d_1 = \{\ln\,[249.04/260] + [.077 + (.09/2).0959]\}/.3(.0959)^{0.5}$$
$$= -0.3376$$
$$N(-0.34) = 0.3669$$
$$d_2 = -0.3376 - (.30)(.0959)^{0.5}$$
$$= -0.4305$$
$$N(-0.43) = 0.3336$$

Finally, find the value of the call option:

$$P_c = P_{sd}\,N(d_1) - Ee^{-rt}\,N(d_2)$$
$$= 249.04(0.3669) - 260e^{-(.077)(.0959)}\,(0.3336)$$
$$= 5.27$$

||||

The higher the assumed dividend yield of the index, the lower the premium of any call options on that index, other things being equal. High dividend yields will increase the premium on put options. Dividend yields vary by market index. Specific information on the dividend yields of the Standard and Poor's indexes is readily found in various Standard and Poor's publications.

EXTENDING THE BLACK-SCHOLES MODEL TO PUT OPTIONS

The Black-Scholes models discussed thus far are used only in the valuation of call options. They can, however, be extended to the valuation of puts. The most straightforward extension of Black-Scholes to puts is based upon a relationship called put-call parity.

Put-call parity is a mathematical relationship that exists between put and call options on the same underlying security with the same striking price and maturity date. The impact of this relationship is to establish a market price level for puts (calls), given an existing price of calls (puts). We will examine put-call parity by assuming the following:

1. A long position in one share of common stock.
2. A long position in a put option on that stock.
3. A short position in one call option with the same maturity date and striking price as the put. (Recall that a short position in the options market means that the option has been written.)
4. A loan on this portfolio at the riskless rate *(r)* and with a maturity that coincides with the maturity of the options contracts. The loan principal *(S)* is equal to the present value of the option's striking price, discounted at the loan's interest rate, or $S = E(1 + r)^{-t}$.

The portfolio's current value, V_p, is simply the sum of the long and short positions (with their proper signs):

$$V_p = P_s + P_p - P_c - S(1 + /r)^{-t} \tag{17-9}$$

where

P_c = the current level of the premiums on the
call options

P_s = the current price of the underlying stock

At option maturity, only two conditions could affect the value of this portfolio. Either the option's striking price is greater than the price of the stock $(E > P_s)$, or the striking price is less than the stock's price $(E < P_s)$. In either case, the net cash flows will be $0. Table 17-7 shows how the portfolio's cash flows cancel one another at option maturity.

Because the net cash flows are zero at maturity, the initial value of the portfolio must be zero also. Otherwise, the proverbial "money machine" would exist—a portfolio that creates wealth from nothing!

Consider what would happen if the initial value of the portfolio was not zero. A negative initial portfolio value means the value of the short positions in Equation 17-9 (the loan and the written call option) would be greater than the value of the long positions. In that case, an investor would receive money initially for forming a portfolio that required no subsequent cash flows. If the initial portfolio value were positive, the investor could achieve the same result by reversing all the signs on all

|||| **TABLE 17-7**

Cash Flows upon Option Maturity

Position	Initial Value	Value of Position at Option Expiration if	
		$P_s < E$	$P_s > E$
Common stock (long)	P_s	P_s	P_{s1}
Put option (long)	P_p	$S - P_s$	0
Call option (short)	$-P_c$	0	$-(P_s - S)$
Loan	$-S$	$-S$	$-S$
Totals	$P_s + P_p - P_c - S$	0	0

positions in Equation 17-9. This would simply involve selling the stock and the put option short, while buying the call and a risk-free security. Again, a money machine would be created since a cash inflow is generated from a portfolio that requires no subsequent cash outflows.

Since $V_{po} = 0$, equation 17-9 can be rearranged in terms of the initial values of the put and the call options:

$$P_c = P_p + P_s - E \qquad (17\text{-}10)$$

and

$$P_p = P_c - P_s + E \qquad (17\text{-}10a)$$

These equations define the put-call parity relationships since they define the initial premium of one option given the premium for the other. They are sometimes called synthetic calls or synthetic puts since the cash flows from the right-hand side of these equations replicate those from a call or put option, respectively.

Using put-call parity, the Black-Scholes formula can be adjusted to find the value of put options. Recall that the Black-Scholes model uses continuous compounding for all cash flows, so that the put-call parity formulas must be adjusted as follows:

$$P_p = P_c - P_o - Ee^{-rt} \qquad (17\text{-}10b)$$

Now, substituting the Black-Scholes value for P_c (defined in Equation 17-6) into Equation 17-10b, we obtain the Black-Scholes expression for valuing a put option:

$$P_p = Se^{-rt}\,[1 - N(d_2)] - P_s[1 - N(d_1)] \qquad (17\text{-}11)$$

For most options, this formula will understate the value of a put option by a small amount. That is because the formula is based upon the assumption that we are evaluating options that cannot be exercised early (called *European options*). American options, which do allow early exercise, are worth slightly more, due to the greater flexibility they give their buyers regarding the date of exercise.

The optimal hedge ratio for put options is

$$h = -[N(d_1) - 1.0] \qquad (17\text{-}12)$$

This is the number of shares of common stock that must be held in combination with a put option on one share in order to form a riskless portfolio. If the portfolio contains a long position in the stock, the put option position should also be long. (This involves purchasing a put.) As we have seen earlier, this portfolio should earn the riskless rate of return (r) in order for the securities in the portfolio to be properly priced.

|||| SUMMARY

An option is a contract that gives the holder either the right to buy (a call option) or the right to sell (a put option) a specified asset at a specified price for a specified period of time.

By itself, an option is a highly risky asset. Not only are the premiums extremely volatile, but they tend to erode as the option approaches expiration. When a call option has a remaining life of several months, its premium may include a significant amount of time value. However, the time value gradually erodes until it becomes zero just before the option expires.

The Black-Scholes option valuation formula states that the value of a call option on a common stock is a function of five variables: the price of the underlying stock, the striking price of the option, the time to expiration, the stock's volatility, and the riskless rate of interest. All of these variables except the striking price are subject to change during the life of the option, and these changes can produce relatively large changes in option values.

All variables in the Black-Scholes model except the volatility of the stock's rate of return are easy to observe or measure. The relevant volatility is the volatility that option buyers and sellers are expecting over the remaining life of the option. This is often estimated by measuring the volatility over recent periods. It is sometimes helpful to calculate the volatility that is implied by the current price of closely related options. If the implied volatility is not the same as the investor's own volatility estimate, the option's current premium may be over- or underpriced.

Stock index options have become an extremely important vehicle for speculating on stock prices and hedging against market risk. Index options differ from stock options in three important respects. First, the underlying "asset" is a stock index rather than a common stock. Second, if an index option is exercised, the option writer is required to make a cash payment to the option holder in the amount of the option's intrinsic value (times the option multiplier) instead of delivering stock. Third, index options provide a means of hedging against market risk. This characteristic of index options makes put options on a stock index especially useful to holders of widely diversified stock portfolios.

QUESTIONS

1. Explain the functions of the Options Clearing Corporation.

2. Compare the risk and potential profit from investing in a common stock with the risk and potential profit from investing in a call option on the stock.

3. What creates the leverage in a call option? What is a good measure of the leverage?

4. Explain why the time value of option A below is greater than the time value of option B on the same stock. The two options have the same expiration date.

	Stock Price	Strike Price	Premium	Time Value
A	$42	$40	$ 6	$4
B	42	25	18	1

   Hint: Calculate the rate of return for each of the options if the price of the stock rises to $50 just before the options expire.

5. Compare the risk and potential profit for writing a covered call with the risk and potential profit for writing a naked call.

6. Define time value. Why do options have a time value? Why are options referred to as wasting assets?

7. What factors determine the time value of an option? Explain.

8. Explain how a put option can provide a hedge against the risk of a long position in a stock.

9. Compare the profit and risk of writing a put with those of writing a covered call.

10. Why does the length of time to expiration affect the value of an option?

11. Explain how to estimate the implied volatility of a stock with the Black-Scholes formula. If the implied volatility is greater than the investor's estimate of the true volatility, why might the investor conclude that the option is overvalued?

12. Explain why option premiums are positively correlated with the volatility of the price of the underlying stock.

13. Why does an increase in interest rates tend to increase the value of call options?

14. Compare and contrast stock options and stock index options.

15. Why are index options a better hedging vehicle than stock options for holders of diversified portfolios of common stocks?

16. Compare the profit and risk of writing a put with those of owning the stock.

17. Which of the following options are in the money? Out of the money?

	Stock Price	Strike Price
Calls:		
A	$43	$40
B	38	40
Puts:		
A	$52	$50
B	47	50

18. Explain the nature and extent of the risk reduction and the cost involved in writing covered calls.

19. The current premiums on two call options with striking prices of $40 on stocks that are selling at $38 are 5¼ and 1½. Explain what may account for the difference in premiums.

20. What is the significance of the hedge ratio in valuing options with the Black-Scholes formula?

21. Write a brief explanation of put-call parity, and explain its significance in option valuation.

22. Describe the two methods of adjusting the Black-Scholes formula for dividends, and explain when each might be appropriate for use.

|||| **PROBLEMS**

1. Calculate the break-even prices of the stocks for the following options, excluding transaction costs. Also, calculate the percentage by which the price of the stock would have to rise, in the case of the call options, or fall, in the case of the puts, to reach the break-even level.

	Option A	Option B
Calls:		
Stock price when option was purchased	$38	$56
Strike price	40	60
Premium per share	6	4
Break-even price of stock		
Required percentage increase in price of stock		
Puts:		
Stock price when option was purchased	$46	$72
Strike price	45	75
Premium per share	4	7
Break-even price of stock		
Required percentage decrease in price of stock		

2. Calculate the profit or loss per share on the following call options, before transactions costs.

	Option A	Option B
Stock price when option was purchased	$38	$43
Strike price	40	40
Time value of option when purchased	5	4
Price of stock just before expiration	43	49

3. Calculate the time values and intrinsic values for the following call options:

Price of Stock	Strike Price	Option Premium	Time Value	Intrinsic Value
$52	$55	$4		
56	55	7		

Problems 4–7 utilize the following data.

Assume you run a $4.5 million mutual fund, consisting of a broad range of equities. The beta of your fund is 1.30. Due to recent actions by the Federal Reserve, you believe that the near-term prospects of the stock market are bearish, and, not wanting to dismantle your portfolio, you want to hedge against potential losses over the next 90-day period. Using the most recent edition of the *Wall Street Journal,* answer the following questions.

4. What index option contract would be suitable for such a situation? Why?

5. What maturity month should be selected? Why?

6. Which of the four basic option positions should be assumed?

7. How many contracts should be purchased? Provide detailed calculations.

8. The following are call option quotations for Bethlehem Steel:

NYSE Close	Strike Price	Bethlehem Steel Calls Last		
		November	December	January
20⅝	20	⅞	1½	1¹⁵⁄₁₆
20⅝	22½	r	⁷⁄₁₆	1³⁄₁₆
20⅝	25	r	s	⁵⁄₁₆

r = not traded; s = no option.

Assume the following additional statistics: riskless rate = 7.5% per year, time to option expiration for the January calls = 63 days.

a. Estimate the implied volatility contained in the January/20 calls.

b.   Use this estimate to derive the fair market premium for the January/22½ calls.

9.   Assume it is September 20, and you are interested in evaluating Crunch Computer's November calls with a striking price of 80. The riskless rate is 7%, the standard deviation of the annualized continuously compounded rate of return on the stock is 0.40, the option's time to expiration is 60 days, the latest closing price of the common stock is $77, and the stock pays a $1.25 quarterly dividend with an ex-dividend date 50 days from today. Evaluate the November/80 calls.

10.   Evaluate an index call option, assuming the following:

Striking price	265
Current index close	245
Index standard deviation	0.20
Riskless return	7½%
Time to option expiration	64 days
Continuous dividend yield on index	4½%

11.   According to Equation 17-10a, put-call parity, the value of a put is equivalent to

$$P_p = P_c - P_s + E$$

Use this relationship to evaluate the December/25/puts, given the following information:

Current price of common	$22.50
Standard deviation of stock returns	0.33
Riskless rate of return	7%
Time to option expiration	90 days

Problems 12–17 utilize the following data.

Assume you own 500 shares of MCI common stock. On March 2, 1990, you became worried about the short-term price potential of MCI, so you decided to utilize a portfolio insurance strategy to protect your position. The option quotations for that day, listing March, April, and July option maturities, are as follows:

NYSE Close	Strike Price	Calls March	April	June	Puts March	April	June
	30	s	5⅜	6½	¹⁄₁₆	⅜	r
35	35	¹³⁄₁₆	1¹³⁄₁₆	3¼	1	1⅝	2¼
35	40	r	⁷⁄₁₆	1⅜	r	5¼	r
35	45	r	³⁄₁₆	½	r	r	r
35	50	s	¹⁄₁₆	r	s	r	r

r = not traded; s = no option

12. What MCI option with an April maturity will provide portfolio insurance protection with the least amount of initial cost? (Identify the option by its striking price.)

13. How many of these option contracts should be purchased?

14. What is the total option premium required to open this position?

15. By March 7, the price of MCI had fallen to 33⅝. Calculate the dollar gains/losses on the underlying common stock.

16. Calculate the dollar gains/losses on the option side of this hedge.

17. Does this appear to have been an effective strategy? Why or why not?

|||| **SELECTED REFERENCES**

Black, Fischer. "Fact and Fantasy in the Use of Options." *Financial Analysts Journal* (July/August 1985): 36–72.

Black, Fischer, and Myron Scholes. "The Pricing of Options and Corporate Liabilities." *Journal of Political Economy* (May/June 1973): 637–59.

Cox, J., S. Ross, and M. Rubenstein. "Option Pricing: A Simplified Approach." *Journal of Financial Economics* (September 1979): 229–63.

Evnine, J., and A. Rudd. "Index Options: The Early Evidence." *The Journal of Finance* (July 1985): 743–56.

Galai, Dan. "Empirical Tests of Boundary Conditions for CBOE Options." *Journal of Financial Economics* (June/September 1978): 187–211.

Geske, R., and H. Johnson. "The American Put Option Valued Analytically." *The Journal of Finance* (December 1984): 1511–24.

Johnson, H. "An Analytic Approximation for the American Put Price." *Journal of Financial and Quantitative Analysis* (March 1983): 141–48.

Klemkosky, Robert, and B. Resnick. "Put Call Parity and Market Efficiency." *The Journal of Finance* (December 1974): 1141–45.

MacBeth, J., and L. Merville. "An Empirical Examination of the Black-Scholes Call Option Pricing Model." *The Journal of Finance* (December 1979): 1173–86.

Rendleman, R., and B. Bartter. "Two-State Option Pricing." *The Journal of Finance* (December 1979): 1093–1110.

Ritchken, Peter. "On Option Pricing Bounds." *The Journal of Finance* (September 1985): 1218–29.

Sterk, W. "Test of Two Models for Valuing Call Options on Stocks with Dividends." *The Journal of Finance* (December 1982): 1229–37.

Whaley, R. "On the Valuation of American Call Options on Stocks with Known Dividends." *Journal of Financial Economics* (June 1981): 207–12.

18 WARRANTS, CONVERTIBLES, AND OPTIONS ON FUTURES

Warrants, convertibles, and options on futures can provide investors with unique opportunities. Since these securities are not as common as the basic futures and options contracts, they are little understood and are ignored by many investors. As this chapter will show, warrants, convertibles, and options on futures are all closely related to options. At the same time, all three securities have unique characteristics and provide fascinating risk/reward potential.

WARRANTS

Warrants entitle their holders to purchase a specific number of shares of common stock at a specified price on or before a specified date. Does this sound similar to a call option? Indeed it does. Nevertheless, there are two fundamental differences between a warrant and a call option. First, a warrant is issued by the issuer of the underlying stock, while a call option is written by an independent third party. Second, warrants have longer lives than call options, with maturities that usually range from 3 to 10 years.

PROPERTIES OF WARRANTS

Warrants are typically issued jointly with bonds as "sweeteners" to enhance their price. After the initial sale of the bond-warrant package, warrants can usually be detached and sold as separate securities. Warrant holders do not have the right to vote in a stockholders' meeting, nor are they eligible for dividends.

The number of shares that can be purchased with one warrant is called the exchange ratio. Unlike call options, exchange ratios of warrants vary with the particular issue involved. Exchange ratios of one to one (one share of common stock for one warrant) are common.

The price at which a warrant holder can purchase common shares by exercising the warrant is called the exercise price. This price is fixed at the time the warrant is issued and usually remains constant. However, with some warrants, especially those with longer maturities, the exercise price increases over time. For example, the warrant may be redeemable for five shares of common stock at $65 per share for the first three years, while after that, it may be redeemable for five shares at $75 per share.

|||| CONVERTIBLE BONDS AND CONVERTIBLE PREFERRED STOCK

Convertibles are fixed-income securities that, at the election of the holder, can be exchanged for a specified number of shares of stock. As noted in Chapter 2, the holder of a convertible security has, in effect, both a fixed-income investment and an option on the company's stock that can be exercised by surrendering the convertible. Typically, the price of a convertible reflects both its value as a bond and the value of the option that comes from the right to convert.

Convertibles have four values: par value, market value (or price), bond value, and convertible value. The bond value is an estimate of what the convertible would be worth as a straight bond; and the conversion value is the value of the stock for which the convertible could be exchanged. In an efficient market, the price of a convertible never falls below the higher of these two amounts for any appreciable length of time. If the price falls below the bond value, the yield becomes higher than that of straight bonds with similar qualities, and investors, seeing this, soon bid the price up. If the price falls below the conversion value, investors buy the convertibles and immediately exchange them for common stock. It doesn't take long for this kind of arbitraging to pull the price up to, or above, the conversion value.

Convertibles are often acquired as an alternative to an investment in the stock or straight bonds of the same company. To assess their relative advantages and disadvantages, it is necessary to understand the following definitions and concepts:

1. *Conversion ratio (cr)* is the number of shares of stock for which the convertible can be exchanged.

2. *Conversion price (cp)* is the price at which the stock can be acquired in exchange for the convertible.

   Conversion price and conversion ratio are related as follows:

   $$cr = \text{par value}/cp$$
   $$cp = \text{par value}/cr$$
   $$cp \times cr = \text{par value}$$

   For example, if a convertible bond with a par value of $1,000 has a conversion ratio of 20, the conversion price is $1,000/20, or $50. And if a bond with a par value of $1,000 has a conversion price of $25, the conversion ratio is $1,000/$25, or 40.

3. *Conversion value* is the value of the stock for which the convertible can be exchanged.

   $$cv = cr \times P_s$$

4. *Conversion premium, in dollars,* is the amount by which the price of the convertible exceeds the conversion value.

   $$prem = \text{market price of convertible} - \text{conversion value}$$

For example, if the market price of a convertible is $1,200 and the conversion value is $1,100, the amount of the conversion premium is $100.

5. *Conversion premium, as a percentage,* is the amount of the conversion premium divided by the conversion value. For example, if the amount of the conversion premium is $100 and the conversion value is $1,100, the conversion premium, as a percentage, is $100/$1,100, or 9.1%. An investor who pays $1,200 for the convertible is paying 9.1% more than it is worth in terms of its exchange value for common stock.

6. *Price risk, in dollars,* is the amount by which the market price of a convertible exceeds its estimated bond value. For example, if the market price of a convertible is $1,200 and the estimated bond value is $950, the amount of the price risk is $250.

7. *Price risk, as a percentage,* is the price risk in dollars divided by market price of the convertible. It is the percentage by which the price of the convertible would fall if it fell to the bond value. For example, if the market price of a convertible is $1,200 and the estimated bond value is $950, the price risk, as a percentage, is $250/$1,200, or 20.8%

RELATIONSHIPS BETWEEN MARKET, BOND, AND CONVERSION VALUES

Figure 18-1 and Table 18-1 show the price, estimated bond value, and conversion value for three convertibles. In addition, Table 18-1 shows the price risk and conversion premium. From Figure 18-1 it is apparent that

|||| **TABLE 18-1**
Three Convertible Bonds

	A	B	C
Par value	$1,000	$1,000	$1,000
Coupon rate	10%	10%	10%
Years to maturity	10	10	10
Price	$ 960	$1,120	$1,450
Rating	BBB	BBB	BB
Stock price	$ 20	$ 37	$ 57
Conversion ratio	25	25	25
Conversion value	$ 500	$ 925	$1,425
Estimate of required return for straight bonds	11%	11%	12%
Estimated bond value	$ 940	$ 940	$ 885
Conversion premium			
In dollars	460	195	25
Percentage	92%	21%	2%
Price risk			
In dollars	$ 20	$ 180	$ 565
Percentage	2%	16%	39%
Yield to maturity	10.92%	8.22%	4.39%

|||| **FIGURE 18-1**
Three Convertible Bonds

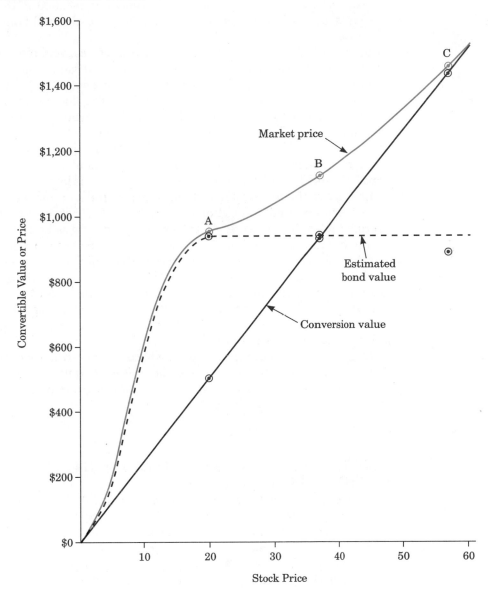

the estimated bond value of a convertible is usually independent of the price of the stock. The example assumes that at all stock prices above $18 to $20, the required return is the same, and the estimated bond value is $940. Only when the price of the stock is very low and the default risk very high due to poor earnings is the required return (therefore the value of the convertible as a straight bond) closely related to the stock price.

When the earnings prospects are favorable enough that the bond payments seem to be well covered, the required return and estimated value of the convertible as a straight bond are largely independent of the stock price. Thus, at stock prices above roughly $20 the estimated bond value levels off at $940.

Figure 18-1 also shows that the market price of a convertible is always equal to or above the higher of the estimated bond value and the conversion value. The conversion value and bond value serve as floors (albeit unsteady ones) under the price of a convertible. The floors provide some support, but are not highly reliable because the conversion value moves up and down with changes in the stock price, and the bond value moves up and down with changes in interest rates or in the quality of the bond.

When the conversion value is far below the bond value (bond A in Figure 18-1 and Table 18-1), the conversion privilege is largely irrelevant, and the price of the convertible is determined entirely, or almost entirely, by its estimated bond value. For bond A, the price risk is low, but the conversion premium is large. At the opposite extreme is bond C, whose conversion value is far above the bond value. Its price is largely determined by the conversion value. The estimated bond value is so low it means little. Bond C is plotted below the bond value line because the horizontal part of the line (at $940) is for bonds like A and B that are rated BBB. Bond C is rated BB and therefore, other things the same, worth less than A and B. For a bond like C, the conversion premium is small, but the price risk is great.

Many convertibles are similar to B, whose price is strongly influenced by both the estimated bond value and the present and prospective future price of the stock. For convertibles like B the price risk and conversion premium are apt to be from 10% to 30% each.

CONVERTIBLES VERSUS COMMON STOCK OR STRAIGHT BONDS

Typically, convertibles have advantages and disadvantages relative to an investment in common stock or straight bonds. Two potential advantages over common stock are less risk (greater price stability as a result of price protection from the bond value, and a stronger claim against the assets in the event of bankruptcy) and, in many cases, a higher yield. The disadvantage is the possibility of smaller capital gains.

The only advantage of a convertible over a straight bond is the possibility of greater price appreciation as a result of the conversion privilege. On the negative side, convertibles are riskier than straight bonds (prices are generally more volatile and they have a subordinated claim against the firm's assets), and the current yield tends to be lower in spite of the fact that they are riskier. Investors are often willing to buy convertibles at lower current yields because of the greater potential for capital gains.

A number of factors should be considered in evaluating a convertible, including the amount of price protection provided by the bond value as

|||| SIDELIGHT
Forcing Conversion of Convertible Bonds: The Case of MCI

Convertibles are usually issued with the intention of later forcing investors to convert their holdings into common stock. Conversion is forced by calling the convertibles when the value of the stock for which they can be exchanged (the conversion value) has risen above the call price. But, to the surprise and dismay of many investors, some issuers have recently called their convertibles, not to force conversion but to redeem the securities with cash. If the market price is higher than the call price, and if the call price is higher than the conversion value, the convertible holders sustain a loss because the market price is immediately driven down to the level of the call price.

For example, MCI recently called its $400 million convertible issue for $1,030 when the market price was $1,090. The price of the convertibles dropped immediately to about $1,030. Investors elected to accept the call price of $1,030 rather than convert because the conversion value was only $990.

SOURCE: Adapted from Barbara Donnelly, "Convertible Bond Game Becomes Riskier," *The Wall Street Journal,* March 7, 1989, p. C1. Reprinted by permission of *The Wall Street Journal,* © Dow Jones & Company, Inc. (1989). All Rights Reserved Worldwide.

measured by the price risk, and the amount of premium being paid for the stock as measured by the conversion premium. Yield comparisons are also important. As noted earlier, convertibles often provide higher current yields than common stock but lower yields than straight bonds. In evaluating convertibles like B and C, where the conversion privilege is an important factor, it would be a mistake not to assess carefully the outlook for the company's stock and the degree to which the price of the convertible is likely to reflect future stock price increases. Since C is selling at only a small premium over the conversion value, its price is sure to keep up, or nearly keep up, with the stock price. For a bond like B, one must consider the probability of a call. B's price will not keep up with the stock price (the conversion premium will shrink) if investors begin to think that an early call is becoming more likely.

|||| **OPTIONS ON FUTURES**

Options on futures (sometimes called *futures options*) are options with a futures contract as their underlying instrument. A call option gives its holder the right to buy the underlying futures contract (which would be assuming a long position in the futures market) at the option's striking price anytime before the option expires. A put option gives its holder the right to sell the underlying futures contract or assume a short position in the futures market. The opposite side of these transactions must be assumed by the writer of the option. The option need not be exercised before it matures. In exchange for assuming the risk of the transaction, the option writer receives the premium, less any commissions and taxes.

The existence of options on futures means that, for some investments, positions can be taken in as many as four levels of securities. Treasury bills, for example, have (1) a spot market, where the bills themselves are purchased and sold; (2) T-bill options; (3) T-bill futures; and (4) options on T-bill futures.

When an investor purchases an option on a futures contract, a series of transactions must occur before that same investor will obtain a position in the underlying asset itself.

EXAMPLE 18-1   AN OPTION ON A GOLD FUTURES CONTRACT

Assume Samantha Speculator purchases a call option on a gold futures contract with a September maturity. This option gives Samantha the right to purchase (go long) one gold futures contract with a September maturity. The cost of this option to Samantha is the premium. If the price of gold rises enough, the options contract will be exercised. Samantha must then meet futures margin requirements commensurate with the normal margin assessed against speculators going long in the gold futures market. Of course, these margin deposits are refunded when the position is liquidated. To this point, Samantha has (1) paid the premium to the option writer for the option on the gold futures contract and (2) met standard margin requirements on the gold futures position after the option was exercised. She still owns no gold. When the futures contract matures, Samantha must pay the futures price for the gold. Only then will she obtain a position in the underlying commodity itself. ||||

Usually, there are just a few weeks between the expiration date of an option on a futures contract and the expiration of the underlying futures contract itself. For example, T-bond options on futures expire the month prior to the expiration of the T-bond futures themselves. In the case of gold, the options on futures and the futures contracts expire in the same month. In any case, the period of time in which an investor can liquidate a futures position after exercising an option on a futures contract is relatively short.

OPTIONS ON INDEX FUTURES

Stock index futures are cash settlement contracts, so *options on index futures* work in a slightly different fashion. Assume that September S&P 500 Index puts have a striking price of 325 and a premium of $7.70. These options give the holder the right to assume a short position on one September S&P 500 Index futures contract at a price of $325.

Recall that each index futures contract has a multiplier, which is 500 for the S&P 500 contract.[1] The current price of the put option (P_p) or the

---

[1]Multipliers for stock index futures are listed with the price quotations on the futures contracts in the *Wall Street Journal*.

price of the call option (P_c) is the listed premium times the contract multiplier:

$$P_c = prem \times \text{multiplier} \qquad (18\text{-}1)$$

or

$$P_p = prem \times \text{multiplier} \qquad (18\text{-}1a)$$

In the case of the September S&P 500 Index put, the price is $3,850 ($7.70 × 500 = $3,850). The put option buyer has the right to sell one futures contract for an amount equal to the option's striking price times the multiplier. In our example, the selling price would be $162,500 ($325 × 500 = $162,500).

The value of the futures contract just before expiration is the index value times the index multiplier. If at expiration of the futures contract the index closes at 295, the futures contract would be worth $147,500 ($295 × 500 = $147,500). Since the short seller has already sold a futures contract for $162,500, the profit is $15,000, and it will be paid by the long to the short upon contract maturity.

The break-even value for the purchase of a put option contract (before transactions costs and taxes) can be found by subtracting the option's premium from its striking price. If, upon expiration of the futures contract, the index closed higher than the difference between the option's striking price and its premium, or 317.30 (325 − 7.70 = 317.30), the short would lose money. The selling price of the futures contract is fixed at $325 by the striking price of the futures option. Possible profits and losses on the purchase of this put option are graphed in Figure 18-2.

‖‖‖ **FIGURE 18-2**

Profits and Losses from S&P 500 Index Put Option on Futures

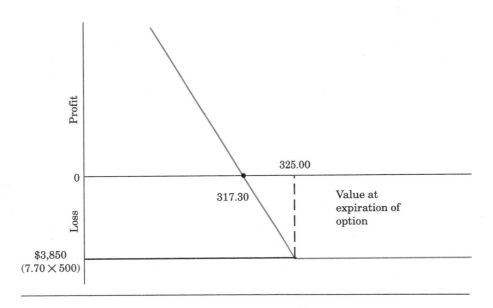

The break-even value for the purchase of an index call can be found by adding the option premium to its striking price. If, upon expiration of the option on the index futures contract, the index value closed higher than the sum of the option premium and striking price, the call option buyer would exercise the option and make a profit. For example, consider September S&P 500 Index calls with a striking price of $325 and a premium of $6.55. In order for the call option buyer to make a profit (before taxes and transactions costs), the index would have to close at 331.55 or higher upon expiration of the option on the index futures. Potential profits and losses on this contract for the call option buyer are graphed in Figure 18-3.

PROPERTIES OF OPTIONS ON FUTURES

Buying options on futures rather than the underlying futures themselves offers the investor several advantages. As with any option, losses for the options buyer are limited, while profits are not. Figure 18-4 compares the profits from holding a call option on gold futures with the profits from the long position in the futures themselves. Note that the losses on the options are limited to the size of the option premium. Profits are also lower for any gold price since the futures buyer participates dollar for dollar in any price increase, while the buyer of calls on gold futures will

||| **FIGURE 18-3**

Profits and Losses from Purchase of March S&P 500 Index Call Option on Futures

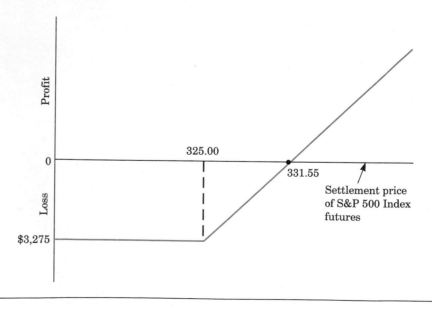

|||| **FIGURE 18-4**

**Profits and Losses from Call Option on Futures versus Long
Position in the Futures Market**

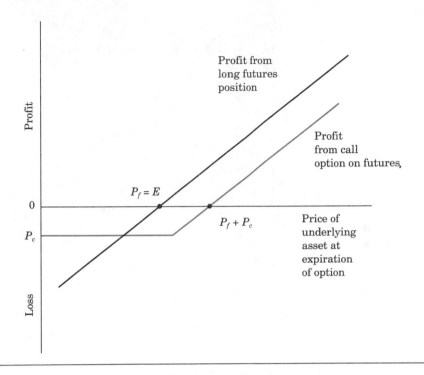

profit only after the price of gold futures increases enough to offset the premium paid for the option.

Figure 18-5 compares profits and losses from purchasing a put option on futures with those from going short in the futures. Again, note that the profits from shorting the futures are larger than those obtained from purchasing a put option on the futures; this is due to the fact that the put option requires an initial premium. With the put, however, losses suffered in the case of an adverse price movement are limited to the premium invested, while losses are unlimited in the futures.

Holders of options on futures do not have to meet margin calls, as they would if they held the underlying futures contract. With options on futures, the option buyer's maximum potential loss is the premium itself. Since this is paid up front, no additional margin requirements are imposed. This gives the options investor "staying power" that the investor in the futures does not possess. Staying power refers to the ability of an investor to sustain adverse price movements without having to meet additional margin calls.

Writers of options on futures, like the writers of any other option, have margin requirements that must be met. The flexibility offered option writers is no greater than that associated with an investment in the

|||| **FIGURE 18-5**

Profits from Put Option on Futures versus Short Position in Futures

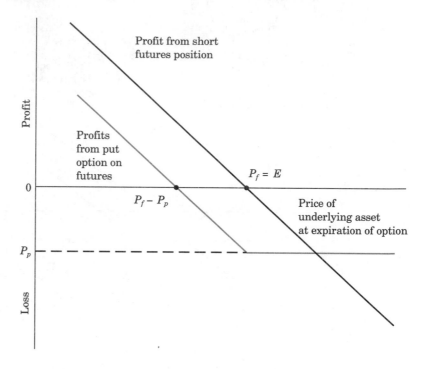

P_p = put option premium
E = exercise price of option
P_f = futures price ($P_f = E$)
$P_f - P_p$ = break even point for put option on futures

underlying futures contract itself. Similar margin requirements are imposed. If the price goes against the option writer, additional margin may have to be supplied.

Greater levels of market liquidity provide an advantage for options on futures over options on the underlying commodity itself. This stems from a large and continuous volume of trading.

Options on commodity futures are easier to exercise than options on the commodities themselves. To exercise an option on the commodity itself, the holder of the option must have funds equal to the entire value of the commodity. In the case of options on futures contracts, the only cash requirement upon exercise is the margin deposit required to carry a position in the futures market. This is normally a fraction of the value of the contract itself. Also, option exercise results simply in a futures market position, which is relatively easy to liquidate. Delivery of the commodity itself is not required.

CALCULATING VALUES OF OPTIONS ON FUTURES

This section explains how to calculate the intrinsic value, time value, and market value of options on futures. We also show how the Black-Scholes option pricing model can be adapted to calculate market values of options on futures.

Intrinsic Value Calculations

The intrinsic value of an option on a futures contract is the maximum of zero or the amount by which the holder of the option would profit if the option were exercised, given current market prices. Intrinsic values for put options on futures (IV_{fp}) and call options on futures (IV_{fc}) are computed as follows:

$$IV_{fp} = \max\{0, E - P_f\} \tag{18-2}$$

and

$$IV_{fc} = \max\{0, P_f - E\} \tag{18-2a}$$

where

$$P_f = \text{the current futures price}$$
$$E = \text{striking price of options on futures}$$

Note that the intrinsic value of options on futures is based upon the price of the underlying futures contract, *not* the price of the underlying commodity in the cash market. This is the only difference between the intrinsic value of straight options and the intrinsic value of options on futures.

Time Value Calculations

Time values of options on futures represent the additional amount, over and above an option's intrinsic value, that investors are willing to pay to speculate on possible future price movements of the underlying contracts. Time values for put options on futures (TV_{fp}) and call options on futures (TV_{fc}) are computed as follows:

$$TV_{fp} = prem - IV_{fp} \tag{18-3}$$

and

$$TV_{fc} = prem - IV_{fc} \tag{18-3a}$$

where

$$prem = \text{option premium}$$

Since IV_{fp} and IV_{fc} are zero for out-of-the-money puts and calls, respectively, the time value of these options equals their premiums.

Adapting the Black-Scholes Pricing Model to Options on Futures

The Black-Scholes pricing model, introduced for straight options in Chapter 17, can also be used to price options on futures. However, it must be modified slightly to take into account some of the differences between options and options on futures.

Although options on futures do not pay dividends, small daily cash flows do originate from the underlying futures contracts. Recall that margin positions on futures are marked to market on a daily basis. Gains in these positions represent small daily cash inflows, while losses represent small daily cash outflows. Daily resettlement of margin positions plays the same role as dividends and complicates the option valuation procedure.

Fortunately, a solution to this problem has been developed by Fischer Black, one of the fathers of the original Black-Scholes pricing model.[2] Call options on futures can be priced with the following model:

$$P_{fc} = e^{-rt}[P_f N(d_1) - EN(d_2)] \tag{18-4}$$

where

P_f = current price of the underlying futures contract

E = striking price of the option

r = continuously compounded riskless rate of return

t = time to expiration of the option, expressed in years

$d_1 = [\ln (P_{fo}/E) + (s^2/2)t]/s(t)^{0.5}$

$d_2 = d_1 - s(t)^{0.5}$

s = annualized variance of returns on the underlying futures contract

Equation 18-4 is similar, but not identical, to the basic Black-Scholes model. It will often give results that are slightly below the actual price for American options due to the possibility that these options can be exercised early.

EXAMPLE 18-2   USING THE BLACK-SCHOLES MODEL TO VALUE OPTIONS ON FUTURES

Assume we want to value the April call options on gold futures with a striking price of 290 and a premium of 5.20. Assume also that the current short-term interest rate is 8.5%, so that $r = \ln (1.085) = 0.0815$; the options on futures have 46 days to maturity, and therefore $T = 46/365 = 0.1260$; and the standard deviation of the underlying futures contract is 0.114.

[2]Fischer Black, "The Pricing of Commodity Contracts," *Journal of Financial Economics* (January/February 1976): 167–79.

Following standard procedure for solving Black-Scholes–type models, we first find $N(d_1)$ and $N(d_2)$:

$$d_1 = [\ln (387.80/390) + (.114^2/2)(0.1260)]/[0.114(.1260)^{0.5}]$$
$$= -0.121$$

$$N(d_1) = 0.4522$$

$$d_2 = -0.121 - 0.114(.1260)^{0.5}$$
$$= -0.1615$$

$$N(d_2) = 0.4364$$

With these results, the value of the call can be found with Equation 18-11 as follows:

$$P_{fc} = e^{(-.0815)(.1260)} (387.8)(.4522) - (390)(.4364)$$
$$= 5.11$$

The call should sell for approximately \$5.11. ||||

EARLY EXERCISE OF OPTIONS ON FUTURES

Options on futures are frequently exercised early. No additional outlay of funds is required. The call option holder receives a long position in the futures market and simply must place a refundable margin deposit with his or her broker. The process works the same way for put options on futures. When exercised, the put option holder receives a short position in the futures market.

|||| **SUMMARY**

In this chapter, we have considered three securities: warrants, convertibles, and options on futures. Although each security is unique, each has valuation characteristics that make it similar to options.

Warrants can be thought of as long-term call options that are issued by the corporation itself. Warrants give their holder the right to purchase a particular number of shares of the sponsoring firm's common stock, on or before a specified date, at a price specified on the warrant contract. They are usually added as a "sweetener" to an issue of preferred stock or bonds. After the purchase of the bond-warrant package, warrants are normally detachable and can be sold as separate securities.

Convertibles are bonds or preferred stocks that can be converted to shares of common stock after a specified future date. A convertible bond can be thought of as a combination of a straight bond and a call option on the firm's stock. The value of a convertible bond, then, is its value as a straight bond plus the value of the option. The conversion ratio is fixed by the issuing firm at the beginning of the bond's life. The choice of whether or not to convert is left to the holder of the convertible security, but corporations often follow certain strategies designed to force conversion at a particular time. Due to the presence of the conversion privilege, these securities normally carry a lower yield than do straight bonds or nonconvertible issues of preferred.

Options on futures are options that have a futures contract as their underlying instrument. Upon exercise, the holder of a call option on a futures contract receives a long position in the futures market, the holder of a put option on a futures contract receives a short position. The writer of the option must assume the offsetting futures position. Options on futures represent limited risk to the option buyer since the most the buyer can lose is the amount of the option premium.

Options on futures represent a relatively straightforward application of the Black-Scholes model, in which the value of the futures contract, rather than the commodity itself, is used to determine the option's current price.

|||| # QUESTIONS

1. Define the following and describe how they apply to warrants:
   a. Exchange ratio
   b. Exercise price
   c. Intrinsic value
   d. Time value

2. Define the following and describe their relationship to convertible bonds:
   a. Conversion ratio
   b. Conversion value
   c. Conversion price
   d. Conversion premium
   e. Bond value
   f. Price risk

3. Summarize the pros and cons of investing in convertible bonds as opposed to straight bonds or stocks.

4. Construct a table that summarizes the futures market positions assumed upon exercise by the buyer and the writer of both puts and calls on options on futures.

5. List the advantages and disadvantages of investing in options on futures rather than the futures themselves.

6. In the mid-1980s, Boeing Company announced it was calling its 8.875% convertible debentures at a price of 106.51, plus accrued interest. The total to be received by the convertible bond holders was $1,076.69 per $1,000 par value.

   The holders of the convertibles were also offered the opportunity to convert their bonds for 35½ shares of common stock. The current price of Boeing common was $43 per share.
   a. Which alternative was better?
   b. Why do you suppose Boeing would make this offer?

|||| PROBLEMS

1. April call options on NYSE Composite Index futures with a striking price of 164 currently have a premium of 5.55. The index multiplier is 500, and its current closing value is 163.94. The options have 48 days remaining to maturity, and the riskless rate is $8\frac{1}{2}\%$. The futures closed at 166.20. Calculate the options' fair market value. Are these options currently overpriced or underpriced?

2. Assume a speculator invests in one of the call options described in Problem 4. Graph the resulting profits and losses (before taxes and commissions) for a range of index futures prices of 150 to 170. Label all possible points and the axes.

3. Assume the same information as in Problem 4. What is the break-even closing index value?

4. Is the option described in Problem 4 an in-the-money option? If so, calculate its intrinsic value. What is the option's time value?

5. A $1,000 convertible bond with a coupon rate of 9% and a 20-year maturity is currently priced at 110. Market yields on similar straight bonds are currently 9%. The conversion ratio on the bond is 25, and the stock's current price is $35. What are the conversion premium and the price risk, in dollars and as a percentage?

6. A convertible bond has a par value of $1,000 and is convertible to 20 shares of common stock. The stock currently has a selling price of $28.
   a. What is the conversion price?
   b. What is the conversion premium?
   c. What is the bond's conversion value?

|||| SELECTED REFERENCES

Courtadon, G. "The Pricing of Options on Default-Free Bonds." *Journal of Financial and Quantitative Analysis* (March 1982): 75–100.

An Introduction to Options on Treasury Bond Futures. (Chicago, Ill.: Chicago Board of Trade, 1986.

Options on Municipal Bond Index Futures: A Research Report. Chicago, Ill.: Chicago Board of Trade.

Schwartz, E. S. "The Valuation of Warrants: Implementing a New Approach." *Journal of Financial Economics* (January 1977): 79–93.

Whaley, R. "Valuation of American Futures Options: Theory and Empirical Tests." *The Journal of Finance* (March 1986): 138.

19 ADVANCED STRATEGIES WITH FUTURES AND OPTIONS

As the markets for futures and options continue to grow, advanced strategies involving these contracts are becoming more common. Two strategies are discussed in this chapter, spreading and straddles. *Spreads* can be formed with either futures or options, while *straddles* are limited to options contracts.

Spreads involve opposite positions in related futures or options contracts. The spreader should buy the contract that is believed to be undervalued and sell the contract that is believed to be overvalued. The purchase and sale of these contracts take place simultaneously. Since opposite positions are taken, risk is controlled, and yet the spreader has an opportunity to receive significant profits if the contracts are truly mispriced.

Spreading involves two positions within the futures (or options) markets. It differs from hedging, in that hedging requires positions in both the futures (or options) market and the cash market. Whereas hedgers are motivated by the opportunity to transfer risk to another party, spreaders are motivated by the opportunity to profit from contracts that are mispriced relative to one another. The actions of spreaders enforce a rational price structure in options and futures markets, and also add important liquidity to these markets.

Spreads can be executed either by traders on the exchange trading floor or by individual investors trading for their own accounts. Once executed, spreads can be held for periods of time ranging from a few days to several months. Spreads are placed when the price difference between two related contracts appears to be abnormal, and they are removed when this differential adjusts back to a more typical level.

Straddles can only be executed with options. Straddles involve the purchase of a call and a put that have the same striking price and the same expiration. This strategy is designed to capitalize on a substantial price movement in either direction, and only price stability will cause losses from a straddle. Straddles are often formed on the eve of major economic announcements, such as quarterly announcements of GNP, the balance of trade, money supply changes, and inflation rates. Straddles can also be formed in anticipation of major corporate announcements, such as quarterly earnings and dividends. Although investors form expectations regarding the content of these announcements, the announced figures may vary widely from those anticipated, causing security prices to respond. It is this response that generates profits for the holder of the straddle.

|||| FUTURES MARKET SPREADS

There are four types of spreads involving futures. An *intramarket spread* (or *time spread*) involves the simultaneous purchase of a futures contract with one delivery month and the sale of a contract for the same item with a different delivery month. Recall that the cost of carry is the variable that relates futures prices over delivery months. Thus, intramarket spreads are executed when futures prices differ over contract maturities by an amount that is not consistent with the cost of carry.

Intermarket spreads involve taking opposite positions on contracts that are sold on more than one exchange. Intermarket spreaders take opposite positions in the same item and the same delivery month, but on different exchanges. An examination of the *Wall Street Journal* will reveal that several items are traded on more than one exchange. Table 19-1 provides a partial list of these assets, along with some of their characteristics. Intermarket spreads can be established on any of these commodities.

An *intercommodity spread* involves the purchase and sale of related items with the same delivery month. For example, a trader could go long in September Treasury bonds and short in September Treasury notes if the prices of these two futures move out of equilibrium. As always, the contract perceived to be overpriced should be sold, and the contract perceived to be underpriced should be purchased.

Finally, *commodity-product spreads* are spreads that involve opposite positions in a commodity and a finished product derived from that commodity. For example, one widely used commodity product spread involves opposite positions in soybean futures and soybean meal or soybean oil futures. The prices of these contracts should be related through the cost of processing the meal or oil. When the difference in these futures prices varies significantly from the processing costs, profits can be made from spreading these commodities. A more detailed discussion of each of these spreads follows.

INTRAMARKET SPREADS

Traders who execute intramarket spreads are attempting to profit from price differences in the same commodity between two different delivery months. The cost of carry is the variable that relates futures prices over time. Understanding the cost of carry is therefore the most important part of understanding intramarket spreads.

As discussed in Chapter 16, the cost of carry is composed of three elements: storage costs, insurance costs, and finance costs. These costs vary over time and across commodities. In comparison to the other two, however, storage costs have remained relatively constant. In the early

|||| **TABLE 19-1**

Selected Futures Contracts Traded on More Than One Exchange

Contract	Exchange*	Contract Size	
Commodities	Corn	CBOT	5,000 bushels
	Corn	MCE	1,000 bushels
	Soybeans	CBOT	5,000 bushels
	Soybeans	MCE	1,000 bushels
	Soybean meal	CBOT	100 tons
	Soybean meal	MCE	20 tons
	Wheat	CBOT	5,000 bushels
	Wheat	KC	5,000 bushels
	Wheat	MPLS	5,000 bushels
	Wheat	MCE	1,000 bushels
	Wheat	WPG	20 metric tons
	Cattle—live	CME	40,000 lbs.
	Cattle—live	MCE	20,000 lbs.
Metals	Gold	COMEX	100 troy oz.
	Gold	CBOT	100 troy oz.
	Gold	MCE	100 troy oz.
	Silver	COMEX	5,000 troy oz.
	Silver	CBOT	1,000 troy oz.
	Silver	CBOT	5,000 troy oz.
	Silver	MCE	1,000 troy oz.
Financial	T-bonds	CBOT	$100,000
	T-bonds	MCE	50,000
	T-bonds	LIFFE	100,000
	5-year T-notes	CBOT	100,000
	5-year T-notes	FINEX	100,000
	Eurodollars	IMM	1 million
	Eurodollars	LIFFE	1 million

*CBOT = Chicago Board of Trade
CME = Chicago Mercantile Exchange
COMEX = Commodity Exchange of New York
FINEX = Financial Exchange of New York
IMM = International Monetary Market
KC = Kansas City Board of Trade
LIFFE = London International Financial Futures Exchange
MCE = MidAmerica Commodity Exchange
MPLS = Minneapolis Grain Exchange
WPG = Winnipeg Commodity Exchange

1980s, the cost of storage for many grains was $0.048 per bushel per month.[1] Over time, this cost has increased with the general price level, but competition among grain elevator operators has kept price increases to a minimum.

Insurance costs are largely a function of the value of the commodity being insured. As commodity prices increase, the cost of insuring these commodities also rises.

[1]*Commodity Trading Manual* (Chicago: Chicago Board of Trade, 1985) p. 128.

In recent years, the most volatile component of storage costs has been the cost of financing. Financing costs are directly related to the prime rate of interest. Since late 1979, when the Federal Reserve changed its strategy for conducting monetary policy, the prime rate has been especially volatile.[2] This volatility has caused the financing component of the cost of carry to be volatile as well.

Consider a grain futures contract. Assume the grain is priced at $4 per bushel, and that the prime rate is 16% per year, as it was in the early 1980s. The cost of financing this commodity would be

$$(\$4.00 \times 0.16)/12 = \$0.0533 \text{ per month}$$

If the prime rate dropped to 9% (as it did during the mid-1980s), the cost of financing this commodity would change to

$$(\$4.00 \times 0.09)/12 = \$0.03 \text{ per month}$$

This represents an approximate 40% change in the monthly cost of financing! Remember, though, that financing costs are only one component of the total cost of carry. Nevertheless, note the magnitude of these changes. Financing costs per bushel are comparable to the cost of storage, and with the recent volatility in interest rates, financing costs are much more unpredictable.

Often, the full cost of carry will not be reflected in the month-to-month spread in commodity futures prices. For example, in April 1989, the spot market price for corn was $2.54 per bushel, and the prime rate was 11.5%. These figures, combined with the storage cost for grains of $.048 per bushel per month, give an implied cost of carry for corn of

$$(\$2.54 \times 0.115)/12 + \$0.048 = \$0.072 \text{ per month}$$

Now examine the data in Table 19-2. As you can see, the price of the July contract is higher than the price of May, but not enough to cover the cost of carry. Then, starting with the September delivery, prices drop, reaching their lowest point with the December contracts. Futures prices for agricultural commodities are typically at their lowest immediately after the harvest season, which for corn is during the fall. As the second column of the table shows, at no point during the year does the month-to-month difference in corn futures prices cover the full cost of carry, which we estimated at $0.072. Figure 19-1 graphs the monthly difference in price and compares this difference to the calculated cost of carry.

---

[2]In October 1979, then Federal Reserve Chairman Paul Volcker appeared on television on a Friday night to make what turned out to be an announcement of historical economic significance. He announced that the focus of the Fed's monetary policy would shift from the stabilization of interest rates to the stabilization of the rate of money supply growth. A rapid escalation of interest rates soon followed, accompanied by the onslaught of a recession. However, economists generally credit this change of focus with breaking the back of the inflationary pressures that dominated our economy during the 1970s, and providing an environment that led to low inflation and a decline in interest rates in the 1980s.

|||| **TABLE 19-2**

Corn Futures Prices, April 1989

Maturity	Futures Price	Change from Prior Month	Implied Monthly Carrying Cost*
May	$2.64	. . . .	. . . .
July	2.67	$.03	$.015
September	2.605	−.065	−.0325
December	2.6025	−.0025	−.00125
March 1990	2.6675	.065	.0325
May	2.6775	.01	.005
July	2.70	.0225	.01125

*Implied monthly carrying cost is calculated by dividing the difference in futures price from the prior month (column 2) by the number of months between futures maturity dates.

SOURCE: *The Wall Street Journal,* April 26, 1989.

Explaining the month-to-month differences in futures prices for a given commodity is a complex task. Only part of these differences are due to the cost of carry. Other factors include expectations of changing production costs, the weather, demand conditions in the marketplace, seasonal patterns in commodity prices, and expectations regarding economic variables such as interest rates and the rate of inflation. Successful intramarket spreading requires analysis of all these factors, plus a good deal of luck.

The July-November Soybean Spread

Since the soybean crop is harvested in the fall, the July-November soybean spread incorporates futures from two different soybean crop years. July soybean futures are typically the last pure "old crop" contracts, while the November contracts are the first pure "new crop" contracts. A September maturity in soybeans is traded, but it occurs during harvest, and September prices are difficult to classify as either old crop or new crop prices. Grain prices are typically lowest immediately after the harvest month and rise thereafter due to the cost of carry. Thus, the July futures contract is typically the highest priced contract in the soybean crop year, while November is typically the lowest.

The July-November spread is calculated by subtracting the November futures price from the price of July futures. Spread values of approximately $1 per bushel are not uncommon, although in 1973 the July-November soybean spread reached levels above $5 per bushel. Some years have negative spreads, indicating either a surplus in the old crop year or an expected shortage in the coming crop year.

An important factor in this spread is the carryover from one crop to another. The carryover consists of unsold soybeans from the current crop year that are left in storage through the coming harvest in expectation that they will be sold in the subsequent crop year. Carryover is a function of the strength of both current and future markets, as well as the current cost of storage.

⫿⫿⫿⫿ **FIGURE 19-1**

Implied versus Actual Cost of Carry

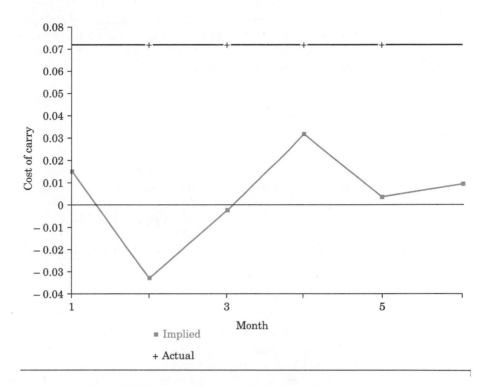

Opposite positions in the two maturity months are assumed in this spread. The exact positions taken are a function of the current spread level and the outlook for the market during the time in which the spread is held.

EXAMPLE 19-1   JULY-NOVEMBER SOYBEAN SPREADS
Assume it is April 10 and soybean futures prices are as follows:

Maturity	Futures Price
July	$8.25
November	6.81

The July-November spread is

$$\$8.25 - \$6.81 = 1.44 \text{ per bushel}$$

After checking this year's soybean demand and the expected crop carryover, you feel a spread of approximately $1 per bushel is warranted. What action should be taken?

As with all spreads, the underpriced contract should be purchased and the overpriced contract sold. Since the current spread is perceived to be too large, the November contract is underpriced relative to July. Therefore, take a long position in the November contract and go short the July contract.

Profits on this spread do not depend upon the direction of soybean prices, but upon the spread moving back to more normal levels (in this case, back to approximately $1). Assume that, within a month, soybean futures exhibit the following prices:

Maturity	Futures Price
July	$7.15
November	6.15

Both contracts fell in price, but the spread moved to a more normal $1 per bushel. Profits from the spread are as follows:

		Action Regarding the	
Date	July Contract	November Contract	**Net Cash Flow**
4/10	+8.25	−6.81	+1.44
5/10	−7.15	+6.15	−1.00
Net	+1.10	−0.66	+0.44

You sold July futures at $8.25 in April and covered this sale in May at $7.15, resulting in a profit on this transaction of $1.10 per bushel, or $5,500 ($1.10 × 5,000 = $5,500) per contract.

You purchased November futures at $6.81 per bushel in April and covered this purchase at $6.15 per bushel in May, resulting in a loss of $0.66 per bushel, or $3,300 ($0.66 × 5,000 = $3,300) per contract. The net profit of $2,200 ($5,500 − $3,300 = $2,200) is the same as the amount by which the July–November spread was initially mispriced [(1.44 − 1.00) × 5,000 = 2,200].

Since opposite positions are taken in the two contracts, the risk of the spread should be lower than that of a single long or short position, although it is possible for *both* positions in the spread to have price movements that create losses for the trader. Due to the expected lower risk levels, margins for spreads are usually lower than those required for outright short or long soybean positions.||||

INTERMARKET SPREADS

Intermarket spreads involve the simultaneous purchase and sale of the same commodity on two different futures exchanges. As always, the higher-priced commodity should be sold, and the cheaper commodity purchased. Since opposite positions are taken in the two markets, the spreader is afforded protection against price level changes. The only thing needed to generate a profit is price convergence. When convergence is complete, the spread is liquidated.

EXAMPLE 19-2 INTERMARKET SILVER SPREAD

Assume the price of December silver futures on the COMEX (Commodity Exchange of New York) is $6.10 per ounce, while the December futures price on the Chicago Board of Trade is only $6.02. Each contract is for 5,000 ounces, and assume there is no reason for the contract prices to vary. Intermarket spreaders would sell the expensive silver (the COMEX contract) and purchase the cheaper silver (the CBOT contract). Both transactions should involve an equal number of contracts. The spread anticipates prices converging. Whether they rise or fall during the life of the spread is immaterial, since the long and short positions are of equal size.

Assume that, over the next three trading days, market conditions force the price of silver up to $6.12 per ounce, and prices in New York and Chicago converge as expected. Once this convergence occurs, the spread should be liquidated since no further profits can be made. At liquidation, the following profits would be realized:

Market	Purchase	Sale	Profits per Ounce	Profits per Contract
New York (COMEX)	$6.12	$6.10	− $0.02	− $100
Chicago	6.02	6.12	0.10	500

Assume now that the price of silver falls to $5.95 instead of rising to $6.12, but again, prices converge before liquidation. The profits from the spread would now be as follows:

Market	Purchase	Sale	Profits per Ounce	Profits per Contract
New York (COMEX)	$5.95	$6.10	$0.15	$750
Chicago	6.02	5.95	− 0.07	− 350

Note that in both cases, the profit from the spread was $400, or the size of the contract (5,000 ounces) multiplied by the initial price discrepancy ($0.08 per ounce). This was true whether the price of silver rose or fell during the period of time in which the spread was held. It is important to remember that profits from assuming an intermarket spread are generated from contracts that are initially mispriced relative to one another.‖‖

In reality, you will seldom find instances like the situation described in Example 19-2, where profits of $400 per contract can be generated by simply initiating an intermarket spread. Normally, small temporary price discrepancies evoke an immediate response from traders that bring the prices back to equilibrium. Intermarket spreads are too easy to execute, and prices seldom move far out of line.

It would be dangerous to assume that any price discrepancy between markets represents an opportunity to profit from an intermarket spread. Sometimes, equilibrium conditions call for the same commodity to sell for different prices in different locations. There are several reasons for this, the most obvious being the presence of transportation costs. Wheat futures traded on the Chicago Board of Trade call for wheat to be delivered to a storage facility in the Chicago area, and futures traded on the Kansas City Board of Trade call for delivery in the Kansas City area. Differences in transportation costs to Chicago versus Kansas City would account for a normal difference in price between these two contracts.

Other price differences are caused by differences in the characteristics of the futures contracts themselves. For example, wheat futures traded on the Minneapolis exchange call for #2 northern spring wheat to be delivered against the contract. In Kansas City, several types of wheat may be delivered, but prices usually reflect #2 hard red winter wheat, which is common to the area. Four classes of wheat can be delivered against Chicago Board of Trade wheat futures, but the price in Chicago often reflects the prices of spring wheats. To the extent that these types of wheat are not substitutes for one another, prices may be expected to vary from one exchange to another.

Spreads on Stock Index Futures

Futures can be traded against four stock market indexes. Differences in the composition and price movements of these indexes can create profitable spreading opportunities. Table 19-3 lists the indexes upon which futures contracts are traded.

Value Line is the broadest based index and is the most sensitive to price movements of smaller firms. Value Line is composed of approximately 80% New York Stock Exchange, 14% over-the-counter, and 6% American Stock Exchange stocks. The S&P 500 Index has approximately 93% NYSE representation, with the balance being AMEX and OTC stocks.

Price movements in blue-chip firms often tend to lead the rest of the market in both bull and bear markets. When a bull market starts, individual investors are attracted to equities. These investors tend to purchase the smaller AMEX and OTC firms included on the Value Line and

|||| **TABLE 19-3**

Major Stock Index Futures

Index	Contract Size	Composition
Major Market	$250 × index	20 NYSE blue chips (parallels Dow Jones Industrial)
S&P 500	$500 × index	500, mostly NYSE
NYSE Composite	$500 × index	All NYSE stocks
Value Line	$500 × index	1,700 stocks from NYSE, AMEX, and OTC

S&P 500 Indexes, causing the prices of these smaller firms to increase after the larger, blue-chip firms.

Blue chips also tend to lead in bear markets. Sometimes, as a bear market matures, the blue chips start to rally again as individual investors seek higher-quality stocks. The Major Market Index (MMI), which consists of blue-chip firms, has been more volatile throughout its history in both bull and bear markets than the other indexes. The statistics from Table 19-4 confirm this observation.

Spreads with index futures almost always involve a position in the MMI and one of the other stock index futures. The specific positions taken depend on the investor's expectations for the direction of the market and the current prices of the respective index futures.

If the market is expected to trend upward, an investor might go long on MMI futures and short on either the S&P 500 or Value Line contract. The spread is based upon the assumption that the MMI will lead the other indexes and will be more volatile. Since opposite positions are taken in the two index contracts, the investor has some protection against adverse price movements. Both initial positions are normally offset with reversing trades before contract maturity.

Executing orders for index spreads can be a problem because the two contracts are traded in different locations. Delays in filling one or the other leg of the spread can mean that the investor opens a position at a vastly different price than he or she originally planned. Some brokers eliminate this problem by quoting a spread price to their customers (e.g., MMI versus Value Line at 60 points) as well as quoting prices on the

|||| **TABLE 19-4**

Stock Index Volatility* (Absolute average weekly change, in percent)

Market Type/Time Period	MMI	S&P 500	NYSE	Value Line
Bear market 1/3/73–12/23/74	2.6169%	2.4814%	2.5303%	N/A
Bull market 12/24/74–6/30/75	2.6112	2.3165	2.3050	2.2164%
Sideways market 7/1/75–8/9/82	1.6102	1.5701	1.5777	1.6309
Bull market 8/10/82–10/10/83	2.2072	2.1480	2.0834	2.0088
Sideways market 10/11/83–10/10/85	1.3174	1.3374	1.3055	1.3420
Bull market 10/11/85–8/25/87	1.9055	1.7958	1.7090	1.4771
Bear market 8/26/87–10/19/87	3.5782	3.2039	3.0342	2.4782
Sideways market 10/20/87–4/22/88	3.3000	3.1974	3.0356	3.6196

Source: "MMI Intermarket Spreads" (MMI Trading Strategies Series, Chicago Board of Trade, July 1988), Table 3.

individual contracts. This, of course, helps the trader evaluate spreading opportunities at any given time.

INTERCOMMODITY SPREADS

Intercommodity spreads involve taking opposite positions in related, but not identical, items. For example, one obvious intercommodity spread might involve going long in Treasury bill futures and short in Treasury bond futures. It is important that the items be related in some fashion, so that an equilibrium pricing relationship between the two exists. When the pricing relationship moves away from equilibrium, there are opportunities to profit from intercommodity spreads. As always, the trader would go long in the perceived low-priced item and short in the other. Once the pricing relationship returns to a more normal level, the spread is liquidated. Some of the more common intercommodity spreads are described in the next paragraphs.

The Corn-Wheat Spread

One of the basic intercommodity spreads involving agricultural commodities is the corn-wheat spread. Both corn and wheat are used as livestock feed. Both corn and wheat futures contracts are sold by the bushel, not by weight. A bushel of wheat is 7% heavier than a bushel of corn, and wheat has a 5% greater feed value than corn. Thus, for agricultural feed purposes, the price of wheat should be at least 12% higher than the price of corn. When the price difference is greater or less than 12%, opportunities for wheat-corn spreading might exist.

The Gold-Silver Ratio Spread

The gold-silver ratio spread involves taking opposite positions on kilo gold and 1,000-ounce silver futures contracts traded on the CBOT. The specific positions taken depend upon the ratio of gold futures prices to silver futures prices. Historically, the gold-silver ratio has varied from a high of 60 to a low of 17, and the average for the last hundred years is 32½.[3]

As with other spreads, profits from this position are a function of changes in the spread, not movements in the level of metals prices. Since opposite positions are taken in the two contracts, this spread can involve lower risk levels than those that would be experienced with outright positions in either metal alone. This is because, historically, gold and silver prices have tended to move in concert. In recognition of the risk-reduction potential this spread offers, most brokers offer lower margin requirements for the spread than are required for holding a position in either metal by itself.

Historically, the spread has widened with negative economic news. This news could consist of, but is not limited to, larger trade deficits, declining dollar values, larger budget deficits, and threats of recession or inflation.

[3]*The Gold-Silver Ratio Spread* (Chicago: Chicago Board of Trade, 1988).

The NOB Spread

NOB stands for "notes over bonds," and the *NOB spread* refers to the difference in price between 10-year Treasury note futures and Treasury bond futures. The NOB spread is simply the price of T-note futures minus the price of T-bond futures. As with other spreads, traders assume opposite positions in the two contracts.

Profits from NOB trading strategies depend upon shifts in the yield curve and the extent to which these shifts are nonparallel.[4] As a brief review, a parallel shift in the yield curve means that, during a period of rising interest rates, all bond maturities rise by an equal amount. Likewise, during a period of falling interest rates, all bond maturities fall by an equal amount. Nonparallel shifts mean that interest rate changes vary across the differing bond maturities.

For parallel shifts in the yield curve, the NOB spread widens when interest rates rise, and it falls when interest rates fall. When interest rates rise, the price of both the T-note and T-bond futures will fall, but the T-bond futures will fall more than the T-note futures because the bonds have longer maturities.

With this principle in mind, NOB strategies can be divided into two categories, long NOB strategies and short NOB strategies. Long NOB strategies involve going short bond futures and long note futures. This position would generate a profit when interest rates increase. A short NOB strategy would involve going long bond futures and short note futures, and this position would generate profits when interest rates decrease.

Normally, the yield curve does not shift equally across all maturities, and this can cause problems when trading NOB spreads. For example, assume you expect interest rates to rise over the near-term future. Since prices of the bond futures are expected to fall more (due to their longer maturities), you would normally execute a long NOB spread, buying notes and selling bonds. But if the yield curve shifts in a nonparallel fashion, so that the rates for intermediate-term securities rise more than those for long-term securities, this strategy can backfire. The prices of the 10-year note futures could actually fall more than prices for longer-maturity bonds. This type of shift, although relatively common, is difficult to predict in advance, and it adds significant risks to the NOB spread.

COMMODITY-PRODUCT SPREADS

In a commodity-product spread, a trader takes opposite positions in a futures contract on a raw commodity and on a product derived from that raw commodity. By definition, these spreads involve only commodities that can be processed.

A common commodity-product spread involves futures on soybeans and soybean meal or soybean oil. Other possible commodity-product

---

[4]See Chapter 14 for a discussion of the factors causing yield curve shifts and the impact of shifts in the yield curve on bond prices.

spreads involve futures on hogs and futures on pork bellies, or futures on crude oil and futures on gasoline or on #2 heating oil.

Evaluating commodity-product spreads requires knowledge of the gross processing margin (GPM), which in turn involves rather detailed knowledge about commodity processing itself. The GPM is the difference between the cost of the raw material and the income derived from sales of the finished (or processed) product.

EXAMPLE 19-3 THE GPM OF SOYBEANS

A 60-pound bushel of soybeans can yield 47 pounds of soybean meal and 11 pounds of soybean oil. The remaining 2 pounds are processing loss and waste. (These figures vary from processor to processor and over time, but they can be used as a rule of thumb.) Assume that July soybeans sell for $7.3625 per bushel.* Also assume July soybean meal sells for $223.10 per ton (or $0.11155 per pound), and July soybean oil sells for $0.2348 per pound. The GPM can be calculated as follows:

GPM = oil proceeds + meal proceeds − per-bushel soybean cost

where

$$\text{oil proceeds} = 11 \times \text{value of soybean oil (per pound)}$$
$$= 11 \times \$0.2348 = \$2.5828$$

$$\text{meal proceeds} = 47 \times \text{value of soybean meal (per pound)}$$
$$= 47 \times \$0.11155 = \$5.24285$$

Therefore, the GPM is

$$\text{GPM} = \$2.5828 + \$5.24285 - \$7.3625 = \$0.46315$$

*The prices used in this example are taken from the *Wall Street Journal,* April 26, 1989.

Processing soybeans with a GPM of less than $0.15 per bushel is generally considered uprofitable. When the GPM falls below this figure, it is a sign that soybean futures are overpriced relative to the futures on meal and oil, and the appropriate commodity-product spread can be initiated at that point. ||||

In Example 19-3, the GPM exceeds the minimum value. Whether it is excessive is difficult to determine. Frequently, GPM figures follow a seasonal pattern, with high margins early in the crop year, followed by declining margins later on. (Recall that the soybean crop year runs from September to September.) Also, a large soybean crop will usually mean high processing margins, while a smaller crop produces lower margins.

|||| **OPTION SPREADS**

Spreads can also be executed with options. Option spreads take on two general forms: (1) the money or price spread (sometimes called a vertical spread) and (2) the time or calendar spread (sometimes called a horizontal spread).[5] Money spreads involve the purchase and sale of options that differ only by the striking (exercise) price of the option. Time spreads involve the purchase and sale of options that differ only by expiration month.

Before going any further, some notation needs to be introduced to identify the wide variety of money and time spreads that are possible. Following generally accepted practice in the financial press, we will refer to these spreads by month and then by striking price, always listing the option purchased first. For example, a June 100/110 spread is a money spread, involving the purchase of June options with a striking price of 100 and the sale of June options with a 110 striking price. A June/September 110 spread is a time spread, involving the purchase of June options with a 110 striking price and the sale of September options with a 110 striking price. A September/June 110 spread is also a time spread, but in this case, the September options were purchased and the June options sold.

MONEY SPREADS

Money spreads can be subdivided into three categories: bull spreads, bear spreads, and butterfly spreads. As their names imply, *bull spreads* are money spreads that generate profits when the underlying security moves up in price, while *bear spreads* are spreads that generate profits when the price of the underlying security falls. *Butterfly spreads* produce profits when prices are stable.

Bull Spreads

Consider the options of du Pont Chemical Corporation, whose quotations appear in Table 19-5. A July 110/115 bull spread is formed by purchasing the July call with a 110 striking price for $5\frac{5}{8}$ and selling the July call with a 115 striking price for $3\frac{1}{4}$. This yields an initial net cash flow of $-2\frac{3}{8}$ per share ($3\frac{1}{4} - 5\frac{5}{8} = -2\frac{3}{8}$).

Now assume the spread is held to option expiration. Three kinds of outcomes could occur. First, both options in the spread could be out of the money. This outcome occurs when the stock price at option expiration is less than the lower of the two striking prices in the spread (in this case, less than 110). Since both options expire out of the money, neither is exercised, and the losses from the spread equal the negative cash flow when the spread was initiated, or $-2\frac{3}{8}$ per share.

Second, both options could expire in the money. This would occur if the stock price at expiration was greater than the higher of the two striking prices included in the spread (in this example, greater than 115). The holder of the 115 call (which was sold) would exercise this call,

[5]Vertical spreads and horizontal spreads get their name from the layout of price quotations on options in the financial press. Options included in vertical (or money) spreads vary only by striking price, which appears vertically in option price quotations. Options included in horizontal (or time) spreads vary only by maturity month, which appears horizontally in option price quotations.

|||| **TABLE 19-5**
Prices of du Pont Chemical Options

Option and NYSE Close	Striking Price	Calls Last:			Puts Last:		
		May	June	July	May	June	July
duPont	95	r	s	r	r	s	¼
110⅝	100	12⅝	r	12¼	⅛	½	¾
110⅝	105	6⅜	8	9	¾	1⅜	1⅞
110⅝	110	2⅝	4	5⅝	2⅝	3	3¾
110⅝	115	¹⁵⁄₁₆	2	3¼	r	r	r
110⅝	120	⁵⁄₁₆	1	1¾	r	r	r

Note: r = not traded; s = no option.
SOURCE: *The Wall Street Journal,* April 26, 1989.

and it would be filled by exercising the 110 call (which was bought). This dual exercise would generate income of $5 per share (the difference in the striking prices of the two options), which is more than enough to offset the initial negative cash flow of the spread. Net income from the spread would be $2.625 per share (5 − 2⅜ = 2⅝). A bull spread will always generate a profit when both options in the bull spread are exercised.

The third case occurs when the stock price at option expiration falls between the striking prices of the two options. Assume, for example, that the stock price settles at $111 when the options expire. The gain on the 110 call would not be large enough to offset the initial −2⅜ cash flow.

If the stock price settles at $112, the gain on exercising the $110 call would be $2, but there would still be a net loss of ⅜. Profits and losses at various stock prices are listed in Table 19-6 and graphed in Figure 19-2.

If the stock price settles at a level of $112.375 the spread breaks even before transaction costs. The break-even stock price *(BEP)* can be calculated with equation 19-1.

$$BEP = E_l + (P_{cl} - P_{ch}) \qquad (19\text{-}1)$$

where

> *BEP* = break-even price, or the stock price level upon option expiration that allows the bull spread to recover its initial costs

> *E* = option striking price (E_l refers to the lower of the two striking prices included in the spread)

> P_{cl} and P_{ch} = premiums on the call options with the lower and the higher striking prices, respectively.

The size of any profits generated from a bull spread held to expiration is a function of the price of the underlying stock at expiration. If this price

|||| **TABLE 19-6**
Profits and Losses from the du Pont Bull Call Spread

Stock price at expiration	$109	$110	$111	$112	$113	$114	$115	$116
Profits from exercise of 110 call	N/A	0	1.00	2.00	3.00	4.00	5.00	6.00
Initial cash outflow	−2.38	−2.38	−2.38	−2.38	−2.38	−2.38	−2.38	−2.38
Loss from exercise of 115 call							0	−1.00
Net profits	−2.38	−2.38	−1.38	−.38	.62	1.62	2.62	2.62

Note: All figures are rounded to the nearest dollar.

is higher than the break-even price, profits will be realized. Prices lower than the break-even price will generate losses.

Gombola, Roenfeldt, and Cooley compared the returns generated from option spreads with the returns obtained from simply buying or writing calls.[6] All spreads were held until the options matured, either three, six, or nine months from formation. Average spread returns, after commissions, were 10.2%, 3.3%, and 23.5% for the three-, six- and nine-month maturities, respectively, compared to returns of −6.2%, 1.5%, and 8.5%, from holding the calls. Furthermore, the standard deviation of returns on the spreads was less than that of the calls. These results indicate that, when held to maturity, bull spreads sometimes offer greater returns at less risk than the purchase of call options.

Bear Spreads

A bear spread is a money spread formed by writing the call with the low striking price and buying the call with the high striking price. Since the call option with the higher striking price will have the lower premium, formation of bear spreads results in a positive cash flow for the trader. Bear spreads generate further profits if the price of the underlying stock falls while the spread is held.

Look again at the price quotations for du Pont options found in Table 19-5. The July 115/105 bear spread would be formed by buying the July 115 call and writing the July 105 call. The cash inflow upon formation of the spread is as follows:

Proceeds per share from writing July 105 call	$9.00
Cost per share of buying July 115 call	3.25
Net cash inflow per share	5.75

[6]Michael J. Gombola, Rodney L. Roenfeldt, and Philip L. Cooley, "Spreading Strategies in CBOE Options: Evidence on Market Performance," *Journal of Financial Research* (Winter 1978): p 35−44.

|||| **FIGURE 19-2**

Profits and Losses from the du Pont Bull Call Spread

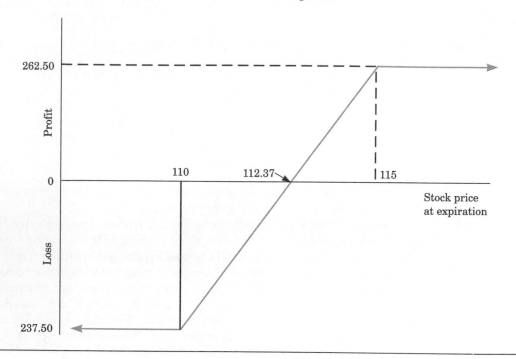

As with the bull spread, the outcomes of this spread can be analyzed by considering what would happen if (1) both options expire out of the money, (2) both options expire in the money, or (3) one option expires out of the money and one expires in the money.

Both options expire out of the money if at option expiration the price of the underlying stock is below both striking prices included in the spread. In this case, nothing happens at expiration because neither option is exercised, and the spread generates a profit of $5.75 per share, equal to the cash inflow at its origination.

Both options expire in the money if, at option expiration, the price of the underlying stock is above the higher striking price (115 in this example). In this case, the holder of the 105 call, which was originally written, exercises the call, and this obligation is filled by exercising the 115 call, which was originally purchased. This generates a loss of $10 per share, which is the difference in the option striking prices. The net loss on the spread is thus

$$\begin{aligned} \text{net loss} &= \text{initial cash inflow} - \text{loss at maturity} \\ &= \text{difference in premiums} - \text{difference in striking prices} \quad (19\text{-}2) \\ &= (P_{cl} - P_{ch}) - (E_l - E_h) \end{aligned}$$

$$= (9.00 - 3.25) - (115 - 105)$$
$$= -4.25$$

In the third case, the underlying stock price at expiration falls between the striking prices of the two options. In this case, the 105 call (which was written) would be exercised, while the 115 call (which was purchased) would go unexercised. Assume, for example, that the stock price upon option expiration is $113. The exercise of the 105 call produces a loss of $8.00 per share, which is deducted from the initial cash inflow of $5.75 to generate a net loss. If the stock price winds up at $111, exercise of the 105 call generates a loss of $6.00 per share, which still produces a net loss for the position. Table 19-7 and Figure 19-3 show the profits and losses from this spread in the event the stock price closes between the striking prices of the two options.

Only if the stock price is less than $110.75 (the sum of the lower striking price and the cash flow generated upon spread formation) will the spread generate a profit. The formula for finding the break-even price on a bear call spread is identical to that of a bull call spread (Equation 19-1). In the case of the bear spread, however, profits are generated if the underlying stock settles at prices *below* the break-even point.

Butterfly Spreads

Butterfly spreads enable the option trader to generate profits when the price for the underlying stock is stable. A butterfly spread involves buying two calls, one with a high striking price and one with a low striking price, and writing two calls with striking prices in the middle. A butterfly spread is a combination of a bull and a bear spread.

For example, examine the du Pont option prices in Table 19-5. A butterfly spread can be constructed by buying July calls with striking prices of 115 and 105. The total outlay required would be 12¼ (3¼ + 9 = 12¼). Also, two July calls are written with striking prices of 110, which is between the striking prices of the calls purchased. The proceeds from writing these calls would be 11¼ (5⅝ × 2 = 11¼). The net cash flow upon spread formation is −$1 per share. Negative cash flows at the initiation of butterfly spreads are typical.

||||| **TABLE 19-7**

Profits and Losses from du Pont July 115/105 Bear Spread

	$115	$113	$111	$109	$107	$105
Stock price at expiration						
Initial cash inflow	5.75	5.75	5.75	5.75	5.75	5.75
Losses from exercise of 105 call	−10.00	−8.00	−6.00	−4.00	−2.00	0
Net profits	−4.25	−2.25	−0.25	1.75	3.75	5.75

Note: Option premiums were obtained from Table 19-5. All figures are quoted on a per-share basis.

|||| **FIGURE 19-3**

Profits and Losses from du Pont July 115/105 Bear Spread

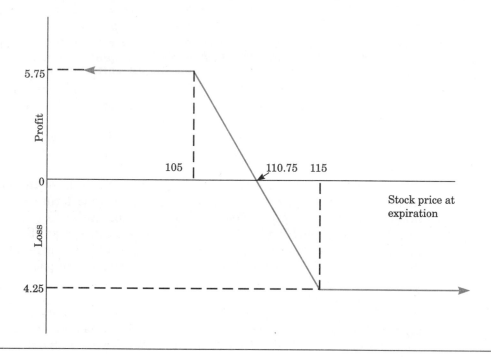

Possible outcomes when the spread is held until option maturity fall into four categories. As these categories are described below, refer to Table 19-8 for the numerical results. Profits and losses from the spread are graphed in Figure 19-4.

First, all options could expire out of the money. This would occur if the price of du Pont stock settled lower than the striking prices of any of the options involved in the spread (lower than $105). If this occurs, no options are exercised at expiration, and the profits from the spread equal the negative cash flow at spread formation.

Second, the option with the lowest striking price is in the money at expiration, and the others are not. This outcome would occur if the price of du Pont settled between $105 and $110 at option maturity. In this case, the 105 call, which was purchased, would be exercised at a profit. The size of this profit may be large enough to offset the losses incurred at spread formation, and thus the spread may or may not earn a profit.

Third, the price of the underlying stock is above the striking price of the two options written ($110), but below the striking price ($115) of the highest call that was purchased. In this case, both the options that were written would be exercised, causing losses on these positions. Profits continue to be generated with the lower call, but these profits must be large enough to offset both the initial loss and the loss incurred on the two calls written. The net outcome can be either a profit or a loss.

ⅠⅠⅠⅠ **TABLE 19-8**

Profits and Losses from the du Pont Butterfly Spread

	The spread consists of the following positions:						
	Position			**Premium**			
	Buy one du Pont July 105 call			−9.00			
	Write two du Pont July 110 calls			+11.25			
	Buy one du Pont July 115 call			−3.25			
	Net cash flow at spread formation			−1.00			
Closing stock price	$104	$106	$108	$110	$112	$114	$116
Profits from exercise of 105 call	N/A	1.00	3.00	5.00	7.00	9.00	11.00
Profits from exercise of 115 call	N/A	N/A	N/A	N/A	N/A	N/A	1.00
Losses from exercise of 2 calls written	N/A	N/A	N/A	0	−4.00	−8.00	−12.00
Initial cash flow	−1.00	−1.00	−1.00	−1.00	−1.00	−1.00	−1.00
Net profits	−1.00	0	2.00	4.00	2.00	0	−1.00

Note: Option premiums are from Table 19-5.

ⅠⅠⅠⅠ **FIGURE 19-4**

Profits and Losses from du Pont Butterfly Spread

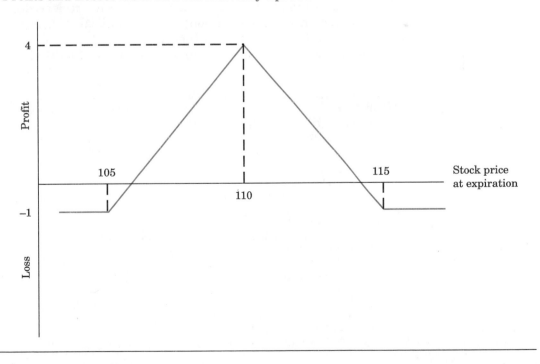

In the fourth case, the price of the underlying stock settles above the striking price of all options in the spread, that is, above $115. Profits result from the exercise of both options purchased, but the losses from the two options written plus the negative cash flow at the outset produce a net loss.

Note from Figure 19-4 that, although profits are generated as long as the underlying stock price settles anywhere between $106 and $114 (the lower striking price plus the initial cash outflow, and the higher striking price minus the initial cash outflow), the maximum profit from the spread comes when the stock price settles at $110, which is the same value as the striking price of the written calls. For this reason, butterfly spreads are best formed with stocks that have a stable price outlook. Furthermore, it is often a good strategy to "center" the spread with at-the-money calls, as we did here.

TIME SPREADS

Time spreads involve the purchase and sale of options that differ only by maturity month. For example, a du Pont July/June 110 spread is a time spread that involves the purchase of the July option with a 110 striking price and the sale of the June option with a 110 striking price. Since the option with the longer maturity will have the larger premium, this particular time spread will have a negative cash flow upon formation.

Time spreads are based upon the relationship between time to maturity and the premium of an option. The rate of decline in the premium as the time to expiration becomes shorter is uneven, accelerating as the option's maturity approaches. Options lose a great deal of their premium value during the last two weeks of their lives.

Table 19-9 shows the decline in premiums for the July/June 110 call

|||| **TABLE 19-9**

du Pont July/June 110 Time Spread

	Cash Flow	Profits
Open time spread		
April 26		
Buy July 110 call	$5.625	
Sell June 110 call	4.000	
Net cash flow	1.625	
Reverse initial position (two possible dates shown)		
June 1		
Buy June 110 call	2.000	
Sell July 110 call	3.940	
Net cash flow	1.940	$0.315
June 16		
June 110 call expires unexercised		
Sell July 110 call	3.450	
Net cash flow	3.450	1.825

spread in du Pont options. The right-hand column in Table 19-9 depicts the difference in premiums between the June and July options, and this difference steadily increases as time progresses. For this reason, time spreads usually involve the purchase of the longer-maturity option and the sale of the shorter-maturity option. Of course, these initial positions are reversed upon liquidation of the spread, and profits (if any) are normally earned only upon liquidation.

In the July/June 110 time spread, the initial premiums are $4.00 for the June option and $5.625 for the July option. Since the July option is purchased and the June option is written, these premiums result in a negative cash flow of −$1.625 per share upon spread formation.

The maximum holding period for a time spread is only until the expiration of the earliest option. Here, this would occur during mid-June. At that time, the spread can be reversed in either of two ways. First, the June option can be allowed to expire unexercised, and the July option can be sold on the same date. Using the premiums calculated in Table 19-9, this strategy would result in a profit of approximately $3.45 per share upon option expiration and a net profit for the time spread of $1.825 per share. (The net profit for the spread was obtained by subtracting the negative cash outflow of $1.625 upon option formation of $3.45 from the profit upon liquidation.

Alternatively, if the spread holder feels the risk of the time spread is too great, both positions in the spread can be canceled before option maturity. This would be done by selling the July call and purchasing the June call. Assuming this is done 16 days before the maturity of the June option, the profits upon liquidation would be $1.94 per share (from Table 19-9), and the net profit for the time spread would be $1.94 − $1.625 = $0.315 per share.

Stable stock prices are the key to generating profits with time spreads. If the price of the underlying stock remains constant, holders of time spreads benefit from the inevitable decline in option premiums as option maturity approaches. The risk of time spreads, however, is the possibility that the price of the underlying security will change too much. Time spreads can generate losses if the price of the underlying security moves substantially in either direction.

When Gombola, Roenfeldt, and Cooley studied returns from time spreads, they found that, before transactions costs the average profit from time spreads was large (122%), while the risks were about the same as with holding call options.[7] However, when transactions costs were taken into account, the profits from time spreads became negative. This should not be too surprising, considering that time spreads involve at least three, and possibly four, transactions, depending on how liquidation of the spread is handled. Brokerage commissions must be paid on each purchase and each sale of an options contract.

---

[7] Gombola, Roenfeldt, and Cooley, "Spreading Strategies in CBOE Options."

|||| OPTION STRADDLES

A straddle involves a put and a call on the same stock, with identical striking prices and maturities. Straddles can be either purchased, where the investor has a long position in both options, or written, where the investor has a short position in both options. Since writing straddles involves very high risks, it is relatively rare, and the remainder of this section will focus on the purchase of straddles.

BASIC STRADDLES

Basic straddles involve one put and one call on the same option. Figure 19-5 shows profits and losses from a typical straddle. Figure 19-5a shows the returns that would be generated from individual investments in du Pont 110 puts and calls maturing in June. Of course, these returns are a function of the price of the underlying stock. Here again, the option premiums are taken from Table 19-5.

Figure 19-5b shows how the returns from the individual options are combined to form the profit and losses from the straddle. Note that the largest loss that could be incurred from holding a straddle is the sum of the two option premiums. Profits are generated if the stock price moves in either direction from the striking price by more than the amount of the two premiums. If the stock price moves up, the call options generate profits; if the price of the stock drops, profits are generated from the put.

As Figure 19-5b indicates, the straddle will not generate a profit unless the price of the underlying stock moves at least $7, the sum of the two premiums, from the striking price of the options in the straddle.

One way to put this figure in perspective is to consider that a $7 price change on a stock that sells for $110.625 is a 6.33% price movement. Given the current du Pont option premiums, the implied volatility (or the annualized standard deviation of returns) of du Pont stock is approximately 0.20. Since the options in this example have about a two-month life (the option quotations are dated April 25, and the straddle is composed of options with a June maturity), the annualized standard deviation for this period can be estimated as $[(2/12)(0.20^2)]^{0.5} = 0.0816$, or 8.16%. If this is a good estimate and if the returns from du Pont stock are normally distributed, the stock's price can be expected to move within a range $\pm 8.16\%$ (one standard deviation) of its current price approximately two-thirds of the time. This compares favorably with the 6.33% price movement required to produce a profit from the straddle. For many straddles, however, this type of analysis will reveal that the required price movement is very unlikely, and that the straddle is probably doomed to generate losses for its investors.

The odds of profiting from a straddle can be improved with the judicious use of timing in the formation of straddles. For example, straddles involving options on individual stocks can be formed on the eve of earnings or dividend announcements for these stocks. The stock's price will move in response to unexpected changes in earnings or dividends, and the

‖‖‖ **FIGURE 19-5**

Straddle Analysis: Using du Pont June 110 Options

(a) Put and Call Profits Graphed Separately

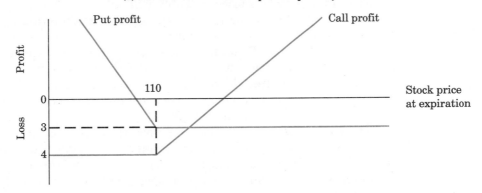

(b) Straddle Profit

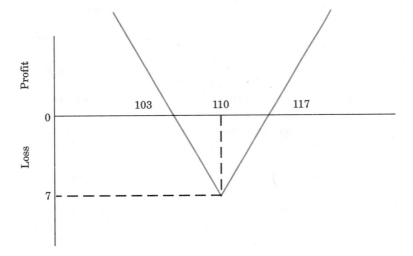

holder of a straddle can profit from stock price movements in either direction. Straddles involving options on stock indexes can be formed on the eve of major economic announcements that have an impact on the market as a whole. Examples of such announcements might include quarterly balance of trade figures, money supply announcements, and announcements of GNP figures.

A word of caution must be added at this point. As discussed in Chapter 8, stock markets are largely "efficient," meaning that available information is embedded in the current price of the stock. Included in this information is the consensus estimate of investors regarding upcoming events and announcements as well as the impact these announcements will have on the stock's price. If the actual information turns out to be as expected, the stock's price probably will not move in response to the announcement. Only if the announced figures contain *unanticipated* information will the stock's price move.

For example, if du Pont announces a $0.50 increase in dividends, and this increase was anticipated, the price of the stock will probably not change very much after the dividend increase. However, if du Pont announces an increase in dividends when none was expected, the price of the shares will respond immediately.

Thus, straddle investors look for opportunities to capitalize on unanticipated changes in company operating results or on situations where they feel that the market consensus regarding these announcements is incorrect. The mere announcement of operating results or of a significant economic event is not sufficient to produce profits.

STRIPS

Strips are variations on the basic straddle. Strips include two puts and one call, all purchased on the same option with the same maturity month and striking price. As this suggests, the motivation behind investing in strips is similar to that of investing in straddles—to take advantage of any volatility in the price of the underlying security. Since two puts are involved, however, the strip investor will profit more from a decline in price than from an increase in price. Thus, strips should be formed when the investor wants to capitalize on *any* price movement in the underlying security, but feels that the direction of this movement is likely to be downward.

The purchase of a strip involves purchasing three options contracts (two puts and a call). Thus, the total premiums involved in the strip are larger than those involved in a straddle, and potential losses from strips are also greater. If the price changes in the anticipated direction (downward), however, the profits from strips can mount up faster than those from simple straddles.

STRAPS

Straps are also variations on the basic straddle. Straps involve two calls and one put, all on the same option, with the same striking price and maturity date. While straps can generate profits in response to any movement in the price of the underlying security, strap investors will profit more from upward movements in price, since two calls are included in the strap and only on put. As with the strip, three options are involved in a strap. This means that the initial investment required for the strap is larger than that required for a simple straddle, and therefore the investor is exposed to larger potential losses. If the price of the underlying security moves in the anticipated direction (upward), however, profits will accrue faster with the strap than with a basic straddle.

In Figure 19-6, the profits and losses from straddles, strips, and straps are compared. For each, the June du Pont options with a striking price of 110 were used. Option premiums were obtained from Table 19-5.

|||| SUMMARY

This chapter examined futures spreads, option spreads, and option straddles. Futures market spreads can be divided into four categories. Intra-market spreads involve opposite positions in futures contracts that differ only by maturity month. Intermarket spreads involve opposite positions on the same contract sold on different exchanges. Intercommodity spreads involve opposite positions on the same delivery month on related commodities. And, finally, commodity-product spreads involve taking opposite positions in futures contracts that are related to one another because they are based on a basic commodity and products derived from it, such as soybean futures and futures on soybean oil and meal.

Several variations of each of these futures spreads are available. Of these, the NOB spread is one of the most widely traded.

|||| **FIGURE 19-6**

Profits and Losses from Straddles, Strips, and Straps Compared

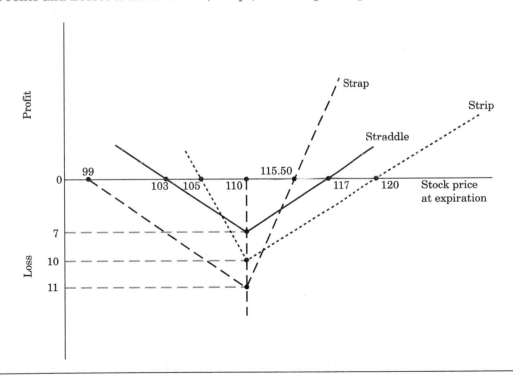

Option spreads fall into two categories, money spreads and time spreads. Money spreads include options that differ only by striking price, while time spreads include options that differ only by expiration month. Money spreads can be further subdivided into bull spreads, so named because they generate profits in bull markets; bear spreads, which generate profits in bear markets; and butterfly spreads, which generate profits during periods of stable prices.

Straddles involve both a put and a call on the same option with the same striking price and expiration month. Straddles are designed to take advantage of extreme price volatility in either direction. Two variations of the straddle are the strip, which is designed to take advantage of price declines, and the strap, which is designed to take advantage of price increases. Strips include two puts for each call, while straps include two calls for each put.

|||| QUESTIONS

1. In what ways are intramarket spreads in futures similar to time spreads with options? How do they differ?

2. Using Table 19-1 as a guide, check the current futures price quotations to see if any profitable intermarket spread opportunities seem to exist.
   a. What factors (other than contract mispricing) may be responsible for any price discrepancies that exist?
   b. If price discrepancies are present, what positions should be taken on each contract involved?
   c. What profit levels are expected for each spread in part (b)?
   d. Follow these contracts daily for a period of at least three to five trading days. What happened to the price differences noted in part (a)? If the prices did not converge, look up the features of each contract involved to try and explain the discrepancy in the price level.

3. Why is rapid execution of buy and sell orders a special problem for intermarket spreads?

4. The average value for the gold-silver ratio spread is 32½. Check the current prices of gold and silver futures in the financial section of your newspaper. Does it appear that profit opportunities for this spread currently exist? If so, what positions should be taken in each contract? Follow these contracts until the spread returns to a more normal level, or, if it remains at its current level, do some research on current market conditions to determine why the ratio is high or low.

5 a. Define the NOB spread.
   b. Assume that investors begin to expect a parallel shift downward in the yield curve. What would you expect to happen to the values of the NOB spread? Explain why.

6. Distinguish between a bull spread and a bear spread. Give an example of each, using options on Dow Chemical with striking prices of 90 and 95.

7. Under what conditions will a butterfly spread generate a profit?

8. In an option time spread, why is the option with the longest maturity usually purchased upon spread formation? (*Hint:* When are the profits from a time spread usually earned?)

9. a. Under what conditions would a time spread be liquidated before expiration of the earliest option.
   b. What is the principal risk of time spreads?

10. a. Should straddles be formed with options on stable or volatile stocks? Why?
    b. What is the maximum loss that can be sustained with a straddle?

11. Straddles are often formed prior to major corporate announcements or economic events. Why? What impact does market efficiency have on this strategy?

12. Distinguish between strips, straps, and straddles. When should each be used?

||| PROBLEMS

1. Assume that the cost of storage and insurance for wheat is currently $0.055 per bushel per month. Look up the current prime rate of interest in the *Wall Street Journal*.
   a. What is the monthly cost of carry for wheat futures?
   b. Examine the current wheat futures price quotations. Are there any contract maturities in which the price difference is large enough to cover the full cost of carry? If so, what action should those who are long in the commodity itself take in regard to these contracts?

2. a. Track the prices for the MMI versus the Value Line stock index spread for the most recent 10 trading days. What was the average spread over this period?
   b. Assume that the MMI leads movements in the Value Line Index. Identify the current market cycle (bull or bear) and explain what position should be taken in each contract.
   c. What are the risks in your recommendation in part *(b)*?

3. a. Using the *Wall Street Journal* (or another publication containing a complete set of financial quotations), look up the futures prices for soybeans, soybean meal, and soybean oil.
   b. Now, assume that a 60-pound bushel of soybeans can yield 47 pounds of soybean meal and 11 pounds of soybean oil. What is the current gross processing margin?
   c. What are the risks in your recommendation in part (b)?

4. You form an August 45/50 money spread with call options on Warner Communications. The stock's current market price is 48⅛, and the premiums on the two options are 5½ and 2⅜, respectively.
    a. Is this a bull, bear, or butterfly spread?
    b. What is the initial cash flow of the spread?
    c. Calculate profits from the spread, assuming the options expire with the following prices for the underlying stock:

    $43.50 per share

    $46.00 per share

    $48.00 per share

    $52.00 per share

    d. What price of Warner Communications common stock will result in a break-even outcome from this spread?

5. Repeat all parts of Problem 4 using an August 50/45 money spread in your analysis.

6. a. Using the current price quotations for Dow Chemical options, construct a butterfly spread. Use the at-the-money calls for the options you write. What options are included in your spread, and what is the spread's initial cash flow?
    b. Calculate profits if the price of Dow Chemical rises by $5 per share before option expiration.
    c. Calculate the upper and lower break-even points (in terms of Dow's closing stock price) for the spread.

7. Assume the following options quotations for Dow Chemical on the dates indicated:

		Calls	
April 25		June	September
95⅝	95	4⅛	6⅝
June 17*			
88½	95	⅟₁₆	1¾

*Last trading day for June options

    a. What is the cash flow upon formation of a September/June 95 spread?
    b. Assuming the spread is liquidated on June 17, what would be the cash flow on that date? What is the profit or loss from the spread?
    c. What had an influence on the net income from this spread?

8. On April 25, Dow Chemical June calls with a striking price of 95 sell for 4⅛, and puts with the same striking price and expiration date sell for 2¼. On June 17, the last trading day for June options, the price of Dow common stock was 88½, while the calls and puts had premiums of ⅟₁₆ and 6⅛, respectively.

a. Form a long straddle on April 25. What is your initial cash outflow?

b. What action should you take on June 17? Calculate your profits/losses (ignore commissions).

9. Examine the following price quotations for Lotus Development:

		Calls		Puts	
April 25		June	July	June	July
22¼	22½	⅞	1½	1⅛	1⅜

a. Assume you are interested in forming straddles for both the June and July maturities. What is your initial cash outflow for each?

b. How far must the price of Lotus Development common move before the June straddle becomes profitable? How about the July straddle? What percentage price movement does each of these represent?

c. Using the software supplied with this text, or a similar program, calculate the implied volatility (the annualized standard deviation) of both the June and the July call options. In your calculations, assume that the riskless rate of interest is 8¾% per year, and that the June and July options have 52 and 84 days left until maturity, respectively.

d. Now, assuming there are two months remaining in the June options and three months remaining in the July options, calculate the volatility that can be expected over each option's remaining life.

e. Comparing your results from parts *(c)* and *(d)*, does it look as if either straddle will be profitable? Which one would be preferable (*Note:* The price of Lotus common stock rose to 26 by the time the June options expired.)

|||| SELECTED REFERENCES

Commodity Trading Manual, Chicago: Chicago Board of Trade, 1985. Chapters 10 and 11.

Frankfurter, George, Richard Stevenson, and Allan Young. "Option Spreading: Theory and Illustration." *Journal of Portfolio Management* (Summer 1979): 59–63.

Gold-Silver Ratio Spread. Chicago: Chicago Board of Trade, 1988.

Gombola, Michael J., Rodney L. Roenfeldt, and Philip L. Cooley. "Spreading Strategies in CBOE Options: Evidence on Market Performance." *Journal of Financial Research* (Winter 1978): 35–44.

July-November Soybean Spread. Chicago: Chicago Board of Trade, 1986.

MMI Intermarket Spreads. Chicago: Chicago Board of Trade, 1988.

Ritchken, Peter H., and Harvey M. Salkin. "Safety First Selection Techniques for Option Spreads." *Journal of Portfolio Management* (Spring 1981): 61–67.

Slivka, Ronald. "Call Option Spreading." *Journal of Portfolio Management* (Spring 1981): 71–76.

Trading the Option NOB. Chicago: Chicago Board of Trade, 1988.

6 PORTFOLIO THEORY AND MANAGEMENT

20 PORTFOLIO MANAGEMENT

Even in a world of highly efficient markets where few investors are able to earn exceptional returns on a consistent basis, portfolio managers have important work to do. They must still identify efficient portfolios and must face the challenge of assembling portfolios that are optimal for their clients.[1] An *optimal portfolio* is the efficient portfolio that, in technical terms, maximizes the investor's utility. In simpler terms, it offers the investor the most satisfying combination of risk and expected return.

PORTFOLIO OBJECTIVES AND CONSTRAINTS

The first task of a portfolio manager is to determine the investor's financial objectives and to learn of any constraints that should be observed in working toward those objectives. Investment objectives are goals; investment constraints are limits placed on the portfolio manager's discretion in attempting to achieve those goals.

Investment objectives are usually stated in terms of risk and return, the amount of risk the investor is willing to assume for a given amount of expected return. For example, the investor's objective for a common stock portfolio might be an annual before-tax return of at least 13% with an annual standard deviation of not more than 15%. It is up to the portfolio manager to determine how much risk the investor can tolerate for a given level of expected return.

Investment constraints relate to matters such as the minimum amount to be invested in highly safe and liquid assets and the maximum amounts to be invested in certain other assets, such as equity securities, real estate, and metals such as gold and silver. The investor's objectives and constraints determine the location of his or her optimal portfolio on the capital market line of Figure 20-1, which is similar to Figure 6-6. An individual with an extremely high aversion to risk may have an optimal portfolio consisting entirely of the risk-free asset; in that case it will be at point *A* on the graph. Obviously, such investors have little need for a portfolio manager. The risk/return preferences of most investors probably

---

[1] An efficient portfolio, you may recall from Chapter 6, is one that offers the highest expected return at a given level of risk or, alternatively, the least amount of risk at a given level of return.

|||| **FIGURE 20-1**

Risk-Return Trade-off: Capital Market Line

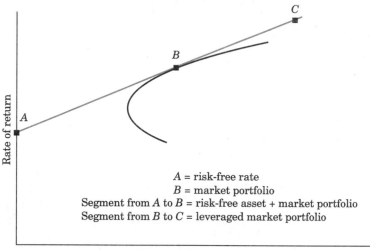

A = risk-free rate
B = market portfolio
Segment from A to B = risk-free asset + market portfolio
Segment from B to C = leveraged market portfolio

Risk (standard deviation)

place their optimal portfolios somewhere between points A and B, a region where portfolios are composed of a combination of the risk-free asset and the market portfolio.[2] Investors with little aversion to risk may choose to hold only risky assets and to finance part of their holdings with borrowed funds. The lower the aversion to risk, the closer the portfolios will be to point C on Figure 20-1.

THE INVESTOR'S TOLERANCE FOR RISK

To assemble an optimal portfolio, the investment manager must have a clear understanding of the investor's attitude toward risk and return. One way to assess investors' *risk tolerance* is to ask them to examine subjective probability distributions for various portfolios and to indicate which combination of risk and return is most appealing. Suppose an investor has only two possible choices: a well-diversified portfolio of common stocks (portfolio A) or a balanced portfolio of common stocks and corporate bonds (portfolio B). Estimates of the possible returns for the two portfolios for the next 12 months are shown in Table 20-1.

An investor with a moderate tolerance for risk might prefer portfolio B over A in spite of the lower expected return. He might be willing to give up three percentage points of expected return in order to reduce the estimated maximum loss from 30% to 10%. A more aggressive investor

[2]Recall from Chapter 6 that the market portfolio contains every risky asset, each in proportion to its total market value. Standard & Poor's 500 Index is often used as a surrogate for the market portfolio.

|||| **TABLE 20-1**

Probability Distributions of Portfolio Returns

	Portfolio A (Common Stocks)			Portfolio B (Stocks and Bonds)	
Probability	Return	Expected Return	Probability	Return	Expected Return
.10	30%	3%	.10	20%	2%
.20	20	4	.20	15	3
.40	15	6	.40	10	4
.20	10	2	.20	5	1
.10	−30	−3	.10	−10	−1
Expected return		12%			9%

might prefer portfolio A for the higher expected return, notwithstanding the possibility of a larger loss.

A similar way to evaluate an investor's attitude toward risk and return is by simulation. The portfolio manager can show the investor what the risk and return of various combinations of assets would have been during certain periods in the past. For example, suppose it has been decided that the investor's portfolio will be composed of three types of assets—common stocks, high-grade corporate bonds, and a risk-free asset—but the appropriate proportions need to determined. Through simulation, the investor can be shown how portfolios with various combinations of these three types of assets would have performed during past periods. This information may help the investor decide how to allocate her own funds among the three types of assets.

|||| # GENERAL PORTFOLIO SELECTION STRATEGIES

Portfolios can be managed actively or passively. Active management implies an effort to beat the market, either by selecting assets that are perceived to be underpriced or by changing the asset mix, which usually means increasing or decreasing the proportion of fixed-income securities in a portfolio of fixed-income securities and common stocks. The decision as to how much of a portfolio's total funds will be allocated to each type of asset is know as the *asset allocation* decision. Active managers of portfolios containing both common stocks and fixed-income securities often change the allocations because of changed expectations about the relative future performance of these two types of assets.

Changing the asset mix in an effort to beat the market is called "timing the market." Another method of market timing involves shifting from low- or medium-beta stocks to high-beta stocks when the market is expected to rise, and shifting from high betas to lower betas when the market seems likely to fall. With passive management, the mix of stocks and bonds or high- and low-beta stocks is changed only in response to a change in the investor's attitude toward risk and return.

ACTIVE MANAGEMENT

Many portfolio managers believe it is possible to outperform the market, and many are paid large fees for attempting to do so. History indicates, however, that few professional managers of common stock portfolios have been able to beat the market on a consistent basis. Since the value of common stocks managed by mutual funds, insurance companies, bank trust departments, and investment advisers is a large percentage of the value of all publicly owned stocks, one can hardly expect their overall performance to be better than the market's.

Table 20-2 shows the annualized rates of return earned by 298 bank pooled stock funds, 65 insurance company common stock accounts, 310 common stock mutual funds, and 300 investment advisers for periods of one, three, five, and ten years ending with the year 1985. In 1985 these organizations were managing approximately $400 billion of common stock assets. Since the returns in Table 20-2 are before deduction of management fees and transactions costs, they are roughly one to two percentage points higher than the returns actually received by the investors.

On the whole, the differences among the returns for the various types of investment managers were not very large, especially for periods of 5 and 10 years. Most of the returns were lower than the return on the S&P 500 Index, even before deduction of management fees and transactions costs. Experience indicates that few managers who have beaten the market over a period of 5 or 10 years have been able to repeat that performance over the next 5- or 10-year period.

Anyone who attempts to outperform the market by selecting stocks that seem to be underpriced should recognize that this strategy often leads to a poorly diversified portfolio. With poor diversification, investors are exposed to a significant amount of avoidable unsystematic risk for which they cannot expect to be compensated, except by chance, in an efficient market. Attempts to select underpriced stocks should be made

|||| TABLE 20-2

Annualized Returns Earned by Various Types of Investment Managers, 1976–1985

| | Annualized Rate of Return | | | |
	One Year	Three Years	Five Years	Ten Years
Banks	30.7%	18.8%	14.5%	13.8%
Insurance companies	31.8	18.9	14.6	14.1
Mutual funds	27.9	16.3	13.4	14.3
Investment advisers	32.8	17.4	13.4	N/A
S&P 500	31.7	17.6	14.6	14.2

SOURCE: Robert A. Levy, "Equity Performance from 1976–85: How Bank Trust Departments Measure Up," *Trusts and Estates* (May 1986): 28–30.

only when there is good reason to believe that the increase in portfolio return will more than offset the increase in risk. Assuming market efficiency and a borrowing rate that is well below the expected return on common stocks, investors who can tolerate more than market risk should invest in a diversified portfolio of stocks and leverage their position rather than hold a portfolio that is subject to a significant amount of unsystematic risk. With a leveraged, highly diversified portfolio, the investors' wealth will move up and down more than the market, but they will not be paying the price of inadequate diversification.

PASSIVE MANAGEMENT

Because of the small chance of finding an investment manager who can beat the market consistently, and because of the sizable fees active investment managers are paid, a number of institutions and other large investors are now using passive management for at least a portion of their funds. With passive management, there is no attempt to beat the market, either by selecting securities that are underpriced or by "timing the market."

Index Funds

The most common method of passive management is to build a portfolio composed of every stock in a broad index of the market or a representative sample of those stocks.[3] Portfolios managed in this manner are called *index funds*. Usually, stocks are removed from an index fund only if they have been removed from the index itself, and they are added only if they have been added to the index. The potential advantages of index funds (or other passively managed funds) are lower management fees, lower transactions costs, low unsystematic risk, and, in many cases, better performance than would be achieved with a managed portfolio.

Indexing services are now provided by a number of banks, investment advisory firms, and mutual funds. Total assets managed in this way amount to billions of dollars. The most widely held mutual funds are the Vanguard Index–500 Portfolio and the Colonial U.S. Equity Index Trust. Both of these passively managed funds are designed to track the Standard & Poor's 500 Index.

A great majority of U.S. index funds use the S&P 500 as their model. Some hold virtually all of the stocks in the index, while others select a sample that may contain as few as 50 stocks or as many as 300 or 400. With the sampling approach, the fund may not track the index as closely, but it will have the advantage of lower transactions costs.

Passive management implies a naïve buy-and-hold policy. Stocks are selected in some manner that assures good diversification and are held more or less indefinitely. Market indexing, however, is not a pure buy-and-hold policy because stocks are added and deleted from the fund as

---

[3]Managers of some index funds have policies that exclude certain stocks. For example, the Wells Fargo Index Fund based on Standard & Poor's 500 excludes the few stocks with a high bankruptcy risk.

the composition of the index changes. Many of these changes are caused by acquisitions, mergers, and bankruptcies and are therefore unavoidable. When a fund is designed to track the S&P 500, its composition is based on the judgement of a small committee in Standard & Poor's Corporation. Stocks may be removed from the index if they have "lost investment favor," and stocks may be added if they have "favorable historical records." Sometimes the index reflects the investment fads of the time, as in the fall of 1980 when 30 to 40% of the weight of the S&P 500 was in energy and energy-related stocks. Any index fund based on the S&P 500 had a heavy concentration in the energy sector at that time.

Passive Funds Based on Attributes

A second approach to passive management of common stock portfolios is to select and hold stocks with certain attributes. As an example, consider a portfolio consisting of stocks with dividend yields of more than 5% or stocks with estimated betas of more than 1.20. Stocks with certain attributes are selected not because they are expected to beat the market, but because they have certain characteristics that are desired by the investor. For instance, some investors want stocks with high dividend yields because they prefer current income over possible future price appreciation. Others may prefer stocks with high beta coefficients because they are long-term investors and expect that over a long period of time stocks with greater systematic risk will provide higher returns.

RISK AND TIME DIVERSIFICATION

A diversified portfolio of common stocks is less risky for a long-term investor (one with a long planning horizon) than for a short-term investor.[4] Long-term investors receive the benefit of time diversification, which means that if a diversified portfolio of common stocks is held for many years, the investor can be quite sure the good performance in the up years will more than offset the bad performance of the down years. The risk of loss is small. In contrast, investors who try to time the market by moving into and out of common stocks on the basis of changes in expectations about future stock prices take the risk that they will be in and out of the market at the wrong times.

The Risk of Market Timing

By definition, the market has few exceptionally good years. Anyone who times the market takes the risk of being out of the market during those years. In the 25-year period from 1966 through 1990, there were just four years in which the return on the S&P 500 was more than 25%. The

---

[4]Some writers disagree with this statement. For example, Richard McEnally has explained that the longer risky assets are held, the greater the variability of the accumulated values, or total returns. In that sense, it is true, the risk is greater for longer holding periods. If risk is viewed in terms of the probability of sustaining a loss, however, the longer the holding period, the smaller the risk. Richard W. McEnally, "Time Diversification: Surest Route to Lower Risk?" *Journal of Portfolio Management* 11, (Summer 1985): 24–26.

compound annual rate of return for the entire period was 9.5%. Leaving out the four best years, the annual return drops to 5.5%, or by more than 40%. It is apparent that the performance of a common stock portfolio can be seriously impaired if an investor moves into and out of the market on the basis of poor market forecasts.

There is much less risk (in terms of the probability of a loss) in holding a diversified portfolio of stocks for a period of, say, 10 years than in holding stocks for just one year. If an investor had purchased a representative sample of the stocks in the S&P 500 at the beginning of each year from 1926 through 1990 and sold the stocks at the end of the year, she would have sustained a loss in 20 of the 65 years, or nearly one-third of the time. But, if an investor had purchased a sample of the S&P 500 at the beginning of each year from 1926 through 1980 and sold the stocks that were purchased each year 10 years later, a loss would have been sustained in only 2 of the 55 overlapping 10-year periods, or less than 4% of the time. Both of the 10-year loss periods ended in the 1930s.

DOLLAR-COST AVERAGING

For investors who are gradually acquiring a portfolio of common stocks over a period of years (whether directly or through the purchase of shares in one or more mutual funds), the risk or poor timing can be minimized by investing equal amounts at frequent, regular intervals. With this procedure, know as *dollar-cost averaging,* investors can be sure of making some purchases when the market is depressed, assuming that the purchases are spaced no more than several months apart. Since more shares are acquired per dollar invested when prices are low than when prices are high, the average cost of the shares acquired is lower than the average price paid, as illustrated in Table 20-3.

Some investors use modified versions of dollar-cost averaging. Their objective is to invest greater amounts when the market is in a slump than when it is near a peak. For example, an individual might plan to double the amount of her periodic investment whenever the market is at least 15% below its high of the latest 24 months. This implies that funds

---

|||| **TABLE 20-3**
Dollar-Cost Averaging

Periodic Investment	Total Investment	Price	Number of Shares Purchased	Number of Shares Owned	Value of Shares Owned
$1,000	$1,000	$20	50.0	50.0	$1,000
1,000	2,000	26	38.5	88.5	2,301
1,000	3,000	16	62.5	151.0	3,416
1,000	4,000	29	34.5	185.5	5,467
1,000	5,000	28	35.7	221.2	6,194
Average price		23.80			
Weighted average cost		22.60			

will be accumulated in other investments that can be liquidated to buy a greater than usual amount of common stocks from time to time. Of course, dollar-cost averaging does not assure investment success over any particular period of time. If the last price in Table 22-3 were $20 instead of $28, the ending total value would have been only $4,710, or $290 less than the total amount invested.

|||| # SPECIFIC PORTFOLIO SELECTION STRATEGIES

Chapters 5, 6, and 7 introduced models and principles that can be used to identify efficient portfolios. In this section the Sharpe portfolio-generating algorithm, which is based upon beta, the systematic measure of risk will be demonstrated.[5] The optimal portfolio solution is surprisingly easy to obtain and provides a reasonable approximation of an efficient set of a limited number of risky securities.

DATA REQUIREMENTS

The inputs for the model may be derived from any reasonable security analysis. As we have seen in previous chapters, the expected return, variance of the return, and beta are three important statistical measures that come from security analysis.

In addition, we have seen that it is necessary to relate security return to the return of a broad-based market portfolio. Thus, additional inputs necessary to the portfolio-building process include the identification of an appropriate market portfolio along with its expected return and variation.

Finally, it should be clear that the risk-free rate of return plays an important part in classical portfolio theory. Therefore, a final input is an estimate of an appropriate risk-free rate.

THE DEFINITION OF RISK

In Chapter 5, we demonstrated that the total risk of a security is the sum of the systematic and unsystematic risk as shown in Equation 20-1:

$$\sigma_i^2 = \beta_i^2 \sigma_m^2 + \sigma_\epsilon^2 \qquad (20\text{-}1)$$

In a well-diversified portfolio, unsystematic risk can be reduced to approximately zero. In this case Equation 20-1 may be written as

$$\sigma_p^2 \approx \beta_p^2 \sigma_m^2 \quad \text{or} \quad \sigma_p \approx \beta_p \sigma_m \qquad (20\text{-}2)$$

Since σ_m is a constant for both securities and portfolios, the standardized portfolio risk for a diversified portfolio may be written as

$$\beta_p = \sigma_p / \sigma_m \qquad (20\text{-}3)$$

[5]W. Sharpe, *Portfolio Theory and Capital Markets* (New York: McGraw-Hill Book Company, 1970), pps. 131, 139, 300–302.

That is, when dealing with a well-diversified portfolio, β_p is an appropriate measure of risk. A portfolio with as few as 15 to 20 securities may allow this specification of risk.[6]

THE INVESTMENT OBJECTIVE AND CONSTRAINTS

Figure 20-2a shows an efficient frontier in the expected return and beta space. As usual, only those portfolios on the frontier provide the highest return for a given level of risk (beta).

A useful investment objective function that implicitly includes the trade-off between systematic risk and return is

$$\max Z = (1 - \lambda)E(R_p) - \lambda\beta_p \qquad (20\text{-}4)$$

where

$$\lambda = \text{measure of investor risk preference } (0 \leq \lambda \leq 1)$$

[6]Investors should be wary of such general specifications on portfolio size. It is not true that every portfolio of 15 or 20 securities will significantly reduce unsystematic risk.

|||| **FIGURE 20-2**

Efficient Frontier

(a) Efficient Frontier
in $E(R_p)$ β_p Space

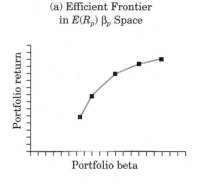

(b) Portfolio that Maximizes
Z Value When
$\lambda = 0.0$

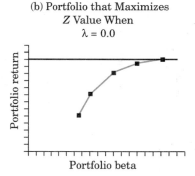

(c) Portfolio that Maximizes
Z Value When
$\lambda = 1.0$

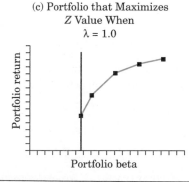

(d) Portfolio that Maximizes
Z Value When
$\lambda = 0.5$

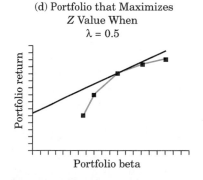

Lambda defines the importance of return relative to risk for an investor. At its extremes, 0 and 1, an investor is, respectively, risk indifferent and risk averse.

When λ is equal to zero, Z equals $E(R_p)$. In this case, maximizing the investment function is the same as maximizing expected return.

Figure 20-2b shows the linear plot of the objective function and the efficient frontier. When λ equals zero, the portfolio that maximizes the investment function Z is at the right-hand end of the efficient frontier.

Figure 20-2c shows the investment situation when λ equals one. In this case Z equals $-\beta$ and the investment objective is to minimize beta. Note that in this case the optimal Z value occurs at the left-hand end of the efficient frontier.

When λ equals 0.5, return and risk are equally important. The plot of the Z function in this case is a 45-degree line. As in the previous cases, the portfolio with the largest value of Z is the efficient portfolio that is tangent with the Z function (see Figure 20-2d).

The relationship between the objective function and the individual securities under consideration may be seen by substituting the usual definitions for $E(R_p)$ and β_p into Equation 20-4. That is, since

$E(R_p) = \Sigma X_i R_i$ = weighted average of the individual security returns
$E(\beta_p) = \Sigma X_i \beta_i$ = weighted average of the individual security betas

then the objective function may be written as

$$\max Z = (1 - \lambda)(X_1 E(R_1) + X_2 E(R_2) + \cdots + X_n E(R_n)) \quad (20\text{-}5)$$
$$- \lambda(X_1 \beta_1 + X_2 \beta_2 + \cdots + X_n \beta_n)$$

where

X_i = the proportion of an investor's available wealth invested in security i

Regrouping to simplify the notation results in an objective function of the following form:

$$\max Z = X_1[(1 - \lambda)E(R_1) - \lambda\beta_1]$$
$$+ X_2[(1 - \lambda)E(R_2) - \lambda\beta_2]$$
$$+$$
$$. \qquad\qquad (20\text{-}6)$$
$$.$$
$$.$$
$$+ X_n[(1 - \lambda)E(R_n) - \lambda\beta_n]$$

The investment objective Z may be written as a function of individual security risk and return trade-off objectives that are defined as

$$z_i = (1 - \lambda)E(R_i) - \lambda\beta_i \quad (20\text{-}7)$$

Thus, Equation 20-6 may be written as

$$\max Z = X_1 z_1 + X_2 z_2 + \cdots + X_n z_n \quad (20\text{-}6a)$$

Note that z_i is the risk-return trade-off function for a security, while Z is the risk-return trade-off function for a portfolio.

The constraint of the objective function is both a minimum security and a maximum wealth allocation constraint. The simplest specification of the constraint occurs when the proportion allocated to the individual securities is limited to the minimum number of securities permitted in a portfolio. The constraint may be written as

$$X_j \leq 1/m \tag{20-8}$$

where

m = the minimum number of securities included in the portfolio

DEFINING THE EFFICIENT FRONTIER

It is now possible to determine the securities to be included in the optimal efficient set of securities. All that is required is to maximize Z for any value of λ when the proportion invested in each security is defined as in Equation 20-8. This involves computing the investment objective for every security and then selecting the m largest values of z_i.

For problems of reduced size, the securities to be included in the efficient portfolio can be determined graphically. A "figure of merit" represents the plots of the individual investment objectives shown in Equation 20-7. Since Equation 20-7 is linear, the computations necessary to create the figure of merit are very simple. For example, if the expected return and beta for security 1 are 26% and 2.0, respectively, then z_1 is 0.26 when $\lambda = 0$ and z_1 is -2 when $\lambda = 1$, calculated as follows:

$$z_1 = (1 - \lambda) \times .26 - \lambda \times 2.0$$
$$\text{If } \lambda = 0.0, \text{ then } z_1 = 0.26.$$
$$\text{If } \lambda = 1.0, \text{ then } z_1 = -2.0.$$

Connecting these two points [(.26, 0.0), $(-2.0, 1.0)$] and similar points for every security under consideration allows the portfolio selection problem to be solved graphically. Figure 20-3a illustrates this procedure for security 1. Figure 20-3a is really nothing more than an XY coordinate axis. The X-axis plots the values of λ, and the Y-axis plots the values of the objective function z_i. Observe that any point on the Y-axis occurs only when $\lambda = 0$, that is, when $z_i = E(R_i)$. The second vertical axis (labeled z = beta in Figure 20-3a) is a graphical aid. This axis still represents the objective function z_i. However, since it is positioned at $\lambda = 1.0$, the values of z_i on this axis will always equal $-\beta_i$.

Figure 20-3b presents a complete figure of merit for security 1 and four other securities. The data inputs are shown in Table 20-4.

For any level of λ, the optimal portfolio of m securities may be determined from the figure of merit. It consists of the securities with the m highest z_i scores; that is, the top m lines in the graph. For example, in Figure 20-3b, when $\lambda = 0$, the top three lines correspond to securities 1, 2, and 3. When $\lambda = 1$, the top three lines/securities are 5, 4, and 3. The mth line from the top over the whole range of λ is referred to as the border line. All lines contained within and including the border line rep-

|||| **FIGURE 20-3a**
Figure of Merit for One Security

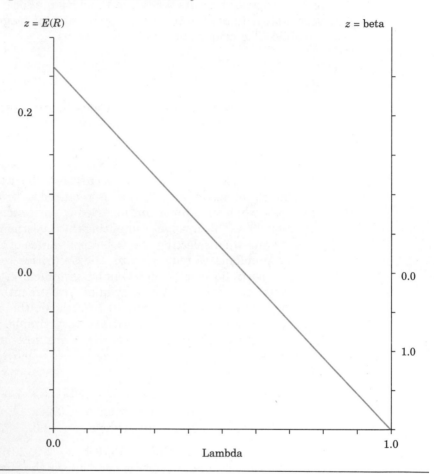

resent the optimal m-security portfolios for various levels of λ. In Figure 20-3b the color line indicates the border line for $m = 3$.

The border line bends when it intersects steeper lines that are above the existing border or flatter lines that are below the border. If the border line is intersected from below, both the border line and the composition of the optimal portfolio change. These intersections represent corner portfolios, where one security will drop out and another security will enter the optimal portfolio. If the intersection is from above, only the border line will change. The composition of the efficient portfolio will remain the same since the intersecting line represents a security that is already in the portfolio.

Each of the corner portfolios in Figure 20-3b can be identified. The expected return and the betas for each of the corner portfolios can be calculated using the following relations:

$$E(R_p) = \sum_{j=1}^{m} X_j E(R_j) \tag{20-9}$$

|||| **FIGURE 20-3b**
Figure of Merit for Five Securities, $m = 5$

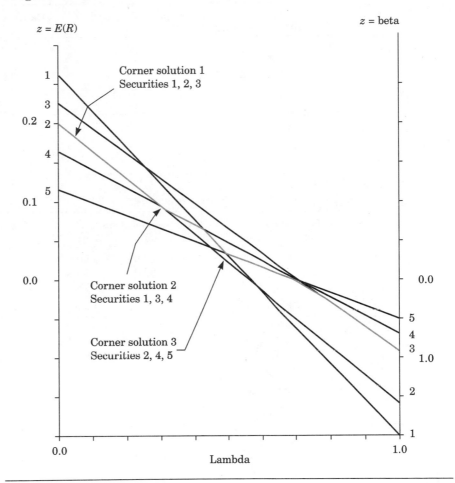

and

$$\beta_p = \sum_{j=1}^{m} X_j \beta_j \qquad (20\text{-}10)$$

The expected return for the first corner portfolio is

$$E(R_p) = (\tfrac{1}{3})(.20) + (\tfrac{1}{3})(.22) + (\tfrac{1}{3})(.26) = .227$$

The beta of the portfolio is

$$\beta_p = (\tfrac{1}{3})(.94) + (\tfrac{1}{3})(1.47) + (\tfrac{1}{3})(2.0) = 1.47$$

The expected return and beta for each of the corner solution portfolios are shown in Table 20-5 and are plotted in Figure 20-4. This figure is the efficient frontier of the five risky securities.

The portfolios shown in Table 20-5 completely identify the efficient frontier of the five securities. They can do so because the constraints and the objective function are linear. Consequently, the efficient frontier is

|||| **TABLE 20-4**
Security Data

Security	Expected Return (R_i)	Expected Beta (β_i)
1	0.26	2.00
2	0.20	1.47
3	0.22	0.94
4	0.16	0.72
5	0.11	0.51

|||| **TABLE 20-5**
Corner Solution Portfolios for Five Securities

| | Corner Solution 1 | | | Corner Solution 2 | | | Corner Solution 3 | |
Stock	Return	Beta	Stock	Return	Beta	Stock	Return	Beta
1	26.0%	2.00	1	26.0%	2.00	3	22.0%	0.94
2	20.0	1.47	3	22.0	0.94	4	16.0	0.72
3	22.0	0.94	4	16.0	0.72	5	11.0	0.51
Portfolio	22.7%	1.47		21.3%	1.22		16.3%	0.72

|||| **FIGURE 20-4**
Efficient Frontier of Five Securities

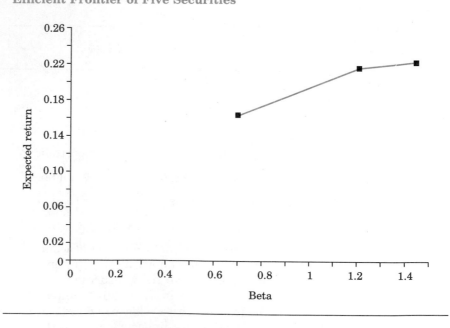

simply a series of linear segments. A point on the frontier between any two adjacent corner portfolios is simply a linear combination of the two portfolios.

The optimal corner solution portfolio can be determined by the risk-free lending or borrowing rate. For a rate of 10%, the optimal combination of the risk-free asset with the optimal risky portfolio is shown in Figure 20-5. Observe that the point of tangency of a line originating at the risk-free rate and the efficient frontier defines the optimal risky portfolio (T), in this case, portfolio 2. Any point along the line represents the best combination of the optimal risky portfolio and the risk-free asset.

The only problem left is to define the investor's preferred combination of risk and return. This is shown in Figure 20-6 by introducing an investor's indifference curve.[7] The point of tangency between the indifference curve and the line segment defines the preferred combination of the risky portfolio and the risk-free asset.

Recall that the expected return of a portfolio made up of the risk-free asset and the risky portfolio is defined as

$$E(R_p) = X_f R_f + (1 - X_f)E(R_T) \qquad (20\text{-}11)$$

where

X_f = the proportion of the investor's portfolio invested in the risk-free asset

[7]See Chapter 6 for a discussion of indifference curves.

||| **FIGURE 20-5**

Selection of the Optimal Portfolio

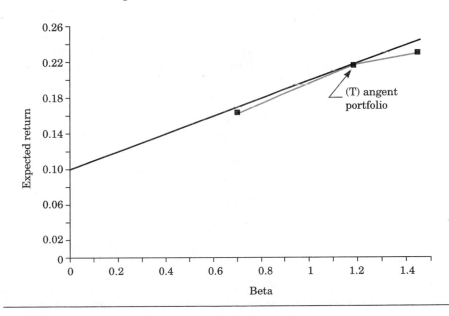

|||| **FIGURE 20-6**

An Investor's Preferred Combination of Risk and Return

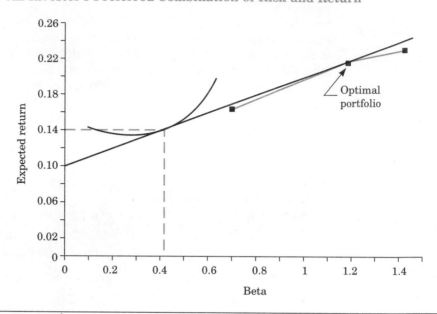

For an investor who requires a 15% rate of return the proportions to invest in the risk-free asset and the risky portfolio can be determined as follows:

$$.15 = X_f(.10) + (1 - X_f)(.213)$$
$$.063 = X_f(.113)$$
$$X_f = .557$$
$$1 - X_f = .443$$

This is a lending portfolio, where the investor commits 55.7% to the risk-free asset and invests 44.3% in the risky portfolio. The investment in each of the risky securities will be

$$.443(\tfrac{1}{3}) = .148 \text{ or } 14.8\% \text{ in security 1}$$
$$.433(\tfrac{1}{3}) = .148 \text{ or } 14.8\% \text{ in security 2}$$
$$.433(\tfrac{1}{3}) = .148 \text{ or } 14.8\% \text{ in security 4}$$

The systematic risk of the portfolio is determined with the following formula:

$$\beta p = X_f\beta_f + (1 - X_f)\beta_T \qquad (20\text{-}12)$$

For the present case, the systematic risk is

$$\beta p = .557(0) + .433(1.22)$$
$$\beta p = .53$$

If an investor specifies a preferred level of risk, the investment proportions can be obtained with Equation 20-12; and the expected return can be found with Equation 20-11.

DIVERSIFICATION ISSUES

A limitation of this portfolio generation model is the assumption that β_p is the appropriate measure of risk. This assumption is invalid when the portfolio contains few securities. Beta becomes a better measure of total risk as the number of securities under consideration and in the portfolio increase. In addition, the number of corner portfolios increases, giving rise to a curve with the more classical shape of the efficient frontier.[8]

Table 20-6 shows the regression statistics for the optimal risky portfolio chosen in the previous section. The table shows that if total risk is described by the systematic risk of the portfolio ($\sigma_p^2 = \beta_p \sigma_m^2$), the total risk is .005. Note, however, that the R^2 (percentage of total risk that is systematic) is only 59.2%. This means that 40.8% $(1 - R^2)$ of the risk is unsystematic. The actual total risk of the portfolio is .00904. This risk can be partitioned into its systematic and unsystematic risk components using Equation 20-1:

$$\sigma_p^2 = \beta_p^2 \sigma_m^2 + \sigma_\epsilon^2$$
$$.00904 = (1.222)^2(00358) + .00368 \qquad (20\text{-}13)$$
$$= .00536 + .00368$$

These results indicate that the unsystematic risk for a small portfolio chosen from a small universe of securities is likely to be unacceptably high.[9]

---

[8]Note, however, that the efficient frontier will still be comprised of straight lines.

[9]The confidence interval for the optimal portfolio can be determined with the following equation:

$$CI = E(R_p) \pm \sigma_\epsilon = [\alpha + \beta_p E(R_m)] \pm \sigma_\epsilon$$

If the expected monthly return is .0178, then the monthly confidence interval is

$$CI = .0178 \pm .0606 = .0784 \text{ to } -.0428.$$

On an annual basis, this interval is

$$CI = .9408 \text{ to } -.5136$$

Obviously, such a wide interval is not very useful for prediction.

||| **TABLE 20-6**

Regression Statistics for the Optimal Risky Portfolio

Regression Output	
Alpha	0.004497
Beta	1.221860
Annual expected return	0.214305
Standard error of Y estimate (σ_ϵ)	0.060695
Variance of Y estimate (σ_ϵ^2)	0.003683
R-squared	0.592352
Number of observations	60
Degrees of freedom	58
Total risk (σ_i^2)	0.009036
Systematic risk (β_{am}^{22})	0.005352
Unsystematic risk (σ_ϵ^2)	0.003683

The portfolio procedure described above illustrates many of the components of *mean-variance portfolio analysis*. However, the graphical procedure for solving for the optimal risky portfolio can be very tedious, to say the least. Fortunately, with the advent of personal computers, this problem is no longer serious. It is relatively easy to program the procedure, and two such programs are provided on the computer disk accompanying this book.

Table 20-7 presents a set of data for 25 securities from which an optimal portfolio of 12 securities was chosen. The data in this table were derived from the Compustat[10] database. The expected return is the annualized average monthly return over the period September 1983 to August 1988. The betas were obtained by regressing the monthly returns of the securities against the monthly returns of the Standard & Poor's 500 Index. The unadjusted slope coefficient of the regression is the beta of the security.[11]

[10]Standard & Poor's Compustat Services, Inc.

[11]For a discussion of the determination of beta and various beta adjustments, see Chapter 5.

|||| **TABLE 20-7**

Selection Pool of 25 Securities

Company	E(R)	Beta
American Brands	17.59%	0.812
Boeing	19.65	0.729
Browning-Ferris	21.12	1.152
Bristol-Myers	19.41	0.553
Anheuser Busch	22.45	0.617
Citicorp	10.92	0.970
Emerson Electric	12.08	0.994
Heinz (H. J.)	24.44	0.651
IBM	1.96	0.707
International Minerals	2.25	0.839
K mart	10.44	1.067
McDonald's	19.03	0.709
McDermott	3.37	1.118
Marriott Corporation	11.99	0.839
Martin-Marietta	11.20	1.101
Quaker Oats	32.43	0.545
Pitney Bowes	24.53	1.034
Raytheon	9.48	0.724
Security Pacific	10.65	0.902
Thomas and Betts	11.75	0.987
TWA	23.74	1.130
Texaco	10.73	0.513
U.S. Shoe	6.96	1.292
U.S. Steel	4.60	0.808
Zurn Industries	15.11	0.740

|||| **FIGURE 20-7**

Optimal Portfolio Selection from 25 Securities

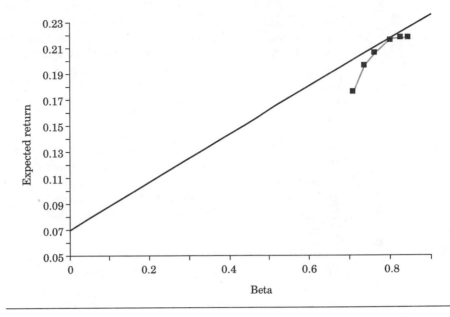

|||| **TABLE 20-8**

Optimal Portfolio from 25 Securities

Company	E(R)	Beta
Quaker Oats	32.43%	0.55
Heinz (H. J.)	24.44	0.65
Anheuser Busch	22.45	0.62
Bristol-Myers	19.41	0.55
Boeing	19.65	0.73
McDonald's	19.03	0.71
Pitney Bowes	24.53	1.03
American Brands	17.59	0.81
Texaco	10.73	0.51
TWA	23.74	1.13
Zurn Industries	15.11	0.74
Browning-Ferris	21.12	1.15
Portfolio	20.85%	0.77

Figure 20-7 shows the plot of the efficient frontier for risky 12-security portfolios along with the tangent line originating from a presumed risk-free rate of 7%. The composition of the optimal or tangent risky 12-security portfolio on the efficient frontier is shown in Table 20-8 along with the returns and betas of the individual securities and the portfolio.

|||| SEEKING BROADER DIVERSIFICATION

It is often assumed that the S&P 500 represents a well-diversified portfolio of risky assets. If it did represent the best possible diversification of risky assets, nothing could be gained by combining other assets with the S&P 500 to reduce the risk or increase the expected return, or both. The portfolio would be on the efficient frontier. No other portfolio of assets would provide a higher expected return at the same level of risk, and no other portfolio would offer the same expected return at a lower level of risk.

It is now well know that the S&P 500 is not an efficient portfolio. By diversifying more widely, investors can acquire more efficient portfolios. Two methods of achieving wider diversification are by investing in common stocks of foreign countries or investing in real estate. These are not the only methods of achieving broader diversification (and they can, of course, both be used in the same portfolio), but they are two that offer a great deal of promise.

INTERNATIONAL DIVERSIFICATION

If a diversified portfolio of foreign stocks offers the same expected return (in U.S. dollars) at the same level of risk as a diversified portfolio of U.S. stocks, a combination of the two portfolios will offer the same expected return as the individual portfolios but at a lower level of risk, assuming that the returns of the U.S. and foreign portfolios are not perfectly positively correlated. We observed in Chapter 6 that the risk of a portfolio depends not only on the risk of the individual assets and their relative weights in the portfolio but on the amount of correlation between the returns of each pair of assets. If any of the correlations are less than 1.0, the risk of the portfolio will be less than a weighted average of the risks of the individual assets. Thus, we can be sure that the risk of an internationally diversified portfolio of common stocks will be lower than a weighted average of the risks of the U.S. and foreign portfolios. But whether the risk of the internationally diversified portfolio will be lower than the risk of the U.S. portfolio depends on the comparative risk of the U.S. and foreign portfolios as well as the correlation between the returns of the two portfolios and their relative weights in the international portfolio.

Even if the expected return for the foreign stocks in a portfolio is below the expected return for the U.S. stocks, the international portfolio will be more efficient than a U.S. portfolio if the reduction in risk is great enough. If the foreign stocks have a higher expected return than the U.S. stocks, so much the better.

Solnik and Noetzlin Study

In an interesting study, Solnik and Noetzlin demonstrated that on the basis of actual returns for the 10-year period from 1971 through 1980, a passively managed portfolio of internationally diversified stocks produced

||| SIDELIGHT
Diversify, but Really Do Spread the Bread

Every investor has heard about how crucial it is to diversify, but many people—even some with varied stock and bond holdings—probably don't realize how undiversified they really are.

"Individuals rarely take an overall view" when it comes to diversification, says Michael Lipper, who heads Lipper Analytical Services. "They think of it in terms of different chunks of money" they have invested in stocks, bonds, cash, and other assets. In reality, "securities are only one part of the total (diversification) picture—and not even the most important one at that."

Take the case of a young Wall Street executive with a mortgaged cooperative apartment in lower Manhattan. A diversified stock portfolio would actually compound, not lessen, such an individual's risk because all those "assets"—job, home, and savings—are heavily exposed to the vagaries of the stock market.

In a similar vein, Lawrence Manchester, head of the private-client group at Standish, Ayer & Wood, says he would advise a client who owns a car agency to avoid long-term bonds, utilities, and insurance stocks. Those investments, just like the car business, are "very interest-rate sensitive," he says. For that client, diversification means "fixing it so that when his company goes in the dumper every four years, he's protected in his portfolio."

The way the professionals see it, diversification for individuals isn't driven by fancy theories about market volatility. Instead, they say, it starts with a basic grasp of personal economic risk.

"I'd always ask myself at the start of the analysis, 'What's the worst that could happen to me? And the next worst?—and build a portfolio strategy based on that," says Russell Fogler of Aronson & Fogler, a Philadelphia money-management firm. "It's a sequential process."

At different points in an individual's lifetime, diversification has two roles to play, the pros say. Initially, its function is to protect the individual from being hit hard by losses in basic "assets," such as job, home, and purchasing power. "Most people don't think of their job as their No. 1 investment," says Mr. Lipper. "But over their lifetime, it's salary, insurance, and pension benefits that will wind up setting their whole investment picture."

The second purpose of diversification is to protect against the long-term risk of "outliving one's capital" once the job ends, says Mr. Lipper. In this context, says Owen Quattlebaum, head of personal financial services at Brown Brothers Harriman & Co., diversification means "branching out into other, risky assets" such as stocks and bonds. In other words, it becomes "something genuinely defined as a way to make money," he says.

SOURCE: Barbara Donnelly, "Diversify, but Really Do Spread the Bread," *The Wall Street Journal*, September 14, 1989. Reprinted by permission of *The Wall Street Journal*, © Dow Jones & Company, Inc. (1989). All Rights Reserved Worldwide.

a higher return at a lower level of risk than the S&P 500.[12] The international portfolio was composed of value-weighted stock indexes for each of 12 countries: the United States and Canada, six European countries (Belgium, France, Germany, the Netherlands, Switzerland, and the United Kingdom), and four Pacific zone markets (Australia, Hong Kong, Japan, and Singapore). Broad-based indexes were used as proxies for the stocks of each country or market. The study also used two multicountry indexes: the Capital International Europe, Australia, and Far East Index (EAFE) and the Capital International World Index, which is composed of EAFE plus indexes for the United States and Canada.

Total returns and standard deviations of the returns for the 10-year period were compared for EAFE stocks (based on the indexes for the six European countries and four Pacific zone markets), U.S. stocks (based on the S&P 500 Index), and world stocks (based on the indexes for all 12 countries). The U.S. stocks accounted for more than half of the world stock index. The compound annual returns (in U.S. dollars) and the standard deviations of the returns are reported in Table 20-9.

Passive international diversification during the period 1971 through 1980, as carried out by Solnik and Noetzlin on the basis of market capitalizations, provided substantially better performance than U.S. stocks alone, as represented by the S&P 500 Index. The risk was lower (14.2% versus 16.0%), and the return nearly 50% higher (9.4% versus 6.8%). But that is history. We do not know what the effects of diversifying internationally will be over any particular period in the future.

Solnik and Noetzlin went a step further and constructed an *ex post* efficient frontier based on the actual returns for the internationally diversified common stock portfolio for the years 1971 through 1980.[13] The stocks of each country were treated as a distinct asset class. The frontier was located by finding those mixes of the 12 asset classes that provided the highest return at each level of risk. The frontier and the returns for the world, EAFE, and U.S. stocks are plotted in Figure 20-8.

[12]Bruno Solnik and Bernard Noetzlin, "Optimal International Asset Allocation," *Journal of Portfolio Management* 9 (Fall 1982): 11–21. The authors excluded the stocks of some foreign countries (e.g., Spain and Italy) on the grounds that the markets in those countries lacked adequate liquidity.

[13]Solnik and Noetzlin also constructed an efficient frontier for internationally diversified portfolios of stocks and bonds.

|||| **TABLE 20-9**

Performance of Foreign and U.S. Stocks, 1971–1980

	Compound Annual Return	Standard Deviation of Returns
EAFE stocks	13.4%	17.3%
U.S. stocks	6.8	16.0
World stocks	9.4	14.2

SOURCE: Bruno Solnik and Bernard Noetzlin, "Optimal International Asset Allocation," *Journal of Portfolio Management* 9 (Fall 1982):11–21.

|||| **FIGURE 20-8**
Efficient Frontier: U.S. and Foreign Stocks

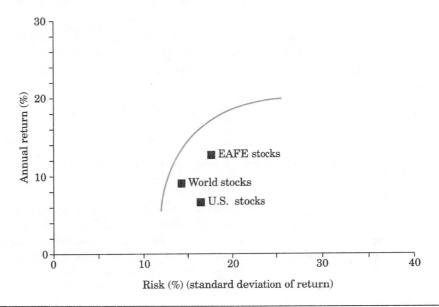

Observe that the efficient frontier is to the left of the plotted risk and return for the world stocks, EAFE stocks, and U.S. stocks, which indicates that none of these three portfolios was efficient. Figure 20-8 demonstrates graphically that during this particular 10-year period international diversification was superior to diversification based on U.S. stocks alone.

It is, of course, much more difficult to construct forward-looking efficient portfolios, based on forecasts of returns, standard deviations, correlations, and exchange rates, than to construct efficient portfolios based on historical data. The forecasting problems can be avoided, however, by taking a passive approach and building international portfolios on the basis of relative market capitalizations, after excluding the stocks of countries where the economic outlook is unfavorable. For example, if German stocks are to be included in the portfolio, and if they represent 20% of the market capitalization of all foreign stocks that might be included, 20% of the foreign portion of the portfolio will be German stocks. And, if the value of the stock of German company X represents 15% of the market capitalization of all stocks in an index of German stocks, 15% of the German portfolio will consist of stock in company X.

DIVERSIFYING WITH REAL ESTATE

The results of four studies comparing the risk and returns of real estate and common stocks are reported in Table 20-10.[14] On the whole, real estate returns have compared favorably with common stock returns in

[14]Robert H. Zerbst and Barbara R. Cambon, "Real Estate: Historical Returns and Risks," *Journal of Portfolio Management* 10 (Spring 1984): 5–20.

|||| **TABLE 20-10**

Real Estate and Common Stocks: Comparisons of Risk and Rates of Return

Author	Kind of Real Estate or Type of Organization	Period	Return		Standard Deviation	
			Real Estate	Stocks	Real Estate	Stocks
Brachman	Commingled funds	1970–79	10.3%	4.7%	4.9%	19.6%
Ibbotson & Fall	Farms and residential housing	1947–78	8.1	10.3	3.5	18.0
McMahan	Multifamily and nonresidential	1951–78	13.9	11.4	3.8	18.3
Smith	Equity REITS	1965–77	9.8	4.6	22.1	18.4

SOURCE: Robert H. Zerbst and Barbara R. Cambon, "Real Estate: Historical Returns and Risks," *Journal of Portfolio Management* 10 (Spring 1984):5–20.

the post–World War II era. Real estate investments performed especially well during the highly inflationary 1970s. Generally, the returns on real estate have also been less volatile than common stock returns. Comparisons of real estate and common stock returns depend, of course, on the periods over which the comparisons are made, the kinds of real estate involved, and the stock index used.

Raising the Efficient Frontier by Adding Real estate

It has been said that "A small amount of asset diversification goes a long way. . . . The first 5 percent, 10 percent, or 15 percent of an asset class added to a portfolio causes the most dramatic diversification possible, assuming this asset is relatively independent of the other assets in the mix."[15] Since real estate returns seem to be quite independent of the returns on stocks and bonds (as indicated by small, often negative correlations), adding real estate to a portfolio containing stocks and bonds may produce significant benefits.

To estimate the potential gains from adding real estate to a portfolio containing stocks, bonds, and Treasury bills, Fogler constructed a number of efficient portfolios based on the following assumptions:

1. Expected returns and standard deviations of the returns for the four classes of assets:

	Expected Return	Annual Standard Deviation of Return
Common stocks	13%	20%
Real estate	11	20
Corporate bonds	8	5
Treasury bills	6	0

2. Zero correlations between the returns for all possible pairs of assets.

[15]Russell H. Fogler, "20% in Real Estate: Can Theory Justify It?" *Journal of Portfolio Management* 10 (Winter 1984): 6–13.

The assumptions were intentionally biased against real estate to minimize the possibility of overstating the potential gains from including real estate in a portfolio. The expected return for real estate was assumed to be two percentage points below the expected return for common stocks even though the assumed standard deviations were the same; and the correlation of real estate returns with common stock returns and bond returns was assumed to be zero even though experience indicates that it might be negative.

Table 20-11 contains a sample of the efficient portfolios constructed by Fogler based on these assumptions. In all but the safest portfolio (portfolio 1 with 91% Treasury bills) and the riskiest (portfolio 7 with 100% common stocks), real estate was an important component. Between these two extremes, the presence of a significant amount of real estate in the portfolio made the expected return higher at a given level of risk, or the risk lower at a given level of expected return, than would have been attained by a portfolio composed only of stocks, bonds, and Treasury bills.

On the whole, real estate can be expected to improve the performance of a portfolio even though it performs poorly during some periods, as does every other type of investment. Real estate is especially attractive as a hedge against inflation. Fogler found a positive correlation of approximately 0.50 between real estate returns (represented by two different proxies) and the rate of inflation for the 63-year period from 1915 to 1978.

‖‖ PORTFOLIO MANAGEMENT ACCORDING TO ARBITRAGE PRICING THEORY

The arbitrage pricing theory (APT) is similar to the capital asset pricing model (CAPM) in certain important respects and remarkably different in others. Both theories assert that expected returns always (and actual returns in the long run) vary directly with systematic risk. Both

‖‖ **TABLE 20-11**

Sample of Efficient Portfolios of Bills, Bonds, Stocks, and Real Estate

| | Portfolio | | | | | | |
	#1	#2	#3	#4	#5	#6	#7
Risk and return:							
Mean return	6.3%	7.5%	9.1%	9.8%	10.4%	10.9%	13.0%
Standard deviation	0.6	2.8	5.6	7.0	8.6	10.0	20.0
Asset mix:							
Treasury bills	91%	54%	9%	0%	0%	0%	0%
Corporate bonds	6	31	61	57	43	32	0
Common stock	2	9	17	26	35	42	100
Real estate	1	6	13	17	22	26	0

SOURCE: Russell H. Fogler, "20% in Real Estate: Can Theory Justify It?" *Journal of Portfolio Management* 10 (Winter 1984): 6–13.

theories also recognize that since unsystematic risk can be diversified away, investors cannot expect to be compensated through higher returns for accepting such risk. Therefore, all portfolios should be highly diversified.

One of the key differences between the APT and the CAPM is in the definition of systematic risk. According to the CAPM, the systematic risk of an asset or portfolio of assets is measured, in relative terms, by the sensitivity of its return to changes in the market return. (Typically, the return on the S&P 500 is used as a surrogate for the market return.) In contrast, the APT asserts that systematic risk is measured in terms of the sensitivity of an asset or portfolio to several economic factors.

Roll and Ross identified the following economic variables as important sources of systematic risk: (1) the rate of inflation; (2) the level of industrial production; (3) the risk premium, as measured by the spread between low-grade and high-grade bond yields; and (4) the slope of the term structure of interest rates.[16] The current price of an asset reflects investor expectations about the future levels of these variables. Price changes occur when the actual values of one or more of these key factors differ from the expected values. It is the unanticipated changes in these factors that cause prices to change.

The APT uses a beta coefficient for each of the important economic variables as opposed to the one beta coefficient of the CAPM. Thus, under the APT, systematic risk is measured in terms of an asset's sensitivity to several factors. If these sensitivities can be estimated with reasonable reliability for a portfolio of assets, the APT may provide a better description of reality and a better basis for forecasting risk and return than the CAPM.

Stocks differ widely in their sensitivities to unexpected changes in economic variables. For example, a food processing company's stock might have a positive sensitivity to unanticipated increases in the rate of inflation because higher inflation may lead to higher nominal earnings. In contrast, the stock of a furniture manufacturer might have a negative sensitivity to an unexpected increase in the rate of inflation because higher inflation usually means higher interest rates, and higher interest rates tend to discourage homebuilding and the purchase of furniture.

Portfolio building under the APT involves the selection of assets whose collective sensitivities to key economic factors will come closest to satisfying the investor's needs. For example, if an investor such as a college endowment fund is vulnerable to unexpected increases in the rate of inflation, its portfolio should have a positive sensitivity to increases in that variable. Higher inflation rates would tend to increase the portfolio's nominal returns.

[16]Richard Roll and Stephen A. Ross, "The Arbitrage Pricing Theory Approach to Strategic Portfolio Planning," *Financial Analysts Journal* 40 (May/June 1984): 14–26.

|||| SUMMARY

The chapter began with a discussion of portfolio objectives and constraints, the investor's tolerance for risk, and methods of estimating risk tolerance. We then noted the difference between active and passive portfolio management and observed that active management can involve either selecting securities that seem to be underpriced or changing the composition of the portfolio from time to time in an effort to "time the market."

There has been a trend toward passive portfolio management. Passive management implies a buy-and-hold policy, with no attempt to beat the market. A passively managed common stock portfolio is constructed in one of two ways: so it will closely track a broad index of the market, or so it will have a certain attribute, such as a high dividend yield or a high average beta, that is attractive to the investor. The desired attribute is not necessarily expected to lead to abnormally high risk-adjusted returns.

We observed that common stocks are less risky, in the sense of a lower risk of loss, for investors who hold a diversified portfolio for a long period of time than for investors with short time horizons. For example, an investor who holds a diversified portfolio of stocks for 10 years is less likely to sustain a loss than an investor whose average holding period for a diversified portfolio is only one year.

Using portfolio principles developed earlier in the book, we have introduced an optimal portfolio-building model. The model is very useful since it makes practical, in relatively simple steps, most of the components of mean-variance analysis.

The principal focus of the chapter was on methods of assembling optimal portfolios for specific investors. Based on historical returns, it seems likely that the efficiency of a common stock portfolio (or a stock and bond portfolio) can be increased by adding foreign stocks, real estate, or both. Sometimes the addition of foreign stocks or real estate to a portfolio will both raise the expected return and lower the risk. The optimal mixture of assets for a given investor depends on four variables: the expected return for each class of assets; the estimated standard deviations of the returns; the estimated correlations between the returns; and the investor's tolerance for risk. The optimal proportions will change with changes in these variables. Sometimes the optimal portfolio will contain only one or two classes of assets.

The arbitrage pricing theory (APT) provides another approach to the construction of optimal portfolios. The goal is to find a portfolio whose collective sensitivities to such factors as the rate of inflation, the level of industrial production, the risk premium required by investors, and the term structure of interest rates come closest to satisfying the investor's needs. For example, if the investor's needs are likely to increase in proportion to any increase in the rate of inflation, his or her portfolio should have a positive sensitivity to inflation.

|||| **QUESTIONS**

1. How are investment objectives related to the capital market line?

2. Explain how to evaluate an investor's tolerance for risk through simulation.

3. What is meant by "active management" of a portfolio? What are the two principal methods of actively managing a portfolio of stocks and bonds?

4. What does "timing the market" mean?

5. What did Levy's analysis show with respect to the results achieved by institutional managers of common stock portfolios on the average?

6. What is passive management? What is an index fund? What are the potential advantages of an index fund over an actively managed portfolio?

7. What is "a naïve buy-and-hold" policy? Why is indexing not a pure buy-and-hold policy?

8. What is the nature of passive management based on stock attributes? Why doesn't this amount to active management?

9. In what sense does the risk of common stock investing vary inversely with the length of the investor's planned holding period or investment horizon? In what sense does the risk of common stock investing, as compared to bond investing, become greater with a longer holding period?

10. Comment on the relative performance of common stocks over 1-year holding periods and overlapping 10-year holding periods from 1926 through 1990.

11. What is dollar-cost averaging? What are the potential advantages of using this strategy for timing stock purchases? Give an example of modified dollar-cost averaging.

12. Explain why the S&P 500 is not an efficient portfolio.

13. Why is the risk of an internationally diversified portfolio less than a weighted average of the risks of the stocks from each country represented in the portfolio?

14. Explain why the risk of an internationally diversified portfolio of common stocks can be greater than the risk of a portfolio of U.S. stocks.

15. Can international diversification of a common stock portfolio be a good thing even if the expected return is lower than the expected return of a well-diversified portfolio of U.S. stocks?

16. Why did Solnik and Noetzlin's study fail to prove that international diversification of a common stock portfolio is always a good thing?

17. Explain how international diversification can be achieved in a passive manner.

18. Why is it likely that adding real estate to a portfolio of stocks and bonds will reduce the risk of the portfolio?

19. Why is it difficult to make generalizations about the relative risk and returns of common stocks and real estate?

20. Explain Fogler's finding as to the effects of adding real estate to a portfolio of Treasury bills, corporate bonds, and common stocks. What were his assumptions?

21. Explain, in general terms, how portfolios are constructed in accordance with the arbitrage pricing theory.

|||| PROBLEMS

1. Using the information for the first 10 securities in Table 20-7, create a figure of merit.

2. On your figure of merit from Problem 1, show the border line for four securities.

3. Identify all of the corner solution portfolios for your figure of merit from Problem 1.

4. Determine the expected return and beta for each of the corner portfolios in Problem 3.

5. Plot the corner solution portfolios from Problem 3 on a graph where the X-axis is beta and the Y-axis is expected return.

6. Assuming that the risk-free rate is 8%, show how you would identify the optimal portfolio of four securities on your expected return and beta graph from Problem 5.

7. Assume that you wish to achieve a rate of return of 16% by investing in both the risk-free asset and the optimal risky portfolio. How much of your available wealth will you invest in each of the securities of the risky portfolio?

8. Explain how you would determine if your optimal portfolio in Problem 7 is well diversified.

|||| PROJECT
Portfolio Construction and Evaluation

Available in the library are information sources that will allow you to obtain return and risk estimates for a large universe of common stocks. These sources *may* include the Compustat and CRSP databases.

Your assignment is to perform the following tasks:

1. Using a specific stock selection strategy, select 20 securities and determine their risk and expected return characteristics for the 1988 calendar year.

2. Define the efficient frontier of 9 securities from your universe of 20 securities.

3. Determine a reasonable estimate of the risk-free rate of return as of January 1989.

4. Determine the optimal risky portfolio from your set of efficient portfolios, i.e., define the security market line relevant to your efficient frontier.

5. Determine whether your optimal risky portfolio is well diversified. Show that adding securities to a portfolio increases the level of diversification.

6. Given your preference for risk, determine what proportion of your investment capital you would invest in the risk-free asset and each of the risky assets.

7. Given that you bought your portfolio on January 2, 1989, and sold the portfolio on December 31, 1989, calculate the three measures of *ex post* performance. Compare your performance to the market and to others in the class. Which measure would be most appropriate for you and why?

|||| **PROJECT**
Portfolio Algorithms

The written literature on portfolio management includes numerous portfolio-building strategies such as the one discussed here.

Locate a portfolio-building algorithm in either a text or a journal. Then, create a user's guide to the algorithm similar to the one in this chapter. If possible, design either a BASIC program or a Lotus spreadsheet that will aid in the portfolio-building process. You should be prepared to turn in the following:

1. Your guide to the portfolio-buidling procedure.

2. Any computer aids.

3. A complete set of reference materials.

MICROCOMPUTER ASSET ALLOCATION SYSTEMS

Two steps are usually involved in assembling a portfolio of securities. The first is to determine an optimal allocation of the investor's funds among various major classes of securities. The second is to select specific securities within each class contained in the optimal portfolio. A brief description of Asset Allocation Tools (AAT), which is one of several asset allocation programs designed for microcomputers, will indicate how that program serves the portfolio manager.[17] It is designed to help the user determine the optimum allocation of an investor's funds among various classes of assets, given the investor's attitude toward risk and return.

The principal elements of AAT are an optimizing program and 17 databases containing monthly returns on more than 150 classes of assets, as well as foreign exchange rates and the rate of inflation. AAT also includes a multiple regression program and a program to facilitate the process of adding data from other computer sources to the AAT database.

The first task of the AAT user is to select from the databases the return series that will serve as proxies for the kinds of assets that might be included in the investor's portfolio. For example, if plausible candidates are common stocks of large U.S. companies, high-grade corporate bonds, real estate, and the stocks of German, Japanese, and British companies, the return series shown in Table 20A-1 can be used to calculate the historical returns, standard deviations, and correlations that may be useful in estimating the future values of these variables.

DATA NEEDED TO FIND OPTIMAL PORTFOLIO

The optimizing program requires six inputs, of which five (all except the upper and lower bounds for each asset) must be estimated. The five estimated inputs are expected return and standard deviation of the returns for each asset, correlation of the returns of each asset with the returns of every other asset, the risk tolerance of the investor, and transaction costs. Users of the program are apt to rely heavily on the historical data in estimating future standard deviations and correlations, but pay less attention to the historical returns in estimating future returns.

---

[17]The explanation of AAT in this section is based on William F. Sharpe, *AAT: Asset Allocation Tools* (Palo Alto, Calif.: The Scientific Press, 1985).

|||| **TABLE 20A-1**
Data Sources

Class of Assets	Publisher of Database	Return Series
Stocks of large U.S. corporations	Ibbotson Associates	Common stocks (S&P 500)
High-grade corporate bonds	Ibbotson Associates (from Salomon Brothers index)	High-grade long-term corporate bond index
Real estate	Asset Allocation Tools	Equity real estate investment trusts
Stocks of German, Japanese, and United Kingdom companies	Capital International	Stock indexes for Germany, Japan, and the United Kingdom

|||| ## ESTIMATION OF INVESTOR'S RISK TOLERANCE

The investor's risk tolerance is expressed as a number from 0 to 100 that "indicates the amount of added risk (in terms of the variance of the returns) the investor is willing to take on to increase the expected return by one percent." An example will illustrate one method of arriving at an estimate of the risk tolerance. Suppose an investor would be willing to accept an increase in risk from 12% to 14% in terms of the standard deviation, or from 144 to 196 in terms of the variance, to attain an increase from 10% to 11% in the expected return. His risk tolerance is calculated by subtracting the lower variance (144) from the higher variance (196) and dividing the difference by the increase in the expected return:

$$(14^2 - 12^2)/(11 - 10) = (196 - 144)/1 = 52$$

An investor's risk tolerance represents, roughly, the percentage of the portfolio she would choose to invest in common stocks if her only choices were common stocks and U.S. Treasury bills. An investor with a risk tolerance of 60 would want 60% of her portfolio to be invested in common stocks and 40% in Treasury bills.

|||| ## AN EXAMPLE

To illustrate how AAT operates (with the aid of Lotus 1-2-3), we will assume that the user wants to assemble an optimal portfolio composed of four classes of securities: stocks that will track the S&P 500 closely, stocks that represent a good sample of those in Capital International's Europe, Australia, and Far East Index (EAFE), U.S. Treasury securities maturing in three to five years, and U.S. Treasury securities maturing in 9 to 11 years. The investor can use the following databases: Wells Fargo's Standard & Poor's 500 Index Fund (composed of all S&P 500 stocks except those with high risk of bankruptcy), Capital International's EAFE; and Salomon Brothers' total rate of return indexes for U.S. government bonds maturing in 3 to 5 years and 9 to 11 years.

After the program has been supplied with the required information (as itemized earlier), it provides the user with the following output: (1) the percentage of the portfolio that must be allocated to each type of asset if the portfolio is to be optimal, that is, if it is to maximize the investor's net utility; (2) the expected return and standard deviation of the optimal portfolio; (3) the risk penalty[18]; and (4) the net utility, which is calculated by subtracting the risk penalty and transaction costs from the expected return. The optimal portfolio is the combination of assets that maximizes the investor's net utility.

The following is a sample calculation of a portfolio's net utility for an investor with a risk tolerance of 80, where the expected return is 18%, the variance of the return is 225, and the estimated transaction costs are 0.75%:

Expected return		18.00%
Decrements from utility:		
Risk penalty	2.81%	
Transaction costs	0.75	
Total		3.56
Portfolio net utility		14.44%

Table 20A-2 is an example of an AAT information worksheet containing all information, except the risk tolerance and risk penalty, required to determine the optimal asset allocation for a specific investor.

Table 20A-3 shows the optimal asset allocations based on the date of Table 20A-2 and a risk tolerance of 50, and it compares the net utility of the optimal portfolio to that of a portfolio where equal amounts are allocated to each asset. With AAT and Lotus 1-2-3, the results can also be displayed in graphical form. The net utility is sometimes called the portfolio risk-adjusted expected return. Roughly, the optimum portfolio is as good for this investor as 8.81% for certain. Another term for portfolio utility is the portfolio's "certainty equivalent."

One of the attractive features of AAT is its ability to provide a number of iterations in a short period of time. If the user wants to see how the optimum portfolio would change if the standard deviation of asset were increased to 20% from 18%, he can find out very quickly. By running a number of iterations with various standard deviations, he can determine the sensitivity of the composition of the portfolio, as well as the portfolio risk and expected return, to changes in the estimated risk of one or more

[18]The risk penalty is the variance of the portfolio's return divided by the risk tolerance of the investor. The smaller the variance and the greater the investor's tolerance for risk, the smaller the risk penalty. If, for example, the variance is 225 and the investor's risk tolerance is 80, the risk penalty is 2.81%, or 225/80.

|||| **TABLE 20A-2**
Information Worksheet for Asset Allocation

	Long-Term Government Bonds	Short-Term Government Bonds	EAFE Stocks	U.S. Stocks
Expected annual return	10.000	9.000	13.500	13.500
Standard deviation	12.822	8.442	16.000	16.000
Correlations:				
Long-term government bonds	1.000	0.969	0.224	0.300
Short-term government bonds	0.969	1.000	0.256	0.257
EAFE stocks	0.224	0.256	1.000	0.523
U.S. stocks	0.300	0.257	0.523	1.000
Bound—upper	100.0	100.0	100.0	100.0
Bound—lower	0.0	0.0	0.0	0.0
Transaction costs—buy	0.50	0.50	0.50	0.50
Transaction costs—sell	0.50	0.50	0.50	0.50

|||| **TABLE 20A-3**
Optimum Portfolio Based on Data in Table 20A-2 Compared to a Portfolio of Equal Allocations

	Funds Allocated Equally	Optimal Portfolio
Asset holdings:		
Long-term government bonds	25.00	15.08
Short-term government bonds	25.00	5.00
EAFE stocks	25.00	33.88
U.S. stocks	25.00	46.06
Portfolio characteristics:		
Expected return	11.50	12.61
Standard deviation	9.79	11.76
Investment objectives:		
Risk tolerance	50	50
Contributions to utility:		
Expected return	11.50	12.61
Decrements from utility:		
Risk penalty	1.92	2.80
Transaction costs	1.00	1.00
Portfolio utility:		
Net utility	8.58	8.81

classes of assets. Similar "what if" types of analysis can be made using various values for the expected returns and the correlations between the returns.

|||| MULTIPLE OPTIMIZATION

If the user wants to see optimum portfolios for a range of risk tolerances, the program will provide this information in a single operation. This feature of the program is especially useful when there is uncertainty about the investor's risk tolerance. For each risk tolerance, the program provides a different optimum portfolio, with a different standard deviation and different expected return. A plot of the expected return against the standard deviation for a set of optimal portfolios based on different risk tolerances, as in Figure 20A-1, make it easy to see how the expected return varies with changes in the risk of the portfolio.

|||| APPENDIX QUESTIONS

1. What can be accomplished by using the microcoputer program called Asset Allocation Tools?

2. How are the databases in AAT used?

3. What are the five inputs to the AAT optimizing program that must be estimated? How are the databases used in making such estimates?

|||| FIGURE 20A-1
Expected Return and Risk

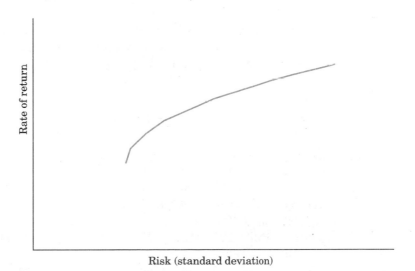

4. Calculate the investor's risk tolerance (as defined by AAT), given that the investor is willing to accept an increase in the variance of 56 for an increase of 2.25 percentage points in the expected return. Explain what the risk tolerance (from 0 to 100) means in terms of the proportion of a portfolio of Treasury bills and common stocks the investor would want to invest in common stocks.

5. What is the output of AAT?

6. How is the risk penalty calculated? How is it reflected in the output of AAT?

7. Explain why AAT's ability to make iterations quickly can be very helpful to the user.

8. Comment on the usefulness of multiple optimization with AAT.

|||| SELECTED REFERENCES

Adler, Michael, and David Simon. "Exchange Risk Surprises in International Portfolios." *Journal of Portfolio Management* 12 (Winter 1986): 44–53.

Brealey, Richard A. "How to Combine Active Management with Index Funds." *Journal of Portfolio Management* 12 (Winter 1986): 4–10

Curley, Anthony J., and Robert M. Bear. *Investment Analysis and Management*. New York: Harper & Row, 1979.

Dunn, Patricia, and Rolf D. Theisen. "How Consistently Do Active Managers Win?" *Journal of Portfolio Management* 9 (Summer 1983): 47–50.

Fielitz, Bruce D., and Frederick L. Muller. "The Asset Allocation Decision." *Financial Analysts Journal* 39 (July/August 1983): 45–50.

Figlewski, Stephen, and Stanley J. Kohn. "Portfolio Management with Stock Index Futures." *Financial Analysts Journal* 38 (January/February 1982): 56–60.

Fogler, Russell H. "20% in Real Estate: Can Theory Justify It?" *Journal of Portfolio Management* 10 (Winter 1984): 6–13.

Good, Walter R., Roy W. Hermansen, and T. Kirkham Barnaby. "Opportunity: Actively Managed Investment Universes." *Financial Analysts Journal* 42 (January/February 1986): 17–21.

Grauer, Robert R., and Nils H. Hakanson. "Higher Return, Lower Risk: Historical Returns on Actively Managed Portfolios of Stocks, Bonds and Bills, 1936–1978." *Financial Analysts Journal* 38 (March/April 1982): 39–53.

Levy, Robert A. "Equity Performance from 1976–85: How Bank Trust Departments Measure Up." *Trusts and Estates* (May 1986): 28–30.

Lloyd, William P., and Naval K. Modani. "Stocks, Bonds, Bills and Time Diversification." *Journal of Portfolio Management* 9 (Spring 1983): 7–11.

McEnally, Richard W. "Latane's Bequest: The Best of Portfolio Strategies." *Journal of Portfolio Management* 12 (Winter 1986): 21–30.

————— "Time Diversification: Surest Route to Lower Risk?" *Journal of Portfolio Management* 11 (Summer 1985): 24–26.

Roll, Richard, and Stephen A. Ross. "The Arbitrage Pricing Theory Approach to Strategic Portfolio Planning." *Financial Analysts Journal* 40 (May/June 1984): 14–26.

Rudd, Andrew. "Optimal Selection of Passive Portfolios." *Financial Management* 9 (Spring 1980): 57–66.

Sharpe, William F. *AAT: Asset Allocation Tools*. Palo Alto, Calif: Scientific Press, 1985.

————— *Portfolio Theory and Capital Markets*. New York: McGraw-Hill Book Company, 1970.

Solnik, Bruno, and Bernard Noetzlin. "Optimal International Asset Allocation." *Journal of Portfolio Management* 9 (Fall 1982): 11–21.

Wilcox, Jarrod W. "Practice and Theory in International Equity Investment." *Financial Analysts Journal* 42 (January /February 1986): 17–21.

Zerbst, Robert H., and Barbara R. Cambon. "Real Estate: Historical Returns and Risks." *Journal of Portfolio Management*: 10 (Spring 1984): 5–20.

MEASURING PORTFOLIO PERFORMANCE

At some point, every active investor realizes the need for a technique to measure portfolio performance. This chapter describes several such techniques and the advantages and disadvantages of each. Unfortunately, portfolio performance measurement is not as straightforward as it might at first appear, and a realistic discussion of the pros and cons of the various techniques takes us to the very heart of asset pricing theory.

All investment decisions contain two important components—risk and return. The measurement techniques described in this chapter, which blend both risk and return into a single index of performance, are called composite performance indexes.

Composite performance indexes are most frequently used in *ex post* reviews of portfolio performance. Mutual fund managers, pension fund managers, and trust account managers regularly get together with performance review committees to review and discuss the performance of their portfolios. Individual investors can also use these measures to monitor their own portfolio returns.

Composite indexes of performance can also be useful in *ex ante* security selection. Using estimates of future risk and return, investors can compare the risk-adjusted returns from a variety of investments with widely differing characteristics.

COMPOSITE PERFORMANCE MEASURES

Proper evaluation of portfolio performance requires that differences in risk be taken into account. Three widely-used portfolio performance measures, the Sharpe index, the Treynor index, and the Jensen index, adjust for risk in different ways.

THE SHARPE INDEX

The Sharpe index, developed by William F. Sharpe, is often referred to as a reward-to-volatility measure because the risk adjustment is made with the standard deviation of the return, a measure of variability or volatility. The Sharpe index is derived from the equation for the capital market line.

$$R_p = R_f + [(R_m - R_f)/\sigma_m]\sigma_p$$

where

$$R_p = \text{portfolio return}$$
$$R_f = \text{risk-free rate}$$
$$R_m = \text{market return}$$
$$\sigma_m \text{ and } \sigma_p = \text{standard deviation of market return and portfolio return, respectively}$$

Rearranging terms, the equation becomes

$$(R_p - R_f)/\sigma_p = (R_m - R_f)/\sigma_m \qquad (21\text{-}1)$$

Equation 21-1, which assumes an efficient market, states that the excess return per unit of risk for an efficient portfolio equals the excess return per unit of risk for the market portfolio.

The left-hand side of equation 21-1 (portfolio excess return adjusted for risk) is the Sharpe index (S_p).

$$S_p = (R_p - R_f)/\sigma_p \qquad (21\text{-}2)$$

where

R_p = portfolio p's average holding period return over the evaluation period

R_f = average risk-free rate over the evaluation period

For a well-diversified portfolio, the expected value of the Sharpe index is the excess return per unit of risk for the market. That is,

$$E(S_p) = (R_m - R_f)/\sigma_m$$

Throughout this chapter, the returns of the Fidelity Magellan Fund will be used to illustrate the portfolio performance techniques being discussed. The Fidelity Magellan Fund is one of the largest mutual funds in the United States. For several years in the 1970s and 1980s, it was ranked as the leading fund in *Barron's* review of mutual fund performance.

The monthly returns of the Magellan Fund for an 18-month period are given in Table 21-1. Also listed are the returns from the market index selected for this example (the NYSE Composite Index) and the monthly returns for 91-day Treasury bills, which represent the risk-free rate of return.

A word of caution—the return statistics used here should not be viewed as indicative of the overall performance of the Magellan Fund in the recent past. It is unwise to make generalizations from an observation period as short as 18 months. The number of observations has been kept to a minimum in order to make replication of the calculations as easy as possible.

Using Equation 21-2 and the return statistics from Table 21-1, the Sharpe index for this particular fund (S_i) is

$$S_i = (-0.0048 - 0.0050)/0.0755 = -0.13\%$$

|||| **TABLE 21-1**
Performance Statistics for the Magellan Fund and the NYSE
Composite Index

Month	Fund Returns	NYSE Composite Index Returns	Risk-Free Return
1	0.0741	0.0378	0.0045
2	0.0128	0.0239	0.0048
3	−0.0172	−0.0183	0.0048
4	−0.0149	0.0038	0.0048
5	0.0415	0.0464	0.0049
6	0.0488	0.0443	0.0051
7	0.0401	0.0325	0.0052
8	−0.0244	−0.0228	0.0056
9	−0.2581	−0.2188	0.0048
10	−0.0370	−0.0091	0.0048
11	−0.0370	−0.0091	0.0049
12	0.0395	0.0427	0.0049
13	0.0609	0.0439	0.0048
14	−0.0028	−0.0257	0.0049
15	0.0178	0.0087	0.0049
16	−0.0027	0.0011	0.0052
17	0.0684	0.0435	0.0054
18	−0.0064	−0.0073	0.0057
Mean	−0.0048	0.0010	0.0050
Standard deviation	0.0755	0.0589	0.0003

Note: All returns are in decimal form.

This means that the Magellan Fund's monthly excess return per unit of risk (per 1% of standard deviation) is a negative 0.13%[1].

THE TREYNOR INDEX

The *Treynor index* is a composite performance measure that indicates the excess returns per unit of systematic risk. In an *ex post* application, it is measured with the following formula:

$$T_i = (R_i - R_f)/\beta_i \qquad (21\text{-}3)$$

where

$$T_i = \text{the Treynor index for portfolio } i$$
$$\beta_i = \text{the beta of portfolio } i$$

The Treynor index is derived from the capital asset pricing model, which, in *ex post* form, is

$$R_p = R_f + (R_m - R_f)\beta_p$$

Rearranging terms, the following result is obtained:

$$(R_p - R_f)/\beta_p = (R_m - R_f)/\beta_m$$

---

[1]The negative composite performance of this fund is probably due in large part to the fact that the observation period over which fund returns were measured includes the month of October 1987, in which the "crash of '87" occurred.

This expression simply states that the excess return per unit of systematic risk of the portfolio equals the excess return per unit of systematic risk for the market. The term on the left-hand side of the expression is the Treynor index.

Ordinary least squares regression was used to calculate the beta of the Magellan Fund. Results from the regression output are given in Table 21-2. Using Equation 21-3 and the results of the beta calculation in Table 21-2, the Treynor index for the Magellan Fund (T_i) can be calculated as

$$T_i = (-0.0048 - 0.0050)/1.181 = -0.83\%$$

The negative Treynor score means that the Magellan Fund's monthly excess return per unit of systematic risk was a negative 0.83%.

In both the Sharpe and Treynor indexes, positive values indicate superior performance. An ordinal ranking of portfolio performance can easily be obtained by calculating Sharpe and Treynor scores for a number of portfolios and listing the portfolios from high to low in numerical order. Many investors want to outperform the market averages. A measure of performance relative to this goal can be obtained by calculating the Sharpe or Treynor index for the overall market with 21-4 or 21-4a and comparing it with the values of individual portfolios.

$$S_m = (R_m - R_f)/\sigma_m \tag{21-4}$$

or

$$T_m = (R_m - R_f)/\beta_m \tag{21-4a}$$

where

S_m and T_m = Sharpe and Treynor index values for the market as a whole, using the returns from a widely accepted market index as a proxy

R_m = average holding period returns from the market index

σ_m = standard deviation of returns of the market index

β_m = the market index beta, assumed to be 1.0

Calculating the performance index value for the market as a whole gives the analyst a benchmark with which to compare the Sharpe and Treynor indexes. Thus, not only can portfolio performance be ranked, but the Sharpe or Treynor index for the overall market can be used to define superior and inferior performance.

The Sharpe and Treynor scores for the market based on the data in Table 21-1 are

$$S_m = (.0010 - .0050)/.0589 = -0.0679$$
$$T_m = (.0010 - .0050)/1.0 = -0.4000$$

Although the scores for the market are negative, they have a smaller negative value than the scores for the Magellan Fund, indicating again that the fund's performance was inferior to that of the market over this time period. However, as we will point out later in the chapter, care must

|||| **TABLE 21-2**

Sample Regression Output from Calculation of the Magellan Fund's Beta

Regression output:	
Constant	−0.00596
X coefficient	1.18098
Standard error of coefficient	0.12389
Standard error of Y estimate	0.03097
R-squared	0.85029
Number of observations	18
Degrees of freedom	16

be taken in interpreting negative composite performance scores. Reserve final judgment until later in the chapter.

THE JENSEN INDEX

The *Jensen index,* developed by Michael Jensen, provides investors with a more direct way to determine if they have been able to "beat the market." This performance index is developed from the notion that, in equilibrium, all securities are priced at a level consistent with the security market line, or

$$\text{actual return} = \text{expected return}$$
$$R_p = R_f + \beta_p(R_m - R_f) \qquad (21\text{-}5)$$

Subtracting R_f from both sides of the equation it becomes

$$R_p - R_f = \beta_p(R_m - R_f) \qquad (21\text{-}6)$$

Equations 21-5 and 21-6 are both expected to hold if securities are priced in equilibrium. Equation 21-6 says that a security's excess return equals the product of its beta and the excess return of the market. If the equality implied by Equation 21-6 does not hold, the security or portfolio must be earning a return that is not consistent with its equilibrium price as defined by the security market line. The equality can be restored by adding a new variable, called Jensen's *alpha,* to the right-hand side of Equation 21-6:

$$R_p - R_f = \beta_p(R_m - R_f) + \alpha_p \qquad (21\text{-}7)$$

where

α_p = Jensen's alpha, the indicator of superior or inferior performance

A positive alpha implies superior portfolio performance; a negative alpha implies inferior portfolio performance. The expected value of alpha is zero, since that is the value that will result if the portfolio is earning its equilibrium return.

A portfolio manager can always attain a zero alpha (before transactions costs) by simply buying and holding a portfolio equivalent to the market index. Such a portfolio would have a beta of 1.0 and a return equal to the average market return. Under these conditions, the two sides of Equation 21-6 would be equal, and Jensen's alpha would be zero. Only through superior security selection or successful market timing will an investor generate alphas that are positive.

Table 21-3 lists the excess returns of the Magellan Fund and the market index, calculated by subtracting the risk-free return from the fund and market returns, respectively. Jensen suggests estimating the values of Equation 21-7's variables through regression. The regression results are given in Table 21-3b. The key value in Table 21-3b is the alpha statistic, the regression intercept.

TESTS FOR STATISTICAL SIGNIFICANCE

One of the advantages of using a regression procedure in fitting Equation 21-7 is that a measure of dispersion is calculated for all of the variables. The dispersion measure of interest in this case is the standard error of

|||| **TABLE 21-3**
Calculation of Jensen's Alpha for the Magellan Fund

(a) Excess Returns for Fund and Market Index		
Month	$(R_i - R_f)$	$(R_m - R_f)$
1	0.0696	0.0333
2	0.0080	0.0192
3	−0.0220	−0.0231
4	−0.1098	−0.0010
5	0.0366	0.0416
6	0.0438	0.0392
7	0.0349	0.0273
8	−0.0300	−0.0284
9	−0.2629	−0.2236
10	−0.0417	−0.0139
11	−0.0418	−0.0140
12	0.0347	0.0378
13	0.0561	0.0391
14	−0.0077	−0.0305
15	0.0126	0.0035
16	−0.0081	−0.0043
17	0.0628	0.0379
18	−0.0121	−0.0129
Mean	−0.0098	−0.0041
Standard deviation	0.0754	0.0589

(b) Regression Output	
Constant	−0.00505
Standard deviation of constant	0.00732
X coefficient	1.18060
Standard deviation of coefficient	0.12400
Standard error of Y estimate	0.03098
R-squared	0.84998
Number of observations	18
Degrees of freedom	16

alpha (the regression intercept) in Equation 21-7. With this statistic, the significance of alpha can be measured through a t-test, with $df = n - 2$, where n = the number of observations. By hypothesizing an expected value of zero, the analyst can determine whether any nonzero value of alpha is statistically significant.

The calculations required for this test are given in Table 21-4. The statistics used in these calculations can be obtained from a variety of regression programs on both a microcomputer and mainframe.[2] The value of the t-statistic is computed by dividing the regression coefficient by its associated standard deviation. For Jensen's alpha (the regression intercept), the value is -0.6899. The t-test's critical value, taken from the table of t-statistics in the appendix at the end of the book, is 2.12 where $df = n - 2 = 16$, and the significance level is 5%. Since the absolute value of the calculated t-statistic is less than the t value with $df = 16$, the value of the intercept is not significantly different from zero. This means that the inferior performance of the fund is not statistically significant at the 5% level.

Significance testing is also possible with the Sharpe and Treynor measures, but the procedure is more complex. The test, along with a numerical example, is described in the appendix to this chapter.

BIAS IN THE PERFORMANCE MEASURES

To be valid, composite performance measures should be independent of their corresponding measures of risk. Friend and Blume have found that composite performance values are dependent on risk.[3] The relationship they found is usually inverse, meaning that stronger composite performance scores are found overall with portfolios that have low levels of risk. The statistical significance of this relationship is high.

This bias can be attributed to several factors, the most important of which is the invalidity of the traditional market model assumption of equal borrowing and lending rates for all investors. Since, in practice,

[2] The t-test is reviewed in any standard statistics text. For example, see David Anderson, Dennis Sweeney, and Thomas Williams, *Introduction to Statistics*, 2d ed. (St. Paul, Minn.: West Publishing Co., 1991).

[3] Irwin Friend and Marshall Blume, "Measurement of Portfolio Performance under Uncertainty," *American Economic Review* (September 1970): 561–74.

|||| **TABLE 21-4**

t-Test Calculations for Magellan Fund Alpha

Variable	Coefficient	Standard Deviation of Coefficient	t-Ratio*
Intercept (alpha)	-0.00505	0.00732	-0.6899
Beta	1.18060	0.12400	9.5210

*The t-ratio is the coefficient divided by its standard deviation.

With a 5% significance level, the critical t value is 2.12. Alpha, with a t-ratio of -0.6899, is not statistically significant at the 5% level.

the borrowing rates are much higher, leveraged (and therefore risky) portfolios are at a disadvantage. During periods of strong bull markets, however, Friend and Blume found that the direction of the bias in composite performance scores actually reverses and becomes positive. This reversal may be due to the differences between actual and expected returns that occur during strong bull markets.

Klemkosky also studied portfolio performance and the potential bias in the composite performance measures.[4] He found a positive relationship between risk and the level of performance indicated by the composite performance measures and suggested this was contrary to Friend and Blume's inverse relationship. However, Klemkosky's observation period was during the late 1960s and early 1970s, a period with a generally strong bull market.

PROBLEMS WITH NEGATIVE EXCESS RETURNS

The Sharpe and Treynor indexes have mathematical properties that make them difficult to interpret if their values are negative. Negative scores occur when the security's returns are lower than the risk-free rate of return that prevailed over the observation period. Uncertainties surrounding the level of return of most investments make negative returns a likely possibility, so a reliable system of evaluating securities under these conditions is a necessity.

Consider the following statistics generated by the S&P 500 Index and the Canadian Fund over the period 1974–1982;

	Canadian Fund	Market Index
Average monthly return	0.53%	0.54%
Standard deviation	5.08	3.32
Average monthly risk-free return		0.83

As these statistics indicate, the market index had both a higher return and a lower standard deviation than the Canadian Fund, and thus it dominated the fund in a mean-variance sense. However, the Canadian Fund had a Sharpe index score of -0.0591, while the market index had a score of -0.0873. Thus, even though the fund was dominated by the market index, its Sharpe performance score was better. This interpretation problem exists only for portfolios with negative returns, and only when securities with similar levels of return and differing levels of risk are compared.[5]

For example, consider the four portfolios in Figure 21-1, all of which would have negative composite performance scores. The lines connecting points J and K and points L and M with point r_f have slopes equal to the value of the composite performance index for each of these portfolios,

[4]Robert C. Klemkosky, "The Bias in Composite Performance Measures," *Journal of Financial and Quantitative Analysis* (June 1973): 505–14.

[5]Dennis Proffitt and Keith L. Taylor, "Evaluating Negative Composite Performance Scores," *Journal of Financial Education* (Fall 1985): 17–21.

|||| **FIGURE 21-1**

Negative Composite Performance

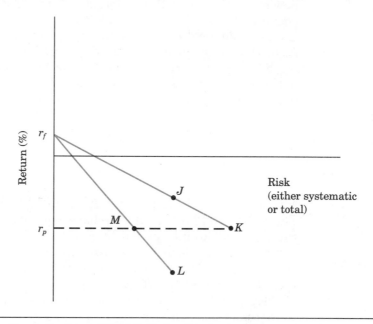

SOURCE: Dennis Proffitt and Keith L. Taylor, "Evaluating Negative Composite Performance Scores," *Journal of Financial Education* 14 (Fall 1985): 17–21.

since the slope is defined as the rise (excess returns) over the run (risk). Portfolios L and M have the same composite performance scores, but L is clearly the worse performer since it has a higher risk and a lower return than M. Portfolio K has a better performance score (flatter slope) than portfolio M even though M has the same return and lower risk. Fortunately, these ranking errors can be resolved with the same performance statistics already gathered in the calculation of the Sharpe and Treynor indexes.

In the lower quadrant of Figure 21-1, both risk *and* return worsen as the distance from the vertical intercept (point r_f) increases. The greater this distance, the worse the performance of the portfolio. Now envision points r_f, K, and r_p as being the three corners of a right triangle. The hypotenuse of this triangle *(r_f-K)* represents the distance (in terms of negative returns and risk) that the portfolio's performance places it from point r_f. As mentioned before, the greater this distance, the worse the performance of the portfolio.

Using the Pythagorean theorem, the squared length of the hypotenuse of a right triangle can be expressed as the sum of the squared length of the remaining two sides. With risk and return already given, the following formula can be used to measure this distance:

$$CI_p = [(r_p - r_f)^2 + (\sigma_p)^2]^{0.5} \qquad (21\text{-}8)$$

where

CI_p = composite performance index for portfolios with negative excess returns

σ_p = risk (either beta or standard deviation) of portfolio i with negative excess returns

Since large distances are associated with higher levels of both risk and negative excess returns, large values of CI in Equation 21-8 are associated with poor portfolio performance.

The negative returns of the Magellan Fund (CI_p) and the NYSE Composite Index (CI_m) can be compared with this technique. Table 21-5 shows the necessary calculations. Since the CI score for the fund is .0761 and that of the market index is .0591, the fund's performance is judged inferior. With this index, large scores indicate inferior performance, since both return and risk worsen as the distance from the vertical intercept increases.

|||| # COMPONENTS OF INVESTMENT PERFORMANCE

Portfolio managers and their clients often want to know why a portfolio has performed better or worse than the market or other portfolios. Differences in performance are due to differences in security selection, or market timing, or both.[6]

SECURITY SELECTION ABILITY

Security selection ability (SSA) refers to the ability of the investor to select securities that are underpriced. The following formula can be used to measure this ability.

[6]The measures presented in this section are adapted from the more detailed expressions in Eugene F. Fama, "The Components of Investment Performance," *The Journal of Finance* (June 1972): 551–67.

|||| **TABLE 21-5**

Calculation of the *CI* Score (for Negative Sharpe and Treynor Scores)

	Magellan Fund	Market Index
R_i	-0.0048	0.0010
R_f	0.0050	0.0050
σ_i	0.0755	0.0589

$$CI_i = [(R_i - R_f)^2 + (\sigma_i)^2]^{0.5}$$
$$CI_i \text{ (fund)} = [(-.0048 - .0050)^2 + (.0755)^2]^{0.5}$$
$$CI_i = 0.0761$$
$$CI_m \text{ (index)} = [(.0010 - .0050)^2 + (.0589)^2]^{0.5}$$
$$CI_m = 0.0590$$

$$SSA_p = \text{actual returns} - \text{expected returns} \qquad (21\text{-}9)$$
$$SSA_p = R_p - [R_f + \beta_p(R_m - R_f)]$$

The formula is used below to calculate the security selection ability for the three porfolios of Figure 21-2.

$$SSA_S = .15 - [.07 + 1.25(.12 - .07)] = 0.0175$$
$$SSA_M = .12 - [.07 + 1.0(.12 - .07)] = 0.0$$
$$SSA_I = .08 - [.07 + .60(.12 - .07)] = -0.02$$

Positive *SSA* scores imply superior security selection ability, whereas negative scores imply inferior security selection ability. Note that portfolio *S* whose risk and return place it above the market line in Figure 21-2 earns a positive *SSA* score, and that portfolio *I*, which falls below the market line, earns a negative *SSA* score.

The security selection score of the Magellan Fund is -0.0050, which indicates inferior selection ability. The calculation of this score is found in Table 21-6.

|||| **FIGURE 21-2**

Security Selection Ability

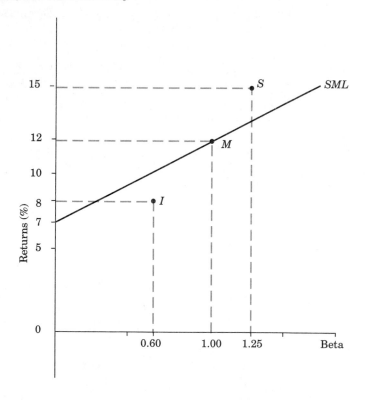

|||| **TABLE 21-6**

Security Selection Ability of the Magellan Fund

Given:
$$R_p = -0.0048$$
$$R_m = 0.0009$$
$$R_f = 0.0050$$
$$\beta_p = 1.18$$
$$SSA_p = R_i - [R_f + \beta_p(R_m - R_f)]$$
$$SSA_p = -0.0050$$

MARKET TIMING ABILITY

Additional profits can be earned by the investor who correctly anticipates the future movement of the overall market and adjusts his or her portfolio's beta to take advantage of these future market movements. The prices of high-beta securities rise faster than others in a bull market, but also fall faster than others in a bear market.

Market timing ability refers to the ability of the investor to earn these extra profits by correctly forecasting changes in market returns and adjusting the risk (by changing the portfolio's beta) in anticipation of these market swings. To illustrate, assume you anticipate the market trending upward over the next 18 months. Figure 21-3 shows the current market condition, as well as the condition anticipated at the end of 18 months. As this figure shows, the slope of the security market line increases when market returns are expected to rise. If they do in fact rise, investors who increased their portfolio betas before the rise are likely to earn high returns.

Market timing ability can be measured only if the following information is available:

β_T = the target beta of the portfolio (Unless the portfolio objectives have changed, this can be defined as the average portfolio beta over the recent past.)

$E(R_m)$ = the level of market returns anticipated at the beginning of the period

$E(R_f)$ = the level of risk-free returns anticipated at the beginning of the period

At the end of the measurement period, the following values must be obtained:

β_i = the actual beta for portfolio i

R_m = actual market returns during the period

R_f = actual risk-free returns during the period

Market timing ability (MTA_i) for portfolio i over a given period is the change in the risk level times the change in risk premium:

$$MTA_i = (\beta_i - \beta_T) \times \{(R_m - R_f) - [E(R_m) - E(R_f)]\} \quad (21\text{-}10)$$

|||| **FIGURE 21-3**

Current and Anticipated Market Conditions

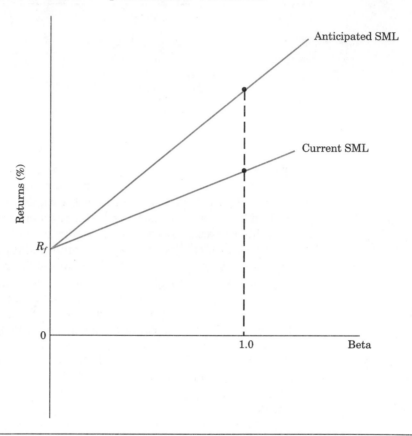

High, positive values of MTA_i indicate superior market timing ability.

For example, assume an investor (Teresa Timer) is particularly astute at market timing. Recently, she increased the beta of her portfolio from 0.9 to 1.75 during a period in which market returns increased from an expected level of 12% to a level of 20%. The interest rate on short-term government securities also rose from 9% to 10% during this period. Using Equation 21-12, Teresa's market timing ability (MTA_{TT}) would be

$$MTA_{TT} = (1.75 - 0.90) \times [(0.20 - 0.10) - (0.12 - 0.09)]$$

$$MTA_{TT} = 0.0595$$

The positive value indicates successful timing ability. Had Teresa lowered the beta of her portfolio during this period, or had the market returns fallen relative to what was expected at the beginning of the period, the sign of one of the terms in the equation would have changed, yielding a negative MTA score.

The timing ability of the Magellan Fund can be measured if we assume the fund's target beta is the beta it maintained in the past. The Magellan Fund is advertised as an aggressive stock fund for investors who are willing to assume above-average levels of risk. Its beta, calculated with data from the past five years, is 1.53. Assuming this to be the fund's target risk level, the timing ability of the Magellan Fund is 0.0040, as calculated in Table 21-7. The positive market timing score indicates successful market timing ability of the fund's manager. The fund's beta was reduced from its target of 1.53 to 1.18 during a period in which market returns were falling.

|||| ROLL'S CRITICISMS OF PERFORMANCE MEASURES

Richard Roll has criticized many of the composite performance measures described in the preceding sections.[7] While his criticisms do not completely negate the use of composite performance indexes, it is necessary to understand the basis for Roll's criticisms in order to interpret the composite performance measures properly.

THE BENCHMARK ERROR

Roll's basic criticism centers on what is called the *benchmark error*. Essentially, the benchmark error says that without a unique, efficient market proxy to use as a standard of comparison, the only conclusions that can be drawn from performance testing relate to the efficiency of the market proxy itself. Empirical problems abound when trying to identify a market proxy that is *ex ante* efficient. Theoretically, it should include not only securities from all the world's equity markets, but also bonds, real estate, art, coins, other collectibles, and other assets that offer the

[7]Roll's criticisms are described in detail in his articles: "A Critique of the Asset Pricing Theory's Tests," *Journal of Financial Economics* (March 1977): 129–76; "Ambiguity When Performance Is Measured by the Security Market Line," *The Journal of Finance* (September 1978): 1051–69; "Performance Evaluation and Benchmark Errors (I)," *Journal of Portfolio Management* (Summer 1980): 5–12; and "Performance Evaluation and Benchmark Errors (II)," *Journal of Portfolio Management* (Winter 1981): 17–22.

|||| TABLE 21-7
Market Timing Ability of the Magellan Fund

Given:
$\beta_i = 1.18$ $\beta_T = 1.53$
$R_m = 0.0009$ $E(R_m) = 0.0125$ (15% per year)
$R_f = 0.0050$ $E(R_f) = 0.0050$ (6% per year)
$MTA_i = (\beta_i - \beta_T) \times \{(R_m - R_f) - [E(R_m) - E(R_f)]\}$
$MTA_i = (1.18 - 1.53) \times [(.0009 - .0050) - (.0125 - .0050)]$
$= 0.0041$

promise of returns to their owners. Such a market proxy does not exist, and at present, the steps necessary to construct one are unknown. For this reason, any performance ranking obtained from a composite index based upon the security market line is suspect.

The Treynor and Jensen indexes are based upon the security market line and thus fall into this category. The Sharpe index, which utilizes total risk, is not subject to the benchmark error.

The genesis of the benchmark error stems from the fact that there is nothing unique about the market index as a point on the efficient frontier, nor is there anything unique about the risk-free return. In fact, even if no true risk-free security existed, it would be possible to derive the security market line as a combination of the market return and a zero-beta security that is uncorrelated with the market index.[8] The zero-beta security would have many of the same properties as, and fulfill the same role as, the risk-free security in the traditional security market line. However, the zero-beta security does not necessarily have a return equivalent to the return on short-term Treasury securities. The zero-beta model describes security returns as a linear function of the market index and the zero-beta security as follows:

$$E(R_i) = E(R_z) + \beta_i[E(R_m) - E(R_z)]$$

where

R_z = the return on the zero-beta security, which is an artificial security derived from the market portfolio

Most empirical tests of the zero-beta model indicate that it is slightly superior to the traditional CAPM (using short-term Treasuries as a proxy for the risk-free rate) in explaining security returns.

In the absence of a unique, well-defined risk-free security, as well as a well-specified market index to use as a proxy, a number of security market lines may exist and be entirely consistent with a given efficient frontier. Figure 21-4 illustrates just this possibility. Note that the position of the market portfolio on the efficient frontier varies with the location of the risk-free return.

Without a unique, well-defined security market line, performance measures based on that line are suspect. As Figure 21-4 indicates, the proper ranking of portfolios represented by points X and Y relative to the market index depends on the security market line selected.

The benchmark error is not a criticism of the general ability of the CAPM to explain security returns, but only of empirical tests of the CAPM and CAPM-based performance measures. The security market line continues to be used in performance measurement; nevertheless, the results of such measurements should be interpreted with caution.

---

[8]Fischer Black, "Capital Market Equilibrium with Restricted Borrowing," *Journal of Business* (July 1972): 444–55.

|||| **FIGURE 21-4**
Possible Security Market Lines without Specification of a Unique
Risk-Free Security

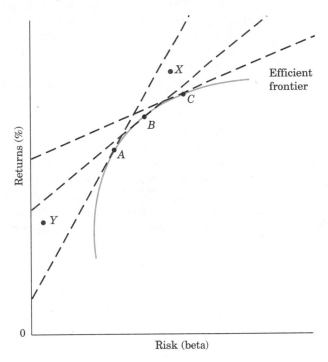

OTHER STATISTICAL PROBLEMS

In addition to the benchmark error, statistical problems include the presence of sampling error and of nonstationarity of returns over time.

Sampling error refers to the variation in sample means that can be
expected when repeated samples are taken from a given population. Obviously, since the samples do not include every element present in the
population, their means and standard deviations will change from one
sample to the next. The amount of change is a function of the dispersion
of values in the original population. The width of the confidence interval
that surrounds a given sample mean can be regarded as a good indicator
of the level of sampling error that is likely to exist.

Sampling error depends on the length of the sampling period when
estimating a security's mean return and variance. Roll found that, for a
stock with an expected return of 10%, almost 30 years of monthly data
are required before the 95% confidence interval of an individual stock's
return does not include zero.[9] Since only 3 to 10 years of data are typically
employed in practice, the width of the resulting confidence interval is so
large that it makes the results almost meaningless. The dispersion of

[9]Roll, "Performance Evaluation and Benchmark Errors (II)."

sample standard deviations is equally wide. The only cure for the sampling error problem is to employ large numbers of observations—much larger than the 3 to 10 years of data commonly employed in practice.

A second statistical problem is the *nonstationarity of returns* exhibited by many stocks. Nonstationarity of returns refers to the fact that, over time, the mean and standard deviation of a stock's returns change. Changes in these values obviously affect the values of the variables needed for composite performance indexes. These changes should not surprise anyone, since they occur as a result of changes in management policies, competitive conditions, and a changing economic climate. If, in order to minimize sampling error, the observation period is lengthened (as recommended above), the probability increases that nonstationarity of returns will be encountered. Under such a scenario, actions taken to reduce one statistical problem simply exacerbate the other.

There is no easy way to resolve this issue. Nonstationarity of returns does lessen the reliability of the results of performance measurement. Roll has proposed a procedure for performance measurement that incorporates the benchmark error, sampling error, and nonstationarity of returns, but it employs statistical methodology that is beyond the scope of this text.[10]

MEASURING BOND PORTFOLIO PERFORMANCE

Like equity investors, bond investors need to evaluate their portfolios. In today's market, active bond portfolio strategies, such as sector swaps and rate anticipation swaps, are commonplace. Increased interest rate volatility has made the realization of large capital gains a real possibility for bond investors. With the greater volatility of bond prices and the accompanying use of active bond strategies in recent years, the need for composite measures of bond performance has increased.

Composite measures of bond performance were developed after the equity measures, and as of this date, they have unresolved theoretical and empirical problems. Nevertheless, the need to evaluate bond portfolios persists. The best course of action for the bond analyst is to proceed with one or more of the evaluation techniques described in this section, remembering always that certain problems and theoretical issues are associated with each technique.

THE BOND MARKET LINE

The *bond market line* depicts the relationship between bond risk and returns.[11] Development of the bond market line begins with the selection of an index to represent the risk and return of the bond market. Two

[10]Ibid.

[11]Wayne H. Wagner and Dennis A. Tito, "Definitive New Measures of Bond Performance . . . and Risk," *Pension World* (May 1977): 10–12.

popular indexes are the Salomon Brothers High-Grade Corporate Bond Index and the Kuhn Loeb Bond Index. Both of these broadly–based, value-weighted indexes are widely reported in the financial press.

The next step in the development of the bond market line is to select a measure to represent risk. In some ways, duration for bonds can be regarded as analogous to beta for stocks. Duration is a measure of the sensitivity of a bond's price to changes in market interest rates. Recall that bond prices move inversely to changes in interest rates. Assuming an equal shift in interest rates among all maturities (this equates to a parallel movement, either up or down, of the yield curve), the relationship between duration and bond prices is roughly

$$\text{percentage change in bond price} = D(\text{YTM}_1 - \text{YTM}_2) \quad (21\text{-}11)$$

where

$$D = \text{bond duration}$$

$(\text{YTM}_1 - \text{YTM}_2) = $ the shift in interest rates, as measured by the original and the new bond yield to maturity, respectively

For example, if the duration of a bond is 10 years, and interest rates rise by 1% (as measured by an increase of 1% in the yield to maturity of the bond), the resultant price change for this bond will be approximately $10(-1\%) = -10\%$.[12] The duration of a portfolio of bonds can be calculated by taking a value-weighted average of the duration of the individual bonds in the portfolio.

The bond market line, then, is formed by connecting points in the risk-return space that represent short-term Treasury securities (the classic "risk-free" security) and one of the widely accepted bond market indexes. Duration, on the horizontal axis, is a surrogate for risk. An example of the bond market line is depicted in Figure 21-5. In this figure, the Kuhn Loeb Index represents the bond market, and its duration was calculated to be 9.75 years.[13]

If a given bond portfolio possesses a yield to maturity above the bond market line at the portfolio's risk, that portfolio has "outperformed" the market and is a superior portfolio. Likewise, yields below the level depicted by the bond market line are underperforming the market and are inferior portfolios.

This representation of the bond market line is subject to two criticisms. First, duration captures only one dimension of bond risk, namely, interest rate risk.[14] Other major sources of bond risk (default risk, for example) are omitted. In fact, several bond market lines may exist at any given time, one for each level of default risk. The slope of these lines is significantly different, indicating that the omission of default risk in the

[12] See Chapter 14 for a more accurate method of calculating the price change.

[13] Wagner and Tito, "Definitive New Measures of Bond Performance . . . and Risk."

[14] Frank Reilly and Rupinder S. Sidhu, "The Many Uses of Bond Duration," *Financial Analysts Journal* (July/August 1980): 58–72.

FIGURE 21-5

The Bond Market Line

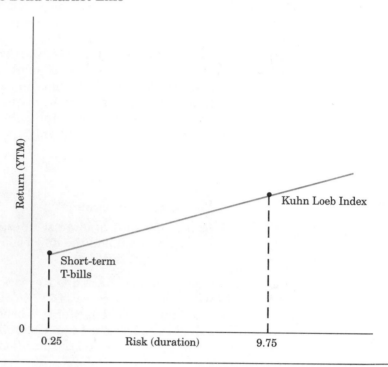

SOURCE: Wayne M. Wagner and Dennis A. Tito, "Definitive New Measures of Bond Performance . . . and Risk," *Pension World* (May 1977): 10–12.

calculation of the bond market line is a significant error. Using a single bond market index to represent all risky bonds (and thereby omitting default risk) can lead to important errors in representing the risk-return trade-off in the bond market.

The other criticism of the bond market line concerns the hypothesized straight-line relationship between bond duration and return.[15] Empirically, it has been found that the relationship is curvilinear. As Figure 21-6 shows, if the bond market is assumed to be linear, bond portfolio managers can "beat" the market by keeping the duration of their portfolios shorter than that of the bond market index. For example, point *A* on the graph represents a portfolio that simply earns an average return given its level of risk, despite the fact that its return is above the required return indicated by the hypothesized linear bond market line.

In view of these criticisms, how are we to proceed in evaluating bond portfolios? Does the bond market line have any value whatsoever? It does, if constructed properly and used with care.

[15] Peter Dietz, H. Russell Fogler, and Anthony U. Rivers, "Duration, Non-Linearity, and Bond Portfolio Performance," *Journal of Portfolio Management* (Spring 1981): 37–41.

|||| **FIGURE 21-6**

The Empirical Relationship between Bond Duration and Returns

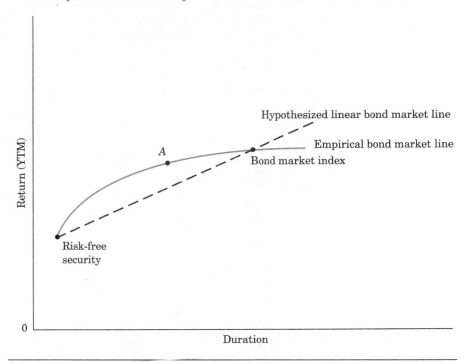

SOURCE: Peter Dietz, H. Russell Fogler, and Anthony U. Rivers, "Duration, Non-Linearity, and Bond Portfolio Performance," *Journal of Portfolio Management* (Spring 1981): 37–41.

First, rather than a comprehensive bond market index, a specialized bond index such as those provided by Salomon Brothers should be used. These specialized bond indexes are broken down into bond market sectors (such as corporates, municipals, and so forth) as well as into various default rating categories.

The use of these specialized bond indexes should overcome the criticism that the bond market line has several slopes, depending on the default rating of the bonds being analyzed. For portfolios of bonds, such as bond mutual funds, the rating that best represents the objectives of the portfolio should be selected. For example, conservative bond funds would probably be evaluated using Moody's AAA Index, while more aggressive bond funds would be evaluated using Moody's A Index. Specific information on the ratings of the bonds in a given fund can almost always be found in the fund's prospectus.

The curvilinear relationship between bond yields and duration has to be incorporated subjectively into bond portfolio analysis. Recall that it is biased toward portfolios with durations shorter than that of the bond index and against portfolios with durations longer than the index. The degree of nonlinearity varies with the time period under observation, but usually it is small and is statistically significant in only about half of the cases.[16] Thus, a small, subjective correction in the portfolio's returns needs to be made. This correction would be positive when duration is greater than the market proxy and negative when duration is less than the market proxy. Furthermore, conclusions regarding bond portfolio performance should be very tentative until performance is measured over several periods.

COMPONENTS OF BOND PORTFOLIO PERFORMANCE

Often, a more detailed breakdown of overall portfolio performance can be helpful in analyzing the sources of superior or inferior returns. Bond portfolio performance can be thought of as a function of factors both controllable and uncontrollable by the portfolio manager, as follows:[17]

$$R = I + C \qquad (21\text{-}12)$$

where

R = overall return

I = effect of the interest rate environment on bond returns (not controllable by the portfolio manager)

C = contribution of the portfolio manager's efforts

Treasury securities are used to measure the interest rate environment (I) because they are the only true "fixed-income" securities. Promised payments for Treasury securities are certain. All other debt securities involve some level of default risk in exchange for the promise of higher yields.

The effect of the interest rate environment (I) can be further broken down into

$$I = E + U \qquad (21\text{-}13)$$

where

E = the return on default-free securities (Treasuries) that would occur with no change in interest rates during the observation period

U = the return on default-free securities attributable to a change in interest rates during the observation period

The variable E can be thought of as the return on Treasuries at the beginning of the period (the expected return for that period). The variable U is then the unexpected return, which is due to interest rate changes during the period.

The contribution of the bond portfolio manager's efforts (C) is the sum of three types of activities:

---

[16] Ibid., p. 38.

[17] Gifford Fong, Charles Pearson, and Oldrich Vasicek, "Bond Performance: Analyzing Sources of Return," *Journal of Portfolio Management* (Spring 1983): 46–50.

$$C = M + S + B \qquad \text{(21-14)}$$

The first of these is *maturity management (M)*, which is the ability to adjust the average portfolio maturity upward (or downward) in the face of decreasing (or increasing) levels of interest rates. Sector/quality management *(S)* refers to the ability of the portfolio manager to invest in sectors of the bond market that are undervalued or in bonds with certain issuers, quality ratings that are undervalued. Bond market sectors refer to the types of such as utilities or municipalities, and quality ratings refer to the default ratings given by Moody's or Standard & Poor's. Sector/quality management involves monitoring the degree of "spread," or the difference in the average interest rates between different types of bonds. When the spread is unusually wide, a buy opportunity is indicated.

Finally, selectivity *(B)* refers to the ability of the bond manager to select individual bond issues *within* a market sector or default quality rating. The goal of selectivity is to pick individual bonds that promise returns over and above the average for their sector or their default rating.

|||| SUMMARY

This chapter has examined the issues surrounding the evaluation of portfolio returns. Initially, portfolio evaluation seemed a rather simple process, as suggested by the straightforward calculation of the Sharpe, Jensen, and Treynor composite performance indexes. However, it soon became apparent that several theoretical and empirical problems are associated with each of these measures. These problems include the benchmark error, nonstationarity of returns, and the large degree of sampling error typically present in the distribution of security returns.

Bond portfolio performance measures were also examined. The simplest of these, the bond market line, was also found to contain theoretical and empirical problems. These problems include the inability of duration to fully represent bond portfolio risk and the nonlinearity of the relationship between bond returns and duration.

Despite these problems with the existing measures, the need for portfolio performance evaluation persists. In view of this need, the best course of action for the investor is not to abandon all attempts to evaluate performance, but to become aware of the existing measurement tools and their problems so that the results of performance evaluation efforts can be interpreted as accurately as possible.

21a TESTING FOR STATISTICAL SIGNIFICANCE WITH THE SHARPE AND TREYNOR MEASURES

When the Jensen composite performance index was first developed, it appeared to hold a significant advantage over the Sharpe and Treynor measures in that it allowed for a test of statistically significant performance differences. Recently, however, a test for statistical significance has been developed in association with the Sharpe and Treynor composite performance indexes.[18]

The test procedure involves calculating the following Z-type statistics for portfolios i and n:

$$Z(S_{in}) = S_{in}/(t)^{0.5} \quad \text{(for Sharpe index)} \tag{21A-1}$$

and

$$Z(T_{in}) = (T_{in})/(g)^{0.5} \quad \text{(for Treynor Index)} \tag{21A-2}$$

where

$S_{in} = \sigma_n R_i - \sigma_i R_n$, a Sharpe index transformation (the necessity for transformed values is explained below)

σ = sample standard deviation for portfolio n or i

R = average excess returns (over the risk-free rate) for portfolio n or i

$T_{in} = (s_{nm}R_i)/\sigma_m^2 - (s_{im}R_n)/\sigma_m^2$, a Treynor index transformation (see explanation below)

s_{im} = sample covariance of excess returns between portfolio i or n and the market (m)

σ_m^2 = sample variance of excess market returns

The risk measures t and g, for the Sharpe and Treynor Z-scores, respectively, are calculated as follows:

$$t = (1/T)\{2\sigma_i^2\sigma_n^2 - 2\sigma_i\sigma_n S_{in} + \tfrac{1}{2}(R_i^2\sigma_n^2) + \tfrac{1}{2}(R_n^2\sigma_i^2) \\ - [(R_iR_n/2\sigma_i\sigma_n)](s_{in}^2 + \sigma_i^2\sigma_n^2)\} \tag{21A-3}$$

$$g = (1/T)[\sigma_i^2 s_{nm}^2 + \sigma_n^2 s_{im}^2 - 2s_{im}s_{nm}\sigma_{in} + r_i^2(\sigma_n^2\sigma_m^2 - s_{nm}^2) \\ + r_n^2(\sigma_i^2\sigma_m^2 - s_{im}^2) - 2r_i r_n(s_{in}\sigma_m^2 - s_{im}s_{nm})] \tag{21A-4}$$

---

[18]J. D. Jobson and Bob M. Korkie, "Performance Hypothesis Testing with the Sharpe and Treynor Measures," *The Journal of Finance* (September 1981): 889–908.

where

$$T = \text{number of observations}$$

Although Equations 21A-3 and 21A-4 look quite formidable, they use relatively straightforward statistical measures that are easily output by a variety of statistical packages.

The usual procedure to test for significant differences between portfolios i and n would be to test the following null hypotheses:

$$\text{Sharpe test:} \quad H_0: S_i - S_n = 0$$

$$\text{Treynor test:} \quad H_0: T_i - T_n = 0$$

However, transformations of the Sharpe and Treynor scores (denoted as S_{in} and T_{in}, respectively) improve the statistical properties of the test. The presence of the estimated covariance term in the denominator of the Treynor index causes large, unpredictable fluctuations in the statistic. The Sharpe transformation provides an improvement when the sample size is small. The nature of the Sharpe and Treynor transformations was indicated in the definitions of the terms S_{in} and T_{in}, respectively (see Equations 21A-1 and 21A-2).

|||| **TABLE 21A-1**

Significance Testing with Sharpe Performance Scores

Basic formula (testing for performance differences between portfolios i and n)

$Z = $ transformed measure of return/square root of risk

$$Z(S_{in}) = S_{in}/(t)^{0.5}$$

Steps

1. Calculate the return transformation:

$$S_{in} = \sigma_n R_i - \sigma_i R_n$$

where

$R_i = $ excess mean returns of fund $= -0.0098$

$R_n = $ excess mean returns of NYSE Index $= -0.0041$

$\sigma_i = $ standard deviation of excess fund returns $= 0.0754$

$\sigma_n = $ standard deviation of excess index returns $= 0.0589$

$$S_{in} = (.0589)(-.0098) - (.0754)(-.0041)$$

$$= 0.00027$$

2. Calculate the risk measure:

$$t = (1/T)\{2\sigma_i^2 s_n^2 - 2\sigma_i \sigma_n s_{in} + \tfrac{1}{2}(R_i^2 \sigma_n^2) + \tfrac{1}{2}(R_n^2 \sigma_i^2 - [(R_i R_n/2\sigma_i \sigma_n)](s_{in}^2 + \sigma_i^2 \sigma_n^2)\}$$

where

$T = $ number of observations $= 18$

$\sigma_i^2 = 0.0057$

$\sigma_n^2 = 0.0035$

$s_{in} = $ covariance of excess returns between fund and index $= 0.50$ (assumed)

$$t = (1/18)\{2(.0057)(.0035) - 2(.0754)(.0589)(.50)$$

$$+ (.50)(-0.0098)^2(.0035) + (.50)(-.0041)^2(.0057)$$

$$- [(-.0098)(-.0041)]/[(2)(.0754)(.0589)]$$

$$[.50^2 + (.0057)(.0035)]\}$$

$$t = -0.00024$$

3. Calculate Z-score

$$Z = (0.00027)/(-0.00024)^{0.5}$$

$$= 0.0174$$

The Sharpe Z-statistic, defined in Equation 21A-1, is generally unbiased. Due to variance overestimation, the Treynor Z-statistic, defined in Equation 21A-2, requires a sample size of at least $T = 60$ to produce an unbiased estimate.

An example of the Sharpe performance test appears in Table 21A-1. The calculated Z-score is 0.0174. Since the normal 95% confidence interval includes the range of Z-scores from $+1.96$ to -1.96, the null hypothesis (no significant performance differences) is not rejected. The Magellan Fund's inferior performance is not statistically significant.

QUESTIONS

1. The Sharpe index, which uses total risk measure in its denominator, is preferred when measuring the performance of an investor's entire investment portfolio. The Treynor index, which uses systematic risk, is the preferred measure when the performance being measured is for only a portion of the investor's portfolio. Why is this the case?

2. Write a brief interpretation of Jensen's alpha as a performance statistic.

3. Why is the expected value of Jensen's alpha always zero?

4. What biases have been found in the Sharpe and Treynor performance measures during bull and bear markets, respectively?

5. Under what conditions are the interpretation problems associated with negative values of the Sharpe and Treynor scores likely to occur?

6. Distinguish between security selection ability and market timing ability.

7. Most mutual fund managers evaluate the performance of their funds against the performance of other funds with comparable objectives. How does the selection of this performance standard involve the benchmark error?

8. What is sampling error and how does it affect the measurement of portfolio performance? What can be done to minimize sampling error when measuring portfolio performance?

9. Would you expect a stock's mean return and standard deviation to be constant over a period of several years? Why or why not? How does this influence the measurement of portfolio performance?

10. What is the bond market line, and how is this concept used in the measurement of bond performance?

11. What measure of risk is typically used when developing a bond market line? Why does the choice of this risk measure subject the bond market line to criticism?

12. Describe the relationship between bond returns and duration. How should an analyst incorporate this relationship into bond performance measurement?

13. List and describe the components of bond portfolio performance measurement.

‖‖‖ PROBLEMS

Monthly returns for the Fidelity Trend Fund are listed below. Returns from the NYSE Composite Index and 91-day T-bill rates for the same months are given in Table 21-1. Use these data to answer Problems 1–4. (All returns are in decimal form.)

Month	Fund Returns	Month	Fund Returns
1	0.0444	10	−0.0636
2	0.0137	11	−0.0631
3	−0.0155	12	0.0498
4	−0.0108	13	0.0806
5	0.0394	14	0.0123
6	0.0627	15	0.0303
7	0.0314	16	−0.0214
8	−0.0254	17	0.0731
9	−0.2958	18	−0.0211

1. What is the value of the Sharpe index for the Fidelity Trend Fund? Has the fund outperformed the NYSE Composite Index over the same period?

2. Calculate the values of the Treynor index for the Fidelity Trend Fund and the market index, and indicate whether the fund has outperformed the market over this time period.

3. a. Using the program diskette that came with this text (or any other suitable statistical package), calculate the value of the Jensen index for the Fidelity Trend Fund, and explain whether it indicates performance superiority or inferiority relative to the market. (*Remember: Excess* fund returns are regressed against the *excess* returns of the market.)

   b. Is the value of Jensen's alpha statistically significant at the 5% significance level?

4. Calculate measures for security selection and market timing ability for the Fidelity Trend Fund. Indicate the role they play in the overall performance score of the fund.

5. In their article "Definitive New Measures of Bond Performance and Risk," Wayne Wagner and Dennis A. Tito indicate the duration of the Kuhn Loeb Bond Market Index is approximately 9.75 years and is relatively constant over time. Assume its return is currently 10%. The duration of 91-day T-bills is 0.25 years, since these T-bills are discount instruments. Their return is currently 6.5% per year. Using these performance statistics, evaluate the following bond portfolios:

   a. A portfolio with a duration of 6 years and a return of 8.5%.

    b. A portfolio with a duration of 11.5 years and a return of 11%.

    c. What return would a short-term bond fund with a duration of four years require in order to match market performance?

*6. The Retired Fund is an open-ended mutual fund composed of $500 million in U.S. bonds and Treasury bills. This fund has a portfolio duration (including the T-bills) of between three and nine years. Retired has shown first quartile (top 25% of all funds) performance over the past five years. However, the directors of the fund would like to measure the market timing skill of the fund's sole bond investment manager. An external consulting firm suggests the following three methods:

    a. Measure the value of the bond portfolio at the beginning of each year, then calculate the return that would have been achieved had that same portfolio been held throughout the year. Then compare this return with the return actually obtained by the fund.

    b. Calculate the average weighting of the portfolio in bonds and T-bills for each year. Construct a benchmark using the same actual bond/bill weighting and the returns on a long bond market index and a T-bill index. Compare this return with the return the portfolio actually earned.

    c. Examine the net bond purchase activity (market value of purchases less sales) for each quarter of the year. If net purchases were positive (negative) in any quarter, the performance of the bonds would be evaluated until the net purchase activity became negative (positive). Positive (negative) net purchases would be viewed as a bullish (bearish) view being taken by the manager. The correctness of this view would be measured.

        Critique *each* method with regard to market timing measurement problems.

7. The Toxic Waste Fund and a broad-based market index had the following performance statistics over the decade of the 1980s:

	Fund	Market
Mean annual return	12%	10%
Beta	1.4	1.0
Standard deviation	0.46	0.30

If the average T-bill rate during the decade was 7½%, calculate the Sharpe and Treynor measures for both the fund and the market. Comment on your results.

8. Assume the following performance statistics:

---

*Note: Problem preceded by an asterisk is in part from a Chartered Financial Analyst (CFA) examination.

Year	Fund Returns	Market Returns
1	-20%	-6%
2	2	-2
3	15	12
4	8	11
5	23	-9
6	7	14
7	-9	11
8	35	12
9	-22	-24
10	8	-3

Assume the average risk-free return was 5% over the period. Calculate the Sharpe, Jensen, and Treynor indexes for the fund and for the market. Evaluate the fund's performance.

9. Assume the fund in Problem 8 is an index fund, and thus has a target beta of 1.0. Measure its security selection ability.

10. Assume that, over the time period specified, the expected risk-free return was 7% and the expected market return was 12%. Evaluate the market timing ability of the fund in Problem 8.

|||| **SELECTED REFERENCES**

Fama, Eugene. "The Components of Investment Performance." *The Journal of Finance* (June 1972): 551–67.

Friend, Irwin, and Marshall Blume. "Measurement of Portfolio Performance under Uncertainty." *American Economic Review* (September 1970): 561–74.

Roll, Richard. "Performance Evaluation and Benchmark Errors (I)." *Journal of Portfolio Management* (Summer 1980): 5–12; Part II (Winter 1981): 17–22.

Wagner, Wayne H., and Dennis A. Tito. "Definitive New Measures of Bond Performance . . . and Risk." *Pension World* (May 1977): 10–12.

_____. "Is Your Bond Manager Skillful?" *Pension World* (June 1977): 9–13.

22 INVESTMENT COMPANIES

Many investors own securities indirectly through shares of investment companies. An *investment company* is a corporation or trust whose business consists solely of attracting capital and investing it in financial assets of various kinds. Investment companies provide investors with a way to acquire a portion of a large, diversified portfolio of securities at minimal cost. As we shall see, however, not all investment companies are well diversified. Managers of investment company portfolios often concentrate their investments in certain types of stocks and bonds in an effort to achieve superior performance.

A number of investment companies offer "families" of mutual funds. Each *mutual fund,* in turn, is a unique investment portfolio, usually with its own investment objectives and mix of securities. Through these funds, firms offer their customers considerable flexibility, allowing them to move money from one fund to another. The transactions costs associated with these fund "switches" are usually lower than the costs of a similar trade executed through a broker.

The number of mutual funds has mushroomed in recent years. From 1977 through the end of 1988, the number offered in the United States grew from 477 to 2,718, for an increase of more than 17% per year. Meanwhile, the value of the assets controlled by these funds grew from $48.5 billion to $810.2 billion, for an annual growth rate of 29%.[1]

What are the reasons for this rapid growth? At least three factors stand out. First, the funds offer investors a chance to diversify for a minimal investment. Diversification provides important risk reduction benefits. For an investor with only a small amount to invest, diversification may otherwise be an unattainable goal. Mutual funds offer these investors a chance to obtain a portion of a diversified investment portfolio.

Second, families of funds offer flexibility, giving investors an opportunity to move money from one fund to another, thereby enabling them to try to take advantage of expected price movements in different market sectors.

Third, they offer convenience. Although an investor must still follow the fortunes of the fund itself, tracking the returns of a few mutual funds is far easier than following the ups and downs of many individual stocks.

One factor that is *not* a contributor to mutual fund growth is an ability to generate excess risk-adjusted returns. Fund performance will be dis-

---

[1]Investment Company Institute, *Mutual Fund Fact Book* (various editions).

cussed in greater depth later in this chapter. For now, however, note that an ability to realize returns over and above the level generated by the market as a whole is not typically one of the advantages of investing in mutual funds.

MUTUAL FUND BASICS

Several properties of mutual funds give their portfolios entirely different risk and return characteristics than individual stocks and bonds. In order to understand the funds as investments, it is necessary to understand these properties and how they affect the results.

NET ASSET VALUE

The net asset value of a mutual fund is the basic measure of the fund's per-share value. It is calculated with the following formula:

$$NAV_i = (mv_i - d_i)/s_i \qquad (22\text{-}1)$$

where

NAV_i = the net asset value per share of fund i

mv_i = total market value of all securities in the fund's portfolio

d_i = debt incurred by the portfolio manager in purchasing securities

s_i = number of shares held by the fund's shareholders

Thus, the net asset value is basically the per-share value of the fund's total holdings, less any debt incurred by the fund manager in purchasing securities on margin.

THE COSTS OF INVESTING IN FUNDS

The costs of investing in mutual funds consist of load charges, management fees, and 12b–1 fees.

A mutual fund can be classified as a load fund, or a no-load fund, or a *low-load fund*. Load funds and low-load funds assess a special charge (over and above the net asset value) on the purchase or sale of the fund's shares. The Securities and Exchange Commission (SEC) regulates the size of the load charges that can be assessed and currently limits these charges to a maximum of 8½% of the price of the fund's shares. A *no-load fund* has no sales charge, so its shares can be bought or sold at the fund's net asset value. *Low-load funds* typically have load charges in the range of 3% to 5.5%.

Sales charges, or front-end loads, are paid when the investor purchases the fund's shares. Redemption charges, or back-end loads, are paid when the investor sells the fund's shares. Seldom will a load fund have both a sales charge and a redemption charge.

In recent years, with the growth in popularity of mutual funds, many have instituted load charges for the first time. Load charges are disclosed in the prospectus of the fund and can also be calculated from mutual fund quotations in the financial press. Table 22-1 depicts mutual fund quotations from the pages of the *Los Angeles Times* in a format typical of fund price quotations in newspapers across the country.

Among others, the table lists quotations of selected Evergreen Group funds. The quotations include, from left to right, the name of the fund, the fund's net asset value, its offering price, and the change in net asset value from the close of trading the previous day. The offering price is the price at which the fund's shares can be purchased. For no-load funds, the offering price is the same as the net asset value; thus, the entry in the offering price column for these funds is simply NL.

In addition to load charges, mutual funds charge annual management fees, which are usually a fraction of 1% of the fund's total portfolio value. No-load funds often have slightly larger management fees than load funds, but exceptions are common.

⫿⫿⫿ **TABLE 22-1**

Mutual Fund Quotations

HOW TO READ MUTUAL FUND TABLES—The following quotations, supplied by the NASD, New York, via the Associated Press, are the prices at which these securities could have been sold (net asset value) or bought (value plus sales charge). "**Chg.**" means the change from the previous day's "sell" quotation. "**NL**" means "no load", only used for funds for which there is no sales commission to buy into the fund or to redeem shares. **x** means ex-dividend, **e**—ex-distribution of capital gains, **s**—stock split or stock dividend, **r**—redemption charge may apply, **t**—redemption charge may apply and charges an annual fee to cover marketing expenses, **p**—charges an annual fee to cover marketing expenses not included in the sales fee, **f**—previous day's quotation, a fund's redemption price, **NAV**—net asset value per share.

Funds	NAV	Offer Price	NAV. Chg.	Funds	NAV	Offer Price	NAV. Chg.	Funds	NAV	Offer Price	NAV. Chg.
AAL Mutual:				Inco	16.07	16.87 +	.04	Gwth p	7.49	7.86 −	.04
CaGr p	12.45	13.07 −	.12	Social p	27.49	28.86 −	.08	HYBd p	9.31	9.77	...
Inco p	9.76	10.25 +	.01	SocBd	16.06	16.86 +	.03	IntlGr p	13.60	14.28 +	.03
MuBd p	10.08	10.58	...	SocEq	18.73	19.66 −	.16	PrcM p	10.41	10.93	...
AARP Invst:				TxF Lt	10.63	10.85 +	.01	**Equitable Funds:**			
CaGr	28.96	NL −	.04	TxF lg	15.56	16.34 +	.02	GovScB t	9.95	9.95 +	.01
GiniM	15.38	NL	...	UsGov	14.84	15.58 +	.01	BalB t	14.23	14.23 −	.10
GthInc	26.07	NL −	.05	WshA p	11.83	12.42 +	.03	GwthB t	17.12	17.12 −	.11
HQBd	15.24	NL +	.01	**Capstone Group:**				STWI p	9.67	9.97 −	.03
TxFBd	16.83	NL +	.03	CshFr	9.95	10.45 −	.12	TxEB t	10.15	10.15 +	.02
TxFSh	15.25	NL +	.01	Fd SW	15.25	16.01 −	.12	**Equitec Siebel:**			
ABT Funds:				GvtInc	4.60	4.60 +	.01	AgGth t	14.26	14.26 −	.10
Emrg p	9.83	10.32 −	.06	MedRs	17.73	18.61 −	.05	HiYld t	6.68	6.68	...
FLTF	10.31	10.82 +	.02	PBHG	11.70	12.28 −	.05	TotRt t	15.80	15.80 −	.06
GthIn p	9.54	10.02 −	.09	Ray El	6.80	7.14 −	.04	USGv t	8.94	8.94 −	.01
SecIn p	9.45	9.92	...	Trend	13.95	14.65 −	.15	EqStrat	27.81	NL −	.79
UtilIn p	11.91	12.50 −	.04	CarilCa	11.92	12.55 −	.03	**Evergreen Funds:**			
AdsnCa p	19.40	20.00 −	.22	**Carneg Cappielo:**				Evgrn	12.57	NL −	.06
AEGON USA:				EmGr p	10.40	10.89 +	.03	TotRtn	18.07	NL −	.08
CapApp	4.07	4.27 −	.03	Grow p	18.20	19.06 −	.21	ValTm	12.19	NL −	.02
HiYld	9.64	10.12 +	.01	TRetn p	11.25	11.78 −	.09	LtdMk	18.61	NL −	.07
Gwth	5.77	6.06 −	.04	**Carnegie Funds:**				ExcelMid	2.54	2.66	...
AFAN Av	10.58	11.11 −	.08	Govl p	9.28	9.72 +	.03	ExcHY p	6.47	6.79 +	.02
AFA Tele	15.38	16.15 −	.18	TEOhG	9.17	9.60 +	.01	FBL Glh t	11.59	11.59 −	.01
AHA Bal	11.17	NL −	.09	TENHi	9.61	10.06 +	.01	**FPA Funds:**			
AHA LIM	10.15	NL +	.01	Cardnl	11.33	12.38 −	.12	Capit	15.30	16.36 +	.06
AIM Funds:				CrdnlGv	8.87	9.29	...	NwInc	10.04	10.51 +	.03
Chart p	7.78	8.23 −	.08	Cnl Shs	20.05	NL −	.18	Parmt	13.64	14.59 −	.01
Const p	10.14	10.73 −	.09	ChartBC	10.99	10.99 −	.16	Peren	20.87	22.32 −	.02
CvYld p	11.30	11.86 −	.03	Chestnt	107.49	NL −	1.45	Fairmt	15.70	NL +	.04

SOURCE: *Los Angeles Times* (April 6, 1991).

Investors may believe that load charges or high management fees are correlated with superior returns. Some may feel that the investment company uses these extra sources of income to support more extensive security research, thereby generating superior returns for the customers of the fund. However, this does not seem to be the case. In general, studies investigating fund performance have found no relationship between the returns generated by funds and the level of the management fees or load charges. Details of these studies are reviewed later in this chapter.

A number of funds changed their fee structure after the SEC passed rule 12b–1 in 1980. With the passage of this rule, funds were allowed to charge an annual distribution fee (called a 12b–1 fee) equal to 1% of their portfolio value. These funds can be identified in the price quotations by the designation "p," which appears after the name of the fund (see Table 22-1).

Often, the distribution fee is supplemented by an exit charge (similar to a back-end load) for shareholders who withdraw from the fund within a few years after purchasing their shares. A typical exit charge starts at 4% in the first year and declines to zero after the fourth year from the time of the initial investment. Funds with this type of arrangement are sometimes said to have "hidden load charges." The sponsors of these funds sometimes pay the seller an annual fee as long as the customer continues to be a shareholder. Distribution (12b–1) fees are designed to reimburse the investment company for these fees and for commissions paid to brokerage houses at the time of the sale.

BASIC ORGANIZATIONAL FORMS

There are two types of investment company organizations: open-end funds (or mutual funds) and closed-end funds. Mutual funds have a variable number of shares. The price of a fund's shares is the net asset value, plus any load fees. The main disadvantage of open-end funds is the fluctuation in the number of shares that occurs over time. These fluctuations often work to the fund's disadvantage, since there are typically heavy fund redemptions during market slumps. Redemptions during bear markets force the fund manager to sell securities when the market is down, thereby locking in losses for the fund.

A *closed-end investment company* issues a fixed number of shares. After the fund is fully subscribed, new investors who desire shares must purchase them from an existing investor, usually through a broker. After the initial subscription, the sales of closed-end fund shares are handled just like the shares of any other corporation. The shares are listed on a stock exchange, trades are executed through brokers, and the price fluctuates daily through the interaction of supply and demand. Typically, the shares of closed-end funds sell at a discount from their net asset value. These discounts are one of the true enigmas in the field of finance. Implications of discounts for closed-end funds are explored later in the chapter.

|||| OPEN-END FUNDS

By far, the most common form of investment company is the open-end fund, or mutual fund. These range from conservative, short-term money market funds to aggressive equity funds and option funds. The various types are described in this section.

EQUITY FUNDS

Mutual funds that invest largely or partly in common stocks are classified into a number of types.[2] Some are classified by their specialty, such as health care stocks, but a majority are classified by objectives, as follows:

1. Aggressive growth funds. Seek maximum capital gains, often by investing in stocks that either pay no dividend or a small dividend. They are apt to do a lot of short-term trading.
2. Growth funds. Primary emphasis is on capital gains. They invest in stocks of well-established companies.
3. Growth and income funds. Objective is long-term capital gains with a steady stream of income. They invest mainly in the stocks of growing companies that have been paying substantial dividends.
4. Income funds. Objective is high level of current income. They invest in stocks of companies with good dividend-paying records.
5. Balanced funds. Seek current income and long-term growth by investing in common stocks, bonds, and preferred stocks.
6. Option/income funds. Seek high current returns by investing largely in dividend-paying stocks on which they sell call options.
7. Asset allocation funds. Are essentially balanced funds that attempt to increase their income through market timing.

A number of funds, called sector funds, specialize in the stocks of certain industries or groups of industries. These include funds that specialize in health care stocks, or stocks of financial service companies, or stocks of public utilities, or stocks of companies that mine precious metals. Because of their lack of diversification, sector funds tend to be riskier than the average. Other funds that specialize in certain groups of stocks include small company funds; global funds, which invest in a mix of U.S. and foreign securities; and foreign stock funds, which are U.S. based funds with predominantly foreign portfolios.

Finally, for investors who believe that it is unrealistic to try to "beat the U.S. market" over a long period of time, the mutual fund industry

---

[2]*Mutual Fund Fact Book* (Washington, D.C.: Investment Company Institute, 1986).

offers index funds, which attempt to mimic the performance of a specified stock index such as Standard & Poor's 500. Typically, index funds are classified as growth and income funds.

BOND FUNDS

Bond funds are specialized by both bond type and by maturity. Investors can select bond funds specializing in corporate bonds, U.S. government and government agency securities, Government National Mortgage Association (GNMA or Ginnie Mae) mortgage-backed securities, or state and municipal securities. Within each class, funds holding longer-term maturities often offer a better yield, but are also riskier.

Bond funds do not have the same risk and return characteristics as the underlying bonds themselves. With bond funds, default risk is minimized through the portfolio effect. The default of a single bond issue has only a small impact on the value of a fund that contains many different bond issues. Perhaps this partly explains the popularity of junk bond funds, which specialize in low-rated, high-yielding corporate bonds.

Interest rate risk manifests itself differently for bond funds than it does for investments in individual bonds. With individual bonds, an investor can be guaranteed a particular series of cash flows (and thus, a particular level of yield) simply by holding the bond until maturity. Even though interest rates may rise or fall, the investor can lock in a level of current income. Bond funds, however, do not provide this assurance. Their net asset value rises and falls on a daily basis, and since, as portfolios of bonds, they have no single maturity date, each bond fund investor is faced with an uncertain cash flow at redemption. Also, the current yield of the fund will change as the fund manager reinvests the principal from maturing bonds or from bonds that are sold before maturity. This means that all cash flows generated by bond funds are uncertain at the time of purchase. Unlike single bond investments, both the yield of a bond fund and the cash flows at redemption are unknown.

A special word of caution applies to GNMA funds. These funds specialize in securities that are backed by GNMA insured mortgages. Most of these mortgages represent long-term, fixed-rate obligations that are prepayable at the option of the borrower. As GNMA bond investors have found out in recent years, during periods of falling interest rates, when most bond investors enjoy an appreciation in the market value of their holdings, a significant proportion of GNMA mortgages have been refinanced at new, lower interest rates. Rather than appreciating in value, the mortgage-backed securities are simply redeemed.

MONEY MARKET FUNDS

Money market funds specialize in short-term securities, usually maturing in 90 days or less. Examples are negotiable certificates of deposit (CDs), U.S. Treasury or government agency securities, Eurodollar deposits, bankers' acceptances, and repurchase agreements negotiated with commercial banks. A proxy for the risk of a money market fund is the average maturity of the fund's portfolio. This maturity, along with the current yield for the fund, is listed in *Barron's* money market fund quotations. Average maturities for most funds fluctuate with market conditions, but usually stay in a range of 30 to 55 days.

Money market funds often provide lower yields than bond funds, but have less interest rate risk. Securities with an average maturity of only a few weeks simply do not fluctuate in value like the longer-term securities found in bond funds. Traditionally, fund yields have been comparable to the yields of CDs from commercial banks, and banks compete with the funds for deposit dollars. While bank CDs offer the advantage of federal deposit insurance, money market funds offer the convenience of withdrawal at any time and do not assess a penalty if funds are withdrawn before a certain minimum time period.

ASSET ALLOCATION FUNDS

Asset allocation funds are mutual funds that maintain holdings in a wide variety of investments, including equities, bonds, real estate, foreign securities, and precious metals. As such, they offer important diversification potential beyond that of even the most well-diversified stock and bond portfolios. For example, from 1966 through 1987, a highly diversified portfolio of investments grew faster than the S&P 500 Index, and the variability of the diversified portfolio was less than half that of the S&P 500 Index.[3] Thus, the portfolio provided investors with both increased returns and lower risk.

Perhaps the acid test for these funds came on October 19, 1987, during the largest single-day market drop in history. On that day, when the Dow fell by more than 23%, none of the asset allocation funds lost more than 9%. A list of selected asset allocation funds, along with their portfolio composition, is given in Table 22-2.

[3]Andrew Evan Serwer, "Spreading Your Wealth Around," *Fortune,* June 20, 1988, pp. 109–110.

|||| **TABLE 22-2**
Asset Allocation Funds

	Proportion of Assets in				
	Stocks	Bonds	Real Estate	Precious Metals	Cash
Blanchard Strategic Growth	43%	11%	0%	12%	34%
BBK Diversa	34	37	6	6	17
USAA Cornerstone	40	15	20	20	5
Permanent Portfolio	22	20	8	25	25

SOURCE: *Fortune,* June 20, 1988, p. 109.

CLOSED-END FUNDS

As mentioned earlier, closed-end funds operate with a fixed number of shares. Consequently, their investment capital is fixed, and the fund manager is free from the worry of having to generate cash to meet unanticipated share redemptions.

At the present time, *Barron's* provides weekly quotations on approximately 112 publicly traded closed-end funds. These include 22 diversified common stock funds, 45 specialized equity and convertible funds, and about 24 bond funds. Three-fourths of the bond funds are selling at a premium over the net asset value, and approximately 80% of the common stock and specialized equity and convertible funds are selling at a discount. Since the premiums and discounts change over time, an investor's return may be either greater or smaller than the return on the investment company's portfolio. *Barron's* and the *Wall Street Journal* list closed-end funds and their current premiums or discounts.

CLOSED-END BOND FUNDS

The stated goals of the various closed-end funds differ widely. Even among the bond funds, some have more aggressive policies than others. Among the tactics used by aggressive funds are short-term trading for capital gains, lending debt securities to brokers in return for cash collateral that is invested by the fund to earn income (the fund also receives the income from the loaned securities), and borrowing from commercial banks to leverage the fund's investments. Most bond funds are more conservative. The goal of the John Hancock Trust, for example, is to earn interest income, with capital appreciation as an additional consideration. It does not engage in leveraging or short-term trading to improve the yield. In spite of the differences in investment policies, however, betas for bond funds (as estimated by Value Line) all lie within a narrow range of 0.55 to 0.65.

Bond funds provide a convenient means of acquiring an interest in a diversified portfolio composed primarily of fixed-income securities. The premiums for most bond funds indicate that investors either expect the funds to earn higher rates of return than the investors themselves could earn on portfolios of comparable risk, or that they are willing to pay something for the diversification that would be difficult for many investors to attain by investing directly.

CLOSED-END COMMON STOCK FUNDS

Most closed-end common stock funds sell at a discount much of the time. There is no simple explanation as to why closed-end common stock funds sell at a discount from net asset value when mutual funds sell at prices equal to their net asset values (or net asset value plus a load charge, in the case of load funds).

Some observers believe that the discounts reflect a lack of interest by brokers in selling shares in closed-end funds when they can earn much higher commissions by selling shares in load funds. A second possibility is that investors discount closed-end shares because of the taxes the investment company will have to pay on the sale of any assets that have appreciated in value since the time of purchase. It is possible, too, that the discounts reflect investor opinion that the funds will not perform very well in the future. The discounts for closed-end stock funds have changed considerably over time.

Some enterprising individuals have profited from the discounted prices of closed-end investment company shares by converting a number of these companies into open-end funds. After conversion, the shares of the fund can be sold for full net asset value, providing a quick profit equal to the size of the original closed-end fund discount. From 1962 through 1982, the shareholders of 15 closed-end funds that were selling at an average discount of 24% voted either to liquidate or convert the company into an open-end fund, usually at a significant gain for the shareholders.[4] A recent closed-end fund conversion attempt by Tom Pickens, the son of T. Boone Pickens, is chronicled in the Sidelight.

Closed-End Specialized Equity and Convertible Funds

Specialized funds usually invest either in the shares of companies in a single industry or cluster of industries (e.g., ASA, which invests in South African gold mining stock, and the Petroleum and Resources Fund, which invests in oil and other natural resource stocks) or in foreign companies, as in the case of the Korea Fund. The 21.50% discount for the stock of ASA in Table 22-3 no doubt reflects widespread pessimism about the

[4]James A. Brickley and James S. Schallheim, "Lifting the Lid on Closed-End Investment Companies: A Case of Abnormal Returns," *Journal of Financial and Quantitative Analysis* (March 1985): 107–17.

||| SIDELIGHT

Leave It to T. Boone's Son to Sniff Out a Bargain: Pickens III Is Heating Up the Race for "Closed-End" Funds

His famous father has earned tens of millions raiding Big Oil's behemoths to unlock cheap energy assets. And as far as T. Boone Pickens III is concerned, "You do what you learn while you're growing up." His bargain-priced target: Japan Fund, Inc., a venerable investment company whose shares have sold for about 20% below book value lately.

Pickens, a Dallas-based private investor, and several New York partners disclosed on March 2 that they have bought 5.5% of Japan Fund's shares and want to take over the company for about $525 million. Such an attack on a closed-end investment company has been a rarity. But it may not be for long: A new breed of raiders may have discovered a way to buy company assets on the cheap.

SOURCE: *Business Week*, March 16, 1987, p. 113. Reprinted by permission of *Business Week*.

future of the South African government and the poor outlook for private industry in that country. The 79.53% premium for the shares of the Korea Fund may have reflected three things: (1) a belief that the stocks held by the fund were undervalued in South Korea; (2) an expectation that the South Korean currency (the won) would increase in value relative to the U.S. dollar; and (3) an extraordinary demand for shares of the fund because they were the only means by which investors in the United States could acquire an interest in South Korean stocks.

DUAL-PURPOSE FUNDS

Dual-purpose funds are special closed-end funds that offer two kinds of shares to the investing public: income shares for those who prefer current income over capital gains and capital shares for those who prefer long-term capital gains over current income. The stock issue consists of equal, or approximately equal, amounts of income shares and capital shares. The income shares are similar to cumulative preferred stock in that they offer the holders a guaranteed minimum yield. The income shareholders receive all of the dividend and interest income, net of expenses, and also participate in any capital appreciation necessary to bring the dividends up to the minimum level specified by the fund.

Dual-purpose funds have a limited life—usually only 10 to 15 years. At the end of that time, the income shareholders are paid a specified amount for their stock, plus any dividends that may be in arrears. The shareholders then decide whether to liquidate the company or convert it into a mutual fund. If the fund is converted, the capital shareholders become the initial shareholders in the new mutual fund. If not, they receive a distribution from the liquidated value of the portfolio.

The several dual-purpose funds that were created in the 1960s have all matured. Two newer funds—Gemini II and Quest Value (shown in Table 22-3)—are currently quoted in *Barron's* weekly report on publicly traded closed-end funds. The premiums for Gemini II Income and Quest Value Income indicate that the expected dividends on those shares provide a much higher return on the net asset values than the expected rates of return on other investments of comparable risk. The capital shares were selling at a discount because investors apparently judged the present

|||| **TABLE 22-3**

Selected Dual Purpose Funds

	Net Asset Value	Market Value	Premium (+) or Discount (−) from NAV
Gemini II—Capital	$16.25	$13.25	−18.46%
Gemini II—Income	9.52	13.00	+36.55%
Quest Value—Capital	19.81	14.25	−28.07%
Quest Value—Income	11.68	13.50	+15.58%

SOURCE: *Barron's,* June 10, 1991

value of the expected future payments from these shares to be less than their current net asset value. The anticipated cash payments to the capital shareholders are discounted over a longer period and—because of greater risk—probably at a higher rate than the payments to the income shareholders.

|||| UNIT INVESTMENT TRUSTS

A unit investment trust is a fixed portfolio of securities that is created for a finite life. Investors purchase shares, called units, in these portfolios and receive periodic income plus a final liquidation payment when the trust is terminated. The trusts are created by brokerage firms, bond dealers, and investment banking firms, who transfer a large package of securities (usually from 10 to 30 different newly issued bonds) to the trust department of a bank in exchange for units, which are sold to investors. The creator of the trust receives a fee of about 2% on the transfer of the securities to the trust and an additional 3% to 5% for selling the units.

Unit trusts are essentially unmanaged portfolios, which means no securities are bought or sold during the life of the trust. The sponsors usually have authority to sell any bonds whose default ratings fall below certain predefined levels. All cash receipts of the trust, other than amounts needed to cover expenses, must be distributed to the holders of the units. The sponsors have no authority to purchase any additional securities for the trust.

Unit trusts are classified in one of three categories. Tax-exempt trusts hold state and local government securities. Corporate income trusts hold corporate bonds, preferred stocks, mortgage-backed securities, and high dividend yield stocks. Government securities trusts hold GNMA mortgage-backed securities. The tax-exempt trusts have been extremely popular. Several sponsors have created trusts that hold the bonds of a single state. Income from these bonds is exempt from state and local taxes for residents of that state, as well as the federal income tax.

The minimum investment in a unit trust varies from $1,000 to $5,000, and the maturities range from 3 to 30 years. In some trusts the bonds mature gradually, while in others all of the bonds mature about the same time. The trustee collects all interest and principal payments and distributes the cash at regular intervals—usually monthly—to the holders of the units.

Most sponsors of unit investment trusts make a secondary market for the units they have created. This makes it easy for investors to liquidate their units before the trust is terminated, and it makes units in older trusts available to investors. The trust assets are monitored daily by agencies such as Standard & Poor's, and this evaluation becomes the basis for the sponsor's bid and asked prices. Some sponsors redeem shares at the asked price, but most redeem at the bid price, which is usually about a 2% discount.

The principal competitors of tax-exempt unit trusts are tax-exempt mutual funds, particularly no-load funds, which can be purchased without paying a sales commission. Unit trusts have the advantage of lower annual expenses (usually less than 0.2% compared to about 0.7% for tax-exempt mutual funds). However, they usually have an initial sales charge of 4% or 5%. Also, if the units are redeemed before maturity, the investor must pay a supplemental charge of approximately 2%. Unless the units are held to maturity, investing in a unit investment trust is usually more expensive than investing in a no-load fund due to the high initial charges.

When choosing between a tax-exempt unit investment trust and a tax-exempt no-load mutual fund or between different trusts, an investor will focus on differences in the expected returns and estimated risks. A trust or mutual fund that appears to offer an unusually attractive yield may hold bonds with high credit risk or bonds with high coupon rates that are likely to be called at an early date. Many tax-exempt trusts are composed entirely of insured bonds. This reduces the risk but also reduces the rate of return by one-fourth to one-half a percentage point.

|||| MUTUAL FUND PERFORMANCE

Should an investor expect to attain better results than the market average by investing in a mutual fund? There is a widely shared belief—or hope—that some mutual fund managers are able to assemble portfolios that consistently outperform the market through superior stock selection, or extraordinary market timing, or both. A number of studies, however, have questioned fund performance superiority. The following are the major questions these studies have addressed:

1. When a proper allowance is made for the difference in risk, have common stock funds, as a whole, outperformed the market?

2. Does the past performance of a fund provide a good basis for predicting its future performance?

3. Are differences in the returns among mutual funds positively related to differences in systematic risk?

4. Do the risk and returns of mutual funds correspond to their stated objectives?

5. Have common stock mutual funds diversified their holdings widely enough to eliminate most of the unsystematic risk?

6. Is mutual fund performance related to the amount of the sales commission, the expense ratio, or the size of the fund?

This section reviews mutual fund performance and the findings regarding these questions.

RATES OF RETURN

A variety of studies have examined mutual fund performance. One of the earliest, which has since become a classic, was published by William F. Sharpe in the *Journal of Business*.[5] The 34 funds in his sample had an average Sharpe index score of 0.663, while the Sharpe index score for the Dow Jones Industrial Average during the same period was 0.667. The lower value indicates inferior fund performance relative to the market average.[6] Sharpe also examined gross fund performance by measuring fund returns before deduction of load charges, management fees, and other expenses that the investor must pay. In his sample, 19 of the 34 funds outperformed the market on a gross performance basis. But, on average, the funds were not able to provide investors with better performance than the Dow Jones Industrial Average.

Relationships between fund performance and several other variables were examined. Not surprisingly, the funds with the lowest expense ratios tended to exhibit stronger performance; thus, funds that pay higher fees to management generally do not gain enough in extra returns to offset their increased charges. Also, fund size was found to be only marginally related to performance, with some tendency for the larger funds to outperform the smaller. Perhaps the size factor found in this study is a carryover from the expense ratio factor. Larger funds often have lower expense ratios when expenses are measured as a percentage of total fund assets.

Michael Jensen found similar results.[7] In his sample of 115 funds, the average fund underperformed the market by approximately 1.1 percentage points when fund expenses were deducted from returns. The average performance improved, but was still negative, when expenses were added back into returns. Thus, even though Jensen's methodology was entirely different, his conclusions were the same as Sharpe's.

Other studies have reached the same conclusion as Sharpe and Jensen. Notable among these is one by Chang and Lewellen.[8] They developed an approach based on the arbitrage pricing theory and found that the average fund did not outperform a simple buy-and-hold strategy with a portfolio equivalent to the market index. In their sample, only 2 of 67 funds exhibited statistically significant superior performance, and from 11 to 30 of the 67 funds had significantly worse performance, depending upon the method used to estimate risk.

Thus, there is strong evidence that mutual funds as a group do not outperform the market on a sustained basis. Other studies have examined fund performance in more detail. We turn our attention to them now.

[5]William F. Sharpe, "Mutual Fund Performance," *Journal of Business* (January 1966): 119–38.

[6]The Sharpe index, along with other measures of portfolio performance, was reviewed in Chapter 21.

[7]Michael C. Jensen, "The Performance of Mutual Funds in the Period 1945–1964," *The Journal of Finance* (May 1968): 389–416.

[8]E. C. Chang and Wilbur G. Lewellen, "An Arbitrage Pricing Approach to Evaluating Mutual Fund Performance," *Journal of Financial Research* (Spring 1985): 15–30.

PERFORMANCE CONSISTENCY

While funds as a group have exhibited no tendency to outperform the market, almost every study has found a few mutual funds with significant performance superiority. A question for investors, then, is the consistency of that performance superiority. More specifically, do the funds that outperform the market in one period show a tendency to continue their performance superiority in subsequent periods? If they do, the process of selecting a fund for investment purposes would be greatly simplified!

Sharpe conducted one of the first tests of performance consistency.[9] He found the correlation between fund performance rankings in consecutive four-year periods was +0.36, indicating a significant tendency for fund performance rankings to repeat themselves. However, when he tested consistency with consecutive two-year intervals, the correlation fell dramatically.

Robert Carlson tested performance consistency in 10-year and 5-year intervals.[10] He found no significant difference in fund performance rankings when performance was measured over consecutive 10-year intervals, but only about half of the 5-year intervals in his study showed performance consistency.

Jensen studied performance consistency relative to the market rather than relative to other funds.[11] Using consecutive 10-year intervals, he found that the funds that outperformed the market in one period were likely to continue to exhibit their performance superiority in the subsequent period. However, further analysis indicated that most of the performance consistency was attributable to the consistency of funds with inferior performance.

Robert Klemkosky also studied fund performance and found that the measurement interval was an important variable in performance consistency.[12] When consecutive four-year intervals were used, he found a significant correlation between fund performance rankings. When consecutive two-year intervals were examined, the correlations were positive, but not significantly different from zero.

Thus, a substantial body of evidence indicates that past fund performance can be of some help in predicting future performance, but only when the holding period is at least four to five years. This means that not only does historical performance have to be measured with an interval of this length, but that the investor's expected holding period must be at least four to five years. Also, the relationship between past and future performance is far from perfect. Although selecting a mutual fund on the basis of past performance may improve the odds, it will not lead to a "sure bet."

[9]Sharpe, "Mutual Fund Performance."

[10]Robert S. Carlson, "Aggregate Performance of Mutual Funds, 1948–1967," *Journal of Financial and Quantitative Analysis* (March 1970): 1–31.

[11]Jensen, "The Performance of Mutual Funds in the Period 1945–1964."

[12]Robert C. Klemkosky, "How Consistently Do Managers Manage?" *Journal of Portfolio Management* (Winter 1977): 11–15.

MARKET TIMING AND SECURITY SELECTION

Fama has defined market timing as the ability of the fund manager to adjust beta to changing market conditions. Selectivity refers to the ability of the fund manager to pick stocks with above-average returns, given their level of risk.[13] The evidence regarding timing and selectivity of mutual funds is mixed.

Fabozzi and Francis studied the market timing activities of a sample of 85 funds.[14] They found that, in general, fund betas do not shift with market conditions. In the few cases where they did, the results were generally "perverse," meaning that the shifts hurt the fund's returns.

Why don't managers attempt to time the market? Fabozzi and Francis suggest three possibilities. First, betas for individual stocks are known to be rather unstable. A manager desiring to increase fund beta may purchase a stock with a historical beta of, say, 1.5, only to find the stock's beta slips to 0.7 while held by the fund. Second, managers may not be able to forecast market conditions with any level of certainty and thus may be unwilling to shift the risk of their fund. Third, the costs of changing the fund's beta may be high relative to the level of rewards that can be obtained.

Alexander and Stover examined market timing activities for a sample of 49 mutual funds.[15] They found the average fund *lowered* its beta by a value of 0.003 during bull markets. Only three funds in their sample had beta movements significantly different from zero, and two of these three lowered betas during bull markets. With a sample of 49 funds and a significance level of 5%, these results could be attributable to chance.

One way that a mutual fund can increase its beta is by increasing the proportion of its assets invested in equities and decreasing the proportion invested in fixed-income securities. Ferri, Oberhelman, and Roenfeldt used a methodology that was sensitive to these portfolio changes to determine if fund managers used timing strategies.[16] They found that only 4 of the 69 funds in their sample made significant portfolio changes in anticipation of a market movement: thus, there was little evidence of successful timing ability.

Stanley Kon developed a switching regression technique to examine market timing and security selection ability.[17] He found evidence of superior market timing performance for some funds, but not for the group as a whole. He also found that 23 of 37 funds exhibited superior selectivity. His study stands alone in this finding. Other studies have found little

---

[13]Both timing and selectivity were discussed in more detail in Chapter 21.

[14]Frank Fabozzi and Jack C. Francis, "Mutual Fund Systematic Risk for Bull and Bear Markets: An Empirical Examination," *The Journal of Finance* (December 1979): 1243–50.

[15]Gordon J. Alexander and Roger D. Stover, "Consistency of Mutual Fund Performance during Varying Market Conditions," *Journal of Economics and Business* (Spring 1980): 219–25.

[16]M. G. Ferri, H. D. Oberhelman, and R. L. Roenfeldt, "Market Timing and Mutual Fund Portfolio Performance," *Journal of Financial Research* (Summer 1984): 143–50.

[17]Stanley J. Kon, "The Market-Timing Performance of Mutual Fund Managers," *Journal of Business* 56 (1983): 323–47.

evidence of successful timing ability. Furthermore, their results showed a negative correlation between market timing ability and security selection.[18]

What can we conclude regarding mutual fund performance? First, they cannot, as a group, generate risk-adjusted performance that is better than the market as a whole. Second, historical performance is of little value in predicting future results, unless the measurement period is at least four to five years. Third, given these results, investors may be better off selecting funds with low fees and expense ratios, as they have had a tendency toward superior performance. Fourth, the relationship between fund size and performance is weak, but larger funds have shown a slight tendency to outperform smaller ones. Fifth, there is little evidence that fund managers engage in market timing.

|||| **SUMMARY**

This chapter has described three types of investment companies: mutual funds, closed-end investment companies, and unit investment trusts. Mutual funds are by far the most important of these in terms of aggregate assets. They are classified into three groups with respect to the initial sales charge: load funds, no-load funds, and low-load funds. Load funds are distributed by brokerage firms, banks, insurance companies, financial planners, and others for a sales charge of up to 8½%. No-load funds are offered to investors by the funds themselves, largely through the mail or by telephone, and there is no sales charge. Low-load funds are simply load funds with a small sales charge, usually ranging from 3% to 5%.

Mutual funds are also classified by their investment policies. The broad classifications include common stock funds, balanced funds (common stocks and fixed-income securities), bond funds (both taxable and tax-exempt), and money market funds.

Mutual fund performance varies widely from one fund to another, and past performance is a far from perfect indicator of future performance. However, it does seem that poor performers have a tendency to continue to perform poorly. Also, funds that have performed well for a period of four or five years often perform well over the next four- or five-year period.

In selecting a mutual fund, investors should consider not only their past performance, but their investment policies, expense ratios, and past and future management. Expense ratios vary widely, and there is no indication that a higher expense ratio leads to better performance.

A closed-end investment company is one that makes an initial stock issue, and usually none thereafter. The shares are then traded on the stock exchanges and in the over-the-counter market like any other stock.

---

[18]Eric C. Chang and Wilbur G. Lewellen, "Market Timing and Mutual Fund Investment Performance," *Journal of Business* (January 1984): 57–72; Roy D. Henrikkson, "Market Timing and Mutual Fund Performance: An Empirical Investigation," *Journal of Business* (January 1984): 73–96.

Shares of closed-end common stock funds often sell at a discount from the net asset value.

A unit investment trust is a form of investment company that is created when a securities firm puts a large portfolio of bonds in a trust with a bank and issues shares (called units) to the investing public. The trust has a limited life, no shares are issued after the initial offering, and all or most of the initial bond portfolio is held until the trust is terminated and the assets are distributed.

||| QUESTIONS

1. What are the differences between a closed-end fund and an open-end fund?

2. What is a unit investment trust? How does it differ from a mutual fund?

3. What reasons are suggested for the discounts on closed-end funds?

4. How do shareholders of a closed-end fund profit from the fund's conversion to an open-end fund?

5. What is a dual-purpose fund? What are the features of the two classes of stock in a dual-purpose fund? What typically happens upon maturity?

6. What are 12b–1 charges, and what impact do they have on fund returns?

7. What conclusions can be drawn regarding the stability of fund performance? What are the implications for investment decision making?

8. What relationship exists between a fund's charges to investors and its performance? Are funds with high charges able to use this revenue to support additional security research that enables the funds to generate superior returns?

9. What is meant by market timing? Do most funds engage in this activity? For those that do, what is their likelihood of success?

10. Under what circumstances are the shares of a sector fund likely to be a wise investment? Are these funds well diversified?

11. What investment goals are compatible with investing in index funds? Is this type of investment an aggressive or defensive strategy?

12. On the whole mutual funds do not offer higher returns than a passive buy-and-hold strategy involving the market index. Nevertheless, they have grown in popularity in recent years. Explain some of the possible reasons for this growth.

||| PROBLEMS

1. You have $10,000 to invest. You select a load fund with an 8.5% front-end load. The fund has annual management fees and other expenses of 0.9%, and its net asset value is $20 per share.

    a. How much of your initial principal is actually invested in shares of the fund? How many shares does this amount purchase?

    b. At the end of the first year, the fund pays a dividend of $1.50 per share, which you have asked to be reinvested in the shares of the fund. The securities in its portfolio earn 10% before expenses. What is the total value of your holdings at the end of one year? How many shares do you own at this time? What rate of return would you earn if you sold now?

    c. Assume that at the end of the second year, the fund's net asset value is $21, its dividend distributions for the year are $2 per share (again, these are reinvested at the end of the year), and the management fees and load charges are the same as before. You sell at the end of the second year. What proceeds do you realize from the sale? What has been your realized annual return over the two-year period?

2. You are considering a $5,000 investment in one of three competing mutual funds.

    ■ Fund A is a no-load fund with an annual management fee of 1% and a 12b–1 fee of 1%.

    ■ Fund B is a low-load fund with a front-end load of 3%, a management fee of 0.5% per year, and 12b–1 fees of 1% for the first year, 0.5% for the second, and 0.0% for the third year and thereafter.

    ■ Fund C is a load fund with an 8.5% front-end load and management fees of 0.35% per year.

    If you expect all three funds to earn 10% per year before expenses, and you plan on holding your investment for a period of 10 years, which fund would generate the maximum wealth over your anticipated holding period?

||| SELECTED REFERENCES

Brauer, Gregory A. "Closed-End Fund Shares Abnormal Returns and the Information Content of Discounts and Premiums." *The Journal of Finance* 43 (1988): 113–27.

Brickley, James A., and James S. Schallheim. "Lifting the Lid on Closed-End Investment Companies: A Case of Abnormal Returns." *Journal of Financial and Quantitative Analysis* (March 1985): 107–17.

Golec, Joseph H. "Do Mutual Fund Managers Who Use Incentive Compensation Outperform Those Who Don't?" *Financial Analysts Journal* 44 (1988): 75–79.

Investment Companies. Boston, Mass.: Arthur Weisenberger Services, Inc., annual editions.

Lechman, Bruce N., and David M. Modest. "Mutual Fund Performance Evaluations: A Comparison of Benchmarks and Benchmark Comparisons." *The Journal of Finance* 42 (1987): 233–65.

Perold, Andre, and William F. Sharpe. "Dynamic Strategies for Asset Allocation." *Financial Analysts Journal* 44 (1988): 16–27.

Perritt, Gerald W. "'All Weather' Protection Using Asset Allocation." and "Allocation Approach Seeks Lower Risk, Steady Returns." *AAII Journal* (July 1988).

Veit, E. T., and J. M. Cheney. "Managing Investment Portfolios: A Survey of Mutual Funds." *The Financial Review* (November 1984): 321–38.

23 INTERNATIONAL INVESTING

For many years, the New York Stock Exchange was the world's largest stock market. Today, however, the Tokyo Stock Exchange holds that title. The total value of equities traded on the Tokyo Exchange in 1989 was $2,366.8 billion, more than 50% greater than the $1,542.8 billion traded on the NYSE that same year.[1] The InterSec Research Corporation estimates that U.S. pension funds will hold $180 billion in foreign investments by 1994, up from only $10.8 billion as recently as 1983.[2] The number of foreign stocks listed on the New York Stock Exchange more than tripled during the 1980's.[3] The number of internationally diversified mutual funds available to U.S. investors has increased rapidly in recent years. All this evidence points to the fact that, now more than ever before, U.S. investors are looking worldwide for investment opportunities.

Why are foreign stocks receiving all this attention? The answer is simple: they provide the potential for both increased returns and lower risks. In recent years, their returns in dollars have been magnified by the declining value of the dollar relative to most foreign currencies. At the same time, the low covariance of returns with most domestic securities make these stocks excellent diversification candidates in a portfolio of domestic stocks.

This chapter will examine the opportunities for international diversification currently available to U.S. investors. International diversification requires some knowledge of capital markets overseas as well as the types of securities available, the risks of these securities, and the returns they have generated in recent years.

WORLDWIDE CAPITAL MARKETS

Organized stock exchanges are found on every continent, as shown in Table 23-1. By far the largest, in terms of the market values of listed securities, are Japan and the United States, which were 39% and 31% of

---

[1] *The Business One Irwin Business and Investment Almanac (1991 edition)* edited by Sumner N. Levine (Business One Irwin, Homewood, Illinois, 1991).

[2] *The Guide to International Capital Markets (1990 edition)* edited by Bryan de Caires (Euromoney Publications PLC, London, 1990). Exhibit 22.2.

[3] *Dow-Jones Business and Investment Almanac* (Homewood, Illinois, Dow-Jones Irwin Inc., various editions).

|||| **TABLE 23-1**
Market Capitalization of Selected Stock Markets

	Total Capital ($ Millions)
ASIA AND AUSTRALIA	
Australia	$ 136,626
Hong Kong	77,496
Japan	4,392,597
New Zealand	13,487
Singapore	35,925
Total: Asia and Australia	$ 4,656,131
EUROPE	
Austria	22,261
Belgium	291,328
Denmark	40,152
Finland	30,652
France	364,841
Germany	365,176
Italy	169,417
Luxembourg	79,979
Netherlands	157,789
Norway	25,285
Spain	122,652
Sweden	119,285
Switzerland	104,239
United Kingdom	826,598
Total: Europe	$ 2,719,654
WESTERN HEMISPHERE	
Canada	291,328
United States	3,505,686
Total: Western Hemisphere	$ 3,797,014
OTHER	
Israel	8,227
South Africa	131,059
Total: Other	$ 139,286
WORLD	
Total	$11,312,085

SOURCE: *Emerging Stock Markets Fact Book* (1990 edition) International Finance Corporation, Washington, D.C., 1990.

the world total, respectively. The markets in Europe accounted for another 24%, and the rest of the world 6%.

INSTITUTIONAL BARRIERS

Evidence of the increasing globalization of security trading can be found in almost all of the world's equity markets. Major U.S. securities firms such as Merrill Lynch, Morgan Stanley, and Goldman, Sachs have pur-

|||| **FIGURE 23-1**
Growth of International Investing

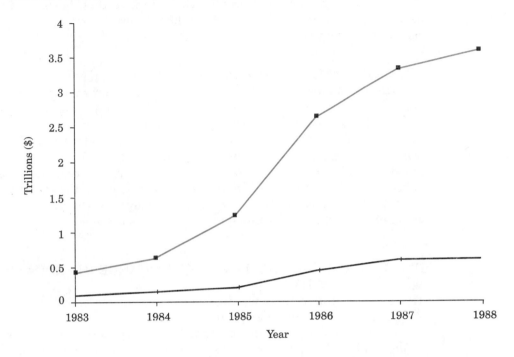

■ Foreign purchases of U.S. securities
+ U.S. purchases of foreign securities

SOURCE: *Treasury Bulletin,* various issues (Treasury Department, Washington, D.C.).

chased seats on the Tokyo Stock Exchange. On the London exchange, more than 40 large institutional traders, including nearly all the major U.S. banks and brokerage houses, have allied themselves with local trading firms.

U.S. firms are utilizing international *syndicates* to market new issues of capital. International syndication is advantageous to the issuer of new stock simply because it provides ready access to a larger pool of potential customers, thereby increasing the probability that the new issue will be successful. Along with international syndication of new capital has come a growing tendency for major international firms to be listed on exchanges outside their home country. All these factors serve to increase the availability of foreign equities to domestic investors. However, there are still significant barriers to the issuance and trading of securities internationally. For example, listing requirements on a number of exchanges are difficult to meet, and disclosure rules are not standardized.

|||| # RATIONALE FOR INVESTING OVERSEAS

"There's no such thing as a free lunch." For investors, however, international portfolio diversification comes close. It has the potential to reduce risk and increase returns.

THE POTENTIAL FOR HIGHER RETURNS

Investors who placed their funds in foreign stocks prospered during the last half of the 1980s, as shown in Table 23-2. To a large degree, this resulted from the decline in the value of the dollar relative to most foreign currencies. Table 23-3 shows the value of the dollar relative to 12 of the world's major currencies at five-year intervals from 1970 to 1990. When the dollar falls in value, overseas investments profit from the greater number of dollars that the U.S. investor receives when the investments are sold. Of course, exchange rates can move against the investor if the value of the dollar rises while foreign securities are held.

EXAMPLE 23-1   BENEFITING FROM A CHANGE IN EXCHANGE RATES

This example illustrates how a decline in the value of the dollar increases the dollar return from a foreign investment.

Table 23-4 lists the price of Komatsu, a Japanese industrial stock traded on the Tokyo Exchange, as of October 1987 and May 1988. Let's see what return a U.S. investor would have earned if he or she had purchased 100 shares of Komatsu in Tokyo in October 1987 and sold them the following May.

|||| **TABLE 23-2**

Returns From the World's Major Equity Markets (March, 1990)

Market	Return in Local Currency		Return in U.S. Dollars	
	One Year	Five Year	One Year	Five Year
New York	15.30%	13.50%	15.30%	13.50%
Tokyo	−9.80%	17.40%	−24.40%	28.60%
London	3.60%	12.90%	1.10%	19.30%
Toronto	6.90%	4.60%	3.70%	10.20%
Frankfurt	45.90%	15.30%	63.40%	29.70%
Sydney	5.30%	13.10%	−3.30%	14.70%
Paris	10.20%	19.10%	23.80%	31.40%
Zurich	13.50%	12.40%	25.90%	25.30%
Hong Kong	−0.20%	16.80%	−0.50%	16.70%
Milan	12.40%	20.30%	25.30%	31.60%
Singapore	24.20%	12.60%	28.60%	16.10%

Note: Returns are calculated as price appreciation only (dividends excluded). Five year data are shown in annual compound rate.

SOURCE: *Tokyo Stock Market Quarterly Review* (New York: Diawa Securities Co. Ltd.), 2, (March 31, 1990).

|||| **TABLE 23-3**

Value of the Dollar Relative to 12 Major Foreign Currencies

Nation and Currency	1970	1975	1980	1985	1990
Canada (dollar)	1.01	1.02	1.17	1.37	1.17
Taiwan (dollar)	40.05	38.00	36.02	39.89	27.41
France (franc)	5.52	4.29	4.23	8.98	5.57
Hong Kong (dollar)	6.06	4.94	4.23	7.79	7.79
India (rupee)	7.58	8.41	7.89	12.33	17.42
Italy (lira)	623.00	653.09	856.20	1,908.90	1,236.23
Japan (yen)	357.60	296.78	226.63	238.47	153.76
South Africa (rand)	139.24	136.47	128.54	45.57	2.66
South Korea (won)	310.57	484.00	607.43	861.89	718.03
Switzerland (franc)	4.32	2.58	1.68	2.46	1.43
United Kingdom (pound)	239.59	222.16	232.43	129.74	170.86
West Germany/Germany (deutsche mark)	3.65	2.46	1.82	2.94	1.68

Note: All figures are given in national currency units per dollar, except South Africa and the United Kingdom, whose values are in U.S. cents per unit of foreign currency.

SOURCE: *Federal Reserve Bulletin,* various issues.

The cost of the 100 shares in yen was Y73,000, and with a dollar-yen exchange rate of .007054, the cost in dollars was $514.94.

$$Y73,000 \times .007054 = \$514.94$$

By the time the stock was sold, in May 1988, the price of Komatsu had risen 50 yen per share, or to 78,000 yen for 100 shares. The investor's holding period return in terms of yen was 6.85%.

$$(Y78,000 - Y73,000)/Y73,000 = 0.0685$$

To find the return in terms of dollars, an adjustment must be made for the change in the exchange rate. This can be done with the following equation, in which x represents the percentage increase in the dollar value of the yen.

$$R = (1 + x)(1 + \text{HPR}) - 1 \qquad (23\text{-}1)$$

where

$$x = (.008043 - .007054)/.007054, \text{ or } 14.02\%.$$

|||| **TABLE 23-4**

Price and Exchange Rate Data for Komatsu

Item	October 1987	May 1988
Price of Komatsu on Tokyo Exchange	Y730	Y780
Exchange rate, yen per dollar	141.77	124.33
Exchange rate, dollars per yen (reciprocal of above)	.007054	.008043

SOURCE: *Wall Street Journal,* various issues.

Thus, the total return in dollars was 21.83%.

$$R = (1.1402)(1.0685) - 1 = 21.83\%$$

The decrease in the yen value of the dollar (or, increase in the dollar value of the yen) transformed a yen return of 6.85% into a dollar return of 21.83.%||||

THE RISK REDUCTION POTENTIAL

The variance, or risk, of a portfolio of securities depends in part on the correlation, or covariance, of the returns of the securities within the portfolio. The formula for the variance of a two-security portfolio is

$$\sigma_p^2 = w_x v_{x\,+} w_y v_y + 2w_x w_y c_{xy}$$

where

σ_p^2 = variance of portfolio returns

w_x = proportion of the total portfolio value invested in security x

v_x = variance of returns of security x

c_{xy} = covariance of returns for x and y

The lower the covariance of returns, the lower the resulting portfolio variance.

Foreign stocks generally exhibit a lower correlation of returns with the U.S. market than do domestic stocks. Thus, one of the principal benefits of these securities is their ability to reduce risk when combined into portfolios with domestic securities. Table 23-5 lists the correlations of returns between several foreign market indexes and the S&P 500. The correlations of the S&P 500 with foreign markets are much lower than among domestic market indexes, which are usually 0.85 or higher.

|||| INTERNATIONAL ASSET PRICING

The principles underlying the capital asset pricing model (CAPM) and the definitions of systematic and non-systematic risk also apply to the pricing of international equities. The application of these principles to international asset pricing depends on the degree to which the markets are integrated.

INTEGRATED CAPITAL MARKETS

As we noted earlier, in integrated capital markets, investment capital flows freely across national borders. With integrated markets worldwide, all assets would be priced relative to a common international market factor, as follows:

|||| **TABLE 23-5**

Correlations Between Selected Equity Markets (Five Year Period Ending December, 1987)

	(1)	(2)	(3)	(4)	(5)	(6)	(7)	(8)	(9)
1. United States	.07	.02	.07	.26	.30	.31	.09	−.08	
2. Japan		.00	.01	.04	−.02	.14	−.06	.11	
3. Argentina			.15	−.03	−.02	.11	.01	.06	
4. Brazil				−.28	.01	−.09	.03	−.03	
5. Greece					.18	.24	.30	−.13	
6. Korea						.08	−.16	−.19	
7. Mexico							.41	−.07	
8. Taiwan								−.20	
9. Venezuela									

SOURCE: *Emerging Stock Markets Factbook* (Washington, D.C.: International Finance Corporation, 1988).

$$R_i = R_f + B_i(R_w - R_f) \qquad (23\text{-}2)$$

where

R_w = returns from the world market portfolio, representing the common international pricing factor

The best-known world market index is the Capital International World Market Index, which is compiled by Capital International Perspectives of Geneva, Switzerland. It could be used to estimate the parameters of Equation 23-2. The values for this index appear in both *Barron's* and the *Wall Street Journal*.

SEGMENTED CAPITAL MARKETS

Institutional barriers and other restrictions often prevent the free flow of investment capital across national boundaries. Under these conditions, asset prices do not move together. The price of a foreign stock on a U.S. exchange is impacted by movements in both the United States and its home-country market. Under these conditions, the following asset pricing model may hold:

$$R_i = R_f + \beta_{i,d}(R_{m,d} - R_f) + \beta_{i,f}(R_{m,f} - R_f) \qquad (23\text{-}3)$$

where

$\beta_{i,d}$ = the beta of stock i when measured against the domestic market index

$\beta_{i,f}$ = the beta of stock i when measured against the foreign, or home-country, market index

$R_{m,d}$ = the return on the domestic market index

$R_{m,f}$ = the return on the foreign, or home-country, index

Equation 23-3 indicates that the return from a foreign stock sold domestically is a linear function of both the domestic and foreign market returns.

Caution should be exercised, however, in using this model. One of the important assumptions of multivariate regression is that each of the independent variables is uncorrelated with the others. When they are not, a problem known as multicollinearity occurs, which distorts the values of the estimated regression coefficients. The growing degree of capital market integration increases the possibility of correlation among the market returns.

A second problem with Equation 23-3 is that it leaves out important independent variables. For example, the prices of foreign stocks are influenced by currency exchange rates, which are not captured in either of the independent variables of Equation 23-3.

|||| COMMON FALLACIES CONCERNING INTERNATIONAL INVESTING

International investing has only recently become popular, and many investors still harbor some mistaken ideas about it. Among these misconceptions are (1) the idea that foreign stocks are riskier than U.S. securities and (2) the belief that currency risks should always be hedged when making foreign investments. Both of these ideas would have some merit if securities were evaluated individually, but not if foreign stocks are to be only a part of an otherwise well-diversified portfolio.

ARE FOREIGN STOCKS RISKIER?

Professionals often refer to foreign security markets as "thin." A thin market is one in which the daily volume of shares traded and the number of buyers and sellers for a given security are small. The lack of market participants creates the potential for large daily price fluctuations (with a corresponding increase in the variance of returns) and a lack of liquidity. However, this thinness leads to increased total risk *only if the foreign security is the investor's entire portfolio*. The low covariance of returns between foreign and U.S. securities represents significant diversification potential (risk *reduction* potential) for foreign stocks even though foreign stocks typically have a high variance.

DO CURRENCY RISKS ALWAYS NEED TO BE HEDGED?

Many investors believe that currency exchange rate risks should be hedged when foreign securities are being purchased. This is advisable when an investor acquires securities that are denominated in only one foreign currency. It is also advisable when an investor is speculating in foreign securities on a short-term basis only.

However, since exchange rate movements are random and relatively independent of one another, when investors include a diversified mix of foreign securities in their portfolio, the marginal risk represented by exchange rate movements is largely diversified away.

Astute investment professionals who manage large portfolios of international securities are well aware of these principles. Jarrod W. Wilcox of Colonial Management Associates believes that "Diversification into foreign investments is clearly not risky, even if we cannot forecast currencies! In fact, currency fluctuations against the U.S. dollar add helpful diversification."[4] Most internationally diversified mutual funds, despite their large size, have not hedged their exchange rate risk with currency futures or options.[5] Research on the stability of the correlations among several major equity markets has found them to be stable over time, even when periods of fixed and floating exchange rates are compared.[6]

|||| ## ALTERNATIVE WAYS TO ACHIEVE INTERNATIONAL DIVERSIFICATION

An investor wishing to diversify with foreign securities has at least three alternatives. They are: (1) the direct purchase or sale on a foreign market, (2) the purchase or sale of American depository receipts (ADRs) on a U.S. exchange, or (3) the purchase of shares in an internationally diversified mutual fund.

DIRECT PURCHASES ON FOREIGN MARKETS

American investors are increasingly turning to overseas markets to acquire part of their investment portfolio, and foreign investment in U.S. markets has also been increasing. Recent figures show that foreign investing in the United States has been increasing at a faster rate than U.S. investment abroad.

A number of problems are involved in foreign investing. Obtaining adequate information on foreign securities is often difficult and sometimes impossible. Foreign securities do not have to meet Securities and Exchange Commission (SEC) disclosure requirements or U.S. accounting standards, and the foreign standards and requirements are often far less stringent. Annual reports of foreign companies, when available, are not directly comparable to those of U.S. firms, and they may not be available in English.

In addition, several institutional barriers are often involved in the purchase or sale of foreign securities. Before purchasing a foreign stock or bond, an investor must convert dollars into units of the foreign currency. That means two commissions must be paid —one for the currency conversion and one for the purchase of the security. Brokerage commissions on the security purchase are sometimes 3 to 10 times higher than

[4]Jarrod W. Wilcox, "Practice and Theory in International Equity Investment," *Financial Analysts Journal* (January/February 1986): 18.

[5]Jon Stein, "How International Funds Hedge Their Currency Exposure," *Futures* (May 1988): 40–41.

[6]G. C. Philippatos, A. Christofi, and P. Christofi, "The Inter-Temporal Stability of International Stock Market Relationships: Another View," *Financial Management* (Winter 1983): 63–69.

in the United States.[8] Trades may take weeks to clear due to settlement delays and/or the thinness of foreign securities markets. News of rights offerings, proxy notices, or special dividend distributions, which may be published only in the foreign press, can easily be missed by U.S. investors.

Governments often impose legal and tax restrictions on international investing. Many foreign governments impose limits on the fraction of a firm's equity that can be purchased by overseas investors.[9] Often, transfer taxes must be paid on foreign investments. Some foreign nations impose withholding taxes on dividends paid to overseas investors. To get a refund, U.S. investors must either file a foreign tax return or request a special tax credit when filing their U.S. return, and the Internal Revenue Service imposes certain limits on the amount of these tax credits.

Due to the special problems of cross-border investing, a number of firms list their shares on several major stock markets worldwide. In 1990, 98 foreign firms were listed on the NYSE.[10] Trading in foreign stocks is also rising in the OTC and AMEX markets.

Multiple listing of international securities allows investors from several nations to purchase shares of foreign firms just like domestic shares. Companies benefit from an ability to sell equity in the most receptive markets worldwide, with only the additional cost of meeting the disclosure standards. Investors gain the benefit of international diversification with lower trading costs and institutional barriers than would otherwise exist. As investor recognition of the benefits of international diversification grows, cross-listing of major multinational firms can be expected to increase.

AMERICAN DEPOSITORY RECEIPTS

American depository receipts (ADRs) are certificates issued by a U.S. bank representing one or more shares of a foreign stock. U.S. investors holding ADRs are entitled to the same dividends and capital gains they would have earned had they purchased the shares directly in a foreign market. ADRs have been traded in this country since the 1920s, and today most are traded over the counter. Like other forms of international trading, they are becoming increasingly popular with investors.

The primary advantage of ADRs to U.S. investors is the ease of purchase and sale. As with any other domestic security, no special transactions costs or taxes are involved. Since they are traded in the U.S., they are bought and sold in U.S. dollars. However, as securities that represent shares of foreign equities, their value is directly associated with the value of the underlying stocks. Thus, investors can obtain the advantages of holding foreign securities without the disadvantage of additional taxes

[8]Alexandra Peers, "International Investing: It's Hot, But Is It Last Year's Good Idea?" *Wall Street Journal,* May 21, 1986, p. 31.

[9]Michael Adler and Bernard Dumas, "International Portfolio Choice and Corporation Finance: A Synthesis," *The Journal of Finance* (June 1983): 925–84.

[10]*Dow Jones Business and Investment Almanac,* (Homewood, Ill.: Dow Jones/Irwin, 1990).

and transactions costs associated with the purchase of shares in a foreign country.

The principal limitation of ADRs is the often limited amount of trading. Although more than 700 ADRs are listed on U.S. exchanges, the trading volume for most is very thin, and the liquidity is poor. The majority of trading activity in ADRs occurs in only the 100 largest issues.[11] However, as interest in ADRs grows, this limitation is becoming less important.

INTERNATIONALLY DIVERSIFIED MUTUAL FUNDS

Internationally diversified mutual funds that specialize in equities are generally divided into three categories: international funds, global funds, and regional funds. International funds invest primarily in non-U.S. equities, global funds invest in a mix of domestic and foreign equities, and regional funds invest in equities from a particular region of the world. The international funds are appropriate for a well-diversified domestic investor who wishes to add foreign securities to his or her holdings. Since they contain both U.S. and foreign securities, the global funds can represent an entire portfolio in themselves. For bond investors, world income funds consist of funds specializing in overseas bonds.

Investor interest in internationally-diversified mutual funds has exploded in recent years. In the early 1980's these funds were a relative oddity, generally considered to be specialty investments and not given serious consideration by most investors. By 1991, however, the number and size of these funds had grown dramatically. The Investment Company Institute, a mutual fund trade association, lists almost 250 internationally diversified funds in its 1991 Directory, including 38 global bond funds, 54 global equity funds, 106 international funds, 20 funds specializing in Asian and Pacific Basin securities, and 26 European stock funds.[12]

A major reason for their growing popularity, no doubt, is their generally good performance. In an analysis of mutual fund performance reported in *Barron's,* all categories of internationally diversified funds (including global funds, international funds, Asian and Pacific Basin funds, and European funds) generated higher returns than the all-equity funds average.[13] This performance superiority held whether returns were measured over a 5-year (1986-1991) or ten-year (1981-1991) period. However, favorable exchange rate movements accounted for a significant part of these returns. Be that as it may, research has shown that the benefits of international diversification outweigh the additional costs of mutual fund investing.[14] International funds can consistently outperform the domestic

[11]*Barron's Finance and Investment Handbook,* John Downes and Jordan Elliot Goodman, eds. (Woodbury, N.Y.: Barron's Educational Services, 1987).

[12]*Directory of Mutual Funds* (1991 edition) Investment Company Institute, Washington, D.C., 1991.

[13]*Barron's* May 13, 1991, page M19.

[14]Dennis Proffitt and Neil Seitz, "The Performance of Internationally Diversified Mutual Funds," *Journal of the Midwest Finance Association* (1983): 39–53.

stock market on a risk-adjusted basis; thus, they provide a service of genuine economic benefit to their investors.

INVESTING IN MULTINATIONAL FIRMS

Agmon and Lessard found potential diversification benefits from investing in a mix of U.S.-based multinational corporations, all of which were listed and regularly traded on U.S. exchanges.[15] However, three other studies soon refuted these findings.[16] It is probably safe to say that investors looking for international diversification benefits should not rely on U.S.-based multinationals, but should concentrate on either foreign stocks listed in the United States, ADRs, or internationally diversified mutual funds.

|||| SUMMARY

The benefits of international diversification are clear. Foreign stocks provide valuable diversification benefits because of the low correlation of their returns with most domestic securities. In addition, through exchange rate movements and foreign government subsidies, international stocks at times provide greater returns than domestic stocks.

Investor interest in international diversification has been growing rapidly. This increased interest has manifested itself in (1) a growing volume of direct, cross-border investing, (2) a growing number of foreign firms listing their stocks on U.S. exchanges, (3) an increase in the number of American depository receipts (ADRs) listed and traded on U.S. exchanges, and finally (4) growing interest in internationally diversified mutual funds.

In the past, high transactions costs and institutional barriers have inhibited the growth of international diversification. As these barriers are eliminated, internationally diversified portfolios are likely to become even more commonplace in the 1990s.

|||| QUESTIONS

1. List the principal benefits of international diversification.
2. Distinguish between segmented and integrated capital markets.
3. What impact does the presence of integrated capital markets have on the diversification benefits of foreign securities? Explain in mathematical terms how this works.

[15]Tamir Agmon and Donald R. Lessard, "Investor Recognition of Corporate International Diversification," *The Journal of Finance* (September 1977): 1049–56.

[16]B. Jacquillat and B. Solnick, "Multinationals Are Poor Tools for Diversification," *Journal of Portfolio Management* (Winter 1978): A.L. Senschak and W.L. Beedles, "Is Indirect International Diversification Desirable?" *Journal of Portfolio Management* (Winter 1980): 49–57; and H.L. Brewer, "Investor Benefits from Corporate International Diversification," *Journal of Financial and Quantitative Analysis* (March 1981): 113–26.

4. The degree of integration among capital markets worldwide is growing. What factors are contributing to this increased level of market integration?

5. How do exchange rate movements affect the returns on foreign investments? Is it advisable to buy or sell foreign stocks during periods when the dollar is falling? Why?

6. Define "thinness" in securities markets. What impact does it have on the total and systematic risk of a security?

7. The financial vice president of a U.S. manufacturing firm makes certain the firm is hedged against foreign currency risk when doing business with a major British customer. The same individual, however, does not hedge against currency risks in her personal investment program. Is this a rational decision?

8. What are the barriers to the direct purchase and sale of foreign equities by U.S. investors?

9. What advantages does the international syndication of new equity issues offer the investor? The issuing firm?

10. What are American depository receipts? What are their principal advantages and limitations to the domestic investor?

11. Discuss the performance of internationally diversified mutual funds. How have these funds performed relative to the domestic market? Why? What could be inferred about the performance of these funds relative to funds limited to domestic securities?

12. Do the stocks of U.S.-based multinational corporations have the same potential to provide diversification benefits as the stocks of foreign firms? What is the evidence, pro and con?

13. A security analyst regresses the returns of an Italian stock against the S&P 500 Index in order to measure the stock's "beta." Interpret the meaning of this beta for the analyst. For whom would this measure be more beneficial, U.S. investors or Italian investors?

|||| **PROBLEMS**

1. You are a U.S. investor with significant holdings in Japanese equities. During the past year, these Japanese equities have increased in value from Y80,000 to Y91,000. During the same period of time, the dollar-to-yen exchange rate has gone from 0.007 to 0.008.
    a. What is the percentage return on these investments, measured in yen?
    b. What is the annual return, measured in dollars?

2. The Japan Fund is a mutual fund specializing in Japanese equities. The Templeton World Fund invests in equities from a wide variety of nations.

a. Find (or calculate) the annual returns earned by both of these funds over each of the past eight (or more) years. Calculate the standard deviation of returns for each of the funds. Which is higher? Is there any reason to expect this result, *a priori?*

b. Use regression or correlation to measure the relationship between the returns of the Japan Fund and the exchange rate changes between the dollar and the yen over the same period. Discuss your findings.

3. Source Perrier sells for 1,460 francs on the Paris Bourse. Suppose you purchase 100 shares, and the exchange rate is 5.36 francs per dollar.

a. What is the dollar price of this stock?

b. In one year, the price of the stock rises to 1,552 francs, and the exchange rate moves to 4.75 francs per dollar. What is the annual return from the stock in francs? In dollars?

4. Companies such as Sony, Unilever, and Mitsubishi are international firms that receive significant attention in the United States. Using *Moody's Manuals* or another comparable source, examine the latest financial statements of these firms. List the items on these statements that appear to be different from those typically found in U.S. firms. What does this indicate to you about the comparability of foreign accounting data with U.S. accounting data? What impact do these items have on U.S. investors wishing to invest in these firms?

Use the data in Table 23-4 for Problems 5–7.

5. Which currency has appreciated the most against the dollar? The least? What implications does this have for international investing over this period?

6. Calculate the standard deviation of the exchange rate *changes*. Which countries have had the largest exchange rate volatility against the dollar? What implications does this have for international investing?

|||| **SELECTED REFERENCES**

Adler, Michael, and Bernard Dumas. "International Portfolio Choice and Corporation Finance: A Synthesis." *The Journal of Finance* (June 1983): 925–84.

Alexander, Gordon J., Cheol S. Eun, and S. Janakiramanan. "International Listings and Stock Returns: Some Empirical Evidence." *Journal of Financial and Quantitative Analysis* 23 (1988): 135–52.

Kaplanis, Evi C. "Stability and Forcasting of the Co-Movement Measures of International Stock Market Returns." *Journal of International Money and Finance* 8 (1988): 63–76.

Solnik, Bruno. "Why Not Diversify Internationally?" *Financial Analysts Journal* (July/August 1974): 48–54.

Stehle, Richard. "An Empirical Test of the Alternative Hypotheses of National and International Pricing of Risky Assets." *The Journal of Finance* (May 1977): 493–502.

Stulz, Rene M. "A Model of International Asset Pricing." *Journal of Financial Economics* (September 1981). 383–406.

Wheatley, Simon. "Some Tests of International Equity Integration." *Journal of Financial Economics* 21 (1988): 177–212.

This appendix describes the software developed for use with the textbook. The programs are designed to help students with some of the more complex computations that may be performed with investment data. The software is intended to aid the educational experience of its users and is not intended as an aid for actual trading applications.

The investment programs were developed using LOTUS 1-2-3 templates and macros. Therefore a basic knowledge of LOTUS conventions is presumed. The programs were developed for use with LOTUS 1-2-3, Release 2.2 or above.[1] In the material to follow, program conventions, brief program descriptions, and detailed program descriptions are provided. The theory and equations used in the programs are described in the textbook. In most cases the programs are written to correspond with examples and problems found in the text.

USING THE PROGRAMS

The software programs are contained on either a 360K or 720K floppy disk. This disk may be copied and used by any student using this textbook. We suggest that, if you do not have a hard disk in your computer, you make a working copy of the disk and put the original in a safe place. If you have a hard disk, you may copy the programs to a directory on your hard disk and then put the original disk in a safe place. Copies of the disk may be made using the DOS COPY command.

We strongly suggest that, if possible, you use these programs on a hard disk machine. This will significantly speed up your access time to the software.

To use the software, load LOTUS 2.2 or higher on to your machine and start the program. Use the LOTUS / FILE DIRECTORY command to specify the default directory for the WEST Investment Programs. If the programs were located in hard disk directory C:\WEST, then the LOTUS command would be:

/FD C:\WEST <Return>

To start the programs use the LOTUS / FILE RETRIEVE command to retrieve the program MENU.WK1.

---

[1] Use of earlier versions of LOTUS may be possible. However the programs have not been tested on versions other than Release 2.2 and Release 3.1.

|||| PROGRAM CONVENTIONS

The programs included on the student diskette employ certain conventions that make the use of the programs fairly straightforward. The following conventions are used in the programs and this reference appendix:

● Each program begins with an introduction screen that provides a brief description of the spreadsheet. The program may be started by pressing ENTER or RETURN key (designated [RTN]).

● All of the programs are controlled by LOTUS 1-2-3 command macros. You can tell if the macro is operational by locating the highlighted CMD indicator at the bottom of the LOTUS 1-2-3 screen.

● The programs are menu driven. In most cases the menus appear above the LOTUS 1-2-3 frame. Selections from the menu may be made by highlighting the item using the arrow keys. As each of the menu items is highlighted, a brief description of the menu function is given. Pressing the [RET] key selects a menu item.

● Data entry in these programs makes use of the LOTUS 1-2-3 /*R*ange *I*nput function. This function allows the entry of data in a range of unprotected cells.[2] You may move between the cells using the arrow keys. After making an entry in a cell, *an arrow key should be pressed to lock in the entry*. Once the data entry is complete, pressing ESCAPE (designated as [ESC]) will return control of the program to a command menu. At times the [ESC] key may have to be pressed twice. Pressing the [RET] key will also lock an entry into a cell. Pressing the [RET] a second time will transfer control back to a menu.

● In some programs, responses to specific questions are solicited from the user. The questions will appear in the command line above the LOTUS 1-2-3 frame. Responses to the questions should be followed by a [RET].

● The user may examine any of the programs or macros by interrupting the command macros. This may be done by simultaneously pressing the CONTROL and BREAK keys ([CNTL][BREAK]). The programs should be interrupted only when a menu is showing above the spreadsheet frame. These keys may have to be pressed several times to interrupt the command macro. When the macro is interrupted, an error code will be displayed in the top right-hand indicator. The error condition may be cleared by pressing the [ESC] key. The spreadsheet will then exist in the normal LOTUS 1-2-3 environment.

● A program that has been intentionally, or unintentionally, interrupted by the user may be restarted, with loss of data, by simultaneously pressing the CONTROL and A keys ([CNTL][A]). This procedure will restart the program from the control screen.

● For those users that wish to examine the command macros, these are located to the right side of the spreadsheet. Most often the macros begin in column AA.

● The main menus of all of the programs contain a QUIT option. This option always returns control to the startup menu program that is used to access each of the programs.

---

[2]On a color monitor, these cells are shown as green entries.

- Additions to the software will be detailed in a file named README.DOC on the student diskette. This file is an ASCII file that may be read with any word processor.

|||| PROGRAM DESCRIPTIONS

The programs and files contained on the student diskette may be copied to the user's hard disk or used on the disk provided. The following files and LOTUS 1-2-3 program templates are contained on the student diskette:

MENU.WK1

This menu program provides access to the other programs on the disk. When the other programs are exited, using the QUIT option from their menus, control is always returned to this program.

DA.WK1

This program allows the user to: (1) enter and save data, (2) calculate returns from price data, (3) calculate data ranges, and (4) calculate means, variances, standard deviations and coefficients of variation for up to 5 data sets.

REGRESS.WK1

The regression program will use data entered with the data analysis program, described above, or entered separately by the user, to create the regression table shown in Table 5-1 of the text.

STOCK.WK1

This program solves for the value of common stock using three dividend discount models. These models are:

1. The Gordon Model—a single period or constant dividend growth model.
2. The multi-stage dividend model—a model for 1 to 5 growth periods. In the last period it is assumed that the growth is normal, i.e., less than the discount rate.
3. The multi-stage Malkiel Model—a model for 1 to 5 growth periods. In the last period it is assumed that the company achieves a market average price/ earning ratio.

BOND.WK1

This program determines the price to maturity, the price to call, the yield to maturity, the yield to call, and the duration of a bond. You may enter either simple bond data (approximate maturity) or exact date information. This program will also allow you to estimate the market rate at which a bond may be called, and examine the price sensitivity of a bond in relation to bonds with lower coupons or longer maturities.

BONDSTRAT.WK1

This program allows the evaluation of the following strategies:

1. Pure Yield Pick Up Swap
2. Substitution Swap
3. Sector Swap
4. Rate Anticipation Swap

In general these strategies are designed to be used with Treasury Securities; however other securities may be used with some minor modifications.

SHARPE.WK1

This program solves for the optimal portfolio from a set of 50 securities using the Sharpe Responsiveness Model. The inputs for the model are: (1) the expected return, and (2) beta. Output includes the optimal portfolio plus the corner solution portfolios and a risk/return graph.

OPTION.WK1

This program solves for the price of an option using the Black/Scholes option pricing model. Values for the implied volatility, delta, gamma, theta, lambda and rho are calculated. The program also performs sensitivity analysis in relation to time, volatility and interest rates. Finally, the program will generate profit profiles for various option strategies.

CBD.WK1

A Treasury Bond future contract will allow the delivery of many different bonds. Prior to the expiration of the contract, the exact bond to be delivered is unknown. It is possible to determine the bond most likely to be delivered, assuming that the market variables remain fairly constant. This program provides an estimate of the cheapest most likely bond to be delivered against a futures contract.

PROGTRAD.WK1

Program trading uses classical arbitrage theory to lock in a profit with minimal risk. Traders buy and sell identical commodities in different markets to take advantage of price disparities. In this program the commodities are the stock and futures of the Major Market Index (MMI).

WESTDAT.WK1

This spreadsheet contains monthly index and price data from July 1980 to July 1990 for:

1. NYSE Composite Index
2. Hewlett-Packard
3. Kimberly Clark

4. IBM

5. McKesson Corporation

6. Boeing

SHARPDAT.WK1

This spreadsheet contains some sample data that may be loaded into the SHARPE.WK1 program.

README.DOC

This document, if it exists, details the changes to the programs since this appendix was written. This file is saved in ASCII format. Thus the file may be read by any word processor or printed out on a screen or printer using DOS commands.

|||| PROGRAM REFERENCE

While the spreadsheets contained on the student diskette are fairly self-explanatory, this section is designed to provide a more detailed look at the programs and clear up any questions concerning appropriate data entries.

PROGRAM MENU (MENU.WK1)

The menu program starts with a logo for the investment programs. Pressing [RET] transfers control to the menu of available programs. As each program is highlighted, using the arrow keys, program descriptions are shown on the screen. An example of the menu screen is shown below. In this example the Sharpe Portfolio program is highlighted and its description is provided. To choose one of the programs you should highlight the program and press [RET].

PROGRAM	PROGRAM DESCRIPTION
Data Analysis Regression Stock Valuation Bond Valuation Bond Strategies Sharpe Portfolio Option Analysis Cheapest Bond Quit	This program solves for the optimal portfolio from a set of 50 securities using the Sharpe Responsiveness Model. The inputs for the model are: (1) the expected return (2) beta. Output includes the optimal portfolio plus the corner solution portfolios and a risk/return graph.

Use the arrow key to move between choices.
Press [RTN] to select a program.

DATA ANALYSIS (DA.WK1)

Following the introduction screen the following menu is displayed above the spreadsheet frame:

```
┌─────────────────────────────────────────────────────────────────┐
│                                                                   │
│  INPUT   RETRIEVE   EDIT   CALCULATE   SAVE   HPY/LOG   QUIT       │
│                                                                   │
└─────────────────────────────────────────────────────────────────┘
```

- Selecting INPUT from the menu transfers control to the data input screen. The user may enter 1 to 5 sets of data, one item (day, month, year) at a time. The arrow keys are used to move between the cells. After entering data in the cell, *press an arrow key to lock the data into the cell.* Zeros should be entered as zeros; blank entries should be left blank. After the line of data is correct, pressing [ESC] will transfer the data to the data base and a second line of data is requested.

  Data entry is concluded by pressing [ESC] without entering any data. A prompt in the command line will question whether you really want to stop entering data. An answer of "Y" will transfer control back to the menu. The data entry table is shown below:

```
┌─────────────────────────────────────────────────────────────────┐
│                                                                   │
│  DATA ENTRY FORM                                                  │
│  ───────────────────────────────────────────────────────────     │
│  Enter data below—enter zeros as zeros                            │
│                                                                   │
│    Use arrow keys to move between entries.                        │
│    Press [ESC] to transfer data to database.                      │
│    Leave data area blank and press [ESC] to stop entering data.   │
│                                                                   │
│    Item     Data Set   Data Set   Data Set   Data Set   Data Set  │
│   Number      #1         #2         #3         #4         #5       │
│  ───────────────────────────────────────────────────────────     │
│      1                                                            │
│  ───────────────────────────────────────────────────────────     │
│                                                                   │
└─────────────────────────────────────────────────────────────────┘
```

- The menu item RETRIEVE copies data from another spreadsheet. The data entered in the spreadsheet must follow a fixed pattern. A maximum of six columns are used for the data. The first column contains a row identifier and the second through sixth columns contain data for up to 5 separate data sets. An example of the data contained in the file WESTDAT.WK1 as shown on page 713 at top:

  The data range, cell A9 to cell F??,[3] must be named DBASE using the LOTUS 1-2-3 /*R*ange *N*ame command. After RETRIEVE has been selected, a prompt asks for the file name containing the data. In our example the name is WEST-DAT. The program then copies the data range DBASE from the data file into the Data Analysis spreadsheet. The spreadsheet is then positioned at the beginning of the data and the menu is displayed.

---

[3] ?? refers to the number of rows in the data set.

	A	B	C	D	E	F
1			MONTHLY INDEX AND PRICE DATA			
2			JUNE 1985 TO JUNE 1990			
3						
4			HEWLETT	KIMBERLY		
5		NYSE	PACKARD	CLARKE	IBM	MCKESSON
6	ITEM	COMPOSITE	Monthly	Monthly	Monthly	Monthly
7	NUMBER	INDEX	Price	Price	Price	Price
8						
9	1	111.11	35	29.56	123.75	23.63
10	2	110.47	37.88	30	131.38	23.25
11	3	109.39	35.5	31.56	126.63	24.44
12	4	105.19	32.5	30.63	123.88	22.63
13	5	109.65	30.25	30.38	129.88	23.81
14	6	116.55	35.88	34.13	139.75	25.69
15	7	121.58	36.75	33.5	155.5	26.19
16	8	122.13	39.38	36.56	151.5	25.88
17	9	130.74	43.88	40.5	150.88	27.63
18	10	137.71	44	43	151.5	30.38
19	11	135.75	45.25	41.25	156.25	28
20	12	142.06	46.25	44.31	152.38	31.13

- The EDIT option allows the data to be examined and changed if necessary. The arrow keys are used to move between the cells. Pressing [ESC] ends the editing session and either transfers control to the menu or allows the entry of additional data items. Data lines cannot be deleted, only changed.

STATISTIC	Data Set #1	Data Set #2	Data Set #3	Data Set #4	Data Set #5
OBSERVATIONS	121	121	121	121	121
RANGE					
HIGH	196.9400	70.5000	76.8750	168.3750	38.3750
LOW	61.5100	17.8120	12.1560	51.5000	14.0620
ARITHMETIC MEAN	120.6163	39.9731	36.6047	109.1932	25.5386
POPULATION					
VARIANCE	1733.2187	158.7257	385.9585	888.8190	56.1180
STD. DEVIATION	41.6319	12.5986	19.6458	29.8131	7.4912
COEF. VARIATION	0.3452	0.3152	0.5367	0.2730	0.2933
SAMPLE					
VARIANCE	1747.6622	160.0484	389.1749	896.2258	56.5856
STD. DEVIATION	41.8050	12.6510	19.7275	29.9370	7.5223
COEF. VARIATION	0.3466	0.3165	0.5389	0.2742	0.2945

- CALCULATE positions the spreadsheet at the output screen shown on at the bottom of page 713 and calculates the various statistics shown. A sub-menu allows you to print the raw data or to print the above output screen to your printer. The printer routines use standard printer functions.

- The SAVE function will store the data into a spreadsheet file. The user is prompted for a file name. The filename chosen may not already exist on the user's default directory. If an error is made that will interrupt the program operation, the SAVE function may be used to save data for use in the regression program (REGRESS.WK1).

- The HPY/LOG option causes price data to be converted into holding period returns or into lognormal returns. The price data is overwritten by the return data. Therefore it is important to save the price data before exercising this menu option. Once the returns have been calculated, they may be edited, printed, saved, or have the statistics calculated as described above.

REGRESSION (REGRESS.WK1)

The following is the first menu of the regression program:

```
 ┌─────────────────────────────────────────────────────────────────┐
 │     A_RETRIEVE      B_RETRIEVE      DATA_INPUT      QUIT           │
 └─────────────────────────────────────────────────────────────────┘
```

- A_RETRIEVE causes the program to retrieve data saved by the Data Analysis (DA. WK1) described above. Once the data has been copied and checked, control of the program is passed to the main program menu. The time it takes to retrieve and check the data depends upon the amount of data and the speed of the computer being used. *PLEASE BE PATIENT*.

- The menu item B_RETRIEVE copies data from a user created spreadsheet. The data entered in the spreadsheet must follow a fixed pattern. The structure of the data file is described above for the Data Analysis (DA.WK1). Once the data has been retrieved, control of the program is transferred to the main program menu.

- If you have not created a data file, this menu choice will transfer control to the data input and statistics program. Using this program a data file may be created.

The main program menu is shown below:

```
 ┌─────────────────────────────────────────────────────────────────┐
 │   EDIT    REGRESS    LOOK    SAVE    PRINT    GRAPH    EXIT        │
 └─────────────────────────────────────────────────────────────────┘
```

- EDIT will allow you to examine and change the data to be regressed. Use the arrow keys to move between cells. To end the edit function, press [ESC].

- The REGRESS function will perform a simple linear regression between two of the sets of data. A prompt will ask which set of data is to be used as the independent or market return variable. You may select sets 1 to 5, or may edit the data, to determine which set to choose. A second prompt will ask which set is to be used as the dependent or security return variable.

The program then creates the regression table. An example of this table for 23 observations is shown below:

Security Return	Market Return	Regression Statistics		Expected Return	Residual Return
−0.0646	0.0128			0.0247	−0.0893
0.0497	0.0259	No. of Observations	23	0.0399	0.0098
−0.0185	0.0158	Degrees of Freedom	21	0.0282	−0.0467
0.2025	0.0970			0.1223	0.0802
−0.0056	−0.0398	Constant (alpha)	0.0099	−0.0362	0.0306
−0.0845	−0.0472	X Coefficient (beta)	1.1588	−0.0448	−0.0397
0.0619	0.0115	Std Err of Coef.	0.3376	0.0232	0.0387
0.0556	0.0409			0.0573	−0.0018
0.0628	−0.0188	Correlation Coeff.	0.5996	−0.0119	0.0748
0.0734	0.0023	R Squared	0.3595	0.0126	0.0608
−0.1083	−0.0111			−0.0030	−0.1053
0.0039	−0.0025	Total Risk*	0.0000	0.0070	−0.0031
−0.0932	−0.0646	Systematic Risk*	−0.0000	−0.0649	−0.0283
−0.0351	−0.0608	Unsystematic Risk or		−0.0606	0.0255
0.0855	0.0529	VAR of Y Est*	0.0043	0.0712	0.0143
−0.1005	0.0379			0.0538	−0.1544
−0.0432	−0.0313	*N−2 degrees of freedom		−0.0264	−0.0169
0.1217	−0.0245			−0.0185	0.1401
−0.0516	−0.0603	Total Risk+	0.0000	−0.0600	0.0084
−0.0513	−0.0125	Systematic Risk+	−0.0000	−0.0046	−0.0468
0.0917	0.0389	Unsystematic Risk+	0.0000	0.0550	0.0367
−0.0114	−0.0123			−0.0044	−0.0070
−0.0290	−0.0501	+N−1 degrees of freedom		−0.0482	0.0192
0.0049	−0.0043	Arithmetic Mean		0.0049	0.0000
0.0067	0.0018	VAR (n−2 degrees of freedom)		0.0024	0.0043
0.0064	0.0017	VAR (n−1 degrees of freedom)		0.0023	0.0041

- The LOOK option allows you to examine the regression output table using the arrow keys. Pressing [ESC] returns to the menu.

- SAVE stores the regression table to a spreadsheet file. You will be prompted for a file name. The file name must not exist on the default directory. If the file name exists, a program error will occur.

- The PRINT function will print the regression table to your default printer. It has been assumed that LOTUS 1-2-3 has been configured for your printer.

- The GRAPH option requires a monitor capable of displaying LOTUS 1-2-3 graphs. The GRAPH function displays the regression line and the regression points. Pressing [RTN] will return the menu. The regression graph for our limited set of data is shown at the top of page 716.

- The EXIT function will erase all of the data in the spreadsheet and will return to the data retrieval menu.

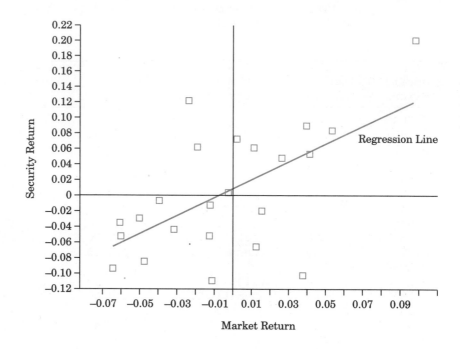

STOCK VALUATION (STOCK.WK1)

The stock program is centered around a single table. You may input or change the data in the table and watch the changes in the pricing cells. The data table with some sample data is shown below:

COMMON STOCK EVALUATION MODELS

Use arrow keys to move between entries—[ESC] to stop entering data

		Growth Period	Growth Rate In Period	Length Of Growth Period
Current Dividend/Shr	$2.00			
Growth periods (5 max)	2			
ROR Discount Rate	15.00%			
CAPM Rate		1	20.00%	5.0
Risk Free Rate	6.00%	2	10.00%	
Beta	1.5			
Market Return	15.00%			
Discount Rate	19.50%			
Current Earning/Shr	$5.00			
Market P/E	8.0			
ROR or CAPM →		Of 15.00%		Of 19.50%
Gordon		NA		NA
Two-period Dividend Model		$65.82		$33.77
Two-period Malkiel Model		$60.87		$50.97

Note from the table that prices are estimated for each of two discount rates. The first rate is a user specified required rate of return. The second rate is derived from the Capital Asset Pricing Model (CAPM).

The current earning per share variable and the market P/E ratio are data necessary for the Malkiel model price estimates. Malkiel assumes that after the period(s) of super-normal growth (growth rate > discount rate) that the market will value the company based on the average market price earning ratio.

The growth rates entered in the table are limited only in the last period of growth. The growth rate must be less than the discount rate.

The menu for this program (shown below) controls the entry of data into the table and allows the table to be printed to the user's default printer. After the selection of each menu item, pressing [ESC] will return to the menu.

NEW_DATA	GROWTH	MARKET	PRINT	QUIT

- NEW_DATA clears the table of existing data and allows the input of a fresh set of data. As the data is input the stock values will change to reflect the data.

- The GROWTH option allows changes to be made in the growth section of the table. The existing data is not cleared. In the last growth period, the growth rate must be less than the discount rate. The length of the growth period, in the last period, does not have to be entered. It is assumed to be infinite.

- The MARKET function allows changes to existing market data, (dividend, interest rates, etc.).

- The PRINT command prints the table to your default printer.

BOND VALUATION (BOND.WK1)

The principles of bond valuation are covered in Chapters 14 and 15. The first menu for BOND.WK1 is shown below:

SIMPLE	EXACT_DATE	CALCULATE	QUIT

- The SIMPLE function allows the calculation of bond price and duration, or yield to maturities and duration, where the approximate term to maturity is known. The data input table is shown on the top of page 718:
Note that 4 cells in the input table are highlighted by arrows. These are values that may be determined by the program. Thus if you wish to solve for the bond price, that cell is left blank while the yield to maturity is entered.
The bond price (assuming call) is the market price of the bond if it is assumed that a call will be made. The call value is the principle of the bond, plus any call premium.
After entering the data and leaving blank those values to be solved, press [ESC] to return control of the program to the menu.

```
┌─────────────────────────────────────────────────────────────────────┐
│                    SIMPLE BOND CALCULATIONS                           │
│                  Assuming $1,000 Face Value Bond                      │
│───────────────────────────────────────────────────────────────────── │
│ Use arrow keys to move between entries                                │
│ Press [ESC] to stop entering data                                     │
│───────────────────────────────────────────────────────────────────── │
│                                                                       │
│ Bond Price                                    →                       │
│ Term To Maturity (Annual Periods)                         10.00       │
│ Coupon Rate (Annual %)                                    12.00%      │
│ Coupon Period (1 or 2)                                        2       │
│ Yield To Maturity (Annual %)                  →            8.00%      │
│                                                                       │
│ Bond Price (Assuming Call)                    →                       │
│ Call Value                                            $1,100.000      │
│ Term To Call                                                5.0       │
│ Yield To Call (Annual %)                      →            8.00%      │
└─────────────────────────────────────────────────────────────────────┘
```

- After the data has been entered, selecting the CALCULATE option from the menu will bring up the following screen with the calculated values highlighted by arrows:

```
┌─────────────────────────────────────────────────────────────────────┐
│                      BOND CALCULATIONS                                │
│───────────────────────────────────────────────────────────────────── │
│ Bond Price                                   →     $1,271.807         │
│ Term To Maturity (Annual Periods)                       10.00         │
│ Coupon Rate (Annual %)                                  12.00         │
│ Coupon Period (1 or 2)                                   2.0          │
│ Yield To Maturity (Annual %)                            8.00%         │
│ Yield To Maturity (Effective Annual %)       →          8.16%         │
│ Duration (annual−maturity)                   →          3.59          │
│                                                                       │
│ Bond Price (Assuming Call)                   →     $1,229.774         │
│ Call Value                                         $1,100.000         │
│ Term To Call                                            5.0           │
│ Yield To Call (Annual %)                                8.00%         │
│ Yield To Call (Effective Annual %)           →          8.16%         │
│ Duration (annual−call)                       →          3.02          │
└─────────────────────────────────────────────────────────────────────┘
```

At this point, control of the program is transferred to the following sub-menu:

```
┌─────────────────────────────────────────────────────────────────────┐
│                                                                       │
│      BOND V. CALL PRICE      MATURITY      COUPON      QUIT            │
│                                                                       │
└─────────────────────────────────────────────────────────────────────┘
```

- Selection BOND V. CALL PRICE locates the spreadsheet on the following table:

BOND PRICE V. CALL PRICE

Bond Data		Market Rates	Bond Value	Call Value	Cost Value
		8.0%	$1,271.81	$1,229.77	($42.03)
Face Value	$1,000.00	9.0%	1,195.12	1,183.08	(12.04)
Coupon Rate	12.00%	10.0%	1,124.62	1,138.61	13.99
Term To Maturity	10	11.0%	1,059.75	1,096.23	36.48
Compounding	2	12.0%	1,000.00	1,055.84	55.84
		13.0%	944.91	1,017.33	72.42
Term To Call	5	14.0%	894.06	980.60	86.54
Call Price	$1,100.00	15.0%	847.08	945.56	98.48

A call should be expected, when the Bond Value equals Par + 1 year's interest. In this case, the market will use the Call Value as the price of the bond.

The Cost Value is the cost to the company for allowing the bond to remain outstanding.

Using the bond data you provided, the above table shows the bond and call values for various interest rates. As a general rule of thumb a call can be expected when the bond price equals par value plus one year's interest.

- The MATURITY option will allow you to examine the price sensitivity of your bond compared to a bond with a longer maturity. The following table is presented:

PRICE SENSITIVITY AND MATURITY

	Bond 1	Bond 2	% Change Market Rate	% Change In Bond 1 Value	% Change In Bond 2 Value
Coupon	12.0%	12.0%	1.0%	−5.5%	−7.1%
Face Value	$1,000.00	$1,000.00	2.0%	−10.6%	−13.3%
Maturity	10	20	3.0%	−15.3%	−18.9%
Compounding	2	2	4.0%	−19.6%	−23.8%
			5.0%	−23.7%	−28.3%
Price @ 12.0%	$1,000.00	$1,000.00	6.0%	−27.4%	−32.3%
			7.0%	−30.8%	−35.9%
			8.0%	−34.1%	−39.1%
			9.0%	−37.0%	−42.1%
			10.0%	−39.8%	−44.8%

Bond maturity increases the sensitivity of the bond to changes in the market interest rate.

- COUPON presents the following table which shows the price sensitivity of your bond to one with a lower coupon rate:

PRICE SENSITIVITY AND COUPON RATES

	Bond 1	Bond 2	% Change Market Rate	% Change In Bond 1 Value	% Change In Bond 2 Value
Coupon	12.0%	6.0%	1.0%	-5.5%	-6.3%
Face Value	$1,000.00	$1,000.00	2.0%	-10.6%	-12.1%
Maturity	10	10	3.0%	-15.3%	-17.5%
Compounding	2	2	4.0%	-19.6%	-22.4%
			5.0%	-23.7%	-26.9%
Price @ 12.0%	$1,000.00	$655.90	6.0%	-27.4%	-31.0%
			7.0%	-30.8%	-34.9%
			8.0%	-34.1%	-38.4%
			9.0%	-37.0%	-41.7%
			10.0%	-39.8%	-44.7%

Bonds with high coupons are less price sensitive to changes in the market interest rate than bonds with low coupons.

- The EXIT option returns control of the program to the main menu.
- The EXACT DATE option, from the first menu, is used to determine bond/call prices or the yield to maturity/call given exact settlement, coupon and

EXACT BOND CALCULATIONS
Assuming $1,000 Face Value Bond

Use arrow keys to move between entries
Press [ESC] to stop entering data

Bond Price	→	
Settlement Date (ex. Mar-15-88)		Mar-15-88
Date Of Last Coupon (ex. Jan-01-88)		jan-01-88
Date Of Next Coupon (ex. Jun-30-88)		JUN-30-88
Maturity Date (ex. Jan-01-2001)		Jan-01-2001
Coupon Rate (Annual %)		12.00%
Coupon Period (1 or 2)		2
Standard Year (360 or 365)		360
Yield To Maturity (Annual %)	→	8.00%
Bond Price (Assuming Call)	→	
Call Value		$1,100.000
Call Date (ex. Jan-01-90)		Jan-01-90
Yield To Call (Annual %)	→	8.00%

maturity date. Such information is commonly available from such sources as Moody's Bond Manual. The input table for the exact date calculations is shown on left at bottom:

Again, 4 cells in the input table are highlighted by arrows. These are values that may be determined by the program. Thus if the user wishes to solve for the yield to maturity, that cell is left blank while the price is provided by the user.

The dates must be entered in the format shown. Months are abbreviated to three letters. The letters may be capitals, lower case, or any combination, as shown. The month name must be followed by a dash (—) and two digits for the day. Days less than 10 must be written as "02". Another dash must follow the day number and then the year is input. Year numbers to 1999 are entered with the last two digits of the year, e.g., 99. Year numbers 2000 and greater use all four year digits.

Pressing [ESC] returns the main menu. You should then select CALCULATE from the menu and the following table is displayed:

BOND CALCULATIONS			
Bond Price + Accrued Interest	$1,301.484	24.667	$1,326.151
Settlement Date			03/15/88
Date Of Last Coupon			01/01/88
Date Of Next Coupon			06/30/88
Maturity Date			01/01/2000
Coupon Rate (Annual %)			12.00%
Coupon Period (1 or 2)			2.00
Standard Year (360 or 365)			360
Yield To Maturity (Annual %)			8.00%
Yield To Maturity (Effective Annual %)			8.16%
Bond Price + Accrued Int. (Call)	$1,152.236	24.667	$1,176.903
Call Value			$1,100.000
Call Date			01/01/90
Yield To Call (Annual %)			8.00%
Yield To Maturity (Effective Annual %)			8.16%

BOND STRATEGY (BONDSTRA.WK1)

The bond strategy program allows the user to evaluate 4 types of bond swaps. The details of these swaps are covered in Chapter 15. The data in the spreadsheet comes from the data in the chapter examples. In this discussion only one of the swaps is shown since the basic format of the menus and tables is the same for each of the swap alternatives.

The first menu for the spreadsheet is shown below:

PICK_UP	SUBSTITUTION	SECTOR	ANTICIPATION	QUIT

● PICK_UP transfers the spreadsheet to the input table for a pure yield pickup swap. That table is shown below:

PURE YIELD PICKUP SWAP

Use arrow keys to move between entries—[ESC] to stop entering data

	Old Bonds	New Bonds
Coupon (%)	10.375	11.250
Face Value	$1,000,000.00	$1,000,000.00
Compounding (1 or 2)	2	2
Transaction Date*	15−SEP−85	15−SEP−85
Maturity Date*	15−MAY−95	5−MAY−95
Bid−Ask**	99.24	104.08
Quoted YTM (%)	10.37	10.54
Reinvestment Rate	10.00	10.00

*Enter date as "5−Sep−91 The quotation mark is required
**Enter bid/ask in 32nds i.e., 99.25 = 99 and 25/32

The dates must be entered as shown in the table. The format of the date entry is "DD-MMM-YY. The quotation market is required. Month names are abbreviated to three letters. Year numbers to 1999 are entered as the last two digits of the year, e.g., 99. Year numbers 2000 and greater use all four year digits.

Once the data is entered, pressing [ESC] transfers control to a sub-menu. The sub-menu is the same for each of the swap alternatives. The sub-menu is shown below:

INPUT	YIELD	SUMMARY	QUIT

● The INPUT command permits you to re-enter the input table and change the information in the table. Pressing [ESC] returns to the sub-menu.

● The YIELD option transfers to a table that shows the yields for the bonds considered in the swap. The yield table for the pure yield pickup swap as shown on page 723 at top:

● SUMMARY transfers to a table that summarizes the net benefits of participating in the swap. An example of the summary table for the pure yield pickup swap follows:

```
                    PURE YIELD PICKUP SWAP
                      YIELD CALCULATIONS
                  Accumulated Value At Maturity
```

	Old Bonds	New Bonds
Par Value	$1,000,000	$952,902
Future Value of Interest		
Payments at a semmiannual		
rate of 5.0%	1,715,296	1,859,960
Total Accumulated Value	$2,715,296	$2,912,861
Value Relative	2.63	2.72
Total Realized Yield		
Realized semiannual yield	5.13%	5.34%
Annual Yield	10.26%	10.67%
Effective Yield	10.52%	10.96%

```
                    PURE YIELD PICK UP SWAP
          Summary At 5.00% Semiannual Reinvestment Rate
```

	Total Accumulated Value	Total Annual Realized Yield	Quoted Yield To Maturity
11.25 Bonds	$2,812,861	10.67%	10.54%
10.38 Bonds	2,715,296	10.26%	10.37%
Difference	$97,565	0.42%	0.17%

- The EXIT function causes the software to return to the main menu for a choice of another swap strategy.

SHARPE MODEL (SHARPE.WK1)

The Sharpe program determines an optimal portfolio of a specified size from a universe of 50 securities. The program is based on Sharpe's Responsiveness Model described in Chapter 20 of the textbook. This program requires graphics capabilities. The main menu of the program is shown below:

```
INPUT  SAVE  GET  OPTIMAL  CORNER  RESTART  PRINT/GRAPH  QUIT
```

- The INPUT option is used to enter the required data for the Sharpe model. These inputs are: 1) a company identifier, 2) the expected return in decimal format, and 3) the beta of the company. As usual, the arrow keys allow movement within the table and pressing [ESC] ends the input session and returns to the main menu.

- GET retrieves data from a user created spreadsheet or from a spreadsheet created by the SAVE command in this program. The format of the data file is fixed. The data table must begin in the A1 cell and can have a maximum of 50 securities. An example of the data is shown below. This data is a subset of the file SHARPDAT.WK1 which may be used with this program.

	A	B	C
1	COMPANY	E(R)	BETA
2			
3	Chrysler	0.178286	1.50
4	Ford	0.193319	1.20
5	General Motors	0.103959	1.00
6	Honda	0.100225	1.00
7	Jaguar	0.140201	1.20
8	Paccar	0.166914	1.00
9	Volvo	0.160514	0.85
10	Champion Spark	0.06973	1.10
11	Echlin	0.083899	1.20
12	Federal–Mogul	0.10462	0.95

Note that the heading and the underline is required. The actual data must start on row 3.

- SAVE is an important menu option. Since this program overwrites the initial data, you should save your data to avoid unnecessary repetitions of data entry. The data will be saved in a spreadsheet whose format is described above. You may choose the file name for the data, however that file name must *not* exist on the LOTUS 1-2-3 default directory. If you select an existing file an error will occur in the program and the data may be lost.

- This is the only program that will not respond to the [ALT][A] program restart command. The reason for this is that the data is continually overwritten in the portfolio creation process. The RESTART option loads a fresh version of the program. Again, the data SAVE command will eliminate a lot of data entry grief, if it is used.

- Once the data is entered, the OPTIMAL option starts the calculation of the Sharpe model. Two prompts will occur in the control panel above the spreadsheet frame. The first prompt asks for the number of securities you wish to include in the optimal portfolio. The second prompt asks for the risk free rate in decimals.

After you have entered the response to the last prompt, the spreadsheet will appear to freeze. The portfolio generation process may take from a few seconds to as long as 20 minutes depending upon: 1) the speed of the user's computer, 2) the number of securities in the security universe, 3) the version

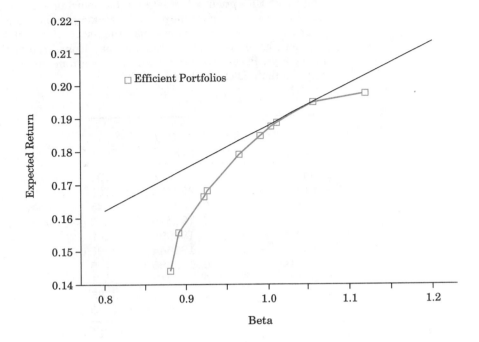

of LOTUS 1-2-3 being used. *Be patient!* The program is finished when a graph of the SHARPE efficient frontier is displayed. An example of this graph is shown above.

Pressing [ESC] at this point will return the main menu and a table showing the optimal portfolio. The optimal portfolio of 10 securities from the universe of securities in the file SHARPDAT.WK1, assuming a risk free rate of 6.0%, is shown below:

COMPANY	OPTIMAL PORTFOLIO E(R)	BETA
Bandag	32.16%	0.95
Maytag	22.33%	1.05
Toro	18.65%	0.95
Ford	19.33%	1.2
Roper Corp	20.43%	1.45
Goodyear Tire	18.90%	1.2
Volvo	16.05%	0.85
Paccar	16.69%	1
Eastman Kodak	15.11%	0.85
E G & G	15.56%	1.05
Portfolio	19.52%	1.055

- The CORNER option will create a table showing each of the corner solution portfolios, that is, each of the portfolios making up the Sharpe efficient frontier. Again this generation process may take several minutes. After the corner solutions have been determined you may look through the table using the arrow keys. Press [ESC] to return to the main menu. A portion of the corner solution table is shown below:

CORNER PORTFOLIO #1

Company	E(R)	Beta
Bandag	0.321619	0.95
Maytag	0.223332	1.05
Roper Corp	0.204299	1.45
Ford	0.193319	1.2
Goodyear Tire	0.188995	1.2
Toro	0.186544	0.95
Chrysler	0.178285	1.5
Paccar	0.166914	1
Volvo	0.160514	0.85
E G & G	0.155563	1.05
Portfolio	0.197938	1.12

Use arrow keys
to move through.
Press [ESC] to quit.

CORNER PORTFOLIO #2

Company	E(R)	Beta
Bandag	0.321619	0.95
Maytag	0.223332	1.05
Toro	0.186544	0.95
Ford	0.193319	1.2
Roper Corp	0.204299	1.45
Goodyear Tire	0.188995	1.2
Volvo	0.160514	0.85
Paccar	0.166914	1
Eastman Kodak	0.151097	0.85
E G & G	0.155563	1.05
Portfolio	0.197938	1.12

- PRINT/GRAPH displays a sub-menu that allows the printing of the optimal portfolio table or the corner solution portfolio table to your default printer. The graph option of the sub-menu will re-display the risk/return graph shown above.

OPTION VALUATION (OPTION.WK1)

The option program consists of three sections. The first section calculates the normal data for the Black-Scholes Option Pricing Model. The second section of the program provides sensitivity analysis of an option position relative to time, volatility, and the risk-free rate. The last section of the program will create the familiar profit diagrams for various option positions.

The main menu is shown below:

ENTER_DATA	IMPLIED_VOLATILITY	SENSITIVITY	PROFIT_GRAPHS	QUIT

● The ENTER_DATA option shifts control of the program to the following table:

BLACK/SCHOLES OPTION PRICING

Use arrow keys to move between entries—[ESC] to stop entering data

Stock Price	$45.00	d1	−0.6204
Exercise Price	$50.00	N(d1)	0.267502
Time to Maturity (days/365)	0.2500	d2	−0.7454
Risk−free Interest Rate (%/year)	8.00%	N(d2)	0.2280
Stock Price Volatility (%/year)	25.00%		
Continuous Dividend Yield (%/year)	0.0%	Stock Price Adjusted	
Call Option Premium	$3.000	For Div. Yield	$45.00

Price and Implied Volatility			Sensitivity Measures		
	Call	Put		Call	Put
Price	$0.862	$4.872	Delta (dC/dS)	0.268	−0.732
			Lambda (dC/dSTD)	0.074	0.074
Implied			Rho (dC/dR)	0.028	−0.095
Volatility	43.09%	43.09%	Theta (dC/dT)	4.596	0.676
			Gamma (dDELTA/dS)	0.059	0.059

As you change the data in the input section of the table the rest of the data changes immediately. The only exception to this rule is that the implied volatility measure must be calculated separately since it must be solved by iteration. As usual pressing [ESC] returns control to the main menu.

● The IMPLIED VOLATILITY function calculates the implied volatility given the call option premium that you provide in the input section of the price table shown above. The call option premium must be in a reasonable price range for the option or else the volatility measure will show as an error.

● The SENSITIVITY option activates the second section of the program. The sensitivity analysis uses the option information you provided in the price table. You are located in an input table where you may define the option position, i.e., the number of calls, puts and amount of stock owned. It should be assumed in these entries that an option controls one share of stock.

Pressing [ESC] brings up a sub-menu that gives you the choice to measure the sensitivity of the position relative to: 1) time, 2) volatility, or 3) the risk-free rate. Since each option follows the same format, we will only demonstrate the sensitivity to time option. Selecting TIME from the sub-menu results in a table showing the sensitivity of the option position to time for various market prices. An example of the position input table and the sensitivity table, which are contained on one screen in the spreadsheet, is shown below:

			SENSITIVITY ANALYSIS				
Use arrow keys to move between entries—[ESC] to stop entering data							
Enter the number of calls, puts and stocks in the option position.							
	Calls		1 Puts	0 Stocks		0	
	Short positions may be entered as negative numbers						
			Time To Expiration				
			0.00	0.19	0.38	0.56	0.75
	M	$35.00	$0.00	$0.00	$0.04	$0.15	$0.34
	A P	$40.00	$0.00	$0.05	$0.33	$0.75	$1.22
	R R	$45.00	$0.00	$0.58	$1.43	$2.24	$3.01
At The Money	K I	$50.00	$0.26	$2.53	$3.80	$4.86	$5.80
	E C	$55.00	$5.01	$6.20	$7.40	$8.46	$9.44
	T E	$60.00	$10.01	$10.82	$11.79	$12.75	$13.67
		$65.00	$15.01	$15.75	$16.57	$17.42	$18.27

The program now transfers to a second sub-menu that allows the sensitivity data to be graphed. Two options exist. The first is a graph of the option position relative to the market price for three selected times to expiration. An example of this graph is shown below:

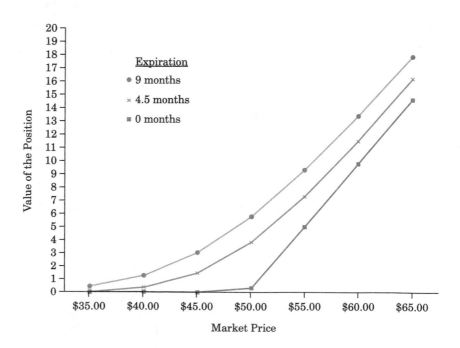

The second option on this sub-menu graphs the option position versus the sensitivity measure, (in this case time), for three stock prices. These prices are: an out of the money price, an at the money price, and an in the money price. An example of this graph is shown:

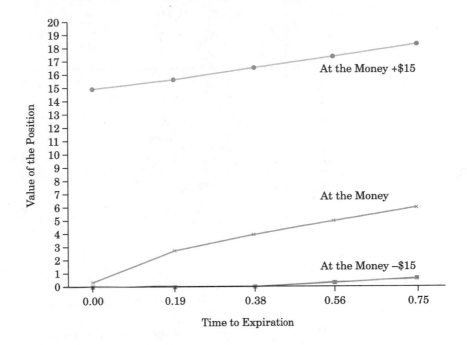

In both sub-menus the EXIT option takes you back to the previous menu. To change the option position, (number of calls, puts, and stocks), you must return to the main menu and again select the SENSITIVITY option.

● The PROFIT/GRAPH option permits you to create option position graphs. You begin in the following input table:

PROFIT PROFILES AT EXPIRATION

Use arrow keys to move between entries—[ESC] to stop entering data

Option Symbol	Strike Price	(S)tock (C)all (P)ut	Number Bought (SOLD)	Premium	Initial Value	Horizontal Spreads		
						Rf Rate	Risk Factor	Time To Expire
POL	$40	C	−1	14	14			
POL	$50	C	2	8	−16			
POL	$60	C	−1	4	4			
					0			
					0			
					0			
					0			

Enter horizontal spread data only for those options with time to expiration when the position is closed.

The data entered in this table will create a butterfly spread. After pressing [ESC] the program displays the profit graph shown below:

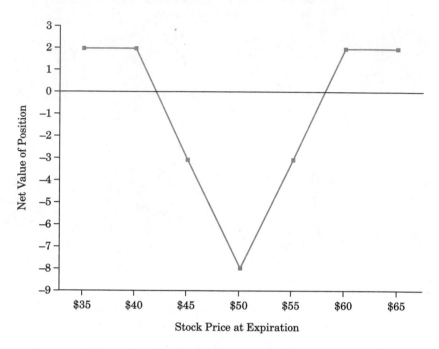

Pressing [ESC] again will display the following profit table:

			PROFIT PROFILE						
			Stock Price At Expiration						
			$35	$40	$45	$50	$55	$60	$65
Initial Value			2.00	2.00	2.00	2.00	2.00	2.00	2.00
POL	$40 C	−1	0	0	−5	−10	−15	−20	−25
POL	$50 C	2	0	0	0	0	10	20	30
POL	$60 C	−1	0	0	0	0	0	0	−5
			0	0	0	0	0	0	0
			0	0	0	0	0	0	0
			0	0	0	0	0	0	0
			0	0	0	0	0	0	0
Net Value			2.00	2.00	−3.00	−8.00	−3.00	2.00	2.00

This table shows the new value of the position at expiration for various stock prices. The initial value is the premium paid or received for the position. The body of the table shows the intrinsic value of each security in the position at expiration.

Again look at the profit/graph input table and note that it has a data input area for horizontal spreads. A horizontal spread involves trading in both long and short term options. At the expiration of the short term option the long term option still has time to expiration. The additional data for the long term option allows an estimate of its price at the expiration of the short term security.

A diagonal spread is created by buying a long-term, low-strike price option and selling a short-term, high-strike price option. For example, if Hewlett Packard were selling at 55 in October, an investor could buy a long term January 50 for $8 and sell a near term October 60 for $1.50. This position, showing the additional data required for the long-term option, is shown:

PROFIT PROFILES AT EXPIRATION

Use arrow keys to move between entries—[ESC] to stop entering data

Option Symbol	Strike Price	(S)tock (C)all (P)ut	Number Bought (SOLD)	Premium	Initial Value	Rf Rate	Risk Factor	Time To Expire
						Horizontal Spreads		
HP	$50	C	1	8	−8	8.00%	25.00%	0.25
HP	$60	C	−1	1.5	1.5			
					0			
					0			
					0			
					0			
					0			

Enter horizontal spread data only for those options with time to expiration when the position is closed.

The profit graph of the diagonal spread and the profit table are shown below:

PROFIT PROFILE

			Stock Price At Expiration						
			$40	$45	$50	$55	$60	$65	$70
Initial Value			(6.50)	(6.50)	(6.50)	(6.50)	(6.50)	(6.50)	(6.50)
HP	$50 C	1	0.1210	0.8623	2.9935	6.6146	11.140	16.019	20.994
HP	$60 C	−1	0	0	0	0	0	−5	−10
			0	0	0	0	0	0	0
			0	0	0	0	0	0	0
			0	0	0	0	0	0	0
			0	0	0	0	0	0	0
			0	0	0	0	0	0	0
Net Value			−6.38	−5.64	−3.51	0.11	4.64	4.52	4.49

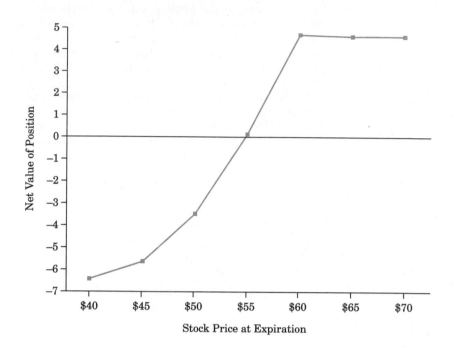

CHEAPEST BOND TO DELIVER (CBD.WK1)

This program determines the most likely bond to be delivered against a Treasury Bond futures contract. A discussion of this principle is covered in Chapter 16. The menu for this program is shown below:

CONTRACT	BOND	SORT	PRINT	QUIT

- The CONTRACT option brings up an input table where the details of the option contract are entered. This table with some sample data is shown below:

```
            CHEAPEST BOND TO DELIVER

Use arrow keys to move between entries—[ESC] to stop
entering data

               YYYY   MM   DD
               ────   ──   ──
Today's Date   1991    8   21 | Futures Price (32nds)*      95.21

Delivery Date  1991   12    1 | Futures Price ($)      95.65625

*Enter bid/ask in 32nds i.e., 99.25 = 99 and 25/32
```

- Choosing BOND, transfers you to a table that allows the input of up to 30 bonds that may be delivered against the contract. As the data is entered other data is automatically calculated in the table. An example of this bond table with 11 entries is shown below:

CHEAPEST BOND TO DELIVER

Use arrow keys to move between entries—[ESC] to stop entering data

Coupon Rate (%)	Maturity YYYY	MM	DD	Ask Price	Accrued Interest	$ Ask Price + Accrued Interest	CBT Factor	Settlement Price	Gain (Loss)
10.75	2005	8	15	122.08	0.18	122.425	1.2245	117.309	(5.1159)
9.375	2006	2	15	111.26	0.15	111.965	1.1146	106.767	(5.1980)
12	2005	5	15	132.16	3.20	135.696	1.3229	129.736	(5.9598)
6.75	1993	2	15	101.04	0.11	101.235	0.9882	94.639	(6.5964)
13.75	2004	8	15	145.29	0.22	146.130	1.4491	138.843	(7.2874)
11.75	2001	2	15	125.27	0.19	126.035	1.2374	118.553	(7.4824)
8.625	1993	8	15	104.10	0.14	104.453	1.0087	96.626	(7.8267)
9	1994	2	15	105.21	0.15	105.803	1.0181	97.539	(8.2639)
12.67	1995	5	15	118.11	3.38	121.719	1.1312	111.581	(10.1381)
3	1995	2	15	94.28	0.05	94.924	0.8689	83.169	(11.7548)
3.5	1998	11	15	95.25	0.93	96.713	0.7687	74.461	(22.2525)

The data required from the user is highlighted in the above table.

- The SORT routine sorts the deliverable bonds in the bond table by the numbers in the gain or loss column. After the sort, the first bond showing in the table has the maximum gain or minimum loss and is the bond most likely to be delivered against the contract. The above table has been sorted.

- The PRINT routine prints both the contract information and the deliverable bond information to your default printer.

PROGRAM TRADING (PROGTRAD.WK1)

The menu of the program trading program is shown below:

DATES/MARGIN	MMI	RESULTS	QUIT

- The DATES/MARGIN option transfers control to a screen in which the purchase date and selling date of the Major Market Index (MMI) may be input. In addition the user indicates the percent of investment funds to be borrowed and the annual borrowing rate. After the data input is complete pressing [ESC] will cause the menu to appear.

- MMI allows the user to input the prices of the MMI on the opening and closing dates and the dividend paid over the open/close interval. There are two data entry screens. The first screen contains the first 11 securities of the MMI.

Pressing [ESC] brings up the second screen. The second screen contains the last 9 securities of the MMI plus the MMI Index value and the MMI futures price. The second screen is shown below:

```
MAJOR MARKET INDEX (MMI) DATA—SCREEN 2
```

Use arrow keys to move between entries—[ESC] to stop entering data

Company	Price Paid On 02/26/86	Price At Closing On 03/24/86	Dividends Paid Over Interval
International Paper	57	60	
Johnson & Johnson	48.375	54	
McDonalds	150.75	161.25	
Merck	97.25	104	0.9
MMM	30.125	29.5	
Mobil Oil	101.125	119.25	
Philip Morris	67	73.5	1.15
Procter and Gamble	42.875	46.125	
Sears	22.625	22.75	
MMI Index	311.74	328.07	
MMI Futures Price	313.55	328.07	

- The RESULTS option transfers to the following screen:

```
PROGRAM TRADING RESULTS
```

Press [ESC] to return to the main menu.

	Stock Position	Futures Position
Shares Of Each MMI Stock Held Long	2,000	
Equity Position In The MMI Shares		$1,374,500
Margin Position In The MMI Shares		$1,374,500
Futures Contracts Sold Short	35	

Profit (Loss) Over 26 Days

	Stock Position	Futures Position
Initial Value of Position	($2,749,000)	$2,743,563
Ending Value Of Position	2,893,000	(2,870,613)
Dividend Income	6,820	
Interest On Margin Loan	(8,438)	
Total	$142,382	($127,050)
Net Profit W/O Transactions Costs	$15,332	
Annualized Return On Equity	15.44%	

The only variable in this screen is the number of shares of each MMI stock held long or sold short. The user may input this value and watch the values on the screen change in response. The determination of whether the shares are held long or sold short is determined by whether the MMI Index is greater or less than the MMI futures price. Pressing [ESC] returns the user to the menu.

PRESENT AND FUTURE VALUE TABLES

TABLE B-1

Present value of \$1 to be received in t periods $= 1/(1 + k)^t$

Period	1%	2%	3%	4%	5%	6%	7%	8%	9%	10%
1	.9901	.9804	.9709	.9615	.9524	.9434	.9346	.9259	.9174	.9091
2	.9803	.9612	.9426	.9246	.9070	.8900	.8734	.8573	.8417	.8264
3	.9706	.9423	.9151	.8890	.8638	.8396	.8163	.7938	.7722	.7513
4	.9610	.9238	.8885	.8548	.8227	.7921	.7629	.7350	.7084	.6830
5	.9515	.9057	.8626	.8219	.7835	.7473	.7130	.6806	.6499	.6209
6	.9420	.8880	.8375	.7903	.7462	.7050	.6663	.6302	.5963	.5645
7	.9327	.8706	.8131	.7599	.7107	.6651	.6227	.5835	.5470	.5132
8	.9235	.8535	.7894	.7307	.6768	.6274	.5820	.5403	.5019	.4665
9	.9143	.8368	.7664	.7026	.6446	.5919	.5439	.5002	.4604	.4241
10	.9053	.8203	.7441	.6756	.6139	.5584	.5083	.4632	.4224	.3855
11	.8963	.8043	.7224	.6496	.5847	.5268	.4751	.4289	.3875	.3505
12	.8874	.7885	.7014	.6246	.5568	.4970	.4440	.3971	.3555	.3186
13	.8787	.7730	.6810	.6006	.5303	.4688	.4150	.3677	.3262	.2897
14	.8700	.7579	.6611	.5775	.5051	.4423	.3878	.3405	.2992	.2633
15	.8613	.7430	.6419	.5553	.4810	.4173	.3624	.3152	.2745	.2394
16	.8528	.7284	.6232	.5339	.4581	.3936	.3387	.2919	.2519	.2176
17	.8444	.7142	.6050	.5134	.4363	.3714	.3166	.2703	.2311	.1978
18	.8360	.7002	.5874	.4936	.4155	.3503	.2959	.2502	.2120	.1799
19	.8277	.6864	.5703	.4746	.3957	.3305	.2765	.2317	.1945	.1635
20	.8195	.6730	.5537	.4564	.3769	.3118	.2584	.2145	.1784	.1486
25	.7798	.6095	.4776	.3751	.2953	.2330	.1842	.1460	.1160	.0923
30	.7419	.5521	.4120	.3083	.2314	.1741	.1314	.0994	.0754	.0573
40	.6717	.4529	.3066	.2083	.1420	.0972	.0668	.0460	.0318	.0221
50	.6080	.3715	.2281	.1407	.0872	.0543	.0339	.0213	.0134	.0085
60	.5504	.3048	.1697	.0951	.0535	.0303	.0173	.0099	.0057	.0033

*The present value is zero to four decimal places.

TABLE B-1 continued

12%	14%	15%	16%	18%	20%	24%	28%	32%	36%
.8929	.8772	.8696	.8621	.8475	.8333	.8065	.7813	.7576	.7353
.7972	.7695	.7561	.7432	.7182	.6944	.6504	.6104	.5739	.5407
.7118	.6750	.6575	.6407	.6086	.5787	.5245	.4768	.4348	.3975
.6355	.5921	.5718	.5523	.5158	.4823	.4230	.3725	.3294	.2923
.5674	.5194	.4972	.4761	.4371	.4019	.3411	.2910	.2495	.2149
.5066	.4556	.4323	.4104	.3704	.3349	.2751	.2274	.1890	.1580
.4523	.3996	.3759	.3538	.3139	.2791	.2218	.1776	.1432	.1162
.4039	.3506	.3269	.3050	.2660	.2326	.1789	.1388	.1085	.0854
.3606	.3075	.2843	.2630	.2255	.1938	.1443	.1084	.0822	.0628
.3220	.2697	.2472	.2267	.1911	.1615	.1164	.0847	.0623	.0462
.2875	.2366	.2149	.1954	.1619	.1346	.0938	.0662	.0472	.0340
.2567	.2076	.1869	.1685	.1372	.1122	.0757	.0517	.0357	.0250
.2292	.1821	.1625	.1452	.1163	.0935	.0610	.0404	.0271	.0184
.2046	.1597	.1413	.1252	.0985	.0779	.0492	.0316	.0205	.0135
.1827	.1401	.1229	.1079	.0835	.0649	.0397	.0247	.0155	.0099
.1631	.1229	.1069	.0930	.0708	.0541	.0320	.0193	.0118	.0073
.1456	.1078	.0929	.0802	.0600	.0451	.0258	.0150	.0089	.0054
.1300	.0946	.0808	.0691	.0508	.0376	.0208	.0118	.0068	.0039
.1161	.0829	.0703	.0596	.0431	.0313	.0168	.0092	.0051	.0029
.1037	.0728	.0611	.0514	.0365	.0261	.0135	.0072	.0039	.0021
.0588	.0378	.0304	.0245	.0160	.0105	.0046	.0021	.0010	.0005
.0334	.0196	.0151	.0116	.0070	.0042	.0016	.0006	.0002	.0001
.0107	.0053	.0037	.0026	.0013	.0007	.0002	.0001	*	*
.0035	.0014	.0009	.0006	.0003	.0001	*	*	*	*
.0011	.0004	.0002	.0001	.0001	*	*	*	*	*

TABLE B-2
Future value of $1 at the end of t periods $= (1 + k)^t$

Period	1%	2%	3%	4%	5%	6%	7%	8%	9%	10%
1	1.0100	1.0200	1.0300	1.0400	1.0500	1.0600	1.0700	1.0800	1.0900	1.1000
2	1.0201	1.0404	1.0609	1.0816	1.1025	1.1236	1.1449	1.1664	1.1881	1.2100
3	1.0303	1.0612	1.0927	1.1249	1.1576	1.1910	1.2250	1.2597	1.2950	1.3310
4	1.0406	1.0824	1.1255	1.1699	1.2155	1.2625	1.3108	1.3605	1.4116	1.4641
5	1.0510	1.1041	1.1593	1.2167	1.2763	1.3382	1.4026	1.4693	1.5386	1.6105
6	1.0615	1.1262	1.1941	1.2653	1.3401	1.4185	1.5007	1.5869	1.6771	1.7716
7	1.0721	1.1487	1.2299	1.3159	1.4071	1.5036	1.6058	1.7138	1.8280	1.9487
8	1.0829	1.1717	1.2668	1.3686	1.4775	1.5938	1.7182	1.8509	1.9926	2.1436
9	1.0937	1.1951	1.3048	1.4233	1.5513	1.6895	1.8385	1.9990	2.1719	2.3579
10	1.1046	1.2190	1.3439	1.4802	1.6289	1.7908	1.9672	2.1589	2.3674	2.5937
11	1.1157	1.2434	1.3842	1.5395	1.7103	1.8983	2.1049	2.3316	2.5804	2.8531
12	1.1268	1.2682	1.4258	1.6010	1.7959	2.0122	2.2522	2.5182	2.8127	3.1384
13	1.1381	1.2936	1.4685	1.6651	1.8856	2.1329	2.4098	2.7195	3.0658	3.4523
14	1.1495	1.3195	1.5126	1.7317	1.9799	2.2609	2.5785	2.9372	3.3417	3.7975
15	1.1610	1.3459	1.5580	1.8009	2.0789	2.3966	2.7590	3.1722	3.6425	4.1772
16	1.1726	1.3728	1.6047	1.8730	2.1829	2.5404	2.9522	3.4259	3.9703	4.5950
17	1.1843	1.4002	1.6528	1.9479	2.2920	2.6928	3.1588	3.7000	4.3276	5.0545
18	1.1961	1.4282	1.7024	2.0258	2.4066	2.8543	3.3799	3.9960	4.7171	5.5599
19	1.2081	1.4568	1.7535	2.1068	2.5270	3.0256	3.6165	4.3157	5.1417	6.1159
20	1.2202	1.4859	1.8061	2.1911	2.6533	3.2071	3.8697	4.6610	5.6044	6.7275
21	1.2324	1.5157	1.8603	2.2788	2.7860	3.3996	4.1406	5.0338	6.1088	7.4002
22	1.2447	1.5460	1.9161	2.3699	2.9253	3.6035	4.4304	5.4365	6.6586	8.1403
23	1.2572	1.5769	1.9736	2.4647	3.0715	3.8197	4.7405	5.8715	7.2579	8.9543
24	1.2697	1.6084	2.0328	2.5633	3.2251	4.0489	5.0724	6.3412	7.9111	9.8497
25	1.2824	1.6406	2.0938	2.6658	3.3864	4.2919	5.4274	6.8485	8.6231	10.834
26	1.2953	1.6734	2.1566	2.7725	3.5557	4.5494	5.8074	7.3964	9.3992	11.918
27	1.3082	1.7069	2.2213	2.8834	3.7335	4.8223	6.2139	7.9881	10.245	13.110
28	1.3213	1.7410	2.2879	2.9987	3.9201	5.1117	6.6488	8.6271	11.167	14.421
29	1.3345	1.7758	2.3566	3.1187	4.1161	5.4184	7.1143	9.3173	12.172	15.863
30	1.3478	1.8114	2.4273	3.2434	4.3219	5.7435	7.6123	10.062	13.267	17.449
40	1.4889	2.2080	3.2620	4.8010	7.0400	10.285	14.974	21.724	31.409	45.259
50	1.6446	2.6916	4.3839	7.1067	11.467	18.420	29.457	46.901	74.357	117.39
60	1.8167	3.2810	5.8916	10.519	18.679	32.987	57.946	101.25	176.03	304.48

*The future value is greater than $100,000.

TABLE B-2 continued

12%	14%	15%	16%	18%	20%	24%	28%	32%	36%
1.1200	1.1400	1.1500	1.1600	1.1800	1.2000	1.2400	1.2800	1.3200	1.3600
1.2544	1.2996	1.3225	1.3456	1.3924	1.4400	1.5376	1.6384	1.7424	1.8496
1.4049	1.4815	1.5209	1.5609	1.6430	1.7280	1.9066	2.0972	2.3000	2.5155
1.5735	1.6890	1.7490	1.8106	1.9366	2.0736	2.3642	2.6844	3.0360	3.4210
1.7623	1.9254	2.0114	2.1003	2.2878	2.4883	2.9316	3.4360	4.0075	4.6526
1.9738	2.1950	2.3131	2.4364	2.6996	2.9860	3.6352	4.3980	5.2899	6.3275
2.2107	2.5023	2.6600	2.8262	3.1855	3.5832	4.5077	5.6295	6.9826	8.6054
2.4760	2.8526	3.0590	3.2784	3.7589	4.2998	5.5895	7.2058	9.2170	11.703
2.7731	3.2519	3.5179	3.8030	4.4355	5.1598	6.9310	9.2234	12.166	15.916
3.1058	3.7072	4.0456	4.4114	5.2338	6.1917	8.5944	11.805	16.059	21.646
3.4785	4.2262	4.6524	5.1173	6.1759	7.4301	10.657	15.111	21.198	29.439
3.8960	4.8179	5.3502	5.9360	7.2876	8.9161	13.214	19.342	27.982	40.037
4.3635	5.4924	6.1528	6.8858	8.5994	10.699	16.386	24.758	36.937	54.451
4.8871	6.2613	7.0757	7.9875	10.147	12.839	20.319	31.691	48.756	74.053
5.4736	7.1379	8.1371	9.2655	11.973	15.407	25.195	40.564	64.358	100.71
6.1304	8.1372	9.3576	10.748	14.129	18.488	31.242	51.923	84.953	136.96
6.8660	9.2765	10.761	12.467	16.672	22.186	38.740	66.461	112.13	186.27
7.6900	10.575	12.375	14.462	19.673	26.623	48.038	85.070	148.02	253.33
8.6128	12.055	14.231	16.776	23.214	31.948	59.567	108.89	195.39	344.53
9.6463	13.743	16.366	19.460	27.393	38.377	73.864	139.37	257.91	468.57
10.803	15.667	18.821	22.574	32.323	46.005	91.591	178.40	340.44	637.26
12.100	17.861	21.644	26.186	38.142	55.206	113.57	228.35	449.39	866.67
13.552	20.361	24.891	30.376	45.007	66.247	140.83	292.30	593.19	1178.6
15.178	23.212	28.625	35.236	53.108	79.496	174.63	374.14	783.02	1602.9
17.000	26.461	32.918	40.874	62.668	95.396	216.54	478.90	1033.5	2180.0
19.040	30.166	37.856	47.414	73.948	114.47	268.51	612.99	1364.3	2964.9
21.324	34.389	43.535	55.000	87.259	137.37	332.95	784.63	1800.9	4032.2
23.883	39.204	50.065	63.800	102.96	164.84	412.86	1004.3	2377.2	5483.8
26.749	44.693	57.575	74.008	121.50	197.81	511.95	1285.5	3137.9	7458.0
29.959	50.950	66.211	85.849	143.37	237.37	634.81	1645.5	4142.0	10143.
93.050	188.88	267.86	378.72	750.37	1469.7	5455.9	19426.	66520.	*
289.00	700.23	1083.6	1670.7	3927.3	9100.4	46890.	*	*	*
897.59	2595.9	4383.9	7370.1	20555.	56347.	*	*	*	*

TABLE B-3

Present value of \$1 per period for t periods $= \dfrac{1 - \dfrac{1}{(1 + k)^t}}{k}$

Number of Payments	1%	2%	3%	4%	5%	6%	7%	8%	9%	10%
1	0.9901	0.9804	0.9709	0.9615	0.9524	0.9434	0.9346	0.9259	0.9174	0.9091
2	1.9704	1.9416	1.9135	1.8861	1.8594	1.8334	1.8080	1.7833	1.7591	1.7355
3	2.9410	2.8839	2.8286	2.7751	2.7232	2.6730	2.6243	2.5771	2.5313	2.4869
4	3.9020	3.8077	3.7171	3.6299	3.5460	3.4651	3.3872	3.3121	3.2397	3.1699
5	4.8534	4.7135	4.5797	4.4518	4.3295	4.2124	4.1002	3.9927	3.8897	3.7908
6	5.7955	5.6014	5.4172	5.2421	5.0757	4.9173	4.7665	4.6229	4.4859	4.3553
7	6.7282	6.4720	6.2303	6.0021	5.7864	5.5824	5.3893	5.2064	5.0330	4.8684
8	7.6517	7.3255	7.0197	6.7327	6.4632	6.2098	5.9713	5.7466	5.5348	5.3349
9	8.5660	6.1622	7.7861	7.4353	7.1078	6.8017	6.5152	6.2469	5.9952	5.7590
10	9.4713	8.9826	8.5302	8.1109	7.7217	7.3601	7.0236	6.7101	6.4177	6.1446
11	10.3676	9.7868	9.2526	8.7605	8.3064	7.8869	7.4987	7.1390	6.8052	6.4951
12	11.2551	10.5753	9.9540	9.3851	8.8633	8.3838	7.9427	7.5361	7.1607	6.8137
13	12.1337	11.3484	10.6350	9.9856	9.3936	8.8527	8.3577	7.9038	7.4869	7.1034
14	13.0037	12.1062	11.2961	10.5631	9.8986	9.2950	8.7455	8.2442	7.7862	7.3667
15	13.8651	12.8493	11.9379	11.1184	10.3797	9.7122	9.1079	8.5595	8.0607	7.6061
16	14.7179	13.5777	12.5611	11.6523	10.8378	10.1059	9.4466	8.8514	8.3126	7.8237
17	15.5623	14.2919	13.1661	12.1657	11.2741	10.4773	9.7632	9.1216	8.5436	8.0216
18	16.3983	14.9920	13.7535	12.6593	11.6896	10.8276	10.0591	9.3719	8.7556	8.2014
19	17.2260	15.6785	14.3238	13.1339	12.0853	11.1581	10.3356	9.6036	8.9501	8.3649
20	18.0456	16.3514	14.8775	13.5903	12.4622	11.4699	10.5940	9.8181	9.1285	8.5136
25	22.0232	19.5235	17.4131	15.6221	14.0939	12.7834	11.6536	10.6748	9.8226	9.0770
30	25.8077	22.3965	19.6004	17.2920	15.3725	13.7648	12.4090	11.2578	10.2737	9.4269
40	32.8347	27.3555	23.1148	19.7928	17.1591	15.0463	13.3317	11.9246	10.7574	9.7791
50	39.1961	31.4236	25.7298	21.4822	18.2559	15.7619	13.8007	12.2335	10.9617	9.9148
60	44.9550	34.7609	27.6756	22.6235	18.9293	16.1614	14.0392	12.3766	11.0480	9.9672

TABLE B-3 continued

12%	14%	15%	16%	18%	20%	24%	28%	32%
0.8929	0.8772	0.8696	0.8621	0.8475	0.8333	0.8065	0.7813	0.7576
1.6901	1.6467	1.6257	1.6052	1.5656	1.5278	1.4568	1.3916	1.3315
2.4018	2.3216	2.2832	2.2459	2.1743	2.1065	1.9813	1.8684	1.7663
3.0373	2.9137	2.8550	2.7982	2.6901	2.5887	2.4043	2.2410	2.0957
3.6048	3.4331	3.3522	3.2743	3.1272	2.9906	2.7454	2.5320	2.3452
4.1114	3.8887	3.7845	3.6847	3.4976	3.3255	3.0205	2.7594	2.5342
4.5638	4.2883	4.1604	4.0386	3.8115	3.6046	3.2423	2.9370	2.6775
4.9676	4.6389	4.4873	4.3436	4.0776	3.8372	3.4212	3.0758	2.7860
5.3292	4.9464	4.7716	4.6065	4.3030	4.0310	3.5655	3.1842	2.8681
5.6502	5.2161	5.0188	4.8332	4.4941	4.1925	3.6819	3.2689	2.9304
5.9377	5.4527	5.2337	5.0286	4.6560	4.3271	3.7757	3.3351	2.9776
6.1944	5.6603	5.4206	5.1971	4.7932	4.4392	3.8514	3.3868	3.0133
6.4235	5.8424	5.5831	5.3423	4.9095	4.5327	3.9124	3.4272	3.0404
6.6282	6.0021	5.7245	5.4675	5.0081	4.6106	3.9616	3.4587	3.0609
6.8109	6.1422	5.8474	5.5755	5.0916	4.6755	4.0013	3.4834	3.0764
6.9740	6.2651	5.9542	5.6685	5.1624	4.7296	4.0333	3.5026	3.0882
7.1196	6.3729	6.0472	5.7487	5.2223	4.7746	4.0591	3.5177	3.0971
7.2497	6.4674	6.1280	5.8178	5.2732	4.8122	4.0799	3.5294	3.1039
7.3658	6.5504	6.1982	5.8775	5.3162	4.8435	4.0967	3.5386	3.1090
7.4694	6.6231	6.2593	5.9288	5.3527	4.8696	4.1103	3.5458	3.1129
7.8431	6.8729	6.4641	6.0971	5.4669	4.9476	4.1474	3.5640	3.1220
8.0552	7.0027	6.5660	6.1772	5.5168	4.9789	4.1601	3.5693	3.1242
8.2438	7.1050	6.6418	6.2335	5.5482	4.9966	4.1659	3.5712	3.1250
8.3045	7.1327	6.6605	6.2463	5.5541	4.9995	4.1666	3.5714	3.1250
8.3240	7.1401	6.6651	6.2402	5.5553	4.9999	4.1667	3.5714	3.1250

TABLE B-4

Sum of $1 per period for t periods $= \dfrac{(1 + k)^t - 1}{k}$

Number of Payments	1%	2%	3%	4%	5%	6%	7%	8%	9%	10%
1	1.0000	1.0000	1.0000	1.0000	1.0000	1.0000	1.0000	1.0000	1.0000	1.0000
2	2.0100	2.0200	2.0300	2.0400	2.0500	2.0600	2.0700	2.0800	2.0900	2.1000
3	3.0301	3.0604	3.0909	3.1216	3.1525	3.1836	3.2149	3.2464	3.2781	3.3100
4	4.0604	4.1216	4.1836	4.2465	4.3101	4.3746	4.4399	4.5061	4.5731	4.6410
5	5.1010	5.2040	5.3091	5.4163	5.5256	5.6371	5.7507	5.8666	5.9847	6.1051
6	6.1520	6.3081	6.4684	6.6330	6.8019	6.9753	7.1533	7.3359	7.5233	7.7156
7	7.2135	7.4343	7.6625	7.8983	8.1420	8.3938	8.6540	8.9228	9.2004	9.4872
8	8.2857	8.5830	8.8923	9.2142	9.5491	9.8975	10.259	10.636	11.028	11.435
9	9.3685	9.7546	10.159	10.582	11.026	11.491	11.978	12.487	13.021	13.579
10	10.462	10.949	11.463	12.006	12.577	13.180	13.816	14.486	15.192	15.937
11	11.566	12.168	12.807	13.486	14.206	14.971	15.783	16.645	17.560	18.531
12	12.682	13.412	14.192	15.025	15.917	16.869	17.888	18.977	20.140	21.384
13	13.809	14.680	15.617	16.626	17.713	18.882	20.140	21.495	22.953	24.522
14	14.947	15.973	17.086	18.291	19.598	21.015	22.550	24.214	26.019	27.975
15	16.096	17.293	18.598	20.023	21.578	23.276	25.129	27.152	29.360	31.772
16	17.257	18.639	20.156	21.824	23.657	25.672	27.888	30.324	33.003	35.949
17	18.430	20.012	21.761	23.697	25.840	28.212	30.840	33.750	36.973	40.544
18	19.614	21.412	23.414	25.645	28.132	30.905	33.999	37.450	41.301	45.599
19	20.810	22.840	25.116	27.671	30.539	33.760	37.379	41.446	46.018	51.159
20	22.019	24.297	26.870	29.778	33.066	36.785	40.995	45.762	51.160	57.275
21	23.239	25.783	28.676	31.969	35.719	39.992	44.865	50.422	56.764	64.002
22	24.471	27.299	30.536	34.248	38.505	43.392	49.005	55.456	62.873	71.402
23	25.716	28.845	32.452	36.617	41.430	46.995	53.436	60.893	69.531	79.543
24	26.973	30.421	34.426	39.082	44.502	50.815	58.176	66.764	76.789	88.497
25	28.243	32.030	36.459	41.645	47.727	54.864	63.249	73.105	84.700	98.347
26	29.525	33.670	38.553	44.311	51.113	59.156	68.676	79.954	93.323	109.18
27	30.820	35.344	40.709	47.084	54.669	63.705	74.483	87.350	102.72	121.09
28	32.129	37.051	42.930	49.967	58.402	68.528	80.697	95.338	112.96	134.20
29	33.450	38.792	45.218	52.966	62.322	73.639	87.346	103.96	124.13	148.63
30	34.784	40.568	47.575	56.084	66.438	79.058	94.460	113.28	136.30	164.49
40	48.886	60.402	75.401	95.025	120.79	154.76	199.63	259.05	337.88	442.59
50	64.463	84.579	112.79	152.66	209.34	290.33	406.52	573.76	815.08	1163.9
60	81.669	114.05	163.05	237.99	353.58	533.12	813.52	1253.2	1944.7	3034.8

*The sum is greater than $100,000.

TABLE B-4 continued

12%	14%	15%	16%	18%	20%	24%	28%	32%	36%
1.0000	1.0000	1.0000	1.0000	1.0000	1.0000	1.0000	1.0000	1.0000	1.0000
2.1200	2.1400	2.1500	2.1600	2.1800	2.2000	2.2400	2.2800	2.3200	2.3600
3.3744	3.4396	3.4725	3.5056	3.5724	3.6400	3.7776	3.9184	4.0624	4.2096
4.7793	4.9211	4.9934	5.0665	5.2154	5.3680	5.6842	6.0156	6.3624	6.7251
6.3528	6.6101	6.7424	6.8771	7.1542	7.4416	8.0484	8.6999	9.3983	10.146
8.1152	8.5355	8.7537	8.9775	9.4420	9.9299	10.980	12.135	13.405	14.798
10.089	10.089	11.066	11.413	12.141	12.915	14.615	16.533	18.695	21.126
12.299	13.232	13.726	14.240	15.327	16.499	19.122	22.163	25.678	29.731
14.775	16.085	16.785	17.518	19.085	20.798	24.712	29.369	34.895	41.435
17.548	19.337	20.303	21.321	23.521	25.958	31.643	38.592	47.061	57.351
20.654	23.044	24.349	25.732	28.755	32.150	40.237	50.398	63.121	78.998
24.133	27.270	29.001	30.850	34.931	39.580	50.894	65.510	84.320	108.43
28.029	32.088	34.351	36.786	42.218	48.496	64.109	84.852	112.30	148.47
32.392	37.581	40.504	43.672	50.818	59.195	80.496	109.61	149.23	202.92
37.279	43.842	47.580	51.659	60.965	72.035	100.81	141.30	197.99	276.97
42.753	50.980	55.717	60.925	72.939	87.442	126.01	181.86	262.35	377.69
48.883	59.117	65.075	71.673	87.068	105.93	157.25	233.79	347.30	514.66
55.749	68.394	75.836	84.140	103.74	128.11	195.99	300.25	459.44	700.93
63.439	78.969	88.211	98.603	123.41	154.74	244.03	385.32	607.47	954.27
72.052	91.024	102.44	115.37	146.62	186.68	303.60	494.21	802.86	1298.8
81.698	104.76	118.81	134.84	174.02	225.02	377.46	633.59	1060.7	1767.3
92.502	120.43	137.63	157.41	206.34	271.03	469.05	811.99	1401.2	2404.6
104.60	138.29	159.27	183.60	244.48	326.23	582.62	1040.3	1850.6	3271.3
118.15	158.65	184.16	213.97	289.49	392.48	723.46	1332.6	2443.8	4449.9
133.33	181.87	212.79	249.21	342.60	471.98	898.09	1706.8	3226.8	6052.9
150.33	208.33	245.71	290.08	405.27	567.37	1114.6	2185.7	4260.4	8233.0
169.37	238.39	283.56	337.50	479.22	681.85	1383.1	2798.7	5624.7	11197.9
190.69	272.88	327.10	392.50	566.48	819.22	1716.0	3583.3	7425.6	15230.2
214.58	312.09	377.16	456.30	669.44	984.06	2128.9	4587.6	9802.9	20714.1
241.33	356.78	434.74	530.31	790.94	1181.8	2640.9	5873.2	12940.	28172.2
767.09	1342.0	1779.0	2360.7	4163.2	7343.8	22728.	69377.	*	*
2400.0	4994.5	7217.7	10435.	21813.	45497.	*	*	*	*
7471.6	18535.	29219.	46057.	*	*	*	*	*	*

t-DISTRIBUTION

Degrees of Freedom	Area in Both Tails Combined			
	0.10	0.05	0.02	0.01
1	6.314	12.706	31.821	63.657
2	2.920	4.303	6.965	9.925
3	2.353	3.182	4.541	5.841
4	2.132	2.776	3.747	4.604
5	2.015	2.571	3.365	4.032
6	1.943	2.447	3.143	3.707
7	1.895	2.365	2.998	3.499
8	1.860	2.306	2.896	3.355
9	1.833	2.262	2.821	3.250
10	1.812	2.228	2.764	3.169
11	1.796	2.201	2.718	3.106
12	1.782	2.179	2.681	3.055
13	1.771	2.160	2.650	3.012
14	1.761	2.145	2.624	2.977
15	1.753	2.131	2.602	2.947
16	1.746	2.120	2.583	2.921
17	1.740	2.110	2.567	2.898
18	1.734	2.101	2.552	2.878
19	1.729	2.093	2.539	2.861
20	1.725	2.086	2.528	2.845
21	1.721	2.080	2.518	2.831
22	1.717	2.074	2.508	2.819
23	1.714	2.069	2.500	2.807
24	1.711	2.064	2.492	2.797
25	1.708	2.060	2.485	2.787
26	1.706	2.056	2.479	2.779
27	1.703	2.052	2.473	2.771
28	1.701	2.048	2.467	2.763
29	1.699	2.045	2.462	2.756
30	1.697	2.042	2.457	2.750
40	1.684	2.021	2.423	2.704
60	1.671	2.000	2.390	2.660
120	1.658	1.980	2.358	2.617
Normal Distribution	1.645	1.960	2.326	2.576

VALUES OF THE STANDARD NORMAL CUMULATIVE PROBABILITY FUNCTION

z	0	1	2	3	4	5	6	7	8	9
−3.	.0013	.0010	.0007	.0005	.0003	.0002	.0002	.0001	.0001	.0000
−2.9	.0019	.0018	.0017	.0017	.0016	.0016	.0015	.0015	.0014	.0014
−2.8	.0026	.0025	.0024	.0023	.0023	.0022	.0021	.0021	.0020	.0019
−2.7	.0035	.0034	.0033	.0032	.0031	.0030	.0029	.0028	.0027	.0026
−2.6	.0047	.0045	.0044	.0043	.0041	.0040	.0039	.0038	.0037	.0036
−2.5	.0062	00.60	.0059	.0057	.0055	.0054	.0052	.0051	.0049	.0048
−2.4	.0082	.0080	.0078	.0075	.0073	.0071	.0069	.0068	.0066	.0064
−2.3	.0107	.0104	.0102	.0099	.0096	.0094	.0091	.0089	.0087	.0084
−2.2	.0139	.0136	.0132	.0129	.0126	.0122	.0119	.0116	.0113	.0110
−2.1	.0179	.0174	.0170	.0166	.0162	.0158	.0154	.0150	.0146	.0143
−2.0	.0228	.0222	.0217	.0212	.0207	.0202	.0197	.0192	.0188	.0183
−1.9	.0287	.0281	.0274	.0268	.0262	.0256	.0250	.0244	.0238	.0233
−1.8	.0359	.0352	.0344	.0336	.0329	.0322	.0314	.0307	.0300	.0294
−1.7	.0446	.0436	.0427	.0418	.0409	.0401	.0392	.0384	.0375	.0367
−1.6	.0548	.0537	.0526	.0516	.0505	.0495	.0485	.0475	.0465	.0455
−1.5	.0668	.0655	.0643	.0630	.0618	.0606	.0594	.0582	.0570	.0559
−1.4	.0808	.0793	.0778	.0764	.0749	.0735	.0722	.0708	.0694	.0681
−1.3	.0968	.0951	.0934	.0918	.0901	.0885	.0869	.0853	.0838	.0823
−1.2	.1151	.1131	.1112	.1093	.1075	.1056	.1038	.1020	.1003	.0985
−1.1	.1357	.1335	.1314	.1292	.1271	.1251	.1230	.1210	.1190	.1170
−1.0	.1587	.1562	.1539	.1515	.1492	.1469	.1446	.1423	.1401	.1379
−.9	.1841	.1841	.1788	.1762	.1736	.1711	.1685	.1660	.1635	.1611
−.8	.2119	.2090	.2061	.2033	.2005	.1977	.1949	.1922	.1894	.1867
−.7	.2420	.2389	.2358	.2327	.2297	.2266	.2236	.2206	.2177	.2148
−.6	.2743	.2709	.2676	.2643	.2611	.2578	.2546	.2514	.2483	.2451
−.5	.3085	.3050	.3015	.2981	.2946	.2912	.2877	.2843	.2810	.2776

(continued)

APPENDIX D
Values of the Standard Normal Cumulative Probability Distribution (continued)

z	0	1	2	3	4	5	6	7	8	9
−3.	.0013	.0010	.0007	.0005	.0003	.0002	.0002	.0001	.0001	.0000
−.4	.3446	.3409	.3372	.3336	.3300	.3264	.3228	.3192	.3156	.3121
−.3	.3821	.3783	.3745	.3707	.3669	.3632	.3594	.3557	.3520	.3483
−.2	.4207	.4168	.4129	.4090	.4052	.4013	.3974	.3936	.3897	.3859
−.1	.4602	.4562	.4522	.4483	.4443	.4404	.4364	.4325	.4286	.4247
−.0	.5000	.4960	.4920	.4880	.4840	.4801	.4761	.4721	.4681	.4641
.0	.5000	.5040	.5080	.5120	.5160	.5199	.5239	.5279	.5319	.5359
.1	.5398	.5438	.5478	.5517	.5557	.5596	.5636	.5675	.5714	.5753
.2	.5793	.5832	.5871	.5910	.5948	.5987	.6026	.6064	.6103	.6141
.3	.6179	.6217	.6255	.6293	.6331	.6368	.6406	.6443	.6480	.6517
.4	.6554	.6591	.6628	.6664	.6700	.6736	.6772	.6808	.6844	.6879
.5	.6915	.6950	.6985	.7019	.7054	.7088	.7123	.7157	.7190	.7224
.6	.7257	.7291	.7324	.7357	.7389	.7422	.7454	.7486	.7517	.7549
.7	.7580	.7611	.7642	.7673	.7703	.7734	.7764	.7794	.7823	.7852
.8	.7881	.7910	.7939	.7967	.7995	.8023	.8051	.8078	.8106	.8133
.9	.8159	.8186	.8212	.8238	.8264	.8289	.8315	.8340	.8365	.8389
1.0	.8413	.8438	.8461	.8485	.8508	.8531	.8554	.8577	.8599	.8621
1.1	.8643	.8665	.8686	.8708	.8729	.8749	.8770	.8790	.8810	.8830
1.2	.8849	.8869	.8888	.8907	.8925	.8944	.8962	.8980	.8997	.9015
1.3	.9032	.9049	.9066	.9082	.9099	.9115	.9131	.9147	.9162	.9177
1.4	.9192	.9207	.9222	.9236	.9251	.9265	.9278	.9292	.9306	.9319
1.5	.9332	.9345	.9357	.9370	.9382	.9394	.9406	.9418	.9430	.9441
1.6	.9452	.9463	.9474	.9484	.9495	.9505	.9515	.9525	.9535	.9545
1.7	.9554	.9564	.9573	.9582	.9591	.9599	.9608	.9616	.9625	.9633
1.8	.9641	.9648	.9656	.9664	.9671	.9678	.9686	.9693	.9700	.9706
1.9	.9713	.9719	.9726	.9732	.9738	.9744	.9750	.9756	.9762	.9767
2.0	.9772	.9778	.9783	.9788	.9793	.9798	.9803	.9808	.9812	.9817
2.1	.9821	.9826	.9830	.9834	.9838	.9842	.9846	.9850	.9854	.9857
2.2	.9861	.9864	.9868	.9871	.9874	.9878	.9881	.9884	.9887	.9890
2.3	.9893	.9896	.9898	.9901	.9904	.9906	.9909	.9911	.9913	.9916
2.4	.9918	.9920	.9922	.9925	.9927	.9929	.9931	.9932	.9934	.9936
2.5	.9938	.9940	.9941	.9943	.9945	.9946	.9948	.9949	.9951	.9952
2.6	.9953	.9955	.9956	.9957	.9959	.9960	.9961	.9962	.9963	.9964
2.7	.9965	.9966	.9967	.9968	.9969	.9970	.9971	.9972	.9973	.9974
2.8	.9974	.9975	.9976	.9977	.9977	.9978	.9979	.9979	.9980	.9981
2.9	.9981	.9982	.9982	.9983	.9984	.9984	.9985	.9985	.9986	.9986
3.	.9987	.9990	.9993	.9995	.9997	.9998	.9998	.9999	.9999	1.000

GLOSSARY

ABNORMAL RETURN The return earned on a stock or other financial asset in excess of the amount required to compensate for the risk involved.

ACCOUNT EXECUTIVE A securities broker who services the accounts of individual investors.

ACCOUNTING EARNINGS, OR REPORTED EARNINGS A firm's revenues less expenses, which, assuming no issuance or repurchase of the company's stock, is the change in the shareholder's equity plus the dividends paid to shareholders.

ACTIVE INVESTMENT STRATEGY Managing a portfolio with the aim of earning positive risk-adjusted returns by selecting mispriced assets or by forecasting the trend of the market.

ACTUAL MARGIN In the case of a margin purchase, the equity in the investor's margin account as a percentage of the account's total market value, or, in the case of a short sale, the equity in the account as a percentage of the margin debt.

AGENCY ISSUES Securities issued by government-sponsored organizations.

ALPHA In estimating beta, the y-intercept of the characteristic line. In estimating future returns, the difference between the expected return, $E(R_i)$, and the equilibrium expected return of the capital asset pricing model, $R_f + B_i(R_m - R_f)$. In evaluating portfolio performance with the capital asset pricing model, the difference between the actual return and the equilibrium expected return.

AMERICAN DEPOSITARY RECEIPTS (ADRs) Certificates issued by U.S. banks that represent indirect ownership of a specified number of shares of a foreign company.

AMERICAN OPTION An option that can be exercised any time before its expiration.

ANNOUNCEMENT DATE The date on which the directors of a corporation announce a corporate action, such as the declaration of a dividend.

ANNUITY A contract under which one party is obligated to pay, and the other party has the right to receive, periodic payments.

ANOMALY A return associated with one or more variables, such as firm size, day of the week, or price/earnings ratio, that is not explained by any known asset pricing model.

ARBITRAGE The simultaneous purchase and sale of the same asset, or similar assets, with the objective of making a riskless profit.

ARBITRAGE PRICING THEORY An asset pricing theory based on the notion that when there are no opportunities to create wealth through risk-free arbitrage, the expected return on a security is a linear function of the security's sensitivity to various common factors.

ARITHMETIC MEAN RETURN An arithmetic average of the periodic returns over two or more periods.

ASK, OR ASKED, PRICE The price at which a specialist or dealer offers to sell a security.

ASSET ALLOCATION The process of determining the optimal allocation of an investor's portfolio among various classes of assets.

AT THE MONEY OPTION An option whose strike, or striking, price is equal to the market value of the underlying asset.

ATTRIBUTE SCREENING Searching through a large number of stocks to find those with attributes that are thought to be associated with positive abnormal returns.

AUCTION MARKET A market, such as the stock exchanges, where the prices of assets are determined by the bidding of buyers and the offerings of sellers.

BANK DISCOUNT YIELD Yield on a U.S. Treasury bill or other short-term discount security calculated by first dividing the discount by the face value, then annualizing with a 360-day year.

BANKER'S ACCEPTANCE A time draft drawn on a bank that is accepted by, and thus becomes an obligation of, the bank.

BARRON'S CONFIDENCE INDEX The spread between the yields of medium- and high-grade corporate bonds. A narrow spread indicates a high degree of confidence in future corporate profitability.

BASIS The difference between the spot, or cash, and futures price of an asset.

BASIS POINT 1/100th of 1%.

BASIS RISK The risk arising from a possible narrowing or widening of the basis.

BEAR SPREAD Writing a call with a low striking price and buying a call on the same stock with a high striking price.

BENCHMARK ERROR Error in portfolio performance evaluation that results from selection of an inappropriate proxy for the market portfolio.

BEST-EFFORTS OFFERING A securities offering in which the investment bankers serve as agents rather than dealers, agreeing only to obtain the best price the market will pay for the securities.

BETA A relative measure of the systematic risk of a security. It reflects the tendency of a security's return to respond to changes in the return on the market portfolio.

BID PRICE The price at which a specialist or dealer offers to buy a security.

BID-ASKED SPREAD The difference between the bid price and the asked price.

BLACK-SCHOLES OPTION PRICING MODEL A formula that values a call option on the basis of the stock price, striking price, risk-free rate of interest, time to maturity, and standard deviation of the stock's return.

BLOCK TRADE A transaction involving 10,000 or more shares.

BLUE SKY LAWS Securities laws of the various states.

BOND A long-term debt instrument that obligates the issuer to pay principal and interest. A *coupon bond* obligates the issuer to make periodic interest payments (called coupon payments) and to repay the principal at maturity.

BOND EQUIVALENT YIELD The yield on a Treasury bill or other short-term discount security calculated by dividing the discount by the price and multiplying the result by the ratio of 365 to the number of days to maturity.

BOND MARKET LINE Typically, shows the relationship between bond duration (as a proxy for interest rate risk) and bond yield.

BOND RATINGS Ratings assigned to bonds to indicate the relative probability of default.

BOND SWAPS A form of active bond management involving the purchase and sale of bonds in an effort to improve the rate of return on the portfolio.

BOOK VALUE The aggregate value of reported common shareholders' equity, which is common stock, plus retained earnings, plus capital contributed in excess of par value.

BROKER An agent who represents buyers and sellers in securities transactions.

BULL SPREAD Writing a call with a high striking price and buying a call on the same stock with a low striking price.

BULLISH, BEARISH Bullish means optimistic and bearish means pessimistic.

BUSINESS RISK The risk associated with unstable operating income, which arises largely from instability in the demand for the firm's products and services, an unstable variable cost ratio, and high fixed operating costs.

BUTTERFLY SPREAD Buying two calls, one with a high striking price and one with a low striking price, and writing two calls with striking prices in the middle.

CALENDAR EFFECT (*see also* January effect *and* weekend effect) The effect of the time of the year or time of the week on common stock returns.

CALL MONEY RATE The interest rate paid by brokerage firms to banks on loans used to finance margin purchases.

CALL OPTION A contract that gives the holder the right to buy from the option writer a specified number of shares of a given stock at a specified price (the striking price) during a specific period of time.

CALL PREMIUM The amount by which the call price of a bond exceeds the par value.

CALL PRICE One or more prices at which an issuer can call bonds prior to the stated maturity.

CALL PROTECTION The protection afforded by a bond covenant that defers the issuer's right to call the bond for a period of years.

CALLABLE BOND A bond that is callable by the issuer before its maturity.

CAPITAL ASSET PRICING MODEL (CAPM) An asset pricing model which states that the expected return on a security is a positive linear function of the security's systematic risk, as measured by its beta.

CAPITAL GAIN (OR LOSS) The amount by which the sale price of an asset exceeds (or is less than) its cost.

CAPITAL MARKET LINE (CML) Shows the expected returns for efficient portfolios as a linear function of their total risk, as measured by the standard deviation of the return.

CAPITAL MARKET SECURITIES Financial assets that either have no maturity or mature in more than one year.

CAPITALIZATION OF EARNINGS Valuation of an asset by applying a multiplier to the expected earnings.

CASH ACCOUNT A brokerage account in which the customer makes only cash transactions.

CASH COLLATERAL In a short sale, the proceeds of the sale of the borrowed stock that are turned over to the broker as collateral for the loan.

CASH EQUIVALENTS Short-term money market securities.

CERTIFICATE OF DEPOSIT A form of time deposit.

CERTIFICATE OF INCORPORATION The corporate charter. Among other things, it establishes the powers of the corporation.

CHARACTERISTIC LINE A plot of the expected return (or excess return) of a security as a function of the expected return (or excess return) of the market.

CLEARINGHOUSE An organization established by an exchange to facilitate the transfer of securities. A clearinghouse for options or futures contracts interposes itself as a third party between the two parties to a trade.

CLOSED-END INVESTMENT COMPANY An investment fund whose shares are traded through brokers at market prices that may be higher or lower than the value of the underlying assets. In contrast to an open-end investment company, or mutual fund, it rarely issues new shares after the initial offering, and it does not stand ready to repurchase its own shares.

COEFFICIENT OF DETERMINATION (R^2) In a regression, the proportion of the variation in the dependent variable associated with (explained by) the independent variable, or variables.

COLLATERAL TRUST BOND A bond that is backed by other securities.

COLLATERALIZED MORTGAGE OBLIGATION (CMO) A mortgage pass-through security under which the principal payments are assigned to maturity groups (or tranches) in succession, with the first group receiving all the principal payments until it has been paid in full, and so on through all the groups.

COMMERCIAL PAPER A type of money market instrument (i.e., short-term unsecured note) issued by corporations.

COMMISSION BROKER A broker on the floor of an exchange who executes orders placed by the public with brokerage firms.

COMMODITY FUND An investment company that deals in commodity futures.

COMMON FACTOR Something, such as a change in the expected rate of inflation, that affects a significant number of stocks or bonds.

COMMON STOCK Equity securities representing an ownership interest in a corporation.

COMPOUND INTEREST Interest on interest.

CONSOLIDATED QUOTATIONS SYSTEM A system that lists current bid-asked prices of specialists on all exchanges, as well as the quotations of certain over the counter dealers.

CONSOLIDATED TAPE A system that reports trades occurring on the national and regional stock exchanges and the NASDAQ system.

CONSTANT GROWTH MODEL A dividend discount (valuation) model based on the assumption that dividends will grow at a constant rate forever.

CONSUMER PRICE INDEX An index of consumer prices prepared by the Department of Labor, Bureau of Labor Statistics.

CONTRARY OPINION A strategy of trading contrary to the opinion of the "crowd."

CONVERSION PREMIUM With convertibles, the amount by which the market price of the security exceeds its conversion value.

CONVERSION PRICE The par value of a convertible divided by the conversion ratio.

CONVERSION RATIO The number of shares of stock for which a convertible can be exchanged.

CONVERSION VALUE The market value of the stock for which a convertible can be exchanged.

CONVERTIBLE SECURITIES Bonds and preferred stocks that, at the holder's option, can be exchanged for a specified number of shares of common stock.

CORPORATE BONDS Long-term debt securities of corporations that typically pay interest semiannually and repay the principal at maturity.

CORPORATE INSIDERS See insiders.

CORRELATION COEFFICIENT A statistic that measures the degree of association between two variables. It scales the covariance to a value between minus one (perfect negative correlation) and plus one (perfect positive correlation).

COUPON PAYMENTS The periodic interest payments on a coupon bond.

COUPON RATE The annual amount of coupon payments on a bond expressed as a percentage of the par value.

COUPON STRIPPING The process of selling separately the individual cash flows (interest payments and maturity value) of a Treasury note or bond.

COVARIANCE An absolute measure of the extent to which two variables tend to be related, or move together.

COVERED CALL WRITING Writing a call option on a security owned by the option writer.

CUMULATIVE AVERAGE ABNORMAL RETURN (CAAR) The total average abnormal return for a number of securities over a specified period.

CURRENCY RISK, OR EXCHANGE RISK The risk in foreign investing that arises from the unpredictability of the rate at which the foreign currency can be converted into the investor's own currency.

CURRENT YIELD The annual coupon payments on a bond divided by its current market price.

DATE OF RECORD The date on which the stockholders of record are determined for the purpose of paying dividends.

DAY-OF-THE-WEEK EFFECT (OR WEEKEND EFFECT) An empirical regularity which indicates that stocks tend to provide lower returns on Mondays than on other days of the week.

DEALER (OR MARKET MAKER) An individual, or firm, who buys and sells securities for his, her, or its own account, thereby facilitating the trading of financial assets.

DEALER'S SPREAD The bid-asked spread quoted by a securities dealer.

DEBENTURE A bond that is not backed, or secured, by specific assets.

DEBIT BALANCE The dollar amount owed a broker as the result of a margin purchase.

DEEP DISCOUNT BOND A bond issued at a price considerably below par because the coupon rate is significantly lower than the required return.

DEFAULT PREMIUM The amount by which the promised yield to maturity exceeds the expected yield to maturity due to the possibility of default.

DEFINED BENEFIT PLAN A pension plan in which the retirement benefits are determined by a formula.

DEFINED CONTRIBUTION PLAN A pension plan in which contributions required by the corporation are determined by formula.

DELTA OF AN OPTION *See* hedge ratio.

DERIVATIVE SECURITIES Securities, such as options and futures, whose payoffs depend on the value of other assets, such as stocks, bonds, or commodities.

DETACHABLE WARRANT A warrant that may be sold separately from the security, usually a bond, with which it was originally issued. *See* Warrant.

DISCOUNT For a debt security or preferred stock, the amount by which the market price is below the face or par value. For the shares of a closed-end investment company, the amount by which market price is below the net asset value.

DISCOUNT BROKER A brokerage firm whose services are limited largely to the execution of orders and whose commissions are generally lower than those of full-service brokerage firms.

DISCOUNT RATE An interest rate that reflects both the time value of money and the riskiness of the flows. It is used to calculate the present value of expected future cash flows.

DISCOUNT SECURITY A fixed-income security that is issued at a discount and promises to make only one payment, the face value.

DIVERSIFIABLE RISK (ALSO FIRM-SPECIFIC, OR NONMARKET, OR UNSYSTEMATIC RISK) Risk associated with factors peculiar to a firm or its industry. Risk that can be avoided by diversifying.

DIVERSIFICATION Investing in more than one asset to reduce the risk.

DIVIDEND DISCOUNT MODEL (DDM) A model based on the assumption that the intrinsic value of a share of stock is the discounted value of all expected future cash dividends.

DIVIDEND PAYOUT RATIO Percentage of earnings paid out as dividends. One minus the earnings retention ratio.

DIVIDEND YIELD The current annualized dividend on a share of common stock divided by the market price of the stock.

DOLLAR-COST AVERAGING Investing equal amounts in common stocks at frequent, regular intervals to reduce the risk of poor timing.

DOW JONES INDUSTRIAL AVERAGE (DJIA) A price-weighted, divisor-adjusted average of 30 large industrial stocks.

DOW THEORY A theory that describes market movements and attempts to predict market trends.

DUAL FUND An investment company with two kinds of shares, income and capital.

DURATION A measure of the average maturity of the payments to be made over the life of a bond or other asset, calculated by weighting the length of time until each payment is expected to be received by the percentage relationship between the present value of the payment and the asset's total present value.

EARNINGS MULTIPLIER *See* P/E ratio.

EARNINGS PER SHARE A company's earnings (actual or predicted) divided by the number of shares outstanding.

EARNINGS/PRICE RATIO (EARNINGS YIELD) Earnings per share divided by price per share. Reciprocal of the price/earnings ratio.

EARNINGS RETENTION RATIO (PLOWBACK RATIO) Percentage of earnings retained in the business. One minus the dividend payout ratio.

EARNINGS YIELD *See* earnings/price ratio.

EFFECTIVE YIELD Annualized return on a Treasury bill, with periodic compounding.

EFFICIENT FRONTIER A graph of portfolios that offer the highest expected return at each level of risk.

EFFICIENT MARKET HYPOTHESIS (EMH) Asserts that the price of every security equals its investment, or intrinsic, value. The weak-form

EMH asserts that the price reflects all information contained in past prices and trading volumes; the semistrong-form asserts that the price reflects all publicly available information; and the strong-form asserts that the price reflects all information, private as well as public.

EFFICIENT PORTFOLIO A portfolio with the highest expected return at a given level of risk, or the least amount of risk at a given level of return.

ELASTICITY OF AN OPTION Percentage change in the price of an option associated with a 1% change in the price of the stock.

EQUIPMENT TRUST CERTIFICATE A bond that is backed (collateralized) by specific pieces of equipment.

EQUITY RISK PREMIUM The difference between the expected (or actual) return on common stocks and the expected (or actual) return on a riskless asset.

EQUITY SECURITIES The nondebt securities (common and preferred stocks) of a corporation.

EQUIVALENT TAXABLE YIELD The pretax yield on a taxable bond that provides an after-tax yield equal to the yield on a tax-exempt bond.

ESTIMATION RISK The degree of uncertainty about the future earnings of a firm, which can be measured by the coefficient of variation of analysts' forecasts of its earnings.

EURODOLLARS Dollar-denominated deposits issued by foreign banks or foreign branches of U.S. banks.

EUROPEAN OPTION An option that can be exercised only at its expiration date.

EVENT STUDIES Studies designed to measure the impact of an event on stocks' returns.

EXCESS RETURN The difference between the return on a security and the return on a riskless asset.

EXCHANGE RATE The price of a unit of one country's currency in terms of one unit of another country's currency.

EXCHANGE RISK *See* currency risk.

EX-DIVIDEND DATE The fourth day before the record date for payment of dividends. Those who purchase shares before the ex-dividend date receive the dividend. Those who purchase on or after the ex-dividend date do not.

EXERCISE PRICE *See* strike price.

EXPECTATIONS THEORY, OR UNBIASED EXPECTATIONS THEORY A theory of the term structure of interest rates which states that a long-term rate is an average of the short-term rates that are expected to prevail over the longer period.

EXPECTED RETURN The probability weighted average of the returns thought possible over some future period.

EXPIRATION DATE The date on which the right to buy or sell under an option contract ceases to exist.

EXTENDABLE NOTES Notes with maturities of 10 to 15 years on which the issuer has the right to change the rate at various times, called election dates, and investors have the right to require redemption at par value whenever the rate is changed.

FACTOR MODEL A model that attributes the return on a security to its sensitivity to factors that affect large numbers of securities. *See* common factors.

FAST-GROWTH STOCK Stocks of companies whose earnings are expected to grow much faster than the economy for at least several years.

FIFO First-in-first-out method of inventory valuation. It assumes that the first items acquired are the first sold.

FILTER RULE A technical rule for timing the market or selecting individual stocks when the price change has been greater than the amount of the filter.

FINANCIAL ANALYST, OR SECURITY ANALYST, OR INVESTMENT ANALYST A person who analyzes financial assets to determine their investment characteristics, including the risk and expected return.

FINANCIAL ASSETS Intangible assets, such as stocks or bonds, that represent a claim against the income generated by real assets or a claim against a government.

FINANCIAL FUTURES Futures contracts on stock indexes or financial assets such as U.S. Treasury securities.

FINANCIAL LEVERAGE The use of debt to fund a portion of the cost of an investment.

FINANCIAL RISK Risk arising from the use of debt.

FIRM-SPECIFIC RISK *See* diversifiable risk.

FIXED-INCOME SECURITIES Securities, such as bonds and preferred stock, that require specified payments.

FLIGHT TO QUALITY The tendency of investors to shift out of higher-risk securities and into lower-risk securities during certain periods, which increases the default premiums on the higher-risk securities.

FLOATING RATE A rate of interest that may change over the life of a bond or other security as the result of a change in a designated interest rate, such as the rate on one-year U.S. Treasury securities.

FLOOR BROKER A member of a securities exchange who assists commission brokers when they are receiving more orders than they can handle.

FLOOR TRADER *See* registered competitive market maker.

FORCED CONVERSION Convertibles are called when the conversion value is well above the call price, causing holders to convert to common stock rather than accept cash.

FORM 10-K Annual report corporations are required to file with the Securities and Exchange Commission.

FORWARD RATE An interest rate for a given maturity that applies, or is expected to apply, to some future period. Explicit forward rates can be seen in the prices for interest rate futures contracts. Implicit forward rates can be calculated from the current rates for securities of different maturities, that is, from the term structure of interest rates.

FOURTH MARKET Market in which exchange-listed securities are traded between investors without the assistance of a broker.

FUNDAMENTAL ANALYSIS Analyzing and predicting the fundamental determinants of stock prices, including earnings, dividends, interest rates, risk, and risk premiums.

FUTURES, OR FUTURES CONTRACT A contract in which one party agrees to buy and the other agrees to sell a specified quantity of a specific asset at a specified price for delivery on a certain future date.

FUTURES OPTION, OR OPTION ON FUTURES An option contract in which the subject of the contract is a futures contract.

GEOMETRIC MEAN The nth root of the product of n numbers.

GEOMETRIC MEAN ANNUAL RETURN The geometric mean of a set of annual returns is the compound annual rate of return.

GENERALLY ACCEPTED ACCOUNTING PRINCIPLES (GAAP) Accounting rules adopted by a recognized authority such as the Financial Accounting Standards Board (FASB).

GENERAL OBLIGATION BOND Bond issued by a state or local government that is backed by the full taxing power of the government.

GINNIE MAE PASS-THROUGH SECURITIES Mortgage-backed pass-through securities that are guaranteed by the Government National Mortgage Association (GNMA, or Ginnie Mae).

HEDGE RATIO FOR AN OPTION, OR THE OPTION'S DELTA The expected change in the value of an option per dollar change in the price of the underlying asset. Thus, the number of shares of stock required to hedge against the price risk of one option.

HEDGING Making an investment in one asset and taking an offsetting position in another asset to reduce the risk of loss.

HOLDING PERIOD The length of time over which an asset has been, or is expected to be, held.

IMMUNIZATION A strategy by which investors try to lock in the total return from a bond portfolio for the period over which they are expected to be held. It involves setting the average duration of the portfolio, rather than the average maturity, equal to the expected holding period. If fully successful, any loss in bond values due to an increase in interest rates will be offset by an increase in reinvestment income, or any loss in reinvestment income due to a decrease in interest rates will be offset by an increase in bond values.

IMPLIED VOLATILITY The standard deviation of a stock's return that is consistent with the price of an option.

IN THE MONEY OPTION In the case of a call (put), an option whose striking price is below (above) the price of the underlying asset.

INDENTURE A contract between the issuer and the bondholders that states the terms of the bond issue.

INDEX ARBITRAGE A strategy designed to take advantage of any mispricing of a stock index futures contract relative to the aggregate value of the underlying stocks. It involves buying a stock index futures contract and selling the individual stocks in the index, or selling a stock index futures contract and buying the individual stocks.

INDEX FUND A mutual fund holding a portfolio that is representative of the stocks in a market index such as Standard & Poor's 500.

INDEX OPTION An option based on a stock market index.

INDIFFERENCE CURVE A curve showing the expected returns and risk of all portfolios that provide an investor with an equal amount of satisfaction.

INFLATION RATE The rate of change in a price index, such as the consumer price index, over a specified period of time.

INITIAL PUBLIC OFFERING (IPO) The initial offering of stock by a company that has been privately owned.

INSIDE INFORMATION Information about a corporation that is known only to corporate officers, directors, and others who have access to nonpublic information about the firm.

INSIDERS In a narrow sense, corporate officers, directors, and major stockholders. More broadly, it includes anyone who has access to nonpublic information about the firm.

INTEREST COVERAGE RATIO, OR TIMES INTEREST EARNED Earnings before interest and taxes (EBIT) divided by interest expense. A measure of financial leverage.

INTEREST RATE FUTURES Futures contracts on fixed-income securities such as U.S. Treasury bills, notes, and bonds.

INTEREST RATE RISK Changes in market interest rates affect bond returns in two ways: through their impact on bond prices and through their effect on reinvestment income. In a narrow sense, interest rate risk refers only to the risk of bond price changes resulting from changes in interest rates, called price risk. In a broader sense, it also includes reinvestment rate risk, which is the risk that income from reinvestment of interest payments will change.

INTERCOMMODITY SPREAD (FUTURES) Taking opposite positions in related commodities, such as corn and wheat. The trader takes a long position in the commodity perceived to be underpriced relative to the other and a short position in the commodity perceived to be relatively overpriced.

INTERMARKET SPREAD (FUTURES) Simultaneous purchase and sale of the same commodity on two different futures exchanges.

INTERNAL RATE OF RETURN Discount rate that equates the present value of the expected cash flows from an investment to its cost.

INTRAMARKET SPREAD (FUTURES) Taking opposite positions in contracts for the same commodity with different delivery months.

INTRAMARKET SWAP, OR SECTOR SWAP (BONDS) Purchase of bonds in one sector and sale of bonds in another in an effort to profit from changes in yield spreads. Sectors are based upon variables such as bond quality, coupon rate, type of issue, and type of issuer.

INTRINSIC VALUE (OPTIONS) The price of the stock minus the striking price, in the case of a call, or the striking price minus the stock price in the case of a put. It cannot be less than zero.

INTRINSIC VALUE, OR INVESTMENT VALUE (STOCKS AND BONDS) The present value of the expected cash flows from an investment.

INVESTMENT BANKERS Provide advice and assistance to the issuers of securities, often serving as both an underwriter and seller of new issues.

INVESTMENT COMPANY An organization that obtains funds from investors and invests those funds in financial assets.

INVESTMENT GRADE BONDS Bonds rated BBB, or Baa, or higher.

INVESTMENT VALUE See intrinsic value.

JANUARY, OR YEAR-END, EFFECT The tendency of stocks to provide higher returns in January than in other months of the year.

JENSEN'S INDEX The alpha of an investment. The difference between the actual return on a security or portfolio and the expected return, given the market return and beta.

JUNK BOND, OR SPECULATIVE BOND A bond rated BB, or Ba, or lower.

LIFO Last-in-first-out method of inventory valuation. It assumes that the last items acquired are the first sold.

LIMIT ORDER An order to buy or sell at a specified, or better, price.

LIMIT ORDER BOOK, OR SPECIALIST'S BOOK A specialist's record showing for each security any limit or stop orders received from brokers.

LIQUIDATION VALUE The amount for which the assets of a firm could be sold, less the amount of its liabilities.

LIQUIDITY (OF AN INVESTMENT) The speed with which an asset can be sold at a price close to that of the preceding transaction.

LIQUIDITY PREFERENCE THEORY A theory which asserts that investors require a liquidity premium for holding longer-term securities and that this premium is reflected in the term structure of interest rates.

LIQUIDITY PREMIUM The expected additional return required by investors on longer-term securities because of their greater interest rate risk.

LISTED SECURITY A security that is listed for trading on an organized exchange.

LISTING REQUIREMENTS The minimum requirements for listing a security.

LOAD FUND A mutual fund that charges a sales commission, or load.

LONDON INTERBANK OFFERED RATE (LIBOR) Rate charged on large interbank loans of Eurodollars in the London market.

LONG HEDGE Hedging against a rise in the price of an asset by purchasing futures.

MACRO EFFICIENCY The degree to which the level of the market as a whole corresponds to the aggregate intrinsic value of the securities.

MAINTENANCE MARGIN The minimum actual margin a brokerage firm allows margin customers to keep in their accounts.

MARGIN The amount or percentage of the cost of securities being bought or sold short that a customer must supply in money or securities, the rest being borrowed from the broker. Margin requirements are set by the Federal Reserve Board.

MARGIN ACCOUNT A brokerage account that permits the customer to do margin trading.

MARGIN CALL A demand by a broker for additional cash or securities when the actual margin falls below the maintenance margin.

MARGINAL TAX RATE The tax rate on an additional dollar of taxable income.

MARKED TO THE MARKET Daily adjustment of the equity in an investor's margin account to reflect price changes.

MARKET ANOMALY *See* anomaly.

MARKET CAPITALIZATION The aggregate market value of a security, especially common stock.

MARKET EFFICIENCY *See* efficient market hypothesis.

MARKET MAKER *See* dealer.

MARKET MODEL Relates the return on each stock linearly to the return on the market. *See* characteristic line.

MARKET ORDER An order to buy or an order to sell immediately at the best available price.

MARKET PORTFOLIO A portfolio of all risky assets in which each is held in proportion to its aggregate market value.

MARKET RISK, OR SYSTEMATIC RISK That part of total risk associated with moves of the market as a whole. To be distinguished from firm-specific, or unsystematic, risk.

MARKET RISK PREMIUM The difference between the expected return for the market as a whole and the risk-free rate of interest.

MARKET SEGMENTATION THEORY, OR SEGMENTED MARKETS THEORY A theory of the term structure of interest rates according to which various investors and borrowers are restricted by law or preference to securities with certain maturities. Thus, rates on each maturity segment are determined by supply and demand conditions in that segment alone.

MARKET TIMING, OR TIMING THE MARKET An active strategy that involves moving funds into and out of stocks and other securities on the basis of changes in their expected near-term performance.

MARKING TO THE MARKET *See* marked to the market.

MICRO EFFICIENCY The degree to which the price of an individual stock or other security corresponds to its intrinsic, or investment, value.

MODERN PORTFOLIO THEORY (MPT) Provides criteria for constructing, revising, and evaluating the performance of portfolios on the basis of the expected return, systematic risk, and total risk.

MOMENTUM INDICATOR Various technical indicators based on past price movements for large groups of stocks.

MONETARY AND STOCK MARKET CREDIT INDICATORS Technical indicators, such as bond yield spreads and margin debt in relation to the amount of new equity financing, that reflect conditions in the financial markets.

MONEY MARKET SECURITIES Securities that mature in one year or less. Usually highly liquid and low risk.

MORTGAGE-BACKED SECURITIES Securities that represent a proportionate ownership claim against a pool of mortgage loans. Also called "pass-throughs" because the holder of the loans passes the borrowers' payments along to the holders of the securities.

MORTGAGE BOND A bond backed by a mortgage on specific property.

MULTIFACTOR CAPM An expanded capital asset pricing model that includes factors such as dividends and stock liquidity in addition to systematic risk.

MUNICIPAL SECURITIES Securities issued by state or local governments or entities, such as airport authorities, created by those governments.

MUTUAL FUND, OR OPEN-END INVESTMENT COMPANY A fund that, as a rule, offers new shares to the public continuously and stands ready to repurchase its shares at any time.

MUTUAL FUND CASH/ASSET RATIO A technical indicator for predicting stock market turning points.

NAKED CALL WRITING Writing a call option on a stock the writer does not own.

NAKED PUT WRITING Writing a put option on a stock when the writer does not have sufficient assets in his or her brokerage account to purchase the stock.

NASDAQ (NATIONAL ASSOCIATION OF SECURITIES DEALERS AUTOMATED QUOTATIONS) An automated communications network operated by the NASD that connects brokers and dealers in the over-the-counter market. It shows the bid and asked prices on thousands of stocks entered into the system by securities dealers.

NASDAQ/NMS (NASDAQ NATIONAL MARKET SYSTEM) A segment of the NASDAQ market consisting of the larger issues. More detailed daily reporting is made for these stocks than for other NASDAQ stocks.

NATIONAL ASSOCIATION OF SECURITIES DEALERS (NASD) A self-regulating organization of brokers and dealers that establishes rules and regulations for the industry and monitors activities of brokers and dealers in the over-the-counter market.

NATIONAL MARKET SYSTEM A fully competitive national market system for securities trading.

NEGLECTED FIRM EFFECT The possible tendency of stocks that are followed by few analysts and held by few institutions to provide abnormally higher returns.

NEGOTIABLE CERTIFICATE OF DE POSIT A certificate of deposit (CD) issued by a bank or other financial institution that can be sold by the holder to another investor.

NET ASSET VALUE The market value of the assets held by an investment company, less any liabilities, divided by the number of shares outstanding.

NEW WAVE THEORY The idea that characteristics (such as a low P/E ratio) that might be used to identify the better-performing stocks of the future are continually changing.

NO GROWTH MODEL, OR ZERO GROWTH, MODEL A dividend discount model that assumes constant annual dividends.

NO-LOAD FUND A mutual fund that does not charge a sales commission.

NOISE TRADING The idea that the prices of securities and other assets respond not only to new information bearing on their value but to information (noise) that has nothing to do with fundamental values.

NOMINAL RETURN The return on an investment unadjusted for inflation. To be distinguished from the real return.

NORMALIZED EARNINGS An estimate of what the company would have earned under normal, mid-cyclical conditions.

ODD-LOT THEORY The notion that those who transact business in odd lots (generally, less than 100 shares) are uninformed and usually do the wrong thing.

OPEN INTEREST The number of a particular futures contract that remain open.

OPEN-END INVESTMENT COMPANY *See* mutual fund.

OPENING PRICE The price at which the first trade of the day takes place.

OPTIMAL PORTFOLIO The efficient portfolio that offers an investor the maximum level of satisfaction. It is at the tangency of the efficient set and the investor's indifference curve.

OPTION A contract between two parties in which one (the writer) grants the other the right to buy (or sell) a specific asset at a specified price over a specified period of time.

OPTION ELASTICITY *See* elasticity of an option.

OPTION ON FUTURES *See* futures option.

ORIGINAL ISSUE DISCOUNT BOND Bonds issued at a discount because the coupon rate is lower than the required return.

OUT OF THE MONEY OPTION In the case of a call (put), an option whose striking price is greater than (less than) the market price of the underlying asset.

OVER-THE-COUNTER (OTC) MARKET A secondary market away from the exchanges in which securities dealers act as the market makers.

OVERPRICED SECURITY A security whose expected return is below the equilibrium expected return, known as the required return.

OVERREACTION HYPOTHESIS The idea that investors tend to overreact to good and bad news, causing stock prices to rise above and fall below their intrinsic values.

PAR VALUE The stated value of par value stock, or the face value of a bond.

PASS-THROUGH SECURITY *See* mortgage-backed security.

PASSIVE INVESTMENT STRATEGY Buying and holding a well-diversified portfolio without attempting to find mispriced securities or time the market.

PAYOUT RATIO *See* dividend payout ratio.

P/E EFFECT The notion that stocks with low P/E ratios tend to provide abnormally high returns.

P/E RATIO, OR PRICE/EARNINGS RATIO Ratio of price per share to earnings per share. Also referred to as the earnings multiplier or price/earnings multiple.

PINK SHEETS Published quotations on over-the-counter stocks that are not in NASDAQ.

PLOWBACK RATIO *See* earnings retention ratio.

POINT-AND-FIGURE CHART A chart that shows only price movements that are considered large enough to be significant.

PORTFOLIO INSURANCE The practice of using put options or predetermined selling prices in an effort to guarantee a minimum rate of return on a risky portfolio while retaining the potential for large gains.

PORTFOLIO MANAGEMENT Utilizing information provided by security analysts to construct and maintain portfolios suitable for their owners.

PORTFOLIO PERFORMANCE EVALUATION Evaluating the risk and return of a portfolio.

POSITIVE FEEDBACK STRATEGY The practice of buying or selling stocks in response to recent price changes.

PREEMPTIVE RIGHT The right of existing shareholders to purchase new shares in a stock offering in proportion to the number of shares they already own.

PREFERRED STOCK A security that has characteristics of both bonds and common stock. Dividends are generally fixed in amount but can be omitted without bankrupting the corporation.

PREMIUM The purchase price of an option; or the amount by which the price of a bond or preferred stock exceeds the par value; or the amount by which the price of a closed-end investment company's shares exceeds the net asset value.

PRICE/EARNINGS RATIO *See* P/E ratio.

PRICE RISK *See* interest rate risk.

PRIMARY MARKET The market for new issues of securities.

PRINCIPAL Same as the face value or par value of a bond.

PRIVATE PLACEMENT The direct sale of a new issue of securities to no more than a few investors.

PROGRAM TRADING The buying or selling of large groups of stocks, usually on the basis of computer-generated orders, with the aim of insuring a portfolio or arbitraging between the stock market and stock index futures.

PROMISED YIELD TO MATURITY The yield to maturity on a bond if all cash flows are received as scheduled. See yield to maturity.

PROSPECTUS The selling circular that must be given to purchasers of new issues of securities before their orders can be accepted.

PROTECTIVE COVENANTS Provisions in a bond indenture relating to such things as sinking fund provisions and limitations on further debt that are for the protection of the bondholders.

PROXY An instrument that empowers someone else to vote in place of a shareholder.

PUBLIC OFFERING An offering of securities in the primary market to the general public.

PURCHASING POWER RISK The risk arising from the uncertainty about the rate of inflation.

PURE YIELD PICKUP SWAP The exchange of one bond for another for the chance of earning a higher long-term yield.

PUT BOND A bond that the holder can surrender for par value at one or more future times.

PUT-CALL PARITY The condition that exists when the price of a call and the price of a put on the same stock, with the same striking price and same expiration date, are such that investors have no opportunity for profitable arbitrage.

PUT OPTION A contract that gives the buyer of the option the right to sell a specified number of shares of a given stock to the seller of the option at a specified price over a specified period of time.

QUALITY OF REPORTED EARNINGS The degree to which reported earnings do not reflect anticipated profits, inventory profits, or understatement of expenses.

RANDOM ERROR TERM, OR RESIDUALS Differences between the actual values of a variable and the values predicted by a model. The parts of the return that are not explained by the explanatory variable, or variables.

RANDOM WALK THEORY, OR RANDOM WALK MODEL Price changes are independent and identically distributed. The size or direction of a security's price change from one period to the next is a matter of chance, which makes it impossible to predict future price changes on the basis of past changes.

RATE ANTICIPATION SWAP An exchange of bonds based on their expected relative performance in the event of an expected change in interest rates.

REAL ASSETS Tangible assets such as land, buildings and equipment that can be used to produce products or deliver services.

REAL ESTATE INVESTMENT TRUST (REIT) An investment fund, similar to an investment company, that primarily holds ownership or creditorship interests in real estate.

REAL RETURN The inflation-adjusted return on an investment.

REAL RISK-FREE RATE The risk-free rate adjusted for inflation.

REALIZED YIELD The actual yield on an investment, including reinvestment income but before adjusting for inflation.

RED HERRING A preliminary prospectus that is subject to revision, does not contain the offering price, and cannot be used to offer the securities for sale.

REGISTERED BONDS Names of the owners are registered with the issuer.

REGISTERED COMPETITIVE MARKET MAKERS Members of an exchange who trade for their own account and assist the specialists in maintaining a fair and orderly market.

REGISTERED REPRESENTATIVE *See* account executive.

REGISTRATION STATEMENT A document filled with the Securities Exchange Commission prior to making a public offering of securities.

REINVESTMENT RATE RISK *See* interest rate risk.

RELATIVE STRENGTH A technical analysis technique that involves plotting the ratio of a stock's price to a market index and studying changes in the ratio.

REPLACEMENT COST The cost of replacing assets.

REPURCHASE AGREEMENT (REPO) A money market instrument that involves the sale of securities (usually U.S. Treasury securities), with the seller agreeing to repurchase the securities at a stated higher price on a specified date.

REQUIRED RATE OF RETURN The minimum acceptable expected rate of return on a particular asset or group of assets at a particular time.

RESIDUAL CLAIM The claim of common shareholders on the assets of a corporation in the event of bankruptcy. It comes after the claims of all creditors and preferred shareholders.

RESIDUALS *See* random error term.

RESISTANCE LEVEL A price level above which it is thought the price of a stock or stock index will have difficulty rising.

RESTRICTED ACCOUNT A margin account in which the actual margin has fallen below the initial margin but is still above the maintenance margin. No additional margin purchases can be made.

RETENTION RATIO *See* earnings retention ratio.

RETURN ON ASSETS (ROA) A measure of profitability: net income divided by total assets or average total assets.

RETURN ON EQUITY (ROE) A measure of profitability: net income divided by common shareholders' equity, or average common shareholders' equity.

RETURN ON SALES (ROS), OR PROFIT MARGIN A measure of profitability: net income divided by net sales.

REVENUE BOND A municipal bond that is backed solely by the revenues from a specific project, or agency, or tax.

REVERSING TRADE The purchase or sale of a futures contract for the purpose of offsetting, and thereby cancelling, a previous sale or purchase of the same contract.

REWARD-TO-VARIABILITY RATIO Ratio of the excess portfolio return (i.e., return minus the risk-free rate) to the standard deviation of the return. Sharpe's measure of portfolio performance.

REWARD-TO-VOLATILITY RATIO Ratio of the excess portfolio return (i.e., return minus the risk-free rate) to beta. Treynor's measure of portfolio performance.

RIDING THE YIELD CURVE Buying securities when the yield curve is upsloping with the intention of selling them at a lower yield before maturity, thereby earning a higher yield than the yield at which they were purchased.

RIGHTS Options issued by a corporation to its shareholders giving them the right to buy at a specified price a specified number of shares of a new issue that is in proportion to the number of shares they already own.

RIGHTS OFFERING A stock offering in which shares are first offered to existing shareholders in proportion to the number of shares they already own.

RISK The chance that the actual return will be different from the expected return.

RISK ARBITRAGE Speculation on securities that are thought to be mispriced, particularly where the arbitrager expects a merger or acquisition.

RISK PREMIUM The amount by which the required return on a risky asset, or group of assets, exceeds the risk-free rate.

RISK TOLERANCE The degree to which an investor is willing to assume greater risk for greater expected returns.

RISK-ADJUSTED RETURN A return that has been adjusted for the difference in risk between two assets or two groups of assets.

RISK-AVERSE INVESTOR An investor who will accept greater risk only if the riskier investment offers a higher expected return.

RISK-FREE ASSET An asset with an assured nominal rate of return; often proxied by short-term U.S. Treasury bills.

RISK-FREE RATE The interest rate (or yield) on a risk-free asset.

RISK-RETURN TRADE-OFF Refers to the positive relationship between risk and the expected return.

RISKY ASSET Any asset whose actual return could be greater or less than expected.

ROUND LOT Usually 100 shares of common stock.

SECONDARY MARKET A market in which previously-issued securities are traded. Includes the exchanges and the OTC market.

SECTOR ROTATION Shifting funds from stocks in one or more industry groups to one or more other groups on the basis of changes in the outlook for the economy and those industries.

SECTOR SWAP *See* intramarket swap.

SECURITIES Instruments that serve as written evidence of ownership or creditorship, such as stocks, bonds, and notes.

SECURITIES AND EXCHANGE COMMISSION (SEC) Federal agency that regulates the issuance and trading of securities.

SECURITIES INVESTOR PROTECTION CORPORATION (SIPC) A corporation that insures brokers' customers against loss resulting from failure of brokerage firms.

SECURITIZATION Securitizing loans, such as residential real estate mortgage loans, by placing them in a pool and issuing securities against the pool.

SECURITY ANALYSIS Analyzing securities to ascertain their risk and estimate their expected returns.

SECURITY ANALYST *See* financial analyst.

SECURITY MARKET LINE (SML) According to the capital asset pricing model, the linear relationship between securities' expected returns and their systematic risk, as measured by beta.

SELF-REGULATION Regulation of the exchanges by the exchanges themselves and regulation of the over-the-counter market by the National Association of Securities dealers, subject to oversight by various federal agencies, including the Securities and Exchange Commission and the Commodity Futures Trading Commission.

SEMISTRONG EFFICIENCY All relevant public information is fully and accurately reflected in security prices at all times.

SENTIMENT INDICATORS Ratios such as the CBOE put/call ratio and the ratio of bearish to bullish investment services that are used by technicians as contrary indicators.

SERIAL BONDS A bond issue with staggered maturities, that is, with different groups of bonds coming due at different times.

SERIAL CORRELATION, OR AUTOCORRELATION The degree of correlation of numbers in a series with lagged numbers in the same series. Positive serial correlation indicates the presence of one or more trends. Negative correlation indicates the existence of more reversals than might occur randomly.

SHELF REGISTRATION SEC allows securities to be registered "and placed on the shelf" for later sale.

SHORT HEDGE Offsetting risk by selling futures contracts.

SHORT INTEREST RATIO A technical indicator. Ratio of total shares sold short to average daily trading volume.

SHORT SALE Sale of stock not owned by the seller, but borrowed from or through a broker. The short seller later purchases identical stock to replace the borrowed shares.

SINGLE INDEX MODEL A model that relates the returns on a stock to the returns on a market index.

SINKING FUND PROVISION A provision in a bond indenture that requires the issuer to repurchase portions of the bond issue before maturity.

SLOW-GROWTH STOCKS Stocks of companies whose earnings are expected to grow no faster than the economy.

SMALL-FIRM (OR SIZE) EFFECT The notion that stocks of small firms provide abnormally high returns.

SPECIALIST A member of a stock exchange who operates as both a broker and a dealer on the floor of the exchange. Specialists act as dealers (buying for inventory and selling from inventory, or selling short) in fulfilling their responsibility to maintain a "fair and orderly market." They act as brokers in facilitating the execution of stop and limit orders.

SPECIALIST'S BOOK *See* limit order book.

SPECIALIST'S SHORT-SALE RATIO A technical indicator. The number of NYSE stocks sold short by specialists during the week divided by the total number of NYSE stocks sold short during the week.

SPECULATIVE GRADE BONDS *See* junk bonds.

SPECULATIVE INDICATORS Technical indicators, for example, the ratio of OTC stock volume to NYSE stock volume. The higher the ratio, supposedly, the greater the amount of speculative activity and the greater the probability of an early downturn.

SPOT MARKET A market in which there is an immediate exchange of an asset for cash.

SPOT PRICE The price of an asset in the spot market.

SPREAD *See* intermarket spread and intramarket spread.

STANDARD DEVIATION A measure of total risk. In a probability distribution, the square root of the expected value of the squared deviation from the mean. Also, the square root of the variance.

STANDARD DEVIATION OF THE RANDOM ERROR TERM, OR RESIDUAL STANDARD DEVIATION A measure of unsystematic risk. *See* Random error term.

STANDARD & POOR'S COMPOSITE INDEX, OR STANDARD & POOR'S 500 An index of stock prices based on the aggregate market values of 500 stocks.

STANDARDIZED UNEXPECTED EARNINGS (SUE) Actual earnings minus expected earnings, divided by the standard deviation of the difference.

STOCK-CHARACTERISTIC STUDIES Tests of the semistrong efficient market hypothesis that look for association between stock characteristics (such as a low P/E ratio or small aggregate market value) and abnormal returns.

STOCK DIVIDEND A dividend in the form of shares of stock that requires a transfer from retained earnings to capital stock and paid-in capital of an amount equal to the market value of the shares issued.

STOCK INDEX FUTURES Futures contracts on a stock index.

STOCK INDEX OPTIONS Options on a stock index.

STOCK PURCHASE WARRANT *See* warrant.

STOCK SPLIT The issuance of a given number of new shares to each shareholder in exchange for the shares already held. In a reverse split the number of new shares is fewer than the number of shares previously held.

STOP ORDER, OR STOP LOSS ORDER An order to sell at a price lower than the current market price or to buy at a price higher than the current price. It becomes a market order if the price reaches or goes beyond the stop price.

STOP PRICE The price set in a stop order.

STRADDLE An option strategy that involves buying both a call and a put on the same asset with the same striking price and same expiration date.

STREET NAME Securities are registered in the name of the investor's brokerage firm.

STRIKE PRICE, OR STRIKING PRICE, OR EXERCISE PRICE The price at which the common stock can be purchased, in the case of a call option, or sold, in the case of a put option.

STRIPS (SEPARATE TRADING OF REGISTERED INTEREST AND PRINCIPAL OF SECURITIES) Zero coupon securities created from new U.S. Treasury notes and bonds by the U.S. Treasury when it is asked to "strip" the securities (i.e., separate the coupons and the principal) so the components can be traded separately.

STRIPS AND STRAPS (OPTIONS) A strip is two puts and one call on the same stock with the same striking price and expiration date; and a strap is two calls and one put on the same stock with the same striking price and expiration date.

STRONG EFFICIENCY All relevant information, private as well as public, is fully and accurately reflected in security prices at all times.

SUBORDINATED DEBENTURES Bonds whose claims are subordinated to those of one or more debts of the corporation.

SUBSTITUTION SWAP Exchange of one bond for another with similar characteristics but a higher yield.

SUPPORT LEVEL A price level below which it is thought the price of a stock or the level of a stock index is unlikely to fall.

SUSTAINABLE EARNINGS The amount of earnings a firm could pay out as dividends without adversely affecting future earnings.

SYNDICATE A group of investment banking firms that is responsible for purchasing a new issue of securities and selling the securities to the public.

SYSTEMATIC RISK *See* market risk.

TAX-EXEMPT BOND A security whose income is exempt from the federal income tax.

TAX SWAP Generally, sale of bonds that are being held at a loss for the purpose of obtaining a tax benefit, followed by the purchase of bonds that differ only slightly from the bonds that were sold.

TECHNICAL ANALYSIS A form of security and market analysis that attempts to predict future price trends on the basis of past price and volume patterns and supposed indicators of future buying and selling pressures.

TERM STRUCTURE OF INTEREST RATES Relationship of interest rates to maturities, all other variables held constant.

TERMINAL, OR ACCUMULATED, VALUE The value of an investment or portfolio of investments at the end of a holding period, with all income reinvested.

THIRD MARKET The over-the-counter market for exchange-listed securities.

THREE-STAGE MODEL A dividend discount model for valuing common stocks that assumes three stages for the dividend growth rate, with the final stage being a perpetual one of constant growth.

TIME-OF-THE-TRADE STUDIES Tests of the semistrong efficient market hypothesis that look for association between abnormal returns and the time of the trade.

TIME SERIES MODEL A model that attempts to represent the pattern of a variable over time and thus facilitate prediction of future values of the variable.

TIME SPREAD Simultaneous purchase and sale of options that differ only in the month of expiration.

TIME VALUE The excess of the market price of an option over its intrinsic value. Arises from the possibility that the intrinsic value of the option may increase before the option expires.

TIMES INTEREST EARNED *See* interest coverage ratio.

TIMING THE MARKET *See* market timing.

TOP-DOWN EARNINGS FORECASTING Forecasting a company's earnings by starting with forecasts for the economy and the firm's industry or industries.

TOTAL REALIZED YIELD *See* realized yield.

TREASURY STOCK Stock that has been repurchased by the issuing corporation and not retired or reissued.

TWO-STAGE MODEL A dividend discount model for valuing common stocks that assumes two stages for the dividend growth rate, the second being a perpetual period of constant growth.

UNBIASED EXPECTATIONS THEORY *See* expectations theory.

UNDERMARGINED ACCOUNT A margin account in which the actual margin has fallen below the maintenance margin.

UNDERPRICED SECURITY A security whose expected return is above the equilibrium expected return, known as the required return.

UNDERWRITING The purchase of a new issue of securities by investment bankers from the issuer and resale to the public.

UNIT INVESTMENT TRUST An unmanaged entity that raises capital through a single issue of securities and invests it in a fixed portfolio of securities, usually bonds.

UNLISTED SECURITY A security that is not listed on an organized exchange.

U.S. SAVINGS BONDS Series EE and Series HH bonds that are issued primarily for the savings of individuals. They are noncallable, nontransferable, and registered. Series EE bonds are issued at a discount and do not pay periodic interest.

U.S. TREASURY BILLS Short-term securities issued by the U.S. Treasury on a discount basis.

U.S. TREASURY BONDS Bonds issued by the U.S. Treasury, usually with an original maturity of more than 10 years.

U.S. TREASURY NOTES Notes issued by the U.S. Treasury with an original maturity of not less than one year nor more than ten.

VALUE-WEIGHTED INDEX A market value index in which each security is weighted according to its aggregate market value.

VARIANCE A measure of total risk. The expected value of the squared deviation from the mean. The square of the standard deviation.

WARRANT, OR STOCK PURCHASE WARRANT A long-term option issued by a corporation on its own stock, usually as an attachment to a new issue of bonds or preferred stock.

WASH SALE Sale at a loss and purchase of a "substantially identical" security within 30 days before or after the sale. Loss is not deductible for tax purposes.

WEAK EFFICIENCY All information obtainable from previous price changes and trading volumes is reflected in the current price of a stock.

WEEKEND EFFECT The apparent tendency of stock returns to be lower on Monday than on any other day of the week.

YIELD CURVE A graphical representation of the term structure of interest rates. Yield to maturity is plotted against time to maturity.

YIELD SPREAD The difference between the promised yields to maturity of two bonds or two classes of bonds. For example, the spread between the yields of AAA (or Aaa) bonds and BBB (or Baa) bonds.

YIELD TO CALL Yield to the earliest call date (calculated as the yield to maturity) for a callable bond.

YIELD TO MATURITY The compound rate that will discount all promised future cash flows from a fixed-income security to its market price. It is the compound rate of return an investor will earn if the security is purchased at the current market price, all payments are made according to schedule, and all interest payments are reinvested at a rate equal to the yield to maturity.

ZERO COUPON BOND A bond that is issued at a discount, makes no periodic interest payments, and pays the face value at maturity.

ZERO GROWTH MODEL *See* no growth model.

Z-STATISTIC The number of standard deviations from the mean in a normal distribution.

NAME INDEX

SUBJECT INDEX